An Introduction to Splines
for use in
Computer Graphics
and
Geometric Modeling

An Introduction to Splines for use in Computer Graphics and Geometric Modeling

By

Richard H. Bartels
John C. Beatty
UNIVERSITY OF WATERLOO

Brian A. Barsky
UNIVERSITY OF CALIFORNIA, BERKELEY

Forewords by
Pierre Bézier
A. Robin Forrest
UNIVERSITY OF EAST ANGLIA

MORGAN KAUFMANN PUBLISHERS, INC.
LOS ALTOS, CALIFORNIA 94022

Editor and President *Michael B. Morgan*
Production Manager *Jennifer M. Ballentine*
Production Assistant *Todd R. Armstrong*
Copyediting *Lee Ballentine*
Book Design *Beverly Kennon-Kelley*
Cover Design *Irene Imfeld*
Composition *ETP Services Company*

Library of Congress Cataloging-in-Publication Data

Bartels, Richard H.
  An introduction to splines for use in computer
graphics and geometric modeling.

  Includes index.
  1. Computer graphics. 2. Spline theory. I. Beatty,
John C. II. Barsky, Brian A., 1954-   .
T385.B365   1986   006.6   86-27650
ISBN 0-934613-27-3

ISBN 0-934613-27-3
Printed in the United States of America

91 90 89 88 87   5 4 3 2 1

Preface

This book began as a set of tutorial notes introducing some of the major concepts in the mathematical literature on splines to people working in computer graphics. We intended to introduce terminology, notation, and basic results in an intuitive fashion, assuming only a background of beginning calculus and a little linear algebra, and selecting material that appeared most applicable to computer graphics. We have tried not to be too formal — the reader will find occasional "arguments," but no proofs. (For rigor, the references by de Boor and Schumaker, given in Chapter 1, are to be studied.) We hoped that such an introduction would enable those working in graphics to make use of the mathematical literature for further study.

In keeping with these introductory and graphics-related goals, we have concentrated on parametric spline curves and parametric, tensor-product spline surfaces. These have become standard tools in the field. More recent subjects, such as multivariate splines and free-form solids modeling, have not been covered, since they are areas of active research beyond the scope of this book.

The easiest decisions were those about the topics to be covered. It proved harder to fix upon a notation that was consistent throughout the book, pedagogically defensible, and in accord with most of the literature. We experimented with at least three distinct schemes. In the end, we settled on a major notational system, used throughout the B-spline and Beta-spline material, and a minor system, used in our discussion of Bézier techniques. This is somewhat in keeping with a similar notational split to be found between the B-/Beta-spline and Bézier literatures.

The most difficult decisions, however, causing the longest discussions, concerned the use of terminology. Not only does the terminology in the graphics literature on splines often conflict with that used in the mathematical literature, but various authors within each field contradict each other in their use of terms. To a mathematician, a "B-spline" is a particular type of spline basis function. To a graphics person, the term "B-spline" suggests a parametric spline, composed of a sum of the mathematician's spline basis functions that have been scaled by a sequence of control vertices. The graphics person's terminology of "B-spline basis function," on the other hand, seems to the mathematician as redundant as "liverwurst sausage." The use of "cardinal" is particularly individual. To one author it denotes a type of basis function; to another author it suggests a constructive technique for producing C^1 interpolating splines, and still another may use it to describe a canonical placement of knots. The reader should be aware that each paper in the literature may be phrased in its own local language. We have done what we could to make choices and remain consistent.

Special thanks are due to many people who helped during the development of the early notes and the subsequent manuscript. Kelly Booth kept our enthusiasm up throughout. Marceli Wein and Ken Evans of the National Research Council of Canada provided the seed money to translate our initial rough draft into our first edition of formal tutorial notes. NSERC of Canada, and NSF and DARPA of the United States, provided financial support for preparation of the first version of the notes and manuscript. The course organizers of Graphics Interface '84, and ACM SIGGRAPH '84, '85, and '86, in allowing us to present tutorials on splines using the notes as a text, provided the forum for extending the notes to include many additional topics. The many attendees of these tutorials have provided a wealth of suggestions, improvements, and encouragement that helped expand the notes into a book manuscript.

The manuscript has been used as the text for CS284 at the University of California, Berkeley, and for CS779 at the University of Waterloo. Students in these courses, together with many of our student colleagues in the graphics laboratories of these two universities, have helped flesh out sections of the book with their theses and projects. We particularly appreciate the help of Eric Bosch, Peter Bumbulis, Tony DeRose, Valerio Franceschin, Dave Forsey, Ines Hardtke, John Jezioranski, Stuart Kingdon, Vic Klassen, Doris Kochanek, Rob Krieger, Dave Martindale, Mike Monagan, Mike Sweeney, and Alan Williams.

We owe debts to Carl de Boor, Ron Goldman, Tim Goodman, Tom Lyche, Rich Riesenfeld, and Larry Schumaker — among many others — from whose papers and discussions we have learned so much.

The VAXIMA, MACSYMA and MAPLE symbolic manipulation systems have been extremely useful in this work, and the authors are grateful to Bruce Char for assisting us in using them effectively. All the manuscript materials were prepared on the Berkeley version of UNIX* document-preparation software (troff, eqn, pic,

---

* UNIX is a trademark of AT&T.

tbl, refer), and we wish to thank Ian! Allen, Dan Field, and Randy Goebel for their assistance with these systems. The text preparation was done on Digital Equipment Corporation VAX computers. Those used at the University of Waterloo were donated by DEC through the WATDEC research agreement; those used at the University of California, Berkeley, were purchased through DARPA support.

Finally, we dedicate these efforts to the late Arthur Barsky and to Audrey Barsky; Virginia, Renate, and Robert Bartels; and Clarissa and Jack Beatty.

Richard H. Bartels
John C. Beatty
Brian A. Barsky
(The Killer B's)
Berkeley and Waterloo
1987

Foreword

The design of complex curved shapes has always posed a problem, and the technology employed has changed radically over the last century. In the past, it was a common practice to lay out the design of a ship or aircraft full-size in a suitable room, conventionally the loft, giving rise to the term *lofting*. Curves were generated using mechanical devices such as sweeps (large French curves) or by bending thin laths of metal or wood round pegs or ducks on the loft floor and were drawn by tracing chalk round the laths or scribing on sheets of aluminum. The laths assumed a shape which was both aesthetically pleasing and mechanically sound, being the curve of minimum strain energy, and they were known as *splines,* an East Anglian dialect word.

In lofting, the shape of a design was represented by a physical artifact, the actual layout, and this was vulnerable to damage. It is said that one of the motivations for a mathematical description came from the realization in the Second World War that a bomb near the loft could disrupt or destroy the master definition of an aircraft. The mathematical method adopted was conic lofting: conic sections were well established mathematically so that geometric constructions for drafting the curves from numerical data or for designing the curves *ab initio* to fit prescribed criteria were available. Several textbooks describing these techniques appeared in the 1940s and make fascinating reading today.

During the same period, the notion of the *mathematical spline* was introduced by Schoenberg, largely for the actuarial fitting of life tables. It was derived from the physical spline by observing that, for small deflections, the shape assumed by the physical spline was a piecewise cubic polynomial. In the early 1960s the limitations of conic lofting became apparent in the civil aircraft industry, and mathematical splines were introduced into lofting by Ferguson at Boeing and later by Sabin at the British Aircraft Corporation, using the interpolatory basis. They made one significant change to Schoenberg's approach: the splines were *vector-valued* rather than *scalar-valued*. This was crucial in two senses: it permitted curves and surfaces to be defined in an axis-independent manner, and it allowed curves to be multi-valued, even closed, and to have slopes of 90°. Unfortunately, it also meant that the spline world split into two camps with the approximation theory community concentrating on *functional* approximation and the geometric design community on *shape* approximation, a totally different problem still today deficient in mathematical underpinnings.

With splines back in the repertoire of the geometric modeller, the next important development lay in the use of vector-valued Bernstein polynomials by Bézier at Renault and de Casteljau at Citroën. Their techniques had the important property, missing in any interpolation method, of guaranteeing that smooth shapes would be generated from smooth data. This variation diminishing property is crucial to the approximation and design of shapes and to the confidence of users. From Bézier curves to B-splines was a natural progression, B-splines being the piecewise analog of the Bernstein polynomials.

I was fortunate to participate in the initial investigation of B-splines for computer-aided geometric design with Riesenfeld and later to supervise (over the Arpanet from Norwich!) Barsky's thesis work on Beta-splines. In Schoenberg's original work the B-spline basis had been cast in terms of truncated power series which, whilst convenient for analysis, was numerically troublesome. The simultaneous appearance, at the start of Riesenfeld's research, of papers by de Boor and Cox giving a numerically stable method for computation of the B-spline basis was fortuitous.

Whilst B-splines and related techniques have made desirable properties for CAGD, not the least in providing excellent human interfaces, explaining in mathematical and computational terms just what they are has proved a difficult task (one that has consistently eluded me) meriting a book rather than a chapter. The Killer B's have written such a volume, tested in the heat of the SIGGRAPH Tutorial cauldron, slaying the impenetrable mystique of curve and surface mathematics, and giving us a text which will serve theoretician and practitioner, implementor and user, and benefit the computer graphics community at large.

A. Robin Forrest
University of East Anglia,
Norwich
1987

Foreword

The first task given to computer-aided design (CAD) was to totally define the shape of an already existing object with the help only of figures.

Before that time, most parts of a figure were drawn with straightedge and compass, and the total shape of objects so drawn was a Boolean combination of so-called "analytic volumes," i. e., cubes, cylinders, cones, tori, and spheres. Then, it became rapidly evident that these objects should be completed with free-form or space surfaces, hence the development of parametric spaces.

When the definition of a shape was obtained, it became possible with the help of a computer, to deal with such phenomena as stress, strain, and fluid dynamics.

Before the advent of the computer, the usual practice was: First, offsets of points located on the surface of a handmade model were measured. Next, those points were traced on a drawing board and interpolated by curves generated either by so-called "French curves," or by flexible lathes. Those lines were then transformed into templates and generatrices of a master-model; interpolation was finally performed by highly skilled operators — pattern-makers or plasterers.

The solutions developed for CAD, and then for CAD/CAM, bear a similarity to this tradition. From offsets previously recorded, some curves are defined, which are supposed to lie on the surface; these form a network, the meshes of which are interpolated, generally with the help of an algorithmic process.

The objects to be represented with these methods belong to one of three categories:

- objects which are part of a technical ensemble, the shapes of which influence their efficacy; they have been obtained by tests and trials, and must be copied with great accuracy, say for instance 10^{-4}.

- aesthetic objects.

- objects which are part of a technical ensemble, but the accuracy of which is not very important, for instance no smaller than 5×10^{-4}.

To define the necessary curves, one can choose between two types of solutions: either the curves must run exactly through the recorded points, or a limit can be assigned to the distance between the curves and the points. The first system is accurate, but each segment of a piecewise curve is limited by two adjacent points. The second system yields a smaller number of segments, since each one can take into account more than two points, with the major advantage of reducing the number of patches making a surface, but at the cost of a certain loss of accuracy. Such representations of curves and surfaces are called "splines" or "lathes."

To have some flexibility, different processes for defining splines have been developed, each having its own advantages as well as limitations.

In this book, Messrs. Richard Bartels, John Beatty, and Brian Barsky describe most of those systems, including a deep study of their properties and potentials. In this respect, this book will be extremely helpful for scientists, students, technicians and engineers. Without a doubt, its authors have performed a good job.

Pierre E. Bézier
Paris 1987

Contents

1
Introduction

The most basic output primitives in every computer graphics library are "LineSegment()" and "Polygon()," or their equivalents. These are, of course, sufficient in the sense that any curved line or surface can be arbitrarily well approximated by straight line segments or planar polygons, but in many contexts that is not enough. Such approximations often require large amounts of data to obtain satisfactory smoothness, and they are awkward to manipulate. Then, too, even with the most sophisticated continuous shading models, polygonal techniques can result in visually objectionable images. Mach bands may be apparent at the borders between adjacent polygons, and there is always a telltale angularity to polygonal silhouettes. Hence many modeling systems are augmented by circles, spheres, cylinders, etc., and allow such simple primitives to be combined to form quite complex objects.

There is a substantial class of curves and surfaces, however, that does not display the sort of regularity that makes such modeling convenient. For these, systems using primitives that can themselves be irregularly curved are more natural. Broadly speaking, these are based either on the interpolation or on the approximation of points that are supplied by the user. In either case a curve is defined by piecing together a succession of *curve segments*, and a surface is defined by stitching together a mosaic of *surface patches*; such a *piecewise* approach is taken for reasons of flexibility and generality.

Such mosaics found one of their first important uses in the automobile industry (Plate I), where car bodies offer an obvious example of *free-form* surfaces. The construction of aircraft, turbomachinery, and automobiles, and recent applications in the advertising and animation industries, have become driving forces behind the research into techniques for surface design.

Interpolatory approaches, most commonly based on cubic splines, are perhaps the more easily understood by users, although less well suited to real-time manipulations. We will see that they lack some of the desirable properties possessed by most approximation techniques. In any case they can provide a convenient means of generating an initial curve or surface from which one can compute other representations based on approximation.

Early work by Coons [Coons64, Coons67] and Bézier [Bézier70, Bézier77] introduced the use of nonlinear parametric polynomial representations for the segments and patches from which we assemble piecewise curves and surfaces. Bézier's work also introduced the techniques of approximating user-specified points, called *control vertices*, rather than interpolating them. We will discuss Bézier techniques in the general context of using *B-splines*, which were introduced to computer graphics more recently by Riesenfeld [Riesenfeld73, Gordon/Reisenfeld74] and are discussed extensively in [de Boor78] and [Schumaker81].

Parametric B-spline curves have many advantages. Among them is the ability to control the degree of continuity at the joints between adjacent curve segments, and at the borders between surface patches, independent of the order of the segments or the number of control vertices being approximated. However, the notion of parametric first or second degree continuity at joints does not always correspond to intuition or to a physically desired effect. For piecewise cubic curves and bicubic surfaces these parametric continuity constraints can be replaced by the more meaningful requirements of continuous unit tangent and curvature vectors, an observation made by [Manning74] and [Barsky81a] among others. Doing so introduces certain constrained discontinuities in the first and second parametric derivatives which are expressed in terms of *bias* and *tension* parameters called β_1 and β_2 in [Barsky81a, Barsky87a]. These provide additional means of locally controlling shape and give rise to Beta-spline curves and surfaces, which we will also discuss.

We end by providing some applications of the material covered to give some examples of how splines have been recently put to use in computer graphics.

1.1 General References

For a general introduction to computer graphics that mentions splines briefly see [Foley/van Dam82] or [Newman/Sproull79]. Foley and van Dam discuss Hermite, cubic Bézier, and cubic B-spline curves and surfaces. They use matrix notation for compactness. Newman and Sproull discuss Bézier and uniform B-spline curves. In both cases the treatment is short and prescriptive, as befits introductory texts.

A general survey of curve and surface representations may be found in [Rogers/Adams76]. A succinct development is generally provided, together with an example or two. The text was not typeset, and as a result the book is often hard to read. Program code is supplied in many cases, but unfortunately in BASIC.

For a work oriented somewhat more toward computer-aided design and manufacturing, [Faux/Pratt79] contains a good treatment of basic analytic and differential geometry and introductions to most of the standard curve and surface techniques, although the treatment of B-splines is again rather summary. More recently [Mortenson85] has appeared, which covers the fundamentals of geometric and analytic properties not only of surfaces but also of solids. It provides a recent introduction to the techniques of solid-model construction.

For an excellent and comprehensive treatment of B-splines from the numerical analyst's point of view, [de Boor78] has served as the standard reference for close to a decade. The material in this book is accessible to anyone with a decent mathematical background willing to read carefully. All the basic algorithms are presented in FORTRAN, and are available on magnetic tape from The International Mathematical and Statistical Library, Inc., in Houston, Texas.

Finally, [Schumaker81] provides an excellent and extensive treatment of splines in great generality, accessible to those with an advanced grounding in mathematical analysis.

There is a wealth of other material we would have liked to cover, were it not for the constraints of time and space. Perhaps foremost among these are the *rational splines*, which are (roughly speaking) a quotient of two splines. A key advantage of this form is the ability to represent conic curves and quadric surfaces, such as cylinders, spheres, and cones. Moreover, the free-form curves and surfaces we discuss are all a special case of the rational splines since the constant function 1 is a prefectly respectable spline, and can be used as the denominator in a rational representation. Another advantage is that the rational formulation is invariant under projective transformations, such as perspective projection.

A good introduction to "nonuniform" rational B-splines, often referred to as *NURB*'s, may be found in [Tiller83]. Thorough understanding of rational splines requires a familiarity with homogeneous coordinates and projective geometry, a detailed treatment of which may be found in [Penna/Patterson86].

2
Preliminaries

It is usually convenient to represent a two-dimensional curve parametrically as

$$\mathbf{Q}(\bar{u}) \;=\; (X(\bar{u}),\, Y(\bar{u}))$$

where $X(\bar{u})$ and $Y(\bar{u})$ are each single-valued functions of the parameter $\bar{u}$. (The significance of the bar over the parameter will be explained shortly.) $X(\bar{u})$ and $Y(\bar{u})$ yield the x- and y-coordinates, respectively, of a point on the curve in question for any value of $\bar{u}$.

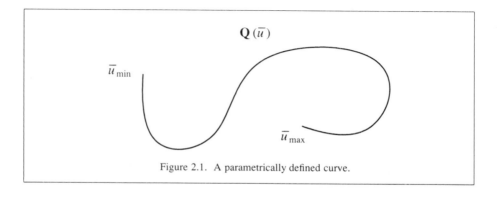

Figure 2.1. A parametrically defined curve.

Although polynomials are computationally efficient and easy to work with, it is not usually possible to define a satisfactory curve using single polynomials for $X(\bar{u})$ and $Y(\bar{u})$. Instead it is customary to break the curve into some number of pieces called *segments*, each defined by separate polynomials, and join the segments together to form a *piecewise polynomial* curve. Thus, as the parameter $\bar{u}$ varies between some initial minimum value $\bar{u}_{\min}$ and some final maximum value $\bar{u}_{\max}$ to define the curve, certain distinguished values of $\bar{u}$, called *knots*, will be encountered that correspond to the *joints* between the polynomial segments. The sequence of knot values is required to be nondecreasing, so that

$$\bar{u}_0 \leq \cdots \leq \bar{u}_j = \bar{u}_{\min} \leq \cdots \leq \bar{u}_\ell = \bar{u}_{\max} \leq \cdots \leq \bar{u}_{\text{last}}.$$

(Note that some of the knots may lie to the left or the right of the range of parameter values defining the curve. Reasons for permitting this will become clear in Chapter 4.) The sequence of knot values

$$\bar{u}_0, \cdots, \bar{u}_j, \cdots, \bar{u}_\ell, \cdots, \bar{u}_{\text{last}}$$

is called the *knot sequence* or the *knot vector*.

Thus the parametric functions $X(\bar{u})$ and $Y(\bar{u})$ are each composed of polynomial pieces, the first covering the interval of $\bar{u}$ ranging from $\bar{u}_j$ to the next distinct knot to the right, the second covering values from this next knot to the subsequent distinct knot further to the right, and so on. Usually $X(\bar{u})$ and $Y(\bar{u})$ are required to satisfy some continuity constraints at the joints between successive polynomial segments; if the 0th through d^{th} derivatives are everywhere continuous (in particular, at the joints), then X and Y are said to be C^d continuous. In Chapter 5 we will discover that issues of continuity can be arranged by admitting *multiple knots*; that is, by letting successive members of the knot sequence be equal, which causes certain of the intervals $[\bar{u}_i, \bar{u}_{i+1})$ to be vacuous. In contrast, sometimes we will assume that the knots are all distinct and a constant distance apart,

$$\bar{u}_{i+1} = \bar{u}_i + \Delta.$$

This is called a *uniform knot sequence*. The frequent choice of convenience will be $\bar{u}_i = i$, for which, clearly, $\Delta = 1$.

It will often be simpler to express X and Y on the interval from $\bar{u}_i$ to $\bar{u}_{i+1}$ as functions of the local parametrization given by

$$u = \frac{\bar{u} - \bar{u}_i}{\bar{u}_{i+1} - \bar{u}_i}$$

rather than as functions of $\bar{u}$. The reparametrization is easily accomplished by substitution, and we will always indicate this local reparametrization in any formula in which it is used by omitting the bar above the u. The presence of the bar will indicate that we are referring to a single parametrization of the entire curve. The absence of the bar indicates we are parametrizing a segment of the curve from the left end of its corresponding knot interval. Thus

$$Y_i(u) = u^2$$

and

$$Y_i(\bar{u}) = \left[\frac{\bar{u} - \bar{u}_i}{\bar{u}_{i+1} - \bar{u}_i} \right]^2$$

are equivalent, each being a reparametrization of the other on the interval from $\bar{u}_i$ to $\bar{u}_{i+1}$.

There are a variety of ways to define a specific curve. Each can be broadly classified as being based on ''interpolation'' or on ''approximation.'' In both cases one begins by specifying a sequence of points, which we will represent in illustrations by a circle ''•'' or a ''+'' sign. In the case of interpolation the curve is required to pass through data points, $\mathbf{P}_i$, in sequence order as shown in Figure 2.2. For those techniques based on approximation the curve is required only to pass ''near'' data points, $\mathbf{V}_i$, in the order shown in Figure 2.3. Exactly what ''near'' means depends on the particular approximation technique used.

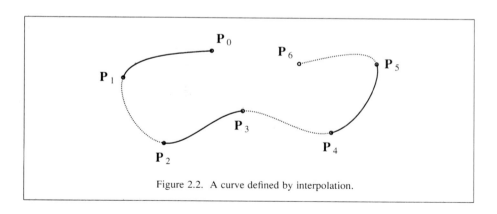

Figure 2.2. A curve defined by interpolation.

In either interpolation or approximation, moving the points alters the curve. We will concentrate on a specific method of approximation, to be introduced in Chapter 4, for which the computational cost of constructing the curve is very low and for which only a portion of the curve changes whenever a single point is moved.

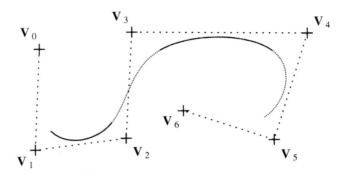

Figure 2.3. An example of a curve that approximates a sequence of points, represented here by "+" signs. The lightly dotted line connecting the points indicates the order in which they are to be approximated. The solid and heavily dotted curves represent distinct curve *segments*. Each is a single parametric cubic. The point at which two successive segments meet is called a *joint*. The value of the parameter $\bar{u}$ which corresponds to a joint is called a *knot*.

3

Hermite and Cubic Spline Interpolation

Suppose that we have $m + 1$ data points $\mathbf{P}_0, \ldots, \mathbf{P}_m$ through which we wish to draw a curve such as that shown in Figure 3.1 (in which $m = 6$).

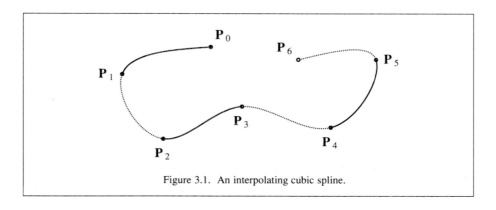

Figure 3.1. An interpolating cubic spline.

Each successive pair of data points is connected by a distinct curve segment. The ith segment runs from $\mathbf{P}_i$ to $\mathbf{P}_{i+1}$, and we will assume that the parameter $\bar{u}$ runs correspondingly from the knot $\bar{u}_i$ to the knot $\bar{u}_{i+1}$ to generate this segment. This corresponds to the knot sequence and parameter range outlined in Chapter 2 with the special choices $\bar{u}_0 = \bar{u}_j = \bar{u}_{\min}$ and $\bar{u}_{\max} = \bar{u}_\ell = \bar{u}_m = \bar{u}_{\text{last}}$. Since each such segment $Q_i(\bar{u})$ is represented parametrically as $(X_i(\bar{u}), Y_i(\bar{u}))$, we are really concerned with how the $X_i(\bar{u})$ and $Y_i(\bar{u})$ are determined by the points

$$\mathbf{P}_i = (x_i, y_i).$$

In general, the x-coordinates $X(\bar{u})$ of points on a curve are determined solely by the x-coordinates $x_0, \ldots, x_m$ of the data points, and similarly $Y(\bar{u})$ is determined solely by the y-coordinates of the data points. Since both $X(\bar{u})$ and $Y(\bar{u})$ are treated in the same way we will discuss only $Y(\bar{u})$; indeed, to obtain curves in three dimensions we simply define a $Z(\bar{u})$ as well and let $\mathbf{Q}_i(u)$ be given by $(X_i(u), Y_i(u), Z_i(u))$.

For ease of computation we will limit ourselves to the use of polynomials in defining $X_i(u)$, $Y_i(u)$ and $Z_i(u)$. Indeed cubic polynomials usually provide sufficient flexibility for many applications at reasonable cost. For the curve in Figure 3.1, then, $Y(\bar{u})$ is shown in Figure 3.2.

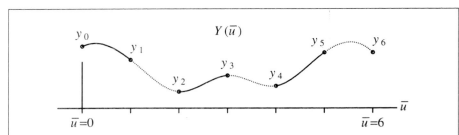

Figure 3.2. $Y(\bar{u})$ for the curve shown in Figure 3.1 above. In this example we have rather arbitrarily chosen to use uniform knot spacing, so that the knot sequence is (0,1,2,3,4,5,6).

It will be easiest to continue the discussion by reparametrizing each segment Y_i separately by substituting u for $\bar{u}$ as was described earlier. This means that $u = \bar{u}_i - i$ for the knot sequence given in Figure 3.2. Each $Y_i(u)$ is a cubic polynomial in the parameter u. We know two things in particular about

$$Y_i(u) = a_i + b_i u + c_i u^2 + d_i u^3,$$

namely that

$$Y_i(0) = y_i \quad = a_i$$

$$Y_i(1) = y_{i+1} \quad = a_i + b_i + c_i + d_i.$$

Because we have four coefficients to determine, we need two other constraints to completely determine a particular $Y_i(u)$. One easy way to do this is to simply pick, arbitrarily, first derivatives D_i of $Y(u)$ at each knot $\bar{u}_i$, so that

$$Y_i^{(1)}(0) = D_i \quad = b_i$$

$$Y_i^{(1)}(1) = D_{i+1} \quad = b_i + 2c_i + 3d_i \ .$$

These four equations can be solved symbolically, once and for all, to yield

$$a_i = y_i$$

$$b_i = D_i$$

$$\tag{3.1}$$

$$c_i = 3(y_{i+1} - y_i) - 2D_i - D_{i+1}$$

$$d_i = 2(y_i - y_{i+1}) + D_i + D_{i+1} \ .$$

Since we use D_i as the derivative at the left end of the ith segment (i.e., as $Y_i^{(1)}(0)$) and at the right end of the $(i-1)^{th}$ segment (as $Y_{i-1}^{(1)}(1)$), $Y(u)$ has a continuous first derivative.

This technique is called *Hermite interpolation*. It can be generalized to higher-order polynomials.

How are the D_i specified? One possibility is to compute them automatically, perhaps by fitting a parabola through y_{i-1}, y_i, and y_{i+1}, and using its derivative at y_i as D_i; arbitrary values (such as 0) can be used at the end points [Kochanek/ et al.82]. Or one can use for D_i the y component of a weighted average of the vector from P_{i-1} to P_i and the vector from P_{i+1} to P_i [Kochanek/Bartels84]. Or the user may specify derivative vectors directly. Some of these possibilities are discussed later in Chapter 21.

It is possible to arrange that successive segments match second as well as first derivatives at joints, using only cubic polynomials. Suppose, as above, that we want to interpolate the $(m+1)$ points $P_0, \ldots, P_m$ by such a curve. Each of the m segments $Y_0(u), \ldots, Y_{m-1}(u)$ is a cubic polynomial determined by four coefficients. Hence we have $4m$ unknown values to determine. At each of the $(m-1)$ interior knots $\bar{u}_1, \ldots, \bar{u}_{m-1}$ (where two segments meet) we have four conditions:

$$Y_{i-1}(1) = y_i \ , \quad Y_{i-1}^{(1)}(1) = Y_i^{(1)}(0)$$

$$Y_i(0) = y_i \ , \quad Y_{i-1}^{(2)}(1) = Y_i^{(2)}(0) \ .$$

Since we also require that

$$Y_0(0) = y_0$$

$$Y_{m-1}(1) = y_m$$

we have a total of $4(m - 1) + 2 = 4m - 2$ conditions from which to determine our $4m$ unknowns. Thus, we need two more conditions. These may be chosen in a variety of ways. A common choice is simply to require that the second derivatives at the endpoints $\bar{u}_0$ and $\bar{u}_m$ both be zero; these conditions yield what is called a *natural cubic spline*. Figure 3.7 is actually a natural cubic spline.

3.1 Practical Considerations — Computing Natural Cubic Splines

We do not need to solve $4m$ equations directly — the problem can be simplified. Notice that a natural cubic spline is actually a special case of Hermite interpolation; we may simply choose first derivative vectors so as to match second derivatives as well. If we can compute the needed D_i, we have already obtained definitions of the a_i, b_i, c_i and d_i in terms of the D_i.

Thus at each internal joint we want to choose D_i so that

$$Y_{i-1}^{(2)}(1) = Y_i^{(2)}(0)$$

or

$$2c_{i-1} + 6d_{i-1} = 2c_i .$$

Substituting in our earlier solutions (3.1) for c_{i-1}, d_{i-1} and c_i, we have

$$2[3(y_i - y_{i-1}) - 2D_{i-1} - D_i] + 6[2(y_{i-1} - y_i) + D_{i-1} + D_i]$$

$$= 2[3(y_{i+1} - y_i) - 2D_i - D_{i+1}].$$

Simplifying, and moving the unknowns to the left, we have

$$D_{i-1} + 4D_i + D_{i+1} = 3(y_{i+1} - y_{i-1}). \tag{3.2}$$

Since there are $m - 1$ internal joints, there are $m - 1$ such equations. Requiring that the second derivative at the beginning of the curve be zero implies that

$$2c_0 = 0$$

$$2[3(y_1 - y_0) - 2D_0 - D_1] = 0$$

$$2D_0 + D_1 = 3(y_1 - y_0).$$

Requiring that the second derivative at the end of the curve be zero similarly results in

$$D_{m-1} + 2D_m \;=\; 3(y_m - y_{m-1}).$$

We now have $m+1$ equations in $m+1$ unknowns. Representing them in matrix form we have

$$
\begin{bmatrix}
2 & 1 & & & & & \\
1 & 4 & 1 & & & & \\
& 1 & 4 & 1 & & & \\
& & 1 & 4 & 1 & & \\
& & & \cdot & \cdot & \cdot & \cdot \\
& & & & 1 & 4 & 1 \\
& & & & & 1 & 2
\end{bmatrix}
\begin{bmatrix}
D_0 \\ D_1 \\ \cdot \\ \cdot \\ \cdot \\ \cdot \\ D_m
\end{bmatrix}
=
\begin{bmatrix}
3(y_1-y_0) \\ 3(y_2-y_0) \\ \cdot \\ \cdot \\ \cdot \\ 3(y_m-y_{m-2}) \\ 3(y_m-y_{m-1})
\end{bmatrix}.
$$

Beginning at the top, the first 1 in each row is eliminated using the row immediately above and the diagonal is scaled:

$$\gamma_0 \leftarrow 1/2$$

for $i \leftarrow 1$ **step** 1 **until** $m-1$ **do**

$$\gamma_i \leftarrow 1/(4-\gamma_{i-1})$$

endfor

$$\gamma_m \leftarrow 1/(2-\gamma_{m-1}).$$

Corresponding operations are carried out on the right-hand-side entries; e.g., for the y components shown above:

$$\delta_0 \leftarrow 3(y_1-y_0)\gamma_0$$

for $i \leftarrow 1$ **step** 1 **until** $m-1$ **do**

$$\delta_i \leftarrow (3(y_{i+1}-y_{i-1})-\delta_{i-1})\gamma_i$$

endfor

$$\delta_m \leftarrow (3(y_m-y_{m-1})-\delta_{m-1})\gamma_m.$$

The result of this *forward elimination* process will be

$$
\begin{bmatrix}
1 & \gamma_0 & & & & & \\
 & 1 & \gamma_1 & & & & \\
 & & 1 & \gamma_2 & & & \\
 & & & \cdot & \cdot & \cdot & \\
 & & & & \gamma_{m-2} & & \\
 & & & & 1 & \gamma_{m-1} & \\
 & & & & & 1 &
\end{bmatrix}
\begin{bmatrix}
D_0 \\ D_1 \\ \cdot \\ \cdot \\ \cdot \\ \cdot \\ D_m
\end{bmatrix}
=
\begin{bmatrix}
\delta_0 \\ \delta_1 \\ \cdot \\ \cdot \\ \cdot \\ \cdot \\ \delta_m
\end{bmatrix}
.
$$

This directly yields the value of D_m, and it is then a simple matter to solve successively for $D_{m-1}, \ldots, D_0$ in a process of *backward substitution*:

$$D_m \leftarrow \delta_m$$

for $i \leftarrow m-1$ **step** -1 **until** 0 **do**

$$D_i \leftarrow \delta_i - \gamma_i D_{i+1}$$

endfor .

The multiplicative factors γ_i that accomplish the forward substitution need only be computed once. The δ_i's must be computed and the backward substitution performed separately for each coordinate. When a data point is moved, the values $\delta_j, \ldots, \delta_m$ must be recomputed and the entire backward substitution again performed.

3.2 Other End Conditions For Cubic Interpolating Splines

There are many other ways in which to determine the additional two constraints needed to define a C^2 continuous interpolating cubic spline fully. These conditions are most commonly applied to the ends of a curve, hence the name *end conditions*; the natural cubic splines offer an example of this. However, all that is really necessary is to provide the missing two conditions. Any two linear equations that are independent of those provided by the interpolation conditions could be used. They could involve data points or derivatives interior to the curve as well as at the ends. Whatever conditions are used, they will have some influence over the shape of the entire curve. For example, instead of fixing the second derivatives at the first and last knot to zero, we may fix the first derivatives there to be zero.

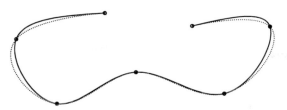

Figure 3.3. The solid line is a natural cubic interpolating spline; that is, the second parametric derivatives at the ends of the solid curve are zero. For the dotted curve the first derivatives at the ends have been set to zero instead.

Another possibility, which de Boor calls the *not-a-knot* condition [de Boor78], is to require C^3 continuity at the second and next-to-last knots u_1 and u_{m-1}. In effect the first two segments are a single polynomial, as are the last two.

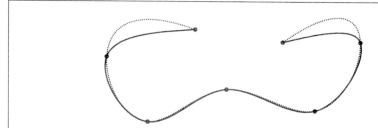

Figure 3.4. The solid line is a natural cubic interpolating spline. For the dotted curve, C^3 continuity has been forced between the first and second segments, and between the last and the next-to-last segments.

Yet another alternative, suggested by Forsythe, Malcolm and Moler [Forsythe/ et al.77], is to use the third derivatives of the cubic polynomials that interpolate the first and last four points as the third derivatives of the first and last segments.

One might allow the user to explicitly supply any two of the first, second, or third derivative vectors at the ends. In any case, we can construct and solve a set of equations very much as we did for the natural cubic splines. Additional discussion of how this can be done, and algorithms, are given in Chapter 4 of [Forsythe/et al.77] and in Chapter 4 of [de Boor78]. For a uniform knot vector, and indeed for any reasonable strictly increasing sequence of knots, these equations are well conditioned and can be solved easily and accurately.

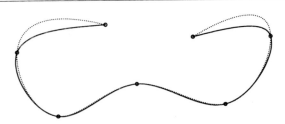

Figure 3.5. The solid line is a natural cubic interpolating spline. For the dotted curve the third derivative of the polynomial that interpolates the first four points is used as the (constant) third derivative of the first segment, and similarly for the last segment.

3.3   Knot Spacing

Although the end conditions discussed above affect the entire curve, their principal influence is felt at the endpoints. Gross changes to a curve's shape can be made anywhere, without moving the interpolation points, by varying the knot spacing. (See Figure 3.6.)

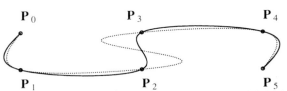

Figure 3.6. The solid line is a natural cubic interpolating spline in which the knots are spaced one unit apart. Unit knot spacing is used also in the dotted curve except for the parametric interval corresponding to the segment between P_2 and P_3, for which the knots are spaced four units apart.

With the single exception of Figure 3.6, we have used a uniform knot sequence in defining the interpolating cubic spline curves discussed above. The knot vector for the solid curve in Figure 3.6 is

0, 1, 2, 3, 4, 5

while the dotted curve interpolates the same data points, but for the knot vector

0, 1, 2, 6, 7, 8.

Thus knot spacing can be used to influence shape; the more difficult question is how that influence can be controlled intuitively.

Uniform knot spacing is one obvious way to define a knot sequence. The Euclidean distance between data points is a second natural choice for the length of the parametric interval over which u varies in defining a segment.

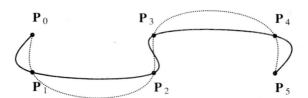

Figure 3.7. The solid line in the above figure is a natural cubic interpolating spline in which the knots are spaced a unit apart. In the case of the dotted curve, the knots corresponding to two successive data points differ in value by the Euclidean distance separating the two points.

3.4 Closed Curves

It is sometimes useful to generate closed curves such as in Figure 3.8. In this case, equation (3.2) applies at each of the m points, with the caveat that indices must be computed modulo $m+1$. The system of equations that results looks a little different:

$$
\begin{bmatrix}
4 & 1 & & & & & & 1 \\
1 & 4 & 1 & & & & & \\
& 1 & 4 & 1 & & & & \\
& & 1 & 4 & 1 & & & \\
& & & \cdot & \cdot & \cdot & \cdot & \\
& & & & & 1 & 4 & 1 \\
1 & & & & & & 1 & 4
\end{bmatrix}
\begin{bmatrix}
D_0 \\
D_1 \\
\cdot \\
\cdot \\
\cdot \\
\cdot \\
D_m
\end{bmatrix}
=
\begin{bmatrix}
3(y_1-y_m) \\
3(y_2-y_0) \\
\cdot \\
\cdot \\
\cdot \\
3(y_m-y_{m-2}) \\
3(y_0-y_{m-1})
\end{bmatrix}
$$

Basically one solves this system as one solved for the D_i for an open curve. During forward elimination, however, it is necessary to compute and save nonzero values for entries in the rightmost column and to successively cancel the leftmost nonzero value in the bottom row. The analogous change must be made to the back substitution process as well.

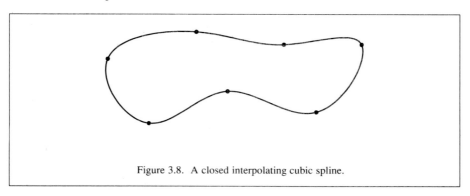

Figure 3.8. A closed interpolating cubic spline.

4

A Simple Approximation Technique — Uniform Cubic B-splines

Later we will develop B-spline curves and surfaces in their full generality. In this section we will introduce them by looking at a simpler and particularly useful special class of B-splines called the *uniform cubic B-splines*. As the name implies, we make use of parametric cubic polynomials on a uniform knot sequence: specifically, on a knot sequence composed of successive integers.

A particular property of the B-spline curves is *local control*, by which we mean that altering the position of a single data point causes only a part of the curve to change. These points will be called *control vertices* since they are usually connected by straight lines to form the vertices and edges of a *control graph* or *control polygon*. While these data points may be interpolated in some constructive techniques (e.g., in Hermite interpolation or in the use of Catmull-Rom splines), we will usually discuss control vertices in situations of approximation rather than interpolation. Figure 4.1 gives the appropriate picture.

Local control makes it possible to modify part of a curve (or surface) without affecting other portions that are already satisfactory, which is often useful in geometric design and modeling. An added benefit of local control is that it minimizes the work required to recompute a curve after a control vertex has been moved since only a small part of the curve has changed.

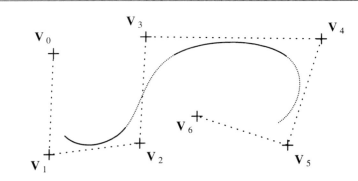

Figure 4.1. An example of a curve defined by a sequence of *control vertices*, represented here by "+" signs, near which the curve passes. The lightly dotted line connecting the control vertices forms the *control polygon*.

4.1   Simple Preliminaries — Linear B-splines

The way in which local control is obtained is most easily explained by considering first a *piecewise linear* interpolation of the control vertices. Consider the "curve" shown in Figure 4.2.

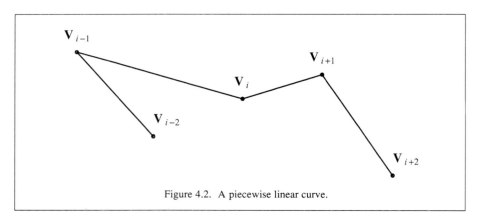

Figure 4.2. A piecewise linear curve.

If we represent the segments of this curve in the obvious way we have

$$
\begin{aligned}
\mathbf{Q}_{i-1}(u) &= (X_{i-1}(u), Y_{i-1}(u)) \\
&= (1-u)\,\mathbf{V}_{i-2} + u\,\mathbf{V}_{i-1} \quad \text{for } u = (\overline{u}-\overline{u}_{i-1})/(\overline{u}_i - \overline{u}_{i-1}) \\
\mathbf{Q}_i(u) &= (X_i(u), Y_i(u)) \\
&= (1-u)\,\mathbf{V}_{i-1} + u\,\mathbf{V}_i \quad \text{for } u = (\overline{u}-\overline{u}_i)/(\overline{u}_{i+1}-\overline{u}_i)
\end{aligned}
$$

$$\mathbf{Q}_{i+1}(u) = (X_{i+1}(u), Y_{i+1}(u))$$
$$= (1-u)\mathbf{V}_i + u\mathbf{V}_{i+1} \qquad \text{for } u = (\bar{u} - \bar{u}_{i+1})/(\bar{u}_{i+2} - \bar{u}_{i+1})$$
$$\mathbf{Q}_{i+2}(u) = (X_{i+2}(u), Y_{i+2}(u))$$
$$= (1-u)\mathbf{V}_{i+1} + u\mathbf{V}_{i+2} \qquad \text{for } u = (\bar{u} - \bar{u}_{i+2})/(\bar{u}_{i+3} - \bar{u}_{i+2})$$

where

$$X_{i-1}(u) = (1-u)x_{i-2} + u\,x_{i-1}$$
$$Y_{i-1}(u) = (1-u)y_{i-2} + u\,y_{i-1}$$

$$X_i(u) = (1-u)x_{i-1} + u\,x_i$$
$$Y_i(u) = (1-u)y_{i-1} + u\,y_i$$

$$X_{i+1}(u) = (1-u)x_i + u\,x_{i+1}$$
$$Y_{i+1}(u) = (1-u)y_i + u\,y_{i+1}$$

$$X_{i+2}(u) = (1-u)x_{i+1} + u\,x_{i+2}$$
$$Y_{i+2}(u) = (1-u)y_{i+1} + u\,y_{i+2}.$$

Altering $\mathbf{V}_i$ clearly affects only the two segments $\mathbf{Q}_i(u)$ and $\mathbf{Q}_{i+1}(u)$ which are adjacent to it: $\mathbf{V}_i$ does not appear in the formulas for any other segments. Let us represent our piecewise linear curve so as to isolate the individual influence of each separate control vertex. Doing this will make straightforward the generalization to higher-order, smoother, piecewise polynomial curves.

If we plot $Y(\bar{u})$ as a function of $\bar{u}$, and represent the contribution of y_i to $Y(\bar{u})$ by a dashed line, we obtain Figure 4.3.

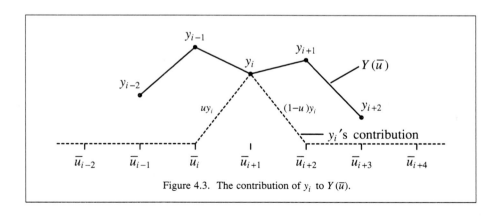

Figure 4.3. The contribution of y_i to $Y(\bar{u})$.

Notice that this contribution is zero both to the left of $\bar{u}_i$ and to the right of $\bar{u}_{i+2}$. Similarly, the contribution of y_{i-1} is shown in Figure 4.4.

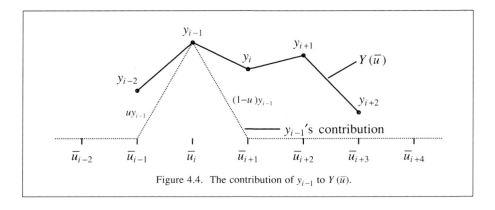

Figure 4.4. The contribution of y_{i-1} to $Y(\overline{u})$.

Plotting these two *hat functions* together gives us, in Figure 4.5, a graphical representation of the fact that $Y_i(u) = (1-u)y_{i-1} + u\,y_i$. (For the sake of clarity we will stop extending these hat functions to the left and right by zero when we draw them because these extensions would all be drawn on top of one another).

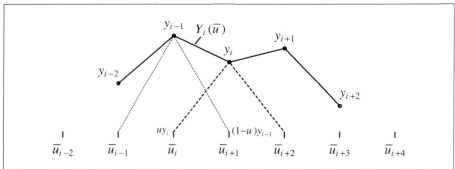

Figure 4.5. A simultaneous look at the contributions of y_{i-1} and y_i to the curve in general, and to $Y_i(\overline{u})$ in particular.

It is useful to think of y_{i-1} and y_i as each *scaling* a corresponding *unit hat function* (see below) whose maximum height is one. These hat functions are all translations of one another. It is also useful to think of y_{i-1} and y_i as each *being weighted by* a corresponding unit hat function. We make the distinction between *weighting* and *scaling* to emphasize that the y's can have any value: positive, negative, or zero. As such, they act like scale factors. The hat functions, on the other hand, are designed to have only a nonnegative value for any value of $\overline{u}$ and, as such, they act like weights.

As $\bar{u}$ increases from $\bar{u}_{i-1}$, the contribution of y_{i-1} grows from nothing at $\bar{u} = \bar{u}_{i-1}$, peaks at $\bar{u} = \bar{u}_i$, and dies away to nothing again at $\bar{u} = \bar{u}_{i+1}$. The contribution of y_i is similar on the interval $\bar{u}_i \leq \bar{u} < \bar{u}_{i+2}$. More profoundly, we have seen that $\mathbf{Q}(\bar{u})$ is entirely determined by $\mathbf{V}_{i-1}$ and $\mathbf{V}_i$ alone in the interval $\bar{u}_i \leq \bar{u} < \bar{u}_{i+1}$. In this interval $Y(\bar{u})$ is just a weighted average of y_{i-1} and y_i, namely

$$Y_i(\bar{u}) = \left[\frac{\bar{u}_{i+1} - \bar{u}}{\bar{u}_{i+1} - \bar{u}_i} \right] y_{i-1} + \left[\frac{\bar{u} - \bar{u}_i}{\bar{u}_{i+1} - \bar{u}_i} \right] y_i$$

$$= (1 - u) y_{i-1} + u\, y_i .$$

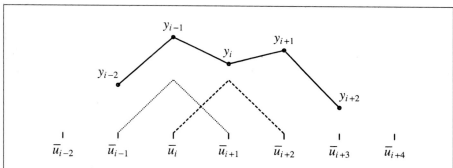

Figure 4.6. Multiplying the two unit (height one) hat functions shown here by y_{i-1} and y_i yields the scaled hat functions shown in Figure 4.5.

If we call the "dotted" unit hat function $B_{i-1}(\bar{u})$ and the "dashed" unit hat function $B_i(\bar{u})$ (to be compatible with later material we name a hat function after the knot at its left extremity), then the line segment attaching y_{i-1} to y_i may be written as

$$Y_i(\bar{u}) = y_{i-1} B_{i-1}(\bar{u}) + y_i B_i(\bar{u}) \quad \text{for } \bar{u}_i \leq \bar{u} < \bar{u}_{i+1} \tag{4.1}$$

where

$$B_i(\bar{u}) = \begin{cases} \dfrac{\bar{u} - \bar{u}_i}{\bar{u}_{i+1} - \bar{u}_i} & \bar{u}_i \leq \bar{u} < \bar{u}_{i+1} \\[2ex] \dfrac{\bar{u}_{i+2} - \bar{u}}{\bar{u}_{i+2} - \bar{u}_{i+1}} & \bar{u}_{i+1} \leq \bar{u} < \bar{u}_{i+2} . \end{cases} \tag{4.2}$$

We can represent the other segments of our piecewise linear curve in the same way; equation (4.1) is quite general. In Figure 4.7 we show all the hat functions

$B_{i-2}(\overline{u})$, ..., $B_{i+2}(\overline{u})$ that define our example "curve." Depending on the point of view we wish to take, we may speak of (4.3) as a *linear combination* of the functions B_i, or as a *weighted sum* of the control vertices V_i. For any particular i, equation (4.3) reduces to equation (4.1) since all the hat functions except $B_{i-1}(\overline{u})$ and $B_i(\overline{u})$ are zero inside the interval from $\overline{u}_i$ to $\overline{u}_{i+1}$. With enough hat functions, we can represent any piecewise linear curve in this way. The unit hat functions $B_i(\overline{u})$ are called *basis functions* for this reason. We may now turn our argument around: any particular vertex V_i contributes to the curve we are defining only where $B_i(\overline{u})$ is nonzero. Since $B_i(\overline{u})$ is nonzero only over the two successive intervals $[\overline{u}_i,\overline{u}_{i+1})$ and $[\overline{u}_{i+1},\overline{u}_{i+2})$, the actual position of V_i can influence only the two corresponding segments $Q_i(\overline{u})$ and $Q_{i+1}(\overline{u})$ of the curve. The result is local control.

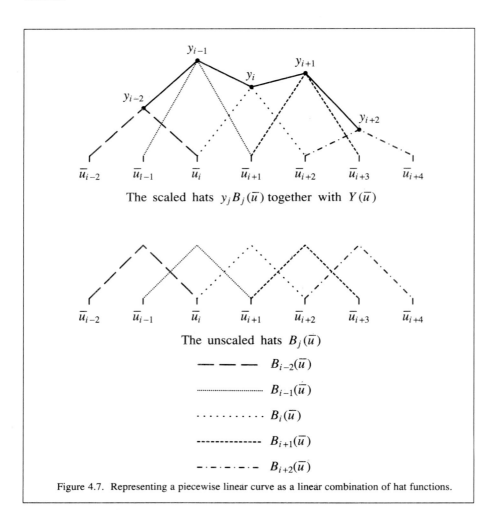

Figure 4.7. Representing a piecewise linear curve as a linear combination of hat functions.

The entire curve can now be written as

$$\mathbf{Q}(\overline{u}) = \sum_i \mathbf{V}_i B_i(\overline{u}) = \sum_i (x_i B_i(\overline{u}),\, y_i B_i(\overline{u}))\,. \tag{4.3}$$

Notice that we have made use of the half-open intervals $[\overline{u}_i, \overline{u}_{i+1})$ and $[\overline{u}_{i+1}, \overline{u}_{i+2})$ so that $\mathbf{Q}_i(\overline{u})$ defines the curve for values of $\overline{u}$ up to but not including $\overline{u}_{i+1}$ because the first interval is open at the right. $\mathbf{Q}_{i+1}(\overline{u})$ then takes over at $\overline{u}_{i+1}$ itself because the second interval is closed at the left.

The hat functions that we have introduced are continuous, although their derivatives usually have jumps at knots (the technical term is C^0 continuous). Consequently, when we use them to weight control vertices and sum them using equation (4.3) we obtain a curve that is continuous, but whose first derivative vector may be discontinuous at knots: a piecewise linear curve, as we knew from the beginning.

4.2   Uniform Cubic B-splines

Our real objective, of course, is to define curves like the one in FIgure 4.8 by assembling pieces that are curved rather than straight. As in Chapter 3, and for the same reasons, we choose to consider piecewise cubic curves.

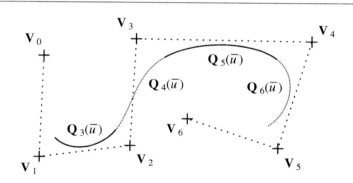

Figure 4.8. The curve shown is constructed from cubic segments so as to approximate the indicated vertices smoothly. The reason for numbering the curve segments as shown will become clear later.

The technique we are now developing does not, in general, interpolate the control vertices — that is a special property of the piecewise linear curves we have considered. Instead, each sequence of control vertices defines a curve that "passes near" those vertices. As before, we may restrict our attention to a single coordinate such as $Y(\bar{u})$, as shown in Figure 4.9.

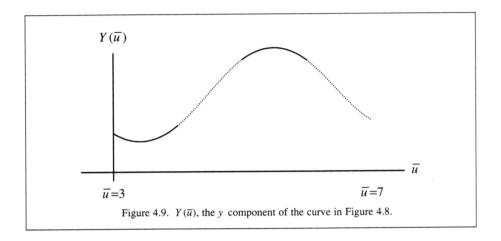

Figure 4.9. $Y(\bar{u})$, the y component of the curve in Figure 4.8.

We focus on piecewise cubic polynomial curves assembled from cubic polynomials $X_i(u)$ and $Y_i(u)$ that have positional, first derivative and second derivative continuity (C^2 continuity) at the joints between successive segments, so that they satisfy the equations

$$\mathbf{Q}_{i-1}(\bar{u}_i) \;=\; \mathbf{Q}_i(\bar{u}_i) \tag{4.4}$$

$$\mathbf{Q}_{i-1}^{(1)}(\bar{u}_i) \;=\; \mathbf{Q}_i^{(1)}(\bar{u}_i) \tag{4.5}$$

$$\mathbf{Q}_{i-1}^{(2)}(\bar{u}_i) \;=\; \mathbf{Q}_i^{(2)}(\bar{u}_i). \tag{4.6}$$

In particular, this implies that

$$Y_{i-1}(\bar{u}_i) \;=\; Y_i(\bar{u}_i)$$

$$Y_{i-1}^{(1)}(\bar{u}_i) \;=\; Y_i^{(1)}(\bar{u}_i)$$

$$Y_{i-1}^{(2)}(\bar{u}_i) \;=\; Y_i^{(2)}(\bar{u}_i)$$

and similarly for $X(\bar{u})$. We can achieve the desired continuity if the basis functions with which we define $X(\bar{u})$ and $Y(\bar{u})$ are themselves C^2 continuous piecewise cubic polynomials with knots at the $\bar{u}_i$, since a linear combination (scaled sum) of such basis functions will also be a C^2 continuous piecewise cubic polynomial. Much as for the piecewise linear case, locality can be obtained if all but a small number of the parametric polynomial segments defining a basis function are identically zero. The basis functions we use will be smoother, and it turns out that this means they have to be nonzero on a somewhat wider interval, but the construction is otherwise quite analogous to the linear case we have already considered. For example, $Y(\bar{u})$ for the curve of Figure 4.8 can be represented in the following way as a sum of scaled C^2 continuous piecewise cubic basis functions.

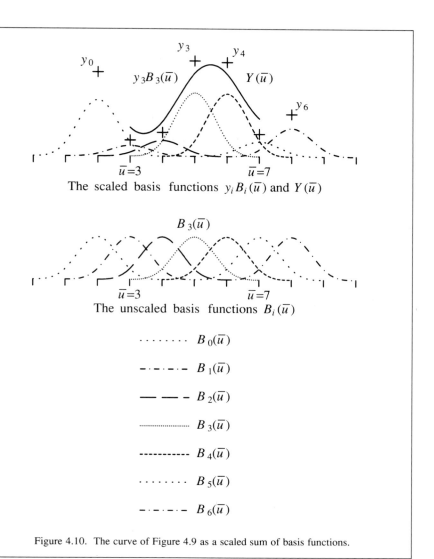

Figure 4.10. The curve of Figure 4.9 as a scaled sum of basis functions.

Figure 4.10 illustrates several conventions. We choose to index control vertices from zero through m (here 6). As we will see, it requires four basis functions to properly define each cubic curve segment. Hence there are three more basis functions (and three more control vertices) than there are curve segments. Each basis function is nonzero over four parametric intervals. The leftmost basis function extends three additional intervals to the left of the curve, and the rightmost basis function extends three additional intervals to the right. Summarizing: there are $m + 1$ control vertices, $m + 1$ basis functions, $m - 2$ curve segments bounded by $m - 1$ knots, and $m - 1 + 3 + 3 = m + 5$ knots altogether. The curve is generated (swept out) as $\bar{u}$ runs from $\bar{u}_3$ to $\bar{u}_{m+1}$. In the notation of Chapter 2

$$\bar{u}_0 < \bar{u}_1 < \bar{u}_2 < \bar{u}_3 = \bar{u}_{\min}$$

$$\bar{u}_{\min} = \bar{u}_3 < \bar{u}_4 < \cdots < \bar{u}_{m+1} = \bar{u}_{\max}$$

$$\bar{u}_{\max} = \bar{u}_{m+1} < \bar{u}_{m+2} < \bar{u}_{m+3} < \bar{u}_{m+4} .$$

Let us see how we might actually define these basis functions. Using a little foresight, we suppose each basis function to be nonzero over four successive intervals (which for convenience we assume all have length one), as shown in Figure 4.11, and ask that within each interval a basis function be defined by a cubic polynomial

$$a_j + b_j u + c_j u^2 + d_j u^3 , \qquad i - 3 \le j \le i .$$

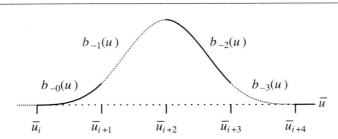

Figure 4.11. The uniform cubic B-spline $B_i(\bar{u})$ is a cubic C^2 basis function centered at $\bar{u}_{i+2}$. It is zero for $\bar{u} \le \bar{u}_i$ and for $\bar{u} \ge \bar{u}_{i+4}$. The nonzero portion of $B_i(\bar{u})$ is composed of the four polynomial segments $b_{-0}(u)$, $b_{-1}(u)$, $b_{-2}(u)$ and $b_{-3}(u)$.

Since the nonzero portion of our cubic basis function $B(\bar{u})$ consists (from left to right) of four *basis segments* $b_{-0}(u)$, $b_{-1}(u)$, $b_{-2}(u)$ and $b_{-3}(u)$, and since each segment has four coefficients, there are sixteen coefficients to determine. By assumption $B_i(\bar{u})$ is identically zero for $\bar{u} \le \bar{u}_i$ and for $\bar{u} \ge \bar{u}_{i+4}$, so the first and second derivatives $B_i^{(1)}(\overline{u})$ and $B_i^{(2)}(\overline{u})$ are also identically zero outside the interval $(\overline{u}_i, \overline{u}_{i+4})$. The requirement that positions, first derivatives, and second derivatives match at each knot $\overline{u}_j$ then implies that

$$
\begin{array}{lll}
0 = b_{-0}(0) & 0 = b_{-0}^{(1)}(0) & 0 = b_{-0}^{(2)}(0) \\
b_{-0}(1) = b_{-1}(0) & b_{-0}^{(1)}(1) = b_{-1}^{(1)}(0) & b_{-0}^{(2)}(1) = b_{-1}^{(2)}(0) \\
b_{-1}(1) = b_{-2}(0) & b_{-1}^{(1)}(1) = b_{-2}^{(1)}(0) & b_{-1}^{(2)}(1) = b_{-2}^{(2)}(0) \qquad (4.7) \\
b_{-2}(1) = b_{-3}(0) & b_{-2}^{(1)}(1) = b_{-3}^{(1)}(0) & b_{-2}^{(2)}(1) = b_{-3}^{(2)}(0) \\
b_{-3}(1) = 0 & b_{-3}^{(1)}(1) = 0 & b_{-3}^{(2)}(1) = 0
\end{array}
$$

where for simplicity each segment is individually parametrized so that $u = 0$ corresponds to its left endpoint and $u = 1$ corresponds to its right endpoint. These constitute fifteen constraints. We will see that it is convenient to require that

$$b_{-0}(0) + b_{-1}(0) + b_{-2}(0) + b_{-3}(0) = 1 . \tag{4.8}$$

Because $b_{-0}(0) = 0$ this simplifies to

$$b_{-1}(0) + b_{-2}(0) + b_{-3}(0) = 1 .$$

Because our knots are equally spaced, this amounts to assuming that when we add together an unscaled sequence of basis functions B_i, each of which is a copy of B shifted so that its *support* (the parameter values for which it is nonzero) begins at $\overline{u}_i$, the three basis functions B_{j-3}, B_{j-2} and B_{j-1} that are nonzero at $\overline{u}_j$ sum to one (Figure 4.12). Such an assumption is said to be a *normalizing condition* and serves to define the function $B(\overline{u})$ uniquely. Rather miraculously, we will see in the next section that this normalizing condition will in fact hold at all other values of $\overline{u}$ as well; that is,

$$b_{-0}(u) + b_{-1}(u) + b_{-2}(u) + b_{-3}(u) = 1, \quad \text{for all } 0 \le u < 1.$$

(Notice that our hat functions also summed to one.)

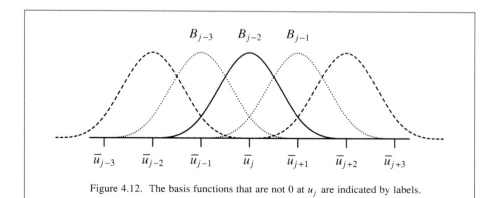

Figure 4.12. The basis functions that are not 0 at u_j are indicated by labels.

We now have sixteen equations in sixteen unknowns (that is why we assumed that our basis function had four cubic segments), and we may solve for the coefficients a_j, b_j, c_j and d_j of the four segments b_{-0}, b_{-1}, b_{-2}, and b_{-3} comprising our basis function B. Doing so yields the polynomials

$$b_{-0}(u) = \frac{1}{6} u^3$$

$$b_{-1}(u) = \frac{1}{6} (1 + 3u + 3u^2 - 3u^3)$$

(4.9)

$$b_{-2}(u) = \frac{1}{6} (4 - 6u^2 + 3u^3)$$

$$b_{-3}(u) = \frac{1}{6} (1 - 3u + 3u^2 - u^3).$$

These four segments define the *uniform cubic B-spline;* again, the term *uniform* means that the knots are equally spaced. The "B" is short for "Basis", which is appropriate because, given a sufficient number of them, they can be used to represent any C^2 spline over a uniform knot sequence. It is easy to verify that these segments have the continuity necessary to qualify them as C^2 splines. Consider, for example, the joint between $b_{-2}(u)$ and $b_{-3}(u)$. So far as positional continuity is concerned, we have

$$b_{-2}(1) = b_{-3}(0) = \frac{1}{6}.$$

Consider the first parametric derivative at their common joint. We have

$$b_{-2}^{(1)}(u) = \frac{1}{6} (-12u + 9u^2)$$

$$b_{-3}^{(1)}(u) = \frac{1}{6} (-3 + 6u - 3u^2)$$

and

$$b_{-2}^{(1)}(1) = b_{-3}^{(1)}(0) = -\frac{1}{2}.$$

Their second parametric derivatives are given by

$$b_{-2}^{(2)}(u) = (-2 + 3u)$$

$$b_{-3}^{(2)}(u) = (1 - u)$$

so that

$$b_{-2}^{(2)}(1) = b_{-3}^{(2)}(0) = 1.$$

However,

$$b_{-2}^{(3)}(u) = 3$$

$$b_{-3}^{(3)}(u) = -1$$

so that their common third parametric derivatives are not equal. Notice that we also have

$$b_{-3}(1) = b_{-3}^{(1)}(1) = b_{-3}^{(2)}(1) = 0.$$

Since the basis function (and consequently all its derivatives) are identically zero to the right of $b_{-3}(1)$, we have positional as well as first and second derivative continuity at the right end of $b_{-3}(u)$ as well.

To determine a curve, we select a set of control vertices $\mathbf{V}_i$ and use them to define the curve

$$\mathbf{Q}(\bar{u}) = \sum_i \mathbf{V}_i B_i(\bar{u}) = \sum_i (x_i B_i(\bar{u}), y_i B_i(\bar{u})) \qquad (4.10)$$

in which each B_i is simply a copy of B, shifted so that its support extends from $\bar{u}_i$ to $\bar{u}_{i+4}$, and the coefficients in the summation are given by the control vertices

$$\mathbf{V}_i = (x_i, y_i).$$

Notice that because the basis functions are nonzero on only four successive intervals, if $\bar{u}_i \le \bar{u} < \bar{u}_{i+1}$ then

$$\mathbf{Q}_i(\bar{u}) = \sum_{r=-3}^{r=0} \mathbf{V}_{i+r} B_{i+r}(\bar{u})$$

$$\qquad (4.11)$$

$$= \mathbf{V}_{i-3} B_{i-3}(\bar{u}) + \mathbf{V}_{i-2} B_{i-2}(\bar{u}) + \mathbf{V}_{i-1} B_{i-1}(\bar{u}) + \mathbf{V}_{i-0} B_{i-0}(\bar{u}).$$

If we replace each basis function $B_j(\bar{u})$ by the particular segment that pertains to the interval $[\bar{u}_i, \bar{u}_{i+1})$, then (4.11) can be written as

$$\mathbf{Q}_i(u) = \sum_{r=-3}^{r=0} \mathbf{V}_{i+r} b_r(u)$$

$$\qquad (4.12)$$

$$= \mathbf{V}_{i-3} b_{-3}(u) + \mathbf{V}_{i-2} b_{-2}(u) + \mathbf{V}_{i-1} b_{-1}(u) + \mathbf{V}_{i-0} b_{-0}(u).$$

Notice that the segments of our basis function are numbered from right to left because that is the order in which they appear when summed to form a curve: the leftmost control vertex scales the rightmost basis segment, and so on. Equation (4.12) also reflects the convenience of parametrizing each basis segment from $u = 0$ at its left end; since the basis functions are all translates of one another, this convention allows us to use the same formulas in defining each basis function, and hence in computing each curve segment.

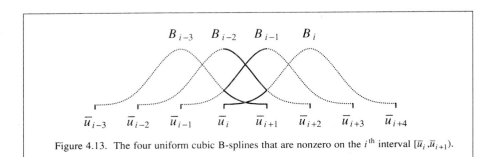

Figure 4.13. The four uniform cubic B-splines that are nonzero on the ith interval $[\bar{u}_i, \bar{u}_{i+1})$.

4.3   The Convex Hull Property

The *convex hull* of a set of control vertices in the plane can be thought of as the region lying inside a rubber band stretched so as to contain the control vertices, and then released so that it "snaps tightly against them."

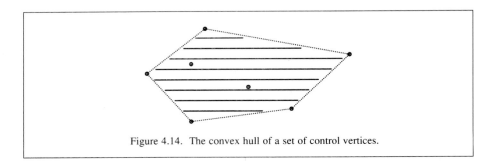

Figure 4.14. The convex hull of a set of control vertices.

Formally, the convex hull defined by the control vertices $\mathbf{V}_i$ consists of all points that can be written as a *convex combination* of those control vertices; that is, of all points that can be expressed in the form

$$\mathbf{Q} = \sum_i w_i \, \mathbf{V}_i$$

for any set of w_i satisfying

$$w_i \geq 0 \text{ for all } i$$

and

$$\sum_i w_i = 1 \, .$$

Note that the line segment joining any two points in a convex hull is also within the convex hull. That is, if

$$\mathbf{Q}_1 = \sum_i w_{i,1} \, \mathbf{V}_i$$

and

$$\mathbf{Q}_2 = \sum_i w_{i,2} \, \mathbf{V}_i \, ,$$

and if $0 \leq \alpha \leq 1$, then

$$\mathbf{Q} = \alpha \, \mathbf{Q}_1 + (1-\alpha) \, \mathbf{Q}_2$$

is also of the form

$$\mathbf{Q} = \sum_i w_i \, \mathbf{V}_i$$

as given above. This can be seen as follows:

$$\begin{aligned}
\mathbf{Q} &= \alpha \, \mathbf{Q}_1 + (1-\alpha) \, \mathbf{Q}_2 \\
&= \alpha \sum_i w_{i,1} \, \mathbf{V}_i + (1-\alpha) \sum_i w_{i,2} \, \mathbf{V}_i \\
&= \sum_i \left[\alpha \, w_{i,1} + (1-\alpha) \, w_{i,2} \right] \mathbf{V}_i \\
&= \sum_i w_i \, \mathbf{V}_i \, .
\end{aligned}$$

The quantities w_i in the last summation are given by

$$w_i = \alpha\, w_{i,1} + (1-\alpha)\, w_{i,2}.$$

It is evident that these quantities are nonnegative. They sum to one because

$$\sum_i \left[\alpha\, w_{i,1} + (1-\alpha)\, w_{i,2} \right] = \alpha \sum_i w_{i,1} + (1-\alpha) \sum_i w_{i,2}$$

$$= \alpha\, 1 + (1-\alpha)\, 1 = \alpha + 1 - \alpha = 1.$$

It is a consequence of the way in which we have constructed the B_i (specifically, a result of their normalization) that the ith segment of a uniform cubic B-spline curve lies within the convex hull of the vertices V_{i-3}, V_{i-2}, V_{i-1} and V_i, as shown in Figure 4.15.

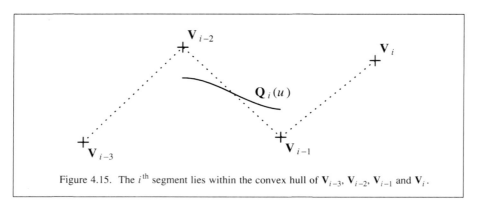

Figure 4.15. The ith segment lies within the convex hull of V_{i-3}, V_{i-2}, V_{i-1} and V_i.

This is true because, although we only required that the basis functions sum to one at the knots, it is easy to verify directly by summing equations (4.9) that

$$\sum_{r=-3}^{r=0} b_r(u) = b_{-3}(u) + b_{-2}(u) + b_{-1}(u) + b_{-0}(u) = 1 \qquad (4.13)$$

for the entire interval $(0 \le u < 1)$. It follows from equation (4.13) and from the fact that the values of the b's are nonnegative that the ith segment of a uniform cubic B-spline curve is created as a convex combination of the control vertices V_{i-3}, V_{i-2}, V_{i-1}, and V_i, with the values of the basis segments acting as the w_i in the discussion above. Hence, the ith segment lies within the convex hull of these control vertices. Thus if four successive control vertices of such a curve are visible on a display screen, just as we would see any straight line segment within the area surrounded by the vertices, we will also see the spline segment they define. An entire curve "follows" the control vertices in the sense that each successive segment lies within the convex hull of the next group of four control vertices; as we go from one segment to the next, the "oldest" is dropped because it no longer contributes to the curve, and a new vertex is picked up.

It also follows from this discussion that we may consider the B-spline curves as a "parameter dependent, varying convex combination" or "running average" of the control vertices.

4.4   Translation Invariance

It is highly desirable that translating all the control vertices by the same amount not change the shape of the curve defined. Like the convex hull property, this is an easy consequence of equation (4.13).

Suppose that we translate the control vertices by $\mathbf{t} = (dx, dy)$. Let $\mathbf{Q}(\overline{u})$ be the curve defined by the control vertices $\mathbf{V}_i$, and let $\mathbf{Q}_t(\overline{u})$ be the curve defined by the control vertices $\mathbf{V}_i + \mathbf{t}$. From (4.10) we have

$$\mathbf{Q}_t(\overline{u}) \;=\; \sum_i (\mathbf{V_i} + \mathbf{t})\, B_i(\overline{u}) \;=\; \sum_i \mathbf{V}_i B_i(\overline{u}) + \mathbf{t} \sum_i B_i(\overline{u}).$$

From (4.13), then, we have

$$\mathbf{Q}_t(\overline{u}) \;=\; \sum_i \mathbf{V_i} B_i(\overline{u}) + \mathbf{t} \;=\; \mathbf{Q}(\overline{u}) + \mathbf{t}.$$

Thus we may either translate the control vertices and then compute the curve they define, or compute the curve first and then translate the points lying on it — the result is the same.

4.5   Rotation and Scaling Invariance

It is also important that we be able to rotate a curve without changing its shape.

Suppose that we rotate the control vertices by some angle θ. Let $\mathbf{R}$ be the matrix accomplishing this rotation. Again $\mathbf{Q}(\overline{u})$ is the curve defined by the control vertices $\mathbf{V}_i$, and let $\mathbf{Q}_r(\overline{u})$ be the curve defined by the control vertices $\mathbf{R} \cdot \mathbf{V}_i$. From (4.10) we have

$$\mathbf{Q}_r(\overline{u}) \;=\; \sum_i (\mathbf{R} \cdot \mathbf{V_i})\, B_i(\overline{u}).$$

Since for any matrix $\mathbf{M}$ and vectors $\mathbf{a}$ and $\mathbf{b}$, $\mathbf{M} \cdot \mathbf{a} + \mathbf{M} \cdot \mathbf{b} = \mathbf{M} \cdot (\mathbf{a} + \mathbf{b})$, we have

$$\mathbf{Q}_r(\overline{u}) \;=\; \mathbf{R} \cdot \sum_i \mathbf{V_i} B_i(\overline{u}) \;=\; \mathbf{R} \cdot \mathbf{Q}(\overline{u}).$$

Thus we may either rotate the control vertices and then compute the curve they define, or compute the curve first and then rotate the points lying on it — the result is the same.

Since scaling can be represented as a matrix operation, a similar argument establishes that the shape of a cubic B-spline curve is not affected by scaling the control vertices — the same curve is obtained if we scale points on the curve instead.

4.6   End Conditions for Curves

Let's consider the beginning of a uniform cubic B-spline curve, shown in Figure 4.16. It is only in the fourth interval $[\bar{u}_3, \bar{u}_4)$ that we have four vertices with which to properly define a curve segment using equation (4.12). We might, of course, choose to define segments in the first three intervals by simply eliminating from equation (4.12) those terms for which we do not have a control vertex. This is not prudent, however, since the resulting curve segments will not necessarily lie within the convex hull of the control vertices defining them. Consider the first interval $[u_0, u_1)$: the corresponding curve segment will necessarily begin at $\mathbf{0}$ since only the one control vertex $\mathbf{V}_0$ is available and at the left end of the interval its corresponding basis function has the value 0.

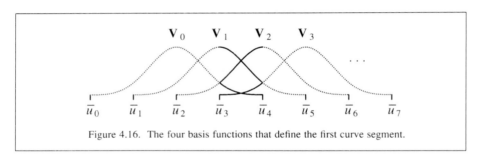

Figure 4.16.   The four basis functions that define the first curve segment.

Similarly, we can continue plotting a curve only so long as we have four control vertices with which to scale B-splines. The last knot is $\bar{u}_{m+4}$, but the last interval on which the curve can be defined is $[\bar{u}_m, \bar{u}_{m+1})$, as indicated in Figure 4.17.

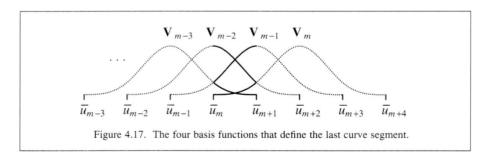

Figure 4.17.   The four basis functions that define the last curve segment.

Thus for a uniform cubic B-spline curve we have three fewer segments than we have control vertices.

Since we often want the beginning or ending of a curve to have some particular property, the behavior of uniform cubic B-spline curves at their end points is of interest. This subject is discussed in [Barsky82], from which the following presentation is drawn.

4.6.1 Curvature

One of the properties in which we are interested is curvature: whether, or how much, a curve "bends" at some point. Curvature is defined quantitatively in the following way.

At a given point **P** on a parametrically defined curve $\mathbf{Q}(\bar{u})$, the circle that has the same first and second derivative vectors as the curve is called the *osculating circle*. The center and radius of this circle are called the *center of curvature* $c(\bar{u})$ and the *radius of curvature* $\rho(\bar{u})$, respectively, at this point; the *curvature* $\kappa(\bar{u})$ at this point is the reciprocal, $1/\rho(\bar{u})$, of the radius of curvature. Thus if the osculating circle has a large radius, the curvature is small, as our intuition tells us. The *curvature vector* $\mathbf{K}(\bar{u})$ has a magnitude equal to the curvature and points from **P** towards the center of curvature.

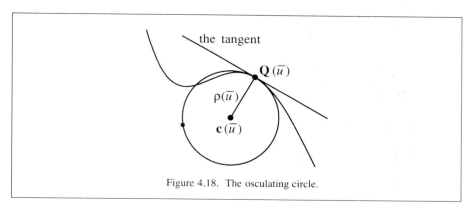

Figure 4.18. The osculating circle.

With the use of a bit of differential geometry it is possible to show (see [Barsky81a, Barsky87a] or pp. 99-101 of [Faux/Pratt79]) that the vector

$$\frac{\mathbf{Q}^{(1)}(\bar{u}) \times \mathbf{Q}^{(2)}(\bar{u})}{|\mathbf{Q}^{(1)}(\bar{u})|^3}$$

has magnitude equal to the curvature. However, this vector is perpendicular to the plane containing the osculating circle (the *osculating plane*). An additional cross-product with

$$\frac{\mathbf{Q}^{(1)}(\bar{u})}{|\mathbf{Q}^{(1)}(\bar{u})|} \qquad (4.14)$$

results in a vector of the same length lying in the osculating plane, which is the curvature vector:

$$K(\overline{u}) = \frac{(Q^{(1)}(\overline{u}) \times Q^{(2)}(\overline{u})) \times Q^{(1)}(\overline{u})}{|Q^{(1)}(\overline{u})|^4}.$$ (4.15)

From (4.15) it follows that:

- if the second derivative vector is zero, then the curvature is zero;

- if the first and second derivative vectors are nonzero but linearly dependent (collinear), then the curvature is zero;

- if the first and second derivative vectors are linearly independent (not collinear), then the curvature is nonzero.

4.6.2   No End Conditions

If we simply evaluate equation (4.12) at $u = 0$ for the vertices V_0, V_1, V_2, and V_3, and at $u = 1$ for the vertices V_{m-3}, V_{m-2}, V_{m-1}, and V_m, using (4.9) to define the basis functions, we find that the curve begins at

$$P_s = Q_3(0) = \frac{1}{6}(V_0 + 4V_1 + V_2)$$ (4.16)

and ends at

$$P_e = Q_m(1) = \frac{1}{6}(V_{m-2} + 4V_{m-1} + V_m).$$

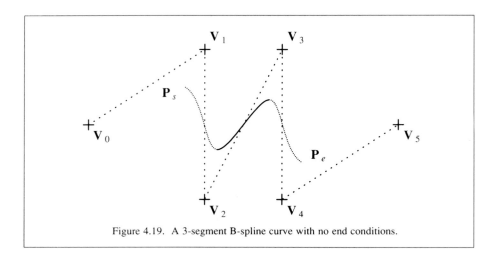

Figure 4.19. A 3-segment B-spline curve with no end conditions.

There are two natural ways in which to better control, among other things, the positions of $\mathbf{P}_s$ and $\mathbf{P}_e$. The first is to simply extend the vertex sequence $\mathbf{V}_0$, $\mathbf{V}_1$, . . . , $\mathbf{V}_{m-1}$, $\mathbf{V}_m$ by repeating the end vertices $\mathbf{V}_0$ and $\mathbf{V}_m$ some number of times; this technique is said to make use of *multiple vertices*. A second technique is to compute additional *phantom vertices* $\mathbf{V}_{-1}$ and $\mathbf{V}_{m+1}$ at either end (instead of having the user specify them), extending the curve by two segments so that $\mathbf{P}_s$ and $\mathbf{P}_e$ satisfy some condition.

4.6.3 Double Vertices

Suppose that we *double* the first and last vertices. That is, the user specifies the sequence of $m + 1$ vertices $\mathbf{V}_0$, $\mathbf{V}_1$, . . . , $\mathbf{V}_{m-1}$, $\mathbf{V}_m$, but we actually compute a curve of m segments from the sequence of $m + 3$ vertices $\mathbf{V}_0$, $\mathbf{V}_0$, $\mathbf{V}_1$, . . . , $\mathbf{V}_{m-1}$, $\mathbf{V}_m$, $\mathbf{V}_m$. By adding a vertex to each end of the curve, we add an additional segment to each end as well. The new segments have the form

$$\mathbf{Q}_2(u) = \mathbf{V}_0 [b_{-3}(u) + b_{-2}(u)] + \mathbf{V}_1 b_{-1}(u) + \mathbf{V}_2 b_{-0}(u) \tag{4.17}$$

$$\mathbf{Q}_{m+1}(u) = \mathbf{V}_{m-2} b_{-3}(u) + \mathbf{V}_{m-1} b_{-2}(u) + \mathbf{V}_m [b_{-1}(u) + b_{-0}(u)]. \tag{4.18}$$

If we evaluate these at $u = 0$ and $u = 1$, respectively, to obtain the first and last points on the curve (or substitute $\mathbf{V}_0$ for $\mathbf{V}_1$ and $\mathbf{V}_1$ for $\mathbf{V}_2$ in (4.16)) we find that

$$\mathbf{P}_s = \mathbf{Q}_2(0) = \frac{1}{6} (5 \mathbf{V}_0 + \mathbf{V}_1) = (1 - \frac{1}{6}) \mathbf{V}_0 + \frac{1}{6} \mathbf{V}_1$$

$$\mathbf{P}_e = \mathbf{Q}_{m+1}(1) = \frac{1}{6} (\mathbf{V}_{m-1} + 5 \mathbf{V}_m) = \frac{1}{6} \mathbf{V}_{m-1} + (1 - \frac{1}{6}) \mathbf{V}_m .$$

Thus the curve begins at a point $\mathbf{P}_s$ that is one-sixth of the way from $\mathbf{V}_0$ to $\mathbf{V}_1$ and ends at a point $\mathbf{P}_e$ that is one-sixth of the way from $\mathbf{V}_m$ to $\mathbf{V}_{m-1}$. Differentiating (4.17) and (4.18) and then evaluating at $u = 0$ and $u = 1$, we find the first derivative vectors at $\mathbf{P}_s$ and $\mathbf{P}_e$ to be

$$\mathbf{Q}_2^{(1)}(0) = \frac{1}{2} (\mathbf{V}_1 - \mathbf{V}_0)$$

$$\mathbf{Q}_{m+1}^{(1)}(1) = \frac{1}{2} (\mathbf{V}_m - \mathbf{V}_{m-1})$$

Thus the curve is tangent at its endpoints to the first and last line segments of the control graph, as shown in Figure 4.20.

If we compute the second derivative vectors at $\mathbf{P}_s$ and $\mathbf{P}_e$, we find that they are collinear with the tangent vectors, so that the curvature at $\mathbf{P}_s$ and $\mathbf{P}_e$ is 0. However, it is not necessary to verify this directly, as it follows from the consideration of triple vertices below.

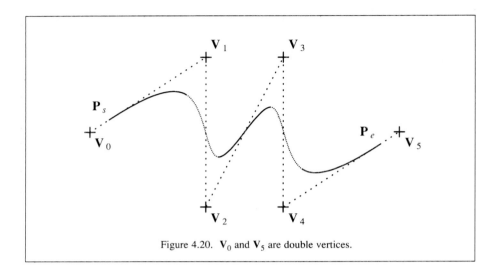

Figure 4.20. V_0 and V_5 are double vertices.

4.6.4   Triple Vertices

Suppose instead that we now *triple* the first and last vertices, so that the curve is computed from the $m+5$ vertices V_0, V_0, V_0, V_1 , . . . , V_{m-1}, V_m, V_m, V_m. This adds two additional segments

$$Q_1(u) = V_0[b_{-3}(u)+b_{-2}(u)+b_{-1}(u)] + V_1 b_{-0}(u)$$

$$Q_2(u) = V_0[b_{-3}(u)+b_{-2}(u)] + V_1 b_{-1}(u) + V_2 b_{-0}(u)$$

(4.19)

to the beginning of the curve and two additional segments

$$Q_{m+1}(u) = V_{m-2}b_{-3}(u) + V_{m-1}b_{-2}(u) + V_m [b_{-1}(u)+b_{-0}(u)]$$

$$Q_{m+2}(u) = V_{m-1} b_{-3}(u) + V_m [b_{-2}(u)+b_{-1}(u)+b_{-0}(u)]$$

(4.20)

to the end of the curve. If we now substitute in equations (4.9) and evaluate $Q_2(0)$ and $Q_{m+3}(1)$ we find that

$$P_s = Q_1(0) = V_0 \quad \text{and}$$

$$P_e = Q_{m+2}(1) = V_m .$$

That is, the curve interpolates the first and last control vertices, as shown in Figure 4.21. The first and last segments of the curve are now straight line segments.

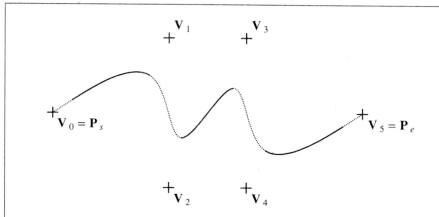

Figure 4.21. $\mathbf{V}_0$ and $\mathbf{V}_m$ are triple vertices, and are interpolated. The control graph has been omitted so that the curve can be seen to reach $\mathbf{V}_0$ and $\mathbf{V}_m$.

We can verify this easily by simplifying (4.19) and (4.20). The equation that results for the first segment is

$$\mathbf{Q}_1(u) = \left[1 - \frac{u^3}{6}\right]\mathbf{V}_0 + \left[\frac{u^3}{6}\right]\mathbf{V}_1$$

or

$$\mathbf{Q}_1(s) = (1-s)\mathbf{V}_0 + s\,\mathbf{V}_1$$

for $s = \frac{1}{6}u^3$, which we recognize as the equation of a line. The last segment of the curve is, analogously,

$$\mathbf{Q}_{m+2}(u) = \left[\frac{1-u^3}{6}\right]\mathbf{V}_{m-1} + \left[1 - \frac{1-u^3}{6}\right]\mathbf{V}_m$$

or

$$\mathbf{Q}_{m+2}(t) = t\,\mathbf{V}_{m-1} + (1-t)\mathbf{V}_m$$

for $t = \frac{1}{6}(1-u^3)$.

The second segment $\mathbf{Q}_2(u)$ and the penultimate segment $\mathbf{Q}_{m+1}(u)$ begin and end, respectively, with a double vertex, and so exhibit the behavior described for double vertices. Thus $Q_2(0)$ lies on the line segment from V_0 to V_1 and the curvature of $Q_2(u)$ is zero at that point, since it has the same first and second derivatives there as $Q_1(u)$, which is a straight line. By the same argument the curvature at $Q_{m+1}(1)$ is zero.

4.6.5   Multiple Interior Vertices

The analysis of double and triple vertices is equally applicable on the interior of a B-spline curve. Triple interior vertices are particularly interesting. So long as the triple vertex and the vertices immediately preceding and succeeding it fail to be collinear, the left and right derivative vectors at the triple vertex also fail to be collinear; the curve is said to be have a *corner*.

At first sight this may seem to contradict the fact that the curve is C^2 continuous. As we will see in the chapter on continuity, the first derivative vector is 0 at the joint and is continuous there. A corner results because the derivative vectors just to the left and right of the joint point in different directions.

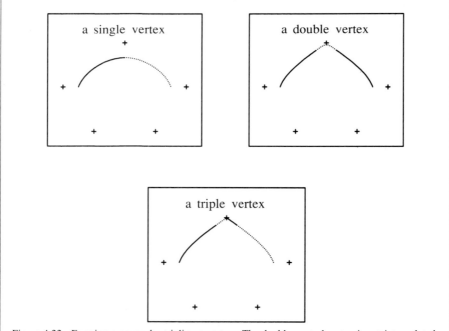

Figure 4.22. Forming a corner by tripling a vertex. The double control vertex is not interpolated, while the triple vertex is.

4.6.6 Collinear Vertices

It is also useful to know that the segment defined by four collinear control vertices V_{i-3}, V_{i-2}, V_{i-1} and V_i is a straight line.

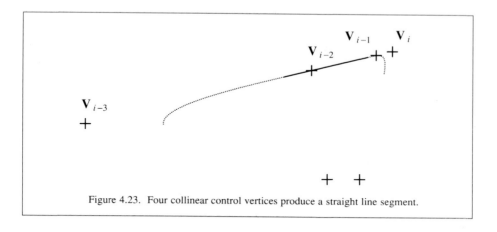

Figure 4.23. Four collinear control vertices produce a straight line segment.

This follows easily from the convex hull property.

4.6.7 Phantom Vertices: Position Specification

The essential idea behind all the *phantom vertex* techniques is to introduce two additional vertices V_{-1} and V_{m+1}, thus defining two additional segments $Q_2(u)$ and $Q_{m+1}(u)$. The positions of V_{-1} and V_{m+1} are obtained by solving some constraint equations expressed in terms of $Q_2(0)$ and $Q_{m+1}(1)$ for V_{-1} and V_{m+1}. For instance, we may allow the user to supply additional points P_s and P_e at which the curve is to begin and end, respectively, and then solve the equations

$$Q_2(0) = P_s = \frac{1}{6} (V_{-1} + 4 V_0 + V_1)$$

$$Q_{m+1}(1) = P_e = \frac{1}{6} (V_{m-1} + 4 V_m + V_{m+1})$$

for

$$V_{-1} = 6 P_s - 4 V_0 - V_1$$

$$V_{m+1} = 6 P_e - 4 V_m - V_{m-1} .$$

$$(4.21)$$

The curvature at $\mathbf{P}_s$ and $\mathbf{P}_e$ is analyzed by computing the first and second derivative vectors at these two points:

$$Q_2^{(1)}(0) = \frac{\mathbf{V}_1 - \mathbf{V}_{-1}}{2} = \mathbf{V}_1 + 2\mathbf{V}_0 - 3\mathbf{P}_s \tag{4.22}$$

$$Q_{m+1}^{(1)}(1) = \frac{\mathbf{V}_{m+1} - \mathbf{V}_{m-1}}{2} = 3\mathbf{P}_e - 2\mathbf{V}_m - \mathbf{V}_{m-1} \tag{4.23}$$

$$Q_2^{(2)}(0) = \mathbf{V}_{-1} - 2\mathbf{V}_0 + \mathbf{V}_1 = 6(\mathbf{P}_s - \mathbf{V}_0) \tag{4.24}$$

$$Q_{m+1}^{(2)}(1) = \mathbf{V}_{m-1} - 2\mathbf{V}_m + \mathbf{V}_{m+1} = 6(\mathbf{P}_e - \mathbf{V}_m). \tag{4.25}$$

Since $\mathbf{V}_1$ appears in (4.22) but not in (4.24), $Q_2^{(1)}(0)$ is not a scalar multiple of $Q_2^{(2)}(0)$, so that the first and second derivative vectors are linearly independent. As we saw earlier, this is sufficient to conclude that the curvature at $\mathbf{P}_s$ is nonzero. Similarly, $\mathbf{V}_m$ appears in (4.23) but not in (4.25), so that the curvature at $\mathbf{P}_e$ is also nonzero.

4.6.8 Phantom Vertices: End Vertex Interpolation

This is really a special case of the position specification described above. Instead of supplying new end points, we ask that phantom vertices $\mathbf{V}_{-1}$ and $\mathbf{V}_{m+1}$ be found that cause the curve to interpolate $\mathbf{V}_0$ and $\mathbf{V}_m$. Substituting $\mathbf{V}_0$ for $\mathbf{P}_s$ and $\mathbf{V}_m$ for $\mathbf{P}_m$ in (4.21) yields the following equations for the phantom vertices $\mathbf{V}_{-1}$ and $\mathbf{V}_{m+1}$.

$$\mathbf{V}_{-1} = 2\mathbf{V}_0 - \mathbf{V}_1$$

$$\mathbf{V}_{m+1} = 2\mathbf{V}_m - \mathbf{V}_{m-1}.$$

For this special case the derivative vectors given in equations (4.22)–(4.25) become

$$Q_2^{(1)}(0) = \mathbf{V}_1 - \mathbf{V}_0$$

$$Q_{m+1}^{(1)}(1) = \mathbf{V}_m - \mathbf{V}_{m-1}$$

$$Q_2^{(2)}(0) = \mathbf{0}$$

$$Q_{m+1}^{(2)}(1) = \mathbf{0}.$$

Thus for end vertex interpolation by means of phantom vertices the curve is tangent to the control graph with zero curvature at its endpoints. Since this case does not usually result in straight line segments for the first and last curve segments, it is distinct from the end vertex interpolation resulting from triple end vertices.

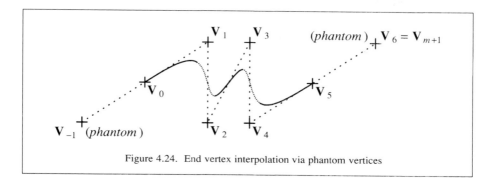

Figure 4.24. End vertex interpolation via phantom vertices

4.6.9   Phantom Vertices: Fixing Derivative Vectors

It is also possible to compute phantom vertices that give the curve selected first or second derivative vectors at its initial and final points. The actual initial and final positions of the curve are fixed as a result of specifying a derivative vector; since they do not coincide with any particularly meaningful positions (such as a control vertex), we will not discuss them. Further details may be found in [Barsky82].

4.6.10   End Conditions: Closed Curves

The curves we have discussed so far are *open* curves, which is to say that the two endpoints do not, in general, coincide. A C^2 continuous *closed* curve whose endpoints do meet, and which is C^2 continuous there as well, is obtained if the first three control vertices are identical to the last three, since if we use the $m+4$ vertex sequence V_0, V_1, V_2, ..., V_{m-1}, V_m, V_0, V_1, V_2 to define $m+1$ segments,

$$P_s = \frac{1}{6} (V_0 + 4V_1 + V_2)$$

and ends at

$$P_e = \frac{1}{6} (V_{m+1} + 4V_{m+2} + V_{m+3}) = \frac{1}{6} (V_0 + 4V_1 + V_2)$$

so that the curve is continuous. To see that the curve is, in fact, C^2 continuous, notice that the last curve segment defined by this vertex sequence is determined by $\mathbf{V}_m$, $\mathbf{V}_0$, $\mathbf{V}_1$ and $\mathbf{V}_2$. If we think of the vertex sequence as wrapping around on itself circularly, with V_m followed by $\mathbf{V}_0$, then the following segment (with which it would join C^2 continuously) would be determined by $\mathbf{V}_0$, $\mathbf{V}_1$, $\mathbf{V}_2$ and $\mathbf{V}_3$. But this is simply the first segment of the curve we have defined, so it is clear that the head and tail of the curve join with first and second derivative continuity.

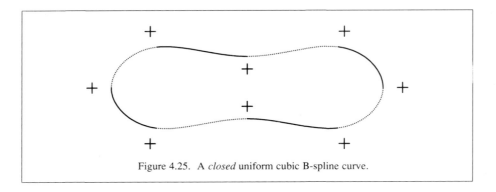

Figure 4.25. A *closed* uniform cubic B-spline curve.

4.7   Uniform Bicubic B-spline Surfaces

We want to form surfaces as a scaled sum of basis functions, as in (4.10), but now X, Y, and Z must be functions of two independent parameters:

$$\sum_r \mathbf{V}_r \, B_r(\overline{u},\overline{v}),$$

and we need basis functions $B_r(\overline{u},\overline{v})$ that are piecewise in the two independent parameters $\overline{u}$ and $\overline{v}$. These basis functions should be bicubic, nonzero only on a local parametric region, nonnegative, and should sum to one. The local-support regions of all the basis functions should cover the $\overline{u},\overline{v}$-plane in some regular fashion, and the indexing scheme used for the control vertices $\mathbf{V}_r$ will have to reflect the geometric arrangement of this covering. Much research is currently appearing on general ways of constructing such basis functions, which are called *multivariate B-splines*. That material is outside the scope of this book, but [Boehm/et al.84] gives a brief introduction.

We will concentrate on a special, classical construction process for surfaces that is a natural and straightforward generalization of the uniform cubic B-spline curves. Recall that a spline curve is formed by piecing together successive curve segments; we will form a spline surface by piecing together *rectangular surface patches* to form a composite surface in much the same way that one constructs a patchwork quilt. We will specify the continuity with which these patches meet, just as we specify the continuity with which curve segments meet.

Our generalization works in the following way. A surface will be formed as a scaled sum of basis functions, using for scale factors the x-, y- and z-coordinates of a *topologically rectangular array* of control vertices, called the *control mesh* or *control graph*, near which the surface is to pass. Since the control vertices are arranged in a rectangular topology, $\mathbf{V}_{i,j}$, the surface can be expressed by a double summation:

$$\mathbf{Q}(\overline{u},\overline{v}) = \sum_i \sum_j \mathbf{V}_{i,j} B_{i,j}(\overline{u},\overline{v})$$

$$= \sum_i \sum_j (\, x_{i,j} B_{i,j}(\overline{u},\overline{v}),\ y_{i,j} B_{i,j}(\overline{u},\overline{v}),\ z_{i,j} B_{i,j}(\overline{u},\overline{v})\,) \,. \tag{4.26}$$

(See Figure 4.26 for an example.)

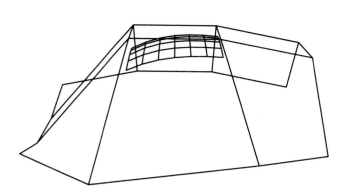

Figure 4.26. A B-spline surface consisting of a single patch, together with its surrounding control graph. Adjacent vertices in the control graph are connected by straight line segments. The control graph is topologically a four by four rectangular mesh. The patch is rendered by drawing seven lines of constant $\overline{u}$ that are equally spaced in $\overline{v}$, and seven lines of constant $\overline{v}$ that are equally spaced in $\overline{u}$. (Not all these lines are visible because of the viewing angle.) Notice how the patch lies close to the central four control vertices.

An easy way to cause the parametric region of locality of the basis functions to be rectangular is to let $B_{i,j}(\overline{u},\overline{v}) = B_i(\overline{u}) B_j(\overline{v})$, where $B_i(\overline{u})$ and $B_j(\overline{v})$ are simply the univariate cubic B-splines defined by (4.9). (See Plate II.) In the mathematical literature the basis function $B_{i,j}(\overline{u},\overline{v})$ formed in this way is called a *tensor-product B-spline*.

There are some details that we need to discuss. We now have two knot sequences — one is a sequence of knot values for $\bar{u}$ and one is a sequence of knot values for $\bar{v}$. Together they form a grid in parameter space. The particular $\bar{u}\,\bar{v}$ grid used to define the single B-spline of Plate II is shown in Figure 4.27. The bivariate B-spline $B_{0,0}(\bar{u},\bar{v})$ of Plate II is formed over the mesh of Figure 4.27 from the univariate B-splines $B_0(\bar{u})$ and $B_0(\bar{v})$. The former is nonzero over the range $(\bar{u}_0,\bar{u}_4)$ and the latter is nonzero over the range $(\bar{v}_0,\bar{v}_4)$, so $B_{0,0}(\bar{u},\bar{v})$ will be nonzero whenever $\bar{u}_0 < \bar{u} < \bar{u}_4$ and $\bar{v}_0 < \bar{v} < \bar{v}_4$ — that is, for the sixteen square *parametric regions* shown in Figure 4.27, and nowhere else.

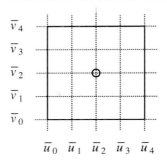

Figure 4.27. The parametric mesh used to construct the bivariate uniform bicubic B-spline $B_{0,0}(\bar{u},\bar{v})$ of Plate II. The "hump" of Plate II lies directly over the 4×4 region outlined with a solid line, falling to zero as it reaches this boundary. Because both the $\bar{u}$ and $\bar{v}$ knots are equally spaced, the peak occurs at $(\bar{u}_2,\bar{v}_2)$ (shown circled).

Because $B_0(\bar{u})$ and $B_0(\bar{v})$ are piecewise functions of $\bar{u}$ and $\bar{v}$ respectively, $B_{0,0}(\bar{u},\bar{v})$ is a piecewise function of both. The parametric region with corners at $(\bar{u}_i,\bar{v}_j)$ and $(\bar{u}_{i+1},\bar{v}_{j+1})$ (a "dotted square" in Figure 4.27) defines an area in which $B_{0,0}(\bar{u},\bar{v})$ is a pure bicubic polynomial. The polynomials for adjacent regions are distinct, but at a shared boundary they agree in position and have identical first and second partial derivatives — that is, they meet with C^2 continuity.

For example, in region A of Figure 4.28, the B-spline $B_{0,0}(\bar{u},\bar{v})$ is the polynomial

$$A(u,v) = \frac{1}{36} u^3 v^3,$$

while in region B it is the polynomial

$$B(u,v) = \frac{1}{36} (1 + 3u + 3u^2 - 3u^3)v^3.$$

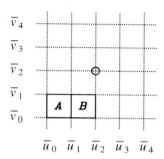

Figure 4.28. For convenience we here name two of the sixteen parametric regions shown in Figure 4.27. In each such region $B_{0,0}(\bar{u},\bar{v})$ is a pure bicubic polynomial of $\bar{u}$ and $\bar{v}$. These regions meet with C^2 continuity.

(We have parametrized each of these regions separately. That is, u and v run from zero to one in both.) The first derivatives with respect to u of $A(u,v)$ and $B(u,v)$ along the boundary between these two regions are

$$\frac{\partial}{\partial u} A(u,v)\Big|_{u=1} = \frac{1}{12} v^3$$

$$\frac{\partial}{\partial u} B(u,v)\Big|_{u=0} = \frac{1}{12} v^3,$$

and the first derivatives with respect to v are

$$\frac{\partial}{\partial v} A(u,v)\Big|_{u=1} = \frac{1}{12} v^2$$

$$\frac{\partial}{\partial v} B(u,v)\Big|_{u=0} = \frac{1}{12} v^2.$$

Hence the two polynomials are C^1 continuous along the boundary $\bar{u}=\bar{u}_1$. The second derivatives with respect to u are

$$\frac{\partial^2}{\partial u^2} A(u,v)\Big|_{u=1} = \frac{1}{6} v^3$$

$$\frac{\partial^2}{\partial u^2} B(u,v)\Big|_{u=0} = \frac{1}{6} v^3,$$

and the second derivatives with respect to v are

$$\frac{\partial^2}{\partial v^2} A(u,v)\Big|_{u=1} = \frac{1}{6} v$$

$$\frac{\partial^2}{\partial v^2} B(u,v)\Big|_{u=0} = \frac{1}{6} v .$$

Hence the two polynomials are C^2 continuous along the boundary $\bar{u} = \bar{u}_1$. On the other hand, the third derivatives with respect to u are

$$\frac{\partial^3}{\partial u^3} A(u,v)\Big|_{u=1} = \frac{1}{6} v^3$$

$$\frac{\partial^3}{\partial u^3} B(u,v)\Big|_{u=0} = -\frac{1}{2} v^3 ,$$

and the third derivatives with respect to v are

$$\frac{\partial^3}{\partial v^3} A(u,v)\Big|_{u=1} = \frac{1}{6}$$

$$\frac{\partial^3}{\partial v^3} B(u,v)\Big|_{u=0} = \frac{1}{6} ,$$

so we see that they are C^2 but not C^3 continuous along this boundary. In the same way we can establish C^2 continuity across all the other region boundaries. (Of course, this also follows directly from the continuity properties of $B_0(\bar{u})$ and $B_0(\bar{v})$ and the fact that $B_{0,0}(\bar{u},\bar{v}) = B_0(\bar{u}) B_0(\bar{v})$.)

We can define another B-spline by adding another value to one of the knot vectors. Suppose that we add a knot $\bar{u}_5$. The resulting parametric grid is shown in Figure 4.29.

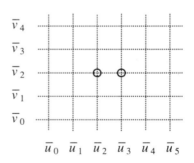

Figure 4.29. This grid allows us to define a second B-spline, centered at $(\bar{u}_3, \bar{v}_2)$ and nonzero for $\bar{u}_1 < \bar{u} < \bar{u}_5$ and $\bar{v}_0 < \bar{v} < \bar{v}_4$.

Adding an additional knot $\bar{v}_5$ to the "vertical" knot sequence would then add two B-splines above the two of Figure 4.29, and so on. So long as we continue using uniform knot sequences, the $B_i(\bar{u})$ and $B_j(\bar{v})$ all have the same shape, and consequently the surface basis functions $B_{i,j}(\bar{u},\bar{v})$ all have the same shape, namely that shown in Plate II. In effect we simply translate the one basis function so that it is centered over a variety of grid intersections.

Now suppose that we extend the knot sequences sufficiently, and ask ourselves how many of the $B_{i,j}(\bar{u},\bar{v})$ will be nonzero four or more regions distant from the ends of the knot sequences. Since each B-spline is nonzero over sixteen regions, sixteen of them will be nonzero on any such region.

Thus exactly sixteen B-splines and their corresponding control vertices are required to define a single surface patch. For example, the parameter grid needed to define the sixteen B-splines that are nonzero when $\bar{u}_3 < \bar{u} < \bar{u}_4$ and $\bar{v}_3 < \bar{v} < \bar{v}_4$ is shown in Figure 4.30.

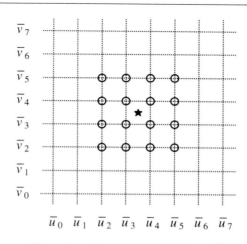

Figure 4.30. The parametric mesh used to construct the sixteen bivariate B-splines that are nonzero when $\bar{u}_0 < \bar{u} < \bar{u}_4$ and $\bar{v}_0 < \bar{v} < \bar{v}_4$. The peaks of these sixteen B-splines are circled. The parametric region in which all sixteen are nonzero is marked with a star.

The sixteen B-splines defined on the grid of Figure 4.30 are shown in Plate III. The result of weighting these by, say, the scale factors

$$
\begin{array}{cccc}
1 & 1 & 1 & 1 \\
1 & 3 & 3 & 1 \\
1 & 3 & 3 & 1 \\
1 & 1 & 1 & 1
\end{array}
$$

and then summing the results is shown in Plate IV. That plate shows one coordinate of a single surface patch — we do the same thing to define the other two coordinates.

In summary, then, since $B_i(\bar{u})$ and $B_j(\bar{v})$ are each nonzero only over four successive intervals, if $\bar{u}_i \leq \bar{u} \leq \bar{u}_{i+1}$ and $v_j \leq \bar{v} \leq v_{j+1}$, and if we adopt the convention that the portion of $\mathbf{Q}(\bar{u},\bar{v})$ defined by this set of values for $\bar{u}$ and $\bar{v}$ is denoted by $\mathbf{Q}_{i,j}(\bar{u},\bar{v})$, we can rewrite (4.26) as

$$\mathbf{Q}_{i,j}(\bar{u},\bar{v}) = \sum_{r=-3}^{0} \sum_{s=-3}^{0} \mathbf{V}_{i+r,j+s} \, B_{i+r}(\bar{u}) B_{j+s}(\bar{v}). \tag{4.27}$$

Or, in terms of u and v,

$$\mathbf{Q}_{i,j}(u,v) = \sum_{r=-3}^{0} \sum_{s=-3}^{0} \mathbf{V}_{i+r,j+s} \, B_{i+r}(u) B_{j+s}(v).$$

This is said to be the *tensor product* of two univariate B-spline curve segments. If we rewrite (4.27) in terms of basis segments instead of basis functions we have

$$\mathbf{Q}_{i,j}(u,v) = \sum_{r=-3}^{0} \sum_{s=-3}^{0} \mathbf{V}_{i+r,j+s} \, b_r(u) b_s(v), \tag{4.28}$$

so that $\mathbf{Q}_{i,j}(u,v)$, the i,j^{th} *patch*, is completely determined by sixteen control vertices. Thus the four-by-four array

$$
\begin{array}{cccc}
\mathbf{V}_{0,3} & \mathbf{V}_{1,3} & \mathbf{V}_{2,3} & \mathbf{V}_{3,3} \\[2ex]
\mathbf{V}_{0,2} & \mathbf{V}_{1,2} & \mathbf{V}_{2,2} & \mathbf{V}_{3,2} \\[2ex]
\mathbf{V}_{0,1} & \mathbf{V}_{1,1} & \mathbf{V}_{2,1} & \mathbf{V}_{3,1} \\[2ex]
\mathbf{V}_{0,0} & \mathbf{V}_{1,0} & \mathbf{V}_{2,0} & \mathbf{V}_{3,0}
\end{array}
$$

of control vertices can be used to define the single patch shown in Figure 4.31.

We emphasize that to create Figure 4.31, the basis functions of Plate III are actually used three times — once to weight x coordinates in forming $X(\bar{u},\bar{v})$, once to weight y coordinates in forming $Y(\bar{u},\bar{v})$, and once to weight z coordinates in forming $Z(\bar{u},\bar{v})$.

Now let us see how two patches are assembled into a composite surface. Return to Figure 4.30. Adding an additional knot $\bar{u}_8$ will create the four additional

B-splines shown in Figure 4.32 and Plate V, which must be weighted by an additional "column" of four control vertices.

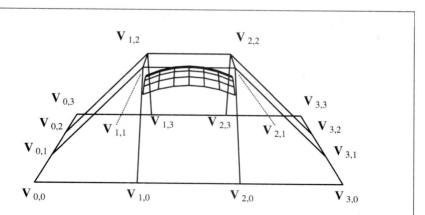

Figure 4.31. Another B-spline surface, consisting of a single patch, with its control graph. Again the patch has been rendered by drawing seven lines of constant $\bar{u}$ which are equally spaced in $\bar{v}$, and seven lines of constant $\bar{v}$ which are equally spaced in $\bar{u}$. Adjacent vertices in the control graph are connected by straight line segments.

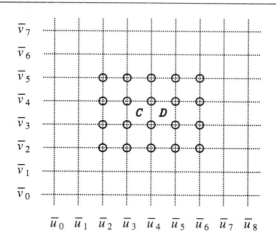

Figure 4.32. The parameter grid which results from adding an additional knot $\bar{u}_8$ to the grid of Figure 4.30. There are now four more B-splines, for a total of twenty. The leftmost sixteen B-splines are used to build a patch over parameter region C, while the rightmost sixteen are used to build a patch over parameter region D. (The middle twelve B-splines contribute to both.)

The coordinate values

$$
\begin{array}{ccccc}
1 & 1 & 1 & 1 & 1 \\
1 & 3 & 3 & 3 & 1 \\
1 & 3 & 3 & 3 & 1 \\
1 & 1 & 1 & 1 & 1
\end{array}
$$

are used to scale the B-splines in Plate V. Again, this represents one of the three coordinate functions needed to define a surface.

In Figure 4.33 we have created a mesh of twenty control vertices in object space to define a two-patch surface. Logically these vertices are arranged as a 4-row by 5-column array of control vertices, in the following rectangular structure

$$
\begin{array}{ccccc}
\mathbf{V}_{0,3} & \mathbf{V}_{1,3} & \mathbf{V}_{2,3} & \mathbf{V}_{3,3} & \mathbf{V}_{4,3} \\
\\
\mathbf{V}_{0,2} & \mathbf{V}_{1,2} & \mathbf{V}_{2,2} & \mathbf{V}_{3,2} & \mathbf{V}_{4,2} \\
\\
\mathbf{V}_{0,1} & \mathbf{V}_{1,1} & \mathbf{V}_{2,1} & \mathbf{V}_{3,1} & \mathbf{V}_{4,2} \\
\\
\mathbf{V}_{0,0} & \mathbf{V}_{1,0} & \mathbf{V}_{2,0} & \mathbf{V}_{3,0} & \mathbf{V}_{4,2} ,
\end{array}
$$

defining two adjacent patches. Columns one, two, three and four together define one patch. Columns two, three, four and five together define the second.

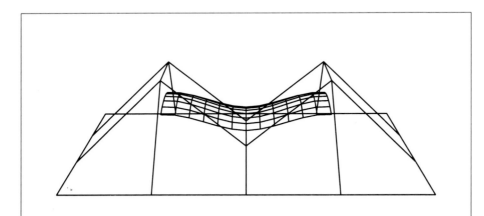

Figure 4.33. This is a B-spline surface consisting of two patches, and the control graph defining it.

More complex surfaces are built up by adding additional rows and columns of control vertices. We emphasize that these vertices must be <u>logically</u> arranged as a rectangular mesh, but that there are <u>no</u> restrictions on their physical positions.

4.8 Continuity for Surfaces

The separability of $B_{i,j}(\bar{u},\bar{v})$ into $B_i(\bar{u})$ and $B_j(\bar{v})$ can be useful. For example, we can expand (4.28) as

$$\mathbf{Q}_{i,j}(u,v) \; = $$

$$[\mathbf{V}_{i-3,j}b_{-3}(u) + \mathbf{V}_{i-2,j}b_{-2}(u) + \mathbf{v}_{i-1,j}b_{-1}(u) + \mathbf{V}_{i,j}b_{-0}(u)]\,b_{-0}(v)$$

$$+\,[\,\mathbf{V}_{i-3,j-1}b_{-3}(u) + \mathbf{V}_{i-2,j-1}b_{-2}(u) + \mathbf{V}_{i-1,j-1}b_{-1}(u) + \mathbf{V}_{i,j-1}b_{-0}(u)]\,b_{-1}(v)$$

$$+\,[\,\mathbf{V}_{i-3,j-2}b_{-3}(u) + \mathbf{V}_{i-2,j-2}b_{-2}(u) + \mathbf{V}_{i-1,j-2}b_{-1}(u) + \mathbf{V}_{i,j-2}b_{-0}(u)]\,b_{-2}(v)$$

$$+\,[\,\mathbf{V}_{i-3,j-3}b_{-3}(u) + \mathbf{V}_{i-2,j-3}b_{-2}(u) + \mathbf{V}_{i-1,j-3}b_{-1}(u) + \mathbf{V}_{i,j-3}b_{-0}(u)]\,b_{-3}(v)$$

From (4.29) it is clear that if we fix u at some arbitrary value between 0 and 1 we can then write (4.29) as

$$\mathbf{Q}_{i,j,u}(v) \; = \; \mathbf{W}_0 b_{-3}(v) + \mathbf{W}_1 b_{-2}(v) + \mathbf{W}_2 b_{-1}(v) + \mathbf{W}_3 b_{-0}(v) \tag{4.30}$$

where the appearance of u in the subscript indicates that its value has been fixed, and

$$\mathbf{W}_3 \; = \; \mathbf{V}_{i-3,j}\ b_{-3}(u) + \mathbf{V}_{i-2,j}\ b_{-2}(u) + \mathbf{V}_{i-1,j}\ b_{-1}(u) + \mathbf{V}_{i,j}\ b_{-0}(u)$$

$$\mathbf{W}_2 \; = \; \mathbf{V}_{i-3,j-1}b_{-3}(u) + \mathbf{V}_{i-2,j-1}b_{-2}(u) + \mathbf{V}_{i-1,j-1}b_{-1}(u) + \mathbf{V}_{i,j-1}b_{-0}(u)$$

$$\mathbf{W}_1 \; = \; \mathbf{V}_{i-3,j-2}b_{-3}(u) + \mathbf{V}_{i-2,j-2}b_{-2}(u) + \mathbf{V}_{i-1,j-2}b_{-1}(u) + \mathbf{V}_{i,j-2}b_{-0}(u)$$

$$\mathbf{W}_0 \; = \; \mathbf{V}_{i-3,j-3}b_{-3}(u) + \mathbf{V}_{i-2,j-3}b_{-2}(u) + \mathbf{V}_{i-1,j-3}b_{-1}(u) + \mathbf{V}_{i,j-3}b_{-0}(u)\,.$$

Thus $\mathbf{Q}_{i,j,u}(v)$ is simply the uniform cubic B-spline curve segment defined by the "control vertices" $\mathbf{W}_0$, $\mathbf{W}_1$, $\mathbf{W}_2$ and $\mathbf{W}_3$. In the same way, the curve segment $\mathbf{Q}_{i,j+1,u}(v)$, in the next patch "up," is given by

$$\mathbf{Q}_{i,j+1,u}(v) \; = \; \mathbf{W}_1 b_{-3}(v) + \mathbf{W}_2 b_{-2}(v) + \mathbf{W}_3 b_{-1}(v) + \mathbf{W}_4 b_{-0}(v)$$

where

$$\mathbf{W}_4 \; = \; \mathbf{V}_{i-3,j+1}\,b_{-3}(u) + \mathbf{V}_{i-2,j+1}\,b_{-2}(u) + \mathbf{V}_{i-1,j+1}\,b_{-1}(u) + \mathbf{V}_{i,j+1}\,b_{-0}(u)\,.$$

This is similarly the second segment in a uniform cubic B-spline curve defined by $\mathbf{W}_0$, $\mathbf{W}_1$, $\mathbf{W}_2$, $\mathbf{W}_3$ and $\mathbf{W}_4$. It follows immediately that this curve is C^2 continuous. Since a completely analogous argument can be made with respect to u by factoring the $b_r(u)$ out of (4.28) instead of the $b_s(v)$, the uniform cubic B-spline surface we have defined is C^2 continuous along lines of constant u and v. It follows from elementary calculus that the uniform cubic B-spline surfaces are therefore C^2 continuous in every direction.

4.9 How Many Patches Are There?

Recall from equation (4.28) and Figure 4.31 that it requires sixteen control vertices to define a single patch. If there are $m + 1$ such columns in the control mesh, each with four vertices, then we can generate $m - 2$ patches.

Similarly, adding a "row" of four vertices enables us to add an adjacent vertical patch; adding n additional rows of four vertices each adds n additional patches, stacked vertically. A total of $n - 2$ such patches result if we have $n + 1$ rows.

In general, then, there are three fewer rows and columns of patches than there are rows and columns of control vertices. Hence an $(m + 1) \times (n + 1)$ array of control vertices defines $(m - 2) \times (n - 2)$ patches.

4.10 Other Properties

The basic properties of B-spline curves that we have discussed in Sections 4.3 through 4.5 carry over easily to B-spline surfaces. Let us sum the basis polynomials which contribute to a patch. (This is a simplification of equation (4.29) in which the control vertices are replaced by the constant 1.)

$$[b_{-3}(u) + b_{-2}(u) + b_{-1}(u) + b_{-0}(u)] \, b_{-0}(v)$$
$$+ [b_{-3}(u) + b_{-2}(u) + b_{-1}(u) + b_{-0}(u)] \, b_{-1}(v)$$
$$+ [b_{-3}(u) + b_{-2}(u) + b_{-1}(u) + b_{-0}(u)] \, b_{-2}(v)$$
$$+ [b_{-3}(u) + b_{-2}(u) + b_{-1}(u) + b_{-0}(u)] \, b_{-3}(v).$$

Each of the bracketed quantities sums to one, as does the resulting sum $b_{-0}(v) + b_{-1}(v) + b_{-2}(v) + b_{-3}(v)$, so the entire expression sums to one. Since each term is nonnegative, it follows immediately that a B-spline patch lies within the convex hull of the control vertices that define it.

The arguments for translation, rotation and scaling invariance are then immediately applicable to surfaces. Moreover, if all the control vertices defining a patch are co-planar, then the patch must lie in that plane — that is, it must be flat.

The perspective transformation, on the other hand, does not preserve the shape of B-spline curves or surfaces. That is, the surface obtained by computing points on a surface and then applying the perspective transformation is not identical to the surface obtained by applying the perspective transformation to the control vertices and then computing points on the surface defined by the transformed control vertices. In fact, the perspective transformation of a cubic curve or surface is not necessarily expressible as a cubic. It is instead a rational polynomial, namely the quotient of two cubic polynomials, and it is easy to construct examples of numerators and denominators that are relatively prime.

4.11 Boundary Conditions for Surfaces

Just as we are interested in specifying end conditions to control the way in which curves terminate, so are we interested in specifying boundary conditions to control the behavior on the periphery of a surface. Indeed we can, in a natural way, define additional boundary patches either by repeating boundary vertices or by defining phantom vertices.

4.11.1 Multiple Vertices

It is easiest to describe and illustrate this process if we start with an array of sixteen control vertices

$$\mathbf{V}_{0,3} \quad \mathbf{V}_{1,3} \quad \mathbf{V}_{2,3} \quad \mathbf{V}_{3,3}$$

$$\mathbf{V}_{0,2} \quad \mathbf{V}_{1,2} \quad \mathbf{V}_{2,2} \quad \mathbf{V}_{3,2}$$

$$\mathbf{V}_{0,1} \quad \mathbf{V}_{1,1} \quad \mathbf{V}_{2,1} \quad \mathbf{V}_{3,1}$$

$$\mathbf{V}_{0,0} \quad \mathbf{V}_{1,0} \quad \mathbf{V}_{2,0} \quad \mathbf{V}_{3,0}$$

defining a single patch that is physically proximate to the four central vertices $\mathbf{V}_{1,1}$, $\mathbf{V}_{2,1}$, $\mathbf{V}_{1,2}$ and $\mathbf{V}_{2,2}$ (as in Figure 4.31). If we double the boundary vertices we obtain the control mesh

$$\mathbf{V}_{0,3} \quad \mathbf{V}_{0,3} \quad \mathbf{V}_{1,3} \quad \mathbf{V}_{2,3} \quad \mathbf{V}_{3,3} \quad \mathbf{V}_{3,3}$$

$$\mathbf{V}_{0,3} \quad \mathbf{V}_{0,3} \quad \mathbf{V}_{1,3} \quad \mathbf{V}_{2,3} \quad \mathbf{V}_{3,3} \quad \mathbf{V}_{3,3}$$

$$\mathbf{V}_{0,2} \quad \mathbf{V}_{0,2} \quad \mathbf{V}_{1,2} \quad \mathbf{V}_{2,2} \quad \mathbf{V}_{3,2} \quad \mathbf{V}_{3,2}$$

$$\mathbf{V}_{0,1} \quad \mathbf{V}_{0,1} \quad \mathbf{V}_{1,1} \quad \mathbf{V}_{2,1} \quad \mathbf{V}_{3,1} \quad \mathbf{V}_{3,1}$$

$$\mathbf{V}_{0,0} \quad \mathbf{V}_{0,0} \quad \mathbf{V}_{1,0} \quad \mathbf{V}_{2,0} \quad \mathbf{V}_{3,0} \quad \mathbf{V}_{3,0}$$

$$\mathbf{V}_{0,0} \quad \mathbf{V}_{0,0} \quad \mathbf{V}_{1,0} \quad \mathbf{V}_{2,0} \quad \mathbf{V}_{3,0} \quad \mathbf{V}_{3,0}$$

which adds a "strip" of boundary patches around the periphery of the original single-patch surface. Notice that the corner vertices $\mathbf{V}_{0,3}$, $\mathbf{V}_{3,3}$, $\mathbf{V}_{0,0}$ and $\mathbf{V}_{3,0}$ are actually replicated three times (once horizontally, once vertically, and once diagonally to define a new corner vertex), while all other boundary vertices are replicated once (doubled). The resulting surface is shown in Figure 4.34, together with a view "from above" of the surface shown in Figure 4.31.

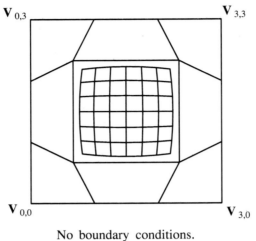

$\mathbf{V}_{0,3}$ $\mathbf{V}_{3,3}$

$\mathbf{V}_{0,0}$ $\mathbf{V}_{3,0}$

No boundary conditions.

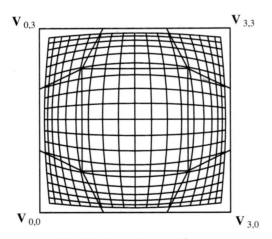

$\mathbf{V}_{0,3}$ $\mathbf{V}_{3,3}$

$\mathbf{V}_{0,0}$ $\mathbf{V}_{3,0}$

Double boundary vertices.

Figure 4.34. The single patch shown on the top has been rendered by drawing 7 equally spaced lines of constant $\bar{u}$ and 7 equally spaced lines of constant $\bar{v}$. An example of double boundary vertices is shown on the bottom. This surface, consisting of 9 patches, has been rendered by drawing 19 equally spaced lines of constant $\bar{u}$ and 19 equally spaced lines of constant $\bar{v}$. Both surfaces are shown from above. Shaded views of these two surfaces are shown in Plates VI and VII.

Suppose that we now triple the boundary vertices, so as to define two additional strips of boundary patches. For our example surface this yields the control mesh

$$\begin{array}{cccccccc}
\mathbf{V}_{0,3} & \mathbf{V}_{0,3} & \mathbf{V}_{0,3} & \mathbf{V}_{1,3} & \mathbf{V}_{2,3} & \mathbf{V}_{3,3} & \mathbf{V}_{3,3} & \mathbf{V}_{3,3} \\[6pt]
\mathbf{V}_{0,3} & \mathbf{V}_{0,3} & \mathbf{V}_{0,3} & \mathbf{V}_{1,3} & \mathbf{V}_{2,3} & \mathbf{V}_{3,3} & \mathbf{V}_{3,3} & \mathbf{V}_{3,3} \\[6pt]
\mathbf{V}_{0,3} & \mathbf{V}_{0,3} & \mathbf{V}_{0,3} & \mathbf{V}_{1,3} & \mathbf{V}_{2,3} & \mathbf{V}_{3,3} & \mathbf{V}_{3,3} & \mathbf{V}_{3,3} \\[6pt]
\mathbf{V}_{0,2} & \mathbf{V}_{0,2} & \mathbf{V}_{0,2} & \mathbf{V}_{1,2} & \mathbf{V}_{2,2} & \mathbf{V}_{3,2} & \mathbf{V}_{3,2} & \mathbf{V}_{3,2} \\[6pt]
\mathbf{V}_{0,1} & \mathbf{V}_{0,1} & \mathbf{V}_{0,1} & \mathbf{V}_{1,1} & \mathbf{V}_{2,1} & \mathbf{V}_{3,1} & \mathbf{V}_{3,1} & \mathbf{V}_{3,1} \\[6pt]
\mathbf{V}_{0,0} & \mathbf{V}_{0,0} & \mathbf{V}_{0,0} & \mathbf{V}_{1,0} & \mathbf{V}_{2,0} & \mathbf{V}_{3,0} & \mathbf{V}_{3,0} & \mathbf{V}_{3,0} \\[6pt]
\mathbf{V}_{0,0} & \mathbf{V}_{0,0} & \mathbf{V}_{0,0} & \mathbf{V}_{1,0} & \mathbf{V}_{2,0} & \mathbf{V}_{3,0} & \mathbf{V}_{3,0} & \mathbf{V}_{3,0} \\[6pt]
\mathbf{V}_{0,0} & \mathbf{V}_{0,0} & \mathbf{V}_{0,0} & \mathbf{V}_{1,0} & \mathbf{V}_{2,0} & \mathbf{V}_{3,0} & \mathbf{V}_{3,0} & \mathbf{V}_{3,0}
\end{array}$$

and defines the surface shown in Figure 4.35.

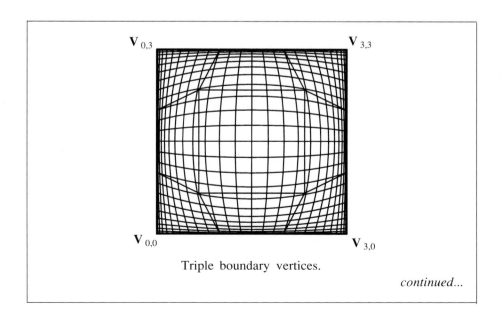

Triple boundary vertices.

continued...

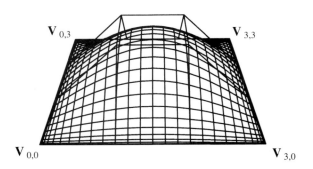

$\mathbf{V}_{0,3}$ $\mathbf{V}_{3,3}$

$\mathbf{V}_{0,0}$ $\mathbf{V}_{3,0}$

The same surface from the front.

Figure 4.35. Triple boundary vertices. This surface, consisting of 25 patches, has been rendered by drawing 31 equally spaced lines of constant $\bar{u}$ and 31 equally spaced lines of constant $\bar{v}$. A shaded version of this surface is shown in Plate VIII.

Doubling and tripling the boundary vertices adds patches that bring the surface closer to the periphery of the control graph. Indeed, for this control graph, tripling the boundary vertices causes the boundary of the surface to interpolate the line segments joining the peripheral boundary vertices. To see why this is so, it is necessary to know that this is a special case; the ''bottom'' four vertices in the control graph are collinear, as are the ''top'' four vertices in the control graph, the leftmost four vertices, and the rightmost four vertices. Let us pick an arbitrary four by four sub-array of the control graph that defines a boundary patch of the ''tripled'' surface, say

$$
\begin{array}{cccc}
\mathbf{V}_{0,3} & \mathbf{V}_{0,3} & \mathbf{V}_{0,3} & \mathbf{V}_{1,3} \\[1.5em]
\mathbf{V}_{0,2} & \mathbf{V}_{0,2} & \mathbf{V}_{0,2} & \mathbf{V}_{1,2} \\[1.5em]
\mathbf{V}_{0,1} & \mathbf{V}_{0,1} & \mathbf{V}_{0,1} & \mathbf{V}_{1,1} \\[1.5em]
\mathbf{V}_{0,0} & \mathbf{V}_{0,0} & \mathbf{V}_{0,0} & \mathbf{V}_{1,0}
\end{array}
$$

and substitute these into equation (4.29) to obtain the patch they define. We have

$$\mathbf{Q}_{1,3}(u,v)$$
$$= [\,\mathbf{V}_{0,3}b_{-3}(u) + \mathbf{V}_{0,3}b_{-2}(u) + \mathbf{V}_{0,3}b_{-1}(u) + \mathbf{V}_{1,3}b_{-0}(u)\,]\,b_{-0}(v)$$
$$\quad [\,\mathbf{V}_{0,2}b_{-3}(u) + \mathbf{V}_{0,2}b_{-2}(u) + \mathbf{V}_{0,2}b_{-1}(u) + \mathbf{V}_{1,2}b_{-0}(u)\,]\,b_{-1}(v) \qquad (4.31)$$
$$\quad [\,\mathbf{V}_{0,1}b_{-3}(u) + \mathbf{V}_{0,1}b_{-2}(u) + \mathbf{V}_{0,1}b_{-1}(u) + \mathbf{V}_{1,1}b_{-0}(u)\,]\,b_{-2}(v)$$
$$\quad [\,\mathbf{V}_{0,0}b_{-3}(u) + \mathbf{V}_{0,0}b_{-2}(u) + \mathbf{V}_{0,0}b_{-1}(u) + \mathbf{V}_{1,0}b_{-0}(u)\,]\,b_{-3}(v).$$

Once again we fix u at some arbitrary value between 0 and 1 and write (4.31) as

$$\mathbf{Q}_{1,3,u}(v) = \mathbf{W}_0 b_{-3}(v) + \mathbf{W}_1 b_{-2}(v) + \mathbf{W}_2 b_{-1}(v) + \mathbf{W}_3 b_{-0}(v)$$

where

$$\mathbf{W}_3 = \mathbf{V}_{0,3}b_{-3}(u) + \mathbf{V}_{0,3}b_{-2}(u) + \mathbf{V}_{0,3}b_{-1}(u) + \mathbf{V}_{1,3}b_{-0}(u)$$

$$\mathbf{W}_2 = \mathbf{V}_{0,2}b_{-3}(u) + \mathbf{V}_{0,2}b_{-2}(u) + \mathbf{V}_{0,2}b_{-1}(u) + \mathbf{V}_{1,2}b_{-0}(u)$$

$$\mathbf{W}_1 = \mathbf{V}_{0,1}b_{-3}(u) + \mathbf{V}_{0,1}b_{-2}(u) + \mathbf{V}_{0,1}b_{-1}(u) + \mathbf{V}_{1,1}b_{-0}(u)$$

$$\mathbf{W}_0 = \mathbf{V}_{0,0}b_{-3}(u) + \mathbf{V}_{0,0}b_{-2}(u) + \mathbf{V}_{0,0}b_{-1}(u) + \mathbf{V}_{1,0}b_{-0}(u).$$

However, these four vertices $\mathbf{W}_3$, $\mathbf{W}_2$, $\mathbf{W}_1$ and $\mathbf{W}_0$ are each points on a uniform cubic B-spline curve segment in which the first three vertices are identical. We already know that such a segment lies on the straight line joining the two distinct control vertices involved, and interpolates the triple vertex. Hence at $u=0$

$$\mathbf{Q}_{1,3,0}(v) = \mathbf{V}_{0,0} b_{-3}(v) + \mathbf{V}_{0,1} b_{-2}(v) + \mathbf{V}_{0,2} b_{-1}(v) + \mathbf{V}_{0,3} b_{-0}(v). \qquad (4.32)$$

But the four control vertices appearing in this equation are exactly the leftmost four vertices in our control graph, which are collinear, and therefore they define a segment of the straight line through $\mathbf{V}_{0,0}$, $\mathbf{V}_{0,1}$, $\mathbf{V}_{0,2}$ and $\mathbf{V}_{0,3}$.

A similar argument establishes that, for this particular surface, all the other boundary curves are straight line segments. Furthermore, since the control vertices along each boundary are collinear, the segments along each boundary are also collinear.

Consider a corner patch, such as the one defined by

$$\begin{array}{cccc}
\mathbf{V}_{0,1} & \mathbf{V}_{0,1} & \mathbf{V}_{0,1} & \mathbf{V}_{1,1} \\[2ex]
\mathbf{V}_{0,0} & \mathbf{V}_{0,0} & \mathbf{V}_{0,0} & \mathbf{V}_{1,0} \\[2ex]
\mathbf{V}_{0,0} & \mathbf{V}_{0,0} & \mathbf{V}_{0,0} & \mathbf{V}_{1,0} \\[2ex]
\mathbf{V}_{0,0} & \mathbf{V}_{0,0} & \mathbf{V}_{0,0} & \mathbf{V}_{1,0}.
\end{array}$$

The left boundary curve of this patch is

$$\mathbf{Q}_{1,1,0}(v) \ = \ \mathbf{V}_{0,0}\, b_{-3}(v) + \mathbf{V}_{0,0}\, b_{-2}(v) + \mathbf{V}_{0,0}\, b_{-1}(v) + \mathbf{V}_{0,1}\, b_{-0}(v)$$

which, for $v = 0$, will interpolate the corner vertex $\mathbf{V}_{0,0}$. Thus the boundary of this surface consists of four straight line segments that join the four corner control vertices.

Unfortunately this behavior is not very general. We have only to arrange that the boundary vertices not be collinear to destroy it, as we illustrate in Figure 4.36, although the boundary of the surface does closely approximate the perimeter of the control graph. It is not hard to see why this failure occurs. If $\mathbf{V}_{0,3}$, $\mathbf{V}_{0,2}$, $\mathbf{V}_{0,1}$ and $\mathbf{V}_{0,0}$ are not collinear then we still have $\mathbf{W}_3 = \mathbf{V}_{0,3}$, $\mathbf{W}_2 = \mathbf{V}_{0,2}$, $\mathbf{W}_1 = \mathbf{V}_{0,1}$ and $\mathbf{W}_0 = \mathbf{V}_{0,0}$, but now (4.32) simply defines an arbitrary uniform cubic B-spline curve segment. The most we can conclude is that the four corner vertices of the control graph will be interpolated by the four corners of the surface, since a similar analysis of the four corner patches yields a boundary curve in which the corner vertex is tripled.

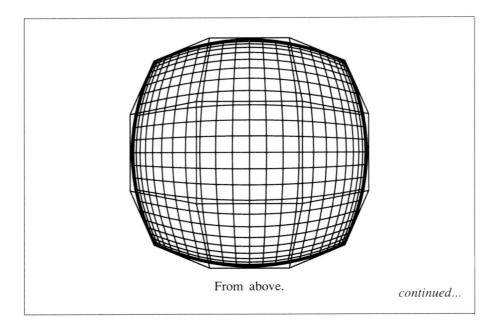

From above.

continued...

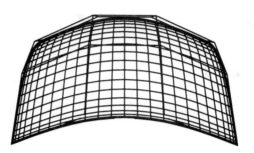

From the front.

Figure 4.36. This is also an example of a 25 patch surface produced from sixteen control vertices by tripling the boundary vertices. Unlike the previous illustrations, however, these boundary vertices are not coplanar. As a result the surface boundary does not interpolate the boundary of the control graph.

One can also define phantom vertices by specifying derivative vectors at the boundaries. However, this is probably too cumbersome to be useful. It may occasionally be useful to define phantom vertices that yield zero curvature around the perimeter of a patch. The details together with some additional analysis of these boundary conditions appear in [Barsky82].

4.11.2 Periodic Surfaces

We can "glue together" opposite edges of a surface, in much the same way that we produced closed curves, by simply wrapping the control graph around on itself. By way of example, let's construct something resembling a cylinder. Suppose that $\bar{u}$ is to increase as we move circularly around the cylinder, and the $\bar{v}$ is to increase as we move down the length of the cylinder. We can get a fairly good approximation to a circle by making a closed curve out of four control vertices laid out in a square, using the control vertex sequence

$$\mathbf{V}_0, \mathbf{V}_1, \mathbf{V}_2, \mathbf{V}_3, \mathbf{V}_0, \mathbf{V}_1, \mathbf{V}_2.$$

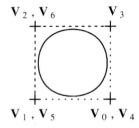

V_2, V_6 V_3

V_1, V_5 V_0, V_4

Figure 4.37. The closed curve defined by four control vertices arranged in a square is approximately a circle. A better approximation can be obtained by distributing more control vertices in a regular circular pattern.

To get an approximate cylinder we simply translate these four control vertices at right angles to the plane in which they lie, making several copies of them as we go. The resulting surface looks like this.

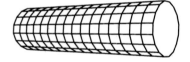

Without the control graph.

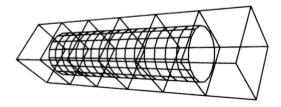

With the entire control graph.

Figure 4.38. "Extruding" the control vertices of Figure 4.37 produces a control graph yielding a reasonable approximation of a cylinder.

Interesting effects can be achieved by pulling some of the "wrapped" points apart. If we take the middle square of control vertices in Figure 4.38 and pull the two vertices V_0 and V_1 at one end away from the two vertices V_5 and V_6 at the other end to yield Figure 4.39 without moving the other control vertices, we obtain the surface shown in Figure 4.40.

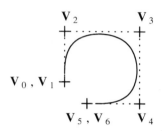

Figure 4.39. Breaking apart the approximate circle of Figure 4.37 produces a gap.

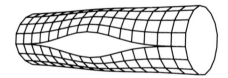

Figure 4.40. If we take the control graph shown in Figure 4.38 and separate the midmost plane of control vertices as in Figure 4.39 so that by themselves they no longer define a closed curve, we open a hole in the approximate cylinder.

We can also "glue" the ends of the control vertex array together at the same time we are wrapping the sides together. If we take the same square of four control vertices, but now revolve it circularly in space at some distance from the origin, we can define an approximation to a torus.

Figure 4.41 represents a transformation of the $\bar{u}, \bar{v}$-rectangle given by $\bar{u}_{min} \leq \bar{u} \leq \bar{u}_{max}$ and $\bar{v}_{min} \leq \bar{v} \leq \bar{v}_{max}$ in the parametric coordinate system into the x, y, z-points of the toroidal object's coordinate system. As $\bar{v}$ progresses from $\bar{v}_{min}$ to $\bar{v}_{max}$, points are traced out along the surface to form a path around the central hole. As $\bar{u}$ progresses from $\bar{u}_{min}$ to $\bar{u}_{max}$, points are traced out perpendicularly to the paths above, circulating from the "equator" of the surface, through the hole, and then back out to the "equator." A shaded version of this surface is shown in Plate IX.

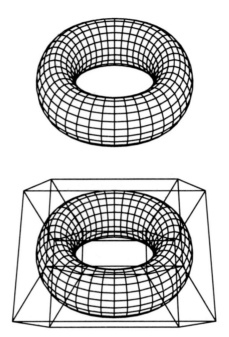

Figure 4.41. This surface is defined by treating the control vertex array periodically in both $\bar{u}$ and $\bar{v}$.

5

Splines in a More General Setting

5.1 Preliminaries

Thus far our treatment of splines has focused on the uniform cubic B-splines. This has enabled us to introduce most of the concepts which interest us in a fairly simple setting that minimizes the complexity of the mathematics involved. Moreover, the uniform cubic B-splines are of substantial interest in their own right since they can be efficiently computed and suffice for many applications.

Nevertheless, there are a number of ways in which we might seek to generalize them to obtain greater flexibility and power:

- we might use polynomials of some other degree;

- we might use an irregularly spaced (*nonuniform*) knot sequence;

- we might wish to impose something other than C^2 continuity at the knots.

In principle we could accomplish all these by simply repeating the development of Chapter 4, defining the appropriate constraint equations and solving them for the coefficients of the basis segments involved. This might be satisfactory for some particularly interesting special cases (such as uniform quintic B-splines). However, it would be terribly cumbersome to carry out every time we wish to see the effect of a different order spline, or to try changing the knot spacing. Fortunately we can do better.

It is a remarkable fact, resulting principally from the work of Isaac Schoenberg, Carl de Boor and Maurice Cox [de Boor72, de Boor78, Cox72], that there exists a single unified algorithm by which all three of the above generalizations of the uniform cubic B-splines can be accomplished.

Our next objective, then, is to develop a general treatment of B-splines of arbitrary order k, defined over irregularly spaced knot sequences, and with any "reasonable" continuity at the joints between segments (or the borders between surface patches). Not surprisingly, this development will be more involved than was our treatment of the uniform cubic B-splines. It does not, however, require anything more than a careful consideration of easily understood properties of polynomials and vector spaces.

By way of introduction we will begin with a few examples, establishing the definitions and nomenclature that we will need later. In the following chapters, much of the development parallels that to be found in [Schumaker81], in [de Boor78], and finally in [Cohen/et al.80], though with a greater emphasis on intuition and at a much lower level of rigor and formality.

We will carry out our theoretical discussions purely in terms of the variable $\bar{u}$, never reparametrizing the separate segment polynomials into [0,1). For example, we will now represent the uniform cubic B-spline of (4.8) on the knot sequence $0, 1, 2, 3, 4$ by

$$
B_0(\bar{u}) = \begin{cases}
& 0 & -\infty < \bar{u} < 0 \\[2mm]
b_{-0}(\bar{u}) = & \dfrac{1}{6}\bar{u}^3 & 0 \le \bar{u} < 1 \\[2mm]
b_{-1}(\bar{u}) = & -\dfrac{1}{6}(3\bar{u}^3 - 12\bar{u}^2 + 12\bar{u} - 4) & 1 \le \bar{u} < 2 \\[2mm]
b_{-2}(\bar{u}) = & \dfrac{1}{6}(3\bar{u}^3 - 24\bar{u}^2 + 60\bar{u} - 44) & 2 \le \bar{u} < 3 \\[2mm]
b_{-3}(\bar{u}) = & -\dfrac{1}{6}(\bar{u}^3 - 12\bar{u}^2 + 48\bar{u} - 64) & 3 \le \bar{u} < 4 \\[2mm]
& 0 & 4 \le \bar{u} < +\infty .
\end{cases}
\tag{5.1}
$$

The splines we have discussed so far have usually involved cubic polynomials, so for variety we will use quadratics in the next few paragraphs. Our first task will be to find out what constitutes reasonable continuity at a knot.

5.2 Continuity

A typical segment polynomial of degree two has the form

$$
p(\bar{u}) = c_0 + c_1\bar{u} + c_2\bar{u}^2 .
$$

If we are to use quadratics, or any other polynomials, to concoct splines, we must carry out, explicitly or implicitly, the sort of construction that we used to form the uniform B-splines. That means, having selected some knot $\bar{u} = \bar{u}_i$ and having decided that

$$p_{left}(\bar{u}) = c_{00} + c_{01}\bar{u} + c_{02}\bar{u}^2$$

and

$$p_{right}(\bar{u}) = c_{10} + c_{11}\bar{u} + c_{12}\bar{u}^2$$

will meet at $\bar{u}_i$ with a certain continuity, we are left with the problem of imposing conditions on the coefficients

$$c_{00}, c_{01}, c_{02}, c_{10}, c_{11}, \text{ and } c_{12}$$

so that the meeting takes place as desired. One possibility, of course, is to request C^2 continuity:

$$p_{left}^{(0)}(\bar{u}_i) = p_{right}^{(0)}(\bar{u}_i)$$
$$p_{left}^{(1)}(\bar{u}_i) = p_{right}^{(1)}(\bar{u}_i)$$
$$p_{left}^{(2)}(\bar{u}_i) = p_{right}^{(2)}(\bar{u}_i).$$

This can only be accomplished by imposing the conditions

$$c_{00} + c_{01}\bar{u}_i + c_{02}\bar{u}_i^2 = c_{10} + c_{11}\bar{u}_i + c_{12}\bar{u}_i^2$$
$$c_{01} + 2c_{02}\bar{u}_i = c_{11} + 2c_{12}\bar{u}_i$$
$$2c_{02} = 2c_{12}.$$

This clearly results in

$$p_{left}(\bar{u}) = p_{right}(\bar{u}).$$

This is surely the highest order of continuity we could expect to specify for quadratics. Both adjoining segments are forced to be the same polynomial, and the knot $\bar{u}_i$ might as well not exist. For the moment, this is an uninteresting outcome, since we wish to concentrate on splines; that is, on piecewise polynomials, not merely polynomials.

The first of the remaining possibilities is C^1 continuity, shown in Figure 5.1. For this we would require

$$p_{left}^{(0)}(\bar{u}_i) = p_{right}^{(0)}(\bar{u}_i)$$
$$p_{left}^{(1)}(\bar{u}_i) = p_{right}^{(1)}(\bar{u}_i),$$

yielding the conditions

$$c_{00} + c_{01}\bar{u}_i + c_{02}\bar{u}_i^2 = c_{10} + c_{11}\bar{u}_i + c_{12}\bar{u}_i^2$$
$$c_{01} + 2c_{02}\bar{u}_i = c_{11} + 2c_{12}\bar{u}_i \ .$$

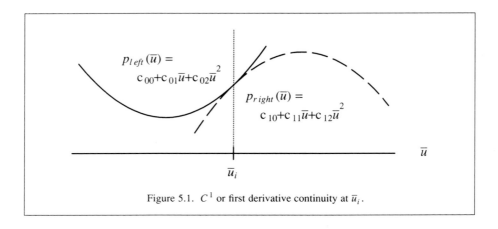

Figure 5.1. C^1 or first derivative continuity at $\bar{u}_i$.

Another possibility is the C^0 continuity of Figure 5.2, for which we would require

$$p_{left}^{(0)}(\bar{u}_i) \ = \ p_{right}^{(0)}(\bar{u}_i) \, ,$$

yielding the conditions

$$c_{00} + c_{01}\bar{u}_i + c_{02}\bar{u}_i^2 = c_{10} + c_{11}\bar{u}_i + c_{12}\bar{u}_i^2 \ .$$

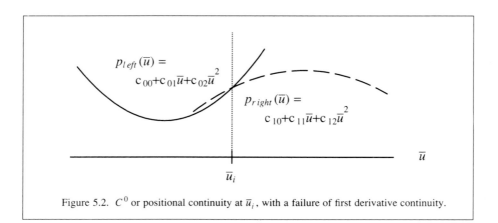

Figure 5.2. C^0 or positional continuity at $\bar{u}_i$, with a failure of first derivative continuity.

Finally, there is the case of no continuity at all (which we will refer to as C^{-1} continuity), for which we would make no requirements and impose no conditions.

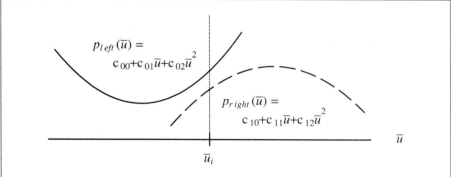

Figure 5.3. A discontinuity at $\overline{u}_i$. $p_{left}(\overline{u})$ and $p_{right}(\overline{u})$ are said to be C^{-1} continuous at $\overline{u}_i$.

In imposing the conditions that force p_{right} to join p_{left} with some degree of continuity, the very fact that three coefficients are involved limits what is possible and what is interesting. In the cubic case there were four coefficients, so C^2 continuity was both interesting and attainable, and we should expect that for polynomials having k coefficients, i.e., having highest power at most $k-1$, only continuities C^{-1} through C^{k-2} are both interesting and attainable. In particular, imposing C^{k-1} continuity forces $p_{left}(\overline{u})$ and $p_{right}(\overline{u})$ to be identical, resulting not only in C^{k-1} continuity, but also C^k, C^{k+1}, ..., C^{∞} continuity.

5.3   Segment Transitions

The process we will ultimately use to construct general B-splines will begin in Chapter 6 by considering precisely what constitutes the transition between two segment polynomials, $p_{left}(\overline{u})$ and $p_{right}(\overline{u})$, that meet at a knot. In this preliminary discussion let us look at some special adjoining segments to get a feel for what is coming. The spline segments that we have already developed are those for the uniform cubic B-spline, so we will use them for illustration. In (5.1) we see that, at the knot $\overline{u} = 0$, the spline $B_0(\overline{u})$ has adjoining segment polynomials

$$p_{left}(\overline{u}) = 0$$

$$p_{right}(\overline{u}) = \frac{1}{6}\overline{u}^3.$$

The approach we will take involves asking whether $B_0(\bar{u})$ can be expressed as a single function over the range $-\infty < \bar{u} < 1$. The answer is "yes"—if we "cheat." $B_0(\bar{u})$ can be expressed on that range as the "single" function

$$B_0(\bar{u}) = p_{left}(\bar{u}) + \Delta_+(\bar{u})$$

$$= 0 + \Delta_+(\bar{u}),$$

where $\Delta(\bar{u})$ denotes the difference polynomial

$$\Delta(\bar{u}) = p_{right}(\bar{u}) - p_{left}(\bar{u}),$$

and the "+" subscript indicates that we only consider the piece of $\Delta(\bar{u})$ on the "positive" side of $\bar{u}=0$. More precisely, $\Delta_+(\bar{u})$ would be, for this pair of segment polynomials,

$$\Delta_+(\bar{u}) = \begin{cases} 0 & \bar{u} < 0 \\ \dfrac{1}{6}\bar{u}^3 & \bar{u} \geq \bar{u}. \end{cases}$$

This, from one point of view, merely hides the piecewise nature of $B_0(\bar{u})$ under a shroud of notation. $\Delta_+(\bar{u})$ has been conjured up to masquerade as a "single" function that helps express $B_0(\bar{u})$ on $-\infty < \bar{u} < 1$. From another point of view, however, this bit of cheating is quite profitable. It leads to the idea of a "one-sided" function, $\bar{u}_+^3$, or more completely $(\bar{u}-0)_+^3$, which we define as

$$(\bar{u}-0)_+^3 = \begin{cases} 0 & \bar{u} < 0 \\ (\bar{u}-0)^3 & \bar{u} \geq 0. \end{cases}$$

This function represents the "essence" of the transition that is made in switching from the identically zero function to the leftmost nonzero segment polynomial of $B_0(\bar{u})$ at the knot $\bar{u}=0$.

Let us consider the next knot, $\bar{u}=1$, using the same form of cheating. We start with

$$B_0(\bar{u}) = 0 + \frac{1}{6}(\bar{u}-0)_+^3,$$

which is valid for the range $-\infty < \bar{u} < 1$, and we ask whether $B_0(\bar{u})$ can be expressed on the range $-\infty < \bar{u} < 2$ by the formula

$$B_0(\bar{u}) = 0 + \frac{1}{6}(\bar{u}-0)_+^3 + \Delta_+(\bar{u})$$

---

for some definition of $\Delta_+(\bar{u})$. The appropriate definition is, clearly,

$$\Delta_+(\bar{u}) \;=\; \begin{cases} 0 & \bar{u} < 1 \\ p_{right}(\bar{u}) - p_{left}(\bar{u}) & \bar{u} \geq 1 \end{cases}$$

$$= \begin{cases} 0 & \bar{u} < 1 \\ -\dfrac{1}{6}\,(3\bar{u}^3 - 12\bar{u}^2 + 12\bar{u} - 4) - \dfrac{1}{6}\,\bar{u}^3 & \bar{u} \geq 1 \end{cases}$$

$$= \begin{cases} 0 & \bar{u} < 1 \\ -\dfrac{4}{6}\,(\bar{u} - 1)^3 & \bar{u} \geq 1. \end{cases}$$

Again, this suggests that the one-sided function

$$(\bar{u}-1)_+^3 \;=\; \begin{cases} 0 & \bar{u} < 1 \\ (\bar{u}-1)^3 & \bar{u} \geq 1 \end{cases}$$

represents the essence of the transition that is made in switching from the leftmost nontrivial segment polynomial of $B_0(\bar{u})$ to the succeeding segment polynomial at $\bar{u} = 1$.

The obvious result of continuing in this fashion is the discovery that it would be handy to define the generic, *one-sided power function*, which is, for any $r = 0, 1, 2 \ldots,$

$$(\bar{u}-t)_+^r \;=\; \begin{cases} 0 & \bar{u} < t \\ (\bar{u}-t)^r & \bar{u} \geq t. \end{cases}$$

We will see in Chapter 6 that a linear combination of these one-sided power functions, for $r = 3$ and $t = 0, 1, 2, 3, 4$, have the capacity to represent $B_0(\bar{u})$ for all values of $\bar{u}$. More profoundly, the one-sided power functions have the capacity to represent any spline over any designated, finite parameter range. They constitute a *basis* for any *space of splines* defined on a finite interval in the same sense that the ordinary shifted powers $(\bar{u}-t)^r$ constitute a basis for any space of polynomials. As such, they provide a mechanism for defining B-splines in general.

This observation hints at the idea that splines constitute a *space*; more precisely, that the terminology and tools of vector spaces can be applied to the study of splines. The remainder of this chapter will explore this idea a bit further in the context of polynomials as well as splines.

5.4 Polynomials

We will focus our attention on k^{th}-*order polynomials*. By this we mean polynomials having precisely k coefficients, with zero coefficients allowed. For example, polynomials of order 4 consist of all functions $p(\bar{u})$ of the variable $\bar{u}$ that can be written in the form

$$p(\bar{u}) = c_0 + c_1\bar{u} + c_2\bar{u}^2 + c_3\bar{u}^3 ,$$

and this is intended to include the cases in which

$$c_3 = 0 \text{ and/or } c_2 = 0 \text{ and/or } c_1 = 0 \text{ and/or } c_0 = 0 .$$

For example, the following are all 4th-order polynomials:

$$p(\bar{u}) = 1 + 2\bar{u} - 7\bar{u}^2 - \bar{u}^3 ,$$

$$p(\bar{u}) = -3 + 4\bar{u} - 1\bar{u}^2 + 0\bar{u}^3 ,$$

and

$$p(\bar{u}) = 2 - 5\bar{u} + 0\bar{u}^2 + 0\bar{u}^3 .$$

Even the polynomial that is constant

$$p(\bar{u}) = 42 + 0\bar{u} + 0\bar{u}^2 + 0\bar{u}^3 ,$$

including the polynomial that is zero everywhere

$$p(\bar{u}) = 0 + 0\bar{u} + 0\bar{u}^2 + 0\bar{u}^3 ,$$

is considered to be a 4th-order polynomial. As a consequence, 4th-order polynomials are the polynomials having at most degree 3. This means that the kth-order polynomials include all polynomials up to and including those of degree $k-1$.

■ Notation

$\mathbf{P}^k$ stands for *the set of all k^{th}-order polynomials*, i.e., all functions of a real variable $\bar{u}$ that can be represented as

$$p(\bar{u}) = \sum_{i=0}^{k-1} c_i \bar{u}^i$$

for any choice of real constants $c_0, \ldots, c_{k-1}$.

■

5.5 Vector Spaces

To be able to treat polynomials and splines more generally, we will draw a great deal from the concept of a vector space. To review: a vector space over the real numbers is any collection of objects for which there are defined operations of

- *vector addition* between any two members of the collection, yielding a member of the collection, and

- *scalar multiplication* between any real number and any member of the collection, yielding a member of the collection.

These operations must satisfy a number of algebraic conditions: Suppose $Z, Y, X, \ldots$ stand for the objects in the collection, suppose $a, b, c, \ldots$ stand for real numbers, and suppose the operations of scalar multiplication and vector addition are denoted in a natural way; i.e., $a X$ and $X + Y$. It is required that the following hold:

- $X + Y = Y + X$ (commutativity of addition);

- $(X + Y) + Z = X + (Y + Z)$ (associativity of addition);

- there is a "zero" vector Θ having the property that $X + \Theta = X$ for all X (the additive identity element);

- $a (X + Y) = (aX) + (aY)$ (distributivity of scalar multiplication over addition);

- $(a + b) X = (aX) + (bX)$ (distributivity of addition over scalar multiplication);

- $(ab) X = a (bX)$ (associativity of scalar multiplication);

- $1 X = X$ for all X (the multiplicative identity element).

The question of what object constitutes the zero vector is of particular interest, because in the answer lies the *de facto* definition of what constitutes the equality (i.e., the equivalence or indistinguishability) of two vectors. This is a remark having particular relevance to splines.

The usual example one has in mind for a vector space is 3-space, i.e., the collection of all objects of the form

$$P = (x, y, z)$$

where x, y, and z are real numbers. Vector addition follows the familiar format:

$$P_1 = (x_1, y_1, z_1)$$
$$P_2 = (x_2, y_2, z_2)$$
$$P_1 + P_2 = (x_1 + x_2, y_1 + y_2, z_1 + z_2).$$

Scalar multiplication (scaling) follows the format

$$P = (x, y, z)$$
$$a P = (a x, a y, a z).$$

The zero vector is, of course,

$$\Theta = (0, 0, 0) = \mathbf{0},$$

which implies that $P_1 = P_2$ if and only if $x_1 = x_2$, $y_1 = y_2$, and $z_1 = z_2$.

One example is 3-space, but there are others. The definition of a vector space is general enough and powerful enough to include many different types of objects. For our deliberations it will be important to observe that k^{th}-order polynomials (and later, k^{th}-order splines on a fixed knot sequence over a fixed parameter range) constitute a vector space.

5.6 Polynomials as a Vector Space

It is easily seen that the set of all k^{th}-order polynomials

$$X(\overline{u}), Y(\overline{u}), Z(\overline{u}), \quad \cdots$$

form a vector space, since the conventional addition of such polynomials

$$X(\overline{u}) + Y(\overline{u}) = (c_0 + \cdots + c_{k-1}\overline{u}^{k-1}) + (d_0 + \cdots + d_{k-1}\overline{u}^{k-1})$$

$$= (c_0 + d_0) + \cdots + (c_{k-1} + d_{k-1})\overline{u}^{k-1}$$

and the conventional scaling of such polynomials

$$a X(\overline{u}) = a (c_0 + \cdots + c_{k-1}\overline{u}^{k-1})$$

$$= (ac_0) + \cdots + (ac_{k-1})\overline{u}^{k-1}$$

satisfy all the rules listed for vector spaces. The polynomial corresponding to Θ is, of course,

$$\Theta(\overline{u}) = 0 + 0\overline{u} + \cdots + 0\overline{u}^{k-1},$$

which implies that $X(\overline{u}) = Y(\overline{u})$ if and only if X and Y have precisely the same coefficients. Stating this formally:

■ **Theorem**

For any $k > 0$, $\mathbf{P}^k$ is a vector space with the usual definitions of polynomial addition and of multiplication by a real number playing the roles, respectively, of vector addition and scalar multiplication.

■

Polynomials can even be written so as to look like ordinary vectors; that is, they can be written as k-*tuples* of numbers. Since a polynomial is completely determined by its *powers of $\bar{u}$ coefficients*, for example, we could write

$$X(\bar{u}) = (c_0, c_1, c_2)$$

with the interpretation that

$$(c_0, c_1, c_2) = c_0(1,0,0) + c_1(0,1,0) + c_2(0,0,1)$$

and, of course,

$$(1,0,0) = 1\bar{u}^0 + 0\bar{u}^1 + 0\bar{u}^2 = \bar{u}^0$$

$$(0,1,0) = 0\bar{u}^0 + 1\bar{u}^1 + 0\bar{u}^2 = \bar{u}^1$$

$$(0,0,1) = 0\bar{u}^0 + 0\bar{u}^1 + 1\bar{u}^2 = \bar{u}^2.$$

The mechanics of this interpretation of polynomials as vectors requires two things:

- that we have chosen a *coordinate system* or, as we will refer to it, a *basis*, and

- that the k-tuple of coefficients given as the description of the polynomial is, in fact, a correct representation in terms of the chosen basis.

These points are worth raising because many coordinate systems (bases) are possible in any given vector space. In the case of polynomials, the following illustration is worth considering. It is easily verified (by expanding the quantities in parentheses and collecting the terms together according to powers of $\bar{u}$) that the polynomial given by

$$5(\bar{u}-1)^2 + 4(\bar{u}-2)^2 + 3(\bar{u}-3)^2$$

is exactly the same as the polynomial given by

$$48\bar{u}^0 - 44\bar{u}^1 + 12\bar{u}^2.$$

In the first case the basis

$$(\bar{u}-1)^2 , \ (\bar{u}-2)^2 , \ (\bar{u}-3)^2$$

and the coefficients

$$5 , \ 4 , \ 3$$

go together. The polynomial can be expressed as the 3-tuple $(5,4,3)$ in the "$(\bar{u}-1)^2 , (\bar{u}-2)^2 . (\bar{u}-3)^2$" coordinate system. In the second case the basis

$$\bar{u}^0 , \ \bar{u}^1 , \ \bar{u}^2$$

and the coefficients

$$48 , \ -44 , \ 12$$

go together. The polynomial can be expressed as the 3-tuple $(48,-44,12)$ in the "$\bar{u}^0 , \bar{u}^1 , \bar{u}^2$" coordinate system.

It would clearly be inappropriate to take the 3-tuple $(5,4,3)$ and to interpret it as a mechanism for describing this polynomial in terms of powers of $\bar{u}$, but it is a valid description of the polynomial in terms of another basis. Thus, we should usually expect to say that some k-tuple $(c_0,...,c_{k-1})$ represents some vector V of some vector space $\mathbf{S}$ with respect to some basis $B_0,...,B_{k-1}$. General practice is often less precise than this. When a basis is not explicitly mentioned, some *canonical* basis is understood by common agreement. Thus, for polynomials, we generally interpret a vector

$$(c_0 , \ldots , \ c_{k-1})$$

as a polynomial in terms of the *powers basis* when no basis is explicitly designated, i.e.,

$$c_0 \bar{u}^0 + \cdots + c_{k-1} \bar{u}^{k-1} ,$$

just as in our usual notion of k-space we use the *unit coordinates*

$$(1,...,0) , \ldots , \ (0,...,1)$$

to interpret a list of numbers

$$(c_0,...,c_{k-1})$$

as a vector

$$c_0 (1,...,0) + \cdots + c_{k-1} (0,...,1) .$$

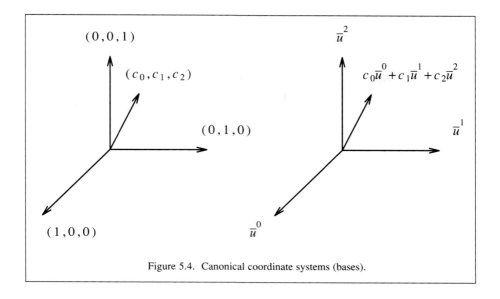

Figure 5.4. Canonical coordinate systems (bases).

In the following section we expand on the notion of a basis and of the relationships between alternative bases.

5.7 Bases and Dimension

To understand what a basis is for a general vector space, it is important to recall the concept of *linear independence*:

Vectors Z , Y , X , ... are *linearly independent* if the only scalars a , b , c , ... for which

$$a X + b Y + \cdots + c Z = \Theta$$

are the trivial ones

$$a = b = \cdots = c = 0.$$

A consequence of this is that if some vector W can be represented in terms of linearly independent vectors X , Y , ..., Z:

$$W = r X + s Y + \cdots + t Z$$

then the coefficients in the combination r , s , ..., t are uniquely defined.

For an arbitrary W and an arbitrary collection $X, Y, \ldots, Z$ we can't guarantee that W has a representation in terms of the collection, even if the collection is linearly independent. For example $\bar{u}^3$ can't be expressed in terms of $\bar{u}^0, \bar{u}^1$, and $\bar{u}^2$ alone. Collections of linearly independent vectors that have the power of representing *every* vector in a space have a special importance.

■ **Definition**

A *basis* of a vector space is a collection of vectors that is linearly independent and that can express any vector in the space as a linear combination.

■

Some spaces are so "rich" that they can only be expressed in terms of infinite collections of vectors. Any space of interest to us, however, will be generated by a finite collection of basis vectors. Bases are not unique, but if one finite basis (containing, say, k vectors) for a space exists, then any other basis for that space must also be comprised of exactly k vectors.

■ **Definition**

The number k (if finite) of the elements in any basis for a vector space, does not depend on the basis. This number is the same for all bases, and it is called the *dimension* of the space.

■

The dimension of 3-space is, of course, 3. The dimension of $\mathbf{P}^k$ is k.

As we have already remarked, we will ultimately discover that splines, as well as polynomials, form vector spaces. The B-splines will form our canonical basis, though we will develop them from the basis of one-sided powers. From the point of view of graphics and the construction of objects using splines or polynomials, the dimension of a space may be thought of as indicating the number of "controls" that may be varied to obtain distinct members of the space. The control variables may be regarded as the coefficients of the basis elements, and each is "independent" in the sense that it can be varied by itself to obtain new vectors not obtainable by using any of the other parameters. Eventually we will associate the dimension of a spline space with the number of control *vertices* that may be used to construct the spline curves or surfaces in that space.

5.8   Change of Basis

The modeling transformations of graphics lead one to confront different bases defining the same space. For example, if 3-space is represented in terms of the basis

$$(1,0,0), (0,1,0), (0,0,1)$$

and this space is subjected to some transformation, $\mathbf{A}$, then the basis undergoes the change

$$(1,0,0)\mathbf{A} \rightarrow (t_{00}, t_{01}, t_{02})$$

$$(0,1,0)\mathbf{A} \rightarrow (t_{10}, t_{11}, t_{12})$$

$$(0,0,1)\mathbf{A} \rightarrow (t_{20}, t_{21}, t_{22}).$$

Under what conditions will

$$(t_{00}, t_{01}, t_{02}), (t_{10}, t_{11}, t_{12}), (t_{20}, t_{21}, t_{22})$$

represent a new coordinate system? The necessary and sufficient condition for these transformed vectors to be a basis is that $\mathbf{A}$ has to be *nonsingular* (that is *invertible*).

More generally, if

$$X_0, \ldots, X_m$$

is one basis for a vector space and

$$Y_0, \ldots, Y_m$$

is another, then each vector in the one basis can be expressed as a linear combination of the vectors in the other basis; e.g.,

$$X_j = a_{0,j} Y_0 + \cdots + a_{m,j} Y_m$$

$$= \sum_{i=0}^{m} a_{i,j} Y_i$$

for $j = 0, 1, \ldots, m$. Conversely, if $Y_0, \ldots, Y_m$ is a basis for a vector space, and if coefficients $a_{i,j}$ are chosen to create linearly independent combinations

$$X_j = a_{0,j} Y_0 + \cdots + a_{m,j} Y_m \quad \text{for } j = 0, \ldots, m$$

then these combinations, X_j, will also be a basis. The constants $a_{i,j}$ appearing in the above assertions make up the *change of basis matrix*

$$\mathbf{A} = \begin{bmatrix} a_{00} & \cdots & a_{0m} \\ \cdot & \cdot & \cdot \\ \cdot & \cdot & \cdot \\ \cdot & \cdot & \cdot \\ a_{m0} & \cdots & a_{mm} \end{bmatrix} ;$$

that is,

$$\begin{bmatrix} X_0, \ldots, X_m \end{bmatrix} = \begin{bmatrix} Y_0, \ldots, Y_m \end{bmatrix} \mathbf{A} .$$

Note: A change of basis matrix <u>must</u> be nonsingular.

Notice that normal 3-space could be represented by the basis

$$X_0 = (1,0,0), \ X_1 = (1,1,0), \ X_2 = (1,1,1)$$

as well as by the basis

$$Y_0 = (1,0,0), \ Y_1 = (0,1,0), \ Y_2 = (0,0,1) .$$

The 3-tuples representing the X's and Y's are to be interpreted in terms of the canonical 3-space coordinates:

$$X_0 \ = \ 1\,(1,0,0) + 0\,(0,1,0) + 0\,(0,0,1)$$

$$X_1 \ = \ 1\,(1,0,0) + 1\,(0,1,0) + 0\,(0,0,1)$$

$$X_2 \ = \ 1\,(1,0,0) + 1\,(0,1,0) + 1\,(0,0,1)$$

and, trivially,

$$Y_0 \ = \ 1\,(1,0,0) + 0\,(0,1,0) + 0\,(0,0,1)$$

$$Y_1 \ = \ 0\,(1,0,0) + 1\,(0,1,0) + 0\,(0,0,1)$$

$$Y_2 \ = \ 0\,(1,0,0) + 0\,(0,1,0) + 1\,(0,0,1) .$$

This means that

$$[\,(1,0,0)\,,\,(1,1,0)\,,\,(1,1,1)\,] = [\,(1,0,0)\,,\,(0,1,0)\,,\,(0,0,1)\,] \begin{bmatrix} 1 & 0 & 0 \\ 1 & 1 & 0 \\ 1 & 1 & 1 \end{bmatrix} ,$$

and conversely,

$$[(1,0,0),(0,1,0),(0,0,1)] = [(1,0,0),(1,1,0),(1,1,1)] \begin{bmatrix} 1 & 0 & 0 \\ -1 & 1 & 0 \\ 0 & -1 & 1 \end{bmatrix}.$$

For another example, the power basis for the quadratic polynomials

$$\bar{u}^0, \ \bar{u}^1, \ \text{and} \ \bar{u}^2$$

could be replaced by

$$(\bar{u}-t)^0, \ (\bar{u}-t)^1, \ \text{and} \ (\bar{u}-t)^2 \ ; \tag{5.2}$$

that is, $(\bar{u}-t)^r$ for $r = 0,1,2$ and any fixed t.

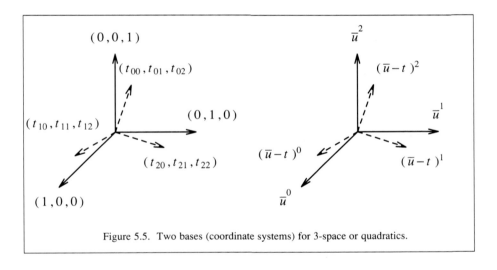

Figure 5.5. Two bases (coordinate systems) for 3-space or quadratics.

The change of basis matrix for this alternative to the power basis for quadratics is given by

$$\mathbf{A} = \begin{bmatrix} 1 & -t & t^2 \\ 0 & 1 & -2t \\ 0 & 0 & 1 \end{bmatrix}.$$

Since this matrix has a determinant equal to 1, it is nonsingular, and this verifies that (5.2) is, indeed, a legitimate basis.

Another important example of an alternative polynomial basis is $(\bar{u}-t)^r$ for a fixed value of r and a sequence of distinct values of t; e.g., $t = \bar{u}_i$, $\bar{u}_{i+1}$, $\bar{u}_{i+2}$:

$$(\bar{u} - \bar{u}_i)^2, \ (\bar{u} - \bar{u}_{i+1})^2, \ \text{and} \ (\bar{u} - \bar{u}_{i+2})^2. \tag{5.3}$$

We will have many occasions to consider extensions of (5.2) and (5.3) to k^{th}-order polynomials in the material that follows.

As a final example, the power basis for the cubics

$$\bar{u}^0, \ \bar{u}^1, \ \bar{u}^2, \ \bar{u}^3$$

could be replaced by the linear combinations

$$
\begin{aligned}
-\bar{u}^3 + 3\bar{u}^2 - 3\bar{u} + 1 &= (1-\bar{u})^3 &&= P_{0,3} \\
3\bar{u}^3 - 6\bar{u}^2 + 3\bar{u} &= 3\bar{u}(1-\bar{u})^2 &&= P_{1,3} \\
3\bar{u}^2 - 3\bar{u}^3 &= 3\bar{u}^2(1-\bar{u}) &&= P_{2,3} \\
\bar{u}^3 &= \bar{u}^3 &&= P_{3,3}
\end{aligned}
$$

to obtain an alternative basis for the cubics. The change of basis equations for this example can be written

$$
\begin{bmatrix} \bar{u}^3 & \bar{u}^2 & \bar{u}^1 & \bar{u}^0 \end{bmatrix}
\begin{bmatrix}
1 & -3 & 3 & -1 \\
0 & 3 & -6 & 3 \\
0 & 0 & 3 & -3 \\
0 & 0 & 0 & 1
\end{bmatrix}
= \begin{bmatrix} P_{3,3} & P_{2,3} & P_{1,3} & P_{0,3} \end{bmatrix}.
$$

(The members of this new basis for the cubics are called the *Bernstein polynomials* — they are used to define *Bézier curves*, which will be discussed in Chapter 10.)

5.9 Subspaces

If any set of ℓ linearly independent vectors is chosen from a space,

$$\mathbf{X} = \{ X_1, \ldots, X_\ell \},$$

and the collection of all vectors formed as linear combinations of this set is considered,

$$\mathbf{W} = \{ W : W = a_1 X_1 + \cdots + a_\ell X_\ell \},$$

then **W** can be seen to be a vector space of dimension ℓ with the members of **X** as a basis. **W** may or may not contain all the vectors of the original space. **W** is referred to as a *subspace* of **X**.

A simple example of a subspace is provided by any of the 2-space planes that are embedded in 3-space and pass through the origin. The x,y plane is a particular instance; it is generated by all linear combinations of the collection

$$(1,0,0) \text{ and } (0,1,0).$$

That is, the x,y plane consists of all linear combinations

$$a\,(1,0,0) + b\,(0,1,0) = (a,b,0).$$

In the same sense, the linear polynomials constitute a subspace of the quadratics. The linear polynomials consist of all linear combinations of the collection

$$\bar{u}^0 \text{ and } \bar{u}^1 \,;$$

that is,

$$a\,\bar{u}^0 + b\,\bar{u}^1 = a + b\,\bar{u}.$$

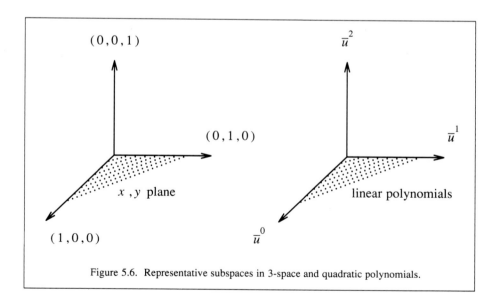

Figure 5.6. Representative subspaces in 3-space and quadratic polynomials.

More profoundly, we will see that the space $\mathbf{P}^k$ is a subspace of the space of kth-order splines.

A basis for a subspace need not be chosen as a subset of the basis for a full space, as was the case in the above two examples. The set of all *linear combinations* of

$$(1,2,3)$$

i.e., all scalar multiples of this vector, forms a subspace (in this case a 1-D subspace — a line) of 3-space. However, if $N_0, \ldots, N_n$ form a basis for a vector space, and $B_0, \ldots, B_m$ ($m < n$) constitutes a basis for one of its subspaces, then we must have the representations

$$B_i = \alpha_{i,0} N_0 + \cdots + \alpha_{i,n} N_n$$

for $i = 0, \ldots, m$ and some (unique) coefficients, $\alpha_{i,0}, \ldots, \alpha_{i,n}$, since each B_i is a member of the space described by the basis $N_0, \ldots, N_n$. That is, the B's may be found from the N's by the use of an $m \times n$ table (matrix) of numbers $\alpha_{i,j}$.

We will show over the course of the next several chapters how the kth-order splines with knots $\{ \bar{u}_0, \ldots, \bar{u}_{m+k} \}$ form a vector space, and how the B-splines constitute a basis. The *Oslo algorithm* for B-spline subdivision, with which we will end this theoretical development, is simply a method for finding the α's for a given N-*basis* spline space and a corresponding B-*basis* spline subspace. The N-space is generated from the B-space by inserting one or more new knots among those that already exist.

5.10   Knots and Parameter Ranges: Splines as a Vector Space

Recall that for cubics ($k = 4$) we required that knots

$$\bar{u}_0, \ \bar{u}_1, \ \bar{u}_2, \ \text{and} \ \bar{u}_3$$

lie "to the left" of the parameter $\bar{u}$ at all times, and that knots

$$\bar{u}_{m+1}, \ \bar{u}_{m+2}, \ \bar{u}_{m+3}, \ \text{and} \ \bar{u}_{m+4}$$

lie "to the right". This meant that, for any value of $\bar{u}$ with which we were dealing, we were in the nonzero domain of four B-splines, whose segment polynomials constituted precisely the basis polynomials needed to define <u>any</u> cubic polynomials as segments of the spline curve we sought to construct.

If we were interested in curves whose "margins" were not composed of general cubics, of course, we could have allowed $\bar{u}$ to pass to the left of $\bar{u}_3$ or to the right of $\bar{u}_{m+1}$. In the extreme case, for example, a curve whose beginning segment could only have zero components would be produced if $\bar{u}$ were allowed to vary to the left of $\bar{u}_0$. Between $\bar{u}_0$ and $\bar{u}_1$, segment components of a curve produced by B-splines can only be multiples of $(\bar{u} - \bar{u}_0)^3$. Each knot to the right of $\bar{u}_0$ brings in one more B-spline, and with it the capacity to provide a "richer" type of cubic as a curve segment. To have general k^{th} order segments for a kth order curve generated from B-splines, we must have

$$\bar{u}_0 , \ldots , \; \bar{u}_{k-1}$$

on the left,

$$\bar{u}_{m+1} , \ldots , \; \bar{u}_{m+k}$$

on the right, and

$$\bar{u}_{k-1} \leq \bar{u} < \bar{u}_{m+1}$$

as the range for the parameter. Strictly speaking, we will see that we only need to constrain ourselves to some fixed parameter range

$$\bar{u}_{\min} \leq \bar{u} < \bar{u}_{\max} ,$$

in order to make use of vector-space results. If $[\bar{u}_{\min}, \bar{u}_{\max})$ includes some knots to the left of $\bar{u}_{k-1}$ or to the right of $\bar{u}_m$, then we may still look upon B-spline combinations as members of a space, and the B-splines as a basis, some k^{th}-order polynomials may not be attainable on some segment intervals. The values of $\bar{u}_{\min}$ and $\bar{u}_{\max}$ do not even have to coincide with knots.

Thus, our view of a spline space will be roughly as shown in Figure 5.7, where $\bar{u}_{\min}$ might even lie to the left of $\bar{u}_0$ or $\bar{u}_{\max}$ might even lie to the right of $\bar{u}_{m+k}$. (Cases where the range $\bar{u}_{\min} \leq \bar{u} < \bar{u}_{\max}$ doesn't contain any of the knots, however, are uninteresting.) We will tend to assume for most of our discussions, however, that $\bar{u}_{\min} = \bar{u}_{k-1}$ and that $\bar{u}_{\max} = \bar{u}_{m+1}$, which constitutes the widest possible parameter range consistent with the use of B-splines as a basis and the attainment of arbitrary k^{th} order polynomials as segment polynomials.

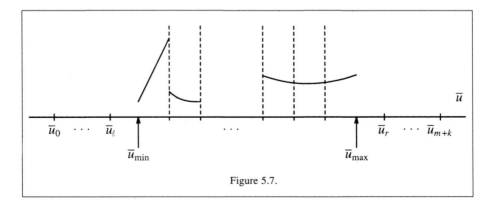

Figure 5.7.

The vector addition of two splines will consist of adding their segment polynomials together piece by piece; i.e., if $s_1(\overline{u})$ is defined in terms of pieces $p_{1,i}(\overline{u})$ on a collection of intervals $[\overline{u}_i,\overline{u}_{i+1})$, and another spline $s_2(\overline{u})$ is defined in terms of pieces $p_{2,i}(\overline{u})$ on the same intervals, and with the same continuity properties between the pieces, then we can set

$$s_1(\overline{u}) + s_2(\overline{u}) \;=\; p_{1,i}(\overline{u}) + p_{2,i}(\overline{u}) \quad \text{on the interval } [\ \overline{u}_i\ ,\overline{u}_{i+1})$$

for each $i = 0,\ldots,\ m+k-1$.

Similarly, the multiplication of a single spline by a scalar can be defined in a piece-by-piece fashion. These definitions satisfy the conditions for vector addition and scalar multiplication.

To completely regard these functions as members of a vector space, it will be necessary to define what we mean by equality. We will say that any two splines $s_1(\overline{u})$ and $s_2(\overline{u})$ are equal if they do not differ for any $\overline{u} \in [\overline{u}_{\min},\overline{u}_{\max})$. This means that the segment polynomials falling outside this parametric interval are of no interest to us when we are comparing two splines. The difference (or identity) of two splines is only a matter to be determined from the segment polynomials within this designated parametric interval. Equivalently, this is a statement about what we consider to be the "zero vector"

$$s_1(\overline{u}) - s_2(\overline{u}) \;=\; \Theta(\overline{u}) \;=\; \text{has value zero for all}\quad \overline{u} \in [\overline{u}_{\min},\overline{u}_{\max})\,.$$

For splines this makes the concept of linear independence a bit more subtle than it was for pure polynomials. Two splines

$$s_1(\overline{u}) \quad \text{and} \quad s_2(\overline{u})$$

are linearly independent if and only if

$$\alpha_1 s_1(\overline{u}) + \alpha_2 s_2(\overline{u}) \;=\; 0$$

implies

$$\alpha_1 \;=\; \alpha_2 \;=\; 0$$

when only the values of $\overline{u}$ on the parameter range of interest are taken into account. As an example, the functions s_1 and s_2 shown below are linearly independent if we are being shown a section of them, and their parameter range for comparison happens to include the interval $[-1,3)$. But viewed as functions to be compared only in the parameter range $[0,2)$, they are linearly dependent — s_2 is a multiple of s_1.

Sometimes it is useful to treat a spline merely as a piecewise function on the real line, with no consideration of its relation to a vector space. Much of what we do in establishing that a B-spline is a divided difference, which is the material in

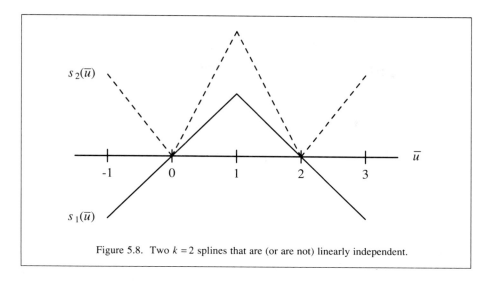

Figure 5.8. Two $k = 2$ splines that are (or are not) linearly independent.

Sections 6.5–6.9, will have this flavor, for example. But whenever we want to justify some result (or gain some insight) about splines derived from properties of vector spaces, we must be prepared to designate a parameter range on which the comparison for equality is to be made.

5.11   Spline Continuity and Multiple Knots

One of our stated intentions is to relax the requirement that a cubic (4th-order) spline need have C^2 continuity across any knot $\bar{u}_i$ or, in general, that a spline involving kth-order polynomial segments have C^{k-2} continuity. One possible suggestion is that we associate an index μ_i with each knot $\bar{u}_i$, indicating what order of continuity is to be imposed at that knot. We could use this index to count the "continuity loss" at the knot $\bar{u}_i$ by the following sort of scheme (remembering that C^{k-1} continuity at a knot implies C^∞ continuity at the knot): let $\mu_i = 1$ indicate that $C^{k-1-\mu_i} = C^{k-2}$ continuity is required, let $\mu_i = 2$ indicate that $C^{k-1-\mu_i} = C^{k-3}$ continuity is required, and so on through $\mu_i = k$ indicating that no continuity at all; i.e., $C^{k-1-\mu_i} = C^{-1}$ continuity, is required at $\bar{u}_i$. This means that we would have to deal with two sequences of numbers to define splines in any generality: the knot sequence

$$\bar{u}_0 , \quad \cdots \quad , \bar{u}_{m+k}$$

and the *index of continuity* sequence

$$\mu_0 , \quad \cdots \quad , \mu_{m+k} .$$

The general picture would be as shown in Figure 5.9.

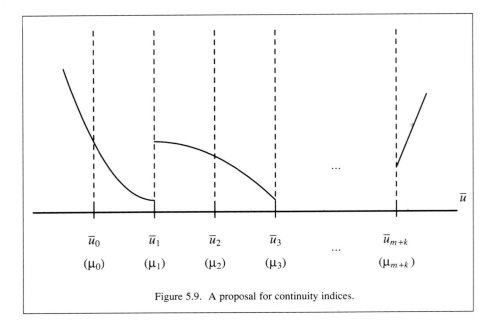

Figure 5.9. A proposal for continuity indices.

This does not turn out to be the best approach. The actual situation is more intricate, because continuity at a knot is influenced by the process of moving knots around. For design purposes we might wish to allow the position of knots to be varied, and this will require the option of allowing knots to be pushed together, e.g.,

$$\bar{u}_i \rightarrow \bar{u}_{i+1} .$$

Suppose that each of these knots is associated with C^{k-2} continuity, and suppose a spline is constructed, for varying choices of $\bar{u}_i$ as it "moves close to" $\bar{u}_{i+1}$; for example:

$$|\bar{u}_i - \bar{u}_{i+1}| = 10^{-1} , \quad |\bar{u}_i - \bar{u}_{i+1}| = 10^{-2} \quad , \ldots, \quad |\bar{u}_i - \bar{u}_{i+1}| = 10^{-j} .$$

When this is tried computationally, and the $(k-2)^{\text{th}}$ derivative of the spline is studied in sequence, this derivative comes closer and closer to being discontinuous as $\bar{u}_i$ moves closer and closer to $\bar{u}_{i+1}$. The following is an example.

Consider the knots

$$\bar{u}_0 = 0 , \ \bar{u}_1 = 1 , \ \bar{u}_2 = 1+d , \ \text{and} \ \bar{u}_3 = 2+d$$

and construct the quadratic spline $(k = 3)$ on the knot intervals

$$[0,1), [1,1+d), \text{ and } [1+d, 2+d)$$

defined by

$$
s(\bar{u}) = \begin{cases}
0 & \bar{u} < 0 \\
\bar{u}^2 & 0 \leq \bar{u} < 1 \\
-\dfrac{2\,\bar{u}\,(\bar{u}-d-2)+d+2}{d} & 1 \leq \bar{u} < 1+d \\
(2+d-\bar{u})^2 & 1+d \leq \bar{u} < 2+d \\
0 & 2+d \leq \bar{u}.
\end{cases}
$$

This spline is shown in Figure 5.10.

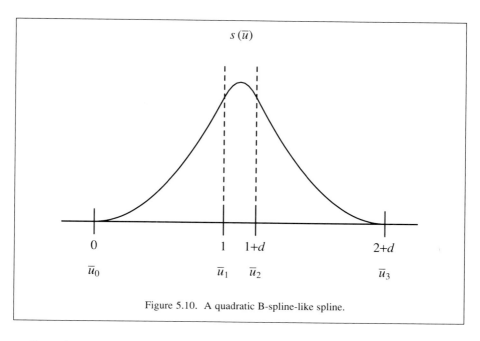

Figure 5.10. A quadratic B-spline-like spline.

Note that this looks very much like a B-spline — it is zero to the left of $\bar{u}=0$, quadratic in each of the three knot intervals, zero to the right of $\bar{u}=2+d$, positive on $(0, 2+d)$, and $C^{3-2}=C^1$ continuous everywhere (i.e., continuous in position and tangent). Its value is 1 at $\bar{u}_1$ and $\bar{u}_2$, and its derivative at these two points is 2 and -2, respectively. Both value and derivative at $\bar{u}_1$ and $\bar{u}_2$ are independent of d. The value of this spline at the midpoint of its support

$$\bar{u} = 1 + \frac{d}{2}$$

is

$$s\left(1 + \frac{d}{2}\right) = \frac{d+2}{2}.$$

If we take the limit of this function as d goes to zero, the result is clearly

$$s(\bar{u}) = \begin{cases} 0 & \bar{u} < 0 \\ \bar{u}^2 & 0 \le \bar{u} < 1 \\ (2-\bar{u})^2 & 1 \le \bar{u} < 2 \\ 0 & 2 \le \bar{u}, \end{cases}$$

which is illustrated in Figure 5.11.

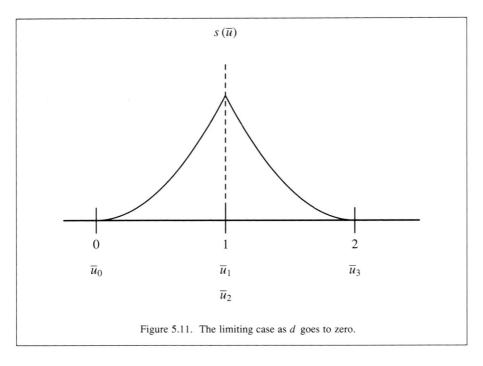

Figure 5.11. The limiting case as d goes to zero.

When this is done more generally, carefully and mathematically with arbitrary splines, then the resulting continuity at a double knot

$$\bar{u}_i = \bar{u}_{i+1}$$

is allowed to be $C^{k-1-2} = C^{k-3}$, which is just what one would have specified by assigning a μ-index of 2 to the knot value represented by the doublet. If a single, simple knot can be regarded as a point at which there can be a single *continuity-loss* for a spline, then this seems to suggest that double knots and double continuity-loss go together. This rule proves true more generally: when more and more knots come together, discontinuities of higher and higher order can result at the rate of one μ count per multiplicity.

As a further example, suppose $\bar{u}_3$ is pushed together with $\bar{u}_1$ and $\bar{u}_2$ in our above quadratic example. The resulting "B-spline-like" object is illustrated in Figure 5.12.

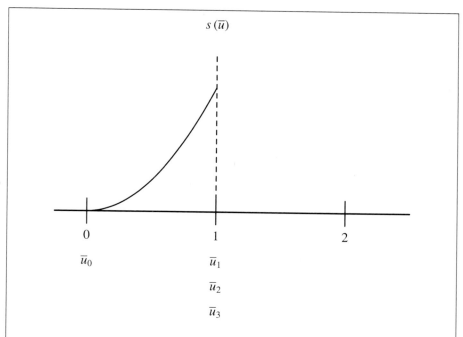

Figure 5.12. A B-spline-like quadratic with three knots put together. $s(\bar{u})$ is zero for $\bar{u} < 0$ and $\bar{u} \geq 1$.

If we move $\bar{u}_0$ into $\bar{u} = 1$ to join $\bar{u}_1$, $\bar{u}_2$, and $\bar{u}_3$, then the spline disappears altogether. Since $k = 3$ for quadratics, and disappearance took place when 4 knots came together, this suggests that we will find it unprofitable in general to push more than k knots together.

More formally, for any $m, k > 0$ we will let $\{\bar{u}_i\}_0^{m+k}$ stand for a chosen *sequence* of $m + k + 1$ knots

$$\{\bar{u}_i\}_0^{m+k} = \{\bar{u}_0, \ldots, \bar{u}_{m+k}\}$$

where

$$\bar{u}_0 \leq \bar{u}_1 \leq \cdots \leq \bar{u}_{m+k}.$$

Notice that more than one knot can fall on the same value. Thus we might have

$$\bar{u}_h < \bar{u}_{h+1} = \cdots = \bar{u}_{i-1} = \bar{u}_i = \bar{u}_{i+1} = \cdots = \bar{u}_{j-1} < \bar{u}_j,$$

a situation depicted in Figure 5.13. We will say that $\bar{u}_i$ is a knot of *multiplicity* $\mu_i = j - h - 1$. (The same is said of any one of the knots $\bar{u}_{h+1}, \ldots, \bar{u}_{j-1}$.) That is, the multiplicity of a knot $\bar{u}_i$ is the count of the knots in the sequence with value equal to $\bar{u}_i$. The multiplicity count includes $\bar{u}_i$ itself. Notice that $\bar{u}_i$ would be a knot of multiplicity 1, if $\bar{u}_{i-1} < \bar{u}_i < \bar{u}_{i+1}$.

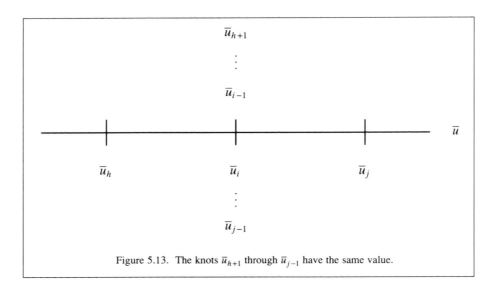

Figure 5.13. The knots $\bar{u}_{h+1}$ through $\bar{u}_{j-1}$ have the same value.

Having suggested the use of μ_i as a continuity-loss index, and then argued that continuity loss is to be associated with knot multiplicity, we will use μ_i to denote the multiplicity of $\bar{u}_i$. The continuity requirement at any knot $\bar{u}_i$ will be $C^{k-1-\mu_i}$, and the number μ_i will be equal to the number of knots in the knot sequence that are equal to $\bar{u}_i$.

As a simple example, consider the knot sequence

$\bar{u}_0$	$\bar{u}_1$	$\bar{u}_2$	$\bar{u}_3$	$\bar{u}_4$	$\bar{u}_5$	$\bar{u}_6$.	
1.0	3.0	3.0	4.0	5.0	5.0	5.0	(5.4)

For this sequence

$$\mu_0 = 1, \quad \mu_1 = 2, \quad \mu_2 = 2, \quad \mu_3 = 1, \quad \mu_4 = 3, \quad \mu_5 = 3, \text{ and } \mu_6 = 3.$$

The set of distinct, consecutive values of $\bar{u}$ across which a spline changes from one polynomial into another are referred to as the *breakpoints* of a spline. In the above example, then, the breakpoints are 1.0, 3.0, 4.0, and 5.0. As a point of terminology, we may speak of a breakpoint as being the location of a certain number of knots. In equation (5.4), 5.0 is the location of 3 knots (a *triple knot*), 4.0 is the location of 1 knot (a *single knot*), and 3.0 is the location of 2 knots (a *double knot*).

Also associated with the breakpoints $\bar{u}_i$ are the *breakpoint intervals*,

$$[\bar{u}_i, \bar{u}_{i+1}),$$

for the values of i for which

$$\bar{u}_i < \bar{u}_{i+1}.$$

These are the half-open intervals over which a spline is merely an ordinary polynomial segment.

There are some subtleties here: the breakpoints are simply *values*. They demarcate the intervals on which a spline is simply a polynomial. The knots, however, are the elements of a *sequence*. They might be viewed as "tokens" that are allocated, in order, to the breakpoint positions along the $\bar{u}$ axis — sometimes one to a breakpoint, but sometimes several in a cluster. To specify a breakpoint, we may simply write down its value. A knot, however, consists of a value and an index, giving the knot's order in a sequence.

There is a need for this pedantry. In previous chapters, knots corresponded to breakpoints and there was nothing unusual about the interval between two knots, $[\bar{u}_i, \bar{u}_{i+1})$. If, however, $\bar{u}_i = \bar{u}_{i+1}$, this half-open interval, which is supposed to consist of all values of $\bar{u}$ satisfying $\bar{u}_i \le \bar{u} < \bar{u}_{i+1}$, is vacuous.

Indeed, the fact that $[\bar{u}_i, \bar{u}_{i+1})$ can be vacuous when $\bar{u}_i$ and $\bar{u}_{i+1}$ are repeated knots leads to a convenient way of designating the breakpoint interval into which a given value of $\bar{u}$ falls. Suppose that $\bar{u}_0 \le \bar{u} < \bar{u}_{m+k}$. Then the sentence,

Let δ be the index such that $\bar{u}_\delta \le \bar{u} < \bar{u}_{\delta+1}$.

is a sentence that uniquely specifies the value of δ. This is easiest to see with an example. Consider the knots of (5.4) and the value of $\bar{u} = 4.0$.

$\delta = 0$ is not such that $\overline{u}_\delta = 1.0 \leq 4.0 < \overline{u}_{\delta+1} = 3.0$

$\delta = 1$ is not such that $\overline{u}_\delta = 3.0 \leq 4.0 < \overline{u}_{\delta+1} = 3.0$

$\delta = 2$ is not (!) such that $\overline{u}_\delta = 3.0 \leq 4.0 < \overline{u}_{\delta+1} = 4.0$

$\delta = 3$ is (!) such that $\overline{u}_\delta = 4.0 \leq 4.0 < \overline{u}_{\delta+1} = 5.0$

etc.

Clearly, $\delta = 3$, and the breakpoint interval containing $\overline{u} = 4.0$ is

$$[\overline{u}_3, \overline{u}_4) = [4.0, 5.0).$$

In summary:

■ **Convention**

Let $\overline{u}$ be any parameter value in the range

$$\overline{u}_0 \leq \overline{u} < \overline{u}_{m+k} .$$

Then the index δ described by

$$\overline{u}_\delta \leq \overline{u} < \overline{u}_{\delta+1}$$

is well-defined and unique, and

$$[\overline{u}_\delta, \overline{u}_{\delta+1})$$

is the breakpoint interval containing $\overline{u}$.

■

If knots remained frozen in place, we would have no reason to separate the concepts of knot and breakpoint; it would suffice to flag each $\overline{u}_i$ with a continuity-loss index μ_i, as was suggested before. The need to distinguish between knots and breakpoints arises when knots are moved about, pushed together, and pulled apart.

We close with a formal notation for a useful set of splines. In this definition $p_{left}(\overline{u})$ is the *segment polynomial* describing $s(\overline{u})$ in the breakpoint interval

$$[\overline{u}_h, \overline{u}_i),$$

where $\bar{u}_h$ is the knot of highest index strictly less than (to the left of) $\bar{u}_i$, and $p_{right}(\bar{u})$ is the segment polynomial describing $s(\bar{u})$ on

$$[\bar{u}_i, \bar{u}_j),$$

where $\bar{u}_j$ is the knot of lowest index strictly greater than (to the right of) $\bar{u}_i$. That is, $[\bar{u}_h, \bar{u}_i)$ and $[\bar{u}_i, \bar{u}_j)$ constitute adjacent breakpoint intervals. Figure 5.13 shows the knot configuration, and Figure 5.14 below shows the segment polynomials in more detail.

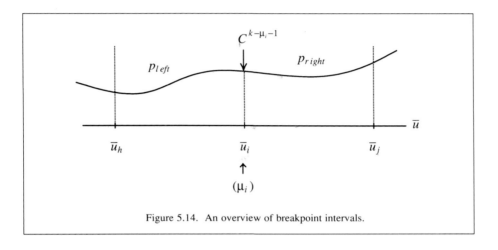

Figure 5.14. An overview of breakpoint intervals.

The ℓth derivative of p_{left} at $\bar{u}_i$ will be denoted by $p_{left}^{(\ell)}(\bar{u}_i)$, and similarly for p_{right}.

The model space that we will will be discussing throughout, the one that constitutes the generator of maximal parametric range for curves and surfaces made up of arbitrary k^{th}-order segments, will be given a short-hand designation. From time to time, other spaces will be brought up, and discussions will touch on other parametric ranges, but the following space will take up much of our attention.

■ **Notation**

Assume that

$$k \geq 1, \quad k-1 < m+1, \quad \bar{u}_{k-1} < \bar{u}_{m+1},$$

and that

$$\bar{u}_i \leq \bar{u}_{i+1} \quad \text{for all } i = 0, \ldots, m+k-1.$$

Then

$$\mathbf{S}(\mathbf{P}^k, \{\bar{u}_i\}_0^{m+k})$$

denotes the set of all k^{th}-order splines with the parameter range

$$\bar{u}_{k-1} \leq \bar{u} < \bar{u}_{m+1}$$

and with the knot sequence

$$\{\bar{u}_i\}_0^{m+k}.$$

This is the set of all functions $s(\bar{u})$ satisfying:

$$s(\bar{u}) \in \mathbf{P}^k$$

for each of the breakpoint intervals

$$[-\infty, \bar{u}_0),$$

$$[\bar{u}_\delta, \bar{u}_{\delta+1}) \text{ for } \delta = 0, \ldots, m+k-1 \text{ such that } \bar{u}_\delta < \bar{u}_{\delta+1},$$

and

$$[\bar{u}_{m+k}, +\infty),$$

and for any knot $\bar{u}_i$, $i \in \{0, \ldots, m+k\}$, with associated multiplicity μ_i,

if

$$s(\bar{u}) = p_{left}(\bar{u}) \in \mathbf{P}^k \quad \text{on } [\bar{u}_h, \bar{u}_i)$$

and

$$s(\bar{u}) = p_{right}(\bar{u}) \in \mathbf{P}^k \quad \text{on } [\bar{u}_i, \bar{u}_j)$$

as shown in Figure 5.14, then

$$p_{left}^{(\ell)}(\bar{u}_i) = p_{right}^{(\ell)}(\bar{u}_i) \text{ for } \ell = 0, \ldots, k-1-\mu_i.$$

No continuity at all is assumed if $k - 1 - \mu_i < 0$.

Two splines are considered to be *identical* if they are equal for all $\bar{u}$ in the parameter range $[\bar{u}_{k-1}, \bar{u}_{m+1})$, even though they may differ outside that range.

■

It is a trivial observation, but one very useful to make, that any k^{th}-order polynomial is a spline in $S(\mathbf{P}^k, \{\bar{u}_i\}_0^{m+k})$. The argument goes like this:

- On each breakpoint interval a kth-order polynomial is, of course, a kth-order polynomial.

- At each breakpoint u_i a kth-order polynomial is C^∞ differentiable; thus it is certainly $C^{k-1-\mu_i}$ differentiable.

There are, obviously, splines in $S(\mathbf{P}^k, \{\bar{u}_i\}_0^{m+k})$ that are not polynomials, so $S(\mathbf{P}^k, \{\bar{u}_i\}_0^{m+k})$ is larger than $\mathbf{P}^k$. The converse of this observation is, clearly, not true: k^{th}-order splines are not, usually, pure polynomials.

A more profound observation is that the sum of any two functions in $S(\mathbf{P}^k, \{\bar{u}_i\}_0^{m+k})$ is also a function in $S(\mathbf{P}^k, \{\bar{u}_i\}_0^{m+k})$, and that any constant times a function in $S(\mathbf{P}^k, \{\bar{u}_i\}_0^{m+k})$ is also a function in $S(\mathbf{P}^k, \{\bar{u}_i\}_0^{m+k})$. Again, a brief argument:

- On any of the breakpoint intervals we are merely dealing with polynomials. The sum of any two k^{th}-order polynomials is still a kth-order polynomial, and a constant times a kth-order polynomial is just a kth-order polynomial.

- At any point in $[\bar{u}_{k-1}, \bar{u}_{m+1})$ we are dealing with functions having the same fixed differentiability properties. At each point of any breakpoint interval that isn't a knot, all derivatives of any k^{th}-order polynomial exist, and so do those of the sums of any two such polynomials or a constant times either one of them. On the other hand, at any knot $\bar{u}_i$, any two members of $S(\mathbf{P}^k, \{\bar{u}_i\}_0^{m+k})$ will have derivatives of order 0 through $k-\mu_i-1$, hence so must their sum or any constant multiple of either.

That is, in short:

■ **Theorem**

$S(\mathbf{P}^k, \{\bar{u}_i\}_0^{m+k})$ is a vector space.

■

■ **Theorem**

$\mathbf{P}^k$ is a (proper) subspace of $S(\mathbf{P}^k, \{\bar{u}_i\}_0^{m+k})$.

■

6

The One-Sided
Basis

6.1 The One-Sided Cubic

This chapter will focus on functions of the form $(\bar{u} - t)_+^r$, on their properties, and on the means by which they are transformed into B-splines. We will begin with an example.

In Figure 6.1, suppose that we have a cubic polynomial $p(\bar{u})$. Let t be some arbitrary position on the $\bar{u}$ axis, and let $\bar{v}$ indicate the displacement from t.

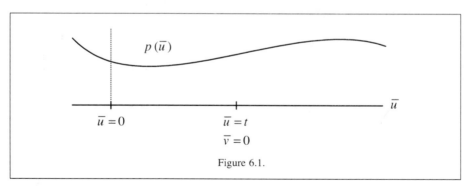

Figure 6.1.

It is easy to see how to express the value of $p(\bar{u})$ in terms of the displacement $\bar{v}$ from the point $\bar{u} = t$, instead of the displacement $\bar{u}$ from the point $\bar{u} = 0$. We know that $\bar{u} = \bar{v} + t$, and we have only to substitute $\bar{v} + t$ for $\bar{u}$ in the expression for $p(\bar{u})$. For example, if

$$p(\bar{u}) = 3 - \bar{u} + \bar{u}^2 - \bar{u}^3$$

and $t = 1$ then

$$p(\bar{v}) = 2 - 2\bar{v} - 2\bar{v}^2 - \bar{v}^3.$$

Since $\bar{v} = \bar{u} - 1$, an alternative representation for $p(\bar{u})$ is

$$p(\bar{u}) = 2 - 2(\bar{u} - 1) - 2(\bar{u} - 1)^2 - (\bar{u} - 1)^3.$$

Thus, if we are given any polynomial $p(\bar{u})$ and constant t, then $p(\bar{u})$ may easily be given in terms of the powers $(\bar{u} - t)$.

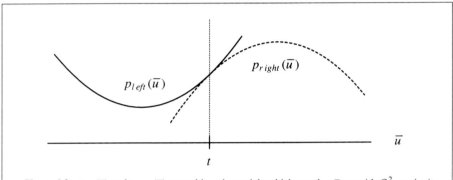

Figure 6.2. $p_{left}(\bar{u})$ and $p_{right}(\bar{u})$ are cubic polynomials which meed at $\bar{u} = t$ with C^2 continuity.

Now suppose that we have two cubic polynomials $p_{left}(\bar{u})$ and $p_{right}(\bar{u})$ which meet with exactly C^2 continuity at the arbitrary parameter value $\bar{u} = t$ (see Figure 6.2). Consider the change

$$\Delta(\bar{u}) = p_{right}(\bar{u}) - p_{left}(\bar{u})$$

as we cross the knot t. Since $\Delta(\bar{u})$ is clearly a cubic polynomial, we know that $\Delta(\bar{u})$ can be represented in terms of an expansion about $\bar{u} = t$, and so we can write

$$\Delta(\bar{u}) = c_0 + c_1(\bar{u} - t) + c_2(\bar{u} - t)^2 + c_3(\bar{u} - t)^3.$$

What are the coefficients c_i? From the expansion of $\Delta(\bar{u})$ in powers of $(\bar{u} - t)$, we see that $\Delta(\bar{u}) = c_0$ at $\bar{u} = t$. Furthermore

$$\frac{d}{d\bar{u}} \Delta(\bar{u}) = c_1 + 2c_2(\bar{u} - t)^1 + 3c_3(\bar{u} - t)^2,$$

so that

$$\frac{d}{d\bar{u}} \Delta(\bar{u}) = c_1 \text{ at } \bar{u} = t.$$

Differentiating again,

$$\frac{d^2}{d\bar{u}^2} \Delta(\bar{u}) = 2c_2 + 6c_3(\bar{u}-t)^1,$$

giving

$$\frac{d^2}{d\bar{u}^2} \Delta(\bar{u}) = 2c_2 \text{ at } \bar{u} = t.$$

Finally,

$$\frac{d^3}{d\bar{u}^3} \Delta(\bar{u}) = 6c_3,$$

and consequently

$$\frac{d^3}{d\bar{u}^3} \Delta(\bar{u}) = 6c_3 \text{ at } \bar{u} = t.$$

The c_i are, essentially, the derivatives of $\Delta(\bar{u})$ at $\bar{u} = t$. But because $p_{left}(\bar{u})$ and $p_{right}(\bar{u})$ are C^2 continuous, we know that they have the same value, first derivative and second derivative at t; that is, derivatives zero, one, and two of $\Delta(\bar{u})$ must be zero at $\bar{u} = t$:

$$\Delta^{(0)}(t) = 0, \quad \Delta^{(1)}(t) = 0, \text{ and } \Delta^{(2)}(t) = 0.$$

So

$$c_0 = 0, \quad c_1 = 0, \text{ and } c_2 = 0,$$

and we have

$$\Delta(\bar{u}) = c_3(\bar{u}-t)^3.$$

In fact, it is clear the value of c_3 is determined by the size of the change in the third derivative of the spline at t; we have

$$c_3 = \frac{1}{6} \left[p_{right}^{(3)}(t) - p_{left}^{(3)}(t) \right].$$

It simplifies things a bit if we use $\Delta_+(\bar{u})$, the one-sided version of $\Delta(\bar{u})$, which leads us to the one-sided version of $(\bar{u}-t)^3$, namely

$$(\bar{u} - t)_+^3,$$

which is zero to the left of $\bar{u} = t$ and acts just like $(\bar{u}-t)^3$ for all $\bar{u} \geq t$. The form of such a function, for $t = \bar{u}_0, \ldots, \bar{u}_8$, is shown in Figure 6.3.

Notice that $(\bar{u}-t)_+^3$ has the value zero at $\bar{u} = t$. So do the first and second derivatives of $(\bar{u}-t)_+^3$. But the third derivative of $(\bar{u}-t)_+^3$ is discontinuous at $\bar{u} = t$:

function value: $(\bar{u}-t)^3 \big|_{\bar{u}=t}$ $= (t-t)^3$ $= 0$

first derivative value: $3 \cdot (\bar{u}-t)^2 \big|_{\bar{u}=t}$ $= 3 \cdot (t-t)^2$ $= 0$

second derivative value: $6 \cdot (\bar{u}-t)^1 \big|_{\bar{u}=t}$ $= 6 \cdot (t-t)^1$ $= 0$

third derivative value: $6 \big|_{\bar{u}=t}$ $= 6$.

This is exactly the sort of discontinuity displayed by C^2 splines in general.

Since $(\bar{u}-t)_+^3$ is zero for $\bar{u} < t$ we can now write

$$p_{left}(\bar{u}) = p_{left}(\bar{u}) + c_3(\bar{u}-t)_+^3$$

and for $\bar{u} \geq t$ we also have

$$p_{right}(\bar{u}) = p_{left}(\bar{u}) + c_3(\bar{u}-t)_+^3 .$$

What we have obtained is a succinct representation, equally valid on either side of t, for the spline represented by $p_{left}(\bar{u})$ and $p_{right}(\bar{u})$. All the foregoing is a special case of Taylor's theorem, in which we have "expanded" $\Delta(\bar{u})$ about $\bar{u} = t$.

Suppose that we have the C^2 cubic spline shown in Figure 6.3.

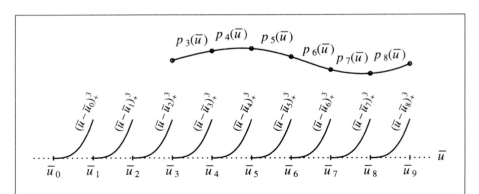

Figure 6.3. A C^2 cubic spline on the range $\bar{u}_3 \leq \bar{u} < \bar{u}_9$ expressed with the aid of *one-sided basis functions*. Each $p_i(\bar{u})$ is a scaled sum of all the basis functions which depart from zero left of, or at, $\bar{u}_i$.

If we identify $p_3(\bar{u})$ with $p_{left}(\bar{u})$ in the above discussion and $p_4(\bar{u})$ with $p_{right}(\bar{u})$, using $t = \bar{u}_4$, then

$$p_4(\bar{u}) = p_3(\bar{u}) + c_{3,4}\,(\bar{u}-\bar{u}_4)_+^3$$

for some constant $c_{3,4}$. It is also important to note that $p_3(\bar{u})$ can be expressed in terms of $(\bar{u}-\bar{u}_0)_+^3$, $(\bar{u}-\bar{u}_1)_+^3$, $(\bar{u}-\bar{u}_2)_+^3$, and $(\bar{u}-\bar{u}_3)_+^3$:

$$p_3(\bar{u}) = c_{3,0}\,(\bar{u}-\bar{u}_0)_+^3 + c_{3,1}\,(\bar{u}-\bar{u}_1)_+^3 + c_{3,2}\,(\bar{u}-\bar{u}_2)_+^3 + c_{3,3}\,(\bar{u}-\bar{u}_3)_+^3 .$$

This is true because

$$(\bar{u}-\bar{u}_0)_+^3 = (\bar{u}-\bar{u}_0)^3 \quad \text{for } \bar{u} \in [\bar{u}_3,\bar{u}_4)$$

$$(\bar{u}-\bar{u}_1)_+^3 = (\bar{u}-\bar{u}_1)^3 \quad \text{for } \bar{u} \in [\bar{u}_3,\bar{u}_4)$$

$$(\bar{u}-\bar{u}_2)_+^3 = (\bar{u}-\bar{u}_2)^3 \quad \text{for } \bar{u} \in [\bar{u}_3,\bar{u}_4)$$

$$(\bar{u}-\bar{u}_3)_+^3 = (\bar{u}-\bar{u}_3)^3 \quad \text{for } \bar{u} \in [\bar{u}_3,\bar{u}_4),$$

and the $(\bar{u}-\bar{u}_0)^3 , \ldots, (\bar{u}-\bar{u}_3)^3$ constitute a basis for the cubics.

If we shift our attention one interval to the right and regard $p_4(\bar{u})$ as $p_{left}(\bar{u})$, then we see that

$$p_5(\bar{u}) = p_4(\bar{u}) + c_{3,5}\,(\bar{u}-\bar{u}_5)_+^3 .$$

Note that this can also be written as

$$p_5(\bar{u}) = p_3(\bar{u}) + c_{3,4}\,(\bar{u}-\bar{u}_4)_+^3 + c_{3,5}\,(\bar{u}-\bar{u}_5)_+^3 ,$$

or even as

$$p_5(\bar{u}) = c_{3,0}\,(\bar{u}-\bar{u}_0)_+^3 + \cdots + c_{3,5}\,(\bar{u}-\bar{u}_5)_+^3 .$$

Continuing in this fashion, we can convince ourselves that the entire cubic spline may be represented on the interval $\bar{u}_3 \le \bar{u} < \bar{u}_9$ as

$$\sum_{i=0}^{8} c_{3,i}\,(\bar{u}-\bar{u}_i)_+^3$$

for some coefficients $c_{3,i}$ that we know how to compute.

Suppose that our ultimate goal were to reproduce the kth order splines on the knot sequence $\{\bar{u}_0, \ldots, \bar{u}_{m+k}\}$ with comparisons for equality restricted to the parameter range $\bar{u}_{k-1} \leq \bar{u} < \bar{u}_{m+1}$; i.e., the splines of the space we have denoted by $S(P^k, \{\bar{u}_i\}_0^{m+k})$. Figure 6.3, for example, gives an illustration with

$$k = 4, \quad m = 8, \quad \{\bar{u}_i\}_0^{m+k} = \{\bar{u}_0, \bar{u}_1, \ldots, \bar{u}_{12}\}$$

and $\bar{u}_{10}, \bar{u}_{11}, \bar{u}_{12}$ not explicitly shown. We might conjecture that this goal could be attained through the use of truncated powers. To see the extent to which this conjecture is true, we will advance the discussion to general order k and to more general knot sequences. We will proceed intuitively; for a rigorous development of this material see [Schumaker81] or [de Boor78].

6.2 The General Case

Consider any spline, $s(\bar{u})$ and its transition from

$$s(\bar{u}) = p_{left}(\bar{u}) \quad \text{for} \quad -\infty < \bar{u} < \bar{u}_0$$

to

$$s(\bar{u}) = p_{right}(\bar{u}) \quad \text{for} \quad \bar{u}_0 \leq \bar{u} < \bar{u}_\lambda$$

at the knot $\bar{u} = \bar{u}_0$. Here we assume that λ is the least index for which $\bar{u}_0 < \bar{u}_\lambda$. This means that the

$$\bar{u}_0, \ldots, \bar{u}_{\lambda-1}$$

are all equal; hence,

$$\mu_0 = \lambda.$$

As $\bar{u}$ crosses the breakpoint represented by $\bar{u}_0$, $s(\bar{u})$ changes from $p_{left}(\bar{u})$, a kth-order polynomial, into $p_{right}(\bar{u})$, also a kth-order polynomial. But $p_{left}(\bar{u})$ and $p_{right}(\bar{u})$ are expected to agree in their first $k - 1 - \mu_0$ derivatives at $\bar{u} = \bar{u}_0$, because of the multiplicity of the knots associated with this breakpoint. Consequently:

$$\begin{aligned}
p_{left}^{(0)}(\bar{u}_0) &= p_{right}^{(0)}(\bar{u}_0) \\
p_{left}^{(1)}(\bar{u}_0) &= p_{right}^{(1)}(\bar{u}_0) \\
&\cdot \qquad \cdot \\
&\cdot \qquad \cdot \qquad\qquad (6.1) \\
&\cdot \qquad \cdot \\
p_{left}^{(k-1-\mu_0)}(\bar{u}_0) &= p_{right}^{(k-1-\mu_0)}(\bar{u}_0).
\end{aligned}$$

Generalizing the argument of the last section we see that

$$\Delta(\bar{u}) = p_{right}(\bar{u}) - p_{left}(\bar{u})$$

$$= \Delta^{(0)}(\bar{u}_0)(\bar{u} - \bar{u}_0)^0 + \Delta^{(1)}(\bar{u}_0)(\bar{u} - \bar{u}_0)^1 + \frac{1}{(k-1)!}\Delta^{(k-1)}(\bar{u}_0)(\bar{u} - \bar{u}_0)^{k-1}.$$

(This representation is an instance of Taylor's Theorem.) Now, for $\bar{u}_0 \le \bar{u} < \bar{u}_\lambda$,

$$s(\bar{u}) = p_{right}(\bar{u}) = p_{left}(\bar{u}) + \Delta(\bar{u}).$$

But, because of (6.1) above,

$$\Delta^{(0)}(\bar{u}_0) = \cdots = \Delta^{(k-1-\mu_0)}(\bar{u}_0) = 0.$$

Hence $\Delta(\bar{u})$ can be written more simply as

$$\Delta(\bar{u}) = c_{k-\mu_0,0}(\bar{u} - \bar{u}_0)^{k-\mu_0} + c_{k-\mu_0+1,0}(\bar{u} - \bar{u}_0)^{k-\mu_0+1} + c_{k-1,0}(\bar{u} - \bar{u}_0)^{k-1}$$

for some some constants $c_{k-\mu_0,0}, \ldots, c_{k-1,0}$. This suggests that we can write $s(\bar{u})$ on the entire range $-\infty < \bar{u} < \bar{u}_\lambda$ as

$$s(\bar{u}) = p_{left}(\bar{u}) + \Delta_+(\bar{u}),$$

where

$$\Delta_+(\bar{u}) = c_{k-\mu_0,0}(\bar{u} - \bar{u}_0)_+^{k-\mu_0} + c_{k-\mu_0+1,0}(\bar{u} - \bar{u}_0)_+^{k-\mu_0+1} + c_{k-1,0}(\bar{u} - \bar{u}_0)_+^{k-1},$$

giving us

$$s(\bar{u}) = \begin{cases} p_{left}(\bar{u}) & -\infty < \bar{u} < \bar{u}_0 \\ p_{right}(\bar{u}) & \bar{u}_0 \le \bar{u} < \bar{u}_\lambda. \end{cases}$$

(This assumes that $\mu_0 \le k$. If $\mu_0 > k$, then we may take 0 as the lowest exponent in the above, i.e., we may use $\min(k, \mu_0)$ in place of μ_0.)

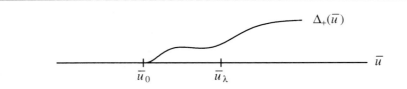

Figure 6.4. $\Delta_+(\bar{u})$ is the amount by which $p_{left}(\bar{u})$ must be changed as we cross $\bar{u}_0$ to obtain $p_{right}(\bar{u})$.

This means that for $\bar{u} \in [\bar{u}_0, \bar{u}_\lambda)$, we have

$$s(\bar{u}) = p_{left}(\bar{u}) + \sum_{r=1}^{\mu_0} c_{k-r,0}(\bar{u} - \bar{u}_0)_+^{k-r}$$

for some constants $c_{k-1,0}, \ldots, c_{k-\mu_0,0}$.

Since we use the one-sided powers only as a means of constructing the general B-splines, which are expected to be zero except on a small number of knot intervals, we can therefore assume that $s(\bar{u})$ is zero on the range $-\infty < \bar{u} < \bar{u}_0$. This simplifies the above to

$$s(\bar{u}) = \sum_{r=1}^{\mu_0} c_{k-r,0}(\bar{u} - \bar{u}_0)_+^{k-r}.$$

Let us number the breakpoints consecutively:

$$\bar{u}_{i_0} = \bar{u}_0, \ \bar{u}_{i_1} = \bar{u}_\lambda, \ \cdots, \bar{u}_{i_L},$$

where $\bar{u}_{i_L}$ is the last breakpoint in the range $[\bar{u}_{k-1}, \bar{u}_{m+1})$. The same argument that we made at the breakpoint given by $\bar{u} = \bar{u}_0$ can be repeated across each successive breakpoint in the parameter range. $s(\bar{u})$ picks up the powers

$$(\bar{u} - \bar{u}_{i_j})^{k-\ell} \quad \text{for} \ \ell = 1, \ldots, \ \mu_{i_j}$$

at each breakpoint $\bar{u}_{i_j}$. This means that $s(\bar{u})$ can be represented across the entire parameter range $\bar{u} \in [\bar{u}_{k-1}, \bar{u}_{m+1})$ by the formula

$$s(\bar{u}) = \sum_{j=0}^{L} \sum_{r=1}^{\mu_{i_j}} c_{k-r,i_j}(\bar{u} - \bar{u}_{i_j})_+^{k-r},$$

where the c's are appropriate coefficients. Note that the summation is doubled, with each breakpoint contributing as many terms (successive powers) as there are knots multiply located on that breakpoint. The simplest version of this formula would be the one in which all knots are simple:

$$s(\bar{u}) = \sum_{j=0}^{m+k} c_{k-1,j} (\bar{u} - \bar{u}_{i_j})_+^{k-1} \quad \text{for all } \bar{u}.$$

Strictly for the $\bar{u}$ on the designated parameter range, the last k of the terms would be zero, reducing this to

$$s(\bar{u}) = \sum_{j=0}^{m} c_{k-1,j} (\bar{u} - \bar{u}_{i_j})_+^{k-1} \quad \text{for } \bar{u}_{k-1} \leq \bar{u} < \bar{u}_{m+1}.$$

This is the formula which describes the curve shown in Figure 6.3, namely

$$s(\bar{u}) = \begin{cases} p_3(\bar{u}) & \text{for} \quad \bar{u} \in [\bar{u}_3, \bar{u}_4) \\ p_4(\bar{u}) & \text{for} \quad \bar{u} \in [\bar{u}_4, \bar{u}_5) \\ p_5(\bar{u}) & \text{for} \quad \bar{u} \in [\bar{u}_5, \bar{u}_6) \\ p_6(\bar{u}) & \text{for} \quad \bar{u} \in [\bar{u}_6, \bar{u}_7) \\ p_7(\bar{u}) & \text{for} \quad \bar{u} \in [\bar{u}_7, \bar{u}_8) \\ p_8(\bar{u}) & \text{for} \quad \bar{u} \in [\bar{u}_8, \bar{u}_9) \end{cases}$$

$$= \sum_{j=0}^{8} c_{3,j} (\bar{u} - \bar{u}_j)_+^3.$$

The functions $(\bar{u} - t)_+^r$, for t = any knot and any power $r = 0, \ldots, k-1$, are worth studying, since the discussion above leads us to believe that they can be used to represent any spline on any collection of knots.

6.3 One-Sided Power Functions

Let us begin with the simplest version of $(\bar{u} - t)_+^r$, the one with $r = 0$. This is the step function given by

$$(\bar{u} - t)_+^0 = \begin{cases} 0 & \bar{u} < t \\ 1 & \bar{u} \geq t. \end{cases} \tag{6.2}$$

This function is an instance of two first order polynomials (constants) tied together with no continuity across the single breakpoint t, which also constitutes a

---

knot of multiplicity 1. This is the simplest possible example of a spline: $k = 1$, $\bar{u}_0 = t$, $\mu_0 = 1$, and we have C^{-1} continuity across the breakpoint. Moreover, it is just what we need to represent functions like $\Delta_+(\bar{u})$ above, where $\Delta(\bar{u})$ is of order 1; $(\bar{u} - \bar{u}_{i_0})^0_+$ is identically zero to the left of $\bar{u}_{i_0}$, and can be used to represent any constant (polynomial of order 1) to the right of $\bar{u}_{i_0}$. Thus

$$\Delta_+(\bar{u}) = \text{constant} \cdot (\bar{u} - t)^0_+ .$$

The "cup and ball" representation given in Figure 6.5 shows that $(\bar{u} - t)^0_+$ has the value 0 from $-\infty$ up to, but not including, $\bar{u} = t$ and the value 1 at $\bar{u} = t$ and thereafter to $+\infty$. This is a convention we will use often in subsequent figures.

■ **Definition**

The rth one-sided power function is given by

$$(\bar{u} - t)^r_+ = (\bar{u} - t)^0_+ (\bar{u} - t)^r$$

$$= \begin{cases} 0 & \bar{u} < t \\ \\ (\bar{u} - t)^r & \bar{u} \geq t , \end{cases} \qquad (6.3)$$

where $r = 0, 1, 2, \cdots$ and $(\bar{u} - t)^0_+$ is given by (6.2) above.

■

It is easily checked that $(\bar{u} - t)^r_+$ is C^{r-1} continuous across any fixed t: there will be a match at $\bar{u} = t$ in value and in the first $r - 1$ derivatives, while the rth derivative will be discontinuous at $\bar{u} = t$.

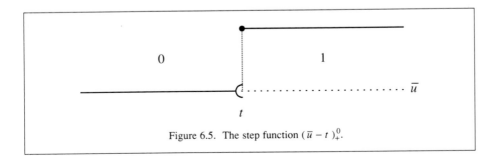

Figure 6.5. The step function $(\bar{u} - t)^0_+$.

6.4 The One-Sided Basis

The discontinuities in any spline we will ever construct are exactly like the discontinuity in

$$(\bar{u}-t)^0_+ ;$$

i.e., all our splines will be "open on the right" in any breakpoint interval. This means that they have one characterization up to, but not including, each breakpoint, and another characterization directly at and to the right of that breakpoint. This follows directly from the way we have defined $\mathbf{S}(\mathbf{P}^k, \{\bar{u}_i\}_0^{m+k})$, and also from the way we will be representing splines using the functions $(\bar{u}-t)^r_+$.

For an arbitrary spline in $\mathbf{S}(\mathbf{P}^k, \{\bar{u}_i\}_0^{m+k})$, when all knots have been considered and all transitions from $p_{left}(\bar{u})$ to $p_{right}(\bar{u})$ have been dealt with, we will have made use of the following one-sided power functions in representing the spline, as shown in Figure 6.6.

$$(\bar{u}-\bar{u}_{i_0})^{k-1}_+, (\bar{u}-\bar{u}_{i_0})^{k-2}_+, \ldots, (\bar{u}-\bar{u}_{i_0})^{k-\mu_{i_0}}_+ \quad \text{for } \bar{u}_{i_0}$$

$$(\bar{u}-\bar{u}_{i_1})^{k-1}_+, (\bar{u}-\bar{u}_{i_1})^{k-2}_+, \ldots, (\bar{u}-\bar{u}_{i_1})^{k-\mu_{i_1}}_+ \quad \text{for } \bar{u}_{i_1}$$

$$\cdots \qquad\qquad \cdots \qquad\qquad (6.4)$$

$$(\bar{u}-\bar{u}_{i_L})^{k-1}_+, (\bar{u}-\bar{u}_{i_L})^{k-2}_+, \ldots, (\bar{u}-\bar{u}_{i_L})^{k-\mu_{i_L}}_+ \quad \text{for } \bar{u}_{i_L} .$$

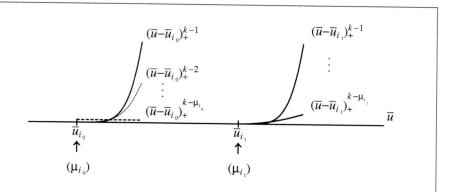

Figure 6.6. We can build, from these functions, an arbitrary spline having the sort of continuity at knots which we desire. (The vertical scale here has been much reduced.)

The functions in (6.4) are linearly independent, and it can easily be seen that each is a member of $S(\mathbf{P}^k, \{\bar{u}_i\}_0^{m+k})$.

■ Theorem

The functions of (6.4) above form a basis for $S(\mathbf{P}^k, \{\bar{u}_i\}_0^{m+k})$.

■

■ Definition

The functions $(\bar{u} - t)_+^r$, are called the *one-sided* or *truncated power basis* for $S(\mathbf{P}^k, \{\bar{u}_i\}_0^{m+k})$.

■

By way of illustrating (6.4), consider the knot sequence

$\bar{u}_0$	$\bar{u}_1$	$\bar{u}_2$	$\bar{u}_3$	$\bar{u}_4$	$\bar{u}_5$	$\bar{u}_6$
1	3	3	5	5	5	5 .

Let us use the one-sided basis to construct quadratic splines ($k = 3$) on the range $\bar{u}_2 \leq \bar{u} < \bar{u}_4$. We have

$$\bar{u}_{k-1} = \bar{u}_2 \quad \text{and} \quad \bar{u}_{m+1} = \bar{u}_4 .$$

If we choose

$$i_0 = 0, \quad i_1 = 1, \quad \text{and} \quad i_2 = i_L = 3$$

then the basis (6.4) would be

$$(\bar{u} - \bar{u}_0)_+^2, \quad (\bar{u} - \bar{u}_1)_+^2, \quad (\bar{u} - \bar{u}_1)_+^1, \quad \text{and} \quad (\bar{u} - \bar{u}_3)_+^2.$$

We needn't restrict ourselves to the interval $[\bar{u}_{k-1}, \bar{u}_{m+1})$, however. One-sided powers have a wider applicability than that. For $-\infty < \bar{u} < +\infty$, consider the uniform cubic B-spline given in (5.1), which we repeat here as (6.5):

$$B_0(\bar{u}) = \begin{cases} 0 & -\infty < \bar{u} < 0 \\[2mm] b_{-0}(\bar{u}) = \dfrac{1}{6}\bar{u}^3 & 0 \le \bar{u} < 1 \\[2mm] b_{-1}(\bar{u}) = -\dfrac{1}{6}(3\bar{u}^3 - 12\bar{u}^2 + 12\bar{u} - 4) & 1 \le \bar{u} < 2 \\[2mm] b_{-2}(\bar{u}) = \dfrac{1}{6}(3\bar{u}^3 - 24\bar{u}^2 + 60\bar{u} - 44) & 2 \le \bar{u} < 3 \\[2mm] b_{-3}(\bar{u}) = -\dfrac{1}{6}(\bar{u}^3 - 12\bar{u}^2 + 48\bar{u} - 64) & 3 \le \bar{u} < 4 \\[2mm] 0 & 4 \le \bar{u} < +\infty. \end{cases} \tag{6.5}$$

Consider the one-sided powers

$$(\bar{u} - 0)_+^3, \ (\bar{u} - 1)_+^3, \ (\bar{u} - 2)_+^3, \ (\bar{u} - 3)_+^3, \ \text{and} \ (\bar{u} - 4)_+^3.$$

It is straightforward to verify that

$$B_0(\bar{u}) = \frac{1}{6}(\bar{u} - 0)_+^3 - \frac{2}{3}(\bar{u} - 1)_+^3 + 1(\bar{u} - 2)_+^3$$

$$- \frac{2}{3}(\bar{u} - 3)_+^3 + \frac{1}{6}(\bar{u} - 4)_+^3. \tag{6.6}$$

This is true, since for $0 \le \bar{u} < 1$ all terms in (6.6) after the equal sign are zero save the first, and (6.6) becomes

$$B_0(\bar{u}) = \frac{1}{6}(\bar{u} - 0)_+^3 = \frac{1}{6}\bar{u}^3.$$

For the range $1 \le \bar{u} < 2$:

$$p_{left}(\bar{u}) = b_{-0}(\bar{u}),$$

$$p_{right}(\bar{u}) = b_{-1}(\bar{u}),$$

the knot at which these segment polynomials join is

$$\bar{u} = 1.$$

Our previous discussions lead us to believe that

$$b_{-1}(\bar{u}) = b_{-0}(\bar{u}) + c\,(\bar{u} - 1)^3$$

for some constant c. Indeed,

$$c = \frac{b_{-1}(\bar{u}) - b_{-0}(\bar{u})}{(\bar{u} - 1)^3}$$

$$= \frac{-\dfrac{3}{6}\bar{u}^3 + \dfrac{12}{6}\bar{u}^2 - \dfrac{12}{6}\bar{u} + \dfrac{4}{6} - \dfrac{1}{6}\bar{u}^3}{(\bar{u} - 1)^3}$$

$$= -\frac{2}{3}.$$

The verification follows this pattern for the remaining breakpoint intervals.

We can, in fact, construct any B-spline we have ever seen as a linear combination of one-sided power functions. Why do we choose to use the B-splines instead of the simpler power functions? Because the one-sided power functions are computationally unsatisfying. Their utility to us is not in constructing splines; for that purpose they suffer from two severe shortcomings: *numerical instability* and *lack of local control*. The utility of the one-sided basis is that it can be easily described and understood. From it we will define the basis we really want to use, namely the B-spline basis.

To elaborate on these shortcomings, consider the preceding example. The uniform B-spline we constructed is representative of the curves and surfaces that we encounter in graphics: they do not behave wildly. Indeed, the uniform B-spline goes to zero to the left and to the right; a more randomly-chosen spline can be expected merely to maintain bounded behavior throughout the region of interest. The one-sided basis, on the other hand, blows up as $\bar{u}$ increases. Hence if the one–sided basis is used to express "reasonable" spline curves and surfaces, the coefficients required to do this can be expected to alternate between large positive and negative values to force *numerical cancellation* of the basis function values as $\bar{u}$ increases. Cancellation is computationally undesirable.

A second shortcoming, from the point of view of graphics, is that the one-sided basis functions do not have *local support*; they are all nonzero on at least half the real line. If one represents a curve or surface in the usual way as a scaled sum of basis functions, the lack of local support translates into a lack of *local control*: the adjustment of any scale factor has an influence over the shape of the rest of the curve. A change in the first scale factor will affect the entire curve. As a result, the adjustment of any scale factor will give rise to a system of linear equations that must be solved to determine the effect of the adjustment on the curve or surface. The system of equations will be large, involving data from all the control vertices. The continual need to solve such systems whenever vertices are adjusted is a bottleneck in real-time interactive graphical design. It is precisely because the uniform B-spline goes to zero outside of a closed, bounded interval that it is of such interest to us.

Finally, there is no intuitive relationship between the scale factors weighting the one-sided basis functions and the shape of the curve they define. On the other hand, we have already seen that the scale factors weighting the B-spline representation of a spline curve have a direct physical interpretation as control vertices.

6.5   Linear Combinations and Cancellation

The key to constructing a desirable basis from the less desirable (but conceptually simple) one-sided basis is to recognize that cancellation can occur and local support can be achieved analytically, by a symbolic process, before any numerical computation is begun. To this end we will rearrange the one-sided basis functions in the above example by taking linear combinations of them to produce new functions that behave in a much more bounded fashion.

Our game plan is as follows. We will begin with

$$(\bar{u}-0)_+^3,$$

which grows cubically for $\bar{u} \geq 0$, and

$$(\bar{u}-1)_+^3,$$

which grows cubically for $\bar{u} \geq 1$. By taking an appropriate linear combination

$$c_0(\bar{u}-0)_+^3 + c_1(\bar{u}-1)_+^3$$

of these two functions, we can produce a third (combined) function whose $\bar{u}^3$ term is cancelled away for $\bar{u} \geq 1$. The three functions

$$(\bar{u}-0)_+^3$$

$$(\bar{u}-1)_+^3$$

and

$$c_0(\bar{u}-0)_+^3 + c_1(\bar{u}-1)_+^3$$

are linearly dependent, but any two of them will be linearly independent. That is, any one of these three functions can be written as a linear combination of the other two, but no single one of them is merely a multiple of one of the others. Since any two of them can represent the third, any two of them can represent anything that could have been represented by the original two basis functions. Since

$$c_0(\bar{u}-0)_+^3 + c_1(\bar{u}-1)_+^3$$

is better behaved than either of the original two functions, i.e., it has no $\bar{u}^3$ term for $\bar{u} \geq 1$ and consequently "grows more slowly" as $\bar{u} \geq 1$, we would like to use this combined function as a replacement for one of the original two to obtain a revised basis. Arbitrarily, we will use it to replace

$$(\bar{u}-0)_+^3 .$$

This combination process can be repeated for the pairs

$$(\bar{u}-1)_+^3 \quad \text{and} \quad (\bar{u}-2)_+^3$$

$$(\bar{u}-2)_+^3 \quad \text{and} \quad (\bar{u}-3)_+^3$$

and

$$(\bar{u}-3)_+^3 \quad \text{and} \quad (\bar{u}-4)_+^3$$

to yield functions that can be substituted for

$$(\bar{u}-1)_+^3$$

$$(\bar{u}-2)_+^3$$

and

$$(\bar{u}-3)_+^3 .$$

More precisely, we see that

$$(\bar{u}-1)_+^3 - (\bar{u}-0)_+^3 = \begin{cases} 0 & \bar{u} < 0 \\ -\bar{u}^3 & 0 \leq \bar{u} < 1 \\ -3\bar{u}^2 + 3\bar{u} - 1 & 1 \leq \bar{u}, \end{cases}$$

which grows *quadratically* for $\bar{u} \geq 1$.

Note that $(\bar{u}-1)_+^3 - (\bar{u}-0)_+^3$ goes negative at $\bar{u} = 0$, and continues to $-\infty$ as $\bar{u}$ increases. From Figure 6.7 it is clear why this is so: $(\bar{u}-0)_+^3$ is positive between 0 and 1, so $-(\bar{u}-0)_+^3$ is negative between 0 and 1. Since $(\bar{u}-1)_+^3$ is zero in this interval, the entire expression is negative on $[0,1)$.

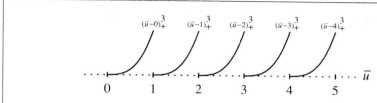

Figure 6.7. The one-sided basis functions for a uniform C^2 cubic spline.

Will this work more generally? Observe that

$$(\bar{u} - \bar{u}_{i+1})_+^3 - (\bar{u} - \bar{u}_i)_+^3$$

$$= \begin{cases} 0 & \bar{u} < \bar{u}_i \\ \\ -(\bar{u} - \bar{u}_i)^3 & \bar{u}_i \le \bar{u} < \bar{u}_{i+1} \\ \\ -3\bar{u}^2(\bar{u}_{i+1} - \bar{u}_i) + 3\bar{u}(\bar{u}_{i+1} - \bar{u}_i)(\bar{u}_{i+1} + \bar{u}_i) & \bar{u}_{i+1} \le \bar{u}. \\ \quad -(\bar{u}_{i+1} - \bar{u}_i)(\bar{u}_{i+1}^2 + \bar{u}_{i+1}\bar{u}_i + \bar{u}_i^2) \end{cases} \qquad (6.7)$$

We are left, as for uniform knot spacing, with a function that grows only quadratically for $\bar{u} \ge \bar{u}_{i+1}$.

6.6 Cancellation as a Divided Difference

We will now try to take two such "quadratically-growing" combinations of the one-sided power functions and combine them further so as to cancel away any $\bar{u}^2$ behavior as $\bar{u} \to \infty$. It was easy to remove the $\bar{u}^3$ terms, for $\bar{u} \ge \bar{u}_{i+1}$, by combining the two one-sided power functions

$$(\bar{u} - \bar{u}_{i+1})_+^3 = \bar{u}^3 + \cdots$$

and

$$(\bar{u} - \bar{u}_i)_+^3 = \bar{u}^3 + \cdots$$

because their dominating $(\bar{u}^3)$ terms had the same, constant coefficient (namely 1). The coefficient of the dominating term (as $\bar{u} \to \infty$) in the rightmost segment of (6.7), however, is troublesome — it depends on i. But notice that the factor $(\bar{u}_{i+1} - \bar{u}_i)$ occurs in every term of the function for $\bar{u} \ge \bar{u}_{i+1}$. We will divide this factor out (for the moment) assuming that all the knots are distinct so that this divisor cannot be zero. That is, we will consider the *divided difference*

$$\frac{(\bar{u}-\bar{u}_{i+1})_+^3 - (\bar{u}-\bar{u}_i)_+^3}{\bar{u}_{i+1}-\bar{u}_i}$$

$$= \left[+\frac{1}{\bar{u}_{i+1}-\bar{u}_i}\right](\bar{u}-\bar{u}_{i+1})_+^3 + \left[-\frac{1}{\bar{u}_{i+1}-\bar{u}_i}\right](\bar{u}-\bar{u}_i)_+^3 \tag{6.8}$$

$$= \begin{cases} 0 & \bar{u} < \bar{u}_i \\[2ex] -\dfrac{(\bar{u}-\bar{u}_i)^3}{(\bar{u}_{i+1}-\bar{u}_i)} & \bar{u}_i \le \bar{u} < \bar{u}_{i+1} \\[2ex] \begin{aligned} & -3\bar{u}^2 + 3\bar{u}(\bar{u}_{i+1}+\bar{u}_i) \\ & \quad - (\bar{u}_{i+1}^2 + \bar{u}_{i+1}\bar{u}_i + \bar{u}_i^2) \end{aligned} & \bar{u}_{i+1} \le \bar{u} \end{cases}$$

because for $\bar{u} \ge \bar{u}_{i+1}$ this difference cancels the cubic term and also ensures that the remaining quadratic term will have the constant coefficient 3. This means that we set

$$c_0 = \left[-\frac{1}{\bar{u}_{i+1}-\bar{u}_i}\right]$$

and

$$c_1 = \left[+\frac{1}{\bar{u}_{i+1}-\bar{u}_i}\right].$$

So as to have a short-hand notation for this expression we will write

$$[\bar{u}_i, \bar{u}_{i+1} : t](\bar{u}-t)_+^3 = \frac{(\bar{u}-\bar{u}_{i+1})_+^3 - (\bar{u}-\bar{u}_i)_+^3}{\bar{u}_{i+1}-\bar{u}_i} \tag{6.9}$$

to indicate the operations of (a) selecting the two values $\bar{u}_{i+1}$ and $\bar{u}_i$, (b) substituting them for t in two copies of $(\bar{u}-t)_+^3$, (c) subtracting the results, and (d) dividing by $\bar{u}_{i+1}-\bar{u}_i$. Thus our original divided difference for uniformly spaced knots is

$$[0,1:t](\bar{u}-t)_+^3 = \frac{(\bar{u}-1)_+^3 - (\bar{u}-0)_+^3}{1-0}$$

$$= (+1)(\bar{u}-1)_+^3 + (-1)(\bar{u}-0)_+^3.$$

We emphasize that this divided difference function (6.9) is a *linear combination* of the one-sided power functions $(\bar{u} - \bar{u}_i)_+^3$ and $(\bar{u} - \bar{u}_{i+1})_+^3$ and that it can be used to *substitute* for either of these one-sided power functions in the collection of basis functions. Because it is a linear combination of $(\bar{u} - \bar{u}_i)_+^3$ and $(\bar{u} - \bar{u}_{i+1})_+^3$, its differentiability properties will be the "union" of those possessed by the two functions individually: C^2 at $\bar{u}_i$ and $\bar{u}_{i+1}$ and fully differentiable elsewhere.

We choose to let

$$[\,0,1:t\,](\bar{u} - t)_+^3$$

(shown in Figure 6.8) replace

$$(\bar{u} - 0)_+^3,$$

and in doing so we have modified our basis into one which is "nicer" in the sense that its first one-sided member grows only quadratically as $\bar{u} \to \infty$.

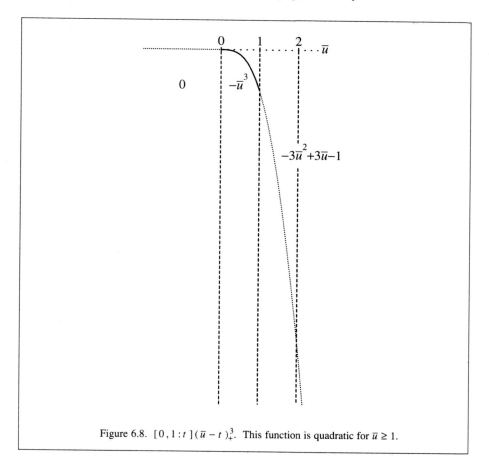

Figure 6.8. $[\,0,1:t\,](\bar{u} - t)_+^3$. This function is quadratic for $\bar{u} \geq 1$.

In like fashion it may be verified that

$$[1,2:t](\bar{u}-t)_+^3 = \frac{(\bar{u}-2)_+^3 - (\bar{u}-1)_+^3}{2-1}$$

$$= \begin{cases} 0 & \bar{u} < 1 \\ -(\bar{u}-1)^3 & 1 \le \bar{u} < 2 \\ -3\bar{u}^2 + 9\bar{u} - 7 & 2 \le \bar{u}, \end{cases}$$

that

$$[2,3:t](\bar{u}-t)_+^3 = \frac{(\bar{u}-3)_+^3 - (\bar{u}-2)_+^3}{3-2}$$

$$= \begin{cases} 0 & \bar{u} < 2 \\ -(\bar{u}-2)^3 & 2 \le \bar{u} < 3 \\ -3\bar{u}^2 + 15\bar{u} - 19 & 3 \le \bar{u}, \end{cases}$$

and that

$$[3,4:t](\bar{u}-t)_+^3 = \frac{(\bar{u}-4)_+^3 - (\bar{u}-3)_+^3}{4-3}$$

$$= \begin{cases} 0 & \bar{u} < 3 \\ -(\bar{u}-3)^3 & 3 \le \bar{u} < 4 \\ -3\bar{u}^2 + 21\bar{u} - 37 & 4 \le \bar{u}. \end{cases}$$

That is, the technique that worked with respect to the first and second knots will work with respect to the remaining adjacent pairs of knots, and we may use the above three functions to substitute for $(\bar{u}-1)_+^3$, $(\bar{u}-2)_+^3$, and $(\bar{u}-3)_+^3$, respectively.

Thus we can replace some of the "eventually-cubic" functions in our original basis with these "eventually-quadratic" functions. In particular,

$$[0,1:t](\bar{u}-t)_+^3 \quad \text{replaces} \quad (\bar{u}-0)_+^3$$
$$[1,2:t](\bar{u}-t)_+^3 \quad \text{replaces} \quad (\bar{u}-1)_+^3$$
$$[2,3:t](\bar{u}-t)_+^3 \quad \text{replaces} \quad (\bar{u}-2)_+^3$$
$$[3,4:t](\bar{u}-t)_+^3 \quad \text{replaces} \quad (\bar{u}-3)_+^3.$$

The original basis appears on the left in Figure 6.9, consisting of one-sided power functions which grow as $\bar{u}^3$ for $\bar{u} \rightarrow +\infty$. The new basis appears on the right, and consists of four functions that begin to go negative cubically but eventually grow as $-\bar{u}^2$ for $\bar{u} \rightarrow +\infty$, together with one of the original truncated cubics which cannot be replaced because there is no truncated cubic to its right with which it can be differenced.

6.7 Cancelling the Quadratic Term — The Second Difference

In the previous section we saw that dividing by the knot spacing $\bar{u}_{i+1} - \bar{u}_i$ set us up to repeat the cancellation process by ensuring that the coefficient of the quadratic term for the rightmost segment was the constant 3. What does the difference

$$[\,\bar{u}_{i+1}, \bar{u}_{i+2} : t\,]\,(\bar{u} - t\,)_+^3 - [\,\bar{u}_i, \bar{u}_{i+1} : t\,]\,(\bar{u} - t\,)_+^3$$

look like for sufficiently large $\bar{u}$? The first term is a spline with breakpoints at $\bar{u}_{i+1}$ and $\bar{u}_{i+2}$, while the second term is a spline with breakpoints at $\bar{u}_i$ and $\bar{u}_{i+1}$. The difference will therefore have breakpoints at $\bar{u}_i$, $\bar{u}_{i+1}$ and $\bar{u}_{i+2}$. Since we are interested in the asymptotic behavior of this difference as $\bar{u} \rightarrow +\infty$, it is sufficient for our purposes to compute the difference of the rightmost segments for these two terms. From (6.8) we see that

$$[\,\bar{u}_i, \bar{u}_{i+1} : t\,]\,(\bar{u} - t\,)_+^3 = -3\bar{u}^2 + 3\bar{u}(\bar{u}_{i+1} + \bar{u}_i) - (\bar{u}_{i+1}^2 + \bar{u}_{i+1}\bar{u}_i + \bar{u}_i^2),$$

from which it is clear that

$$[\,\bar{u}_{i+1}, \bar{u}_{i+2} : t\,]\,(\bar{u} - t\,)_+^3 = -3\bar{u}^2 + 3\bar{u}(\bar{u}_{i+2} + \bar{u}_{i+1}) - (\bar{u}_{i+2}^2 + \bar{u}_{i+2}\bar{u}_{i+1} + \bar{u}_{i+1}^2).$$

Hence

$$[\,\bar{u}_{i+1}, \bar{u}_{i+2} : t\,]\,(\bar{u} - t\,)_+^3 - [\,\bar{u}_i, \bar{u}_{i+1} : t\,]\,(\bar{u} - t\,)_+^3$$
$$= 3\bar{u}(\bar{u}_{i+2} - \bar{u}_i) - (\bar{u}_{i+2} - \bar{u}_i)(\bar{u}_{i+2} + \bar{u}_{i+1} + \bar{u}_i).$$

The quadratic term has disappeared, as expected. To obtain a constant coefficient for the linear term, it is clear that we need to divide by $\bar{u}_{i+2} - \bar{u}_i$. What we want to compute, then, is

$$\frac{\dfrac{(\bar{u} - \bar{u}_{i+2})_+^3 - (\bar{u} - \bar{u}_{i+1})_+^3}{\bar{u}_{i+2} - \bar{u}_{i+1}} - \dfrac{(\bar{u} - \bar{u}_{i+1})_+^3 - (\bar{u} - \bar{u}_i)_+^3}{\bar{u}_{i+1} - \bar{u}_i}}{\bar{u}_{i+2} - \bar{u}_i}$$

$$= 3\bar{u} - \bar{u}_{i+2} - \bar{u}_{i+1} - \bar{u}_i \qquad \text{for } \bar{u} \geq \bar{u}_{i+2}.$$

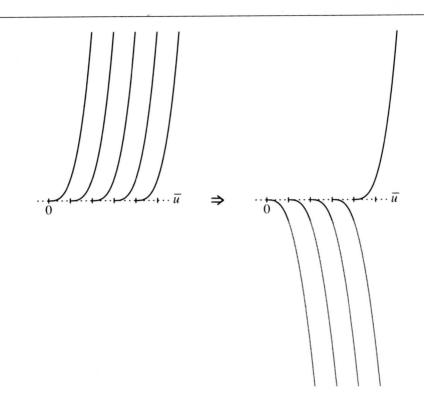

Figure 6.9. All five of the functions shown on the left are cubic. The first four are replaced by four eventually-quadratic functions on the right. Each eventually-quadratic function consists of three polynomial segments: the first is identically zero, begins at $-\infty$, and is not plotted; the second, drawn as a solid line, is cubic; the third, drawn dotted, is quadratic and continues indefinitely to $-\infty$. The fifth function on the left cannot be replaced by an eventually-quadratic function because there is no one-sided cubic to its right with which it can be differenced. We will deal with this technicality later.

Expanding our short-hand notation, we write this as

$$[\, \overline{u}_i \,, \overline{u}_{i+1} \,, \overline{u}_{i+2} : t \,]\, (\overline{u} - t\,)_+^3 \,.$$

This *second difference* goes positive at $\overline{u}_i$. It is easy to figure out why: we saw earlier that $[\,\overline{u}_i \,, \overline{u}_{i+1} : t\,]\,(\overline{u} - t\,)_+^3$ goes negative, so $-[\,\overline{u}_i \,, \overline{u}_{i+1} : t\,]\,(\overline{u} - t\,)_+^3$ goes positive. Since $[\,\overline{u}_{i+1} \,, \overline{u}_{i+2} : t\,]\,(\overline{u} - t\,)_+^3$ is zero between $\overline{u}_i$ and $\overline{u}_{i+1}$ (and $\overline{u}_{i+2} > \overline{u}_i$, so that the denominator is positive), the difference (6.10) is initially positive, and, in fact, it remains so.

Notice that

$$[\,\bar{u}_i\,,\bar{u}_{i+1}\,,\bar{u}_{i+2}:t\,]\,(\,\bar{u}-t\,)_+^3 \qquad\qquad (6.10)$$

$$= \frac{[\,\bar{u}_{i+1}\,,\bar{u}_{i+2}:t\,]\,(\,\bar{u}-t\,)_+^3 - [\,\bar{u}_i\,,\bar{u}_{i+1}:t\,]\,(\,\bar{u}-t\,)_+^3}{\bar{u}_{i+2}-\bar{u}_i}.$$

This suggests a recursive definition for divided differences — such a definition is to be the subject of Chapter 7.

Our second difference, then, is a function which grows only linearly as $\bar{u}\to\infty$. Such functions can be used to replace the functions of (6.9), which in turn replaced certain of the original one-sided power functions, to yield an even "nicer" basis containing functions which grow only linearly as $\bar{u}\to+\infty$.

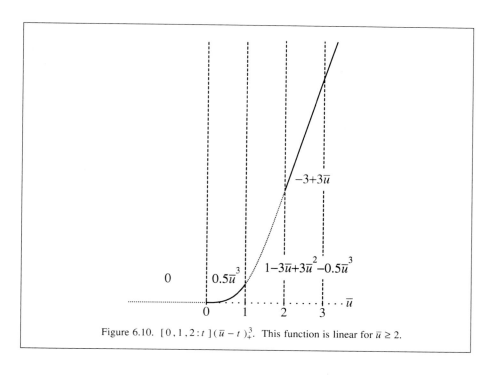

Figure 6.10. $[\,0\,,1\,,2:t\,]\,(\,\bar{u}-t\,)_+^3.$ This function is linear for $\bar{u}\geq 2.$

In the case of our example,

$$[0,1,2:t](\bar{u}-t)_+^3 \;=\; \frac{\dfrac{(\bar{u}-2)_+^3-(\bar{u}-1)_+^3}{2-1} - \dfrac{(\bar{u}-1)_+^3-(\bar{u}-0)_+^3}{1-0}}{2-0}$$

$$=\; \begin{cases} 0 & \bar{u} < 0 \\[2mm] \dfrac{1}{2}(\bar{u}^3) & 0 \le \bar{u} < 1 \\[2mm] -\dfrac{1}{2}(\bar{u}^3 - 6\bar{u}^2 + 6\bar{u} - 2) & 1 \le \bar{u} < 2 \\[2mm] \dfrac{1}{2}(6\bar{u}-6) & 2 \le \bar{u}. \end{cases}$$

As expected, this function is linear for $\bar{u} \ge 2$ (see Figure 6.10). Now that we know how to cancel the quadratic term, we can do this for each successive pair of eventually-quadratic basis functions:

$$[0,1,2:t](\bar{u}-t)_+^3 \quad \text{replaces} \quad [0,1:t](\bar{u}-t)_+^3$$
$$[1,2,3:t](\bar{u}-t)_+^3 \quad \text{replaces} \quad [1,2:t](\bar{u}-t)_+^3$$
$$[2,3,4:t](\bar{u}-t)_+^3 \quad \text{replaces} \quad [2,3:t](\bar{u}-t)_+^3.$$

Figure 6.11 illustrates this process.

6.8 Cancelling the Linear Term — The Third Difference

In the preceding section we accomplished the replacement of $(\bar{u}-\bar{u}_i)_+^3$ by

$$[\bar{u}_i,\bar{u}_{i+1},\bar{u}_{i+2}:t](\bar{u}-t)^{3+} \;=\; 3\bar{u}-\bar{u}_{i+2}-\bar{u}_{i+1}-\bar{u}_i \quad \text{for } \bar{u} \ge \bar{u}_{i+2}.$$

In the same way we replaced $(\bar{u}-\bar{u}_{i+1})_+^3$ by

$$[\bar{u}_{i+1},\bar{u}_{i+2},\bar{u}_{i+3}:t](\bar{u}-t)_+^3 \;=\; 3\bar{u}-\bar{u}_{i+3}-\bar{u}_{i+2}-\bar{u}_{i+1} \quad \text{for } \bar{u} \ge \bar{u}_{i+3},$$

and so on. Since

$$[\bar{u}_{i+1},\bar{u}_{i+2},\bar{u}_{i+3}:t](\bar{u}-t)_+^3 - [\bar{u}_i,\bar{u}_{i+1},\bar{u}_{i+2}:t](\bar{u}-t)_+^3 \;=\; -(\bar{u}_{i+3}-\bar{u}_i),$$

we now replace $[\bar{u}_i,\bar{u}_{i+1},\bar{u}_{i+2}:t](\bar{u}-t)_+^3$ by the *third difference*

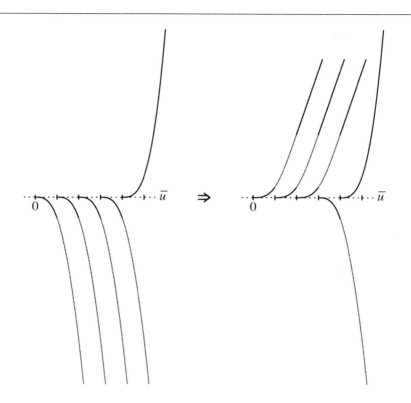

Figure 6.11. Taking a second divided difference of two eventually-quadratic functions allows us to obtain eventually-linear functions. Since we only have four eventually-quadratic functions on the left, we can only do this three times.

$$[\,\overline{u}_i\,,\overline{u}_{i+1}\,,\overline{u}_{i+2}\,,\overline{u}_{i+3}:t\,]\,(\overline{u}-t\,)^3_+$$

$$= \frac{[\,\overline{u}_{i+1}\,,\overline{u}_{i+2}\,,\overline{u}_{i+3}:t\,]\,(\overline{u}-t\,)^3_+ - [\,\overline{u}_i\,,\overline{u}_{i+1}\,,\overline{u}_{i+2}:t\,]\,(\overline{u}-t\,)^3_+}{\overline{u}_{i+3} - \overline{u}_i}$$

$$= \frac{3\overline{u} - \overline{u}_{i+3} - \overline{u}_{i+2} - \overline{u}_{i+1} - 3\overline{u} + \overline{u}_{i+2} + \overline{u}_{i+1} + \overline{u}_i}{\overline{u}_{i+3} - \overline{u}_i}$$

$$= -1 \quad \text{for } \overline{u} \ge \overline{u}_{i+3},$$

which we will denote by

$$[\,\bar{u}_i\,,\bar{u}_{i+1}\,,\bar{u}_{i+2}\,,\bar{u}_{i+3}:t\,]\,(\bar{u}-t\,)^3_+\,.$$

In a like manner we replace $[\,\bar{u}_{i+1}\,,\bar{u}_{i+2}\,,\bar{u}_{i+3}:t\,]\,(\bar{u}-t\,)^3_+$ by

$$[\,\bar{u}_{i+1}\,,\bar{u}_{i+2}\,,\bar{u}_{i+3}\,,\bar{u}_{i+4}:t\,]\,(\bar{u}-t\,)^3_+$$

$$=\frac{[\,\bar{u}_{i+2}\,,\bar{u}_{i+3}\,,\bar{u}_{i+4}:t\,]\,(\bar{u}-t\,)^3_+ - [\,\bar{u}_{i+1}\,,\bar{u}_{i+2}\,,\bar{u}_{i+3}:t\,]\,(\bar{u}-t\,)^3_+}{\bar{u}_{i+4}-\bar{u}_{i+1}}$$

$$=\frac{3\bar{u}-\bar{u}_{i+4}-\bar{u}_{i+3}-\bar{u}_{i+2}-3\bar{u}+\bar{u}_{i+3}+\bar{u}_{i+2}+\bar{u}_{i+1}}{\bar{u}_{i+4}-\bar{u}_{i+1}}$$

$$=-1\quad\text{for }\bar{u}\geq\bar{u}_{i+4}\,,$$

and so on.

Returning to our example, we have

$$[\,0,1,2,3:t\,]\,(\bar{u}-t\,)^3_+\;=\;\frac{[\,1,2,3:t\,]\,(\bar{u}-t\,)^3_+ - [\,0,1,2:t\,]\,(\bar{u}-t\,)^3_+}{3-0}$$

$$=\cfrac{\cfrac{\cfrac{(\bar{u}-3)^3_+-(\bar{u}-2)^3_+}{3-2}-\cfrac{(\bar{u}-2)^3_+-(\bar{u}-1)^3_+}{2-1}}{3-1}-\cfrac{\cfrac{(\bar{u}-2)^3_+-(\bar{u}-1)^3_+}{2-1}-\cfrac{(\bar{u}-1)^3_+-(\bar{u}-0)^3_+}{1-0}}{2-0}}{3-0}$$

$$=\begin{cases} 0 & \bar{u}<0 \\[6pt] -\dfrac{1}{6}(\bar{u}^3) & 0\leq\bar{u}<1 \\[6pt] \dfrac{1}{6}(2\bar{u}^3-9\bar{u}^2+9\bar{u}-3) & 1\leq\bar{u}<2 \\[6pt] -\dfrac{1}{6}(\bar{u}^3-9\bar{u}^2+27\bar{u}-21) & 2\leq\bar{u}<3 \\[6pt] -1 & 3\leq\bar{u}. \end{cases}$$

(See Figure 6.12.) As expected, it is constant for $\bar{u}\geq 3$.

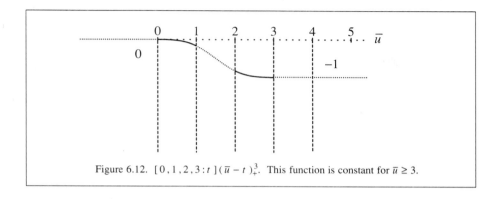

Figure 6.12. $[\,0,1,2,3:t\,]\,(\overline{u}-t\,)_+^3$. This function is constant for $\overline{u}\geq 3$.

As before, we can now replace successive pairs of eventually-linear functions with eventually-constant functions:

$$[\,0,1,2,3:t\,]\,(\overline{u}-t\,)_+^3 \quad \text{replaces} \quad [\,0,1,2:t\,]\,(\overline{u}-t\,)_+^3$$
$$[\,1,2,3,4:t\,]\,(\overline{u}-t\,)_+^3 \quad \text{replaces} \quad [\,1,2,3:t\,]\,(\overline{u}-t\,)_+^3.$$

Figure 6.13 illustrates the result.

6.9 The Uniform Cubic B-spline — A Fourth Difference

The third divided differences are constant, in fact -1, for sufficiently large $\overline{u}$. This avoids the need to cancel large positive values with large negative values. To obtain locality, that is, to obtain functions that return all the way to zero, requires the computation of one more difference. To be consistent with earlier steps we compute

$$\frac{1}{\overline{u}_{i+4}-\overline{u}_i}\left\{[\,\overline{u}_{i+1},\overline{u}_{i+2},\overline{u}_{i+3},\overline{u}_{i+4}:t\,]\,(\overline{u}-t\,)_+^3\right.$$

$$\left.-\,[\,\overline{u}_i,\overline{u}_{i+1},\overline{u}_{i+2},\overline{u}_{i+3}:t\,]\,(\overline{u}-t\,)_+^3\right\} \;=\; 0 \quad \text{for } \overline{u}\geq \overline{u}_{i+4}, \tag{6.11}$$

although the division by $\overline{u}_{i+4}-\overline{u}_i$ is actually superfluous. We denote the ratio (6.11) by

$$[\,\overline{u}_i,\overline{u}_{i+1},\overline{u}_{i+2},\overline{u}_{i+3},\overline{u}_{i+4}:t\,]\,(\overline{u}-t\,)_+^3. \tag{6.12}$$

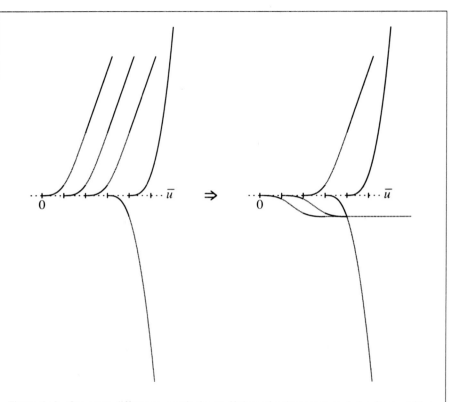

Figure 6.13. One more difference cancels the coefficient of a linear term to 0, leaving us with a constant function -1 for sufficiently large values of $\bar{u}$. Since we have three eventually-linear functions, we can do this twice to produce two eventually-constant functions.

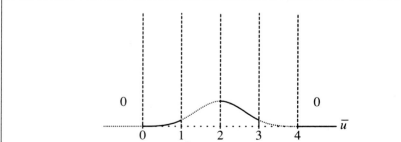

Figure 6.14. $[\,0,1,2,3,4:t\,]\,(\bar{u}-t\,)_{+}^{3}$. This looks like the uniform cubic B-spline we met in Chapter 4.

For the uniform knot sequence we have been using as an example, $[0,1,2,3,4{:}t](\overline{u} - t)_+^3$ is exactly the spline of equation (5.1) — the uniform cubic B-spline for the knots $\{0,1,2,3,4\}$ (see Figure 6.14).

We can use this eventually-zero function as a substitute for an eventually-constant function (see Figure 6.15), which substituted for the eventually-linear function, which substituted for an eventually-quadratic function, which substituted for the original cubic function $(\overline{u} - \overline{u}_i)_+^3$. We arrive at this eventually-zero function by combining differences of

$$(\overline{u} - 0)_+^3, \ (\overline{u} - 1)_+^3, \ (\overline{u} - 2)_+^3, \ (\overline{u} - 3)_+^3, \ (\overline{u} - 4)_+^3$$

so as to cancel, in succession, the powers

$$\overline{u}^3, \ \overline{u}^2, \ \overline{u}^1, \ \overline{u}^0 .$$

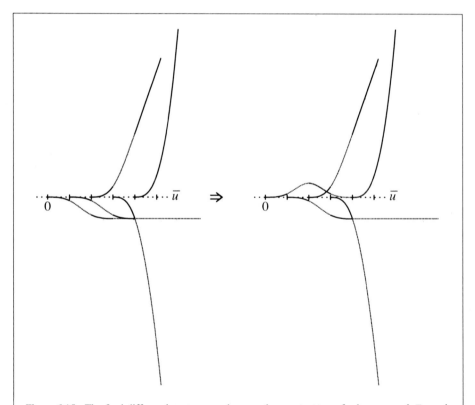

Figure 6.15. The final differencing step cancels away the constant term for large enough $\overline{u}$, resulting in a piecewise polynomial which is nonzero for only four intervals. The two eventually-constant functions on the left are exactly what we need to produce the single eventually-zero function on the right that has been our objective.

For future reference we note that because (6.12) involves an even number of differences it will go positive at $\bar{u}_i$.

We emphasize that for the knot sequences we have been considering, the divided difference notation we have been using is simply shorthand. If we let $f_i = (\bar{u} - \bar{u}_{i+j})_+^3$ then

$$[\bar{u}_i, \bar{u}_{i+1}, \bar{u}_{i+2}, \bar{u}_{i+3}, \bar{u}_{i+4} : t](\bar{u} - t)_+^3 =$$

$$\frac{\dfrac{\dfrac{\dfrac{f_1 - f_0}{\bar{u}_1 - \bar{u}_0} - \dfrac{f_2 - f_1}{\bar{u}_2 - \bar{u}_1}}{\bar{u}_2 - \bar{u}_0} - \dfrac{\dfrac{f_2 - f_1}{\bar{u}_2 - \bar{u}_1} - \dfrac{f_3 - f_2}{\bar{u}_3 - \bar{u}_2}}{\bar{u}_3 - \bar{u}_1}}{\bar{u}_3 - \bar{u}_0} - \dfrac{\dfrac{\dfrac{f_2 - f_1}{\bar{u}_2 - \bar{u}_1} - \dfrac{f_3 - f_2}{\bar{u}_3 - \bar{u}_2}}{\bar{u}_3 - \bar{u}_1} - \dfrac{\dfrac{f_3 - f_2}{\bar{u}_3 - \bar{u}_2} - \dfrac{f_4 - f_3}{\bar{u}_4 - \bar{u}_3}}{\bar{u}_4 - \bar{u}_2}}{\bar{u}_4 - \bar{u}_1}}{\bar{u}_4 - \bar{u}_0}.$$

This is a rather complicated expression, but we have seen why each of the terms appears. It is also clear from this expression that all we have done is replace $(\bar{u} - \bar{u}_i)_+^3$ by a particularly desirable linear combination of $(\bar{u} - \bar{u}_i)_+^3$, $(\bar{u} - \bar{u}_{i+1})_+^3$, $(\bar{u} - \bar{u}_{i+2})_+^3$, $(\bar{u} - \bar{u}_{i+3})_+^3$ and $(\bar{u} - \bar{u}_{i+4})_+^3$.

Our development has shown us how to obtain the single eventually-zero basis function shown in Figure 6.15. In actual fact we start with a larger number of one-sided cubics, and replace as many as we can at each step. Six truncated cubics would have allowed us to compute two eventually-zero basis functions, and so on. So as to be able to replace all the truncated cubics needed to represent the curve in question, we add four more one-sided cubics, positioned arbitrarily to the right of $\bar{u}_m$ (see Figure 6.16).

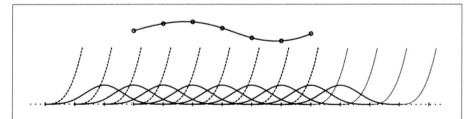

Figure 6.16. The dotted curves on the right are truncated cubics. They make it possible to difference the rightmost of the original cubics (which are drawn dashed) to replace all the original truncated power functions by B-splines. Notice that there are an equal number of each.

Thus it appears that B-splines can be constructed by differencing one-sided power functions. This proves to be the case, but a little more preparation is needed if we are going to handle completely arbitrary knot sequences: the differencing process we have developed breaks down if two or more knots move together. If we had encountered a situation in which $\bar{u}_i = \bar{u}_{i+1}$, we would at some point have divided by zero. The remedy for this difficulty becomes clear if we watch what happens as $\bar{u}_i$ and $\bar{u}_{i+1}$ move "close together":

$$\lim_{\bar{u}_i \to \bar{u}_{i+1}} \frac{(\bar{u} - \bar{u}_{i+1})^{k-1} - (\bar{u} - \bar{u}_i)^{k-1}}{\bar{u}_{i+1} - \bar{u}_i} = \frac{d}{dt}(\bar{u} - t)^{k-1}\Big|_{t = u_i}.$$

This suggests that it would be useful to study derivatives of one-sided power functions, and to expand the idea of differencing to include differentiation when multiple knots are encountered. We take this direction in the next chapter. There we will digress briefly from splines to formally introduce the divided difference operation, to study its relationship to differentiation, and to consider the properties of one-sided power functions under differencing and differentiation.

7

Divided Differences

In the previous section three important things occurred: we introduced the one-sided basis for the splines $S(\mathbf{P}^k, \{\bar{u}_i\}_0^{m+k})$, we suggested the consideration of divided differences, and we claimed that uniform B-splines can be represented as divided differences of the one-sided power functions. To proceed logically from this background:

- $S(\mathbf{P}^k, \{\bar{u}_i\}_0^{m+k})$ is a vector space, and we know a set of functions that form a basis for that space.

- Any basis for a vector space can be obtained from suitable linear combinations of the elements of any other basis.

- The divided difference operation, at least in the uniform-knot case, is a mechanism for (a) constructing linear combinations of functions, and (b) manufacturing the B-splines. We should, therefore, investigate the extent to which, for nonuniform knot sequences, functions like B-splines can be produced by differencing the one-sided power functions.

- We should further investigate the extent to which these difference-manufactured B-splines can be used to generate all the splines in $S(\mathbf{P}^k, \{\bar{u}_i\}_0^{m+k})$.

Such an investigation is our next objective. To begin we must develop a collection of results about the one-sided power functions and their interactions with derivative and difference operations.

7.1 Differentiation and One-Sided Power Functions

We will begin with differentiation. Notice that $(\bar{u} - t\,)_+^r$ suffers a discontinuity (as a function of $\bar{u}$ for fixed t) in the rth derivative when $\bar{u} = t$, where it is a C^{r-1} function, and that it is at least C^r continuous everywhere else. In fact, even the discontinuity is not too serious. The discontinuity in any derivative of any spline in $S(\mathbf{P}^k, \{\bar{u}_i\}_0^{m+k})$ derives ultimately from the behavior of the function $(\bar{u} - t\,)_+^0$, and since this function is *open on the right*, we will easily verify that a right-handed derivative of $(\bar{u} - t\,)_+^r$ with respect to $\bar{u}$ does exist at the point $\bar{u} = t$. Moreover, at all other values of $\bar{u}$ the right-handed derivative exists and is equivalent to the standard derivative of the function.

■ **Definition**

The derivative

$$D_{\bar{u}} f(\bar{u})$$

of any function $f(\bar{u})$ is said to be taken in the *right-handed* sense, if

$$D_{\bar{u}} f(\bar{u}) = \lim_{\substack{\varepsilon \to 0 \\ \varepsilon > 0}} \frac{f(\bar{u} + \varepsilon) - f(\bar{u})}{\varepsilon}.$$

■

Note that the limit is approached from the *positive* side. Since ε is positive, $\bar{u} + \varepsilon$ lies to the *right* of $\bar{u}$.

■ **Convention**

The derivatives of the one-sided power function $(\bar{u} - t\,)_+^r$ with respect to $\bar{u}$ for fixed t are:

for the zeroth derivative,

$$D_{\bar{u}}^{(0)} (\bar{u} - t\,)_+^r = (\bar{u} - t\,)_+^r;$$

for the first derivative,

$$D_{\bar{u}}^{(1)} (\bar{u} - t\,)_+^r = D_{\bar{u}} (\bar{u} - t\,)_+^r = \lim_{\substack{\varepsilon \to 0 \\ \varepsilon > 0}} \frac{(\bar{u} + \varepsilon - t\,)_+^r - (\bar{u} - t\,)_+^r}{\varepsilon};$$

and recursively,

$$D_{\bar{u}}^{(\ell)} (\bar{u} - t)_+^r = D_{\bar{u}} [D_{\bar{u}}^{(\ell-1)} (\bar{u} - t)_+^r]$$

for all the succeeding derivatives, $\ell = 2, 3, \ldots$ (understood in the right-handed sense).

∎

Consider what this means for $r = 0$ and $\ell = 1$. For any chosen $\bar{u} < t$,

$$(\bar{u} + \varepsilon - t)_+^0 - (\bar{u} - t)_+^0 = 0 - 0 = 0$$

for all $\varepsilon > 0$ small enough. Hence the limit defined above for $\varepsilon \to 0$ is equal to zero. On the other hand, for any chosen $\bar{u} \geq t$,

$$(\bar{u} + \varepsilon - t)_+^0 - (\bar{u} - t)_+^0 = 1 - 1 = 0$$

for all $\varepsilon > 0$. (Note: $0^0 = 1$ by convention.) Since the limit defined above is zero, the one-sided power function $(\bar{u} - t)_+^0$, for variable $\bar{u}$ and fixed t, behaves exactly like a constant (a polynomial of order 1) under the application of right-handed differentiation with respect to $\bar{u}$. Since $(\bar{u} - t)_+^0$ is a simple spline of order 1, this is very appealing. Furthermore, for higher orders the product rule for differentiation may be applied, giving

$$D_{\bar{u}} (\bar{u} - t)_+^r = D_{\bar{u}} [(\bar{u} - t)_+^0 (\bar{u} - t)^r]$$

$$= [D_{\bar{u}} (\bar{u} - t)_+^0] \cdot (\bar{u} - t)^r + (\bar{u} - t)_+^0 \cdot [D_{\bar{u}} (\bar{u} - t)^r]$$

$$= 0 \cdot (\bar{u} - t)^r + (\bar{u} - t)_+^0 \cdot [r (\bar{u} - t)^{r-1}]$$

$$= r (\bar{u} - t)_+^{r-1}.$$

(7.1)

Hence we have the following theorem.

∎ **Theorem**

For all $r, \ell \geq 0$,

$$D_{\bar{u}}^{(\ell)} (\bar{u} - t)_+^r = \begin{cases} \dfrac{r!}{(r-\ell)!} (\bar{u} - t)_+^{r-\ell} & \text{for } \ell \leq r \\[2ex] 0 & \text{for } \ell > r. \end{cases}$$

∎

This is also very appealing. It means, under the agreement that we consider only right-handed derivatives whenever $(\bar{u} - t)_+^r$ is being regarded as a function of $\bar{u}$ for fixed t, that $(\bar{u} - t)_+^r$ behaves just like the ordinary polynomial $(\bar{u} - t)^r$.

Notice that $(\bar{u} - t)_+^r$ is also a function of t. As such, for fixed $\bar{u}$, it is at least a C^r function of t, except when $t = \bar{u}$, and at that critical value of t it has a left-handed derivative with respect to t. We can see this best by turning the equations (6.2) and (6.3) around to look at them from the "t point of view." Equation (6.2) becomes

$$(\bar{u} - t)_+^0 = \begin{cases} 1 & t \le \bar{u} \\ 0 & t > \bar{u}, \end{cases}$$

(6.3) becomes

$$(\bar{u} - t)_+^r = (\bar{u} - t)_+^0 (\bar{u} - t)^r$$

$$= \begin{cases} (\bar{u} - t)^r & t \le \bar{u} \\ 0 & t > \bar{u}, \end{cases}$$

and Figure 6.5 becomes Figure 7.1.

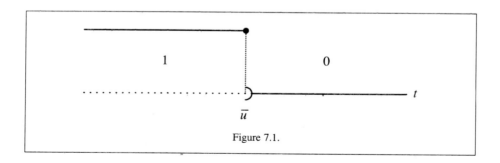

Figure 7.1.

Somewhat later we will begin dealing with $(\bar{u} - t)_+^r$ as a function of t. Observe that, as such, it is *open on the left*. Consequently our intuition with respect to $\bar{u}$ can be applied to t as well. For example:

■ Definition

The derivative

$$D_t \, g(t)$$

of any function $g(t)$ is said to be taken in the *left-handed* sense if

$$D_t \, g(t) \;=\; \lim_{\substack{\varepsilon \to 0 \\ \varepsilon > 0}} \frac{g(t-\varepsilon) - g(t)}{-\varepsilon} \; ,$$

■

Note that the limit is approached from the <u>negative</u> side. Since ε is positive, $t - \varepsilon$ lies to the <u>left</u> of t.

■ Convention

The derivatives of the one-sided power function $(\bar{u} - t)_+^r$ with respect to t for fixed $\bar{u}$ are:

for the zero-th derivative,

$$D_t^{(0)} (\bar{u} - t)_+^r \;=\; (\bar{u} - t)_+^r;$$

for the first derivative,

$$D_t^{(1)} (\bar{u} - t)_+^r \;=\; D_t \, (\bar{u} - t)_+^r$$

$$=\; \lim_{\substack{\varepsilon \to 0 \\ \varepsilon > 0}} \frac{(\bar{u} - (t-\varepsilon))_+^r - (\bar{u} - t)_+^r}{-\varepsilon} \; ;$$

and recursively,

$$D_t^{(\ell)} (\bar{u} - t)_+^r \;=\; D_t \, [D_t^{(\ell-1)} (\bar{u} - t)_+^r]$$

for all the succeeding derivatives, $\ell = 2, 3, \ldots$ (understood in the left-handed sense).

■

Results similar to those of (7.1) hold for $D_t^{(\ell)}(\bar{u}-t)_+^r$.

■ **Theorem**

For all r, $\ell \geq 0$,

$$
D_t^{(\ell)}(\bar{u}-t)_+^r = \begin{cases} (-1)^\ell \dfrac{r!}{(r-\ell)!}\,(\bar{u}-t)_+^{r-\ell} & \text{for } \ell \leq r \\[2ex] 0 & \text{for } \ell > r \,. \end{cases}
$$

■

Divided differences are close relatives of derivatives. In the previous chapter we took the function $(\bar{u}-t)_+^r$, evaluated it at some knot $t = \bar{u}_i$, evaluated it again at some other knot $t = \bar{u}_{i+1}$, and formed the combination

$$
\frac{(\bar{u}-\bar{u}_{i+1})_+^r - (\bar{u}-\bar{u}_i)_+^r}{\bar{u}_{i+1} - \bar{u}_i} \,.
$$

We can only write this if we assume that $\bar{u}_{i+1}$ and $\bar{u}_i$ are distinct. However, if we should let $\bar{u}_i$ approach and join $\bar{u}_{i+1}$, the above combination would be consistent with the left-handed derivative. (That is, letting $\varepsilon = u_{i+1} - u_i > 0$.)

$$
\lim_{\bar{u}_i \to \bar{u}_{i+1}} \frac{(\bar{u}-\bar{u}_{i+1})_+^r - (\bar{u}-\bar{u}_i)_+^r}{\bar{u}_{i+1} - \bar{u}_i} = \lim_{\bar{u}_i \to \bar{u}_{i+1}} \frac{(\bar{u}-\bar{u}_i)_+^r - (\bar{u}-\bar{u}_{i+1})_+^r}{\bar{u}_i - \bar{u}_{i+1}}
$$

$$
= \lim_{\substack{\varepsilon \to 0 \\ \varepsilon > 0}} \frac{(\bar{u}-(\bar{u}_{i+1}-\varepsilon))_+^r - (\bar{u}-\bar{u}_{i+1})_+^r}{-\varepsilon}
$$

$$
= D_t\,(\bar{u}-t)_+^r\big|_{t=\bar{u}_{i+1}} \,.
$$

It is this observation that will provide us with a definition for divided differences that includes the case of repeated values, namely, that distinct values are handled by differencing and dividing, while repeated values are handled by differentiation.

7.2 Divided Differences in a General Setting

Let us work up to a definition for general divided differences gradually, reminding ourselves a little about calculus along the way. Forgetting about the specific form of the one-sided power functions for a moment, we will frame our discussion in terms of general functions, f, g, h, ..., of general variables, x, y, z, ... We will come back to our specific functions $(\bar{u} - t)_+^r$ in a short while.

Consider any differentiable function. Recall that differentiation is an *operator* which provides a *mapping* of differentiable functions onto other functions; e.g.,

$$D_x f(x,y) = g(x,y)$$

and

$$D_y f(x,y) = h(x,y).$$

The "source" function, $f(x,y)$, and the "target" function, $g(x,y)$ or $h(x,y)$, have the same number of variables. In like fashion we can regard the divided difference as an operator, which provides us with a mapping:

$$[z_1,z_2:x]f(x,y) = \frac{f(z_2,y) - f(z_1,y)}{z_2 - z_1} = G(z_1,z_2,y)$$

or

$$[z_1,z_2:y]f(x,y) = \frac{f(x,z_2) - f(x,z_1)}{z_2 - z_1} = H(x,z_1,z_2).$$

These mappings convert the source function, f, of two variables, into target functions, G or H, of three variables. If the appropriate two of these variables are permitted to merge to a common value,

$$z_1 \rightarrow z \leftarrow z_2$$

then we obtain a function of two variables again. In fact,

$$[z,z:x]f(x,y) = \lim_{\substack{z_1 \to z \\ z_2 \to z}} G(z_1,z_2,y) = D_x f(x,y)\big|_{x=z} = g(z,y)$$

or

$$[z,z:y]f(x,y) = \lim_{\substack{z_1 \to z \\ z_2 \to z}} H(x,z_1,z_2) = D_y f(x,y)\big|_{y=z} = h(x,z).$$

For higher differences this becomes slightly more complicated, so it will be worthwhile to economize on notation for the purpose of clarity. All except the one variable undergoing the differencing will now be suppressed; i.e., $f(x,y) = f(x)$, if we are differencing with respect to x.

Consider

$$[z_1, z_2, z_3 : x] f(x) = \frac{[z_2, z_3 : x] f(x) - [z_1, z_2 : x] f(x)}{z_3 - z_1}$$

$$= \frac{\dfrac{f(z_3) - f(z_2)}{z_3 - z_2} - \dfrac{f(z_2) - f(z_1)}{z_2 - z_1}}{z_3 - z_1}.$$

Using a Taylor series expansion we have

$$\frac{f(z_3) - f(z_2)}{z_3 - z_2} = f^{(1)}(z_2) + \frac{1}{2}(z_3 - z_2) f^{(2)}(z_2) + \mathbf{O}((z_3 - z_2)^2)$$

where the expression $\mathbf{O}((z_3 - z_2)^2)$ indicates that the remainder of the series will behave like a constant times $(z_3 - z_2)^2$ (will have the same "order of behavior" as $(z_3 - z_2)^2$) if the values of z_3 and z_2 approach each other. Similarly

$$-\frac{f(z_2) - f(z_1)}{z_2 - z_1} = \frac{f(z_1) - f(z_2)}{z_2 - z_1}$$

$$= -f^{(1)}(z_2) - \frac{1}{2}(z_1 - z_2) f^{(2)}(z_2) + \mathbf{O}((z_1 - z_2)^2).$$

Consequently

$$\frac{\dfrac{f(z_3) - f(z_2)}{z_3 - z_2} - \dfrac{f(z_2) - f(z_1)}{z_2 - z_1}}{z_3 - z_1}$$

$$= \frac{1}{2(z_3 - z_1)} [(z_3 - z_2) - (z_1 - z_2)] f^{(2)}(z_2) + \frac{\mathbf{O}((z_3 - z_2)^2) + \mathbf{O}((z_1 - z_2)^2)}{(z_3 - z_1)}$$

$$= \frac{1}{2} f^{(2)}(z_2) + \frac{\mathbf{O}((z_3 - z_2)^2) + \mathbf{O}((z_1 - z_2)^2)}{(z_3 - z_1)}.$$

If z_1, z_2, z_3 are allowed to approach a common value, z, in a reasonable way, then the trailing expression will go to zero. This motivates the following interpretation:

$$[z, z, z : x] f(x) = \lim_{\substack{z_1 \to z \\ z_2 \to z \\ z_3 \to z}} [z_1, z_2, z_3 : x] f(x)$$

$$= \frac{1}{2} D_x^{(2)} f(x)\big|_{x = z = z_1 = z_2 = z_3}.$$

And in general, not surprisingly:

$$[z_1, \ldots, z_{1+\ell} : x] f(x) = \frac{1}{\ell!} D_x^{(\ell)} f(x)\big|_{x = z_1 = \cdots = z_{1+\ell}}$$

when $z_1 = \cdots = z_{1+\ell}$.

With these preliminaries, we will give a recursive definition of the *divided difference operator*. The definition begins by regarding the zero[th] divided difference as the operation that evaluates a function at a specified value of a variable. This corresponds roughly to the zero[th] differentiation operator; i.e.,

$$D_x^{(0)} f(x)\big|_{x = z_1} = f(z_1).$$

■ **Definition**

For any values $z_i \leq \cdots \leq z_{i+\ell}$ the ℓth *divided difference* is given by

$$[z_i : x] f(x) = f(z_i)$$

for $\ell = 0$, and for $\ell \geq 1$ by

$$[z_i, \ldots, z_{i+\ell} : x] f(x)$$

$$= \frac{[z_{i+1}, \ldots, z_{i+\ell} : x] f(x) - [z_i, \ldots, z_{i+\ell-1} : x] f(x)}{z_{i+\ell} - z_i}$$

if $z_{i+\ell}$, or else

$$[z_i, \ldots, z_{i+\ell} : x] f(x) = \frac{1}{\ell!} D_x^{(\ell)} f(x)\big|_{x = z_i}$$

if $z_{i+\ell} = z_i$.

■

Observe that the notation

$$[z_i : x], [z_i, z_{i+1} : x], [z_i, z_{i+1}, z_{i+2} : x], \text{ etc.}$$

is reasonably suggestive for low-order divided differences. However, something like

$$[z_i, \ldots, z_{i+r} : x]$$

is often more confusing than helpful. Thus we will sometimes use the more compact form below.

■ **Notation**

$$[z_i, \ldots, z_{i+r} : x] = [z_i(r) : x].$$

■

The intent of this definition is to express, in shorthand, that z_i followed by the next r z's in sequence define the rth order divided difference.

Two comments are worth making before we proceed:

- Once we move back to the specific case of the one-sided power functions, we will only be interested in the divided differences of $(\bar{u} - t)_+^r$ with respect to $\bar{u}$ or with respect to t, rather than the divided differences of general functions. In this case, the differentiation in the above definition will either be right-handed, for differences with respect to $\bar{u}$, or left-handed, for differences with respect to t.

- The definition was motivated by the idea that divided differences could be equated with derivatives when any two or more of the values, $z_i, \ldots, z_{i+\ell}$, join together. The discussion about this was only motivational, but it can be made rigorous. It is proven in [Schumaker81] that, if $z_{i+r}(\varepsilon)$, for $r = 0, 1, \ldots, \ell$, is any sequence of points with $z_{i+r}(\varepsilon) \to z_{i+r}$ as $\varepsilon \to 0$, then it is true for any sufficiently smooth function, $p = p(t)$ (e.g., $(\bar{u} - t)_+^r$), that:

$$\lim_{\varepsilon \to 0} [z_i(\varepsilon), z_{i+1}(\varepsilon), \ldots, z_{i+\ell}(\varepsilon) : t] p(t)$$

$$= [z_i, z_{i+1}, \ldots, z_{i+\ell} : t] p(t).$$

In particular, the divided difference over an arbitrary set of points $z_i, \ldots, z_{i+\ell}$ that contains repetitions is the limit of divided differences over distinct points. Until now we have thought of the knots $\bar{u}_i$ in

$S(\mathbf{P}^k, \{\bar{u}_i\}_0^{m+k})$ as being fixed, and usually we have regarded them as distinct. This gives us the option to regard knots as movable and, at times, confluent.

7.3   Algebraic and Analytic Properties

We have reminded ourselves that differentiation can be regarded as an operator that maps functions into functions, and we have taken this same view in the case of the divided difference. We close by establishing a few of the algebraic properties of these operators.

Let us recall that the differentiation operator is a *linear operator*; i.e.,

$$D_x \{ \alpha f(x) \} = \alpha \{ D_x f(x) \}$$

for any scalar α, and

$$D_x \{ f_1(x) + f_2(x) \} = \{ D_x f_1(x) \} + \{ D_x f_2(x) \}$$

for any two functions $f_1(x)$ and $f_2(x)$. This holds for right-handed and left-handed differentiation as well as for ordinary, unrestricted differentiation. This means that, for any sum,

$$D_x \{ \sum_j \alpha_j f_j(x) \} = \sum_j \alpha_j \{ D_x f_j(x) \}.$$

It is just as easily seen that the simple divided difference operation (6.9) also behaves linearly. For example:

$$[z_1, z_2 : x] \{ \alpha f(x) \} = \frac{\alpha f(z_2) - \alpha f(z_1)}{z_2 - z_1}$$

$$= \alpha \frac{f(z_2) - f(z_1)}{z_2 - z_1}$$

$$= \alpha \{ [z_1, z_2 : x] f(x) \}$$

for any scalar α. Similarly,

$$[z_1, z_2 : x] \{ f_1(x) + f_2(x) \}$$

$$= \{ [z_1, z_2 : x] f_1(x) \} + \{ [z_1, z_2 : x] f_2(x) \}$$

for any two functions, $f_1(x)$ and $f_2(x)$. As a result of the definition above and some of our preceding observations, we have the following.

■ **Theorem**

The divided difference is a linear operator; i.e.,
for each fixed ℓ, if

$$[z_i\,(\ell):x\,]f_j(x)$$

exists for each j in some set of indices **J**, then

$$[z_i\,(\ell):x\,]\left\{\sum_{j\in \mathbf{J}}\alpha_j\,f_j(x)\right\}\ =\ \sum_{j\in \mathbf{J}}\alpha_j\,\{\,[z_i\,(\ell):x\,]f_j(x)\,\}$$

for any scalars α_j , $j\in \mathbf{J}$.

■

This provides us with a final observation. Notice that the order in which we perform differencing and differentiation can be swapped whenever these operations act on different variables.

■ **Corollary**

$$D_x^{(r)}\,[\,z_i\,(\ell):y\,]\,f\,(x\,,y\,)\ =\ [\,z_i\,(\ell):y\,]\,D_x^{(r)}f\,(x\,,y\,)$$

■

PLATE I. An automobile body designed as a composite of bicubic patches. Courtesy of Fred Krull, General Motors Research Laboratory.

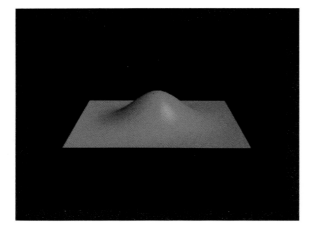

PLATE II. The non-zero portion of
a single uniform bicubic B-spline
$B_{0,0}(\bar{u},\bar{v})$, formed by taking the
product of the two univariate uni-
form cubic B-splines $B_0(\bar{u})$ and
$B_0(\bar{v})$. We show here the central
"peak" of the B-spline hump —
like the univariate B-splines, it
continues to infinity in all directions with the value zero.

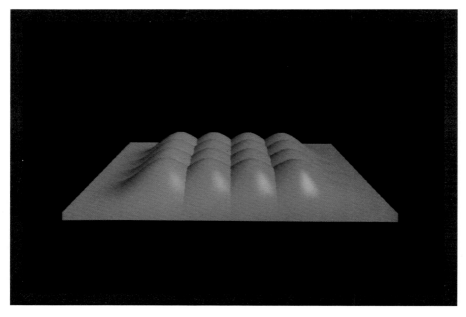

PLATE III. The sixteen uniform bicubic B-splines that are non-zero when $\bar{u}_3 < \bar{u}+ \quad \bar{u}_4$ and $\bar{v}_3 < \bar{v} < \bar{v}_4$.

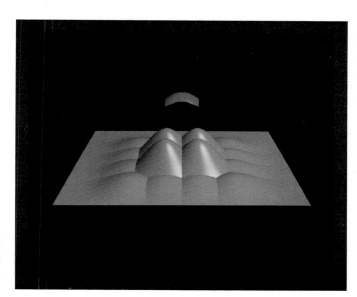

PLATE IV.
Scaling the B-splines of Plate
III to define one coordinate
of a single surface patch.
This is, say, $Y(\bar{u}, \bar{v})$.

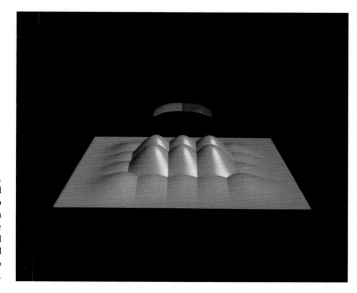

PLATE V.
Scaling the B-splines defined
on the grid of Figure 4.32 to
define one coordinate of a
two-patch surface. The
patches have been colored
differently and separated
slightly to make them easy to
distinguish.

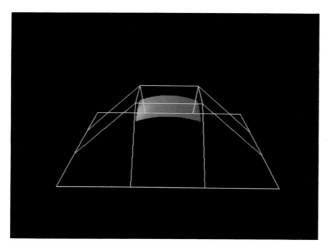

PLATE VI.
A shaded version of the surface
displayed in wire-frame format
on the left of Figure 4.34.

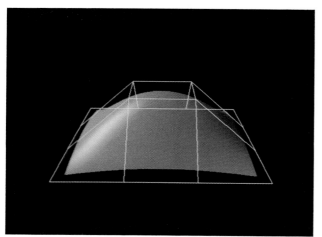

PLATE VII.
A shaded version of the surface
displayed in wire-frame format
on the right of Figure 4.34.

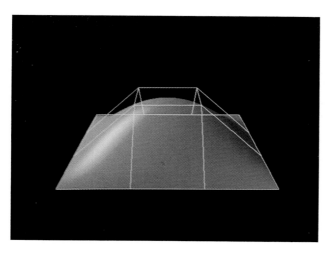

PLATE VIII.
A shaded version of the surface
displayed in wire-frame format
in Figure 4.35.

PLATE IX.
A shaded version of the "torus" of
Figure 4.41.

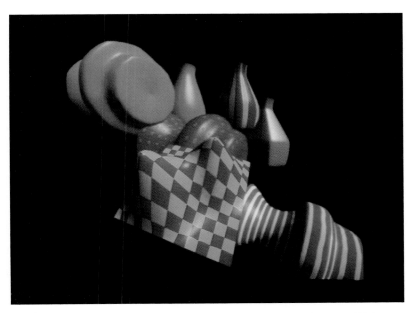

PLATE X. Christmas at Macy's. An example of creative rendering. Courtesy of Brian
Barsky, Mark D. Dippé, and Tony de Rose, University of California, Berkeley.

PLATE XI. A set of goblets designed as Beta-spline surfaces. Varying amounts of tension are shown. Courtesy of Brian Barsky, Mark D. Dippé, and Tony de Rose, University of California, Berkeley.

PLATE XII.
Dali Vases — Three B-spline vases; ray-traced with certain rays permitted to "leak through." Courtesy of Mike Sweeney, Abel Image Research.

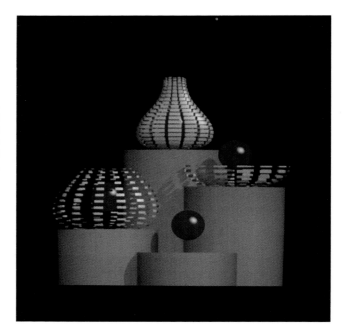

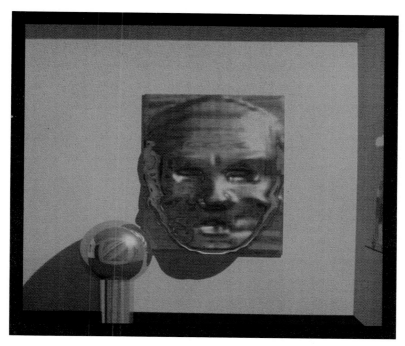

PLATE XIII. View of a gallery room with a B-spline mask. The mask is rendered in copper and the cylinder and sphere are rendered in stainless steel. The metallic effects are due in part to an adaptation of the Cook-Torrence illumination model for ray tracing and in part to secondary reflections. The mask and sphere reflect each other, as well as a tapestry and doorway behind the viewer, pictures on the side walls, and the blue rug on the floor. Courtesy of Mike Sweeney, Abel Image Research.

PLATE XIV.
Flamingos — "One curve, three definitions." Courtesy of Maureen Stone, Xerox Palo Alto Research Center.

PLATE XV.
A milk drop. This image is one of the early examples of strobe photography. It was taken at the Massachusetts Institute of Technology by Harold Edgerton. The raster version of the image was distibuted courtesy of the University of Southern California Image Processing Lab.

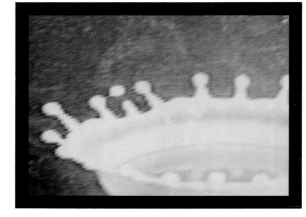

PLATE XVI.
The milk drop, interpolated by a B-spline "surface" and evaluated at knot positions as well as midway between knot positions to achieve a doubling of the image size. Courtesy of Vic Klassen, University of Waterloo.

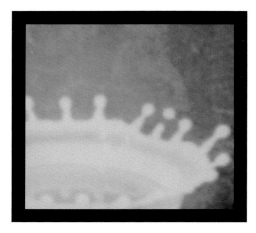

PLATE XVII.
The milk drop data used as control vertices to create a B-spline surface. The image has been doubled. Courtesy of Vic Klassen, University of Waterloo.

8

General
B–splines

In Chapter 6 we found that

$$[\,0\,,1\,,2\,,3\,,4:t\,]\,(\,\overline{u}-t\,)^3_+$$

looks exactly like the uniform cubic B-spline of Chapter 4. More generally, we found that

$$[\,\overline{u}_0\,,\overline{u}_1\,,\overline{u}_2\,,\overline{u}_3\,,\overline{u}_4:t\,]\,(\,\overline{u}-t\,)^3_+$$

yielded an eventually-zero function. Of course, any scalar multiple of an eventually-zero function is also eventually-zero, and we will see that if we use

$$(\overline{u}_4-\overline{u}_0)\,[\,\overline{u}_0\,,\overline{u}_1\,,\overline{u}_2\,,\overline{u}_3\,,\overline{u}_4:t\,]\,(\,\overline{u}-t\,)^3_+\;=\;(\overline{u}_4-\overline{u}_0)\,[\,\overline{u}_0\,(4):t\,]\,(\,\overline{u}-t\,)^3_+$$

as our cubic B-spline then the curves we define will have the convex hull and translation invariance properties. We will denote this function by

$$B_{0,4}(\overline{u})\,.$$

The notation is intended to remind us of the following.

- $B_{0,4}(\overline{u})$ is a member of $S(\mathbf{P}^4,\{\overline{u}_i\}_0^{m+k})$; the second subscript of B indicates its order.

- $B_{0,4}(\overline{u})$ is positive for $\overline{u}$ between $\overline{u}_0$ and $\overline{u}_4$; the two subscripts together indicate its support, i.e., the range of parameter values for which it is nonzero.

For B-splines in general, including those with unequally spaced or multiple knots, this notation will continue to indicate order and support.

■ **Definition**

Given knots $\bar{u}_0, \ldots, \bar{u}_m, \ldots, \bar{u}_{m+k}$, and assuming that $i \leq m$, the *B-spline of order k associated with the knots $\bar{u}_i, \ldots, \bar{u}_{i+k}$ is given by*

$$B_{i,k}(\bar{u}) = (-1)^k (\bar{u}_{i+k} - \bar{u}_i) [\bar{u}_i(k):t](\bar{u}-t)_+^{k-1}.$$

It should be observed that $B_{i,k}(\bar{u})$ is vacuous if $\bar{u}_i = \bar{u}_{i+k}$.

■

In Chapter 6 we saw that odd divided differences of $(\bar{u}-t)_+^{k-1}$ were negative. The term $(-1)^k$, which is -1 for odd values of k and $+1$ for even values of k, is therefore introduced so that $B_{i,k}(\bar{u})$ will be positive for all k.

Our earlier observations about the cubic B-splines can be generalized as follows.

- $B_{i,k}(\bar{u})$ is a member of $\mathbf{S}(\mathbf{P}^k, \{\bar{u}_i\}_0^{m+k})$; it is composed of segment polynomials having order k.

- Knot multiplicities greater than k are of no interest in constructing splines, and in their absence we have $\bar{u}_{i+k} > \bar{u}_i$ for every i. As we will see later, it follows that $B_{i,k}(\bar{u}) > 0$ for $\bar{u}$ between $\bar{u}_i$ and $\bar{u}_{i+k}$.

- $B_{i,k}(\bar{u}) = 0$, for $\bar{u} < \bar{u}_i$ or $\bar{u}_{i+k} \leq \bar{u}$. Thus i, k indicates the interval of support. (The value of $B_{i,k}(\bar{u})$ at $\bar{u} = \bar{u}_i$ will depend upon the multiplicity of $\bar{u}_i$ and upon the value of k. Notice particularly that $\bar{u}_i$ is *included* and $\bar{u}_{i+k}$ is *excluded*. This is a result of the fact that $B_{i,k}(\bar{u})$ is constructed from the functions $(\bar{u}-t)_+^r$ and is open on the right.)

8.1 A Simple Example — Step Function B-splines

Let us recall how we arrived at the preceding definition by examining the B-spline representation of piecewise linear functions. First consider

$$B_{i,1}(\bar{u}) = (-1)(\bar{u}_{i+1} - \bar{u}_i)[\bar{u}_i(1):t](\bar{u}-t)_+^0$$

$$= (-1)(\bar{u}_{i+1} - \bar{u}_i)[\bar{u}_i, \bar{u}_{i+1}:t](\bar{u}-t)_+^0.$$

Since $k = 1$, only multiplicities of 1 are interesting, and we must have $\bar{u}_i < \bar{u}_{i+1}$. The definition of a divided difference tells us that

$$B_{i,1}(\bar{u}) = (-1)(\bar{u}_{i+1} - \bar{u}_i) \frac{(\bar{u} - \bar{u}_{i+1})_+^0 - (\bar{u} - \bar{u}_i)_+^0}{(\bar{u}_{i+1} - \bar{u}_i)}$$

$$= (\bar{u} - \bar{u}_i)_+^0 - (\bar{u} - \bar{u}_{i+1})_+^0$$

$$= \begin{cases} 0 & \text{for} \quad \bar{u} < \bar{u}_i \\ 1 & \text{for} \quad \bar{u}_i \leq \bar{u} < \bar{u}_{i+1} \\ 0 & \text{for} \quad \bar{u}_{i+1} \leq \bar{u}. \end{cases}$$

Figure 8.1 illustrates the differencing process from which this function is constructed. This very simple example shows the idea of combining two adjacent one-sided functions to obtain a function that is zero to the left of $\bar{u}_i$ and dies away to zero on the right of $\bar{u}_{i+1}$.

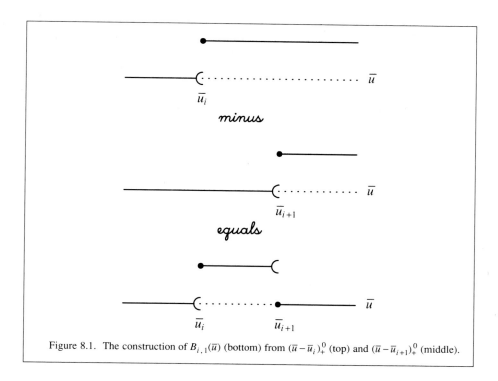

Figure 8.1. The construction of $B_{i,1}(\bar{u})$ (bottom) from $(\bar{u} - \bar{u}_i)_+^0$ (top) and $(\bar{u} - \bar{u}_{i+1})_+^0$ (middle).

This B-spline serves just as well to construct piecewise, first-order, C^{-1} polynomials (i.e., step functions) as did the one-sided functions $(\bar{u} - \bar{u}_i)_+^0$ and $(\bar{u} - \bar{u}_{i+1})_+^0$.

Let us consider the simple case in which the knots are

$$\begin{array}{cccc} \bar{u}_0 & \bar{u}_1 & \bar{u}_2 & \bar{u}_3 \ , \\ 0 & 2 & 4 & 5 \end{array}$$

our designated parameter range is

$$\bar{u}_{k-1} \ = \ \bar{u}_0 \ \leq \ \bar{u} \ < \ \bar{u}_3 \ = \ \bar{u}_{m+1} \ ,$$

and the randomly chosen step function to be represented (see Figure 8.2) is:

$$s_1(\bar{u}) \ = \ \begin{cases} 0.25 & \bar{u} < 0 \\ 0.50 & 0 \leq \bar{u} < 2 \\ 0.75 & 2 \leq \bar{u} < 4 \\ 1.25 & 4 \leq \bar{u} < 5 \\ 2.00 & 5 \leq \bar{u} \ . \end{cases}$$

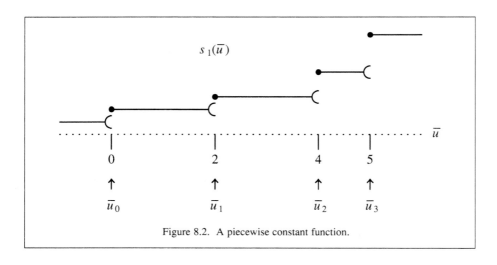

Figure 8.2. A piecewise constant function.

This step function is a member of the space

$$\mathbf{S}(\ \mathbf{P}^1 \ , \{0,2,4,5\}\ )\ ,$$

for which the designated parameter range was defined to be [0,5) and for which the appropriate one-sided basis is

$$(\bar{u}-\bar{u}_0)^0_+ = (\bar{u}-0)^0_+ = \begin{cases} 0 & \bar{u} < 0 \\ 1 & \bar{u} \geq 0 \end{cases}$$

$$(\bar{u}-\bar{u}_1)^0_+ = (\bar{u}-2)^0_+ = \begin{cases} 0 & \bar{u} < 2 \\ 1 & \bar{u} \geq 2 \end{cases}$$

$$(\bar{u}-\bar{u}_2)^0_+ = (\bar{u}-4)^0_+ = \begin{cases} 0 & \bar{u} < 4 \\ 1 & \bar{u} \geq 4 \end{cases}$$

(see Figure 8.3). Note that there is no one-sided power function in the basis that could possibly account for the behavior of the step function outside [0,5). That region of the $\bar{u}$ axis, however, is outside the parameter range associated with the spline space we are considering.

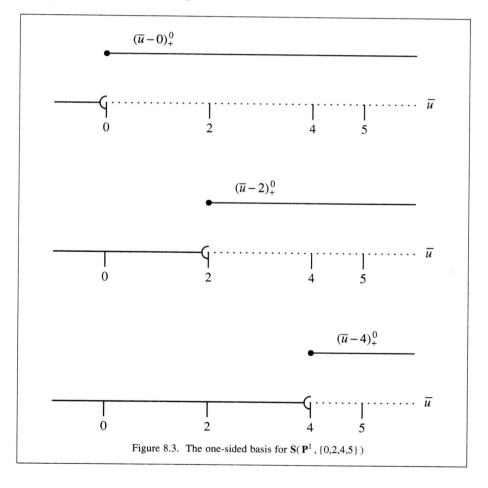

Figure 8.3. The one-sided basis for $\mathbf{S}(\mathbf{P}^1, \{0,2,4,5\})$

The one-sided power functions cannot reproduce $s_1(\overline{u})$ on the entire axis, as we have remarked before, but we can reproduce the behavior of $s_1(\overline{u})$ restricted to the parameter range [0,5) by a function $s_2(\overline{u})$:

$$s_2(\overline{u}) = (0.50)(\overline{u}-0)^0_+ + (0.25)(\overline{u}-2)^0_+ + (0.50)(\overline{u}-4)^0_+ \tag{8.1}$$

(see Figure 8.4).

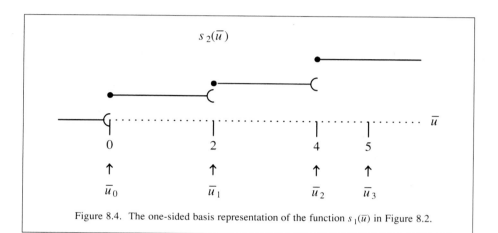

Figure 8.4. The one-sided basis representation of the function $s_1(\overline{u})$ in Figure 8.2.

Again, notice that the representation $s_2(\overline{u})$ differs from the given step function $s_1(\overline{u})$ outside $[\overline{u}_0,\overline{u}_3) = [0,5)$, a fact which is not at all disturbing: recall that members of $S(\mathbf{P}^1, \{0,2,4,5\})$ are indistinguishable if they only differ outside the designated parameter range.

The obvious divided differencing process to be considered uses

$$(\overline{u}-0)^0_+ \quad \text{and} \quad (\overline{u}-2)^0_+$$

to construct the B-spline

$$B_{0,1}(\overline{u}) = (-1)(2-0)[0,2{:}t](\overline{u}-t)^0_+ = \begin{cases} 0 & \overline{u} < 0 \\ 1 & 0 \le \overline{u} < 2 \\ 0 & 2 \le \overline{u} \end{cases}$$

which is substituted for $(\overline{u}-0)^0_+$, and uses

$$(\overline{u}-2)^0_+ \quad \text{and} \quad (\overline{u}-4)^0_+$$

to construct the B-spline

$$B_{1,1}(\bar{u}) = (-1)(4-2)[2,4{:}t](\bar{u}-t)_+^0 = \begin{cases} 0 & \bar{u} < 2 \\ 1 & 2 \le \bar{u} < 4 \\ 0 & 4 \le \bar{u} \end{cases}$$

which is substituted for $(\bar{u}-2)_+^0$. Finally, the one-sided power function

$$(\bar{u}-5)_+^0,$$

which was not needed for the one-sided basis representation, can be differenced with

$$(\bar{u}-4)_+^0,$$

to produce the final B-spline:

$$(\bar{u}-\bar{u}_3)_+^0 = (\bar{u}-5)_+^0 = \begin{cases} 0 & \bar{u} < 5 \\ 1 & 5 \le \bar{u} \end{cases}$$

$$B_{2,1}(\bar{u}) = (-1)(5-4)[4,5{:}t](\bar{u}-t)_+^0 = \begin{cases} 0 & \bar{u} < 4 \\ 1 & 4 \le \bar{u} < 5 \\ 0 & 5 \le \bar{u}, \end{cases}$$

which substitutes for $(\bar{u}-4)_+^0$. Figure 8.5 depicts this basis. Note that this B-spline basis, like the one-sided basis, cannot account for the behavior of the step function outside the designated parameter range. This allows us to represent $s_1(\bar{u})$, restricted to [0,5), by the functions $s_3(\bar{u})$:

$$s_3(\bar{u}) = (0.50)B_{0,1}(\bar{u}) + (0.75)B_{1,1}(\bar{u}) + (1.25)B_{2,1}(\bar{u})$$

(see Figure 8.6). Compare this B-spline representation $s_3(\bar{u})$ (shown in Figure 8.6) with the original step function $s_1(\bar{u})$ (given by (8.1) and shown in Figure 8.2), and with its one-sided representation $s_2(\bar{u})$ (shown in Figure 8.4). All three are identical on the parameter range [0,5). They are consequently, by convention, the same spline with respect to the space $S(\mathbf{P}^1, \{0,2,4,5\})$.

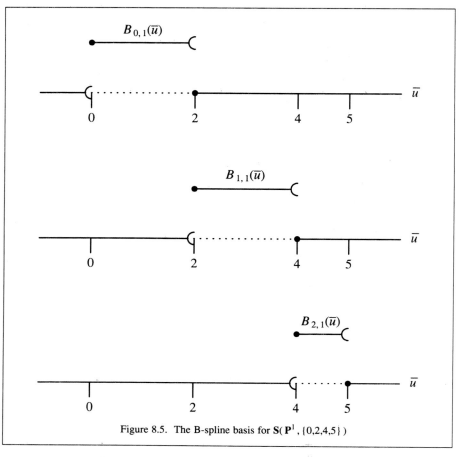

Figure 8.5. The B-spline basis for $S(\mathbf{P}^1, \{0,2,4,5\})$

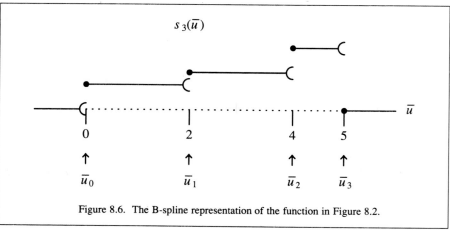

Figure 8.6. The B-spline representation of the function in Figure 8.2.

8.2 Linear B-splines

The reader should be cautious about following us too far without objection. The above example was chosen to have unequally spaced knots, so it is a bit more general than the uniform case. But it is possible that any inferences we might draw from this example break down in the presence of multiple knots. Let us introduce another knot at $\bar{u} = 4$ to see what can be learned. To do this, we will go to order $k = 2$, since knots of multiplicity 2 are uninteresting for $k = 1$. So that this multiplicity falls strictly within the designated parameter range and contributes to the "significant" portion of any spline, we will add the knot

$$\bar{u}_5 = 7$$

so that the knot sequence is

$$\begin{array}{cccccc} \bar{u}_0 & \bar{u}_1 & \bar{u}_2 & \bar{u}_3 & \bar{u}_4 & \bar{u}_5 . \\ 0 & 2 & 4 & 4 & 5 & 7 \end{array}$$

Consider $S(\mathbf{P}^2, \{0,2,4,4,5,7\})$. The elements of this space are:

linear   for $\bar{u} < 0$

C^0 at $\bar{u} = 0$

linear   for $0 \leq \bar{u} < 2$

C^0 at $\bar{u} = 2$

linear   for $2 \leq \bar{u} < 4$

C^{-1} at $\bar{u} = 4$

linear   for $4 \leq \bar{u} < 5$

C^0 at $\bar{u} = 5$

linear   for $5 \leq \bar{u} < 7$

C^0 at $\bar{u} = 7$

linear   for $7 \leq \bar{u}$.

A representative spline from this space is shown in Figure 8.7. We take the parameter range of this space to be

$$\bar{u}_{k-1} = \bar{u}_1 \leq \bar{u} < \bar{u}_4 = \bar{u}_{m+1} .$$

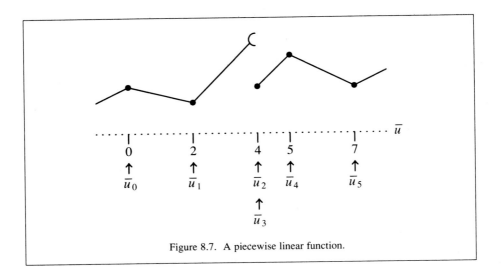

Figure 8.7. A piecewise linear function.

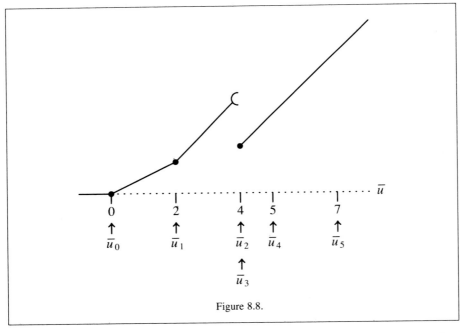

Figure 8.8.

The parameter range begins with $\bar{u}_1$ because we need two linearly independent functions to define the first segment. The knot $\bar{u}_5$ is added to the right of the parameter range so that there will be a one-sided function to difference with $(\bar{u} - \bar{u}_4)_+^1$.

The one-sided basis for this space is

$$(\bar{u}-0)_+^1, \ (\bar{u}-2)_+^1, \ (\bar{u}-4)_+^0, \ (\bar{u}-4)_+^1.$$

The one-sided representation for the spline shown in Figure 8.7 is shown in Figure 8.8.

We use

$$(\bar{u}-0)_+^1, \ (\bar{u}-2)_+^1, \ (\bar{u}-4)_+^1,$$

together with the extra one-sided power functions

$$(\bar{u}-5)_+^1 \ \text{and} \ (\bar{u}-7)_+^1,$$

to construct the B-splines

$$
\begin{aligned}
B_{0,2}(\bar{u}) &= (-1)^2 (\bar{u}_2 - \bar{u}_0) [\, \bar{u}_0, \bar{u}_1, \bar{u}_2 : t \,](\bar{u}-t)_+^1 \\[2mm]
&= (\bar{u}_2 - \bar{u}_0) \left[\frac{[\, \bar{u}_1, \bar{u}_2 : t \,](\bar{u}-t)_+^1 - [\, \bar{u}_0, \bar{u}_1 : t \,](\bar{u}-t)_+^1}{\bar{u}_2 - \bar{u}_0} \right] \\[2mm]
&= \frac{[\, \bar{u}_2 : t \,](\bar{u}-t)_+^1 - [\, \bar{u}_1 : t \,](\bar{u}-t)_+^1}{\bar{u}_2 - \bar{u}_1} \\[2mm]
&\quad - \frac{[\, \bar{u}_1 : t \,](\bar{u}-t)_+^0 - [\, \bar{u}_0 : t \,](\bar{u}-t)_+^1}{\bar{u}_1 - \bar{u}_0} \\[2mm]
&= \frac{(\bar{u}-\bar{u}_2)_+^1 - (\bar{u}-\bar{u}_1)_+^1}{\bar{u}_2 - \bar{u}_1} - \frac{(\bar{u}-\bar{u}_1)_+^1 - (\bar{u}-\bar{u}_0)_+^1}{\bar{u}_1 - \bar{u}_0} \\[2mm]
&= \frac{(\bar{u}-4)_+^1 - (\bar{u}-2)_+^1}{4-2} - \frac{(\bar{u}-2)_+^1 - (\bar{u}-0)_+^1}{2-0} \\[4mm]
&= \begin{cases}
0 & \bar{u} < 0 \\[2mm]
\dfrac{\bar{u}-0}{2-0} & 0 \leq \bar{u} < 2 \\[2mm]
\dfrac{2-\bar{u}}{4-2} + 1 & 2 \leq \bar{u} < 4 \\[2mm]
0 & 4 \leq \bar{u}
\end{cases}
\end{aligned}
$$

$$B_{1,2}(\overline{u}) \;=\; (-1)^2\,(\overline{u}_3 - \overline{u}_1)\,[\,\overline{u}_1,\overline{u}_2,\overline{u}_3 : t\,]\,(\overline{u} - t\,)_+^1$$

$$=\; (\overline{u}_3 - \overline{u}_1)\left[\frac{[\,\overline{u}_2,\overline{u}_3 : t\,]\,(\overline{u} - t\,)_+^1 \;-\; [\,\overline{u}_1,\overline{u}_2 : t\,]\,(\overline{u} - t\,)_+^1}{\overline{u}_3 - \overline{u}_1}\right]$$

$$=\; D_t^{(1)}(\overline{u} - t\,)_+^1\Big|_{t=\overline{u}_2=\overline{u}_3} \;-\; \frac{[\,\overline{u}_2 : t\,]\,(\overline{u} - t\,)_+^1 - [\,\overline{u}_1 : t\,]\,(\overline{u} - t\,)_+^1}{\overline{u}_2 - \overline{u}_1}$$

$$=\; -(\overline{u} - \overline{u}_2)_+^0 \;-\; \frac{(\overline{u} - \overline{u}_2)_+^1 - (\overline{u} - \overline{u}_1)_+^1}{\overline{u}_2 - \overline{u}_1}$$

$$=\; -(\overline{u} - 4)_+^0 \;-\; \frac{(\overline{u} - 4)_+^1 - (\overline{u} - 2)_+^1}{4 - 2}$$

$$=\; \begin{cases} 0 & \overline{u} < 2 \\[2mm] \dfrac{\overline{u} - 2}{4 - 2} & 2 \le \overline{u} < 4 \\[2mm] 0 & 4 \le \overline{u} \end{cases}$$

$$B_{2,2}(\overline{u}) \;=\; (-1)^2\,(\overline{u}_4 - \overline{u}_2)\,[\,\overline{u}_2,\overline{u}_3,\overline{u}_4 : t\,]\,(\overline{u} - t\,)_+^1$$

$$=\; \begin{cases} 0 & \overline{u} < 4 \\[2mm] \dfrac{4 - \overline{u}}{5 - 4} + 1 & 4 \le \overline{u} < 5 \\[2mm] 0 & 5 \le \overline{u} \end{cases}$$

$$B_{3,2}(\overline{u}) \;=\; (-1)^2\,(\overline{u}_5 - \overline{u}_3)\,[\,\overline{u}_3,\overline{u}_4,\overline{u}_5 : t\,]\,(\overline{u} - t\,)_+^1$$

$$=\; \begin{cases} 0 & \overline{u} < 4 \\[2mm] \dfrac{\overline{u} - 4}{5 - 4} & 4 \le \overline{u} < 5 \\[2mm] \dfrac{5 - \overline{u}}{7 - 5} + 1 & 5 \le \overline{u} < 7 \\[2mm] 0 & 7 \le \overline{u}. \end{cases}$$

These B-splines are plotted in Figure 8.9. Pay particular attention to the B-splines $B_{1,2}(\overline{u})$ and $B_{2,2}(\overline{u})$, which contain a discontinuity at the breakpoint $\overline{u} = 4$. Multiplying these B-splines by the appropriate scale factors results in a curve indistinguishable from that of Figure 8.7 on the parameter range [2,5).

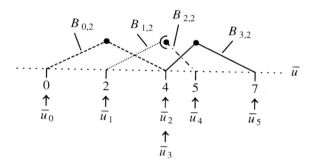

Figure 8.9. The B-splines of order 2 with which we can represent the piecewise linear curve shown in Figure 8.7.

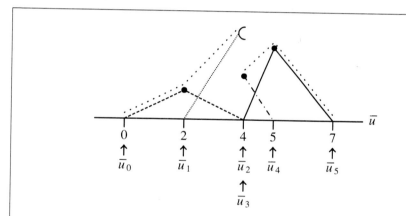

Figure 8.10. The piecewise linear curve of Figure 8.7 (shown with a lightly dotted line) represented as a linear combination of B-splines of order 2. Notice how the double knot at $\bar{u} = 4$ allows us to represent a discontinuity in the curve at this point.

Any spline of the sort shown in Figure 8.7 can be represented by this collection of B-splines on the parameter range $[\bar{u}_1, \bar{u}_4) = [2,5)$.

8.3 General B-spline Bases

The previous example suggests how a pure B-spline basis can be constructed for the spline space $\mathbf{S}(\mathbf{P}^k, \{\bar{u}_i\}_0^{m+k})$.

■ **Construction**

For any given knot sequence $\{\bar{u}_i\}_0^{m+k}$, let

$$B_{i,k}(\bar{u}) = (-1)^k (\bar{u}_{i+k} - \bar{u}_i) [\bar{u}_i(k):t](\bar{u}-t)_+^{k-1}$$

for $i = 0, \ldots, m$.

■

■ **Theorem**

The functions $B_{0,k}(\bar{u}), \ldots, B_{m,k}(\bar{u})$ constructed in this fashion form a basis for $\mathbf{S}(\mathbf{P}^k, \{\bar{u}_i\}_0^{m+k})$.

■

This is a result due to Curry and Schoenberg, and a proof may be found in [de Boor78]. It implies that the dimension of $\mathbf{S}(\mathbf{P}^k, \{\bar{u}_i\}_0^{m+k})$ is $m+1$, provided no knot has multiplicity greater than k, which would result in some of the B-splines being vacuous. Recall that we are considering the parameter range to be $[\bar{u}_{k-1}, \bar{u}_{m+1})$.

8.4 Examples — Quadratic B-splines

The divided difference formulation could be used directly to evaluate the B-splines (though we will discourage this from the standpoint of numerical accuracy in some subsequent remarks). We will illustrate this process of evaluation with a couple of examples. First, consider $B_{0,3}(\bar{u})$ with $\bar{u} = 2$ on the knots

$$\bar{u}_0 \quad \bar{u}_1 \quad \bar{u}_2 \quad \bar{u}_3,$$
$$0 \quad 1 \quad 3 \quad 4$$

shown in Figure 8.11.

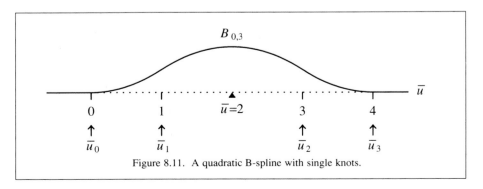

Figure 8.11. A quadratic B-spline with single knots.

In the table below, beginning at the second column, each entry is the divided difference of the entry to its left in the preceding column and the entry just above that. That is, for each pattern

$$
\begin{array}{ll}
A & \\
B & C
\end{array}
$$

we have

$$
C = \frac{B - A}{\bar{u}_{i_1} - \bar{u}_{i_2}}
$$

for some appropriate knots $\bar{u}_{i_1}$ and $\bar{u}_{i_2}$.

$\bar{u}_i$	$(\bar{u} - \bar{u}_i)_+^2$	$[*,*]$	$[*,*,*]$	$[*,*,*,*]$
0	$(2-0)_+^2 = 4$			
1	$(2-1)_+^2 = 1$	$\dfrac{1-4}{1-0} = -3$		
3	$(2-3)_+^2 = 0$	$0 - \dfrac{1}{3} - 1 = -\dfrac{1}{2}$	$\dfrac{-\dfrac{1}{2}+3}{3} - 0 = \dfrac{5}{6}$	
4	$(2-4)_+^2 = 0$	$0 - \dfrac{0}{4} - 3 = 0$	$\dfrac{0+\dfrac{1}{2}}{4} - 1 = \dfrac{1}{6}$	$\dfrac{\dfrac{1}{6} - \dfrac{5}{6}}{4-0} = -\dfrac{1}{6}$

The above differencing process establishes that

$$
B_{0,3}(2) = (-1)^3(4-0)(-\frac{1}{6})
$$

$$
= \frac{2}{3}
$$

for the knot sequence

$$
\{\bar{u}_i\}_0^{m+k} = \{0,1,3,4\}.
$$

A more involved example is given by the computation of $B_{0,3}(2)$ if the knot sequence is

$$
\begin{array}{cccc}
\bar{u}_0 & \bar{u}_1 & \bar{u}_2 & \bar{u}_3, \\
0 & 1 & 1 & 3
\end{array}
$$

shown in Figure 8.12.

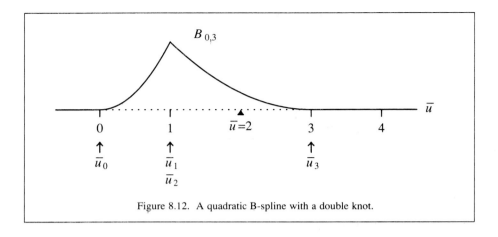

Figure 8.12. A quadratic B-spline with a double knot.

The table for the divided difference computation is given below. Note that the repeated knot requires the computation of a derivative.

$\bar{u}_i$	$(\bar{u} - \bar{u}_i)_+^2$	$[*,*]$	$[*,*,*]$	$[*,*,*,*]$
0	$(2-0)_+^2 = 4$			
1	$(2-1)_+^2 = 1$	$\dfrac{1-4}{1-0} = -3$		
1	$(2-1)_+^2 = 1$	$D_t(2-t)^2\mid_{t=1} = -2$	$\dfrac{-2+3}{1} - 0 = 1$	
3	$(2-3)_+^2 = 0$	$0 - \dfrac{1}{3} - 1 = -\dfrac{1}{2}$	$\dfrac{-\dfrac{1}{2} + 2}{3} - 1 = \dfrac{3}{4}$	$\dfrac{\dfrac{3}{4} - 1}{3} - 0 = -\dfrac{1}{12}$

This table establishes that

$$B_{0,3}(2) = (-1)^3(3-0)\left[-\frac{1}{12}\right] = \frac{1}{4}.$$

This example raises another issue we should consider. Our preliminary discussions introduced the operation of divided differencing in the context of simple knots. We motivated the use of divided differences informally on the grounds that, when

$$\bar{u}_i < \cdots < \bar{u}_{i+k},$$

this operation was precisely what was needed to form linear combinations of

$$(\bar{u} - \bar{u}_i)_+^{k-1}, \ldots, (\bar{u} - \bar{u}_{i+k})_+^{k-1}$$

having compact support. That is, the differencing process is a means of finding coefficients $d_i, \ldots, d_{i+k}$ for which

$$B_{i,k}(\bar{u}) = d_i (\bar{u} - \bar{u}_i)_+^{k-1} + \cdots + d_{i+k} (\bar{u} - \bar{u}_{i+k})_+^{k-1}$$

had the property that

$$B_{i,k}(\bar{u}) = 0 \text{ for } \bar{u} \geq \bar{u}_{i+k}.$$

This informal explanation does not apply when knots become multiple, yet we proceeded to define the divided difference operator in general, including the case of multiple knots, and then claim, or at least imply, that the functions

$$B_{i,k}(\bar{u}) = (-1)^k (\bar{u}_{i+k} - \bar{u}_i)[\bar{u}_i(k):t](\bar{u}-t)_+^{k-1}$$

would have this property of compact support. We will give empirical evidence below that this is true. Let us look at the example of the knots $\{0,1,1,3\}$ to see what happens.

The one-sided power functions that are appropriate for this knot sequence are

$$(\bar{u}-0)_+^2, \ (\bar{u}-1)_+^2, \ (\bar{u}-1)_+^1, \ \text{and } (\bar{u}-3)_+^2. \tag{8.2}$$

Note that there are two powers of $(\bar{u}-1)$ associated with the double knot $\bar{u}=1$, a first power and a square. Recall that $(\bar{u}-1)_+^2$ allows us to alter the second derivative as we cross a knot; in the same way, the truncated power function $(\bar{u}-1)_+^1$ allows us to alter the first derivative as we cross a knot. To develop any spline basis suitable for this knot sequence we must restrict our attention to linear combinations of these functions.

The divided difference table above, for general $\bar{u}$, would be

$\bar{u}_i$	$(\bar{u} - \bar{u}_i)_+^2$	$[*,*]$	$[*,*,*]$	$[*,*,*,*]$
0	$(\bar{u}-0)_+^2$			
1	$(\bar{u}-1)_+^2$	$\dfrac{(\bar{u}-1)_+^2 - (\bar{u}-0)_+^2}{1-0}$		
1	$(\bar{u}-1)_+^2$	$D\ (\bar{u}-t)^2\|_{t=1} = -2(\bar{u}-1)_+^1$	A	
3	$(\bar{u}-3)_+^2$	$\dfrac{(\bar{u}-3)_+^2 - (\bar{u}-1)_+^2}{3-1}$	B	C

where

$$A = \frac{-2(\bar{u}-1)_+^1 - \dfrac{(\bar{u}-1)_+^2 - (\bar{u}-0)_+^2}{1-0}}{1-0}$$

$$B = \frac{\dfrac{(\bar{u}-3)_+^2 - (\bar{u}-1)_+^2}{3-1} + 2(\bar{u}-1)_+^1}{3-1}$$

and

$$C = \frac{B-A}{3-0}.$$

Clearly, we are still producing linear combinations of the one-sided power functions (8.2). Indeed, the derivative that arises when a multiple knot is encountered reduces the order of the one-sided function just enough to introduce the appropriate lower-degree continuity.

What is more, the compact support property (locality) also holds. If the expression for C above is written out, and then simplified symbolically under the assumption that $\bar{u} > 3$ so that the "+" subscripts are no longer relevant, then all terms in the numerator cancel to zero.

We end this section with a cautionary remark. Both computational tables above, for $B_{0,3}(2)$ with single knots and for a double knot, involve arithmetic with a mixture of positive and negative numbers. This implies that cancellations can take place in floating-point to produce inaccurate results. These inaccuracies will be pronounced in cases where knots are <u>nearly</u> but <u>not</u> exactly multiple. The divided difference definition of a B-spline is <u>not</u> the recommended formula to use in numeric computations. We will establish more viable methods of computation in a later chapter.

8.5 The Visual Effect of Knot Multiplicities — Cubic B-splines

We will end this chapter with a few more examples of B-splines, chosen now from the more useful cubic case. Most of the material in this and the following section is taken from [Barsky/Beatty83b].

Let us begin with the knots we have been using for the uniform B-spline discussions:

$$\bar{u}_0 \quad \bar{u}_1 \quad \bar{u}_2 \quad \bar{u}_3 \quad \bar{u}_4.$$
$$\phantom{\bar{u}_0}0 \quad\;\; 1 \quad\;\; 2 \quad\;\; 3 \quad\;\; 4$$

We will progressively increase the multiplicity of the knot at $\bar{u} = 1$ to watch what happens. As a reminder, we give the description of the uniform B-spline on these knots once again:

$$B_{0,4}(\bar{u}) = (-1)^4 (\bar{u}_4 - \bar{u}_0) [\bar{u}_0(4):t] (\bar{u} - t)_+^3$$

$$= (-1)^4 (\bar{u}_4 - \bar{u}_0) [\bar{u}_0, \bar{u}_1, \bar{u}_2, \bar{u}_3, \bar{u}_4 : t] (\bar{u} - t)_+^3$$

$$= (4-0)[0,1,2,3,4:t](\bar{u} - t)_+^3$$

$$= \begin{cases} b_{-0}(\bar{u}) & 0 \leq \bar{u} < 1 \\ b_{-1}(\bar{u}) & 1 \leq \bar{u} < 2 \\ b_{-2}(\bar{u}) & 2 \leq \bar{u} < 3 \\ b_{-3}(\bar{u}) & 3 \leq \bar{u} < 4, \end{cases}$$

where the segment polynomials are given by

$$b_{-0}(\bar{u}) = \frac{\bar{u}^3}{6}$$

$$b_{-1}(\bar{u}) = -\frac{3\bar{u}^3 - 12\bar{u}^2 + 12\bar{u} - 4}{6}$$

$$b_{-2}(\bar{u}) = \frac{3\bar{u}^3 - 24\bar{u}^2 + 60\bar{u} - 44}{6}$$

$$b_{-3}(\bar{u}) = -\frac{\bar{u}^3 - 12\bar{u}^2 + 48\bar{u} - 64}{6}.$$

Figure 8.13 shows the graph of $B_{0,4}(\bar{u})$.

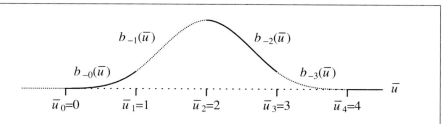

Figure 8.13. $B_{0,4}(\bar{u})$, a uniform cubic B-spline, with each of the segment polynomials making up the basis function labeled and distinguished by the alternating use of dotted and solid lines.

If the knot at $\bar{u} = 1$ is doubled, then $B_{0,4}(\bar{u})$ is as shown in Figure 8.14.

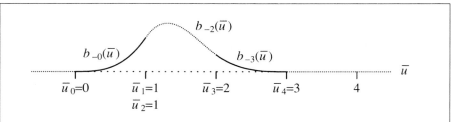

Figure 8.14. The double knot at $\bar{u} = 1$ eliminates second-derivative continuity there, although first-derivative continuity remains. Notice that the basis function is no longer symmetric.

Notice that the support of this function (the region on which it is different from zero) is still $(\bar{u}_0, \bar{u}_4)$, but this now represents the interval

$$0 < \bar{u} < 3$$

because the knots $\bar{u}_1$ and $\bar{u}_2$ have "moved together." The segment polynomials $b_{-0}(\bar{u})$ and $b_{-2}(\bar{u})$ have only their value and first derivative in common at $\bar{u} = 1$; i.e., $B_{0,4}(\bar{u})$ has C^1 continuity at the breakpoint $\bar{u}_1$. The segment polynomials are given by

$$b_{-0}(\bar{u}) = \frac{\bar{u}^3}{2}$$

$b_{-1}(\bar{u})$ *is vacuous*

$$b_{-2}(\bar{u}) = \frac{5\bar{u}^3 - 27\bar{u}^2 + 45\bar{u} - 21}{4}$$

and

$$b_{-3}(\bar{u}) = -\frac{\bar{u}^3 - 9\bar{u}^2 + 27\bar{u} - 27}{4}.$$

Since there are now only three segments to the B-spline instead of four, we have had to choose a new numbering of the segment polynomials. Our choice reflects the idea that, since the interval between $\bar{u}_1$ and $\bar{u}_2$ has now disappeared, we should dispense with $b_{-1}(\bar{u})$. The first derivatives of the remaining segment polynomials are

$$b_{-0}^{(1)}(\bar{u}) = \frac{3\bar{u}^2}{2}$$

$$b_{-2}^{(1)}(\bar{u}) = \frac{15\bar{u}^2 - 54\bar{u} + 45}{4}$$

and

$$b_{-3}^{(1)}(\bar{u}) = -\frac{3\bar{u}^2 - 18\bar{u} + 27}{4}.$$

Notice that $b_{-0}^{(1)}(1) = b_{-2}^{(1)}(1) = 1.5$ and that $b_{-2}^{(1)}(2) = b_{-3}^{(1)}(2) = -0.75$, thus establishing first derivative continuity at $\bar{u} = 1$ and $\bar{u} = 2$. The second derivatives are

$$b_{-0}^{(2)}(\bar{u}) = 3\bar{u}$$

$$b_{-2}^{(2)}(\bar{u}) = \frac{30\bar{u} - 54}{4}$$

and

$$b_{-3}^{(2)}(\bar{u}) = -\frac{6\bar{u} - 18}{4}.$$

We see that $b_{-0}^{(2)}(1) = 3$ while $b_{-2}^{(2)}(1) = -6$, so that $B_{i,k}(\bar{u})$ has a discontinuous second derivative at $\bar{u} = \bar{u}_1$. Observe however, that $b_{-2}^{(2)}(2) = b_{-3}^{(2)}(2) = 1.5$, so $B_{i,k}(\bar{u})$ does have a continuous second derivative at $\bar{u} = \bar{u}_3$. This follows, of course, from the fact that we have not increased the knot multiplicity at $\bar{u} = 2$, and the discontinuity that we have introduced at the breakpoint $\bar{u} = \bar{u}_1 = \bar{u}_2 = 1$ has no influence on the other breakpoints.

Figure 8.15 contains a knot of multiplicity three (C^0, or positional continuity) and Figure 8.16 a knot of multiplicity four (no continuity). Notice that in each case the basis function, which is cubic, is nonzero over the span of four knots, namely for $u \in [\bar{u}_0, \bar{u}_4)$. The two cubics that meet at the triple knot in Figure 8.15 meet only with C^0 (that is, $C^{4-1-\mu}$ continuity). Each additional time a knot

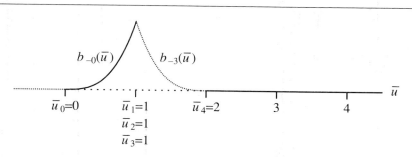

Figure 8.15. A knot of multiplicity 3, which reduces the cubic B-spline to positional continuity at $\bar{u} = 1$.

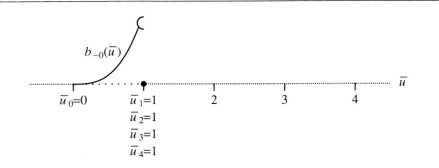

Figure 8.16. A knot of multiplicity 4, which eliminates even positional continuity at $\bar{u} = 1$.

is repeated, the parametric continuity of the underlying basis functions, and hence the parametric continuity of any curve they might construct, is reduced by one order. The segment polynomials for the triple-knot case are:

$$b_{-0}(\bar{u}) \;=\; \bar{u}^3$$

$$b_{-1}(\bar{u}) \;\; is \; vacuous$$

$$b_{-2}(\bar{u}) \;\; is \; vacuous$$

$$b_{-3}(\bar{u}) \;=\; -\bar{u}^3 + 6\bar{u}^2 - 12\bar{u} + 8 \,.$$

Finally, the segment polynomials for the quadruple-knot case are:

$$b_{-0}(\bar{u}) \;=\; \bar{u}^3$$

$$b_{-1}(\bar{u}) \;\; is \; vacuous$$

$$b_{-2}(\bar{u}) \;\; is \; vacuous$$

$$b_{-3}(\bar{u}) \;\; is \; vacuous \,.$$

Figure 8.17 shows some of the ways in which multiplicities may be assigned to one of the breakpoints defining a cubic B-spline in which the nonvacuous intervals all have unit length.

The following set of figures illustrates the effect that multiple knots have on the shape of a parametric curve.

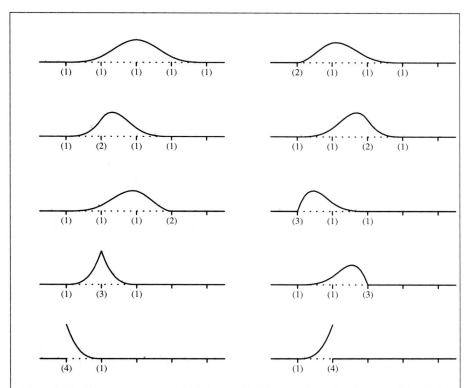

Figure 8.17. The various ways in which knot multiplicities can be assigned to one of the breakpoints defining a cubic B-spline. The multiplicities are indicated in parentheses.

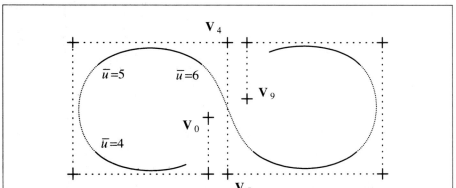

Figure 8.18. This is a uniform cubic B-spline curve. The knots are equally spaced and of multiplicity 1.

Figure 8.18 shows a simple curve obtained from ten control vertices using uniform cubic B-splines.

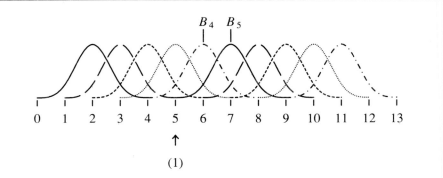

Figure 8.19. These are the B-splines used in constructing the curve of Figure 8.18. They are all translates of one another.

We have flagged the B-splines as follows in Figure 8.19:

$$B_{4,4}(\bar{u}) \rightarrow B_4 \quad \text{and} \quad B_{5,4}(\bar{u}) \rightarrow B_5.$$

These particular B-splines are distinguished because we will be increasing the multiplicity of the knot at $\bar{u} = 5$, and these basis functions are the ones that will show the most effect. The curve will likewise display the largest change in the interval between the control vertices $\mathbf{V}_4$ and $\mathbf{V}_5$.

The space of splines under consideration is

$$\mathbf{S}(\mathbf{P}^4, \{\bar{u}_i\}_0^{13})$$

and the dimension of this space is 10, which is just what we need to manage ten control vertices. The parameter range is taken to be $[3, 10)$, by our definition of this space, and as $\bar{u}$ travels from 3 to 10, it passes through the seven intervals

$$[3,4), [4,5), [5,6), [6,7), [7,8), [8,9), \text{ and } [9,10).$$

The portions of the curve generated as $\bar{u}$ runs through these segments are indicated by alternating solid and dotted lines.

Consider now what happens if we double the knot at $\bar{u} = 5$. To retain the same dimension, i.e., to use the same control vertices, we have now to use the knot sequence

$$\{0, 1, 2, 3, 4, 5, 5, 6, 7, 8, 9, 10, 11, 12\}$$

so that the parameter range becomes $[3, 9)$. This means that $\bar{u}$ will now travel through only the six intervals

$$[3,4), [4,5), [5,6), [6,7), [7,8), \text{ and } [8,9)$$

as the curve is traced out. That is, there are six curve segments. Figures 8.20 and 8.21 show what happens.

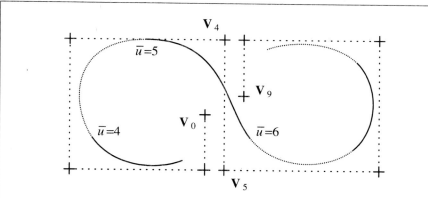

Figure 8.20. The breakpoints defining this curve are equally spaced, but there is a double knot at $\bar{u} = 5$. (See Figure 8.21.)

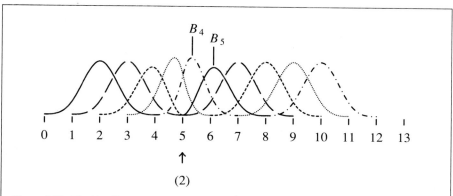

Figure 8.21. The B-splines used to construct the curve of Figure 8.20. There is a double knot at $\bar{u} = 5$.

When the knot at $\bar{u} = 5$ is tripled, the knot sequence becomes

$$\{0, 1, 2, 3, 4, 5, 5, 5, 6, 7, 8, 9, 10, 11\},$$

the parameter range becomes $[3, 8)$, and there are five segments. The fact that some of the underlying B-splines have discontinuities in the first derivative is apparent in Figures 8.22 and 8.23.

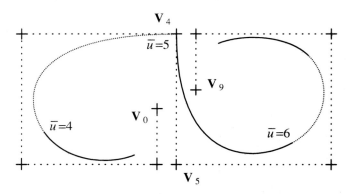

Figure 8.22. The breakpoints defining this curve are equally spaced, but there is a triple knot at $\bar{u} = 5$. Since this is a cubic B-spline, we are only left with positional continuity at the triple knot. (See Figure 8.23.)

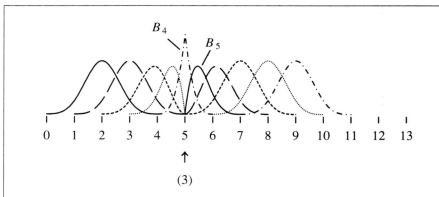

Figure 8.23. The B-splines used to construct the curve of Figure 8.22. There is a triple knot at $\bar{u} = 5$.

Finally, quadrupling the knot at $\bar{u} = 5$ yields the knot sequence

$$\{\, 0\,,1\,,2\,,3\,,4\,,5\,,5\,,5\,,5\,,6\,,7\,,8\,,9\,,10\,\},$$

the parameter range $[\,3\,,7\,)$, and four segments. Some of the underlying B-splines in Figure 8.25 are now discontinuous, as is the curve in Figure 8.22 which results.

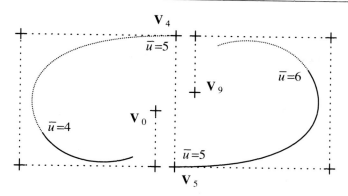

Figure 8.24. The breakpoints defining this curve are equally spaced, but there is a quadruple knot at $\bar{u} = 5$. Since this is a cubic B-spline, we are left with no continuity whatsoever at the multiple knot. (See Figure 8.25.)

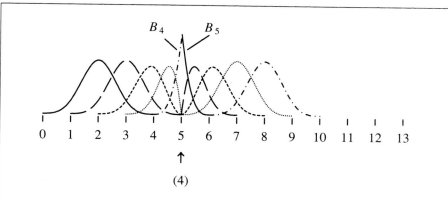

Figure 8.25. The B-splines used to construct the curve of Figure 8.24. There is a quadruple knot at $\bar{u} = 5$. Although $B_{4,4}$ and $B_{5,4}$ both have the value 1 at $\bar{u} = 5$, they are scaled by distinct control vertices and so a positional discontinuity will result in the curve so long as the control vertices scaling them are not identical.

8.6 Altering Knot Spacing — More Cubic B-splines

It is also interesting to see what effect results from changing the knot spacing rather than knot multiplicity. Figure 8.26 shows the original uniform cubic B-spline curve of Figure 8.18, generated by the B-splines of Figure 8.19, superimposed on the curve obtained when the knot interval $[\bar{u}_6, \bar{u}_7) = [6, 7)$ defining the middle curve segment in Figure 8.18 is shrunk to 0.2 units in length.

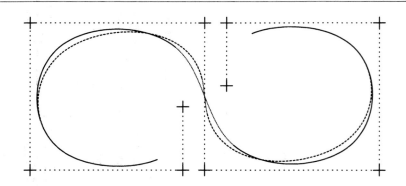

Figure 8.26. The middle segment in both curves is dotted. The remainder of the uniform cubic B-spline is drawn with a solid line while the remainder of the nonuniformly spaced curve is drawn dashed. The parametric length of the dotted segment is here being changed from 1.0 to 0.2.

Figure 8.27 illustrates what happens when the same interval is instead expanded to 5 units in length.

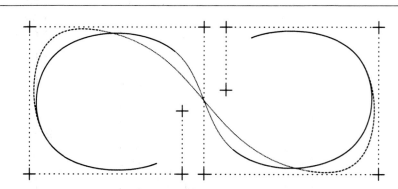

Figure 8.27. The middle segment in both curves is dotted. The remainder of the uniform cubic B-spline is drawn with a solid line while the remainder of the nonuniformly spaced curve is drawn dashed. The parametric length of the dotted segment is here being changed from 1.0 to 5.0.

9

B-spline
Properties

The previous chapter has given the basic definition of B-splines in general terms
and showed the manner in which they can be used to construct parametric spline
curves and surfaces. To proceed further, it will be necessary to discuss a few
more of the theoretical properties that B-splines possess. We want to know, for
example,

- whether every B-spline constructed according to the general definition is positive on the interval of its associated knots (something we surely want it to
  be if it is to be used as a weighting function for constructing curves from
  control vertices);

- whether the general B-splines have compact support (local control);

- whether the general B-splines sum to one (which will mean, together with
  the property of positivity, that general B-splines have the convex hull property);

- what constitutes a good way of evaluating the B-splines.

This section will establish some results in these areas.

9.1 Differencing Products — The Leibniz Rule

We will begin by establishing that B-splines satisfy a recurrence. This is a fact
that was established independently by Carl de Boor [de Boor72] and Maurice Cox
[Cox72].

Let us try the following exercise in creative algebra, and see where it leads. First, recall that

$$B_{i,k}(\bar{u}) = (-1)^k \, (\bar{u}_{i+k} - \bar{u}_i) \, [\, \bar{u}_i\,(k): t\,]\,(\bar{u}-t\,)_+^{k-1}.$$

But note the obvious fact that

$$(\bar{u}-t\,)_+^{k-1} = (\bar{u}-t\,)\cdot(\bar{u}-t\,)_+^{k-2},$$

at least for $k \geq 2$. This means that $B_{i,k}(\bar{u})$ is constructed by differencing a product, for $k > 1$. If the difference operator were a differentiation operator instead, it would be natural for us to follow this observation by an application of the product rule; for example,

$$
\begin{aligned}
D_t\,(\bar{u}-t\,)\cdot(\bar{u}-t\,)_+^{k-2} &= \left[(-1)(\bar{u}-t\,)_+^{k-2}\right] \\
&\quad + \left[(\bar{u}-t\,)\cdot(-1)(k-2)(\bar{u}-t\,)_+^{k-3}\right] \\
&= \left[-(\bar{u}-t\,)_+^{k-2}\right] + \left[-(k-2)(\bar{u}-t\,)_+^{k-2}\right].
\end{aligned}
$$

Although this might not seem very productive, it would, in effect, have split a kth-order B-spline, constructed from $(\bar{u}-t)_+^{k-1}$, into a combination of two terms involving $(\bar{u}-t)_+^{k-2}$, from which we might attempt to draw a connection with B-splines of order $k-1$. By this route, perhaps a recurrence could be established. That is, if we can relate the kth-order B-splines to those of order $k-1$, then we can relate those of order $k-1$ to those of order $k-2$, and so on down to 1st-order B-splines (the simple step functions).

This is precisely the approach we will take. To pursue this, we will have to establish a product rule for the divided difference operator.

We begin by recalling the *product rule for differentiation*:

$$D_x\{f_1(x)\cdot f_2(x)\} = \{D_x f_1(x)\}\cdot f_2(x) + f_1(x)\cdot\{D_x f_2(x)\}.$$

A more general version of the product rule is the *Leibniz rule*:

$$D_x^{(\ell)}\{f_1(x)\cdot f_2(x)\} = \sum_{r=0}^{\ell} \begin{bmatrix} \ell \\ r \end{bmatrix} \{D_x^{(r)}f_1(x)\}\cdot\{D_x^{(\ell-r)}f_2(x)\},$$

where

$$\begin{bmatrix} \ell \\ r \end{bmatrix} = \frac{\ell!}{r!\,(\ell-r)!}$$

is the binomial coefficient. That is, for example (using superscript notation for derivatives in the interest of succinctness),

$$\{f_1(x)f_2(x)\}^{(2)} = f_1^{(2)}(x)f_2^{(0)}(x) + 2f_1^{(1)}(x)f_2^{(1)}(x)$$

$$+ f_1^{(0)}(x)f_2^{(2)}(x),$$

and

$$\{f_1(x)f_2(x)\}^{(3)} = f_1^{(3)}(x)f_2^{(0)}(x) + 3f_1^{(2)}(x)f_2^{(1)}(x)$$

$$+ 3f_1^{(1)}(x)f_2^{(2)}(x) + f_1^{(0)}(x)f_2^{(3)}(x),$$

and so on through Pascal's triangle of binomial coefficients.

The corresponding Leibniz rule for divided differences is as follows.

■ Theorem

For any $z_i, \ldots, z_{i+\ell}$ and any appropriately differentiable functions $f_1(x)$ and $f_2(x)$:

$$[z_i(\ell):x]\{f_1(x)f_2(x)\}$$

$$= \sum_{r=0}^{\ell} \{[z_i(r):x]f_1(x)\}\{[z_{i+r}(\ell-r):x]f_2(x)\}.$$

■

Note that this is virtually the same as the rule for differentiating a product, save that the binomial coefficients do not appear. For example if $\ell = 2$,

$$[z_i(2):x]\{f_1(x)\cdot f_2(x)\} = [z_i(0):x]f_1(x)\cdot[z_i(2):x]f_2(x)$$

$$+ [z_i(1):x]f_1(x)\cdot[z_{i+1}(1):x]f_2(x)$$

$$+ [z_i(2):x]f_1(x)\cdot[z_{i+2}(0):x]f_2(x).$$

This result is important enough that we owe ourselves the struggle of seeing how it can be established.

■ Argument

Assume, for convenience, that $z_i \leq \cdots \leq z_{i+\ell}$.
We proceed by induction on ℓ.

$\ell = 0$:

$$[z_i(0):x]\{f_1(x)f_2(x)\} = f_1(z_i)f_2(z_i)$$

$$= \sum_{r=0}^{0}\{[z_i(0):x]f_1(x)\}\{[z_i(0):x]f_2(x)\}$$

by definition (trivially).

$\ell > 0$ and $z_i = z_{i+\ell}$:

In this case the Leibniz rule for derivatives applies:

$$[z_i(\ell):x]\{f_1(x)f_2(x)\}$$

$$= \frac{1}{\ell!}D_x^{(\ell)}\{f_1(x)f_2(x)\}\big|_{x=z_i}$$

$$= \frac{1}{\ell!}\sum_{r=0}^{\ell}\frac{\ell!}{r!(\ell-r)!}\{D_x^{(r)}f_1(x)\}\{D_x^{(\ell-r)}f_2(x)\}\big|_{x=z_i}$$

$$= \sum_{r=0}^{\ell}\{\frac{1}{r!}D_x^{(r)}f_1(x)\}\{\frac{1}{(\ell-r)!}D_x^{(\ell-r)}f_2(x)\}\big|_{x=z_i}$$

$$= \sum_{r=0}^{\ell}\{[z_i(r):x]f_1(x)\}\{[z_{i+r}(\ell-r):x]f_2(x)\}.$$

$\ell > 0$ and $z_i < z_{i+\ell}$:

Now we make use of the inductive assumption that the theorem holds for $\ell-1$. Then

$$[z_i(\ell):x]\{f_1(x)f_2(x)\}$$

$$= \frac{[z_{i+1}(\ell-1):x]\{f_1(x)f_2(x)\} - [z_i(\ell-1):x]\{f_1(x)f_2(x)\}}{z_{i+\ell} - z_i}$$

$$= \left[\sum_{r=0}^{\ell-1} \{[z_{i+1}(r):x]f_1(x)\}\{[z_{i+1+r}(\ell-1-r):x]f_2(x)\} \right.$$

$$\left. - \sum_{r=0}^{\ell-1} \{[z_i(r):x]f_1(x)\}\{[z_{i+r}(\ell-1-r):x]f_2(x)\} \right] \Bigg/ (z_{i+\ell} - z_i).$$

We can add and subtract

$$\sum_{r=0}^{\ell-1} \{[z_i(r):x]f_1(x)\}\{[z_{i+r+1}(\ell-1-r):x]f_2(x)\}$$

in the numerator to obtain

$$\left[\sum_{r=0}^{\ell-1} \{[z_{i+1}(r):x]f_1(x)\}\{[z_{i+r+1}(\ell-1-r):x]f_2(x)\} \right.$$

$$- \sum_{r=0}^{\ell-1} \{[z_i(r):x]f_1(x)\}\{[z_{i+r+1}(\ell-1-r):x]f_2(x)\}$$

$$+ \sum_{r=0}^{\ell-1} \{[z_i(r):x]f_1(x)\}\{[z_{i+r+1}(\ell-1-r):x]f_2(x)\}$$

$$\left. - \sum_{r=0}^{\ell-1} \{[z_i(r):x]f_1(x)\}\{[z_{i+r}(\ell-1-r):x]f_2(x)\} \right] \Bigg/ (z_{i+\ell} - z_i).$$

The first and the second terms in the numerator can be combined, as can the third and fourth, to change the numerator into the following:

$$\sum_{r=0}^{\ell-1} \left[[z_{i+r+1}(\ell-1-r):x]f_2(x) \right] \left[[z_{i+1}(r):x]f_1(x) - [z_i(r):x]f_1(x) \right]$$

$$+ \sum_{r=0}^{\ell-1} \left[[z_i(r):x]f_1(x) \right] \left[[z_{i+r+1}(\ell-1-r):x]f_2(x) \right. \qquad (9.1)$$

$$\left. - z_{i+r}(\ell-1-r):x]f_2(x) \right].$$

But in the first term the recursive definition of the divided difference provides the substitution

$$[z_{i+1}(r):x]f_1(x) - [z_i(r):x]f_1(x) = [z_i(r+1):x]f_1(x) \cdot (z_{i+r+1} - z_i).$$

(This, in itself, deserves a short argument. Two cases present themselves: in the first, $z_i < z_{i+r+1}$, and in the second $z_i = z_{i+r+1}$. In the former case, the substitution is obvious. In the latter, because of the assumed ordering of the z values, $z_i = \cdots = z_{i+r+1}$, and consequently both

$$[z_{i+1}(r):x\,]f_1(x)$$

and

$$[z_i(r):x\,]f_1(x)$$

are equal to

$$D_x^{(r+1)}f_1(x)\big|_{x=z_i}.$$

Hence their difference is zero. On the other hand

$$[z_i(r+1):x\,]f_1(x)\cdot(z_{i+r+1}-z_i) = \{D_x^{(r+2)}f_1(x)\big|_{x=z_i}\}\cdot(z_{i+r+1}-z_i),$$

which is also zero because of the second factor.)

In the second term of (9.1) we have the similar substitution

$$[z_{i+r+1}(\ell-1-r):x\,]f_2(x) - [z_{i+r}(\ell-1-r):x\,]f_2(x)$$

$$= [z_{i+r}(\ell-r):x\,]f_2(x)\cdot(z_{i+\ell}-z_{i+r}).$$

After making these substitutions, we can multiply out the factors $(z_{i+r+1}-z_i)$ and $(z_{i+\ell}-z_{i+r})$ to obtain

$$\left[\sum_{r=0}^{\ell-1} z_{i+r+1}[z_i(r+1):x\,]f_1(x)[z_{i+r+1}(\ell-1-r):x\,]f_2(x)\right.$$

$$-\sum_{r=0}^{\ell-1} z_i[z_i(r+1):x\,]f_1(x)[z_{i+r+1}(\ell-1-r):x\,]f_2(x)$$

$$+\sum_{r=0}^{\ell-1} z_{i+\ell}[z_i(r):x\,]f_1(x)[z_{i+r}(\ell-r):x\,]f_2(x)$$

$$\left.-\sum_{r=0}^{\ell-1} z_{i+r}[z_i(r):x\,]f_1(x)[z_{i+r}(\ell-r):x\,]f_2(x)\right]\Big/(z_{i+\ell}-z_i).$$

The first and the last sum collapse, leaving only the two terms

$$+ z_{i+\ell} [z_i (\ell):x] f_1(x) [z_{i+\ell}(0):x] f_2(x)$$

and

$$- z_i [z_i (0):x] f_1(x) [z_i (\ell):x] f_2(x).$$

The second of these terms can be put into the second sum, and the first of these terms can be put into the third sum, to yield

$$\left[z_{i+\ell} \sum_{r=0}^{\ell} [z_i (r):x] f_1(x) [z_{i+r} (\ell-r):x] f_2(x) \right.$$

$$\left. - z_i \sum_{r=0}^{\ell} [z_i (r):x] f_1(x) [z_{i+r} (\ell-r):x] f_2(x) \right] \Big/ (z_{i+\ell} - z_i).$$

And, finally, the term $(z_{i+\ell} - z_i)$ can be divided out to give

$$\sum_{r=0}^{\ell} [z_i (r):x] f_1(x) [z_{i+r} (\ell-r):x] f_2(x).$$

∎

This completes our discussion of the Leibniz rule for divided differences.

9.2 Establishing a Recurrence

To repeat the observations made at the beginning of this chapter, the definition of a general B-spline is:

$$B_{i,k}(\bar{u}) = (-1)^k (\bar{u}_{i+k} - \bar{u}_i) [\bar{u}_i (k):t] (\bar{u}-t)_+^{k-1}.$$

We observe that

$$(\bar{u}-t)_+^{k-1} = (\bar{u}-t) \cdot (\bar{u}-t)_+^{k-2},$$

at least for $k \geq 2$. Thus, for $k \geq 2$, $B_{i,k}(\bar{u})$ is constructed by differencing a product. We apply the Leibniz rule:

$$[\bar{u}_i (k):t] (\bar{u}-t)_+^{k-1}$$

$$= [\bar{u}_i (k):t] \{ (\bar{u}-t) (\bar{u}-t)_+^{k-2} \}$$

$$= \sum_{j=0}^{k} \{ [\bar{u}_i (j):t] (\bar{u}-t)\} \cdot \{ [\bar{u}_{i+j} (k-j):t] (\bar{u}-t)_+^{k-2} \}$$

$$= [\bar{u}_i\,(0):t\,](\bar{u}-t\,)[\bar{u}_i\,(k):t\,](\bar{u}-t\,)_+^{k-2}$$

$$+\ [\bar{u}_i\,(1):t\,](\bar{u}-t\,)[\bar{u}_{i+1}\,(k-1):t\,](\bar{u}-t\,)_+^{k-2}$$

$$+\ [\bar{u}_i\,(2):t\,](\bar{u}-t\,)[\bar{u}_{i+2}\,(k-2):t\,](\bar{u}-t\,)_+^{k-2}$$

$$+\ \cdots\ +\ [\bar{u}_i\,(k):t\,](\bar{u}-t\,)[\bar{u}_{i+k}\,(0):t\,](\bar{u}-t\,)_+^{k-2}.$$

But note that

$$[\bar{u}_i\,(0):t\,](\bar{u}-t\,)\ =\ (\bar{u}-\bar{u}_i\,).$$

Note that

$$[\bar{u}_i\,(1):t\,](\bar{u}-t\,)\ =\ \frac{(\bar{u}-\bar{u}_{i+1})-(\bar{u}-\bar{u}_i\,)}{\bar{u}_{i+1}-\bar{u}_i}$$

$$=\ \frac{\bar{u}_i-\bar{u}_{i+1}}{\bar{u}_{i+1}-\bar{u}_i}\ =\ -1$$

(and similarly for differentiation, if $\bar{u}_i=\bar{u}_{i+1}$). Note that

$$[\bar{u}_i\,(2):t\,](\bar{u}-t\,)\ =\ \frac{[\bar{u}_{i+1}\,(1):t\,](\bar{u}-t\,)-[\bar{u}_i\,(1):t\,](\bar{u}-t\,)}{\bar{u}_{i+2}-\bar{u}_i}$$

$$=\ \frac{(-1)-(-1)}{\bar{u}_{i+2}-\bar{u}_i}\ =\ 0$$

(and similarly for differentiation, if $\bar{u}_i=\bar{u}_{i+1}$, or $\bar{u}_{i+1}=\bar{u}_{i+2}$, or both). Finally, note that all further differences of $(\bar{u}-t\,)$ are also zero. It is useful to observe that the kth divided-difference operator has the same property as does the kth differentiation operator in that it will cancel to zero any k^{th}-order polynomial. So

$$[\bar{u}_i\,(k):t\,](\bar{u}-t\,)_+^{k-1}$$

$$=\ (\bar{u}-\bar{u}_i\,)[\bar{u}_i\,(k):t\,](\bar{u}-t\,)_+^{k-2}-[\bar{u}_{i+1}\,(k-1):t\,](\bar{u}-t\,)_+^{k-2}.$$

From the recursive definition of divided differences, the first term can be written as

$$(\bar{u}-\bar{u}_i\,)[\bar{u}_i\,(k):t\,](\bar{u}-t\,)_+^{k-2}$$

$$=\ (\bar{u}-\bar{u}_i\,)\frac{[\bar{u}_{i+1}\,(k-1):t\,](\bar{u}-t\,)_+^{k-2}-[\bar{u}_i\,(k-1):t\,](\bar{u}-t\,)_+^{k-2}}{\bar{u}_{i+k}-\bar{u}_i}.$$

We assume that this expression is legal, i.e., the denominator is not zero, since if $\bar{u}_i = \bar{u}_{i+k}$, this means that $\bar{u}_i$ would have multiplicity greater than k, making $B_{i,k}(\bar{u})$ vacuous and leaving us nothing to prove. Consequently,

$$B_{i,k}(\bar{u}) = (-1)^k (\bar{u}_{i+k} - \bar{u}_i)[\bar{u}_i(k):t](\bar{u}-t)_+^{k-1}$$

$$= (-1)^k (\bar{u}_{i+k} - \bar{u}_i) \frac{\bar{u} - \bar{u}_i}{\bar{u}_{i+k} - \bar{u}_i}[\bar{u}_{i+1}(k-1):t](\bar{u}-t)_+^{k-2}$$

$$- (-1)^k (\bar{u}_{i+k} - \bar{u}_i) \frac{\bar{u} - \bar{u}_i}{\bar{u}_{i+k} - \bar{u}_i}[\bar{u}_i(k-1):t](\bar{u}-t)_+^{k-2}$$

$$- (-1)^k (\bar{u}_{i+k} - \bar{u}_i)[\bar{u}_{i+1}(k-1):t](\bar{u}-t)_+^{k-2}.$$

The first and last terms can be combined to give

$$B_{i,k}(\bar{u}) = (-1)^k (\bar{u} - \bar{u}_{i+k})[\bar{u}_{i+1}(k-1):t](\bar{u}-t)_+^{k-2}$$

$$- (-1)^k (\bar{u} - \bar{u}_i)[\bar{u}_i(k-1):t](\bar{u}-t)_+^{k-2}.$$

Note that

$$(-1)^k (\bar{u} - \bar{u}_{i+k}) = (-1)^{k-1} (\bar{u}_{i+k} - \bar{u})$$

and that

$$-(-1)^k (\bar{u} - \bar{u}_i) = +(-1)^{k-1} (\bar{u} - \bar{u}_i).$$

This means that

$$B_{i,k}(\bar{u}) = (-1)^{k-1} (\bar{u}_{i+k} - \bar{u})[\bar{u}_{i+1}(k-1):t](\bar{u}-t)_+^{k-2}$$

$$+ (-1)^{k-1} (\bar{u} - \bar{u}_i)[\bar{u}_i(k-1):t](\bar{u}-t)_+^{k-2}. \tag{9.2}$$

But, in this expression, it is easy to recognize two lower-order B-splines. Let us look carefully at the first term. If

$$\bar{u}_{i+1} = \bar{u}_{i+k}$$

then, by the definition of the divided difference,

$$[\bar{u}_{i+1}(k-1):t](\bar{u}-t)_+^{k-2} = \frac{1}{(k-1)!} D_t^{(k-1)}(\bar{u}-t)_+^{k-2}\big|_{t=\bar{u}_{i+1}} = 0.$$

On the other hand, if

$$\bar{u}_{i+1} < \bar{u}_{i+k} ,$$

then, since by the definition of the B-splines we would have

$$B_{i+1,k-1}(\bar{u}) = (-1)^{k-1} (\bar{u}_{i+k} - \bar{u}_{i+1}) [\bar{u}_{i+1}(k-1):t] (\bar{u}-t)_+^{k-2},$$

it follows that the first term equals

$$\frac{\bar{u}_{i+k} - \bar{u}}{\bar{u}_{i+k} - \bar{u}_{i+1}} B_{i+1,k-1}(\bar{u}) . \tag{9.3}$$

That is, the first term is zero if $\bar{u}_{i+1} = \cdots = \bar{u}_{i+k}$ and it equals the expresion given in (9.3) if $\bar{u}_{i+1} < \bar{u}_{i+k}$. A similar discussion applies to the second term. This means that we can reasonably write the equation

$$B_{i,k}(\bar{u}) = \frac{\bar{u} - \bar{u}_i}{\bar{u}_{i+k-1} - \bar{u}_i} B_{i,k-1}(\bar{u}) + \frac{\bar{u}_{i+k} - \bar{u}}{\bar{u}_{i+k} - \bar{u}_{i+1}} B_{i+1,k-1}(\bar{u}) \tag{9.4}$$

provided that we interpret the terms

$$\frac{\bar{u} - \bar{u}_i}{\bar{u}_{i+k-1} - \bar{u}_i} B_{i,k-1}(\bar{u}) \quad \text{and} \quad \frac{\bar{u}_{i+k} - \bar{u}}{\bar{u}_{i+k} - \bar{u}_{i+1}} B_{i+1,k-1}(\bar{u})$$

as zero, respectively, whenever

$$\bar{u}_{i+k-1} - \bar{u}_i = 0 \quad \text{and} \quad \bar{u}_{i+k} - \bar{u}_{i+1} = 0 .$$

That is, we have discovered that the B-splines satisfy a *recurrence relation*.

9.3   The Recurrence and Examples

■ **Theorem**

For any $i \in \{0, 1, \ldots, m\}$

$$B_{i,1}(\bar{u}) = \begin{cases} 1 & \bar{u}_i \le \bar{u} < \bar{u}_{i+1} \\ \\ 0 & \text{otherwise} \end{cases}$$

and

$$B_{i,r}(\bar{u}) = \frac{\bar{u} - \bar{u}_i}{\bar{u}_{i+r-1} - \bar{u}_i} B_{i,r-1}(\bar{u}) + \frac{\bar{u}_{i+r} - \bar{u}}{\bar{u}_{i+r} - \bar{u}_{i+1}} B_{i+1,r-1}(\bar{u})$$

for $r = 2, 3, \ldots, k$,

where we interpret the terms

$$\frac{\bar{u} - \bar{u}_i}{\bar{u}_{i+r-1} - \bar{u}_i} B_{i, r-1}(\bar{u}) \quad \text{and} \quad \frac{\bar{u}_{i+r} - \bar{u}}{\bar{u}_{i+r} - \bar{u}_{i+1}} B_{i+1, r-1}(\bar{u})$$

as zero, respectively, whenever

$$\bar{u}_{i+r-1} - \bar{u}_i = 0 \quad \text{and} \quad \bar{u}_{i+r} - \bar{u}_{i+1} = 0.$$

■

Figure 9.1 gives a functional picture of the recurrence producing a quadratic B-spline. The hat function $B_{i, 2}(\bar{u})$ results from adding together a linear factor times the step function $B_{i, 1}(\bar{u})$ and a linear factor times the step function $B_{i+1, 1}(\bar{u})$. The hat function $B_{i+1, 2}(\bar{u})$ is produced similarly from linear factors and the step functions $B_{i+1, 1}(\bar{u})$ and $B_{i+2, 1}(\bar{u})$. Finally, the quadratic hump $B_{i, 3}(\bar{u})$ results from adding together a linear factor times $B_{i, 2}(\bar{u})$ and a linear factor times $B_{i+1, 2}(\bar{u})$.

At any stage of the recurrence, the linear factor

$$\frac{\bar{u} - \bar{u}_i}{\bar{u}_{i+r-1} - \bar{u}_i}$$

has value 0 at $\bar{u} = \bar{u}_i$ and value 1 at $\bar{u} = \bar{u}_{i+r-1}$. This factor is applied to

$$B_{i, r-1}(\bar{u}),$$

which has $\bar{u}_i$ and $\bar{u}_{i+r-1}$ as the left and right knots, respectively, of its nonzero support, as shown in Figure 9.2. Similarly, the linear factor

$$\frac{\bar{u}_{i+r} - \bar{u}}{\bar{u}_{i+r} - \bar{u}_{i+1}}$$

varies from 1 at $\bar{u}_{i+1}$ to 0 at $\bar{u}_{i+r}$. The B-spline

$$B_{i+1, r-1}(\bar{u})$$

to which this factor is applied has $\bar{u}_{i+1}$ and $\bar{u}_{i+r}$ as the left and right knots, respectively, of its nonzero support, as Figure 9.3 illustrates. Applying the two factors to the two B-splines yields two splines of order r, which are added together to produce the B-spline $B_{i, r}(\bar{u})$.

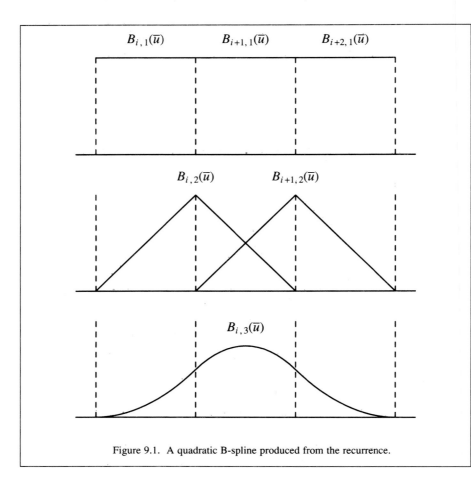

Figure 9.1. A quadratic B-spline produced from the recurrence.

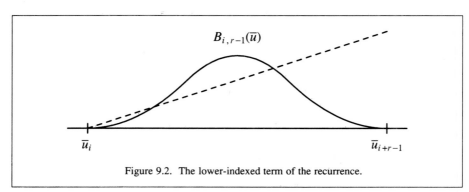

Figure 9.2. The lower-indexed term of the recurrence.

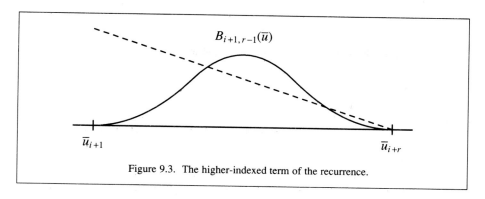

$$B_{i+1,r-1}(\bar{u})$$

$\bar{u}_{i+1}$ $\bar{u}_{i+r}$

Figure 9.3. The higher-indexed term of the recurrence.

To get a further feeling for this recurrence, we will use it to construct all the possible linear B-splines. Consider the general case of three knots

$$\bar{u}_i \ , \ \ \bar{u}_{i+1} \ , \ \ \text{and} \ \ \bar{u}_{i+2} .$$

If these three knots are distinct, then according to the recurrence

$$B_{i,2}(\bar{u}) \ = \ \frac{\bar{u}-\bar{u}_i}{\bar{u}_{i+1}-\bar{u}_i} \ B_{i,1}(\bar{u}) + \frac{\bar{u}_{i+2}-\bar{u}}{\bar{u}_{i+2}-\bar{u}_{i+1}} \ B_{i+1,1}(\bar{u})$$

$$= \ \frac{\bar{u}-\bar{u}_i}{\bar{u}_{i+1}-\bar{u}_i} \left\{ \begin{array}{ll} 1 & \bar{u}_i \ \leq \bar{u} < \bar{u}_{i+1} \\ \\ 0 & \text{otherwise} \end{array} \right\}$$

$$+ \ \frac{\bar{u}_{i+2}-\bar{u}}{\bar{u}_{i+2}-\bar{u}_{i+1}} \left\{ \begin{array}{ll} 1 & \bar{u}_{i+1} \leq \bar{u} \ \ \bar{u}_{i+2} \\ \\ 0 & \text{otherwise} \end{array} \right\}.$$

That is, according to the recursive formula,

$$B_{i,2}(\bar{u}) \ = \ \left\{ \begin{array}{ll} \dfrac{\bar{u}-\bar{u}_i}{\bar{u}_{i+1}-\bar{u}_i} & \bar{u}_i \ \leq \bar{u} < \bar{u}_{i+1} \\ \\ \dfrac{\bar{u}_{i+2}-\bar{u}}{\bar{u}_{i+2}-\bar{u}_{i+1}} & \bar{u}_{i+1} \leq \bar{u} < \bar{u}_{i+2} \\ \\ 0 & \text{otherwise} . \end{array} \right.$$

This is just the familiar "hat function" pictured in Figure 9.4.

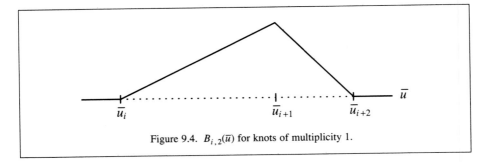

Figure 9.4. $B_{i,2}(\bar{u})$ for knots of multiplicity 1.

Suppose that the right-hand two knots are pushed together; i.e.,

$$\bar{u}_i < \bar{u}_{i+1} = \bar{u}_{i+2}.$$

Then the recursive formula becomes

$$B_{i,2}(\bar{u}) = \frac{\bar{u} - \bar{u}_i}{\bar{u}_{i+1} - \bar{u}_i} B_{i,1}(\bar{u}) + 0$$

$$= \frac{\bar{u} - \bar{u}_i}{\bar{u}_{i+1} - \bar{u}_i} \left\{ \begin{array}{ll} 1 & \bar{u}_i \le \bar{u} < \bar{u}_{i+1} \\ \\ 0 & \text{otherwise} \end{array} \right\},$$

which leaves us with

$$B_{i,2}(\bar{u}) = \left\{ \begin{array}{ll} \dfrac{\bar{u} - \bar{u}_i}{\bar{u}_{i+1} - \bar{u}_i} & \bar{u}_i \le \bar{u} < \bar{u}_{i+1} \\ \\ 0 & \text{otherwise}. \end{array} \right.$$

This function has the form given in Figure 9.5.

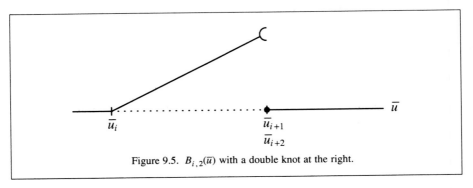

Figure 9.5. $B_{i,2}(\bar{u})$ with a double knot at the right.

Finally, if

$$\bar{u}_i = \bar{u}_{i+1} < \bar{u}_{i+2},$$

then the recursive formula becomes

$$B_{i,2}(\bar{u}) = 0 + \frac{\bar{u}_{i+2} - \bar{u}}{\bar{u}_{i+2} - \bar{u}_{i+1}} B_{i+1,1}(\bar{u})$$

$$= \frac{\bar{u}_{i+2} - \bar{u}}{\bar{u}_{i+2} - \bar{u}_{i+1}} \left\{ \begin{array}{ll} 1 & \bar{u}_{i+1} \le \bar{u} < \bar{u}_{i+2} \\ 0 & \text{otherwise} \end{array} \right\},$$

leaving us with

$$B_{i,2}(\bar{u}) = \left\{ \begin{array}{ll} \dfrac{\bar{u}_{i+2} - \bar{u}}{\bar{u}_{i+2} - \bar{u}_{i+1}} & \bar{u}_{i+1} \le \bar{u} < \bar{u}_{i+2} \\[2ex] 0 & \text{otherwise}, \end{array} \right.$$

which is shown in Figure 9.6.

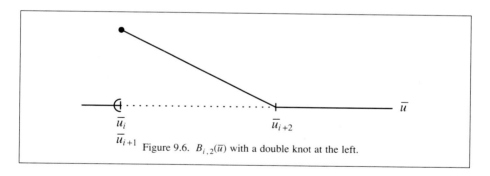

Figure 9.6. $B_{i,2}(\bar{u})$ with a double knot at the left.

9.4 Evaluating B-splines Through Recurrence

The evaluation of general B-splines may be carried out directly by this recurrence. We will explore this in more detail in Chapter 20. Here, merely to provide an illustration, we will find the value of $B_{0,3}(2)$ on the knot sequence $0,1,3,4$ and on the knot sequence $0,1,1,3$. These are the two examples that we used to illustrate the divided-difference evaluation of a B-spline in Chapter 8, and the pictures were as shown in Figures 9.7 and 9.8.

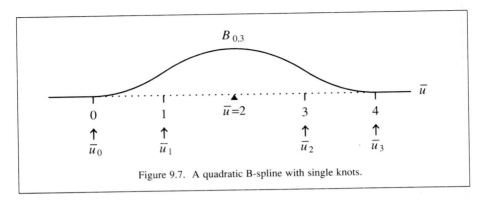

Figure 9.7. A quadratic B-spline with single knots.

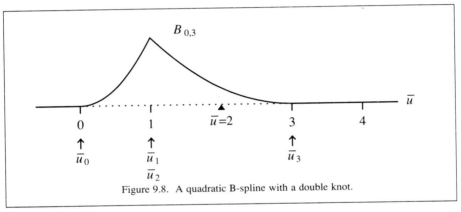

Figure 9.8. A quadratic B-spline with a double knot.

The tables have the same flavor as those used in the divided difference illustration, namely that an entry in one column is obtained by performing a computation on the adjacent entries to its left. Note that $\bar{u}_i$ is needed in the computation for $i = 0, \ldots, 3$, but we only need the values of $B_{i,1}(\bar{u})$ for $i = 0, \ldots, 2$. For the distinct-knot example we have

$\bar{u}_i$	$B_{i,1}(\bar{u})$	$B_{i,2}(\bar{u})$	$B_{i,3}(\bar{u})$
0	0		
		$\dfrac{(2-0)}{(1-0)} 0 + \dfrac{(3-2)}{(3-1)} 1 = \dfrac{1}{2}$	
1	1		$\dfrac{(2-0)}{(3-0)} \dfrac{1}{2} + \dfrac{(4-2)}{(4-1)} \dfrac{1}{2} = \dfrac{2}{3}$
		$\dfrac{(2-1)}{(3-1)} 1 + \dfrac{(4-2)}{(4-3)} 0 = \dfrac{1}{2}$	
3	0		
4			

and for the double-knot example we have

$\bar{u}_i$	$B_{i,1}(\bar{u})$	$B_{i,2}(\bar{u})$	$B_{i,3}(\bar{u})$
0	0		
		$\dfrac{(2-0)}{(1-0)}\,0+0=0$	
1	0		$\dfrac{(2-0)}{(1-0)}\,0+\dfrac{(3-2)}{(3-1)}\dfrac{1}{2}=\dfrac{1}{4}$
		$0+\dfrac{(3-2)}{(3-1)}\,1=\dfrac{1}{2}$	
1	1		
3			

In all instances in the above two computational tables, arithmetic was carried out entirely with nonnegative numbers. The implication of this is that the recurrence computation of the values of a B-spline will be numerically <u>stable</u> and accurate.

9.5 Compact Support, Positivity, and the Convex Hull Property

We will end by disposing of the remaining questions that were raised at the beginning of this chapter.

■ **Theorem**

$$B_{i,k}(\bar{u}) > 0 \quad \text{for} \quad \bar{u}_i < \bar{u} < \bar{u}_{i+k}$$

and

$$B_{i,k}(\bar{u}) = 0 \quad \text{for} \quad \bar{u} < \bar{u}_i \quad \text{and} \quad \bar{u} \geq \bar{u}_{i+k}$$

■

The value of $B_{i,k}(\bar{u}_i)$ will depend upon the multiplicity of $\bar{u}_i$ and upon the value of k. In particular, $B_{i,k}(\bar{u}_i) = 1$ when the multiplicity of $\bar{u}_i$ is k, and is otherwise zero.

■ **Argument**

The recurrence provides the simplest means for seeing that $B_{i,k}(\bar{u})$ is zero for values of $\bar{u}$ less than $\bar{u}_i$ or greater than $\bar{u}_{i+k}$. If we follow the recurrence for

$B_{i,k}(\bar{u})$ through the successively lower orders $k-1, k-2, \ldots, 1$, ending at the step functions, we see that $B_{i,k}(\bar{u})$ can be expressed in the form

$$B_{i,k} = p_{i,k}(\bar{u}) B_{i,1}(\bar{u}) + \cdots + p_{i+k-1,k}(\bar{u}) B_{i+k-1,1}(\bar{u}),$$

where each $p_{j,k}$ is a kth order polynomial. The step functions $B_{j,1}(\bar{u})$ appearing in the sum are all seen to be zero for the values of $\bar{u}$ in question.

To establish positivity for $\bar{u}_i < \bar{u} < \bar{u}_{i+k}$, we work inductively from the recurrence.

$k = 1$:

In this case the B-spline is just the step function whose value is 1 on the interval $[\bar{u}_i, \bar{u}_{i+1})$ and zero everywhere outside that interval.

Assumed true for $k - 1$:

We have

$$B_{i,k}(\bar{u}) = \frac{\bar{u} - \bar{u}_i}{\bar{u}_{i+k-1} - \bar{u}_i} B_{i,k-1}(\bar{u}) + \frac{\bar{u}_{i+k} - \bar{u}}{\bar{u}_{i+k} - \bar{u}_{i+1}} B_{i+1,k-1}(\bar{u}).$$

Notice that both factors

$$\bar{u}_{i+k} - \bar{u} \quad \text{and} \quad \bar{u} - \bar{u}_i$$

are positive for $\bar{u}_i < \bar{u} < \bar{u}_{i+k}$. By the induction hypothesis, each of the ratios

$$\frac{B_{i+1,k-1}(\bar{u})}{\bar{u}_{i+k} - \bar{u}_{i+1}}$$

and

$$\frac{B_{i,k-1}(\bar{u})}{\bar{u}_{i+k-1} - \bar{u}_i}$$

is either positive or zero. They cannot both be zero, since this would imply

$$\bar{u}_i = \bar{u}_{i+k-1} \quad \text{and} \quad \bar{u}_{i+1} = \bar{u}_{i+k},$$

which would force

$$\bar{u}_i = \bar{u}_{i+k},$$

and we have been working under the assumption that $\bar{u}_i < \bar{u} < \bar{u}_{i+k}$, which disallows this. Hence, $B_{i,k}(\bar{u})$ is the sum of two positive quantities (or one positive and one zero quantity) on the interval in question.

■

This result establishes at least the plausibility of using the general B-splines as weighting functions to construct curves and surfaces. A more important result is that the general B-splines sum to one. In Chapter 4 we pointed out that summation to one was necessary for translation invariance, and the two properties of positivity and summation to one, together, give us the convex hull property. For B-splines of order k this means that, if $\mathbf{Q}$ is any curve constructed from control vertices $\mathbf{V}_i$,

$$\mathbf{Q}(\bar{u}) \;=\; \sum_i \mathbf{V}_i \, B_{i,k}(\bar{u}),$$

then each point on the curve lies in the convex hull of at most k successive control vertices (and, in the case of multiple knots, even fewer than k).

■ **Theorem**

For any fixed value of $\bar{u} \in [\,\bar{u}_{k-1}, \bar{u}_{m+1})$.

$$\sum_{i=0}^{m} B_{i,k}(\bar{u}) \;=\; 1.$$

■

■ **Argument**

$k = 1$:

In this case the result is trivial. On any breakpoint interval for which $\bar{u}_i$ is the last knot in a multiplicity cluster $B_{i,1}(\bar{u})$ appears as is given below.

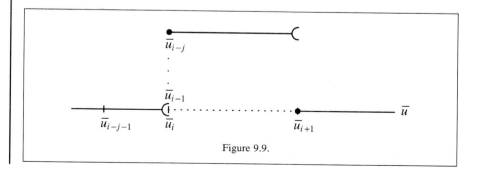

Figure 9.9.

$B_{i-r,1}(\bar{u})$ is vacuous for $r = 1, \ldots, j$.

Assume that the theorem is true for $k - 1$; then

$$\sum_{i=0}^{m} B_{i,k}(\bar{u}) = \sum_{i=0}^{m} \left\{ \frac{\bar{u} - \bar{u}_i}{\bar{u}_{i+k-1} - \bar{u}_i} B_{i,k-1}(\bar{u}) + \frac{\bar{u}_{i+k} - \bar{u}}{\bar{u}_{i+k} - \bar{u}_{i+1}} B_{i+1,k-1}(\bar{u}) \right\}$$

$$= \sum_{i=0}^{m} \frac{\bar{u} - \bar{u}_i}{\bar{u}_{i+k-1} - \bar{u}_i} B_{i,k-1}(\bar{u}) + \sum_{i=1}^{m+1} \frac{\bar{u}_{i+k-1} - \bar{u}}{\bar{u}_{i+k-1} - \bar{u}_i} B_{i,k-1}(\bar{u}),$$

where the sum has been broken into two parts, and then the index has been shifted by one in the second summation.

Consider the quantity

$$\frac{\bar{u}_{i+k-1} - \bar{u}}{\bar{u}_{i+k-1} - \bar{u}_i} B_{i,k-1}(\bar{u})$$

which appears in the second sum. Suppose we set the index value to $i = 0$. Then this quantity would become

$$\frac{\bar{u}_{k-1} - \bar{u}}{\bar{u}_{k-1} - \bar{u}_0} B_{0,k-1}(\bar{u}).$$

But $\bar{u} \in [\bar{u}_{k-1}, \bar{u}_{m+1})$, which means that $\bar{u} \geq \bar{u}_{k-1}$. On the other hand, $B_{0,k-1}(\bar{u})$ has to be zero for $\bar{u} \geq \bar{u}_{k-1}$. This means that we can add this term to the first sum without changing the value of that sum. A similar argument shows that we can add the term

$$\frac{\bar{u} - \bar{u}_{m+1}}{\bar{u}_{m+k} - \bar{u}_{m+1}} B_{m+1,k-1}(\bar{u})$$

to the second sum, since $B_{m+1,k-1}(\bar{u})$ will be zero for all values of $\bar{u} < \bar{u}_{m+1}$. This gives

$$\sum_{i=0}^{m} B_{i,k}(\bar{u}) = \sum_{i=0}^{m+1} \frac{\bar{u}_{i+k-1} - \bar{u}_i}{\bar{u}_{i+k-1} - \bar{u}_i} B_{i,k-1}(\bar{u}) = \sum_{i=0}^{m+1} B_{i,k-1}(\bar{u}) = 1$$

by the induction assumption.

∎

9.6   Practical Implications

Now that we have generalized the uniform cubic B-splines to arbitrary order, let us see how the properties of corresponding curves generalize. The material through Section 9.6.4 is taken from [Barsky/Beatty83b].

9.6.1   B-splines of Different Order

We begin with a uniform cubic B-spline curve like the one shown in Figure 9.10. Because it requires four vertices — and basis functions — to define a segment, there are three fewer segments than there are control vertices in a cubic B-spline curve; for a curve of order k there are $k - 1$ fewer segments than control vertices. If we increase the order of the B-splines for a fixed set of control vertices, we therefore reduce the number of segments, and we have consequently placed a large number of initial and final vertices in the control graph for Figure 9.10.

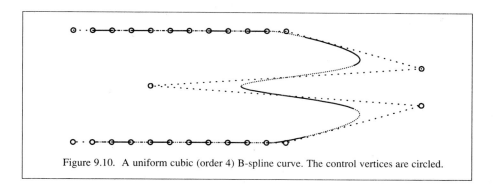

Figure 9.10. A uniform cubic (order 4) B-spline curve. The control vertices are circled.

Figure 9.11 illustrates what happens when we use tenth order B-splines. There are six fewer segments than in the fourth order curve of Figure 9.10: three fewer at the beginning and three fewer at the end. Also, the curve "oscillates less;" the influence of a given control vertex on any particular segment has been reduced. This follows from the fact that there are more vertices influencing the segment, since each B-spline has larger support. Each segment also lies within the convex hull of ten control vertices now instead of four.

Conversely, if we reduce the order of the B-splines then each vertex influences fewer segments; however, its influence on these arguments is stronger. For second order B-splines each segment is determined by two control vertices. Since it must lie within the convex hull of the two vertices, and the basis functions go to zero at either end, the segment is simply a straight line from the first vertex to the second. Figure 9.12 illustrates this.

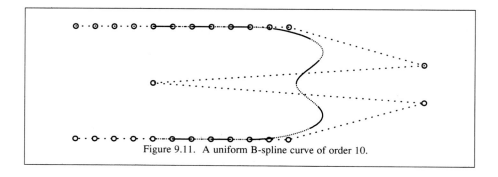

Figure 9.11. A uniform B-spline curve of order 10.

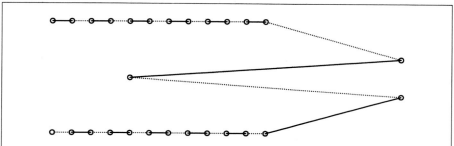

Figure 9.12. A uniform B-spline curve of order 2 (the control graph is not shown). A B-spline curve of order 1 would consist simply of the control vertices.

To facilitate comparison, we show several curves of differing order in the Figure 9.13. The second order curve is shown with a dotted line, and connects the control vertices with straight line segments. The curve of order 20 is shown with a solid line. Intermediate curves are drawn dashed. Higher order curves are, of course, more expensive to compute.

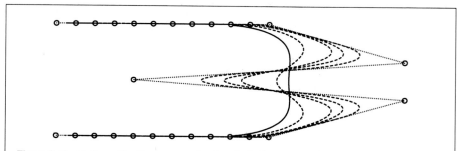

Figure 9.13. Uniform B-spline curves of orders 2, 3, 4, 5, 10 and 20 for the same control vertices.

9.6.2 Multiple Knots

In a B-spline of order k, we may usefully associate a breakpoint with at most k knots. Figure 9.14 illustrates why, as do Figures 8.24 and 8.25.

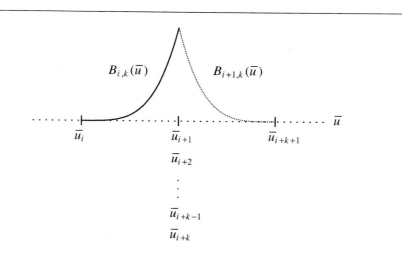

Figure 9.14. Since $\bar{u}_{i+1}$ is a knot of multiplicity k, $B_{i,k}(\bar{u})$ and $B_{i+1,k}(\bar{u})$ span only one nonvacuous interval each, as shown. All other basis functions must be zero at $\bar{u}_{i+1}$. $B_{i,k}(\bar{u})$ approaches the value one from the left as $\bar{u}$ approaches $\bar{u}_{i+1}$, and $B_{i+1,k}(\bar{u})$ must attain the value one at $\bar{u}_{i+1}$. Consequently $\mathbf{V}_{i+1}$ will be, and $\mathbf{V}_i$ will appear to be, interpolated at $\bar{u}_{i+1}$, and the curve $\mathbf{Q}(\bar{u})$ constructed from the control vertices $\{\,...\,,\mathbf{V}_i\,,\mathbf{V}_{i+1}\,,...\,\}$ will, in general, be discontinuous.

Since the jth B-spline $B_{j,k}(\bar{u})$ spans the k intervals from $\bar{u}_j$ to $\bar{u}_{j+k}$, there are only two B-splines whose support is associated with the breakpoint at $\bar{u}_{i+1}$. If $\bar{u}_{i+1}$ were of multiplicity $k+1$, then $B_{i+1,k}(\bar{u})$ would span the zero length interval from $\bar{u}_{i+1}$ to $\bar{u}_{i+k+1}$. The right hand or dotted B-spline in Figure 9.14 would then be called $B_{i+2,k}(\bar{u})$. Greater multiplicity would simply introduce additional vacuous B-splines.

For the breakpoint $\bar{u} = \bar{u}_{i+1}$ we have $C^{k-1-k} = C^{-1}$ continuity, i.e., no continuity at all. Moreover,

$$\lim_{\bar{u}\to\bar{u}_{i+1}} B_{i,k}(\bar{u}_{i+1}) = 1.$$

Consider any infinitesimal step to the left of $\bar{u}_{i+1}$:

$$\bar{u}_{i+1} - \varepsilon \quad \text{for } \varepsilon > 0,$$

and consider the B-splines,

$$B_{i-1,k}(\overline{u}), \ldots, B_{i-k+1,k}(\overline{u}),$$

that have support on $[\overline{u}_i, \overline{u}_{i+1})$ and that, together with $B_{i,k}(\overline{u})$, contribute to a curve segment $\mathbf{Q}(\overline{u})$ for $\overline{u}$ in this interval. First, we shall have

$$B_{i,k}(\overline{u}_{i+1}-\varepsilon) \approx 1.$$

The next B-spline to the left, $B_{i-1,k}(\overline{u})$, has a knot of multiplicity $k-1$ at $\overline{u}_{i+1}$, and is consequently C^0 there. Since

$$B_{i-1,k}(\overline{u}_{i+1}) = B_{i-1,k}(\overline{u}_{i+k}) = 0,$$

we shall have

$$B_{i-1,k}(\overline{u}_{i+1}-\varepsilon) \approx 0.$$

Similarly

$$B_{i-k+1,k}(\overline{u}_{i+1}-\varepsilon) \approx \cdots \approx B_{i-2,k}(\overline{u}_{i+1}) \approx 0.$$

Since

$$B_{i-k+1,k}(\overline{u}_{i+1}-\varepsilon) + \cdots + B_{i,k}(\overline{u}_{i+1}-\varepsilon) = 1$$

for all small, positive values of ε, we must be able to make $\mathbf{Q}(\overline{u}_{i+1}-\varepsilon)$ arbitrarily close to

$$\mathbf{V}_{i-k+1}B_{i-k+1,k}(\overline{u}_{i+1}-\varepsilon) + \cdots + \mathbf{V}_i B_{i,k}(\overline{u}_{i+k}-\varepsilon) \approx \mathbf{V}_i$$

as $\varepsilon > 0$ is made arbitrarily close to zero. As $\overline{u}$ becomes equal to $\overline{u}_{i+1}$, $B_{i,k}(\overline{u})$ drops abruptly to zero and $B_{i+1,k}(\overline{u})$ jumps abruptly to one. Since $\mathbf{Q}(\overline{u}_{i+1})$ is given by

$$\mathbf{V}_{i-k+2}B_{i-k+2,k}(\overline{u}_{i+1}) + \cdots + \mathbf{V}_i B_{i,k}(\overline{u}_{i+1}) + \mathbf{V}_{i+1}B_{i+1,k}(\overline{u}_{i+1}) + ,$$

and since all these B-spline values are zero save $B_{i+1,k}(\overline{u}_{i+1})$, which is 1,

$$\mathbf{Q}(\overline{u}_{i+1}) = \mathbf{V}_{i+1},$$

and there will be a jump in the curve from $\mathbf{V}_i$ to $\mathbf{V}_{i+1}$ (assuming $\mathbf{V}_i \neq \mathbf{V}_{i+1}$).

A slight adaptation of this argument can be used to show that a knot of multiplicity $k-1$ will result in a positionally continuous B-spline curve $\mathbf{Q}(\overline{u})$ which interpolates $\mathbf{V}_i$. This is because $B_{i,k}(\overline{u})$ will be a function like that shown in

Figure 9.15 which rises to one and then falls back to zero continuously, while all "surrounding" B-splines whose intervals of support are associated with the knot $\overline{u}_{i+1}$ will have the value zero at $\overline{u}_{i+1}$.

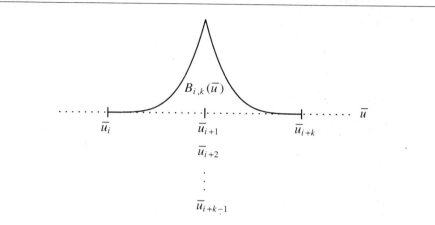

Figure 9.15. Since $\overline{u}_{i+1}$ is a knot of multiplicity $k-1$, $B_{i,k}(\overline{u})$ is the only B-spline among $B_{i-k+1,k}(\overline{u})$, $B_{i-k+2,k}(\overline{u})$, ..., $B_{i,k}(\overline{u})$ that is nonzero at $\overline{u}_{i+1}$, and it therefore attains the value one there. Thus $\mathbf{V}_i$ will be interpolated in this situation.

9.6.3 Collinear Control Vertices

If k successive control vertices are collinear then they define a straight line segment. This follows easily from the convex hull property. If the knot sequence is such as to require the adjoining segments to meet this straight line with C^2 continuity (i.e., the breakpoint corresponding to that joint has multiplicity at most $k-3$) then the ends of those segments must have zero curvature there. Hence if a control graph ends in $k-1$ collinear control vertices and the terminating breakpoint has multiplicity at most $k-3$ (one for a cubic) then the curve will end with zero curvature.

9.6.4 Multiple Vertices

Just as we can repeat values in the knot sequence underlying a B-spline curve, so we can repeat vertices in the control graph. First let us recall that the ith segment in a B-spline curve of order k is defined by control vertices $\mathbf{V}_{i-k+1}$, ..., $\mathbf{V}_i$. Furthermore, since $B_{i-k+1}(\overline{u})$ is zero at $\overline{u}_{i+1}$, $\mathbf{V}_{i-k+1}$ does not affect the last point $\mathbf{Q}_i(\overline{u}_{i+1})$ of the ith segment. $\mathbf{Q}_i(\overline{u}_{i+1})$ is therefore entirely determined by $\mathbf{V}_{i-k+2}$, ..., $\mathbf{V}_i$. If these $k-1$ vertices are identical we have

$$Q_i(\overline{u}_{i+1}) = \sum_{r=-k+1}^{0} V_{i+r} B_{i+r,k}(\overline{u}_{i+1}) = \sum_{r=-k+2}^{0} V_{i+r} B_{i+r,k}(\overline{u}_{i+1})$$

$$= V_i \sum_{r=-k+1}^{0} B_{i+r,k}(\overline{u}_{i+1}) = V_i.$$

Thus a control vertex of multiplicity $k-1$ is interpolated, regardless of the knot sequence at hand. Moreover, $Q_i(\overline{u})$ is guaranteed to be a straight line segment, since in this case we can factor the equation for $Q_i(\overline{u}_i)$ as

$$V_{i-k+1}B_{i-k+1,k}(\overline{u}) + V_i \sum_{r=-k+2}^{0} B_{i+r,k}(\overline{u})$$

$$= V_{i-k+1}B_{i-k+1,k}(\overline{u}) + V_i \left[1 - B_{i-k+1,k}(\overline{u}) \right].$$

This is a convex combination of V_{i-k+1} and V_i and so defines a straight line segment. V_{i-k+1} and V_i are not, in general, interpolated.

Unless the knot $\overline{u}_{i-1}$ has multiplicity $k-2$ or greater, the previous curve segment, namely $Q_{i-1}(\overline{u})$, will be at least C^2 continuous with $Q_i(\overline{u})$ at $\overline{u}_{i-1}$, and must therefore have a zero second derivative and zero curvature there since $Q_i(\overline{u})$ is a straight line segment. Moreover, $Q_{i-1}(\overline{u})$ must terminate somewhere on the line segment connecting V_{i-k+1} and $V_{i-k+2} = \cdots = V_i$. A similar argument establishes that $Q_{i+1}(\overline{u})$ begins with zero curvature at a point lying between $V_{i-k+2} = \cdots = V_i$ and V_{i+1}.

9.6.5   End Conditions

Our description of multiple knots and multiple vertices is applicable to any part of the curve, but is particularly useful in controlling behavior at the ends of a curve. In general the most we can say about these endpoints is that they lie within the convex hull of the first and last $k-1$ control vertices, respectively. From earlier results it follows that either an initial knot of multiplicity $k-1$ (or of multiplicity k), or an initial control vertex of multiplicity $k-1$, will cause the curve to interpolate its first control vertex. In the latter case the first curve segment is a short straight line. Moreover, an initial vertex of multiplicity $k-2$ will cause the curve to begin somewhere on the line segment joining the first and second control vertices with zero curvature. The end of a curve may be similarly controlled. A more detailed discussion may be found in [Barsky82].

9.6.6 Interpolating the Endpoints of a Simple Cubic B-spline Curve

Because of their usefulness, we shall take a closer look at the family of cubic curves based on a knot sequence with uniform spacing except at the endpoints, which have multiplicity 4. It is a feature of this family that the tangent vector at the beginning of a curve lies along the line segment connecting the first and second control vertices (and similarly at the end of a curve).

These curves are nearly as simple as the uniform cubic B-splines; they differ only near the ends. We shall see that only the first two and the last two intervals require special treatment. It is a possible complication that, because of the way B-splines are built from an underlying knot sequence, we would expect curves of one, two, three and four segments all to involve distinct B-splines. As it happens, however, only two additional segment polynomials are needed to handle these special cases. The easiest way to see this is simply to work out the segment polynomials for all these cases and look for repetition, which we shall now do. For simplicity, and to emphasize symmetry, the following equations are expressed in terms of both u and $v = 1 - u$.

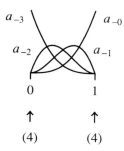

Figure 9.16. The knots at 0 and 1 have multiplicity 4. The initial and final control vertices for curves drawn with these basis functions are interpolated — see Figure 9.17, for example. Each basis polynomial is labeled in correspondence with equations (9.5) below.

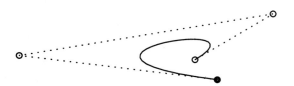

Figure 9.17. A curve drawn using the basis functions of Figure 9.16. The first and last control vertices are interpolated. We shall see in Chapter 10 that this is a Bézier curve.

For a curve consisting of one segment (see Figures 9.16 and 9.17) we have

$$a_{-3}(u,v) = v^3$$

$$a_{-2}(u,v) = 3uv^2$$

$$a_{-1}(u,v) = 3u^2v \qquad (9.5)$$

$$a_{-0}(u,v) = u^3.$$

Notice the symmetry in u and v, which is actually symmetry in u and $1-u$.

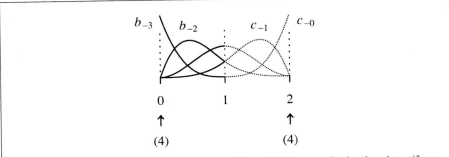

Figure 9.18. The knots at 0 and 2 have multiplicity 4. The knot spacing is otherwise uniform.

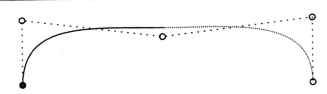

Figure 9.19. A curve drawn using the basis functions of Figure 9.18. The first and last control vertices are interpolated. Unlike the curve of Figure 9.17, the curve shown here is not a Bézier curve.

When there are two segments in the curve (see Figures 9.18 and 9.19) we have

$$b_{-3}(u,v) = v^3$$

$$b_{-2}(u,v) = \frac{1}{4}u(1+4v+7v^2)$$

$$b_{-1}(u,v) = \frac{1}{2} u^2 (1 + 2v)$$

$$b_{-0}(u,v) = \frac{1}{4} u^3$$

$$c_{-3}(u,v) = \frac{1}{4} v^3$$

$$c_{-2}(u,v) = \frac{1}{2} v^2 (1 + 2u)$$

$$c_{-1}(u,v) = \frac{1}{4} v (1 + 4u + 7u^2)$$

$$c_{-0}(u,v) = u^3 .$$

Again notice the symmetry in u and v.

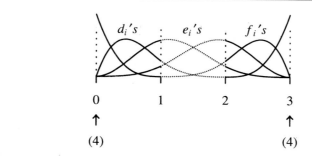

Figure 9.20. The knots at 0 and 3 have multiplicity 4. The knot spacing is otherwise uniform.

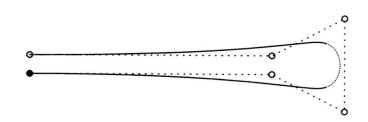

Figure 9.21. A curve drawn using the basis functions of Figure 9.20. The first and last control vertices are interpolated.

When there are three segments in the curve (see Figures 9.20 and 9.21) we have

$$d_{-3}(u,v) = v^3$$

$$d_{-2}(u,v) = \frac{1}{4} u (1+4v+7v^2)$$

$$d_{-1}(u,v) = \frac{1}{12} u^2 (7+11v)$$

$$d_{-0}(u,v) = \frac{1}{6} u^3$$

$$e_{-3}(u,v) = \frac{1}{4} v^3$$

$$e_{-2}(u,v) = \frac{1}{12} (2+6v+6v^2-7v^3)$$

$$e_{-1}(u,v) = \frac{1}{12} (2+6u+6u^2-7u^3)$$

$$e_{-0}(u,v) = \frac{1}{4} u^3$$

$$f_{-3}(u,v) = \frac{1}{6} v^3$$

$$f_{-2}(u,v) = \frac{1}{12} v^2 (7+11u)$$

$$f_{-1}(u,v) = \frac{1}{4} v (1+4u+7u^2)$$

$$f_{-0}(u,v) = u^3 .$$

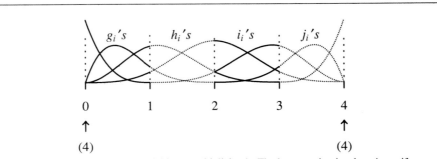

Figure 9.22. The knots at 0 and 4 have multiplicity 4. The knot spacing is otherwise uniform.

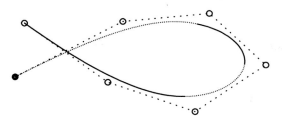

Figure 9.23. A curve drawn using the basis functions of Figure 9.22. The first and last control vertices are interpolated.

When there are four segments in the curve (see Figures 9.22 and 9.23), we have

$$g_{-3}(u,v) = v^3$$

$$g_{-2}(u,v) = \frac{1}{4} u \, (1 + 4v + 7v^2)$$

$$g_{-1}(u,v) = \frac{1}{12} u^2 (7 + 11v)$$

$$g_{-0}(u,v) = \frac{1}{6} u^3$$

$$h_{-3}(u,v) = \frac{1}{4} v^3$$

$$h_{-2}(u,v) = \frac{1}{12} (2 + 6v + 6v^2 - 7v^3)$$

$$h_{-1}(u,v) = \frac{1}{6} (4 - 6v^2 + 3v^3)$$

$$h_{-0}(u,v) = \frac{1}{6} u^3$$

$$i_{-3}(u,v) = \frac{1}{6} v^3$$

$$i_{-2}(u,v) = \frac{1}{6} (4 - 6u^2 + 3u^3)$$

$$i_{-1}(u,v) = \frac{1}{12}(2+6u+6u^2-7u^3)$$

$$i_{-0}(u,v) = \frac{1}{4}u^3$$

$$j_{-3}(u,v) = \frac{1}{6}v^3$$

$$j_{-2}(u,v) = \frac{1}{12}v^2(7+11u)$$

$$j_{-1}(u,v) = \frac{1}{4}v(1+4u+7u^2)$$

$$j_{-0}(u,v) = u^3.$$

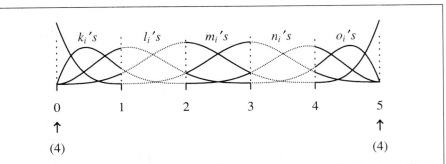

Figure 9.24. The knots at 0 and 5 have multiplicity 4. The knot spacing is otherwise uniform. Basis polynomials for the middle interval, namely [2,3], are those of a uniform cubic B-spline. In longer knot sequences of this sort the additional intervals (i.e. all those more than two from either end) are all uniform as well.

When there are five segments in the curve (see Figures 9.24 and 9.25) we have

$$k_{-3}(u,v) = v^3$$

$$k_{-2}(u,v) = \frac{1}{4}u(1+4v+7v^2)$$

$$k_{-1}(u,v) = \frac{1}{12}u^2(7+11v)$$

$$k_{-0}(u,v) = \frac{1}{6}u^3$$

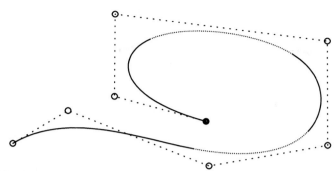

Figure 9.25. A curve drawn using the basis functions of Figure 9.24. The first and last control vertices are interpolated.

$$l_{-3}(u,v) = \frac{1}{4} v^3$$

$$l_{-2}(u,v) = \frac{1}{12} (2 + 6v + 6v^2 - 7v^3)$$

$$l_{-1}(u,v) = \frac{1}{6} (4 - 6v^2 + 3v^3)$$

$$l_{-0}(u,v) = \frac{1}{6} u^3$$

$$m_{-3}(u,v) = \frac{1}{6} v^3$$

$$m_{-2}(u,v) = \frac{1}{6} (4 - 6u^2 + 3u^3)$$

$$m_{-1}(u,v) = \frac{1}{6} (4 - 6v^2 + 3v^3)$$

$$m_{-0}(u,v) = \frac{1}{6} u^3$$

(9.6)

$$n_{-3}(u,v) = \frac{1}{6} v^3$$

$$n_{-2}(u,v) = \frac{1}{6} (4 - 6u^2 + 3u^3)$$

$$n_{-1}(u,v) = \frac{1}{12}(2+6u+6u^2-7u^3)$$

$$n_{-0}(u,v) = \frac{1}{4}u^3$$

$$o_{-3}(u,v) = \frac{1}{6}v^3$$

$$o_{-2}(u,v) = \frac{1}{12}v^2(7+11u)$$

$$o_{-1}(u,v) = \frac{1}{4}v(1+4u+7u^2)$$

$$o_{-0}(u,v) = u^3.$$

There are several things to notice about these equations. First, the m_i are the segment polynomials for a uniform cubic B-spline — the multiple knots at either end are sufficiently distant from this segment not to influence its shape. (Substituting $1-u$ for v in equations (9.6) and expanding makes this clear.) Thus, in a curve having five or more segments, the first two segments and the last two segments are defined by the k_i, l_i, n_i and o_i, while the remaining interior segments are all uniform cubic B-splines, defined by the m_i.

Second, there is a great deal of repetition. Curves of one, two, three and four segments can be expressed, for the most part, in terms of the segment polynomials for a five segment curve. Thus the segment polynomials of a one segment curve can be expressed as

$$a_{-3}(u,v) = k_{-3}(u,v)$$

$$a_{-2}(u,v) = 3uv^2(u,v)$$

$$a_{-1}(u,v) = 3u^2v(u,v)$$

$$a_{-0}(u,v) = o_{-0}(u,v),$$

the segment polynomials for a two segment curve can be expressed as

$$b_{-3}(u,v) = k_{-3}(u,v)$$

$$b_{-2}(u,v) = k_{-2}(u,v)$$

$$b_{-1}(u,v) = \frac{1}{2}u^2(1+2v)$$

$$b_{-0}(u,v) = n_{-0}(u,v)$$

$$c_{-3}(u,v) = l_{-3}(u,v)$$

$$c_{-2}(u,v) = \frac{1}{2} v^2 (1 + 2u)$$

$$c_{-1}(u,v) = o_{-1}(u,v)$$

$$c_{-0}(u,v) = o_{-0}(u,v),$$

the segment polynomials for a three segment curve can be expressed as

$$d_{-3}(u,v) = k_{-3}(u,v)$$

$$d_{-2}(u,v) = k_{-2}(u,v)$$

$$d_{-1}(u,v) = k_{-1}(u,v)$$

$$d_{-0}(u,v) = k_{-0}(u,v)$$

$$e_{-3}(u,v) = l_{-3}(u,v)$$

$$e_{-2}(u,v) = l_{-2}(u,v)$$

$$e_{-1}(u,v) = n_{-1}(u,v)$$

$$e_{-0}(u,v) = n_{-0}(u,v)$$

$$f_{-3}(u,v) = o_{-3}(u,v)$$

$$f_{-2}(u,v) = o_{-2}(u,v)$$

$$f_{-1}(u,v) = o_{-1}(u,v)$$

$$f_{-0}(u,v) = o_{-0}(u,v),$$

and the segment polynomials for a four segment curve are simply

$$g_{-3}(u,v) = k_{-3}(u,v)$$

$$g_{-2}(u,v) = k_{-2}(u,v)$$

$$g_{-1}(u,v) = k_{-1}(u,v)$$

$$g_{-0}(u,v) = k_{-0}(u,v)$$

$$h_{-3}(u,v) = l_{-3}(u,v)$$

$$h_{-2}(u,v) = l_{-2}(u,v)$$

$$h_{-1}(u,v) = l_{-1}(u,v)$$

$$h_{-0}(u,v) = l_{-0}(u,v)$$

$$i_{-3}(u,v) = n_{-3}(u,v)$$

$$i_{-2}(u,v) = n_{-2}(u,v)$$

$$i_{-1}(u,v) = n_{-1}(u,v)$$

$$i_{-0}(u,v) = n_{-0}(u,v)$$

$$j_{-3}(u,v) = o_{-3}(u,v)$$

$$j_{-2}(u,v) = o_{-2}(u,v)$$

$$j_{-1}(u,v) = o_{-1}(u,v)$$

$$j_{-0}(u,v) = o_{-0}(u,v).$$

Third, the equations for each curve are symmetric. Thus

$$g_{-3}(u,v) = g_{-3}(u,1-u) = j_{-0}(1-u,u) = j_{-0}(v,u),$$

$$g_{-2}(u,v) = g_{-2}(u,1-u) = j_{-1}(1-u,u) = j_{-1}(v,u),$$

. . .

$$h_{-1}(u,v) = h_{-1}(u,1-u) = i_{-2}(1-u,u) = i_{-2}(v,u),$$

$$h_{-0}(u,v) = h_{-0}(u,1-u) = i_{-3}(1-u,u) = i_{-3}(v,u)$$

so that

$$j_{-1}(u,v) = j_{-1}(u,1-u) = \frac{1}{4}(1-u)(1+4u+7u^2)$$

can be computed by evaluating

$$g_{-2}(v,u) = g_{-2}(1-u,u) = \frac{1}{4}(1-u)(1+4u+7u^2).$$

That is, $j_{-1}(u,1-u)$ can be computed by evaluating $g_{-2}(1-u,u)$. Considering both repetition and symmetry, there are in fact only twelve distinct polynomials (including the uniform cubic basis segments). Another way of looking at this is to realize that handling the special cases — curves with fewer than five segments — involves the manipulation of only two additional polynomials.

If the segment polynomials are evaluated once and tabulated, then the symmetry amounts simply to indexing either from the beginning of the knot sequence or from the end, depending on whether $g_{-2}(u,1-u)$ or $j_{-1}(u,1-u) = g_{-2}(1-u,u)$ is desired.

It might be thought that a curve of seven segments is necessary before the middle segment reduces to the uniform cubic B-spline segment polynomials, on the grounds that for curves of fewer segments there is at least one B-spline in each interval whose definition involves a knot of multiplicity greater than one. That the middle segment of a five segment curve is already a uniform cubic B-spline can be deduced from the fact the segment polynomials on any given segment must sum to 1 — a precise argument is left to the reader.

Is there a difference between multiplicity k and multiplicity $k-1$ knots at the ends? Consider Figures 9.26 and 9.27, for example. A B-spline is completely determined by the knot spacing over which it is differenced. Hence the only B-splines which differ between Figures 9.26 and 9.27 are those defined by the knots [0,0,0,0,1] and [1,2,2,2,2] in Figure 9.26 and by [−1,0,0,0,1] and [1,2,2,2,3] in Figure 9.27; these are the dotted and dashed B-splines, respectively. The solidly drawn B-splines are differenced over exactly the same knots, and must therefore be identical. But the B-splines defined on [0,1) in Figure 9.26 sum to one on that interval, as do the B-splines defined on [0,1) in Figure 9.27, so it must be the case that dotted B-spline from Figure 9.26 and the dotted B-spline from Figure 9.27 are also identical on [0,1). A similar argument applies to the end of the curve.

This argument is easily generalized to handle curves with one, three, four or more segments, so it is in fact true that it makes no difference whether we use multiplicity 3 or multiplicity 4 knots at the ends of a cubic, and we can generalize further in the obvious way to curves of arbitrary order k.

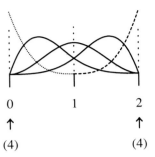

0   1   2

↑   ↑

(4)   (4)

Figure 9.26. The knots at 0 and 2 have multiplicity 4. The dotted B-spline is defined on the knots [0,0,0,0,1]; the dashed B-spline is defined on the knots [1,2,2,2,2]. Compare these B-splines with those of Figure 9.27.

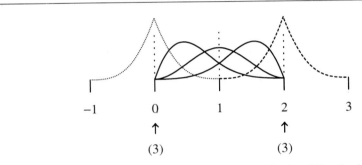

−1   0   1   2   3

↑   ↑

(3)   (3)

Figure 9.27. The knots at 0 and 2 have multiplicity 3. The dotted B-spline is defined on the knots [-1,0,0,0,1]; the dashed B-spline is defined on the knots [1,2,2,2,3]. Compare these B-splines with those of Figure 9.26.

10

Bézier Curves

Bernstein-Bézier curves and surfaces, or more briefly, *Bézier* curves and surfaces [Bézier70, Bézier77, Forrest72] constituted one of the earliest attempts to develop a flexible and intuitive interface for computer aided design, and they have been used for some years by Renault to design the ''skin'' or outer panels of automobiles [Bézier74]. They are interesting in their own right, relate naturally to B-spline curves, and provide a convenient context in which to introduce the ideas of *subdivision* and *refinement*.

Throughout this chapter our notation will be slightly different from that in the foregoing material on B-splines in order to bring our presentation more in line with that of the standard literature on Bézier techniques. We will refer to the *degree*, d, of curves rather than their order, k, and the basis functions with which we work will be denoted by $P_{i,d}$ rather than $B_{i,k}$. Keep in mind, however, that $d = k - 1$. Furthermore, we will show that the basis functions used for Bézier curves and surfaces are, in fact, B-splines, so the material of this chapter is not really a digression.

A degree d Bézier curve is defined, much like a B-spline curve, as

$$\mathbf{Q}(u) = \sum_{i=0}^{d} \mathbf{V}_i P_{i,d}(u) \quad \text{for } 0 \le u \le 1, \tag{10.1}$$

where

$$P_{i,d}(u) = \begin{bmatrix} d \\ i \end{bmatrix} u^i (1-u)^{d-i} \tag{10.2}$$

are the *Bernstein polynomials*, the $\begin{pmatrix} d \\ i \end{pmatrix}$ being the binomial coefficients. Using the Binomial Theorem it is easy to show that a Bézier curve lies within the convex hull of its defining control vertices. First we write

$$
\begin{aligned}
1 &= \left[(1-u) + u \right]^d = \sum_{i=0}^{d} \begin{pmatrix} d \\ i \end{pmatrix} u^i (1-u)^{d-i} \\
&= (1-u)^d + du(1-u)^{d-1} + \cdots + du^{d-1}(1-u) + u^d \\
&= P_{0,d}(u) + P_{1,d}(u) + \cdots + P_{d-1,d}(u) + P_{d,d}(u).
\end{aligned}
\tag{10.3}
$$

Thus the $P_{i,d}(u)$ sum to one. Because $0 \le u \le 1$ the quantities u and $(1-u)$ are both nonnegative; it follows that the $P_{i,d}(u)$ are also nonnegative. Therefore a Bézier curve must lie within the convex hull of its control vertices.

It is a fact, although we will not prove it here, that the Bernstein polynomials of degree d are a basis for the polynomials of degree d. (The argument for the cubic case is indicated at the end of Section 5.8.)

By way of example, for cubic Bézier curves we have

$$
\begin{aligned}
\mathbf{Q}(u) &= \mathbf{V}_0 P_{0,3} + \mathbf{V}_1 P_{1,3} + \mathbf{V}_2 P_{2,3} + \mathbf{V}_3 P_{3,3} \\
&= \mathbf{V}_0 (1-u)^3 + \mathbf{V}_1 3u(1-u)^2 + \mathbf{V}_2 3u^2(1-u) + \mathbf{V}_3 u^3.
\end{aligned}
$$

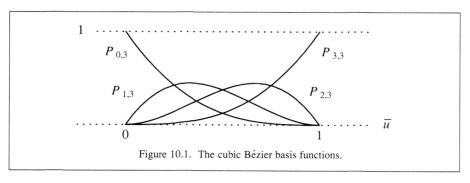

Figure 10.1. The cubic Bézier basis functions.

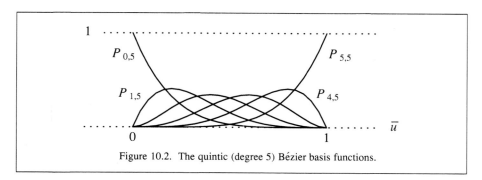

Figure 10.2. The quintic (degree 5) Bézier basis functions.

By inspection it is easy to see from (10.1) and (10.2) that $Q(0) = V_0$ and $Q(1) = V_d$; that is, the first and last control vertices are interpolated.

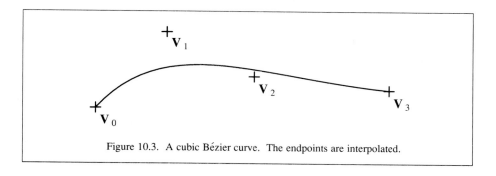

Figure 10.3. A cubic Bézier curve. The endpoints are interpolated.

10.1 Increasing the Degree of a Bézier Curve

Suppose that we are unable to produce a curve of the desired shape with a degree d Bézier curve. One option is to use a Bézier curve of higher degree. Having chosen to work at a higher degree, we may simply define a new curve. On the other hand, a polynomial of degree d is also a polynomial of degree $d + 1$; hence there exists a set of $d + 2$ control vertices W_i that defines a degree d Bézier curve originally defined by $d + 1$ control vertices V_i. The relationship between the V_i and the W_i, which appears in [Forrest72], is given by the following formulas:

$$W_0 = V_0$$

$$W_i = \left[\frac{i}{d+1}\right] V_{i-1} + \left[1 - \frac{i}{d+1}\right] V_i \quad \text{for } i = 1, \ldots, d$$

$$W_{d+1} = V_d .$$

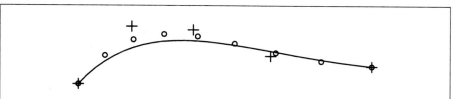

Figure 10.4. This is the curve of Figure 10.3, defined as a degree 4 Bézier curve (with control vertices given by "+") and as a degree 8 Bézier curve (with control vertices given by "o").

10.2 Composite Bézier Curves

Using a higher-degree Bézier curve gives more flexibility, but it also increases the cost of evaluation. Then too, the movement of any one control vertex still alters the entirety of a simple Bézier curve. An alternative is to construct a composite curve from several simple Bézier curves by causing the last vertex of the ith segment to coincide with the first vertex of the $(i+1)^{st}$ segment. Since the first and last vertices of a Bézier curve are interpolated, this results in C^0 continuity. Differentiating (10.1) we see that

$$\mathbf{Q}^{(1)}(0) = d(\mathbf{V}_1 - \mathbf{V}_0) \tag{10.4}$$

and

$$\mathbf{Q}^{(1)}(1) = d(\mathbf{V}_d - \mathbf{V}_{d-1}), \tag{10.5}$$

so that the tangents at either end are collinear with the line segment between the first two and last two control vertices, respectively. Consecutive segments in a composite Bézier curve can therefore be made C^1 continuous simply by arranging that the penultimate control vertex of the first curve, the shared endpoint, and the second vertex of the next curve be collinear and equally spaced. (See Figure 10.5.)

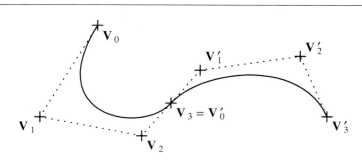

Figure 10.5. A composite cubic Bézier curve. The unprimed vertices define one curve segment and the primed vertices define another. Because $\mathbf{V}_2$, $\mathbf{V}_3 = \mathbf{V}'_0$ and $\mathbf{V}'_1$ are collinear and $|\mathbf{V}_3 - \mathbf{V}_2| = |\mathbf{V}'_1 - \mathbf{V}'_0|$ the composite curve will be C^1 continuous.

The second derivatives at the beginning and end of a simple Bézier curve are given by

$$\mathbf{Q}^{(2)}(0) = d(d-1)\left[(\mathbf{V}_2 - \mathbf{V}_1) - (\mathbf{V}_1 - \mathbf{V}_0) \right]$$

and

$$\mathbf{Q}^{(2)}(1) \;=\; d\,(d-1)\left[\,(\mathbf{V}_{d-2}-\mathbf{V}_{d-1}) - (\mathbf{V}_{d-1}-\mathbf{V}_{d}\,)\,\right].$$

Suppose that we want to link two Bézier curves together with C^2 continuity. If the first segment is defined by the control vertices $\mathbf{V}_0, \mathbf{V}_1, \ldots \mathbf{V}_d$, then: the position of the first control vertex in the second segment is fixed at $\mathbf{V}_d$ by the requirement that the segments join, the requirement for first derivative continuity fixes the position of the second vertex at $\mathbf{V}_d + (\mathbf{V}_d - \mathbf{V}_{d-1})$, and the requirement for second derivative continuity fixes the position of the third vertex at $\mathbf{V}_{d-2} + 4\,(\mathbf{V}_d - \mathbf{V}_{d-1})$. Thus if we are dealing with cubic Bézier curves, when we add another curve segment we are free to position only the last of the control vertices for the new segment. The positions of the first three control vertices are fixed by the requirement of C^2 continuity. The use of higher-degree curves leaves more of the internal control vertices for a segment free of constraints. Requiring higher-degree continuity imposes constraints on additional control vertices neighboring each joint.

If we move the joint between two segments in a composite cubic Bézier curve, the above considerations tell us that if we demand only C^1 continuity then only the segments which meet at the joint in question are altered. Only one or both of the control vertices on either side of the joint must be moved (so as to remain collinear with the joint), and neither affects C^1 continuity at neighboring joints.

If we insist on maintaining C^2 continuity while moving a joint, it is possible to manipulate the control vertices so as to restrict change to the four segments surrounding the altered joint: cubic B-spline curves have this property, and the cubic B-splines can be used to represent all C^2 polynomial curves, so in particular it must be possible for the Bézier curve. (This argument will become clearer after we have discussed how to convert between representations in section 10.9.) However, it is easier to see how locality can be obtained for a C^2 quintic Bézier curve.

Similar observations can be made when considering the movement of other control vertices in a composite cubic Bézier curve. Some of these limitations can be overcome using the more general concept of *geometric continuity* covered in Chapters 13 and 15. For an application of geometric continuity to Bézier curves, the reader is referred to [DeRose/Barsky84, Fournier/Barsky85].

10.3   Local vs. Global Control

When comparing Bézier and B-spline curves it is sometimes said that the former exhibit "global control" while the latter exhibit "local control." This is true, but only in the following sense. When drawing Bézier curves we very often make use of a single segment, adding control vertices (and consequently raising the degree of the curve) when we need more control or when a lower degree is unable to represent the desired shape. Each of the control vertices, then, affects the entire curve. Its effect is "global."

B-spline curves are usually composite because there is no need to satisfy constraints among the control vertices to maintain continuity. In such a curve, moving a given control vertex alters only a few segments of the curve. The effect is "local."

Technically speaking, however, this is misleading. If we restrict ourselves to a curve consisting of a single segment, then moving any control vertex alters the entire segment for both Bézier and B-spline curves. If we look at composite curves, then in either case moving a single control vertex will affect only certain segments of the curve. The real difference between the two is that maintaining C^1 or higher continuity in a composite Bézier curve requires that the positions of the control vertices satisfy certain constraints, while the control vertices of composite B-spline curves may be moved arbitrarily, without constraint, and maintain the same continuity.

10.4   Subdivision and Refinement

As mentioned, composite Bézier shapes provide an alternative to degree-raising to gain more flexibility. Compositing also provides a mechanism for breaking a large curve or surface into smaller chunks, each of which might be easier to render. Thus, the partitioning of curves and surfaces has utility both for design, where flexibility is needed, and for rendering, where "bite-sized" pieces are needed.

One aspect of forming composites is *parametric* and the other is *geometric*. A simple means of breaking a Bézier curve into parts, for example, is to partition the parametric range over which it is defined

$$0 \le u < 1$$

into a composite of subranges

$$0 \le u < \pi_1 , \ \pi_1 \le u < \pi_2 , \ldots, \ \pi_f \le u < 1$$

and to treat each component of the curve,

$$\mathbf{Q}(u) \ \text{ for } \ \pi_j \le u < \pi_{j+1} ,$$

as a separate object. Similar remarks apply to surfaces, of course. Such an approach is *subdivision* in its simplest form.

Simple subdivision may serve for the purpose of rendering, but it is not sufficient for design purposes, since the subranges might not be coordinated in any way with the control vertices, which are the designer's natural means of shaping a curve or surface. Simple subdivision causes a change in the parametric realm without taking any account of geometric realities. We therefore introduce

---

216   Bézier Curves

the concept of *refinement*. This is a process for Bézier curves and surfaces, and more generally for B-spline curves and surfaces, that determines the way in which control vertices must be reorganized in order that a single shape can be regarded as a composite of two or more shapes. The process defines new control vertices and parametric partitions together. It leaves some choice, at least for general B-spline curves and surfaces, about what groups of control vertices and corresponding parametric ranges are to be regarded as the component curves or surfaces. For Bézier curves, however, the process of refinement is little more complicated than the arbitrary selection of some point, u^*, to provide the break between the "left half" of the curve

$$\mathbf{Q}(u) \quad \text{for } 0 \leq u < u^*$$

and the "right half" of the curve

$$\mathbf{Q}(u) \quad \text{for } u^* \leq u < 1 .$$

Bézier surfaces are equally simple. Hence, it is in our presentation of Bézier material that we will first touch on these issues, first for *midpoint refinement and subdivision*, $u^* = 1/2$, in Section 10.5 and later for arbitrary values of u^* between 0 and 1 in Section 10.6.

Historically, subdivision has been used as a kind of "divide-and-conquer" technique in computer-aided geometric modeling and computer graphics for the construction as well as the display of free-form curves and surfaces.

For construction, subdivision has been used as a method of top-down design. The central idea is that the design process is iterative; it starts with a rough overall shape and converges to a final form. At each step, the designer can specify a geometric region that he or she wishes to modify. Through the use of refinement, additional control vertices are created in this geometric region, and a coordinated partitioning of parametric space is defined, without modifying the current shape. The additional control vertices and the parametric partitioning, then, provide the means by which the original shape can be regarded as the composite of two or more smaller shapes.

[Knapp79] describes a design scheme based on the subdivision approach. Subdivision has also been used as a top-down method for the construction of surfaces by fitting from sampled data. The technique in [Schmitt/et al.86] begins with a rough approximating surface and progressively refines it in successive steps to adjust regions where the data is poorly approximated.

For display, simple subdivision, as well as refinement-oriented subdivision, has been used to provide a polygonal approximation (by the control graph) to a spline surface. An adaptive subdivision algorithm recursively splits the curve or surface where the approximation is poor. This may be done arbitrarily at the parametric level, or at each step of the subdivision, a process of refinement may first be used to create a new set of control vertices defining the shape, and then parts of the curve or surface may be identified with subsets of the new control vertices. This process can be used to create a succession of subsurfaces, or a succession of new sets of control vertices that converge to the surface. When the component subsurfaces are small enough and flat enough, or when the refined vertices are sufficiently close to the curve or surface, they can be used as a polygonal approximation of the shape. (Some surfaces that have been rendered in this fashion are shown in Plate X.) Of historical interest are the approaches in [Nydegger72] and [Ramer72]. An early algorithm, introduced by Catmull [Catmull74, Catmull75], subdivides the surface until each piece is no larger than a pixel. More recent algorithms use termination criteria based on *bilinearity* [Clark79] or *flatness* [Lane/Carpenter79, Lane/et al.80, Barsky/De Rose85, Barsky/et al.87, Barsky87]; that is, the recursion stops when the subsurface, or its defining set of control vertices, is planar to within a given tolerance. Another early subdivision algorithm, discovered by Chaikin [Chaikin74], successively chops the corners of a control polygon, yielding a piecewise linear approximation to a quadratic B-spline curve or surface [Riesenfeld75]. A recursive subdivision algorithm, which generates bicubic surfaces of arbitrary topology and which has no closed form, is discussed in [Catmull/Clark78, Doo78, Doo/Sabin78].

The mathematical theory of refinement has been analyzed for various curve and surface representations. An early precursor to the development of the refinement of Bézier curves and surfaces was the work of de Casteljau [deCasteljau59], who developed a recursion formula for the evaluation of a point on a Bézier curve or surface. This recursive algorithm has recently been generalized for rational curves and surfaces in [Piegl85]. Algorithms for both polynomial and rational parametric curves were presented in [Koparkar/Mudor83]. The refinement process that defines the midpoint subdivision of Bézier curves and surfaces was thoroughly analyzed by Lane and Riesenfeld [Lane/Riesenfeld80]. The more general case of the refinement algorithm leading to arbitrary Bézier subdivision (where the subdivision point is not constrained to be the parametric midpoint) was handled in [Hosaka/Kimura80], [Lane/Riesenfeld81, Goldman82, Barsky85], and is covered in Section 10.6. Catmull [Catmull75] derived basis functions that required only additions and shifts to carry out subdivision. In [Lane/Riesenfeld80], Lane and Riesenfeld analyzed the refinement of uniform B-splines. Refinement of the more general nonuniform B-splines has been developed independently by Cohen, Lyche and Riesenfeld in the "Oslo algorithm" [Cohen/et al.80, Riesenfeld/et al.81, Prautzsch84, Prautzsch85, Lee85] and by Boehm in the "knot insertion algorithm" [Boehm80, Boehm85, Boehm/Prautzsch85]. Beta-splines, which we will introduce later, can be subdivided as explained in [Barsky/et al.87], [Joe87], and [Cohen88], while the subdivision of the special case of Beta2-splines is covered in [Barsky/DeRose85]. On a related note, the technique of Wang [Wang84] yields the number of subdivisions necessary to achieve a given tolerance of approximation. However, his technique is not adaptive; that is, a full subdivision tree must be constructed.

10.5   Midpoint Subdivision of Bézier Curves

The easiest refinement/subdivision question to ask is: can we find a way to redefine control vertices so as to break a cubic Bézier curve in half? That is, suppose we have the Bézier curve

$$\mathbf{Q}(u) = \mathbf{V}_0(1-u)^3 + \mathbf{V}_1\,3u\,(1-u)^2 + \mathbf{V}_2\,3u^2(1-u) + \mathbf{V}_3\,u^3$$

for $0 \le u \le 1$. Can we find control vertices

$$\mathbf{S}_0,\ \mathbf{S}_1,\ \mathbf{S}_2,\ \mathbf{S}_3,\ \mathbf{T}_0,\ \mathbf{T}_1,\ \mathbf{T}_2,\ \mathbf{T}_3$$

such that the Bézier curve

$$\mathbf{L}(s) = \mathbf{S}_0(1-s)^3 + \mathbf{S}_1\,3s\,(1-s)^2 + \mathbf{S}_2\,3s^2(1-s) + \mathbf{S}_3\,s^3$$

for $0 \le s \le 1$ is the first half of the curve defined by $\mathbf{V}_0$, $\mathbf{V}_1$, $\mathbf{V}_2$ and $\mathbf{V}_3$ (i.e., $\mathbf{Q}(u)$ for $0 \le u \le 0.5$), and

$$\mathbf{R}(t) = \mathbf{T}_0(1-t)^3 + \mathbf{T}_1\,3t\,(1-t)^2 + \mathbf{T}_2\,3t^2(1-t) + \mathbf{T}_3\,t^3$$

for $0 \le t \le 1$ is the second half of the curve defined by $\mathbf{V}_0$, $\mathbf{V}_1$, $\mathbf{V}_2$ and $\mathbf{V}_3$ (i.e., $\mathbf{Q}(u)$ for $0.5 \le u \le 1$)? Not surprisingly, the answer is yes.

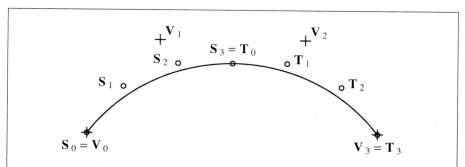

Figure 10.6. Subdivision of a cubic Bézier curve. The original control vertices $\mathbf{V}_0$, $\mathbf{V}_1$, $\mathbf{V}_2$ and $\mathbf{V}_3$ are represented by "+". The new control vertices are represented by "o".

The refinement phase of the operation we wish to carry out consists of creating the vertices $\mathbf{S}_0, \ldots, \mathbf{S}_3$ and $\mathbf{T}_0, \ldots, \mathbf{T}_3$ that (together) define the same curve defined by $\mathbf{V}_0, \ldots, \mathbf{V}_3$. The subdivision phase of the operation consists, trivially, of determining which ranges of the parameter u correspond to the two resulting component curves, which control vertices define the two component curves, and where to put the location of the joint (the geometric point of contact between the curves). It is a particular feature of Bézier curves that the point at which these two subcurves can be separated is geometrically indicated by the common vertex $S_3 = T_0$.

We know that

$$S_0 = V_0$$

$$S_3 = Q(\frac{1}{2}) = \frac{1}{8} \left[V_0 + 3V_1 + 3V_2 + V_3 \right].$$

From (10.4) and (10.5) we know that

$$L^{(1)}(0) = 3(S_1 - S_0)$$

and

$$L^{(1)}(1) = 3(S_3 - S_2).$$

Since we have $s = 2u$, by the chain rule we have

$$\frac{d}{du} L(s(u)) = \frac{d}{ds} L(s) \cdot \frac{d}{du} s(u) = 2L^{(1)}(s),$$

whence

$$L^{(1)}(0) = \frac{1}{2} Q^{(1)}(0) = \frac{3}{2}(V_1 - V_0)$$

and

$$L^{(1)}(1) = \frac{1}{2} Q^{(1)}(\frac{1}{2}) = \frac{3}{8} \left[V_3 + V_2 - V_1 - V_0 \right].$$

We now have four equations, namely

$$S_0 = V_0$$

$$3(S_1 - S_0) = \frac{3}{2}(V_1 - V_0)$$

$$3(S_3 - S_2) = \frac{3}{8} \left[V_3 + V_2 - V_1 - V_0 \right]$$

$$S_3 = \frac{1}{8} \left[V_0 + 3V_1 + 3V_2 + V_3 \right].$$

Solving them yields

$$\mathbf{S}_0 = \mathbf{V}_0$$

$$\mathbf{S}_1 = \frac{1}{2}(\mathbf{V}_0 + \mathbf{V}_1)$$

$$\mathbf{S}_2 = \frac{1}{4}(\mathbf{V}_0 + 2\mathbf{V}_1 + \mathbf{V}_2)$$

$$\mathbf{S}_3 = \frac{1}{8}(\mathbf{V}_0 + 3\mathbf{V}_1 + 3\mathbf{V}_2 + \mathbf{V}_3).$$

In a completely analogous way we can show that

$$\mathbf{T}_0 = \frac{1}{8}(\mathbf{V}_0 + 3\mathbf{V}_1 + 3\mathbf{V}_2 + \mathbf{V}_3)$$

$$\mathbf{T}_1 = \frac{1}{4}(\mathbf{V}_1 + 2\mathbf{V}_2 + \mathbf{V}_3)$$

$$\mathbf{T}_2 = \frac{1}{2}(\mathbf{V}_2 + \mathbf{V}_3)$$

$$\mathbf{T}_3 = \mathbf{V}_3.$$

These vertices are more efficiently computed in the following order:

$$\mathbf{S}_0 = \mathbf{V}_0$$

$$\mathbf{S}_1 = \frac{1}{2}(\mathbf{V}_0 + \mathbf{V}_1)$$

$$t = \frac{1}{2}(\mathbf{V}_1 + \mathbf{V}_2)$$

$$\mathbf{S}_2 = \frac{1}{2}(\mathbf{S}_1 + t)$$

$$\mathbf{T}_3 = \mathbf{V}_3$$

$$\mathbf{T}_2 = \frac{1}{2}(\mathbf{V}_2 + \mathbf{V}_3)$$

$$\mathbf{T}_1 = \frac{1}{2}(t + \mathbf{T}_2)$$

$$\mathbf{S}_3 = \mathbf{T}_0 = \frac{1}{2}(\mathbf{S}_2 + \mathbf{T}_1).$$

There are two benefits we derive from this process. First, it can be shown that the new control graphs lie closer to the curve than the original control graph [Lane/Riesenfeld80]. Thus, one technique for rendering a curve is to continue this process recursively until the control graphs are a sufficiently good approximation to the curve. Then we may simply draw the graphs as an approximation to the curve.

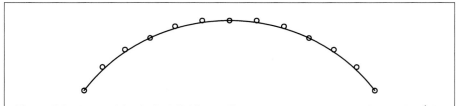

Figure 10.7. A second level of subdivision applied to Figure 10.6. There are four cubic Bézier curves here.

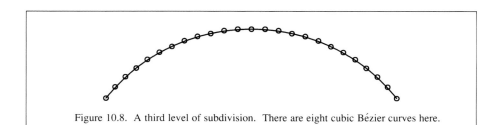

Figure 10.8. A third level of subdivision. There are eight cubic Bézier curves here.

Because a Bézier curve lies within the convex hull of its defining control vertices, one may test to see if the length of the control graph is within some tolerance of the distance between the first and last control vertices [Lane/et al.80], or whether the distance between each pair of control vertices is less than some tolerance, or whether the deviation of internal control vertices from a line segment joining the end vertices is sufficiently small [Lane/Riesenfeld80], etc. The convergence test can be applied to each subdivided curve individually, so that the subdivision process ceases adaptively when the curve has become "locally flat."

Second, subdivision can aid in the design of a curve since it provides more control vertices, whose movement affects the shape of a smaller portion of the curve. Of course one must be careful not to destroy the desired continuity at joints when moving control vertices; as we have seen, this can be a fairly severe restriction unless sufficiently high-degree Bézier curves are used.

Midpoint subdivision of higher-order Bézier curves, having degree d, can be accomplished using the formula

$$\mathbf{S}_i = \sum_{r=0}^{i} \begin{bmatrix} i \\ r \end{bmatrix} \frac{\mathbf{V}_r}{2^i} \quad \text{for } i = 0, 1, \ldots, d$$

derived in [Clark79]. From symmetry we have

$$\mathbf{T}_i = \sum_{r=i}^{d} \begin{bmatrix} d-i \\ d-r \end{bmatrix} \frac{\mathbf{V}_r}{2^{d-i}} \quad \text{for } i = 0, 1, \ldots, d .$$

Clark's proof makes use of the Binomial Theorem and various binomial identities. An induction proof of essentially the same result is given in [Lane/Riesenfeld80], where the following algorithm for efficiently computing the $\mathbf{S}_i$ and $\mathbf{T}_i$ is presented as well.

for $i \leftarrow 0$ **step** 1 **until** d **do**

    $\mathbf{S}_i \leftarrow \mathbf{V}_i$

endfor

$\mathbf{T}_d \leftarrow \mathbf{V}_d$

for $j \leftarrow 1$ **step** 1 **until** d **do**

    tmp2 $\leftarrow \mathbf{S}_{j-1}$

    for $k \leftarrow j$ **step** 1 **until** d **do**

        tmp1 $\leftarrow$ **tmp2**

        tmp2 $\leftarrow \frac{1}{2} (\mathbf{S}_{k-1} + \mathbf{S}_k)$

        $\mathbf{S}_{k-1} \leftarrow$ **tmp1**

    endfor

    $\mathbf{S}_d \leftarrow \mathbf{T}_{d-j} \leftarrow$ **tmp2**

endfor

A general technique for directly subdividing elsewhere than at the parametric midpoint of a Bézier curve appears next.

10.6   Arbitrary Subdivision of Bézier Curves

This section, taken from [Barsky85], generalizes *midpoint subdivision* to *arbitrary subdivision*, enabling the subdivision to be performed at any parametric value, not solely at the midpoint. To develop this material, it helps to expand the notation for a dth degree Bézier curve to include the list of the control vertices that define it, and the parametric range it covers:

$$\mathbf{Q}_d (\mathbf{V}_0, \mathbf{V}_1, \ldots, \mathbf{V}_d ; 0, 1 ; u).$$

10.6.1 Convex Combinations of Lower Degree Curves

Before deriving the equations governing the arbitrary subdivision of Bézier curves, it will be shown that a dth degree Bézier curve is a *convex combination* of a pair of $(d-1)^{\text{st}}$ degree Bézier curves. In particular, the curve for $\mathbf{V}_0, \ldots, \mathbf{V}_d$ is a convex combination of the curves for $\mathbf{V}_0, \ldots, \mathbf{V}_{d-1}$ and $\mathbf{V}_1, \ldots, \mathbf{V}_d$ with coefficients $1-u$ and u, respectively:

$$
\mathbf{Q}_d(\mathbf{V}_0, \mathbf{V}_1, \ldots, \mathbf{V}_d; 0, 1; u)
$$

$$
= (1-u)\,\mathbf{Q}_{d-1}(\mathbf{V}_0, \mathbf{V}_1, \ldots, \mathbf{V}_{d-1}; 0, 1; u) \tag{10.6}
$$

$$
+ u\,\mathbf{Q}_{d-1}(\mathbf{V}_1, \mathbf{V}_2, \ldots, \mathbf{V}_d; 0, 1; u).
$$

To show this [Lane/et al.80], begin with the following expression for the curve $\mathbf{Q}_d(\mathbf{V}_0, \mathbf{V}_1, \ldots, \mathbf{V}_d; 0, 1; u)$:

$$
\mathbf{Q}_d(\mathbf{V}_0, \mathbf{V}_1, \ldots, \mathbf{V}_d; 0, 1; u) = \sum_{i=0}^{d} P_{i,d}(u)\,\mathbf{V}_i,
$$

and substitute the formula for the ith Bernstein polynomial in place of $P_{i,d}(u)$ to obtain

$$
\sum_{i=0}^{d} \binom{d}{i} u^i (1-u)^{d-i}\,\mathbf{V}_i.
$$

Next, expand using a combinatoric identity,

$$
\sum_{i=0}^{d} \left[\binom{d-1}{i} + \binom{d-1}{i-1} \right] u^i (1-u)^{d-i}\,\mathbf{V}_i,
$$

and separate into two sums,

$$
\sum_{i=0}^{d} \binom{d-1}{i} u^i (1-u)^{d-i}\,\mathbf{V}_i + \sum_{i=0}^{d} \binom{d-1}{i-1} u^i (1-u)^{d-i}\,\mathbf{V}_i.
$$

Each of the summations has a term in which the binomial coefficient is zero; specifically,

$$
\binom{d-1}{d} = 0 \quad \text{and} \quad \binom{d-1}{-1} = 0.
$$

When these terms are removed, the limits of the sums are changed as follows:

$$
\sum_{i=0}^{d-1} \binom{d-1}{i} u^i (1-u)^{d-i}\,\mathbf{V}_i + \sum_{i=1}^{d} \binom{d-1}{i-1} u^i (1-u)^{d-i}\,\mathbf{V}_i. \tag{10.7}
$$

Now, the second summation can be rewritten by changing the index of summation. Replacing i with $j = i - 1$ $(i = j + 1)$ in this summation yields:

$$\sum_{i=1}^{d} \begin{bmatrix} d-1 \\ i-1 \end{bmatrix} u^i (1-u)^{d-i} \mathbf{V}_i = \sum_{j=0}^{d-1} \begin{bmatrix} d-1 \\ j \end{bmatrix} u^{j+1} (1-u)^{d-1-j} \mathbf{V}_{j+1}. \qquad (10.8)$$

Finally substituting this new expression (10.8) for the second summation in equation (10.7) yields:

$$\mathbf{Q}_d (\mathbf{V}_0, \mathbf{V}_1, \ldots, \mathbf{V}_d; 0, 1; u)$$

$$= \sum_{i=0}^{d-1} \begin{bmatrix} d-1 \\ i \end{bmatrix} u^i (1-u)^{d-i} \mathbf{V}_i + \sum_{j=0}^{d-1} \begin{bmatrix} d-1 \\ j \end{bmatrix} u^{j+1} (1-u)^{d-1-j} \mathbf{V}_{j+1} \qquad (10.9)$$

$$= (1-u) \sum_{i=0}^{d-1} \begin{bmatrix} d-1 \\ i \end{bmatrix} u^i (1-u)^{d-1-i} \mathbf{V}_i + u \sum_{j=0}^{d-1} \begin{bmatrix} d-1 \\ j \end{bmatrix} u^j (1-u)^{d-1-j} \mathbf{V}_{j+1},$$

which is exactly equation (10.6).

10.6.2 New Vertices and Geometric Construction

Considering equation (10.9) and combining the summations, we have

$$\mathbf{Q}_d (\mathbf{V}_0, \mathbf{V}_1, \ldots, \mathbf{V}_d; 0, 1; u) = \sum_{i=0}^{d-1} P_{i,d-1}(u)[(1-u)\mathbf{V}_i + u \mathbf{V}_{i+1}]. \qquad (10.10)$$

Equation (10.10) can be rewritten as

$$\mathbf{Q}_d (\mathbf{V}_0, \mathbf{V}_1, \ldots, \mathbf{V}_d; 0, 1; u) = \sum_{i=0}^{d-1} P_{i,d-1}(u) \mathbf{V}_i^{[1]}(u),$$

where

$$\mathbf{V}_i^{[1]}(u) = (1-u)\mathbf{V}_i + u \mathbf{V}_{i+1}.$$

In this notation the superscript [1] on $\mathbf{V}_i$ is to remind us that we have performed one interpolation, starting at $\mathbf{V}_i$, to produce $\mathbf{V}_i^{[1]}$. The argument (u) reminds us of the parametric value that was used in the interpolation. Repeating this process recursively r times yields

$$\mathbf{Q}_d (\mathbf{V}_0, \mathbf{V}_1, \ldots, \mathbf{V}_d; 0, 1; u) = \sum_{i=0}^{d-r} P_{i,d-r}(u) \mathbf{V}_i^{[r]}(u), \qquad (10.11)$$

where

$$\mathbf{V}_i^{[r]} = (1-u)\,\mathbf{V}_i^{[r-1]}(u) + u\,\mathbf{V}_{i+1}^{[r-1]}(u)\quad r \geq 1 \tag{10.12}$$

$$\mathbf{V}_i^{[0]} = \mathbf{V}_i \qquad\qquad\qquad\qquad r = 0.$$

When $r = d$, equation (10.11) becomes

$$\mathbf{Q}_d\,(\,\mathbf{V}_0,\mathbf{V}_1,\ldots,\ \mathbf{V}_d\,;0,1\,;u\,) = P_{0,0}(u)\,\mathbf{V}_0^{[d]}(u),$$

which is

$$\mathbf{Q}_d\,(\,\mathbf{V}_0,\mathbf{V}_1,\ldots,\ \mathbf{V}_d\,;0,1\,;u\,) = \mathbf{V}_0^{[d]}(u),$$

because $P_{0,0}(u) = 1$.

Thus, for a given parametric value u^*, the point on the curve at u^* is $\mathbf{V}_0^{[d]}(u^*)$, as defined in equation (10.12). This yields another way to compute a point on the curve; simply compute this vertex recursively using a ratio equal to the parametric value of the desired point. This idea can be used to geometrically construct a Bézier curve. To compute the point $\mathbf{Q}\,(u^*)$, each edge of the control polygon is divided in the ratio of u^* to $1-u^*$, and these points are connected in succession to form $d-1$ edges. This process is repeated, and after d iterations, a single point results which is the desired value. Figure 10.9 illustrates the computation of a point on a cubic Bézier curve. This same process can be performed for various values of the parameter u, and then these points can be connected to generate a piecewise linear approximation to the curve. An example of this process showing a cubic curve is given in Section 10.6.4 and illustrated in Figure 10.10.

In addition, $\mathbf{V}_0^{[d]}(u^*)$ is the common vertex between the two pieces of a subdivided curve, each with its own control polygon. This is derived in the next section and is illustrated in Figure 10.9 for degree $d = 3$.

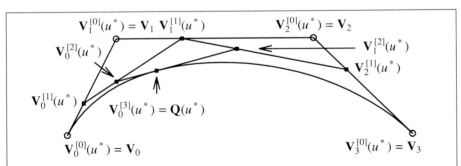

Figure 10.9. $\mathbf{V}_0^{[3]}(u^*)$ is the common vertex between the two pieces that result from subdividing a curve of degree $d = 3$.

10.6.3 The Mathematical Theory of Arbitrary Subdivision

Our notation for a curve has been extended to include the parametric limits corresponding to the initial and terminal points of the curve. (Note that these parametric limits are not necessarily the same as the parametric limits defining the interval over which the parameter is allowed to vary.) We shall now make use of this feature of our notational extension. The curve defined by the $d + 1$ control vertices $\mathbf{V}_0, \ldots, \mathbf{V}_d$ and beginning at $u = a$ and ending at $u = b$ is given by

$$\mathbf{Q}_d (\mathbf{V}_0, \mathbf{V}_1, \ldots, \mathbf{V}_d ; a, b; u).$$

It will now be shown that for $a = 0$ and $b = 1$ the two subdivided curves are

$$\mathbf{Q}_d \left[\mathbf{V}_0^{[0]}(u^*), \mathbf{V}_0^{[1]}(u^*), \ldots, \mathbf{V}_0^{[d]}(u^*); 0, u^*; \frac{u}{u^*} \right] \quad 0 \leq u \leq u^*$$

on the left and

$$\mathbf{Q}_d \left[\mathbf{V}_0^{[d]}(u^*), \mathbf{V}_1^{[d-1]}(u^*), \ldots, \mathbf{V}_d^{[0]}(u^*); u^*, 1; \frac{u - u^*}{1 - u^*} \right] \quad u^* \leq u \leq 1$$

on the right. This means that the refinement process to be established replaces the vertices

$$\mathbf{V}_0, \mathbf{V}_1, \ldots, \mathbf{V}_d$$

by the two sets of vertices

$$\mathbf{V}_0^{[0]}(u^*), \mathbf{V}_0^{[1]}(u^*), \ldots, \mathbf{V}_0^{[d]}(u^*)$$

and

$$\mathbf{V}_0^{[d]}(u^*), \mathbf{V}_1^{[d-1]}(u^*), \ldots, \mathbf{V}_d^{[0]}(u^*).$$

Given the arbitrarily named parameters

$$v = \frac{u}{u^*}$$

and

$$w = \frac{u - u^*}{1 - u},$$

---

it is then the case that for $0 \le v \le 1$, the first set of vertices define the left portion of the original curve, while for $0 \le w \le 1$, the second set of vertices defines the right half of the curve.

As in the case of midpoint subdivision, the special nature of Bézier curves provides that one of the new control vertices be the joint between the two subcurves; in this case it is $\mathbf{V}_0^{[d]}(u^*)$. Figure 10.9 illustrates this for $d = 3$.

In particular, for $d = 1$, we have

$$\mathbf{Q}_1(\mathbf{V}_0, \mathbf{V}_1; 0, 1; u) = (1 - u)\mathbf{V}_0 + u\mathbf{V}_1,$$

and we wish to express this as

$$\mathbf{Q}_1(\mathbf{V}_0, \mathbf{V}_1; 0, 1; u) = \begin{cases} \left(1 - \dfrac{u}{u^*}\right)\mathbf{S}_0 + \dfrac{u}{u^*}\mathbf{S}_1 & 0 \le u \le u^* \\[3ex] \left(1 - \dfrac{u - u^*}{1 - u^*}\right)\mathbf{T}_0 + \dfrac{u - u^*}{1 - u^*}\mathbf{T}_1 & u^* \le u \le 1. \end{cases}$$

We shall show that

$$\mathbf{S}_0 = \mathbf{V}_0^{[0]}(u^*) \quad \text{and} \quad \mathbf{S}_1 = \mathbf{V}_0^{[1]}(u^*),$$

where $\mathbf{V}_0^{[0]}(u^*)$ and $\mathbf{V}_0^{[1]}(u^*)$ are as defined in equation (10.12). The fact that

$$\mathbf{T}_0 = \mathbf{V}_0^{[1]}(u^*) \quad \text{and} \quad \mathbf{T}_1 = \mathbf{V}_1^{[0]}(u^*)$$

can be established in an analogous fashion. By addition and subtraction:

$$\mathbf{Q}_1(\mathbf{V}_0, \mathbf{V}_1; 0, 1; u) = \left(1 - \frac{u}{u^*}\right)\mathbf{V}_0 + \left(\frac{u}{u^*} - u\right)\mathbf{V}_0 + u\mathbf{V}_1$$

$$= \left(1 - \frac{u}{u^*}\right)\mathbf{V}_0 + \left[\frac{u}{u^*}\mathbf{V}_0 - u\mathbf{V}_0 + u\mathbf{V}_1\right]$$

$$= \left(1 - \frac{u}{u^*}\right)\mathbf{V}_0 + \left[\frac{u}{u^*}\mathbf{V}_0 - u\mathbf{V}_0 + u\mathbf{V}_1\right]\frac{u^*}{u}\frac{u}{u^*}$$

$$= \left(1 - \frac{u}{u^*}\right)\mathbf{V}_0 + \left[\mathbf{V}_0 - u^*\mathbf{V}_0 + u^*\mathbf{V}_1\right]\frac{u}{u^*}$$

$$= \left[1 - \frac{u}{u^*}\right]\mathbf{V}_0 + \left[(1-u^*)\mathbf{V}_0 + u^*\mathbf{V}_1\right]\frac{u}{u^*}$$

$$= \left[1 - \frac{u}{u^*}\right]\mathbf{V}_0^{[0]}(u^*) + \frac{u}{u^*}\mathbf{V}_0^{[1]}(u^*)$$

where $\mathbf{V}_0^{[0]} = \mathbf{V}_0$ and $\mathbf{V}_0^{[2]} = (1-u^*)\mathbf{V}_0 + \mathbf{V}_1$.

Now for the general result:

$$\mathbf{Q}_d(\mathbf{V}_0, \mathbf{V}_1, \ldots, \mathbf{V}_d; 0, 1; u)$$

$$= \begin{cases} \mathbf{Q}_d\left[\mathbf{V}_0^{[0]}(u^*), \mathbf{V}_0^{[1]}(u^*), \ldots, \mathbf{V}_0^{[d]}(u^*); 0, u^*; \dfrac{u}{u^*}\right] & 0 \le u \le u^* \\[4mm] & \hspace{1cm}(10.13) \\[2mm] \mathbf{Q}_d\left[\mathbf{V}_0^{[d]}(u^*), \mathbf{V}_1^{[d-1]}(u^*), \ldots, \mathbf{V}_d^{[0]}(u^*); u^*, 1; \dfrac{u-u^*}{1-u^*}\right] & u^* \le u \le 1. \end{cases}$$

Equation (10.13) will be proven inductively on d for $0 \le u \le u^*$; the case of $u^* \le u \le 1$ can be proven in an analogous fashion.

We have already established the basis, $d = 1$. For the induction step, assume that equation (10.13) is true for $r = 1, \ldots, d - 1$. Recall that

$$\mathbf{Q}_d(\mathbf{V}_0, \ldots, \mathbf{V}_d; 0, 1; u)$$

can be written as

$$(1-u)\mathbf{Q}_{d-1}(\mathbf{V}_0, \ldots, \mathbf{V}_{d-1}; 0, 1; u) + u\mathbf{Q}_{d-1}(\mathbf{V}_1, \ldots, \mathbf{V}_d; 0, 1; u).$$

By the induction hypothesis, this becomes

$$(1-u)\mathbf{Q}_{d-1}\left[\mathbf{V}_0^{[0]}(u^*), \mathbf{V}_0^{[1]}(u^*), \ldots, \mathbf{V}_0^{[d-1]}(u^*); 0, u^*; \frac{u}{u^*}\right]$$

$$+ u\mathbf{Q}_{d-1}\left[\mathbf{V}_1^{[0]}(u^*), \mathbf{V}_1^{[1]}(u^*), \ldots, \mathbf{V}_1^{[d-1]}(u^*); 0, u^*; \frac{u}{u^*}\right]$$

for $0 \le u \le u^*$. Since $(1-u) = (1 - \dfrac{u}{u^*} + \dfrac{u}{u^*} - u)$, this can be expanded as follows:

$$\left[1-\frac{u}{u^*}\right]\mathbf{Q}_{d-1}\left[\mathbf{V}_0^{[0]}(u^*),\mathbf{V}_0^{[1]}(u^*),\ldots,\mathbf{V}_0^{[d-1]}(u^*);0,u^*;\frac{u}{u^*}\right]$$

$$+\frac{u}{u^*}\left[u^*\mathbf{Q}_{d-1}\left[\mathbf{V}_1^{[0]}(u^*),\mathbf{V}_1^{[1]}(u^*),\ldots,\mathbf{V}_1^{[d-1]}(u^*);0,u^*;\frac{u}{u^*}\right]\right.$$

$$\left.+(1-u^*)\mathbf{Q}_{d-1}\left[\mathbf{V}_0^{[0]}(u^*),\mathbf{V}_0^{[1]}(u^*),\ldots,\mathbf{V}_0^{[d-1]}(u^*);0,u^*;\frac{u}{u^*}\right]\right].$$

Regrouping, we have

$$\left[1-\frac{u}{u^*}\right]\mathbf{Q}_{d-1}\left[\mathbf{V}_0^{[0]}(u^*),\mathbf{V}_0^{[1]}(u^*),\ldots,\mathbf{V}_0^{[d-1]}(u^*);0,u^*;\frac{u}{u^*}\right]$$

$$+\frac{u}{u^*}\mathbf{Q}_{d-1}\left[(1-u^*)\mathbf{V}_0^{[0]}+u^*\mathbf{V}_1^{[0]}(u^*),\right.$$

$$(1-u^*)\mathbf{V}_0^{[1]}+u^*\mathbf{V}_1^{[1]}(u^*),\ldots,$$

$$\left.(1-u^*)\mathbf{V}_0^{[d-1]}+u^*\mathbf{V}_1^{[d-1]}(u^*);0,u^*;\frac{u}{u^*}\right].$$

By definition (10.12) of $\mathbf{V}_i^{[r]}(u^*)$, this becomes

$$\left[1-\frac{u}{u^*}\right]\mathbf{Q}_{d-1}\left[\mathbf{V}_0^{[0]}(u^*),\mathbf{V}_0^{[1]}(u^*),\ldots,\mathbf{V}_0^{[d-1]}(u^*);0,u^*;\frac{u}{u^*}\right]$$

$$+\frac{u}{u^*}\mathbf{Q}_{d-1}\left[\mathbf{V}_0^{[1]}(u^*),\mathbf{V}_0^{[2]}(u^*),\ldots,\mathbf{V}_0^{[d]}(u^*);0,u^*;\frac{u}{u^*}\right].$$

But from (10.6), this is just

$$\mathbf{Q}_d\left[\mathbf{V}_0^{[0]}(u^*),\mathbf{V}_0^{[1]}(u^*),\ldots,\mathbf{V}_0^{[d]}(u^*);0,u^*;\frac{u}{u^*}\right],$$

which substantiates claim (10.13) for $0\leq u\leq u^*$, the proof for $u^*\leq u\leq 1$ is analogous. Thus, the two sub-curves defined by the new control vertices given in (10.12) together form a curve that is coincident with the original curve.

10.6.4 An Illustration of Arbitrary Subdivision

An example illustrating the arbitrary subdivision process is given in Figure 10.10. In this multipage example, the original control polygon consists of four vertices, as shown in Figure 10.10(i). First, the geometric construction is applied to this polygon.

The parametric value u^*, at which the subdivision is to occur, reflects the lengths of the polygon edges in geometric space. Specifically, it is ratio of the length of the "left half" of the control polygon to its total length; that is,

$$u^* = \frac{|V_0 - V_1| + \frac{1}{2}|V_1 - V_2|}{|V_0 - V_1| + |V_1 - V_2| + |V_2 - V_3|} .$$

The parameter *step* describes the construction process. At step r, the vertices $V_j^{[r]}(u^*)$, $j = 0, \ldots, 3 - r$ are determined. Figure 10.10(i) shows step 0, where the vertices are the four original control vertices. Then, step 1 yields three new vertices (Figure 10.10(ii)) and step 2 yields two new vertices (Figure 10.10(iii)). Finally, Figure 10.10(iv) shows the point on the curve, $V_0^{[3]}(u^*)$, which is determined at step 3. This completes the geometric construction for the point on the curve from the original control graph. Now, the same process is performed recursively on the new control vertices. For this construction, a new value of u^* will be computed in terms of each new set of control vertices.

This recursive subdivision corresponds to a preorder traversal of a tree. For this reason, the subdivision stages can be labeled in correspondence with the nodes in the tree. For each *subdivision* in sequence, *level* and *branch* define the node as follows: level is the depth of the node in the tree and branch indicates which specific node at that level by a left/right code (except at level 0 where branch is undefined).

The depth of the tree determines the precision of the subdivision; the deeper the tree, the closer the new control vertices will be to the true curve. *Flatness* is a natural geometric criterion for quantifying the precision of the approximation [Barsky/et al.87]. For the simplicity of this example, however, the depth of the tree will be cut off at 2 across the entire tree. Note that, in general, the depth of the tree would not be the same at all the leaves. In fact, this arbitrary cutoff yields a very poor final approximation (images (xxiii) and (xxiv) of Figure 10.10) to the curve. Using a reasonable stopping criterion, such as flatness, would remedy this defect.

Since the depth of the tree is 2, it has seven nodes; hence the subdivision numbers range from 0 to 6, the level from 0 to 2, and branch is L or R at level 1, and LL, LR, RL, or RR at level 2. The specific values of each of these parameters, in the order of tree traversal, are given in Table A and the tree is shown in Figure 10.11.

The images in Figure 10.10 show the complete subdivision process. After the geometric construction is completed for the original control graph, the construction is performed on the "left" control graph, $\mathbf{V}_0^{[0]}(u^*)$, $\mathbf{V}_0^{[1]}(u^*)$, $\mathbf{V}_0^{[2]}(u^*)$, $\mathbf{V}_0^{[3]}(u^*)$, as shown in images (v) through (vii) of Figure 10.10. This process is repeated for subdivision 2 in images (viii) through (x). Subdivision 3 is shown in images (xi) through (xiii). Images (xiv) through (xvi) show subdivision 4. Subdivision 5 is shown in images (xvii) through (xix) of Figure 10.10. Images (xx) through (xxii) show subdivision 6. Finally, image (xxiii) shows the approximation to the curve determined by the points $\mathbf{V}_0^{[3]}(u^*)$ produced at each step, and image (xxiv) shows the curve itself.

Table A. Subdivision, number, level, and branch value
for the examples in Figure 10.10.

Subdivision	Level	Branch	Images
0	0	-	(ii)-(iv)
1	1	L	(v)-(vii)
2	2	LL	(viii)-(x)
3	2	LR	(xi)-(xiii)
4	1	R	(xiv)-(xvi)
5	2	RL	(xvii)-(xix)
6	2	RR	(xx)-(xxii)

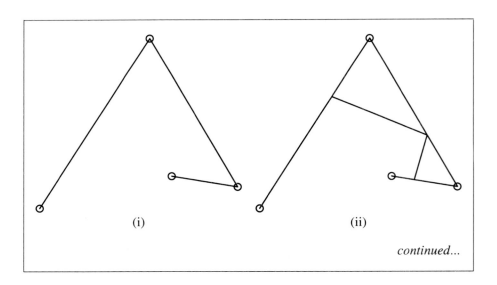

(i) (ii)

continued...

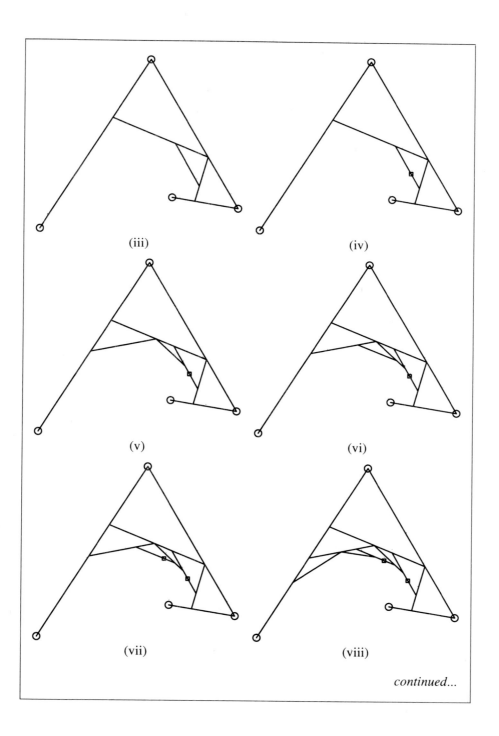

(iii)

(iv)

(v)

(vi)

(vii)

(viii)

continued...

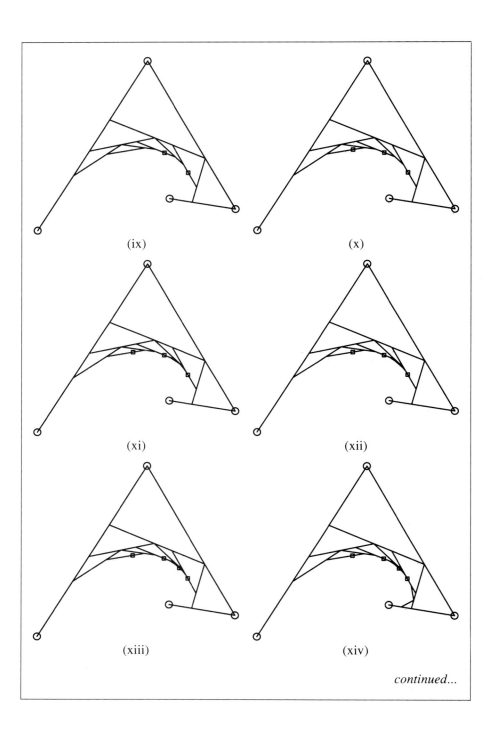

(ix)

(x)

(xi)

(xii)

(xiii)

(xiv)

continued...

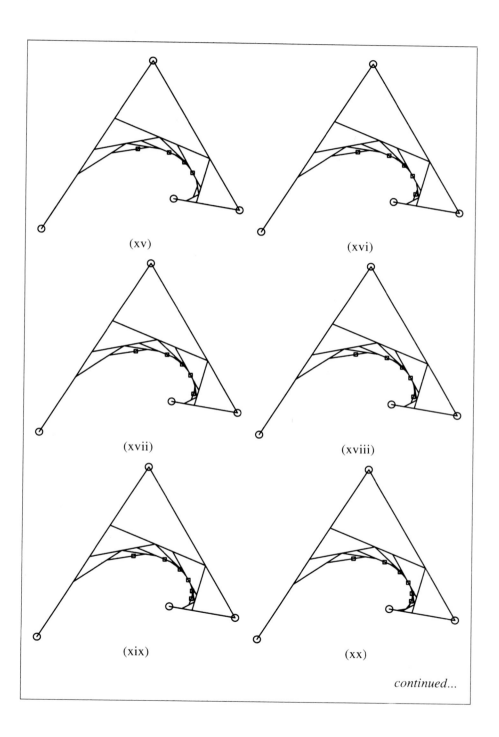

(xv)

(xvi)

(xvii)

(xviii)

(xix)

(xx)

continued...

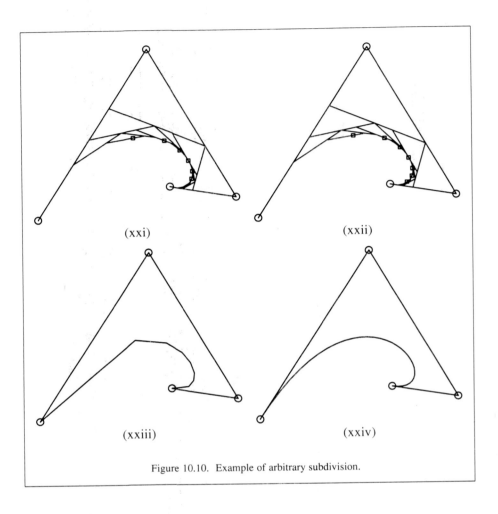

(xxi)

(xxii)

(xxiii)

(xxiv)

Figure 10.10. Example of arbitrary subdivision.

It should be mentioned that although this chapter only concerns itself with Bézier *curves*, the results could be extended for *surfaces* by treating the control vertices in each parametric direction as a control polygon for a curve, and applying the recurrence relation accordingly.

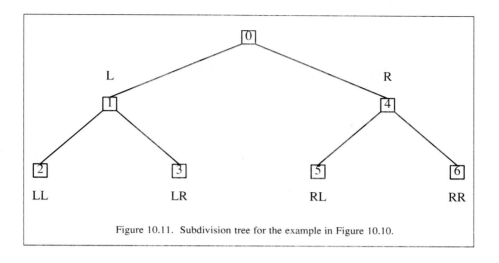

Figure 10.11. Subdivision tree for the example in Figure 10.10.

10.7 Bézier Curves From B-splines

There is an interesting connection between the Bernstein polynomials and the B-splines: the B-splines of order $d + 1$ over a knot sequence in which each break-point has multiplicity $d + 1$ are exactly the Bernstein polynomials of degree d. It is easiest to convey the idea of this connection by considering the simple knot sequence

$$
\begin{array}{cccccccc}
\bar{u}_0 & \bar{u}_1 & \bar{u}_2 & \bar{u}_3 & \bar{u}_4 & \bar{u}_5 & \bar{u}_6 & \bar{u}_7 \\
0 & 0 & 0 & 0 & 1 & 1 & 1 & 1 \;.
\end{array}
$$

Our claim is that the four B-splines $B_{0,4}(\bar{u})$, $B_{1,4}(\bar{u})$, $B_{2,4}(\bar{u})$ and $B_{3,4}(\bar{u})$ over this knot sequence are exactly the Bernstein polynomials $P_{0,3}(\bar{u})$, $P_{1,3}(\bar{u})$, $P_{2,3}(\bar{u})$ and $P_{3,3}(\bar{u})$ given by (10.2).

Recall that

$$
B_{i,k}(\bar{u}) \;=\; \frac{\bar{u} - \bar{u}_i}{\bar{u}_{i+k-1} - \bar{u}_i}\, B_{i,k-1}(\bar{u}) \;+\; \frac{\bar{u}_{i+k} - \bar{u}}{\bar{u}_{i+k} - \bar{u}_{i+1}}\, B_{i+1,k-1}(\bar{u}) \,. \tag{10.14}
$$

Let us expand the B-spline $B_{0,4}(\bar{u})$, which has support $(\bar{u}_0, \bar{u}_4)$, all the way down to the $B_{i,1}(\bar{u})$.

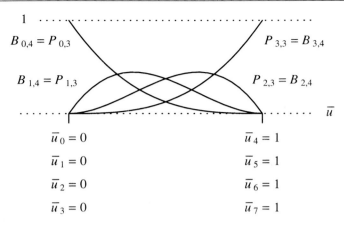

Figure 10.12. The Bernstein polynomials $P_{2,3}(\overline{u})$ are actually the B-splines $B_{i,y}(\overline{u})$ on the knot sequence $(0, 0, 0, 0, 1, 1, 1, 1)$.

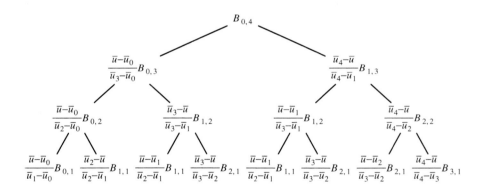

The following points are of interest:

- Since we are evaluating a B-spline of order 4, the tree must have depth 3.

- The value of $B_{0,4}$ is a sum of eight terms. Each term is the product of the coefficients in one of the eight root-leaf paths of this tree.

- A leaf of this tree will be nonzero only if its denominator is $\overline{u}_4 - \overline{u}_3$. In this case only the rightmost leaf is nonzero.

- To arrive at a leaf we begin with the root $B_{0,4}$, which has support $(\bar{u}_0, \bar{u}_4)$, and proceed down the tree. Going left as we leave a node corresponds to following the left term of the recurrence (10.14), and removes one knot interval from the end of the support; going right as we leave a node corresponds to following the right term of the recurrence (10.14), and removes one knot interval from the beginning of the support. The goal is to prune the support down to the two knots $\bar{u}_3$ and $\bar{u}_4$ which immediately surround the only nonvacuous interval.

- The denominators along the path to a nonzero leaf are one since they must include $[\bar{u}_3, \bar{u}_4)$ and $\bar{u}_4 - \bar{u}_3 = 1$. The numerator at a node is $\bar{u}$ if the node is entered by a left branch, and $(1 - \bar{u})$ if the node is entered by a right branch.

- Since in this case we begin with $(\bar{u}_0, \bar{u}_4)$ and must end with $(\bar{u}_3, \bar{u}_4)$, it is clear that we must always take a rightmost branch, pruning $(\bar{u}_0, \bar{u}_1)$, $(\bar{u}_1, \bar{u}_2)$ and $(\bar{u}_2, \bar{u}_3)$ in succession. For future reference we record this tree as being one in which the nonzero leaf is reached by taking zero left branches, and that there are exactly $\binom{3}{0} = 1$ such paths.

- Hence $B_{0,4}(\bar{u}) = \begin{bmatrix} 3 \\ 0 \end{bmatrix} (1 - \bar{u})^3 = (1 - \bar{u})^3$.

Now consider $B_{1,4}(\bar{u})$, which has support $(\bar{u}_1, \bar{u}_5)$.

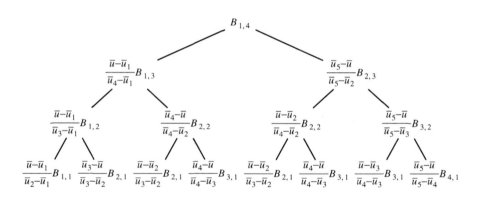

In this case we must prune $(\bar{u}_1, \bar{u}_5)$ down to $(\bar{u}_3, \bar{u}_4)$ to obtain a nonzero leaf. The root-leaf paths that accomplish this are those that involve exactly one left branch, to reduce $\bar{u}_5$ to $\bar{u}_4$, and there are exactly $\binom{3}{1} = 3$ such paths. Hence

$$B_{1,4}(\bar{u}) = \begin{bmatrix} 3 \\ 1 \end{bmatrix} \bar{u}(1 - \bar{u})^2 = 3\bar{u}(1 - \bar{u})^2.$$

Next consider $B_{2,4}(\bar{u})$, which has support $(\bar{u}_2, \bar{u}_6)$.

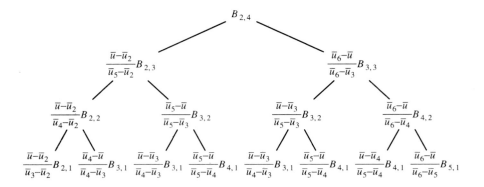

Now we must prune $(\bar{u}_2, \bar{u}_6)$ down to $(\bar{u}_3, \bar{u}_4)$ to obtain a nonzero leaf. The root-leaf paths that accomplish this are those that involve exactly two left branches, thus reducing $\bar{u}_6$ to $\bar{u}_5$ and $\bar{u}_5$ to $\bar{u}_4$, and there are exactly $\binom{3}{2} = 3$ such paths. Hence

$$B_{2,4}(\bar{u}) = \begin{bmatrix} 3 \\ 2 \end{bmatrix} \bar{u}^2 (1 - \bar{u}) = 3\bar{u}^2 (1 - \bar{u}).$$

Finally, consider $B_{3,4}(\bar{u})$, which has support $(\bar{u}_3, \bar{u}_7)$.

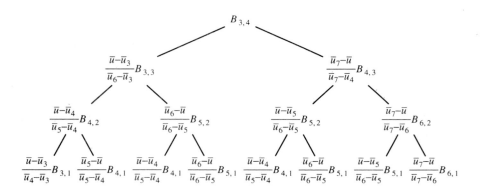

Now we must prune $(\bar{u}_3, \bar{u}_7)$ down to $(\bar{u}_3, \bar{u}_4)$ to obtain a nonzero leaf. The root-leaf paths which accomplish this are exactly those that involve three left branches, to reduce $\bar{u}_7$ to $\bar{u}_6$, $\bar{u}_6$ to $\bar{u}_5$ and $\bar{u}_5$ to $\bar{u}_4$, and there are exactly $\binom{3}{3} = 1$ such paths. Hence

$$B_{3,4}(\bar{u}) = \begin{bmatrix} 3 \\ 3 \end{bmatrix} \bar{u}^3 = \bar{u}^3.$$

Summarizing, we have

$$B_{i,4}(\bar{u}) = \begin{bmatrix} 3 \\ i \end{bmatrix} \bar{u}^i (1-\bar{u})^{3-i}$$

for $i = 0,1,2,3$. By a slight generalization of this argument we have

$$B_{i,d+1}(\bar{u}) = \begin{bmatrix} d \\ i \end{bmatrix} \bar{u}^i (1-\bar{u})^{d-i}$$

for $i = 0, 1, \ldots, d$ if the $B_{i,d+1}$ are defined over a knot sequence with uniformly spaced breakpoints of multiplicity $d+1$. We compare this with (10.2) and conclude that

$$B_{i,d+1}(\bar{u}) = P_{i,d}(\bar{u})$$

in these circumstances.

The Bernstein polynomials take the form

$$P_{i,d}(\bar{u}) = \begin{bmatrix} d \\ i \end{bmatrix} \frac{(\bar{u}-a)^i (b-\bar{u})^{d-i}}{(b-a)^d}$$

if we are interested in the interval $[a,b]$ rather than $[0,1]$. We leave for the reader the exercise of verifying that for the knot sequence consisting of $(d+1)$ knots a followed by $(d+1)$ knots b we have

$$B_{i,d+1}(\bar{u}) = \begin{bmatrix} d \\ i \end{bmatrix} \frac{(\bar{u}-a)^i (b-\bar{u})^{d-i}}{(b-a)^d} = P_{i,d}(\bar{u}).$$

10.8 A Matrix Formulation

It is common to use matrix notation in representing the segments of parametric curves. For example, a cubic Bézier curve segment defined by control vertices $\mathbf{U}_0$, $\mathbf{U}_1$, $\mathbf{U}_2$, and $\mathbf{U}_3$; i.e.,

$$\mathbf{Q}(u) = \mathbf{U}_0(1-u)^3 + \mathbf{U}_1 3u(1-u)^2 + \mathbf{U}_2 3u^2(1-u) + \mathbf{U}_3 u^3,$$

can be written as

$$\mathbf{Q}(u) = \begin{bmatrix} 1 & u & u^2 & u^3 \end{bmatrix} \begin{bmatrix} 1 & 0 & 0 & 0 \\ -3 & 3 & 0 & 0 \\ 3 & -6 & 3 & 0 \\ -1 & 3 & -3 & 1 \end{bmatrix} \begin{bmatrix} \mathbf{U}_0 \\ \mathbf{U}_1 \\ \mathbf{U}_2 \\ \mathbf{U}_3 \end{bmatrix} \tag{10.15}$$

$$= \begin{bmatrix} 1 & u & u^2 & u^3 \end{bmatrix} \cdot Bez \cdot \begin{bmatrix} \mathbf{U}_0 & \mathbf{U}_1 & \mathbf{U}_2 & \mathbf{U}_3 \end{bmatrix}^T,$$

where T is the *transpose* operator, which converts a row vector into a column vector and vice versa. The ith segment of a uniform cubic B-spline curve can be written as

$$\mathbf{Q}_i(u) = \begin{bmatrix} 1 & u & u^2 & u^3 \end{bmatrix} \frac{1}{6} \begin{bmatrix} 1 & 4 & 1 & 0 \\ -3 & 0 & 3 & 0 \\ 3 & -6 & 3 & 0 \\ -1 & 3 & -3 & 1 \end{bmatrix} \begin{bmatrix} \mathbf{V}_{i-3} \\ \mathbf{V}_{i-2} \\ \mathbf{V}_{i-1} \\ \mathbf{V}_i \end{bmatrix}$$

(10.16)

$$= \begin{bmatrix} 1 & u & u^2 & u^3 \end{bmatrix} \cdot Bspl \cdot \begin{bmatrix} \mathbf{V}_{i-3} & \mathbf{V}_{i-2} & \mathbf{V}_{i-1} & \mathbf{V}_i \end{bmatrix}^T ,$$

a cubic segment resulting from the Hermite interpolation formula can be represented by

$$\mathbf{Q}_i(u) = \begin{bmatrix} 1 & u & u^2 & u^3 \end{bmatrix} \begin{bmatrix} 1 & 0 & 0 & 0 \\ 0 & 1 & 0 & 0 \\ -3 & -2 & 3 & -1 \\ 2 & 1 & -2 & 1 \end{bmatrix} \begin{bmatrix} \mathbf{P}_i \\ \mathbf{D}_i \\ \mathbf{P}_{i+1} \\ \mathbf{D}_{i+1} \end{bmatrix}$$

$$= \begin{bmatrix} 1 & u & u^2 & u^3 \end{bmatrix} \cdot Herm \cdot \begin{bmatrix} \mathbf{P}_i & \mathbf{D}_i & \mathbf{P}_{i+1} & \mathbf{D}_{i+1} \end{bmatrix}^T ,$$

and, of course, the power series representation of a parametric cubic segment

$$\mathbf{Q}(u) = \mathbf{a} + \mathbf{b}u + \mathbf{c}u^2 + \mathbf{d}u^3$$

is represented trivially by

$$\mathbf{Q}(u) = \begin{bmatrix} 1 & u & u^2 & u^3 \end{bmatrix} \begin{bmatrix} 1 & 0 & 0 & 0 \\ 0 & 1 & 0 & 0 \\ 0 & 0 & 1 & 0 \\ 0 & 0 & 0 & 1 \end{bmatrix} \begin{bmatrix} \mathbf{a} \\ \mathbf{b} \\ \mathbf{c} \\ \mathbf{d} \end{bmatrix} .$$

The matrices above are all 4×4 because we are dealing with cubic segments. In general we would have to define $k \times k$ matrices for k^{th} order spline segments.

It is worthwhile observing that the row and column ordering of these matrices can be changed as a matter of convenience. If the order of the <u>columns</u> of the matrix is changed, then the entries in the vector of <u>control information</u> (the $\mathbf{U}$'s, $\mathbf{V}$'s, etc.) merely needs to be rearranged correspondingly. For example, the Hermite representation could also be written as

$$
\mathbf{Q}_i(u) = \begin{bmatrix} 1 & u & u^2 & u^3 \end{bmatrix} \begin{bmatrix} 1 & 0 & 0 & 0 \\ 0 & 0 & 1 & 0 \\ -3 & 3 & -2 & -1 \\ 2 & -2 & 1 & 1 \end{bmatrix} \begin{bmatrix} \mathbf{P}_i \\ \mathbf{P}_{i+1} \\ \mathbf{D}_i \\ \mathbf{D}_{i+1} \end{bmatrix}.
$$

If the order of the <u>rows</u> of the matrix is changed, then the entries in the vector of parameter information (the powers of $\bar{u}$) merely needs to be rearranged correspondingly. For example, the Bézier representation could be written as

$$
\mathbf{Q}_i(u) = \begin{bmatrix} u^3 & u^2 & u & 1 \end{bmatrix} \begin{bmatrix} -1 & 3 & -3 & 1 \\ 3 & -6 & 3 & 0 \\ -3 & 3 & 0 & 0 \\ 1 & 0 & 0 & 0 \end{bmatrix} \begin{bmatrix} \mathbf{U}_0 \\ \mathbf{U}_1 \\ \mathbf{U}_2 \\ \mathbf{U}_3 \end{bmatrix}
$$

(which makes the matrix *symmetric*).

As [Smith83] points out, the use of matrices emphasizes the ease with which one can render curves represented in a variety of ways. One need write only a single procedure, whose parameters are a coefficient matrix and a data vector. We have avoided matrix representations because they are less intuitive to the newcomer. Matrices do, however, provide a concise and powerful notation; the survey of surface modeling techniques given in [Barsky84b] illustrates this nicely.

10.9 Converting Between Representations

Another point, which it is convenient to recall here, is that each of the curve representations mentioned above relies on some particular basis for the cubic polynomials, and there is consequently a transformation from each to any of the others that can conveniently be expressed in terms of a matrix. To convert the control vertices for a uniform cubic B-spline curve segment into a Bézier representation we need only equate the coefficients of the u^i (which must be unique, since the u^i are a basis) in (10.15) and (10.16) and solve for

$$
\begin{bmatrix} \mathbf{U}_0 & \mathbf{U}_1 & \mathbf{U}_2 & \mathbf{U}_3 \end{bmatrix}^T = Bez^{-1} \cdot Bspl \cdot \begin{bmatrix} \mathbf{V}_0 & \mathbf{V}_1 & \mathbf{V}_2 & \mathbf{V}_3 \end{bmatrix}^T
$$

$$
= \frac{1}{6} \begin{bmatrix} 1 & 4 & 1 & 0 \\ 0 & 4 & 2 & 0 \\ 0 & 2 & 4 & 0 \\ 0 & 1 & 4 & 1 \end{bmatrix} \begin{bmatrix} \mathbf{V}_0 \\ \mathbf{V}_1 \\ \mathbf{V}_2 \\ \mathbf{V}_3 \end{bmatrix}.
$$

Conversely, to convert the control vertices for a Bézier representation into a B-spline representation we compute

$$\begin{bmatrix} \mathbf{V}_0 \ \mathbf{V}_1 \ \mathbf{V}_2 \ \mathbf{V}_3 \end{bmatrix}^T = Bspl^{-1} \cdot Bez \cdot \begin{bmatrix} \mathbf{U}_0 \ \mathbf{U}_1 \ \mathbf{U}_2 \ \mathbf{U}_3 \end{bmatrix}^T$$

$$= \begin{bmatrix} 6 & -7 & 2 & 0 \\ 0 & 2 & -1 & 0 \\ 0 & -1 & 2 & 0 \\ 0 & 2 & -7 & 6 \end{bmatrix} \begin{bmatrix} \mathbf{U}_0 \\ \mathbf{U}_1 \\ \mathbf{U}_2 \\ \mathbf{U}_3 \end{bmatrix} \cdot$$

To convert from the power series representation to the Bézier control vertices we can compute

$$\begin{bmatrix} \mathbf{U}_0 \ \mathbf{U}_1 \ \mathbf{U}_2 \ \mathbf{U}_3 \end{bmatrix}^T = Bez^{-1} \cdot \begin{bmatrix} \mathbf{a} \ \mathbf{b} \ \mathbf{c} \ \mathbf{d} \end{bmatrix}^T$$

$$= \frac{1}{3} \begin{bmatrix} 3 & 0 & 0 & 0 \\ 3 & 1 & 0 & 0 \\ 3 & 2 & 1 & 0 \\ 3 & 3 & 3 & 3 \end{bmatrix} \begin{bmatrix} \mathbf{a} \\ \mathbf{b} \\ \mathbf{c} \\ \mathbf{d} \end{bmatrix},$$

to convert from the power series representation to the B-spline control vertices involves computing

$$\begin{bmatrix} \mathbf{V}_0 \ \mathbf{V}_1 \ \mathbf{V}_2 \ \mathbf{V}_3 \end{bmatrix}^T = Bspl^{-1} \cdot \begin{bmatrix} \mathbf{a} \ \mathbf{b} \ \mathbf{c} \ \mathbf{d} \end{bmatrix}^T$$

$$= \frac{1}{3} \begin{bmatrix} 3 & -3 & 2 & 0 \\ 3 & 0 & -1 & 0 \\ 3 & 3 & 2 & 0 \\ 3 & 6 & 11 & 18 \end{bmatrix} \begin{bmatrix} \mathbf{a} \\ \mathbf{b} \\ \mathbf{c} \\ \mathbf{d} \end{bmatrix}, \qquad (10.17)$$

and to convert from a B-spline segment to a segment in Hermite representation involves computing

$$\begin{bmatrix} \mathbf{P}_i \ \mathbf{D}_i \ \mathbf{P}_{i+1} \ \mathbf{D}_{i+1} \end{bmatrix}^T = Herm^{-1} \cdot Bspl \cdot \begin{bmatrix} \mathbf{V}_0 \ \mathbf{V}_1 \ \mathbf{V}_2 \ \mathbf{V}_3 \end{bmatrix}^T$$

$$= \frac{1}{6} \begin{bmatrix} 1 & 4 & 1 & 0 \\ -3 & 0 & 3 & 0 \\ 0 & 1 & 4 & 1 \\ 0 & -3 & 0 & 3 \end{bmatrix} \begin{bmatrix} \mathbf{V}_0 \\ \mathbf{V}_1 \\ \mathbf{V}_2 \\ \mathbf{V}_3 \end{bmatrix} \cdot$$

The above discussion tells us only how to convert a single curve segment from one representation to another. This is sufficient if we are translating into the power basis. But what happens if we convert from the power basis to Bernstein

---

polynomials or B-splines? Do the control vertices match up so as to form a single composite curve?

Suppose that we have two consecutive cubic segments $Q_3(u)$ and $Q_4(u)$ that meet with C^2 continuity. Let V_0, V_1, V_2 and V_3 be the B-spline control vertices that define Q_3 and let W_1, W_2, W_3 and W_4 be the B-spline control vertices that define Q_4. Now consider the five B-spline control vertices V_0, V_1, V_2, V_3 and V_4 that define the composite curve $Q(u)$ consisting of $Q_3(u)$ and $Q_4(u)$. Because the B-splines are a basis, we must have $V_1 = W_1$, $V_2 = W_2$ and $V_3 = W_3$. Thus the B-spline control vertices must match up.

It is inefficient to compute all four control vertices for $Q_4(u)$; three of them have already been generated for $Q_3(u)$. We have only to compute W_4, which from (10.17) we see is exactly

$$W_4 = \frac{1}{3} (3\mathbf{a} + 6\mathbf{b} + 11\mathbf{c} + 18\mathbf{d}).$$

This computation is then repeated for each segment to yield all the control vertices.

By the same sort of argument it follows that we can convert uniquely from a C^2 Bézier curve to the (still C^2) unique power representation, and thence to a B-spline representation in which the control vertices must match up. The four control vertices defining the first segment are computed as above. The additional vertex for the second and succeeding segments are given by

$$W_4 = 2\mathbf{U}_1 - 7\mathbf{U}_2 + 6\mathbf{U}_3.$$

If the Bézier curve is not C^2 then the control vertices will not match up since the curve is not, in fact, a uniform cubic B-spline. It is, of course, possible to represent it as a B-spline by using a knot vector containing multiple knots.

Conversion from a B-spline to a Bézier curve proceeds simply by repeated application of the appropriate matrix equation given above. The Bézier control vertices computed will necessarily satisfy the C^2 continuity constraints developed previously.

10.10   Bézier Surfaces

Bézier surfaces are defined from Bézier curves in exactly the same way that B-spline surfaces are built from B-spline curves. We take the *tensor product* of two Bézier curves:

$$Q(u,v) = \sum_{i=0}^{d} \sum_{j=0}^{e} V_{i,j} P_{i,d}(u) P_{j,e}(v).$$

The Bernstein polynomials $P_{i,d}(u)$ and $P_{j,e}(v)$ need not be of the same degree. Indeed, the same is true of the B-splines from which we constructed B-spline surfaces. Techniques for building multipatch Bézier surfaces with C^1 or C^2 continuity at patch boundaries are discussed in [Faux/Pratt79].

11
Knot Insertion

In this chapter and the next we will consider the general subdivision problem for B-splines: suppose we have constructed a curve or a surface using some set of control vertices, and we now wish to express the same curve or surface in terms of a larger number of control vertices. This is precisely what was done in Sections 10.5 and 10.6 when we "broke a Bézier curve in two." The curve of Figure 10.6 was originally constructed in terms of the four control vertices $\mathbf{V}_0$, $\mathbf{V}_1$, $\mathbf{V}_2$, and $\mathbf{V}_3$, and it was re-represented in terms of the seven control vertices $\mathbf{S}_0$, $\mathbf{S}_1$, $\mathbf{S}_2$, $\mathbf{S}_3 = \mathbf{T}_0$, $\mathbf{T}_1$, $\mathbf{T}_2$, and $\mathbf{T}_3$. The more general version, given in Figure 10.9, shows the situation (in different notation) when the Bézier curve is broken at an arbitrary parametric value along its length. What was not stressed at the time, in order to concentrate on the control vertices and to keep the discussion simple, but which we now wish to observe, is that the subdivision process introduced a joint into the middle of the curve by introducing a knot (in fact, of multiplicity 4) into the underlying parameter space. It is this observation, due chiefly to Boehm [Boehm80, Boehm85, Boehm/Prautzsch85] and to Cohen, Lyche, and Riesenfeld [Cohen/ et al.80], that we must expand upon to develop and understand the re-representation of a spline curve by an increased number of control vertices when general B-splines are used rather than the special case of B-splines in the guise of Bernstein polynomials.

Just as two issues, knots and control vertices, must be kept in mind when discussing subdivision for general B-splines, it is also useful to recognize two processes for which the re-representation can be used: *subdivision* and *refinement*. In the Bézier case, the increase in the number of control vertices from four to seven, associated with a process of knot insertion, cleanly split the curve into two separate curves. For general B-spline curves, the knot-insertion process we will discuss, which will be the means of re-representing the curve in terms of more control vertices (refining the control graph), will not necessarily split the curve into two or more cleanly separated parts (subdividing the curve). If the curve is to be considered as a composite of two or more separate parts, it will be necessary to replicate and group the control vertices in some process subsequent to the one that inserts knots.

11.1   Knots and Vertices

We begin by elaborating on the connection between refining the control graph of a curve or surface and inserting knots into the underlying parameter space. Each new control vertex that we might add needs to be weighted by some new B-spline; each new B-spline that we might construct needs some knot at which to become nonzero. For refinement, we want

$$\mathbf{Q}(\bar{u}) \; = \; \sum_{i=0}^{m} \mathbf{V}_i \, B_{i,k}(\bar{u}) \; = \; \sum_{j=0}^{m+n} \mathbf{W}_j \, N_{j,k}(\bar{u}) , \tag{11.1}$$

where

$$n > 0$$

and

$$\{ \, \mathbf{V}_0, \dots, \mathbf{V}_m \, \} \text{ becomes } \{ \, \mathbf{W}_0, \dots, \mathbf{W}_{m+n} \, \} .$$

The process to be described does not attempt to find the vertices $\mathbf{W}$ explicitly. Rather, it finds the new B-splines, $N_{j,k}(\bar{u})$, and uses them to determine the $\mathbf{W}$'s implicitly. We will find that we can construct the new B-splines directly from the old B-splines by inserting new knots into the existing knot sequence, and this insertion process will directly define the new control vertices. This is the approach developed by Cohen, Lyche, and Riesenfeld [Cohen/et al.80].

Let us consider inserting n new knots into the existing sequence $\{\bar{u}_0, \dots, \bar{u}_{m+k}\} = \{\bar{u}_i\}_0^{m+k}$ to obtain a new sequence $\{\bar{w}_0, \dots, \bar{w}_{m+n+k}\}$ $= \{\bar{w}_j\}_0^{m+n+k}$, where $\{\bar{u}_i\}_0^{m+k} \subset \{\bar{w}_j\}_0^{m+n+k}$, as suggested by the following picture.

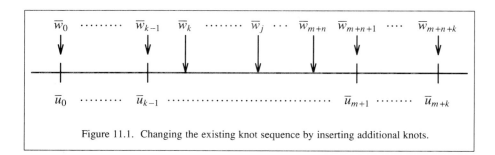

Figure 11.1. Changing the existing knot sequence by inserting additional knots.

This picture is intended to indicate that each $\bar{u}_i$ is identical to one of the $\bar{w}_j$, and that some further $\bar{w}$ knots have been scattered along the parameter range $[\bar{u}_{k-1}, \bar{u}_{m+1})$. We will concentrate on this style of insertion for the sake of discussion. Restricting the introduction of new knots to the range $[\bar{u}_{k-1}, \bar{u}_{m+1})$ is consistent in spirit to the discussion in [Cohen/et al.80] and to the related material on inserting knots in [Schumaker81]. A further convention followed in these references is that whenever new knots are added on top of existing knots $\bar{u}_i$, or are added multiply by themselves, it will be required that

$$\bar{w}_j < \bar{w}_{j+k}$$

for all j. That is, we will prohibit ourselves from adding new knots to any location on the $\bar{u}$ axis where the result of the addition would be to create a cluster (multiple knot) of multiplicity higher than k. If this were not observed, then we would be creating k-segment "knot intervals" of zero length for which the corresponding B-splines would be vacuous, which would be a futile exercise.

■ **Notation**

We will denote the multiplicity of each $\bar{w}_j$ by ν_j.

■

This sets up the convention that, corresponding to $\{\bar{u}_i\}$, μ_i, and $B_{i,k}(\bar{u})$ in the original spline space, we have $\{\bar{w}_j\}$, ν_j, and $N_{j,k}(\bar{u})$ in the refined space.

The sense of the refinement process is that knots are "interspersed" among the knots of the $\{\bar{u}_i\}_0^{m+k}$ sequence, and then the resulting sequence is renamed using $\bar{w}$ "labels," as shown in Figure 11.2.

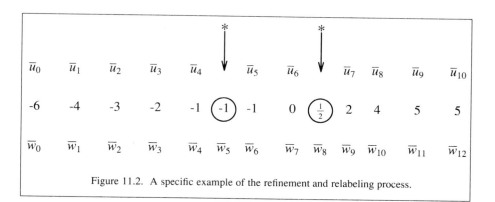

Figure 11.2. A specific example of the refinement and relabeling process.

Observe that a knot (which happens to have the value -1) is inserted between $\overline{u}_4$ and $\overline{u}_5$ (both of which also have the value -1). That new knot could have been inserted before $\overline{u}_4$ (in which case it would have received the label $\overline{w}_4$ and $\overline{u}_4$ would have been relabeled $\overline{w}_5$), or it could have been inserted after $\overline{u}_5$ (in which case it would have received the label $\overline{w}_6$, so that $\overline{u}_4$ and $\overline{u}_5$ would have become $\overline{w}_4$ and $\overline{w}_5$, respectively).

■ Definition

The knot sequence

$$\{\overline{w}_j\}_0^{m+n+k} = \{\overline{w}_0, \ldots, \overline{w}_{m+n+k}\} \quad \text{where} \quad n > 0$$

formed in accord with the above discussion will be called a *refinement of the knot sequence*

$$\{\overline{u}_i\}_0^{m+k} = \{\overline{u}_0, \ldots, \overline{u}_{m+k}\}.$$

■

The convention of locating breakpoint intervals according to the unique index δ satisfying

$$\overline{u}_\delta \leq \overline{u} < \overline{u}_{\delta+1}$$

will extend to the $\{\overline{w}_j\}$ sequence, too:

■ Convention

Let $\overline{u}$ be any parameter value in the range

$$\overline{w}_0 \leq \overline{u} < \overline{w}_{m+n+k-1}.$$

Then the index δ described by

$$\overline{w}_\delta \leq \overline{u} < \overline{w}_{\delta+1}$$

is well-defined and unique, and

$$[\overline{w}_\delta, \overline{w}_{\delta+1})$$

is the breakpoint interval containing $\overline{u}$ in the refined knot sequence.

■

Notice that the δ convention can be used with respect to the $\{\bar{u}_i\}$ sequence to locate the breakpoint interval into which a knot $\bar{w}_j$ in the refined sequence falls:

$$\bar{u}_\delta \le \bar{w}_j < \bar{u}_{\delta+1}.$$

For example, in Figure 11.2, if $j = 4$, then $\delta = 5$, which locates $\bar{w}_4 = -1$ in the breakpoint interval

$$[\bar{u}_5, \bar{u}_6) = [-1, 0).$$

Finally, we introduce an indexing convention that provides a convenient way of relating the knots of $\{\bar{u}_i\}_0^{m+k}$ to the knots of $\{\bar{w}_j\}_0^{m+n+k}$ that represent them in the refinement. We will denote by $\eta(i)$ the index of the knot in $\{\bar{w}_j\}_0^{m+n+k}$ corresponding to $\bar{u}_i$. For example, in Figure 11.2, if $i = 5$, then $\eta(i) = 6$, since $\bar{u}_5$ was relabeled as $\bar{w}_6$.

■ **Notation**

For any index $i \in \{0, \ldots, m+k\}$ chosen to select a knot $\bar{u}_i$,

$$\eta(i)$$

is defined to be the unique index

$$\eta(i) \in \{0, \ldots, m+n+k\}$$

for which $\bar{w}_{\eta(i)}$ is the member of $\{\bar{w}_j\}_0^{m+n+k}$ identified with $\bar{u}_i$.

■

11.2   Representation Results

Recall that the reason for considering knot refinement is to represent any curve defined by the B-splines $B_{0,k}(\bar{u}), \ldots, B_{m,k}(\bar{u})$ in terms of the B-splines $N_{0,k}(\bar{u}), \ldots, N_{m+n,k}(\bar{u})$. Figure 11.3 gives an overview of what happens when $k = 2$ and a single knot is inserted.

The simplicity of this linear-spline example makes it easy to see the main results we wish to bring out. We note first that the B-splines B_0, B_1, B_2, B_3 defined on the knots $\bar{u}_i$ have been replaced by the B-splines N_0, N_1, N_2, N_3, N_4 defined on the knots $\bar{w}_j$. We have not lost the ability to represent curves as linear combinations of B's, however, because each $B_i(\bar{u})$ is itself a linear combination of N's. In fact,

$$B_0(\bar{u}) = 1 \cdot N_0(\bar{u})$$

$$B_1(\bar{u}) = 1 \cdot N_1(\bar{u}) + \frac{1}{2} \cdot N_2(\bar{u})$$

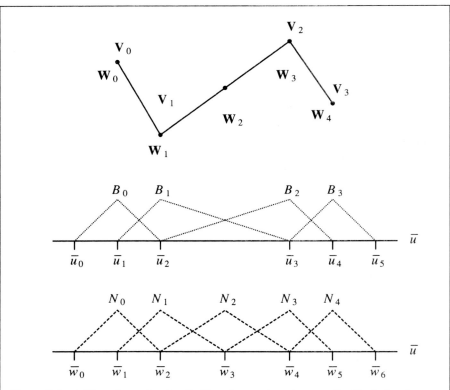

Figure 11.3. Adding a knot when $k = 2$. Note that we show the normalized basis functions — they are not scaled by the corresponding control vertex.

$$B_2(\overline{u}) = \frac{1}{2} \cdot N_2(\overline{u}) + 1 \cdot N_3(\overline{u})$$

$$B_3(\overline{u}) = 1 \cdot N_4(\overline{u}).$$

Consequently, any linear combination of the B's can be reproduced as a linear combination of the N's,

$$\mathbf{V}_0 B_0(\overline{u}) + \mathbf{V}_1 B_1(\overline{u}) + \mathbf{V}_2 B_2(\overline{u}) + \mathbf{V}_3 B_3(\overline{u})$$

$$= \mathbf{V}_0 [1 N_0(\overline{u})] + \mathbf{V}_1 [1 N_1(\overline{u}) + \frac{1}{2} N_2(\overline{u})]$$

$$+ \mathbf{V}_2 [\frac{1}{2} N_2(\overline{u}) + 1 N_3(\overline{u})] + \mathbf{V}_3 [1 N_4(\overline{u})]$$

$$= [\, 1\; \mathbf{V}_0 \,]\, N_0(\overline{u}) \;+\; [\, 1\; \mathbf{V}_1 \,]\, N_1(\overline{u}) \;+\; [\, \frac{1}{2}\, \mathbf{V}_1 \;+\; \frac{1}{2}\, \mathbf{V}_2 \,]\, N_2(\overline{u}) \tag{11.2}$$

$$+\; [\, 1\; \mathbf{V}_2 \,]\, N_3(\overline{u}) \;+\; [\, 1\; \mathbf{V}_3 \,]\, N_4(\overline{u})$$

$$= \mathbf{W}_0 N_0(\overline{u}) \;+\; \mathbf{W}_1 N_1(\overline{u}) \;+\; \mathbf{W}_2 N_2(\overline{u}) \;+\; \mathbf{W}_3 N_3(\overline{u}) \;+\; \mathbf{W}_4 N_4(\overline{u}).$$

This has two implications. The first is that each individual B-spline $B_i(\overline{u})$ can be represented as a linear combination of the B-splines $N_j(\overline{u})$, which implies that the space

$$\mathbf{B} \;=\; \left\{ \text{all linear combinations of } B_0, \ldots, B_3 \right\}$$

is a subspace of

$$\mathbf{N} \;=\; \left\{ \text{all linear combinations of } N_0, \ldots, N_4 \right\}.$$

The second implication is that any curve defined in terms of the B's can also be defined in terms of the N's. We can "substitute" an expression in terms of N's for each B and deduce control vertices $\mathbf{W}$ from the given control vertices $\mathbf{V}$.

The important quantities needed to rewrite "B-curves" as "N-curves" are the coefficients α that express the individual B's in terms of the N's. In our linear-spline example we have

$$B_0(\overline{u}) \;=\; \alpha_0(0)\, N_0(\overline{u})$$

$$B_1(\overline{u}) \;=\; \alpha_1(1)\, N_1(\overline{u}) + \alpha_1(2)\, N_2(\overline{u})$$

$$B_2(\overline{u}) \;=\; \alpha_2(2)\, N_2(\overline{u}) + \alpha_2(3)\, N_3(\overline{u}) \tag{11.3}$$

$$B_3(\overline{u}) \;=\; \alpha_3(4)\, N_4(\overline{u}),$$

where

$$\alpha_0(0) \;=\; 1$$

$$\alpha_1(1) \;=\; 1 \qquad \alpha_1(2) \;=\; \frac{1}{2}$$

$$\alpha_2(2) \;=\; \frac{1}{2} \qquad \alpha_2(3) \;=\; 1$$

$$\alpha_3(4) \;=\; 1.$$

The reason for the unusual indexing scheme for the α's will become clearer in Chapter 12. In view of (11.2) and (11.3) we have

$$\mathbf{W}_0 = \alpha_0(0)\,\mathbf{V}_0$$

$$\mathbf{W}_1 = \alpha_1(1)\,\mathbf{V}_1$$

$$\mathbf{W}_2 = \alpha_1(2)\,\mathbf{V}_1 + \alpha_2(2)\,\mathbf{V}_2$$

$$\mathbf{W}_3 = \alpha_2(3)\mathbf{V}_2$$

$$\mathbf{W}_4 = \alpha_3(4)\,\mathbf{V}_3\,.$$

The quadratic B-spline curve shown in Figure 11.4 provides a less trivial example of knot insertion.

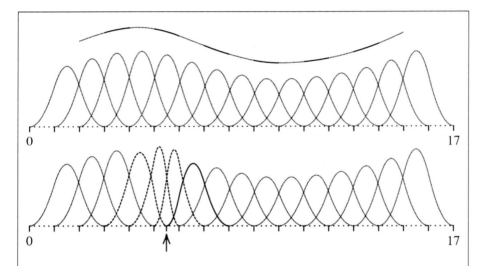

Figure 11.4. A thirteen segment quadratic B-spline curve. The arrow points to $\bar{u} = 5.5$, where a knot has been inserted, splitting the fourth segment from the left in half. That is, the fourth segment is regarded as two distinct quadratic polynomials that meet with first derivative continuity at $u = 5.5$. It follows that this curve can be represented using the lower set of B-splines, as shown.

Both sets of basis functions are shown scaled so that each of their sums, respectively, equals the curve shown. One new basis function is added (drawn as a solid curve), and the shape of three B-splines is changed (drawn as dashed curves). Notice also that since these are quadratic B-splines, each spans three intervals.

The curve in Figure 11.4 is a scaled sum of the B-splines defined on the upper (uniform) knot sequence. The knot inserted at $\bar{u} = 5.5$ causes a new basis function to be added below in Figure 11.4, and causes three basis functions to change shape: namely the basis functions that go positive at 3, 4 and 5, these being the only old basis functions defined by divided differences that now include the new knot at 5.5.

Each of the uniform (upper) B-splines in Figure 11.4 is, of course, itself a piecewise quadratic curve and can therefore be represented as a scaled sum of the B-splines defined on the lower (refined) knot sequence, as shown in Figures 11.6–11.8. (Figure 11.5 locates these three basis functions among those defined on the refined knot sequence in Figure 11.4.)

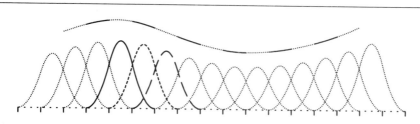

Figure 11.5. Figure 11.6 shows the representation of the solidly drawn basis function in terms of the refined knot sequence of Figure 11.4; Figures 11.7 and 11.8 similarly treat the two basis function drawn dashed here.

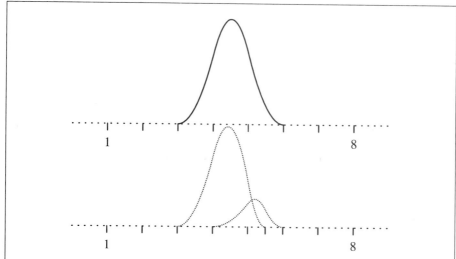

Figure 11.6. A detail from Figure 11.4. The sum of the lower two basis functions is exactly the upper.

To be more general, suppose that we do this for each of the upper basis functions in Figure 11.4. Each lower basis function is needed some (small) number of times. Add up all its contributions, and the result is the scale factor by which it is weighted in representing the curve of Figure 11.4.

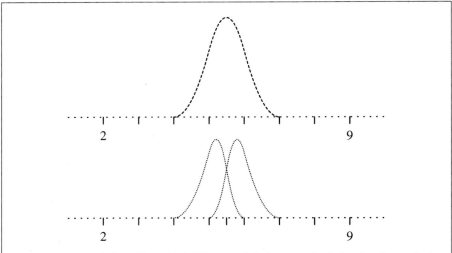

Figure 11.7. A detail from Figure 11.4. The sum of the lower two basis functions is exactly the upper.

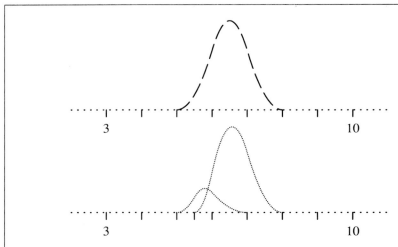

Figure 11.8. Another detail from Figure 11.4. Again, the sum of the lower two basis functions is exactly the upper.

The observations that we have just made with these two examples, inserting a single knot into a linear spline space and inserting a single knot into a quadratic spline space, hold true for general refinements and for general orders. We will close this chapter with some theorems that give precise results. The proofs are omitted, since the intuition developed above is sufficient for our purposes. The interested reader is referred to [Prautzsch85] and the sections on knot refinement in [Schumaker81]. The primary importance of these results to us will be the use to which we can put them in Chapter 12. Each of the results that we state will assume that an order k and a knot sequence $\{\bar{u}_i\}_0^{m+k}$ has been given, and that a new knot sequence $\{\bar{w}_j\}_0^{m+n+k}$ has been derived by refinement; i.e., by the insertion of n new knots. Recall that the insertions are to be made, by convention, within the interval $[\bar{u}_{k-1}, \bar{u}_{m+1})$, and that vacuous B-splines will be avoided by assuming that $\bar{u}_i < \bar{u}_{i+k}$ and $\bar{w}_j < \bar{w}_{j+k}$ for all $i = 0, \ldots, m$ and $j = 0, \ldots, m+n$.

■ **Theorem**

Given the knots $\bar{u}_i$ and their refinement $\bar{w}_j$ as above, the vector space

$$\mathbf{B} = \left\{ \text{all linear combinations of the B-splines } B_{i,k}(\bar{u}) \text{ for } i = 0, \ldots, m \right\}$$

is a proper subspace of the vector space

$$\mathbf{N} = \left\{ \text{all linear combinations of the B-splines} \right.$$

$$\left. N_{j,k}(\bar{u}) \text{ for } j = 0, \ldots, m+n \right\}.$$

■

The above theorem states a result for $-\infty < \bar{u} < +\infty$. Our convention of inserting knots only within $[\bar{u}_{k-1}, \bar{u}_{m+1})$ makes it possible to make the following similar statement for $\bar{u}_{k-1} \le \bar{u} < \bar{u}_{m+1}$.

■ **Theorem**

The vector space $\mathbf{S}(\mathbf{P}^k, \{\bar{u}_i\}_0^{m+k})$ is a proper subspace of $\mathbf{S}(\mathbf{P}^k, \{\bar{w}_j\}_0^{m+n+k})$.
■

■ **Theorem**

For each $i = 0, \ldots, m$

$$B_{i,k}(\overline{u}) = \sum_{j=0}^{m+n} \alpha_{i,k}(j) N_{j,k}(\overline{u})$$

for some coefficients $\alpha_{i,k}(j)$.

■

■ **Theorem**

If

$$\mathbf{Q}(\overline{u}) = \sum_{i=0}^{m} \mathbf{V}_i B_{i,k}(\overline{u})$$

is a curve obtained from $\mathbf{S}(\mathbf{P}^k, \{\overline{u}_i\}_0^{m+k})$, then

$$\mathbf{Q}(\overline{u}) = \sum_{j=0}^{m+n} \mathbf{W}_j N_{j,k}(\overline{u})$$

is the same curve obtained from $\mathbf{S}(\mathbf{P}^k, \{\overline{w}_j\}_0^{m+n+k})$, where

$$\mathbf{W}_j = \sum_{i=0}^{m} \alpha_{i,k}(j) \mathbf{V}_i$$

for each $j = 0, \ldots, m+n$.

■

This last result follows easily, since by substitution

$$\sum_{i=0}^{m} \mathbf{V}_i B_{i,k}(\overline{u}) = \sum_{i=0}^{m} \mathbf{V}_i \sum_{j=0}^{m+n} \alpha_{i,k}(j) N_{j,k}(\overline{u})$$

$$= \sum_{j=0}^{m+n} \left[\sum_{i=0}^{m} \alpha_{i,k}(j) \mathbf{V}_i \right] N_{j,k}(\overline{u}) = \sum_{j=0}^{m+n} \mathbf{W}_j N_{j,k}(\overline{u})$$

and

$$\mathbf{W}_j = \sum_{i=0}^{m} \alpha_{i,k}(j)\mathbf{V}_i$$

by the linear independence of the N's.

In Chapter 12 we will establish precise formulas, derived from the recurrence properties of the B-splines $B_{i,k}(\overline{u})$ and $N_{j,k}(\overline{u})$, for computing the coefficients $\alpha_{i,k}(j)$. We will find that the α's satisfy a simple recurrence of their own.

12

The Oslo Algorithm

This chapter will cover the technical details of the most general refinement algorithm known for B-splines. In the previous chapter we observed that a curve $\mathbf{Q}(\bar{u})$ constructed

- from one set of control vertices, $\mathbf{V}_0, \ldots, \mathbf{V}_m$,

- weighted by one set of B-splines, B_i,

- and defined on one set of knots, $\{\bar{u}_i\}_0^{m+k}$

can be represented in terms of

- a larger set of control vertices, $\mathbf{W}_0, \ldots, \mathbf{W}_{m+n}$,

- weighted by a refined set of B-splines, N_j,

- and defined on a finer mesh of knots, $\{\bar{w}_j\}_0^{m+n+k}$.

The key idea is that the process of knot refinement produces a spline space based upon the refined knot sequence $\{\bar{w}_j\}$ which contains a spline space based upon the original knot sequence $\{\bar{u}_j\}$ [Prautzsch85]. It is directly from these observations, and from B-spline recurrence, that the detailed behavior of the $\alpha_{i,k}(j)$ can be determined, and it is the behavior of the α's upon which the B-spline and control-vertex refinements are based.

12.1   Discrete B-spline Recurrence

We introduced the quantities $\alpha_{i,k}(j)$ that provided a translation from the $\mathbf{V}_i$ to the $\mathbf{W}_j$ via the equation

$$\mathbf{W}_j = \sum_{i=0}^{m} \alpha_{i,k}(j)\,\mathbf{V}_i \quad \text{for } j = 0, \dots, m+n,$$

and from the B_i to the N_j via the equation

$$B_{i,k}(\bar{u}) = \sum_{j=0}^{m+n} \alpha_{i,k}(j)\,N_{j,k}(\bar{u}). \tag{12.1}$$

Our first task in this chapter will be to establish that these coefficients $\alpha_{i,k}(j)$ satisfy a recurrence very much like the one satisfied by the B-splines:

■ **Theorem**

$$\alpha_{i,1}(j) = \begin{cases} 1 & \bar{u}_i \le \bar{w}_j < \bar{u}_{i+1} \\ \\ 0 & \text{otherwise} \end{cases}$$

and

$$\alpha_{i,r}(j) = \frac{\bar{w}_{j+r-1} - \bar{u}_i}{\bar{u}_{i+r-1} - \bar{u}_i}\,\alpha_{i,r-1}(j) + \frac{\bar{u}_{i+r} - \bar{w}_{j+r-1}}{\bar{u}_{i+r} - \bar{u}_{i+1}}\,\alpha_{i+1,r-1}(j) \tag{12.2}$$

for $r = 2, 3, \dots, k$, where k is the order of the spline in question.

■

As usual, we interpret the term involving any ratio

$$\frac{\overline{w}_{j+r-1} - \overline{u}_i}{\overline{u}_{i+r-1} - \overline{u}_i} \quad \text{or} \quad \frac{\overline{u}_{i+r} - \overline{w}_{j+r-1}}{\overline{u}_{i+r} - \overline{u}_{i+1}}$$

to be zero if the respective denominator is zero.

This recurrence, as well as a related recurrence for obtaining the control vertices **W** from the control vertices **V**, was first established in [Cohen/et al.80]; they have recently been established by a much simpler method in [Prautzsch84, Prautzsch85], which is the source of the argument given here, and in [Lee85], which makes use of *dual functionals*, an important theoretical tool. The argument takes place with respect to the parameter range

$$-\infty < \overline{u} < +\infty$$

and involves the spaces

$$\mathbf{B} = \left\{ \text{all linear combinations of the B-splines } B_{i,k}(\overline{u}) \right.$$

$$\left. \text{for } i = 0, \ldots, m \right\}$$

$$\mathbf{N} = \left\{ \text{all linear combinations of the B-splines } N_{j,k}(\overline{u}) \right.$$

$$\left. \text{for } j = 0, \ldots, m+n \right\}.$$

It is worth observing that the functions $B_{i,k}(\overline{u})$ are linearly independent on $(-\infty, +\infty)$, just as they are when we consider our usual range $[\overline{u}_{k-1}, \overline{u}_{m+1})$. Likewise, the functions $N_{j,k}(\overline{u})$ are linearly independent on $(-\infty, +\infty)$. Moreover, [Prautzsch85], **B** is a subspace of **N**. Recall also our usual assumption that

$$\overline{u}_{k-1} \;=\; \overline{w}_{k-1} \;\leq\; \overline{u} \;<\; \overline{w}_{m+n+1} \;=\; \overline{u}_{m+1} \tag{12.3}$$

but note that the recurrence construction for the B-splines is not restricted to (12.3) but holds for any $\overline{u}$. With these preliminary remarks in mind, we are ready to establish the theorem for the α recurrence (12.2).

■ Argument

Consider the identity (12.1). This is a representation formula for $B_{i,k}(\overline{u})$, regarded as an element of the space **N**. We may apply the B-spline recurrence to $B_{i,k}(\overline{u})$ to obtain

$$B_{i,k}(\overline{u}) \;=\; \frac{\overline{u} - \overline{u}_i}{\overline{u}_{i+k-1} - \overline{u}_i} \, B_{i,k-1}(\overline{u}) \;+\; \frac{\overline{u}_{i+k} - \overline{u}}{\overline{u}_{i+k} - \overline{u}_{i+1}} \, B_{i+1,k-1}(\overline{u}) . \tag{12.4}$$

On the other hand, we may apply the B-spline recurrence to $N_{j,k}(\overline{u})$ to obtain

$$N_{j,k}(\overline{u}) \;=\; \frac{\overline{u} - \overline{w}_j}{\overline{w}_{j+k-1} - \overline{w}_j} \, N_{j,k-1}(\overline{u}) \;+\; \frac{\overline{w}_{j+k} - \overline{u}}{\overline{w}_{j+k} - \overline{w}_{j+1}} \, N_{j+1,k-1}(\overline{u}) . \tag{12.5}$$

Both (12.4) and (12.5) are valid for all values of $\overline{u}$.

Combining (12.4) and (12.5) with (12.1) yields the following identity, which is valid for all $\overline{u}$:

$$\frac{\overline{u} - \overline{u}_i}{\overline{u}_{i+k-1} - \overline{u}_i} \, B_{i,k-1}(\overline{u}) \;+\; \frac{\overline{u}_{i+k} - \overline{u}}{\overline{u}_{i+k} - \overline{u}_{i+1}} \, B_{i+1,k-1}(\overline{u})$$

$$=\; \sum_{j=0}^{m+n} \alpha_{i,k}(j) \left[\frac{\overline{u} - \overline{w}_j}{\overline{w}_{j+k-1} - \overline{w}_j} \, N_{j,k-1}(\overline{u}) \right. \tag{12.6}$$

$$\left. +\; \frac{\overline{w}_{j+k} - \overline{u}}{\overline{w}_{j+k} - \overline{w}_{j+1}} \, N_{j+1,k-1}(\overline{u}) \right].$$

Let us begin with the right-hand side of (12.6). The summation can be regrouped in terms of $N_{j,k}(\overline{u})$; doing so, and interchanging terms, we have:

$$
\sum_{j=0}^{m+n} \alpha_{i,k}(j) \left[\frac{\overline{u} - \overline{w}_j}{\overline{w}_{j+k-1} - \overline{w}_j} N_{j,k-1}(\overline{u}) \right.
$$

$$
\left. + \frac{\overline{w}_{j+k} - \overline{u}}{\overline{w}_{j+k} - \overline{w}_{j+1}} N_{j+1,k-1}(\overline{u}) \right]
$$

(12.7)

$$
= \sum_{j=0}^{m+n+1} \left[\frac{\overline{w}_{j+k-1} - \overline{u}}{\overline{w}_{j+k-1} - \overline{w}_j} \alpha_{i,k}(j-1) \right.
$$

$$
\left. + \frac{\overline{u} - \overline{w}_j}{\overline{w}_{j+k-1} - \overline{w}_j} \alpha_{i,k}(j) \right] N_{j,k-1}(\overline{u}).
$$

The second summation of (12.7) contains two spurious α's: $\alpha_{i,k}(-1)$ and $\alpha_{i,k}(m+n+1)$, which we have introduced to unify the summations and which we define to be zero.

Returning to (12.6), consider the left-hand side of the equation. The representation of B's in terms of α's and N's given by (12.1) for k^{th}-order splines can be equally well used for $k-1^{\text{st}}$-order splines. This can be seen from the fact that $\{\overline{w}_j\}_0^{m+n+k}$ is still a refinement of $\{\overline{u}_i\}_0^{m+k}$, so the spline space for which the functions $N_{j,k-1}(\overline{u})$ form a basis still contains the space for which the functions $B_{i,k-1}(\overline{u})$ form a basis. The only peculiarity worthy of mention is the fact that the multiplicity of some of the knots in $\{\overline{u}_i\}_0^{m+k}$ and/or $\{\overline{w}_j\}_0^{m+n+k}$ may be higher than we have usually admitted for $k-1^{\text{st}}$-order spline spaces. This is consistent with the nature of the B-spline recurrence, however; we merely accept terms containing ratios with zero denominators as zero, and we must accept the fact that some of the B-splines that formally appear in our summations will be vacuous.

Applying the representation (12.1) to $B_{i,k-1}(\overline{u})$ and $B_{i+1,k-1}(\overline{u})$ separately transforms the left-hand side of (12.6) into:

$$
\frac{\overline{u} - \overline{u}_i}{\overline{u}_{i+k-1} - \overline{u}_i} \sum_{j=0}^{m+n+1} \alpha_{i,k-1}(j) N_{j,k-1}(\overline{u})
$$

$$
+ \frac{\overline{u}_{i+k} - \overline{u}}{\overline{u}_{i+k} - \overline{u}_{i+1}} \sum_{j=0}^{m+n+1} \alpha_{i+1,k-1}(j) N_{j,k-1}(\overline{u}).
$$

We may define the spurious quantities $\alpha_{i,k}(m+n+1)$ and $\alpha_{i+1,k}(m+n+1)$ to be zero.

The two summations above may be combined to obtain

$$
\sum_{j=0}^{m+n+1} \left[\frac{\bar{u} - \bar{u}_i}{\bar{u}_{i+k-1} - \bar{u}_i} \, \alpha_{i,k-1}(j) \right.
$$

$$
\left. + \frac{\bar{u}_{i+k} - \bar{u}}{\bar{u}_{i+k} - \bar{u}_{i+1}} \, \alpha_{i+1,k-1}(j) \right] N_{j,k-1}(\bar{u}).
$$

(12.8)

Combining (12.7) with (12.8) yields

$$
\sum_{j=0}^{m+n+1} \left[\frac{\bar{u} - \bar{u}_i}{\bar{u}_{i+k-1} - \bar{u}_i} \, \alpha_{i,k-1}(j) + \frac{\bar{u}_{i+k} - \bar{u}}{\bar{u}_{i+k} - \bar{u}_{i+1}} \, \alpha_{i+1,k-1}(j) \right.
$$

$$
\left. - \frac{\bar{w}_{j+k-1} - \bar{u}}{\bar{w}_{j+k-1} - \bar{w}_j} \, \alpha_{i,k}(j-1) - \frac{\bar{u} - \bar{w}_j}{\bar{w}_{j+k-1} - \bar{w}_j} \, \alpha_{i,k}(j) \right] N_{j,k-1}(\bar{u}) = 0
$$

(12.9)

The identity (12.9) is valid for all values of $\bar{u}$.

It is tempting to conclude that the coefficient of $N_{j,k-1}(\bar{u})$ in (12.9), the term in brackets, is zero for all $\bar{u}$; that is:

$$
\frac{\bar{u} - \bar{u}_i}{\bar{u}_{i+k-1} - \bar{u}_i} \, \alpha_{i,k-1}(j) + \frac{\bar{u}_{i+k} - \bar{u}}{\bar{u}_{i+k} - \bar{u}_{i+1}} \, \alpha_{i+1,k-1}(j)
$$

$$
- \frac{\bar{w}_{j+k-1} - \bar{u}}{\bar{w}_{j+k-1} - \bar{w}_j} \, \alpha_{i,k}(j-1) - \frac{\bar{u} - \bar{w}_j}{\bar{w}_{j+k-1} - \bar{w}_j} \, \alpha_{i,k}(j) = 0.
$$

(12.10)

In fact this is true. We will sketch the reasoning for this in the simplest case, that in which there are no multiple knots. A complete justification would require a limiting process to produce multiple knots by the confluence of distinct knots, and that is outside the scope of this work.

Let us, therefore, assume that all the refined knots, $\bar{w}$, are distinct.

For $\bar{u} < \bar{w}_0 = \bar{u}_0$ and $\bar{u} > \bar{w}_{m+n+k} = \bar{u}_{m+k}$ all the terms in all the formulas (12.4 – 12.9) are zero. The equalities are trivially true, and we learn nothing.

With i chosen arbitrarily, let $\overline{w}_0 \leq \overline{u} < \overline{w}_1$. In this interval only $N_{0,k-1}(\overline{u})$ is nonzero. (In fact, it is positive.) This means that (12.4 – 12.9) simplify to yield the single equation

$$
\frac{\overline{u} - \overline{u}_i}{\overline{u}_{i+k-1} - \overline{u}_i} \, \alpha_{i,k-1}(0) \; + \; \frac{\overline{u}_{i+k} - \overline{u}}{\overline{u}_{i+k} - \overline{u}_{i+1}} \, \alpha_{i+1,k-1}(0)
$$

$$
- \frac{\overline{w}_{k-1} - \overline{u}}{\overline{w}_{k-1} - \overline{w}_0} \, \alpha_{i,k}(-1) \; - \; \frac{\overline{u} - \overline{w}_0}{\overline{w}_{k-1} - \overline{w}_0} \, \alpha_{i,k}(0) \; = \; 0
$$

(12.11)

This is a linear expression in $\overline{u}$,

$$
C + D\,\overline{u} = 0,
$$

(12.12)

which holds identically for all $\overline{w}_0 \leq \overline{u} < \overline{w}_1$. This is possible only if the constants C and D are both zero, which implies that the equality is true for all $-\infty < \overline{u} < +\infty$, not merely on the interval $[\overline{w}_0, \overline{w}_1)$. This establishes the validity of (12.10) for $j = 0$ for all i and $\overline{u}$. Consequently, all the terms involving $j = 0$ in (12.4 – 9) are zero; the summations in these equations really begin at $j = 1$.

But we may now consider the interval $\overline{w}_1 \leq \overline{u} < \overline{w}_2$ with arbitrary i. In this interval, only $N_{1,k-1}(\overline{u})$ is nonzero, and the argument just given about $N_{0,k-1}(\overline{u})$ can be applied, appropriately modified, to verify that (12.10) holds for $j = 1$.

Consequently, the summations really begin at $j = 2$.

The induction step that completes the argument should be clear by now. The expression in (12.10) is zero for all values of $\overline{u}$. If we substitute the particular value

$$
\overline{u} \; = \; \overline{w}_{j+k-1}
$$

into (12.10), the result given by (12.2) follows immediately.

To see that the starting values for the recurrence are correct; that is, the definitions for the quantities $\alpha_{i,1}(j)$, it is merely necessary to consider a picture. Since

$$B_{i,k}(\overline{u}) = \sum_{j=0}^{m+n} \alpha_{i,k}(j) N_{j,k}(\overline{u}) \quad \text{for} \quad i = 0, \ldots, m,$$

this tells us what the contribution of a particular B-spline $N_{j,k}(\overline{u})$ is to the B-spline $B_{i,k}(\overline{u})$. For the 1st-order B-splines we see that $B_{i,k}(\overline{u})$ and $N_{j,k}(\overline{u})$ must, in fact, be exactly equal if $\overline{u}_i \leq \overline{w}_j < \overline{u}_{i+1}$ for values of $\overline{u}$ within the interval $[\overline{w}_j, \overline{w}_{j+1})$. This makes sense, as an example will illustrate: the single 1st-order B-spline shown in Figure 12.1 is replaced by the four 1st-order B-splines shown in Figure 12.2 when we insert the knots at 0.20, 0.50 and 0.75.

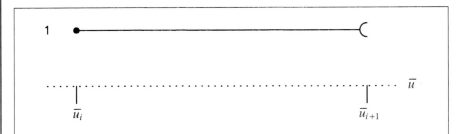

Figure 12.1. The single 1st-order B-spline $B_{i,1}(\overline{u})$ which has the value 1.0 on the interval $[\overline{u}_i, \overline{u}_{i+1})$.

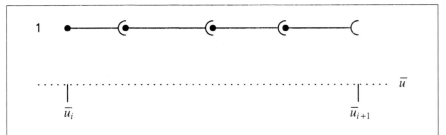

Figure 12.2. The four constant B-splines that replace $B_{i,1}(\overline{u})$ of Figure 12.1 when we insert knots at the values 0.20, 0.50 and 0.75 in the interval $[\overline{u}_i, \overline{u}_{i+1})$.

■

An inspection of (12.2) suggests that $\alpha_{i,k}(j)$ must have the character that the B-spline $B_{i,k}(\overline{u})$ would have if it were defined, not on the continuum of $\overline{u}$ values, but on the discrete collection $\{\overline{w}_j\}_0^{m+n+k}$ instead. This observation is one justification for the name given to the α's; they are known as the *discrete B-splines*.

12.2 Discrete B-spline Properties

We see by the above that the behavior of the α's parallels very closely the behavior of the B-splines. What do the α's look like? Are they "hump-shaped" like the continuous B-splines? Are they local? Are they nonnegative? Do they sum to one? On the following pages we will plot a few low-order discrete B-splines to gain some feeling for them.

For $k = 1$ we are at the bottom of the α recurrence. The discrete B-spline $\alpha_{i,1}(j)$ is a function defined over the indices of the $\overline{w}$ knots, and it is clear from the recurrence that the interval of indices on which this function is nonzero is that corresponding to the $\overline{w}$ values falling in the interval $[\overline{u}_i , \overline{u}_{i+1})$. Example values for $\overline{u}$, $\overline{w}$, and $\alpha_{i,1}$ (for fixed i) are shown in Table A, which produces the graph in Figure 12.3.

Since

$$\mathbf{W}_j = \sum_{i=0}^{m} \alpha_{i,k}(j) \mathbf{V}_i$$

such graphs and tables indicate precisely how many $\mathbf{W}$'s depend in what way upon which $\mathbf{V}$'s. In particular, Table A and Figure 12.3 show that $\mathbf{W}_j$, $\mathbf{W}_{j+1}$, $\mathbf{W}_{j+2}$, and $\mathbf{W}_{j+3}$ are each $1 \times \mathbf{V}_i$, where the index j corresponds to $\overline{w}_j = 0.0000$ and the index i corresponds to $\overline{u}_i = 0.0000$.

For $k = 2$ there are several configurations, depending on multiplicities. We show three examples. Example values of $\overline{u}$, $\overline{w}$ and $\alpha_{i,1}$ for $\overline{u}$ knots of multiplicity 1 are shown in Table B. (Again, i has a fixed value here.) Figure 12.4 contains the corresponding graph.

Observe that Table B and Figure 12.4 specify that

$$\mathbf{W}_j = \frac{1}{5}\mathbf{V}_i + \text{other } \mathbf{V}\text{'s}$$

$$\mathbf{W}_{j+1} = \frac{1}{2}\mathbf{V}_i + \text{other } \mathbf{V}\text{'s}$$

$$. \quad . \quad . \qquad .$$

$$. \quad . \quad . \qquad .$$

$$. \quad . \quad . \qquad .$$

$$\mathbf{W}_{j+6} = \frac{1}{4}\mathbf{V}_i + \text{other } \mathbf{V}\text{'s},$$

where j is the index for which $\overline{w}_j = 0.0000$ and i is the index for which $\overline{u}_i = 0.0000$.

Placing a double knot at $\overline{u}_i$ produces Table C and Figure 12.5, which imply that

$$\mathbf{W}_j = 1\,\mathbf{V}_i$$

$$\mathbf{W}_{j+1} = \frac{4}{5}\mathbf{V}_i + \text{other } \mathbf{V}\text{'s}$$

$$\mathbf{W}_{j+2} = \frac{1}{2}\mathbf{V}_i + \text{other } \mathbf{V}\text{'s}$$

$$\mathbf{W}_{j+3} = \frac{1}{4}\mathbf{V}_i + \text{other } \mathbf{V}\text{'s},$$

where j is the smallest index for which $\overline{w}_j = 0.0000$, and i is likewise the smallest index for which $\overline{u}_i = 0.0000$. A double knot at the next $\overline{u}$ position to the right, on the other hand, produces Table D and Figure 12.6.

Finally, we give a few representative configurations for cubic ($k = 4$) discrete B-splines. The multiplicity one $\overline{u}$ knots that we have been using in these examples yield the table E and Figure 12.7.

Doubling the knot at $\overline{u}_{i+2}$ yields Table F and Figure 12.8, while tripling the knot of $\overline{u}_{i+2}$ yields Table G and Figure 12.9.

In none of the above examples did we explore the effect of increasing the multiplicity of one or more of the $\overline{w}$ knots. The effect of doing this, like the effect of increasing the multiplicity of the $\overline{u}$ knots, is to "shorten" the interval on which one or more of the α's is nonzero.

These figures and tables have served, we hope, to convey a feeling for the behavior of $\alpha_{i,k}(j)$ for fixed i as a function of j. It is equally useful to observe how the α's behave for fixed j and a sequence of successive i's. Since

$$\mathbf{W}_j = \sum_{i=0}^{m} \mathbf{V}_i\,\alpha_{i,k}(j) \quad \text{for} \quad j = 0,\ldots,\,m+n,$$

this tells us how various $\mathbf{V}_i$'s are weighted in computing a particular $\mathbf{W}_j$. The following is an example for $k = 4$ using the $\overline{u}$ and $\overline{w}$ knots of Figure 12.7. Fixing our attention on $\overline{w}_j = 1.0000$, Table H shows the result the result of computing successive α's from $\alpha_{i-3,4}(\overline{w}_j)$, to $\alpha_{i+4,4}(\overline{w}_j)$. The graphs of these α's in a neighborhood of $\overline{w}_j$ are in Figure 12.10. Table H should be read as a "vertical slice" through those plots at the position indicated by the label $\overline{w}_j$.

Table A

$\overline{u}$	$\overline{w}$	$\alpha_{i,1}$
-3.0000 ($\overline{u}_{i-3}$)	-3.0000	0
-2.0000 ($\overline{u}_{i-2}$)	-2.0000	0
	-1.5000	0
-1.0000 ($\overline{u}_{i-1}$)	-1.0000	0
	-0.5000	0
	-0.2500	0
0.0000 ($\overline{u}_i$)	0.0000	1
	0.2000	1
	0.5000	1
	0.7500	1
1.0000 ($\overline{u}_{i+1}$)	1.0000	0
	1.3333	0
	1.6250	0
	1.7500	0
2.0000 ($\overline{u}_{i+2}$)	2.0000	0
	2.5000	0
3.0000 ($\overline{u}_{i+3}$)	3.0000	0
4.0000 ($\overline{u}_{i+4}$)	4.0000	0

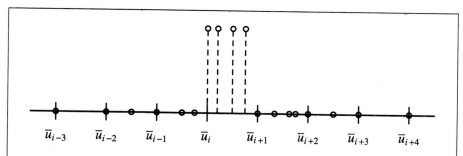

Figure 12.3. The first-order discrete B-spline. We have not explicitly labeled the $\overline{w}$ values; they are visible only as the locations of the values plotted for $\alpha_{i,1}$. Notice that the nonzero α's all fall within one half-open interval.

Table B

$\overline{u}$	$\overline{w}$	$\alpha_{i,2}$
-3.0000 ($\overline{u}_{i-3}$)	-3.0000	0
-2.0000 ($\overline{u}_{i-2}$)	-2.0000	0
	-1.5000	0
-1.0000 ($\overline{u}_{i-1}$)	-1.0000	0
	-0.5000	0
	-0.2500	0
0.0000 ($\overline{u}_i$)	0.0000	1/5
	0.2000	1/2
	0.5000	3/4
	0.7500	1
1.0000 ($\overline{u}_{i+1}$)	1.0000	2/3
	1.3333	3/8
	1.6250	1/4
	1.7500	0
2.0000 ($\overline{u}_{i+2}$)	2.0000	0
	2.5000	0
3.0000 ($\overline{u}_{i+3}$)	3.0000	0
4.0000 ($\overline{u}_{i+4}$)	4.0000	0

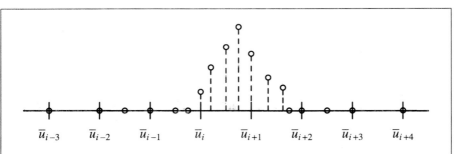

Figure 12.4. Values of the second-order discrete B-spline with no multiplicities. Recall that these values graph the contribution of $\mathbf{V}_i$, which is weighted by the B-spline $B_{i,2}(\overline{u})$, to various $\mathbf{W}_j$'s. This time the nonzero α's all fall within two successive half-open intervals.

Table C

$\overline{u}$	$\overline{w}$	$\alpha_{i,2}$
-3.0000 ($\overline{u}_{i-3}$)	-3.0000	0
-2.0000 ($\overline{u}_{i-2}$)	-2.0000	0
	-1.5000	0
-1.0000 ($\overline{u}_{i-1}$)	-1.0000	0
	-0.5000	0
	-0.2500	0
0.0000 ($\overline{u}_i$)	0.0000	1
0.0000 ($\overline{u}_{i+1}$)	0.0000	4/5
	0.2000	1/2
	0.5000	1/4
	0.7500	0
1.0000 ($\overline{u}_{i+2}$)	1.0000	0
	1.3333	0
	1.6250	0
	1.7500	0
2.0000 ($\overline{u}_{i+3}$)	2.0000	0
	2.5000	0
3.0000 ($\overline{u}_{i+4}$)	3.0000	0
4.0000 ($\overline{u}_{i+5}$)	4.0000	0

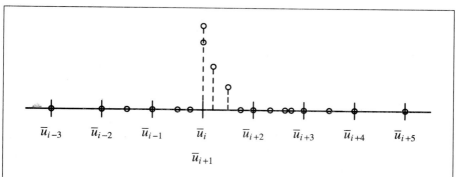

Figure 12.5. The second-order discrete B-spline with $\overline{u}_i = \overline{u}_{i+1}$. The introduction of a double knot means that $\alpha_{i,2}$ will contribute to $\mathbf{W}_i$ and $\mathbf{W}_{i+1}$. Since both of these are weighting refined B-splines become positive at the same breakpoint, our graph shows two α values aligned over that breakpoint.

Table D

$\overline{u}$	$\overline{w}$	$\alpha_{i,2}$
-3.0000 $(\overline{u}_{i-3})$	-3.0000	0
-2.0000 $(\overline{u}_{i-2})$	-2.0000	0
	-1.5000	0
-1.0000 $(\overline{u}_{i-1})$	-1.0000	0
	-0.5000	0
	-0.2500	0
0.0000 $(\overline{u}_i)$	0.0000	1/5
	0.2000	1/2
	0.5000	3/4
	0.7500	1
1.0000 $(\overline{u}_{i+1})$	1.0000	0
1.0000 $(\overline{u}_{i+2})$	1.0000	0
	1.3333	0
	1.6250	0
	1.7500	0
2.0000 $(\overline{u}_{i+3})$	2.0000	0
	2.5000	0
3.0000 $(\overline{u}_{i+4})$	3.0000	0
4.0000 $(\overline{u}_{i+5})$	4.0000	0

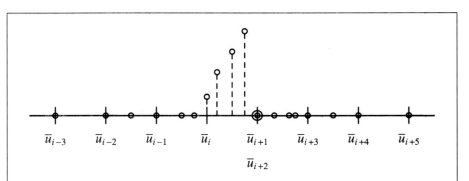

Figure 12.6. The second-order discrete B-spline with $\overline{u}_{i+1} = \overline{u}_{i+2}$. This time the two aligned α values both happen to have the value zero.

Table E

$\overline{u}$	$\overline{w}$	$\alpha_{i,4}$
-3.0000 $(\overline{u}_{i-1})$	-3.0000	0
-2.0000 $(\overline{u}_i)$	-2.0000	1/8
	-1.5000	7/16
-1.0000 $(\overline{u}_{i+1})$	-1.0000	5/8
	-0.5000	41/60
	-0.2500	19/30
0.0000 $(\overline{u}_{i+2})$	0.0000	119/240
	0.2000	5/16
	0.5000	5/32
	0.7500	1/24
1.0000 $(\overline{u}_{i+3})$	1.0000	1/96
	1.3333	0
	1.6250	0
	1.7500	0
2.0000 $(\overline{u}_{i+4})$	2.0000	0
	2.5000	0
3.0000 $(\overline{u}_{i+5})$	3.0000	0
4.0000 $(\overline{u}_{i+6})$	4.0000	0

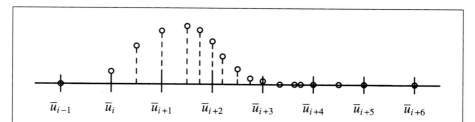

Figure 12.7. The discrete cubic (order 4) B-spline with no multiplicity. This time the nonzero α's span four successive intervals, namely $[\overline{u}_i, \overline{u}_{i+4})$.

Table F

$\bar{u}$	$\bar{w}$	$\alpha_{i,4}$
-3.0000 ($\bar{u}_{i-1}$)	-3.0000	0
-2.0000 ($\bar{u}_i$)	-2.0000	3/16
	-1.5000	21/32
-1.0000 ($\bar{u}_{i+1}$)	-1.0000	3/4
	-0.5000	5/8
	-0.2500	2/5
0.0000 ($\bar{u}_{i+2}$)	0.0000	1/5
0.0000 ($\bar{u}_{i+3}$)	0.0000	1/20
	0.2000	0
	0.5000	0
	0.7500	0
1.0000 ($\bar{u}_{i+4}$)	1.0000	0
	1.3333	0
	1.6250	0
	1.7500	0
2.0000 ($\bar{u}_{i+5}$)	2.0000	0
	2.5000	0
3.0000 ($\bar{u}_{i+6}$)	3.0000	0
4.0000 ($\bar{u}_{i+7}$)	4.0000	0

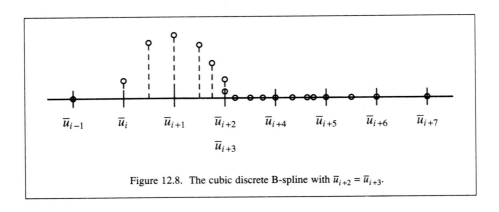

Figure 12.8. The cubic discrete B-spline with $\bar{u}_{i+2} = \bar{u}_{i+3}$.

Table G

$\overline{u}$	$\overline{w}$	$\alpha_{i,4}$
-3.0000 ($\overline{u}_{i-1}$)	-3.0000	0
-2.0000 ($\overline{u}_i$)	-2.0000	3/16
	-1.5000	21/32
-1.0000 ($\overline{u}_{i+1}$)	-1.0000	9/16
	-0.5000	1/4
	-0.2500	0
0.0000 ($\overline{u}_{i+2}$)	0.0000	0
0.0000 ($\overline{u}_{i+3}$)	0.0000	0
0.0000 ($\overline{u}_{i+4}$)	0.0000	0
	0.2000	0
	0.5000	0
	0.7500	0
1.0000 ($\overline{u}_{i+5}$)	1.0000	0
	1.3333	0
	1.6250	0
	1.7500	0
2.0000 ($\overline{u}_{i+6}$)	2.0000	0
	2.5000	0
3.0000 ($\overline{u}_{i+7}$)	3.0000	0
4.0000 ($\overline{u}_{i+8}$)	4.0000	0

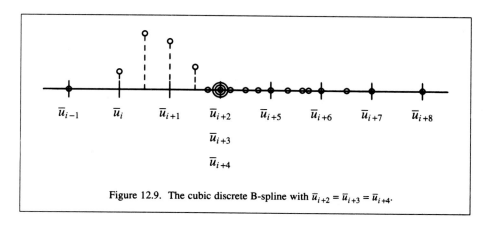

Figure 12.9. The cubic discrete B-spline with $\overline{u}_{i+2} = \overline{u}_{i+3} = \overline{u}_{i+4}$.

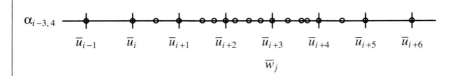

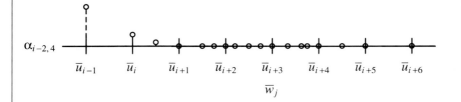

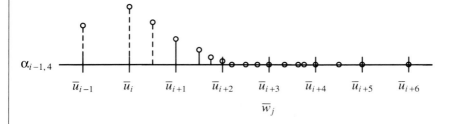

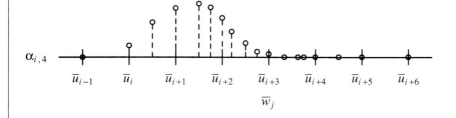

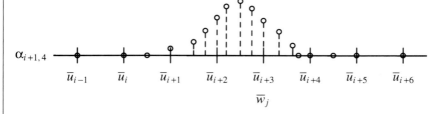

continued...

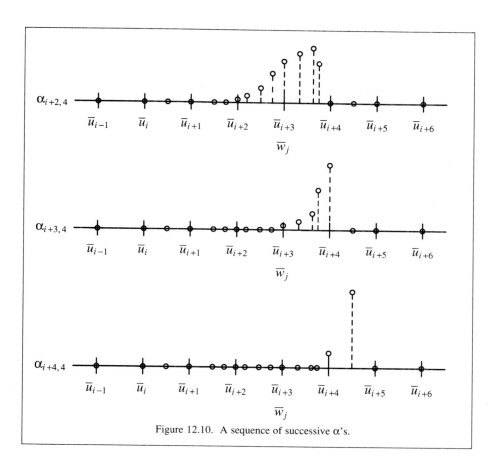

Figure 12.10. A sequence of successive α's.

Table H

$\overline{w}_j = 1.0000$	
$\alpha_{i-3,4}(j)$	0
$\alpha_{i-2,4}(j)$	0
$\alpha_{i-1,4}(j)$	0
$\alpha_{i,4}(j)$	1/96
$\alpha_{i+1,4}(j)$	251/576
$\alpha_{i+2,4}(j)$	19/36
$\alpha_{i+3,4}(j)$	5/192
$\alpha_{i+4,4}(j)$	0

Table H and Figure 12.10, indicate that

$$\mathbf{W}_j = \frac{1}{96}\mathbf{V}_i + \frac{251}{576}\mathbf{V}_{i+1} + \frac{19}{36}\mathbf{V}_{i+2} + \frac{5}{192}\mathbf{V}_{i+3}.$$

The value of $\overline{w}_j$ being considered is $\overline{w}_j = \overline{u}_{i+3}$. Consequently, it falls in the interval

$$\overline{u}_{i+3} \le \overline{w}_j < \overline{u}_{i+4}$$

Letting $\delta = i + 3$ be the index such that $\overline{u}_\delta \le \overline{w}_j < \overline{u}_{\delta+1}$, we observe that

$$\alpha_{0,4}(\overline{w}_j) = \cdots = \alpha_{\delta-4,4}(\overline{w}_j) = 0$$

$$\alpha_{\delta+1,4}(\overline{w}_j) = \cdots = \alpha_{m,4}(\overline{w}_j) = 0$$

and

$$\alpha_{\delta-3,4}(\overline{w}_j),\ \alpha_{\delta-2,4}(\overline{w}_j),\ \alpha_{\delta-1,4}(\overline{w}_j),\ \alpha_{\delta,4}(\overline{w}_j) \ne 0.$$

Remarkably, these nonzero values sum to one.

In the light of these preliminary demonstrations we state the following:

■ Properties

1. For any given j let δ be such that $\overline{u}_\delta \le \overline{w}_j < \overline{u}_{\delta+1}$.
   Then $\alpha_{i,k}(j) = 0$ for $i \notin \{\delta-k+1, \ldots, \delta\}$, for $i = 0, \ldots, m$.

2. $\alpha_{i,k}(j) \ge 0$ for all i, j, k.

3. $\sum_{i=0}^{m} \alpha_{i,k}(j) = 1.$

■

Property 1 establishes the locality of the refinement process by saying that at most k discrete B-splines can be nonzero for any fixed value of j, meaning that the refinement process will produce new control vertices $\mathbf{W}_j$, each of which depends on no more than k of the original control vertices $\mathbf{V}_i$. More specifically, $\mathbf{W}_j$ will depend upon some subset of $\mathbf{V}_{\delta-k+1}, \ldots, \mathbf{V}_\delta$, these being the control vertices that are weighted by the B-splines whose support includes the new knot. In particular, introducing a new knot (and therefore a new control vertex) changes at most k of the old vertices.

Properties 2 and 3 establish a geometric containment property, namely that $\mathbf{W}_j$ will be a weighted average of the members of $\mathbf{V}_{\delta-k+1}, \ldots, \mathbf{V}_\delta$. That is, $\mathbf{W}_j$ will lie in their convex hull. We will establish these properties using, for the most part, the arguments found in [Cohen/et al.80].

■ Argument

We will establish Properties 1 and 2 first, using an induction argument. Property 3 will follow from the fact that the functions $N_{j,k}(\bar{u})$ constitute a basis for $\mathbf{S}(\mathbf{P}^k, \{\bar{w}_j\}_0^{m+n+k})$, that they sum to one, and that the functions $B_{i,k}(\bar{u})$ are representable in terms of the N's. We begin with Property 1.

For first-order α's (that is, for $k = 1$), Properties 1 and 2 may be taken as evident, by inspection, from the consideration of pictures such as Figure 12.3. Alternatively, note from the recurrence that

$$\alpha_{i,1}(j) = 0 \quad \text{for} \quad \bar{w}_j < \bar{u}_i \quad \text{and} \quad \bar{w}_j \geq \bar{u}_{i+1}$$

and that

$$\alpha_{i,1}(j) = 1 \quad \text{for} \quad \bar{w}_j \geq \bar{u}_i \quad \text{and} \quad \bar{w}_j < \bar{u}_{i+1}.$$

In this context it follows directly from the recurrence that

- for fixed j, $\alpha_{i,1}(j) = 0$ when we do not have $\bar{u}_i \leq \bar{w}_j < \bar{u}_{i+1}$ (that is, Property 1 holds);

- $\alpha_{i,1}(j) \geq 0$; that is, Property 2 holds.

We next establish inductively that Properties 1 and 2 hold for higher-order α's. Assume that they hold for $\alpha_{i,k-1}(j)$ for all i and j and for some $k > 1$.

For Property 1 we wish to show that, for fixed j and for δ defined by $\bar{u}_\delta \leq \bar{w}_j < \bar{u}_{\delta+1}$, it is true that $\alpha_{i,k}(j) = 0$ whenever $i \notin \{\delta-k+1, \ldots, \delta\}$.

Recall the recurrence

$$\alpha_{i,k}(j) = \frac{\bar{w}_{j+k-1} - \bar{u}_i}{\bar{u}_{i+k-1} - \bar{u}_i} \alpha_{i,k-1}(j) + \frac{\bar{u}_{i+k} - \bar{w}_{j+k-1}}{\bar{u}_{i+k} - \bar{u}_{i+1}} \alpha_{i+1,k-1}(j).$$

By the induction hypothesis the factor $\alpha_{i,k-1}(j)$ is zero for all $i \notin \{\delta-(k-1)+1, \ldots, \delta\}$; that is, for all $i \notin \{\delta-k+2, \ldots, \delta\}$. Similarly, the factor $\alpha_{i+1,k-1}(j)$ is zero for all $i+1 \notin \{\delta-k+2, \ldots, \delta\}$; that is, for all $i \notin \{\delta-k+1, \ldots, \delta-1\}$. Taking the union of these two index sets, we see that both terms in the recurrence are zero when

$$i \notin \{\delta-k+1, \ldots, \delta\},$$

which establishes Property 1.

To establish Property 2 it is instrumental to establish a stronger version of Property 1. First, however, we need to define some additional notation.

Let $j = \rho(i)$ be the $\bar{w}$-index of the knot $\bar{w}_j$ such that (i) $\bar{u}_i = \bar{w}_j$, and (ii) $\bar{u}_i$ and $\bar{w}_j$ have an identical number of equal knots to their left in the $\bar{u}$- and $\bar{w}$-sequences, respectively. That is:

$$\cdots \quad \bar{u}_{i-s-1} \quad < \bar{u}_{i-s} \quad = \bar{u}_{i-s+1} \quad = \cdots = \bar{u}_i \quad \cdots$$

$$\cdots \quad \bar{w}_{\rho(i)-s-1} < \bar{w}_{\rho(i)-s} = \bar{w}_{\rho(i)-s+1} = \cdots = \bar{w}_{\rho(i)} \cdots$$

$$\uparrow \qquad\qquad\qquad\qquad\qquad \uparrow$$

for any $s \geq 0$. For future use we note that
(1) $j > \rho(i)$ implies that $\bar{w}_j \geq \bar{u}_i$ and
(2) $\rho(i-1) \leq \rho(i)-1$.
We are now ready to argue the

Claim: $\alpha_{i,k}(j) = 0$ if $\bar{w}_j < \bar{u}_i$ or $j+k > \rho(i+k)$

Roughly speaking, this claim tells us that $N_{j,k}(\bar{u})$ does not contribute to the representation of $B_{i,k}(\bar{u})$ if its support "extends" either to the left or to the right of $B_{i,k}(\bar{u})$'s support.

The proof is by induction. For the basis step we take $k = 1$. Recall that

$$\alpha_{i,1}(j) = \begin{cases} 1 & \text{if } \bar{u}_i \leq \bar{w}_j < \bar{u}_{i+1} \\ \\ 0 & \text{otherwise.} \end{cases}$$

Suppose $\bar{w}_j < \bar{u}_i$. Then $\alpha_{i,1}(j)=0$ is immediate.

Suppose $j+1 > \rho(i+1)$. Then $\bar{w}_{j+1} \geq \bar{u}_{i+1}$. On the one hand, if $\bar{w}_{j+1} > \bar{u}_{i+1}$ then $\bar{w}_j \geq \bar{u}_{i+1}$ and $\alpha_{i,1}(j)=0$.

On the other hand, suppose that $\bar{w}_{j+1} = \bar{u}_{i+1}$. If we had $j+1=\rho(i+1)$ then $\bar{w}_{j+1}$ and $\bar{u}_{i+1}$ would have the same number of identically valued knots to their left in the $\bar{w}$- and $\bar{u}$-sequences, respectively. Since we actually have $j+1 > \rho(i+1)$ there must be at least one more such knot in the $\bar{w}$-sequence than in the $\bar{u}$-sequence. Hence we must have $\bar{w}_j = \bar{w}_{j+1} = \bar{u}_{i+1}$, so that $\bar{u}_i \leq \bar{w}_j < \bar{u}_{i+1}$ fails and $\alpha_{i,1}(j)=0$.

For the induction step, assume that the claim is true for $r-1$ such that $1 \leq r-1 \leq k-1$. Then

$$\alpha_{i,r-1}(j) = 0 \text{ if } \bar{w}_j < \bar{u}_i \text{ or } j+r-1 > \rho(i+r-1)$$

$$\alpha_{i+1,r-1}(j) = 0 \text{ if } \bar{w}_j < \bar{u}_{i+1} \text{ or } j+r-1 > \rho(i+1+r-1) = \rho(i+r) \ .$$

Consider

$$\alpha_{i,r}(j) = \frac{\bar{w}_{j+r-1} - \bar{u}_i}{\bar{u}_{i+r-1} - \bar{u}_i} \, \alpha_{i,r-1}(j) + \frac{\bar{u}_{i+r} - \bar{w}_{j+r-1}}{\bar{u}_{i+r} - \bar{u}_{i+1}} \, \alpha_{i+1,r-1}(j) \ .$$

Suppose that $\bar{w}_j < \bar{u}_i$. Then $\bar{w}_j < \bar{u}_i \leq \bar{u}_{i+1}$ and both $\alpha_{i,r-1}(j)$ and $\alpha_{i+1,r-1}(j)$ are zero by the induction hypothesis, so $\alpha_{i,r}(j)=0$.

Suppose that $j+r > \rho(i+r)$. Then $j+r-1 > \rho(i+r)-1 \geq \rho(i+r-1)$. By the induction hypothesis $\alpha_{i,r-1}(j)=0$, and the first term must be zero.

Let us now focus on the second term. The fact that $j+r > \rho(i+r)$ implies that $j+r-1 \geq \rho(i+r)$. If $j+r-1 > \rho(i+r)$ then $\alpha_{i+1,r-1}(j)=0$ immediately from the induction hypothesis.

On the other hand, if $j+r-1 = \rho(i+r)$ then $\overline{w}_{j+r-1} = \overline{u}_{i+r}$, and the numerator of the second term is zero, so that the second term itself is zero.

Our stronger version of Property 1 is now established. Property 2 follows easily. It is trivially true that $\alpha_{i,1}(j) \geq 0$. Suppose that the α's of order $r-1$ are nonnegative, $1 \leq r-1 \leq k-1$, and examine the recurrence. The denominators are clearly nonnegative, and by convention a term is taken as zero if its denominator is zero.

It follows from our claim that for $\alpha_{i,r}(j)$ to be nonzero we must have $\overline{w}_j \geq \overline{u}_i$ and $j+r \leq \rho(i+r)$. Surely $\overline{w}_j \leq \overline{w}_{j+r}$, so $\overline{u}_i \leq \overline{w}_{j+r-1}$ and $(\overline{w}_{j+r-1} - \overline{u}_i) \geq 0$. Moreover, $j+r \leq \rho(i+r)$ implies that $j+r-1 < \rho(i+r)$, whence $\overline{w}_{j+r-1} \leq \overline{u}_{i+r}$, so that $(\overline{u}_{i+r} - \overline{w}_{j+r-1}) \geq 0$.

But then we must have $\alpha_{i,r}(j) \geq 0$ when $\overline{w}_j \geq \overline{u}_i$ and $j+r \leq \rho(i+r)$, as desired, and Property 2 is established.

Property 3 is immediately established for all k by an observation about linear independence. We know that

$$\sum_{j=0}^{m+n} N_{j,k}(\overline{u}) = 1 .$$

Furthermore, by the linear independence of the N's, the only linear combination of $N_{j,k}(\overline{u})$ which can sum to 1 is the combination shown here, i.e., the one having all coefficients equal to 1. But recall that

$$B_{i,k}(\overline{u}) = \sum_{j=0}^{m+n} \alpha_{i,k}(j) N_{j,k}(\overline{u})$$

for each i. Summing both sides of this equation on i yields

$$1 = \sum_{i=0}^{m} B_{i,k}(\overline{u}) = \sum_{i=0}^{m} \sum_{j=0}^{m+n} \alpha_{i,k}(j) N_{j,k}(\overline{u})$$

$$= \sum_{j=0}^{m+n} \left[\sum_{i=0}^{m} \alpha_{i,k}(j) \right] N_{j,k}(\overline{u}) .$$

By the uniqueness of the coefficients which will yield a linear combination of 1 with the $N_{j,k}(\overline{u})$, it follows that

$$\sum_{i=0}^{m} \alpha_{i,k}(j) = 1,$$

which establishes Property 3.

∎

12.3   Control Vertex Recurrence

The final theoretical remark we have to make concerns the control vertices themselves. Recall that

$$\mathbf{W}_j = \sum_{i=0}^{m} \alpha_{i,k}(j)\, \mathbf{V}_i.$$

We now see that

$$\mathbf{W}_j = \sum_{i=\delta-k+1}^{\delta} \alpha_{i,k}(j)\, \mathbf{V}_i,$$

which means that the $\mathbf{W}_j$ "depend locally" on the $\mathbf{V}_i$ in the sense that adding knots in a certain region of $\overline{u}$ will only change the control vertices being weighted by the B-splines whose nonzero intervals are touched by these new knots. Moreover, since

$$\sum_{i=\delta-k+1}^{\delta} \alpha_{i,k}(j) = 1$$

and the α values are nonnegative, $\mathbf{W}_j$ must be a weighted average of the vertices $\mathbf{V}_i$. Like the spline curve which both the $\mathbf{V}$'s and the $\mathbf{W}$'s define, each $\mathbf{W}_j$ lies in the convex hull of k successive vertices $\mathbf{V}_i$.

Finally, note that the recurrence for the α's can be applied to produce

$$\mathbf{W}_j = \sum_{i=\delta-k+1}^{\delta} \alpha_{i,k}(j)\, \mathbf{V}_i \tag{12.13}$$

$$= \sum_{i=\delta-k+1}^{\delta} \left[\frac{\overline{w}_{j+k-1} - \overline{u}_i}{\overline{u}_{i+k-1} - \overline{u}_i}\, \alpha_{i,k-1}(j) + \frac{\overline{u}_{i+k} - \overline{w}_{j+k-1}}{\overline{u}_{i+k} - \overline{u}_{i+1}}\, \alpha_{i+1,k-1}(j) \right] \mathbf{V}_i.$$

This develops into a recurrence for the control vertices themselves. Property 3 of the previous section guarantees that

$$\alpha_{\delta-k+1,k-1}(j) = \alpha_{\delta+1,k-1}(j) = 0,$$

which permits us to rearrange and collect terms in (12.13) to obtain

$$\mathbf{W}_j = \sum_{i=\delta-k+2}^{\delta} \alpha_{i,k-1}(j) \, \mathbf{V}_i^{[k-1]}$$

where

$$\mathbf{V}_i^{[k-1]} = \frac{(\overline{w}_{j+k-1}-\overline{u}_i) \, \mathbf{V}_i + (\overline{u}_{i+k-1}-\overline{w}_{j+k-1}) \, \mathbf{V}_{i-1}}{(\overline{u}_{i+k-1}-\overline{u}_i)}$$

This may be repeated to yield

■ **Control Vertex Recurrence**

Let

$$\mathbf{V}_i^{[k]} = \mathbf{V}_i$$

and

$$\mathbf{V}_i^{[r-1]} = \frac{(\overline{w}_{j+r-1}-\overline{u}_i) \, \mathbf{V}_i^{[r]} + (\overline{u}_{i+r-1}-\overline{w}_{j+r-1}) \, \mathbf{V}_{i-1}^{[r]}}{(\overline{u}_{i+r-1}-\overline{u}_i)}$$

for $r = k, \ldots, 2$ (interpreted as zero when the denominator is zero).

Then

$$\mathbf{W}_j = \mathbf{V}_\delta^{[1]},$$

where δ is the unique index for which $\overline{u}_\delta \le \overline{w}_j < \overline{u}_{\delta+1}$.

■

This permits the direct computation of the $\mathbf{W}$ vertices from the $\mathbf{V}$ vertices using only the knots $\{\overline{u}_i\}_0^{m+k}$ and $\{\overline{w}_j\}_0^{m+n+k}$.

12.4 Illustrations

We close with some examples of this process. For the first example consider the curve of Figure 12.11. The B-splines that weight the nine control vertices are defined on the uniform knots $\bar{u}_i = i$, and the beginning and ending control vertices are repeated once. The coordinates x_i, y_i of the $\mathbf{V}_i$ and the knots $\bar{u}_i$ are given in Table I.

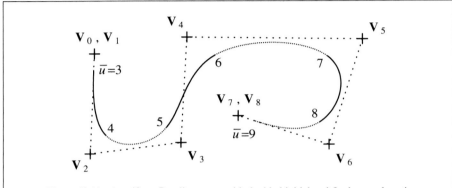

Figure 12.11. A uniform B-spline curve with doubled initial and final control vertices.

Table I

x	y	
0.4568	1.3369	
0.4568	1.3369	
0.4122	0.2562	$\mathbf{V}_2$
1.3482	0.3788	$\mathbf{V}_3$
1.4100	1.5153	
3.2199	1.4930	
2.8746	0.3565	
1.9387	0.6685	
1.9387	0.6685	

We have flagged control vertices $\mathbf{V}_2$ and $\mathbf{V}_3$ because, if we introduce a new knot at $\bar{u} = 4.5$, precisely these vertices change. The new control vertices $\mathbf{W}_j$ are given in Table J, and the corresponding control graph is shown in Figure 12.12. Notice that the three new control vertices $\mathbf{W}_2$, $\mathbf{W}_3$, and $\mathbf{W}_4$ lie closer to the curve than did the two vertices $\mathbf{V}_2$ and $\mathbf{V}_3$ which they replace.

Table J

x	y	
0.4568	1.3369	
0.4568	1.3369	
0.4196	0.4363	$\mathbf{W}_2$
0.8802	0.3175	$\mathbf{W}_3$
1.3585	0.5682	$\mathbf{W}_4$
1.4100	1.5153	
3.2199	1.4930	
2.8746	0.3565	
1.9387	0.6685	
1.9387	0.6685	

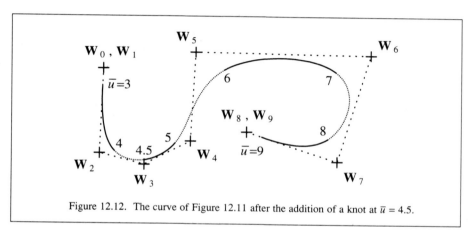

Figure 12.12. The curve of Figure 12.11 after the addition of a knot at $\bar{u} = 4.5$.

For a second illustration of refinement, suppose we consider uniform knots $\bar{u}_i$ and add a new knot at the midpoint of each knot interval of the parameter range $[\bar{u}_i, \bar{u}_{i+1})$, $i = 3, \ldots, m$. For example, the knot vectors for $m = 8$, are shown in Figure 12.13.

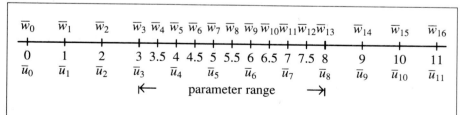

Figure 12.13. The special case of uniform knot spacing and refinement by midpoints.

The **V**'s and **W**'s will then be related as in Figure 12.14, which indicates, for example, that $\mathbf{W}_3$ is a weighted average of the **V**'s given by

$$\mathbf{W}_3 = \alpha_{1,4}(3)\,\mathbf{V}_1 + \alpha_{2,4}(3)\,\mathbf{V}_2 + \alpha_{3,4}(3)\,\mathbf{V}_3$$

$$= \frac{1}{8}\,\mathbf{V}_1 + \frac{3}{4}\,\mathbf{V}_2 + \frac{1}{8}\,\mathbf{V}_3.$$

In Figure 12.15 we see the control graph introduced in Figure 4.31 of Section 4.7, which has triple vertices around its perimeter.

	$\mathbf{W}_0$	$\mathbf{W}_1$	$\mathbf{W}_2$	$\mathbf{W}_3$	$\mathbf{W}_4$	$\mathbf{W}_5$	$\mathbf{W}_6$	$\mathbf{W}_7$	$\mathbf{W}_8$	$\mathbf{W}_9$	$\mathbf{W}_{10}$	$\mathbf{W}_{11}$	$\mathbf{W}_{12}$
$\mathbf{V}_0$	1	$\frac{1}{6}$											
$\mathbf{V}_1$		$\frac{5}{6}$	$\frac{1}{2}$	$\frac{1}{8}$									
$\mathbf{V}_2$			$\frac{1}{2}$	$\frac{3}{4}$	$\frac{1}{2}$	$\frac{1}{8}$							
$\mathbf{V}_3$				$\frac{1}{8}$	$\frac{1}{2}$	$\frac{3}{4}$	$\frac{1}{2}$	$\frac{1}{8}$					
$\mathbf{V}_4$						$\frac{1}{8}$	$\frac{1}{2}$	$\frac{3}{4}$	$\frac{1}{2}$	$\frac{1}{8}$			
$\mathbf{V}_5$								$\frac{1}{8}$	$\frac{1}{2}$	$\frac{3}{4}$	$\frac{1}{2}$		
$\mathbf{V}_6$										$\frac{1}{8}$	$\frac{1}{2}$	$\frac{5}{6}$	
$\mathbf{V}_7$												$\frac{1}{6}$	1

Figure 12.14. The control-vertex chart for the refinement shown in Figure 12.13.

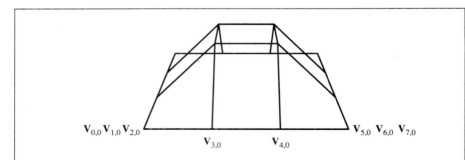

$\mathbf{V}_{0,0}\,\mathbf{V}_{1,0}\,\mathbf{V}_{2,0}$ $\mathbf{V}_{3,0}$ $\mathbf{V}_{4,0}$ $\mathbf{V}_{5,0}\;\mathbf{V}_{6,0}\;\mathbf{V}_{7,0}$

Figure 12.15. The given, unrefined control graph. Only a sampling of the tripled boundary vertices, varying in the first subscript alone, are labeled to keep the picture uncluttered.

If we halve the knot intervals in both parametric directions as illustrated in Figures 12.13 and 12.14, we obtain the control graph of Figure 12.16. The surface defined by this control graph, which is swept out by values of $3 \leq \bar{u} < 8$ and $3 \leq \bar{v} < 8$, can easily be partitioned into four subsurfaces whose parameter ranges are

Surface 1: $3 \leq \bar{u} < 5.5$, $3 \leq \bar{v} < 5.5$

Surface 2: $3 \leq \bar{u} < 5.5$, $5.5 \leq \bar{v} < 8$

Surface 3: $5.5 \leq \bar{u} < 8$, $3 \leq \bar{v} < 5.5$

Surface 4: $5.5 \leq \bar{u} < 8$, $5.5 \leq \bar{v} < 8$

and whose control vertices are, respectively,

$$
\begin{array}{ll}
\text{Surface 1:} &
\begin{matrix}
\mathbf{W}_{0,0} & \cdots & \mathbf{W}_{7,0} \\
\cdot & \cdot & \cdot \\
\cdot & \cdot & \cdot \\
\cdot & \cdot & \cdot \\
\mathbf{W}_{0,7} & \cdots & \mathbf{W}_{7,7}
\end{matrix}
\end{array}
\qquad
\begin{array}{ll}
\text{Surface 2:} &
\begin{matrix}
\mathbf{W}_{0,5} & \cdots & \mathbf{W}_{7,5} \\
\cdot & \cdot & \cdot \\
\cdot & \cdot & \cdot \\
\cdot & \cdot & \cdot \\
\mathbf{W}_{0,12} & \cdots & \mathbf{W}_{7,12}
\end{matrix}
\end{array}
$$

$$
\begin{array}{ll}
\text{Surface 3:} &
\begin{matrix}
\mathbf{W}_{5,0} & \cdots & \mathbf{W}_{12,0} \\
\cdot & \cdot & \cdot \\
\cdot & \cdot & \cdot \\
\cdot & \cdot & \cdot \\
\mathbf{W}_{5,7} & \cdots & \mathbf{W}_{12,7}
\end{matrix}
\end{array}
\qquad
\begin{array}{ll}
\text{Surface 4:} &
\begin{matrix}
\mathbf{W}_{5,5} & \cdots & \mathbf{W}_{12,5} \\
\cdot & \cdot & \cdot \\
\cdot & \cdot & \cdot \\
\cdot & \cdot & \cdot \\
\mathbf{W}_{5,12} & \cdots & \mathbf{W}_{12,12}
\end{matrix}
\end{array} .
$$

This observation lays the foundation for a process of "subdivided refinement." Each of surfaces 1 through 4 can be regarded as totally separate from the other three and can be subjected independently to further applications of the Oslo algorithm. (It is in this manner that the Oslo refinement can be made consistent with the subdivision schemes introduced by Catmull [Catmull74, Catmull75].)

Considering once more the complete surface, the control graph of Figure 12.17 results if we again halve the knot intervals.

This particular sequence of refinements is creating control graphs that are quite clearly converging to the spline surface defined by the graphs (refer to Figure 4.35). In fact, any sequence of refinements in which the spacing between the knots tends to zero throughout the parameter range will show this pattern of convergence.

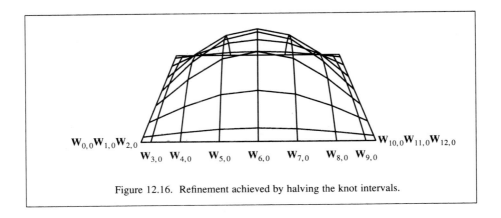

$\mathbf{W}_{0,0}\mathbf{W}_{1,0}\mathbf{W}_{2,0}$ $\mathbf{W}_{10,0}\mathbf{W}_{11,0}\mathbf{W}_{12,0}$

$\mathbf{W}_{3,0}$ $\mathbf{W}_{4,0}$ $\mathbf{W}_{5,0}$ $\mathbf{W}_{6,0}$ $\mathbf{W}_{7,0}$ $\mathbf{W}_{8,0}$ $\mathbf{W}_{9,0}$

Figure 12.16. Refinement achieved by halving the knot intervals.

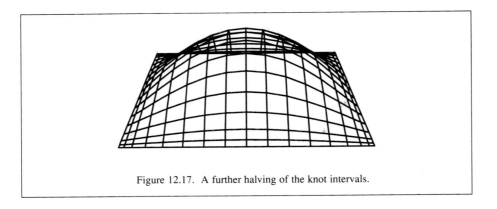

Figure 12.17. A further halving of the knot intervals.

As a final note, we should point out that the "boundary entries" appearing in the table of Figure 12.14 (i.e., the values 1, 1/6, 5/6) are a consequence of our decision to insert knots only on the parametric range $[\bar{u}_3, \bar{u}_8)$. However, we could have regarded our knot sequence as having extended arbitrarily far to the right and to the left, and we could have halved <u>every</u> segment interval. With appropriate attention to a new parametric range after the refinement, the awkward "boundary" values could have been ignored. More specifically, we could have regarded the original space as having some extra B-splines on the left

$$\cdots \; B_{-3,4}(\bar{u}) \, , \; B_{-2,4}(\bar{u}) \, , \; B_{-1,4}(\bar{u})$$

associated with knots

$$\cdots \; \bar{u}_{-3} \, , \; \bar{u}_{-2} \, , \; \bar{u}_{-1}$$

$$\cdots \ \overline{u}_{-3} \ , \ \overline{u}_{-2} \ , \ \overline{u}_{-1}$$

and arbitrary control vertices. Similarly, on the right, we could have had

$$B_{8,4}(\overline{u}) \ , \ B_{9,4}(\overline{u}) \ , \ B_{10,4}(\overline{u}) \ \cdots$$

associated with the knots

$$\overline{u}_8 \ , \ \overline{u}_9 \ , \ \overline{u}_{10} \ \cdots$$

and arbitrary control vertices. The space we had been working in, then, would have been comfortably "interior" to this extended one, and a halving of all the intervals from $\overline{u}_0$ to $\overline{u}_{11}$ would have seemed quite natural. The result would have been that our control vertices, with some arbitrary vertices on the side, would have been refined according to a pleasing

$$\frac{1}{2} \ , \ \frac{1}{2} \ , \ \frac{1}{8} \ , \ \frac{3}{4} \ , \ \frac{1}{8}$$

pattern without any exceptions. The curve itself, however, would then begin at $\overline{w}_{2(k-1)} = \overline{w}_6$ (which was $\overline{u}_{k-1} = \overline{u}_3$ before refinement) and end at $\overline{w}_{2(m+1)}$ ($\overline{u}_{m+1}$ before refinement). The additional control vertices are arbitrary because they do not participate in defining the curve of interest, which is defined on the interval $[\overline{u}_3, \overline{u}_{m+1}) = [\overline{w}_6, \overline{w}_{2(m+1)})$.

13

Parametric vs. Geometric Continuity

Our objective in this chapter is to show that the relationship between the continuity of parametric derivatives and the physically meaningful notions of *unit tangent vector continuity* and *curvature vector continuity* is subtle. This will motivate a generalization of the uniform cubic B-splines, called the *uniformly-shaped cubic Beta-splines*, which we will introduce in the next chapter. Most of what follows may be found in [Barsky81a, Barsky87a, Barsky87b].

13.1 Geometric Continuity

Intuitively, if we consider a parametric curve to be the path of motion of a point, the direction of the first derivative vector tells us the direction of motion of the point at any instant, and the length of this vector tells us the speed of motion. Geometrically, two curves are joined smoothly with respect to their first derivatives if their respective derivative vectors at the joint point in the same direction. The magnitude of the left and right derivative vectors; i.e., the speed at the entry to and the exit from the joint, has no bearing on the issue of directionality. Hence we extract the direction from a parametric first derivative by normalizing its length: the *unit tangent vector* of a curve $\mathbf{Q}(\overline{u})$ is

$$\hat{\mathbf{T}}(\overline{u}) = \frac{\mathbf{Q}^{(1)}(\overline{u})}{|\mathbf{Q}^{(1)}(\overline{u})|}. \tag{13.1}$$

As we have discussed in Section 4.6.1, the *curvature vector* is

$$\mathbf{K}(\overline{u}) \;=\; \kappa(\overline{u})\hat{\mathbf{N}}(\overline{u}) \;=\; \kappa(\overline{u})\frac{\hat{\mathbf{T}}^{(1)}(\overline{u})}{|\hat{\mathbf{T}}^{(1)}(\overline{u})|}$$

where $\kappa(\overline{u})$ is the *curvature* of $\mathbf{Q}(\overline{u})$ at $\overline{u}$ and $\hat{\mathbf{N}}(\overline{u})$ is the *normal vector* at $\overline{u}$; i.e., the unit vector pointing from $\mathbf{Q}(\overline{u})$ towards the center of the osculating circle at $\mathbf{Q}(\overline{u})$. $\mathbf{K}(\overline{u})$ records the extent to which the curve is "bent" away from a straight line; its direction tells us how that bending is oriented with respect to the direction in which the curve is headed.

It is shown in [Manning74, Faux/Pratt79, Barsky81a, Barsky87a, Barsky87b] that

$$\mathbf{K}(\overline{u}) \;=\; \frac{\mathbf{Q}^{(1)}(\overline{u}) \times \mathbf{Q}^{(2)}(\overline{u}) \times \mathbf{Q}^{(1)}(\overline{u})}{|\mathbf{Q}^{(1)}(\overline{u})|^4}. \tag{13.2}$$

We will say that a curve whose unit tangent vector and curvature vector are everywhere continuous has G^2 or *second degree geometric continuity*.

As it turns out, the usual definition of continuity is inconsistent with our perception of continuity. We will see, as in [Barsky84b], that we can manipulate the way in which curve segments are parametrized so as to cause the parametric first and second derivative vectors to violate our intuition about the physical continuity of a curve. Many curves are G^2 continuous but not C^2 continuous, and C^2 continuous curves can fail to appear geometrically continuous.

13.2 Continuity of the First Derivative Vector

First let us see that a first derivative vector may be continuous even though the curve itself has a discontinuous tangent. We have already seen an illustration of this in Figure 4.22, but we can give an even simpler example. The idea is to arrange for the first derivative vector to be $(0,0)$ at the point in question, so that the unit tangent vector is discontinuous even though the first derivative is continuous. In such a case we may easily arrange that, for $\varepsilon > 0$, the limit from the left

$$\lim_{\varepsilon \to 0^+} \frac{\mathbf{Q}^{(1)}(\overline{u} - \varepsilon)}{|\mathbf{Q}^{(1)}(\overline{u} - \varepsilon)|}$$

and the limit from the right

$$\lim_{\varepsilon \to 0^+} \frac{\mathbf{Q}^{(1)}(\overline{u} + \varepsilon)}{|\mathbf{Q}^{(1)}(\overline{u} + \varepsilon)|}$$

be distinct.

Consider the two line segments $Q_1(u)$ and $Q_2(u)$ defined by

$$Q_1(u) = (2u - u^2, 2u - u^2) \qquad 0 \le u \le 1$$

$$Q_2(u) = (1 + u^2, 1 - u^2) \qquad 0 \le u \le 1.$$

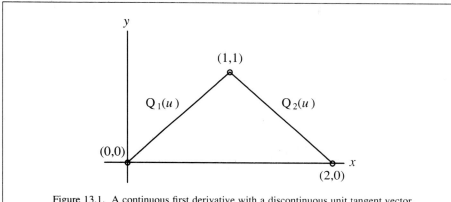

Figure 13.1. A continuous first derivative with a discontinuous unit tangent vector.

These line segments are positionally continuous since $Q_1(1) = Q_2(0) = (1,1)$. Their first derivative vectors are

$$Q_1^{(1)}(u) = (2 - 2u, 2 - 2u) = (2-2u)(1,1)$$

$$Q_2^{(1)}(u) = (2u, -2u) = 2u(1,-1).$$

Since $Q_1^{(1)}(1) = Q_2^{(1)}(0) = (0,0)$, the first derivative vectors are continuous at the joint (as well as being continuous elsewhere), even though the unit tangent vectors for $Q_1(u)$ and $Q_2(u)$, given by

$$\hat{T}_1(1) = \frac{1}{\sqrt{2}}(1,1)$$

$$\hat{T}_2(0) = \frac{1}{\sqrt{2}}(1,-1),$$

clearly point in different directions and are therefore not continuous.

It is also quite possible for the first derivative vector to be discontinuous even though the curve possesses a physically continuous unit tangent vector throughout its length. Consider

$$\mathbf{Q}_1(u) \; = \; (\, 12u\,, 9u \,) \qquad\qquad 0 \le u \le 1$$

$$\mathbf{Q}_2(u) \; = \; (\, 4\,(u+3),\, 3\,(u+3)\,) \qquad 0 \le u \le 1$$

whose first derivative vectors are

$$\mathbf{Q}_1^{(1)}(u) \; = \; (\, 12, 9 \,)$$

$$\mathbf{Q}_2^{(1)}(u) \; = \; (\, 4, 3 \,)\,.$$

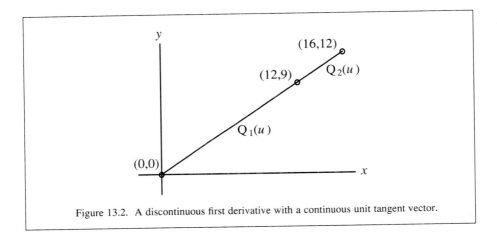

Figure 13.2. A discontinuous first derivative with a continuous unit tangent vector.

These line segments are collinear and have a continuous unit tangent vector, namely $(\frac{4}{5}, \frac{3}{5})$, even though there is a jump in the first derivative vector at the joint.

13.3 Continuity of the Second Derivative Vector

We can find instances of the same sort of phenomena for the second parametric derivative vector as well. First we show that the existence of a continuous second derivative vector need not ensure that the curvature vector is continuous. Consider

$$\mathbf{Q}_1(u) \; = \; \left[\; \cos(\frac{\pi}{2}\,(1-u)^3)\,, \; \sin(\frac{\pi}{2}\,(1-u)^3) \; \right] \qquad 0 \le u \le 1$$

$$\mathbf{Q}_2(u) \; = \; \left[\; 3 - 2\cos(\frac{\pi}{2}\,u^3)\,, \; -2\sin(\frac{\pi}{2}\,u^3) \; \right] \qquad 0 \le u \le 1,$$

which define two circles of radius one and two centered at (0,0) and at (3,0), respectively, which meet at (1,0). Because they have different radii, there is a change in the curvature where they meet, and consequently a jump in the curvature vector.

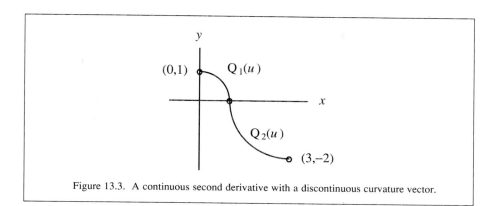

Figure 13.3. A continuous second derivative with a discontinuous curvature vector.

On the other hand, their first derivative vectors are

$$\mathbf{Q}_1^{(1)}(u) = \frac{1}{2}\left[\; 3\pi\sin\left[\frac{\pi(1-u)^3}{2}\right](1-u)^2\;,\; -3\pi\cos\left[\frac{\pi(1-u)^3}{2}\right](1-u)^2\;\right]$$

$$\mathbf{Q}_2^{(1)}(u) = \left[\; 3\pi u^2\sin\left[\frac{\pi u^3}{2}\right]\;,\; -3\pi u^2\cos\left[\frac{\pi u^3}{2}\right]\;\right]$$

and their second derivative vectors are

$$\mathbf{Q}_1^{(2)}(u) = \frac{1}{4}\left[\; -9\pi^2\cos\left[\frac{\pi(1-u)^3}{2}\right](1-u)^4 - 12\pi\sin\left[\frac{\pi(1-u)^3}{2}\right](1-u)\;,\right.$$

$$\left. 12\pi\cos\left[\frac{\pi(1-u)^3}{2}\right](1-u) - 9\pi^2\sin\left[\frac{\pi(1-u)^3}{2}\right](1-u)^4\;\right]$$

$$\mathbf{Q}_2^{(2)}(u) = \frac{1}{2}\left[\; 12\pi u\sin\left[\frac{\pi u^3}{2}\right] + 9\pi^2 u^4\cos\left[\frac{\pi u^3}{2}\right]\;,\right.$$

$$\left. 9\pi^2 u^4\sin\left[\frac{\pi u^3}{2}\right] - 12\pi u\cos\left[\frac{\pi u^3}{2}\right]\;\right].$$

In particular,

$$\mathbf{Q}_1^{(2)}(1) = (0,0)$$

$$\mathbf{Q}_2^{(2)}(0) = (0,0)$$

so that the second derivative vectors for the two curve segments are continuous where they join, even though the curvature vector has a jump at the joint both in direction and in magnitude, since

$$\mathbf{K}_1(1) = (-1.0,0)$$

$$\mathbf{K}_2(0) = (+0.5,0).$$

It is also possible for the curvature vector to be continuous even if the second derivative vector is not. Consider the following two curve segments, which define successive portions of a circle of radius one centered at the origin (so that the curvature vector must be continuous).

$$\mathbf{Q}_1(u) = \left[\sin\left[\frac{\pi}{2}u^2\right] , \cos\left[\frac{\pi}{2}u^2\right] \right] \qquad 0 \le u \le 1$$

$$\mathbf{Q}_2(u) = \left[\cos\left[\frac{\pi}{2}u^2\right] , -\sin\left[\frac{\pi}{2}u^2\right] \right] \qquad 0 \le u \le 1.$$

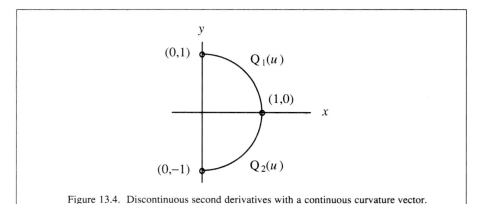

Figure 13.4. Discontinuous second derivatives with a continuous curvature vector.

The first derivative vectors are

$$\mathbf{Q}_1^{(1)}(u) = \left[\pi u \cos\left(\frac{\pi u^2}{2}\right), \; -\pi u \sin\left(\frac{\pi u^2}{2}\right) \right]$$

$$\mathbf{Q}_2^{(1)}(u) = \left[-\pi u \sin\left(\frac{\pi u^2}{2}\right), \; -\pi u \cos\left(\frac{\pi u^2}{2}\right) \right],$$

and the second derivative vectors are

$$\mathbf{Q}_1^{(2)}(u) = \left[\pi \cos\left(\frac{\pi u^2}{2}\right) - \pi^2 u^2 \sin\left(\frac{\pi u^2}{2}\right), \right.$$

$$\left. -\pi \sin\left(\frac{\pi u^2}{2}\right) - \pi^2 u^2 \cos\left(\frac{\pi u^2}{2}\right) \right]$$

$$\mathbf{Q}_2^{(2)}(u) = \left[-\pi \sin\left(\frac{\pi u^2}{2}\right) - \pi^2 u^2 \cos\left(\frac{\pi u^2}{2}\right), \right.$$

$$\left. \pi^2 u^2 \sin\left(\frac{\pi u^2}{2}\right) - \pi \cos\left(\frac{\pi u^2}{2}\right) \right].$$

In particular, the second derivative vectors at the joint between the two segments are

$$\mathbf{Q}_1^{(2)}(1) = (-\pi^2, -\pi)$$

$$\mathbf{Q}_2^{(2)}(0) = (0, -\pi)$$

although the curvature vector is clearly continuous since the two curves together are simply a semi-circle of radius one, centered at the origin. Indeed, the reader may care to verify that the less exotic parametric representation of such a semi-circle as

$$\mathbf{Q}_1(u) = \left[\sin\left(\frac{\pi}{2} u\right), \; \cos\left(\frac{\pi}{2} u\right) \right]$$

$$\mathbf{Q}_2(u) = \left[\cos\left(\frac{\pi}{2} u\right), \; -\sin\left(\frac{\pi}{2} u\right) \right]$$

is C^2 continuous since

$$\mathbf{K}_1(1) = \mathbf{K}_2(0) = (-1, 0).$$

14

Uniformly–Shaped
Beta–splines

We have seen that $\hat{\mathbf{T}}$ and $\mathbf{K}$ capture the physically meaningful notions of direction and curvature. The parametric first and second derivative vectors, on the other hand, may be changed by reparametrization without altering the curve, and moreover their continuity may not reflect the actual ''physical continuity'' of the curve. In this chapter, we will consider whether one can define curves in which geometric rather than parametric continuity is required, drawing upon material which appears in [Barsky81a, Barsky87a, Barsky87b]. In doing so we will see that we can gain additional control over the shape of the cubic piecewise polynomial curves which interest us.

Of course, $\mathbf{Q}$, $\hat{\mathbf{T}}$ and $\mathbf{K}$ are easily seen to be continuous away from the joints of a piecewise polynomial. What we want is to develop a means of enforcing continuity of position, unit tangent, and curvature vector *at* the joint between two successive curve segments as well. Our approach is very much analogous to the way in which we previously derived the uniform cubic B-splines.

Obtaining positional continuity is easy. We have simply to require that

$$\mathbf{Q}_{i-1}(1) = \mathbf{Q}_i(0). \tag{14.1}$$

Next we observe that two curves will have the same unit tangent vector at their joint if their first derivative vectors are collinear and have the same sense, that is, if one is a positive multiple of the other. The following equation captures this notion.

$$\beta_1 \mathbf{Q}_{i-1}^{(1)}(1) = \mathbf{Q}_i^{(1)}(0) \qquad \beta_1 > 0 \tag{14.2}$$

There is an instantaneous change in velocity at the joint, but not a change in direction.

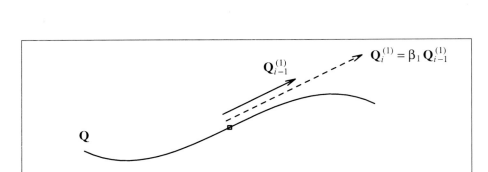

Figure 14.1. The idea behind the notion of G^1 continuity is that the tangent vectors at the joint between two successive segments need only be collinear; their magnitudes may differ by a positive factor which we are calling β_1.

Obtaining continuity of the curvature vector is somewhat more involved. Equation (13.2) gives us a way of computing the curvature vector at an arbitrary point. Let us use it to obtain the curvature of two consecutive segments $\mathbf{Q}_{i-1}(u)$ and $\mathbf{Q}_i(u)$ at their common joint and equate the two expressions.

$$\frac{\mathbf{Q}_{i-1}^{(1)}(1)\times\mathbf{Q}_{i-1}^{(2)}(1)\times\mathbf{Q}_{i-1}^{(1)}(1)}{|\mathbf{Q}_{i-1}^{(1)}(1)|^4} = \frac{\mathbf{Q}_i^{(1)}(0)\times\mathbf{Q}_i^{(2)}(0)\times\mathbf{Q}_i^{(1)}(0)}{|\mathbf{Q}_i^{(1)}(0)|^4}$$

If we substitute for $\mathbf{Q}_i^{(1)}(0)$ using equation (14.2) this becomes

$$\frac{\mathbf{Q}_{i-1}^{(1)}(1)\times\mathbf{Q}_{i-1}^{(2)}(1)\times\mathbf{Q}_{i-1}^{(1)}(1)}{|\mathbf{Q}_{i-1}^{(1)}(1)|^4} = \frac{\beta_1\mathbf{Q}_{i-1}^{(1)}(1)\times\mathbf{Q}_i^{(2)}(0)\times\beta_1\mathbf{Q}_{i-1}^{(1)}(1)}{|\beta_1\mathbf{Q}_{i-1}^{(1)}(1)|^4}$$

$$= \frac{\mathbf{Q}_{i-1}^{(1)}(1)\times\dfrac{\mathbf{Q}_i^{(2)}(0)}{\beta_1^{\,2}}\times\mathbf{Q}_{i-1}^{(1)}(1)}{|\mathbf{Q}_{i-1}^{(1)}(1)|^4}.$$

Clearly equality is ensured if $\beta_1^{\,2}\mathbf{Q}_{i-1}^{(2)}(1)=\mathbf{Q}_i^{(2)}(0)$. However, since the cross product of a vector with itself is zero, $\mathbf{Q}_i^{(2)}(0)$ may have an additional component along $\mathbf{Q}_{i-1}^{(1)}(1)$. Hence equality still results if, for any real numbers β_1 and β_2,

$$\beta_1^{\,2}\mathbf{Q}_{i-1}^{(2)}(1)+\beta_2\mathbf{Q}_{i-1}^{(1)}(1)=\mathbf{Q}_i^{(2)}(0)\qquad\beta_1>0. \tag{14.3}$$

Equation (14.3) has a natural physical interpretation: $\mathbf{Q}_i^{(2)}(0)$ may have an additional component directed along the tangent since acceleration along the tangent does not "deflect" a point traveling along the curve and so does not affect the curvature there.

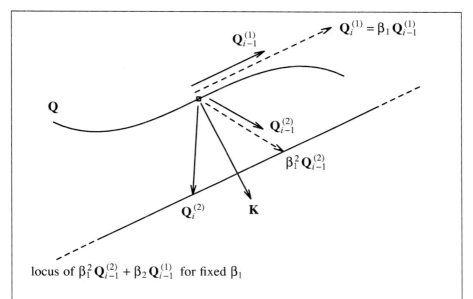

Figure 14.2. The left and right second parametric derivatives at the joint between two segments may differ by an arbitrary component along their common unit tangent since applying force along the direction of motion does not deflect a moving point.

Geometric continuity results, then, if equations (14.1), (14.2) and (14.3) hold at every knot u_i, for any positive β_1 and for any β_2. These equations are, by definition, less restrictive than simple continuity of position and parametric derivatives, which is the special case in which $\beta_1 = 1$ and $\beta_2 = 0$, yielding the uniform cubic B-spline curves.

If $\mathbf{Q}(u)$ is defined using cubic splines, then these equations must hold for the basis functions as well since

$$\mathbf{Q}(u) \;=\; \sum_i \mathbf{V}_i\, B_i(u)$$

$$\mathbf{Q}^{(1)}(u) \;=\; \sum_i \mathbf{V}_i\, B_i^{(1)}(u)$$

and any of the control vertices may be **0**. Conversely, if the basis functions satisfy these equations, as for example

$$\beta_1 \, b_{-0}^{(1)}(u_i) \;=\; b_{-1}^{(1)}(u_i)$$

then so will the curves they define. We will now arrange that this be so.

Let us again consider a basis function composed of four cubic polynomial segments, so that

$$\mathbf{Q}_i(u) \;=\; \mathbf{V}_{i-3} \, b_{-3}(u) + \mathbf{V}_{i-2} \, b_{-2}(u) + \mathbf{V}_{i-1} \, b_{-1}(u) + \mathbf{V}_i \, b_{-0}(u),$$

just as for the uniform cubic B-splines in Chapter 4. This time we ask that they satisfy the geometric constraints (14.1), (14.2) and (14.3) instead of the parametric constraints (4.4), (4.5) and (4.6). The equations which result are

$$
\begin{aligned}
0 &= b_{-0}(0) & 0 &= b_{-0}^{(1)}(0) \\
b_{-0}(1) &= b_{-1}(0) & \beta_1 \, b_{-0}^{(1)}(1) &= b_{-1}^{(1)}(0) \\
b_{-1}(1) &= b_{-2}(0) & \beta_1 \, b_{-1}^{(1)}(1) &= b_{-2}^{(1)}(0) \\
b_{-2}(1) &= b_{-3}(0) & \beta_1 \, b_{-2}^{(1)}(1) &= b_{-3}^{(1)}(0) \\
b_{-3}(1) &= 0 & \beta_1 \, b_{-3}^{(1)}(1) &= 0
\end{aligned}
$$

$$\text{(14.4)}$$

$$
\begin{aligned}
0 &= b_{-0}^{(2)}(0) \\
\beta_1^2 \, b_{-0}^{(2)}(1) + \beta_2 \, b_{-0}^{(1)}(1) &= b_{-1}^{(2)}(0) \\
\beta_1^2 \, b_{-1}^{(2)}(1) + \beta_2 \, b_{-1}^{(1)}(1) &= b_{-2}^{(2)}(0) \\
\beta_1^2 \, b_{-2}^{(2)}(1) + \beta_2 \, b_{-2}^{(1)}(1) &= b_{-3}^{(2)}(0) \\
\beta_1^2 \, b_{-3}^{(2)}(1) + \beta_2 \, b_{-3}^{(1)}(1) &= 0.
\end{aligned}
$$

To obtain sixteen equations we again require, hoping to obtain the convex hull property, that

$$b_{-0}(0) + b_{-1}(0) + b_{-2}(0) + b_{-3}(0) \;=\; b_{-1}(0) + b_{-2}(0) + b_{-3}(0) \;=\; 1,$$

yielding a total of sixteen equations in sixteen unknowns. For any particular values of β_1 and β_2 these equations can be solved numerically (as in the B-spline case) to obtain explicit formulas for the polynomials comprising the basis segments. This is not very practical, however, since we do not want to solve a new system every time we wish to alter one of the β parameters. Instead we can solve this system symbolically, using a symbolic manipulation system such as MACSYMA [Bogen83], to obtain the following symbolic representation of the basis segments for all values of β_1 and β_2.

$$b_{-0}(u) = \frac{1}{\delta} \left[2u^3 \right]$$

$$b_{-1}(u) = \frac{1}{\delta} \left[2 + (6\beta_1)u + (3\beta_2 + 6\beta_1^2)u^2 - (2\beta_2 + 2\beta_1^2 + 2\beta_1 + 2)u^3 \right]$$

$$b_{-2}(u) = \frac{1}{\delta} \left[(\beta_2 + 4\beta_1^2 + 4\beta_1) + (6\beta_1^3 - 6\beta_1)u \right.$$

$$\left. - (3\beta_2 + 6\beta_1^3 + 6\beta_1^2)u^2 + (2\beta_2 + 2\beta_1^3 + 2\beta_1^2 + 2\beta_1)u^3 \right]$$

$$b_{-3}(u) = \frac{1}{\delta} \left[(2\beta_1^3) - (6\beta_1^3)u + (6\beta_1^3)u^2 - (2\beta_1^3)u^3 \right]$$

(14.5)

where

$$\delta = \beta_2 + 2\beta_1^3 + 4\beta_1^2 + 4\beta_1 + 2 \neq 0.$$

Notice that if we substitute $\beta_1 = 1$ and $\beta_2 = 0$ into the Beta-spline constraint equations (14.4) we obtain the B-spline constraint equations (4.7), and that substituting these values into the Beta-spline basis segments (14.5) we obtain the B-spline basis segments (4.9). For other values of β_1 and β_2 the Beta-spline basis segments fail to be C^2 continuous at knots, although they do satisfy equations (14.4) and are therefore G^2 continuous.

Equations (14.5) can, of course, be evaluated more rapidly if they are factored. For any particular values of β_1 and β_2 they are cubic polynomials in u, so forward differencing can also be used where appropriate. The efficient evaluation of these equations is discussed in [Barsky81a, Barsky87b]

We will use the symbol "G" instead of "B" to denote basis functions that are geometrically continuous. Thus, we have

$$G_i(u) = \begin{cases} \frac{1}{\delta} \left[2u^3 \right] \\ \frac{1}{\delta} \left[2 + (6\beta_1)u + (3\beta_2 + 6\beta_1^2)u^2 - (2\beta_2 + 2\beta_1^2 + 2\beta_1 + 2)u^3 \right] \\ \frac{1}{\delta} \left[(\beta_2 + 4\beta_1^2 + 4\beta_1) + (6\beta_1^3 - 6\beta_1)u \right. \\ \left. - (3\beta_2 + 6\beta_1^3 + 6\beta_1^2)u^2 + (2\beta_2 + 2\beta_1^3 + 2\beta_1^2 + 2\beta_1)u^3 \right] \\ \frac{1}{\delta} \left[(2\beta_1^3) - (6\beta_1^3)u + (6\beta_1^3)u^2 - (2\beta_1^3)u^3 \right], \end{cases}$$

over the intervals $[\bar{u}_i, \bar{u}_{i+1})$, $[\bar{u}_{i+1}, \bar{u}_{i+2})$, $[\bar{u}_{i+2}, \bar{u}_{i+3})$ and $[\bar{u}_{i+3}, \bar{u}_{i+4})$, respectively, and

$$Q_i(u) = V_{i-3} G_{i-3}(u) + V_{i-2} G_{i-2}(u) + V_{i-1} G_{i-1}(u) + V_i G_i(u).$$

We will refer to the basis functions whose segments are defined by equations (14.5) as *uniformly-shaped Beta-splines* to distinguish them from the more general Beta-splines, which will be defined subsequently (and also denoted by G_i, or sometimes $G_{i,k}$).

Increasing β_1 increases the "velocity" with which we traverse a curve immediately after a joint, with respect to the "velocity" just previous to the joint, thus serving to *bias* the curve. Values in excess of one cause the unit tangent vector at the joint (which is, of course, continuous) to have greater influence to the right than to the left, in that the curve will "continue in the direction of the tangent" farther in the rightmost segment. Values of β_1 ranging from one down to zero have the reciprocal effect, causing the curve to lie close to the tangent farther to the left of a joint than to the right. (See Figures 14.3 and 14.4.)

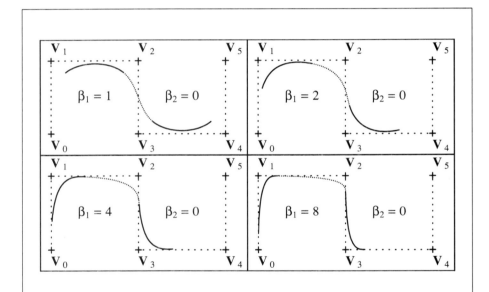

Figure 14.3. This sequence of curves illustrates the effect of increasing β_1 on a uniformly-shaped Beta-spline curve.

Figure 14.4 shows the basis functions used to define the curves pictured in Figure 14.3. Each basis function is computed for a distinct value of β_1, which determines the ratio of the slopes to the left and right of each joint. Notice that since the same basis function is used for each of $X(\overline{u})$ and $Y(\overline{u})$, any continuous basis

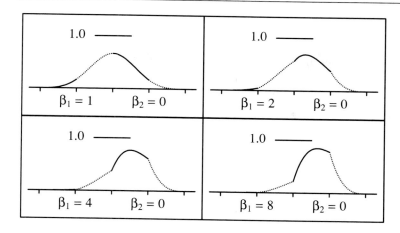

Figure 14.4. These are the basis functions, G_i, corresponding to the curves of Figure 14.3.

function whose first derivative is continuous except for a positive jump of some arbitrary value (β_1) at the knots suffices to define a curve with unit tangent continuity.

The β_2 parameter serves to control *tension* in the curve: altering the value of β_2 moves the joint between $Q_{i-1}(u)$ and $Q_i(u)$ along a vector that passes through control vertex V_{i-2}, and this happens simultaneously for all the joints in a uniformly-shaped curve. For example, increasingly positive values move each joint towards its corresponding control vertex and flatten the curve against the control graph. (See Figures 14.5 and 14.6.)

Notice that as β_2 increases in Figure 14.6, the peak of the basis function approaches one and the "tails" of the basis function, lying in the leftmost and rightmost intervals of its support, approach zero. Since our indexing convention is that the ith basis function is scaled by V_i and has support $[\overline{u}_i, \overline{u}_{i+4})$, this peak is at $\overline{u}_{i+2}$. Again by convention this is the joint between $Q_{i+1}(u)$ and $Q_{i+2}(u)$.

More generally, the curve itself converges to the control graph as β_2 goes to infinity, the joints between segments converging to the control vertices. This behavior may be predicted from equations (14.5). As β_2 is increased, the basis segments converge to

$$b_{-0}(u) = 0$$

$$b_{-1}(u) = (3u^2 - 2u^3)$$

$$b_{-2}(u) = 1 - (3u^2 - 2u^3)$$

$$b_{-3}(u) = 0$$

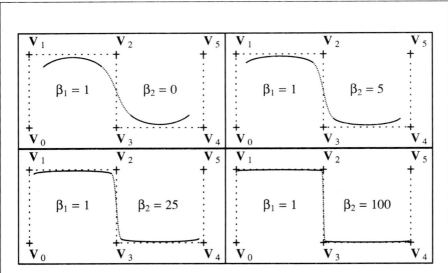

Figure 14.5. This sequence of curves illustrates the effect of increasing β_2 on a uniformly-shaped Beta-spline curve.

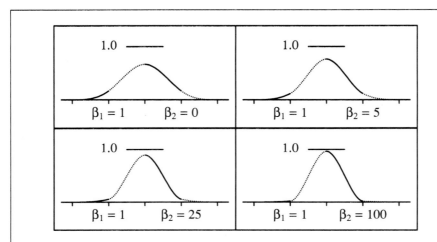

Figure 14.6. These are the basis functions, G_i, corresponding to the curves of Figure 14.5.

for any value of β_1. If we let $t = (3u^2 - 2u^3)$, it is easy to see that in the limit we obtain a curve that varies linearly between each successive pair of control vertices.

β_1 also serves, to some extent, as an "asymmetric tension parameter." If for any value of β_2 we allow β_1 to become arbitrarily large then the basis segments converge to

$$b_{-0}(u) = 0$$

$$b_{-1}(u) = 0$$

$$b_{-2}(u) = (3u - 3u^2 + u^3)$$

$$b_{-3}(u) = 1 - (3u - 3u^2 + u^3).$$

If these are scaled by $\mathbf{V}_i$, $\mathbf{V}_{i-1}$, $\mathbf{V}_{i-2}$ and $\mathbf{V}_{i-3}$, respectively, to define the ith segment $\mathbf{Q}_i(u)$ then this segment of the curve converges to a straight line between $\mathbf{V}_{i-3}$ and $\mathbf{V}_{i-2}$.

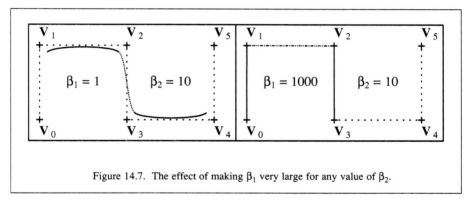

Figure 14.7. The effect of making β_1 very large for any value of β_2.

If β_2 has the value zero and we allow β_1 to approach zero then we obtain symmetrical behavior:

$$b_{-0}(u) = u^3$$

$$b_{-1}(u) = 1 - u^3$$

$$b_{-2}(u) = 0$$

$$b_{-3}(u) = 0.$$

In this case $\mathbf{Q}_i(u)$ is, in the limit, a straight line running from $\mathbf{V}_{i-1}$ to $\mathbf{V}_i$.

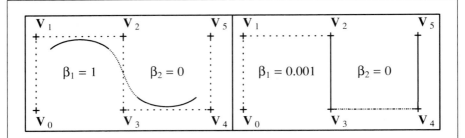

Figure 14.8. Decreasing β_1 to zero does draw the curve flat against the control graph when β_2 is zero.

Curiously enough, however, if β_2 is nonzero then as β_1 approaches zero the basis segments converge to

$$b_{-0}(u) = \frac{1}{\beta_2 + 2} \; 2u^3$$

$$b_{-1}(u) = \frac{1}{\beta_2 + 2} \left[\; 2 + 3\beta_2 u^2 - (2\beta_2 + 2) u^3 \; \right]$$

$$b_{-2}(u) = \frac{1}{\beta_2 + 2} \left[\; \beta_2 - 3\beta_2 u^2 + 2\beta_2 u^3 \; \right]$$

$$b_{-3}(u) = 0.$$

Thus as β_1 approaches zero, $\mathbf{Q}_i(u)$ does not, in general, approach a straight line unless β_2 is zero.

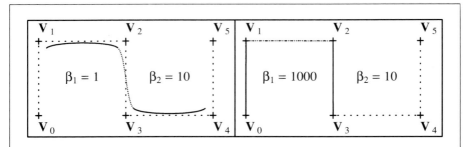

Figure 14.9. If β_2 is not zero the curve does not converge to the control graph as β_1 approaches zero.

β_1 and β_2 may be altered, independent of the control vertices, to change the shape of the curve. In the curves we have been discussing, a single value of β_1 is used for the entire curve, and similarly for β_2. We would prefer, if possible, to specify distinct values of β_1 and β_2 at each joint. Before discussing how this can be done, we indicate briefly how uniformly-shaped Beta-spline surfaces can be constructed from uniformly-shaped Beta-spline curves.

14.1 Uniformly-Shaped Beta-spline Surfaces

The formation of uniformly-shaped Beta-spline surfaces is completely analogous to our earlier construction of uniform cubic B-spline surfaces. Once again our surface is a scaled sum of basis functions in which X, Y and Z are functions of two independent variables:

$$\mathbf{Q}(\overline{u},\overline{v}) = \sum_{i,j} \mathbf{V}_{i,j} G_{i,j}(\overline{u},\overline{v})$$

$$= \sum_{i,j} (\ x_{i,j}\, G_{i,j}(\overline{u},\overline{v}),\ y_{i,j}\, G_{i,j}(\overline{u},\overline{v}),\ z_{i,j}\, G_{i,j}(\overline{u},\overline{v})\ ). \tag{14.6}$$

For coefficients we again use the x-, y- and z-coordinates of a two-dimensional array of control vertices that we have called the control mesh or control graph. To obtain locality we want the new basis functions $G_{i,j}(\overline{u},\overline{v})$ to be nonzero only for a small range of $\overline{u}$ and $\overline{v}$. One way of arranging this is to let $G_{i,j}(\overline{u},\overline{v}) = G_i(\overline{u})\, G_j(\overline{v})$, where $G_i(\overline{u})$ and $G_j(\overline{v})$ are simply the univariate basis functions (14.5) that we developed for the Beta-spline curves. Since each is nonzero only over four successive intervals, if $\overline{u}_i \leq \overline{u} \leq \overline{u}_{i+1}$ and $\overline{v}_j \leq \overline{v} \leq \overline{v}_{j+1}$ we can rewrite (14.6) as

$$\mathbf{Q}_{i,j}(\overline{u},\overline{v}) = \sum_{r=-3}^{0} \sum_{s=-3}^{0} \mathbf{V}_{i+r,j+s}\, G_{i+r}(\overline{u})\, G_{j+s}(\overline{v}). \tag{14.7}$$

If we rewrite this in terms of basis segments instead of basis functions and recall our convention that the portion of $\mathbf{Q}(u,v)$ defined by this set of values for u and v is denoted by $\mathbf{Q}_{i,j}(u,v)$, then we can write

$$\mathbf{Q}_{i,j}(u,v) = \sum_{r=-3}^{0} \sum_{s=-3}^{0} \mathbf{V}_{i+r,j+s}\, b_r(u)\, b_s(v) \tag{14.8}$$

so that $\mathbf{Q}_{i,j}(u,v)$, the i,j^{th} *patch,* is completely determined by sixteen control vertices. As before, the separability of $G_{i,j}(\overline{u},\overline{v})$ into $G_i(\overline{u})$ and $G_j(\overline{v})$ can be used to establish that the resulting surfaces are G^2 continuous across patch boundaries. For example, we can expand (14.8) as

$$\mathbf{Q}_{i,j}(u,v) = \qquad\qquad\qquad\qquad\qquad\qquad\qquad\qquad (14.9)$$

$$[\ \mathbf{V}_{i-3,j}\ b_{-3}(u)\ +\ \mathbf{V}_{i-2,j}\ b_{-2}(u)\ +\ \mathbf{V}_{i-1,j}\ b_{-1}(u)\ +\ \mathbf{V}_{i,j}\ b_{-0}(u)\ ]\ b_{-0}(v)$$

$$+\ [\ \mathbf{V}_{i-3,j-1}b_{-3}(u)\ +\ \mathbf{V}_{i-2,j-1}b_{-2}(u)\ +\ \mathbf{V}_{i-1,j-1}b_{-1}(u)\ +\ \mathbf{V}_{i,j-1}b_{-0}(u)\ ]\ b_{-1}(v)$$

$$+\ [\ \mathbf{V}_{i-3,j-2}b_{-3}(u)\ +\ \mathbf{V}_{i-2,j-2}b_{-2}(u)\ +\ \mathbf{V}_{i-1,j-2}b_{-1}(u)\ +\ \mathbf{V}_{i,j-2}b_{-0}(u)\ ]\ b_{-2}(v)$$

$$+\ [\ \mathbf{V}_{i-3,j-3}b_{-3}(u)\ +\ \mathbf{V}_{i-2,j-3}b_{-2}(u)\ +\ \mathbf{V}_{i-1,j-3}b_{-1}(u)\ +\ \mathbf{V}_{i,j-3}b_{-0}(u)\ ]\ b_{-3}(v).$$

From this it is clear that if we fix u at some arbitrary value between 0 and 1 then we can write (14.9) as

$$\mathbf{Q}_{i,j,u}(v)\ =\ \mathbf{W}_0 b_{-3}(v) + \mathbf{W}_1 b_{-2}(v) + \mathbf{W}_2 b_{-1}(v) + \mathbf{W}_3 b_{-0}(v)$$

where

$$\mathbf{W}_3\ =\ \mathbf{V}_{i-3,j}\ b_{-3}(u)\ +\ \mathbf{V}_{i-2,j}\ b_{-2}(u)\ +\ \mathbf{V}_{i-1,j}\ b_{-1}(u)\ +\ \mathbf{V}_{i,j}\ b_{-0}(u)$$

$$\mathbf{W}_2\ =\ \mathbf{V}_{i-3,j-1}b_{-3}(u)\ +\ \mathbf{V}_{i-2,j-1}b_{-2}(u)\ +\ \mathbf{V}_{i-1,j-1}b_{-1}(u)\ +\ \mathbf{V}_{i,j-1}b_{-0}(u)$$

$$\mathbf{W}_1\ =\ \mathbf{V}_{i-3,j-2}b_{-3}(u)\ +\ \mathbf{V}_{i-2,j-2}b_{-2}(u)\ +\ \mathbf{V}_{i-1,j-2}b_{-1}(u)\ +\ \mathbf{V}_{i,j-2}b_{-0}(u)$$

$$\mathbf{W}_0\ =\ \mathbf{V}_{i-3,j-3}b_{-3}(u)\ +\ \mathbf{V}_{i-2,j-3}b_{-2}(u)\ +\ \mathbf{V}_{i-1,j-3}b_{-1}(u)\ +\ \mathbf{V}_{i,j-3}b_{-0}(u).$$

Thus $\mathbf{Q}_{i,j,u}(v)$ is simply the uniformly-shaped Beta-spline curve segment defined by the "control vertices" $\mathbf{W}_0$, $\mathbf{W}_1$, $\mathbf{W}_2$ and $\mathbf{W}_3$. It is not hard to see that $\mathbf{Q}_{i,j+1,u}(v)$, in the next patch "up", is given by

$$\mathbf{Q}_{i,j+1,u}(v)\ =\ \mathbf{W}_1 b_{-3}(v) + \mathbf{W}_2 b_{-2}(v) + \mathbf{W}_3 b_{-1}(v) + \mathbf{W}_4 b_{-0}(v)$$

where

$$\mathbf{W}_4\ =\ \mathbf{V}_{i-3,j+1} b_{-3}(u) + \mathbf{V}_{i-2,j+1} b_{-2}(u) + \mathbf{V}_{i-1,j+1} b_{-1}(u) + \mathbf{V}_{i,j+1} b_{-0}(u).$$

This is simply the second segment in a uniformly-shaped Beta-spline curve defined by the "control vertices" $\mathbf{W}_0$, $\mathbf{W}_1$, $\mathbf{W}_2$, $\mathbf{W}_3$ and $\mathbf{W}_4$. It follows immediately that this curve is G^2 continuous. Since a completely analogous argument can be made with respect to u by factoring the $b_r(u)$ out of (14.8) instead of the $b_s(v)$, the uniformly-shaped Beta-spline surface we have defined is G^2 continuous along lines of constant u and v.

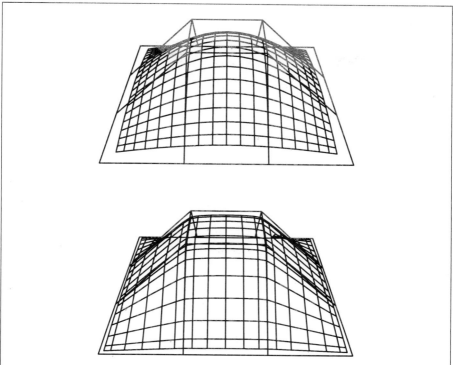

Figure 14.10. Uniformly-shaped Beta-spline surfaces: β_2 is 0 on the top and 25 on the bottom. The control graph has double vertices around its periphery.

Figure 14.10 shows a surface, in wire-frame display, being subjected to the influence of tenstion (β_2). Plate XI gives a more polished view of the effects that can be achieved by varying β_2.

14.3 An Historical Note

Although the term *geometric continuity* was introduced by [Barsky81a], similar ideas had appeared previously in somewhat different contexts. The earliest such public reference appears to have been in [Manning74]. This paper considers the problem of designing what we now call G^2 interpolatory curves, and derives equations 13.2, 14.2 and 14.3. In the same year, a polynomial alternative to the spline under tension {Schweikert66] called the *v-spline* was developed in [Nielson74]. This piecewise polynomial curve is the solution of a minimization problem similar to the one from which natural cubic splines result. [Barsky84a] presents a unified approach to both the spline under tension and the *v*-spline, deriving each one from a variational principle. This derivation emphasizes the relation of the v-spline to the conventional cubic interpolatory spline. From this, it is straightforward to see that the v-spline is a global representation with respect to its defining points. Although the v-spline was not developed from the point of view of continuity conditions, it possesses a combination of C^1 and G^2 continuity. The work in both [Manning74] and [Nielson74] made use of a global interpolatory spline representation, as distinct from the local B-spline-like formulation introduced in [Barsky81a].

15

Geometric Continuity, Reparametrization, and the Chain Rule

Before we begin our first generalization of the uniformly-shaped Beta-spline, we will give a brief outline of the notion of geometric continuity as presented in [Bartels83, Barsky/DeRose84, DeRose/Barsky85, DeRose85].

The issue of geometric continuity arises from changes in parametrization when a transition is made from one segment of a piecewise parametric curve to another. This is indicated by the fact that the technique we invariably used in Chapter 13 to construct our examples involved the change of parametric formulas between segments. The result of this was to alert us about comparing entering and exiting tangent vectors at the joint between the segments. A further simplification involved assigning the same symbol, u, to the parameter on the left and on the right, no matter how differently we constructed the two parametrizations. We then compared

$$\frac{d}{du} \mathbf{Q}_{i-1}(u) \bigg|_{u=1} \quad \text{with} \quad \frac{d}{du} \mathbf{Q}_i(u) \bigg|_{u=0}$$

and ignored the fact that the two instances of u were totally different. This approach did not hurt us in Chapter 4 when we did this between segments of the uniform cubic B-spline to set up the 16 defining equations, since the parameter u on the left differed from the parameter u on the right only by an additive constant. Consequently, derivatives on the left and on the right with respect to u were directly comparable. Problems were avoided for the construction of general B-splines, since for that presentation we always used $\bar{u}$; that is, we never switched parametrizations. Now, however, we wish to do a careful job of reparametrization, and this means that we must pay more attention to the details of comparing derivatives.

The geometric care that we took in Chapters 13 and 14 showed us that the normalized tangent and curvature vectors could overcome our lack of care in comparing derivatives. But geometric entities such as these rapidly grow more complicated for higher derivatives. We need something simpler and more analytic.

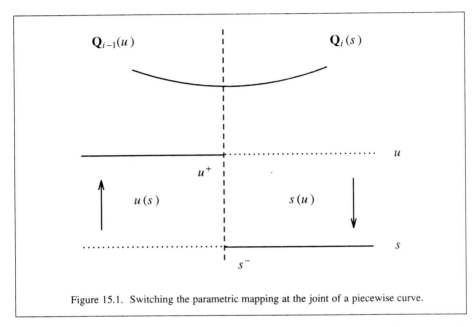

Figure 15.1. Switching the parametric mapping at the joint of a piecewise curve.

Figure 15.1 gives a more precise depiction of what reparametrization is all about. On the left, $\mathbf{Q}_{i-1}$ is given in terms of a parameter, u, which takes on its maximum value of u^+ at the joint. On the right, $\mathbf{Q}_i$ is given in terms of a different parameter, s, which takes on its minimum value of s^- at the joint. We make the basic assumption that s is an ''extension'' of u to the right of the joint in the sense that s could be expressed as a monotone increasing function, $s = s(u)$, of increasing u. Likewise, we assume that u is an ''extension'' of s to the left of the joint in the sense that u could be expressed as a monotone decreasing function, $u = u(s)$, of decreasing values of s. For the reparametrizations that we used in Chapter 4 between segments of the uniform cubic B-spline, for example, this was certainly the case, since these reparametrizations amounted to

$$s = u - 1 \quad \text{and} \quad u = s + 1 .$$

We will also assume that the derivatives of s with respect to u, and of u with respect to s, exist for as high an order as we might need.

Making the correct comparison of derivatives at the joint, to avoid comparing "apples with oranges," requires that we look at the derivatives of $\mathbf{Q}$ on the left and on the right with respect to a common parameter. The reason that the normalized tangent vector is suitable for comparison, for instance, is that it derives from the common arc-length parametrization on the left and on the right. In this case we simply choose one of the two parameters, say s, and use it on both sides of the joint (recall that $D_s^{(1)}$ denotes the first derivative with respect to s of ...):

$$D_s^{(1)} \mathbf{Q}_{i-1}(u(s))\Big|_{\substack{u=u^+ \\ s=s^-}} \quad \text{and} \quad D_s^{(1)} \mathbf{Q}_i(s)\Big|_{s=s^-}.$$

If we demand equality now, we are forced to invoke the chain rule to make the comparison:

$$D_s^{(1)} \mathbf{Q}_{i-1}(u(s)) = \left[D_s^{(1)} u(s) \right] D_u^{(1)} \mathbf{Q}_{i-1}(u).$$

And so, the equality demanded for derivatives to match at the left and right of the joint, in spite of the reparametrization, must be

$$\left[D_s^{(1)} u(s) \right]\Big|_{s=s^-} D_u^{(1)} \mathbf{Q}_{i-1}(u)\Big|_{u=u^+} = D_s^{(1)} \mathbf{Q}_i(s)\Big|_{s=s^-}.$$

In more conventional notation we must have

$$\frac{du}{ds} \frac{dQ_{i-1}(u)}{du} = \frac{dQ_i(s)}{ds},$$

when $u = u^+$ and $s = s^-$. This is precisely

$$\beta_1 \mathbf{Q}_{i-1}^{(1)}(u^+) = \mathbf{Q}_i^{(1)}(s^-),$$

where β_1 represents the derivative of the parameter u with respect to the parameter s taken at the value of s corresponding to the joint.

A careful evaluation of geometric continuity, then, leads to the conclusion that curve segments $\mathbf{Q}_{i-1}$ and $\mathbf{Q}_i$ are joined in a G^1 fashion if *there exists some reparametrization* with respect to which they are joined in a C^1 fashion [Barsky/DeRose84]. The quantity β_1 is simply the derivative

$$\frac{du}{ds}$$

for this reparametrization at the joint.

This insight can be extended. For second derivatives the chain rule gives

$$\left[D_s^{(1)}(u(s)) \right]^2 \Big|_{s=s^-} D_u^{(2)} \mathbf{Q}_{i-1}(u) \Big|_{u=u^+}$$

$$+ \left[D_s^{(2)}(u(s)) \right]^2 \Big|_{s=s^-} D_u^{(1)} \mathbf{Q}_{i-1}(u) \Big|_{u=u^+}$$

$$= D_s^{(2)} \mathbf{Q}_{i-1}(s) \Big|_{s=s^-},$$

or

$$\left[\frac{du}{ds} \right]^2 \frac{d^2 \mathbf{Q}_{i-1}(u)}{du^2} + \frac{d^2 u}{ds^2} \frac{d \mathbf{Q}_{i-1}(u)}{du} = \frac{d^2 \mathbf{Q}_i(s)}{ds^2},$$

when $u = u^+$ and $s = s^-$. In other words,

$$\beta_1^2 \mathbf{Q}_{i-1}^{(2)}(u^+) + \beta_2 \mathbf{Q}_{i-1}^{(1)}(u^+) = \mathbf{Q}_i^{(2)}(s^-).$$

The quantity β_2 represents

$$\frac{d^2 u}{ds^2} \Big|_{s=s^-}$$

for the reparametrization.

The next higher derivative yields

$$\beta_1^3 \mathbf{Q}_{i-1}^{(3)}(u^+) + 3 \beta_2 \beta_1 \mathbf{Q}_{i-1}^{(2)}(u^+) + \beta_3 \mathbf{Q}_{i-1}^{(1)}(u^+) = \mathbf{Q}_i^{(3)}(s^-),$$

where β_3 represents

$$\frac{d^3 u}{ds^3} \Big|_{s=s^-}$$

for the reparametrization.

In this way, formulas defining G^n continuity can be derived [Barsky/DeRose84]. The same technique, namely that of reparametrization, has the additional advantage that it can be used to define geometric continuity for general surfaces (including non-tensor-product surfaces), as explained in [DeRose/Barsky85].

Dyn and Micchelli [Dyn/Micchelli85], extending work by Goodman [Goodman85], have shown that the existence of basis functions of the sort relevant to computer graphics can be inferred from properties of the matrices

$$k = 3: \quad \left[\beta_1 \right]$$

$$k = 4: \quad \begin{bmatrix} \beta_1 & 0 \\ \beta_2 & \beta_1{}^2 \end{bmatrix}$$

$$k = 5: \quad \begin{bmatrix} \beta_1 & 0 & 0 \\ \beta_2 & \beta_1{}^2 & 0 \\ \beta_3 & 3\beta_2\beta_1 & \beta_1{}^3 \end{bmatrix}$$

etc.

Suppose we take the kth matrix and remove any j rows and, independently, any j columns, for $j = 0, \ldots, k-2$, to form a determinant. For example, remove the first and tenth rows and the third and sixth columns, if $j = 2$. The result is known as a *minor* of the kth matrix. All minors of the matrix are obtained for all possible row/column choices for all values of j.

If all the minors of the kth matrix are positive (a property called *total positivity*) then there exist basis functions, $G_{i,k}$, for the corresponding geometrically continuous splines, and the basis functions are nonnegative, have compact support (k knot intervals), and sum to one. The restrictions that $\beta_1 \geq 0$ and $\beta_2 \geq 0$, for example, which make geometric sense for the uniformly-shaped cubic Beta-splines, are a consequence of asking for the total positivity of the matrix for $k = 4$.

With this as background, the next chapters will explore different approaches to the generalization of the uniformly shaped, cubic Beta-spline. We will restrict ourselves to the cubic case, but it will be clear how other degrees of Beta-splines could be achieved. All our generalizations will be computationally (if not necessarily theoretically) different; however, they will all derive from the same underlying chain-rule principle.

One generalization, called the continuously-shaped Beta-splines, parametrizes β_1 and β_2 as functions of u on each segment interval in such a way as to yield seperately-specified bias and tension parameters $\beta_{1,i}$ and $\beta_{2,i}$ at each joint.

Another generalization starts with the knowledge that the cubic basis functions, $G_i = G_{i,4}$, exist, and seeks an efficient computational process for evaluating $G_{i,4}(u)$ that imitates the divided difference. The result is called the *discretely-shaped* Beta-spline.

The equations for geometric continuity are associated with formal discontinuities in first and second derivatives between adjoining segments. This leads to a generalization: the *B-representation* of the Beta-spline. Triple knot B-splines (whose segment polynomials, in fact, are simply the Bernstein polynomials) provide us with the necessary discontinuities, and it is possible to represent cubic Beta-splines in B-spline (or Bézier) terms [Höllig86].

In [Goodman/Unsworth85, Goodman/Unsworth86], explicit formulas are derived for two canonical forms of the Beta-spline: a form that has arbitrary β_1's and β_2's but uniform knot spacing, and a form that has arbitrary β_2's and arbitrary knot spacing but fixes the β_1's to 1. Both of these canonical forms can be transformed to the general case. The explicit formula of one of the canonical forms can be used to build upon the quadratic B-splines, providing a "recurrence" computation for the cubic Beta-splines. This material provides us with the *explicit* Beta-spline.

16

Continuously–Shaped
Beta–splines

Now we want to see how to generalize the uniformly-shaped Beta-splines so as to obtain local control of the shape parameters β_1 and β_2. The material in this chapter is taken from [Barsky/Beatty83a] and is expanded upon in [Barsky87b].

Let $\beta_{1,i}$ and $\beta_{2,i}$ be the values of β_1 and β_2, respectively, to be associated with the joint between $Q_{i-1}(u)$ and $Q_i(u)$. We would like to use the basis segments given by equations (14.5), making β_1 and β_2 functions of u in such a way as to interpolate between the $\beta_{1,i}$'s and $\beta_{2,i}$'s, respectively, at each end of a segment while preserving G^2 continuity of the curve.

To develop our formulas, we will use $\beta(u)$ rather than $\beta_1(u)$ or $\beta_2(u)$ whenever the argument applies to both β's. No confusion can occur because products of β_1 and β_2 do not arise. Similarly, β_i will be used to represent both $\beta_{1,i}$ and $\beta_{2,i}$.

Let us consider the following derivative with respect to u of a representative term of (14.5),

$$\frac{c \, [\beta(u)]^p \, u^q}{\delta(u)} , \tag{16.1}$$

where c is a constant. Its first parametric derivative with respect to u is

$$\frac{c \, q \, [\beta(u)]^p \, u^{q-1}}{\delta(u)} + \frac{c \, p \, [\beta(u)]^{p-1} \, \beta^{(1)}(u) \, u^q}{\delta(u)} \tag{16.2}$$

$$- \frac{c \, [\beta(u)]^p \, \delta^{(1)}(u) \, u^q}{\delta(u)^2} ,$$

where

$$\delta(u) = \beta_2(u) + 2[\beta_1(u)]^3 + 4[\beta_1(u)]^2 + 4\beta_1(u) + 2$$

$$\delta^{(1)}(u) = \beta_2^{(1)}(u) + 6[\beta_1(u)]^2 \beta_1^{(1)}(u) + 8\beta_1(u)\beta_1^{(1)}(u) + 4\beta_1^{(1)}(u).$$

(16.3)

Examination of (16.2) and (16.3) reveals that the second and third terms of (16.2) involve products with $\beta_1^{(1)}(u)$ or $\beta_2^{(1)}(u)$, while the first term of (16.2) would constitute the complete parametric derivative if β_1 and β_2 were not functions of u. If we were to compute $\beta_1(u)$ and $\beta_2(u)$ by interpolating between the $\beta_{1,i}$'s and $\beta_{2,i}$'s in such a way as to cause $\beta_1^{(1)}(u)$ and $\beta_2^{(1)}(u)$ to be zero at each joint then equations (14.2) would hold and G^1 continuity would be preserved.

Similarly, the second parametric derivative of (16.1) is

$$\frac{c(q-1)q[\beta(u)]^p u^{q-2}}{\delta(u)}$$

(16.4)

$$-\frac{c[\beta(u)]^p \delta^{(2)}(u) u^q}{\delta(u)^2} + \frac{2c[\beta(u)]^p \delta^{(1)}(u)^2 u^q}{\delta(u)^3}$$

$$-\frac{2cp[\beta(u)]^{p-1}\beta^{(1)}(u)\delta^{(1)}(u)u^q}{\delta(u)^2} - \frac{2cq[\beta(u)]^p \delta^{(1)}(u)u^{q-1}}{\delta(u)^2}$$

$$+\frac{cp[\beta(u)]^{p-1}\beta^{(2)}(u)u^q}{\delta(u)} + \frac{c(p-1)p[\beta(u)]^{p-2}\beta^{(1)}(u)^2 u^q}{\delta(u)}$$

$$+\frac{2cpq[\beta(u)]^{p-1}\beta^{(1)}(u)u^{q-1}}{\delta(u)},$$

where

$$\delta^{(2)}(u) = \beta_2^{(2)}(u) + 6[\beta_1(u)]^2\beta_1^{(2)}(u) + 8\beta_1(u)\beta_1^{(2)}(u)$$

$$+ 4\beta_1^{(2)}(u) + 12\beta_1(u)\beta_1^{(1)}(u)^2 + 8\beta_1^{(1)}(u)^2.$$

Again, only the first term of (16.4) lacks a product with at least one of $\beta_1^{(1)}(u)$, $\beta_2^{(1)}(u)$, $\beta_1^{(2)}(u)$ or $\beta_2^{(2)}(u)$, and the first term would constitute the complete second parametric derivative if β_1 and β_2 were not functions of u. Thus arranging that all four derivatives have the value zero at joints should be sufficient to preserve G^2 continuity of the curve. This is easily accomplished in the following manner.

Suppose that we use a polynomial $H(\beta_{i-1}, \beta_i; u)$ to interpolate between β_{i-1} and β_i. We have six constraints, since we would like

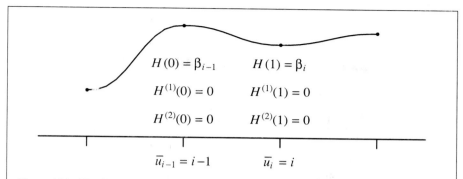

Figure 16.1. The idea is to interpolate the β_i in such a way as to cause the first and second derivatives at the knots to be zero.

$$H(\beta_{i-1}, \beta_i ; 0) = \beta_{i-1}$$

$$H(\beta_{i-1}, \beta_i ; 1) = \beta_i$$

$$H^{(1)}(\beta_{i-1}, \beta_i ; 0) = 0$$

$$H^{(1)}(\beta_{i-1}, \beta_i ; 1) = 0$$

$$H^{(2)}(\beta_{i-1}, \beta_i ; 0) = 0$$

$$H^{(2)}(\beta_{i-1}, \beta_i ; 1) = 0.$$

This suggests the use of a fifth degree polynomial (which has, of course, six coefficients). If

$$H(\beta_{i-1}, \beta_i ; u) = a + b u + c u^2 + d u^3 + e u^4 + f u^5$$

then the above equations take the form

$$H(\beta_{i-1}, \beta_i ; 0) = \beta_{i-1} = a$$

$$H(\beta_{i-1}, \beta_i ; 1) = \beta_i = a + b + c + d + e + f$$

$$H^{(1)}(\beta_{i-1}, \beta_i ; 0) = 0 = b$$

$$H^{(1)}(\beta_{i-1}, \beta_i ; 1) = 0 = b + 2c + 3d + 4e + 5f$$

$$H^{(2)}(\beta_{i-1}, \beta_i; 0) = 0 = 2c$$

$$H^{(2)}(\beta_{i-1}, \beta_i; 1) = 0 = 2c + 6d + 12e + 20f.$$

It is straightforward to obtain the polynomial

$$\beta_i(u) = H(\beta_{i-1}, \beta_i; u) \tag{16.5}$$

$$= \beta_{i-1} + 10(\beta_i - \beta_{i-1})u^3 - 15(\beta_i - \beta_{i-1})u^4 + 6(\beta_i - \beta_{i-1})u^5$$

$$= \beta_{i-1} + (\beta_i - \beta_{i-1})[10u^3 - 15u^4 + 6u^5]$$

which satisfies these equations; this is, in fact, a special case of quintic Hermite interpolation. By the argument just given, the use of (16.5) to interpolate β_1 and β_2 in (14.5) preserves G^2 continuity of the curve.

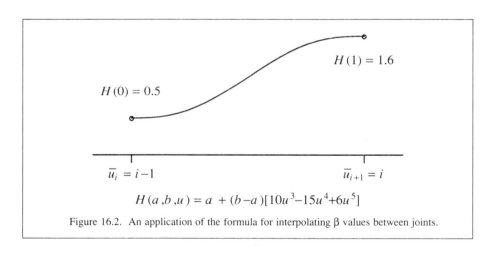

$$H(a, b, u) = a + (b-a)[10u^3 - 15u^4 + 6u^5]$$

Figure 16.2. An application of the formula for interpolating β values between joints.

It is, of course, possible that the derivative terms appearing in (16.1) and (16.4) might sum in such a way as to yield G^2 continuous curves even though the derivatives were nonzero; we have not ruled this out for all other interpolation schemes. However, using MACSYMA [Bogen83] it is not hard to produce examples that demonstrate that neither linear interpolation nor cubic Hermite interpolation works. Moreover, geometric continuity is not necessarily preserved if we use general quintic Hermite interpolation, even if the same two nonzero values are used for the first and second derivatives of $\beta_1(u)$ at the joints, and similarly for $\beta_2(u)$. Thus C^2 continuity of $\beta_1(u)$ and $\beta_2(u)$ is not sufficient to ensure G^2 continuity. See [Barsky82] for an example.

We will refer to the curves whose segments are defined by equations (4.10) and (14.5), where $\beta_1(u)$ and $\beta_2(u)$ are interpolated by equation (16.5), as *continuously-shaped Beta-spline curves*.

16.1 Locality

Just as for the uniformly-shaped Beta-splines, each basis function is nonzero only over four successive intervals. Since each basis function is used to weight a particular control vertex, moving a control vertex will alter only the four corresponding curve segments. These are, of course, consecutive.

The effect of altering a β_i is more localized still. The β_i at a particular joint determines how β is interpolated over the segments that meet at that joint, so that only two curve segments are changed.

16.2 Bias

Figure 16.3 illustrates a few of the effects that can be obtained by altering β_1's.

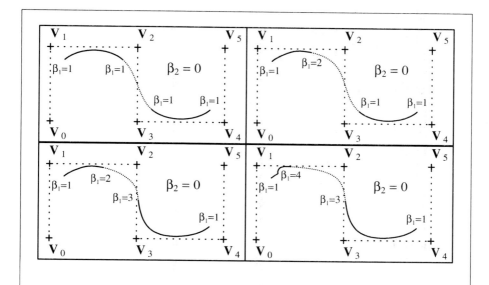

Figure 16.3. For these curves β_2 is held constant at zero while β_1 interpolates the values shown.

Although the resulting curves are often visually satisfying, their extreme locality with respect to changes in the shape parameters can result in "kinks" if there are large differences in the β values for consecutive control vertices. In Figure 16.4, modest reduction in the size of the jumps ameliorates the effect. The effect could also be overcome by using an alternative to equation (16.5) that interpolates the β's at more than two successive knots.

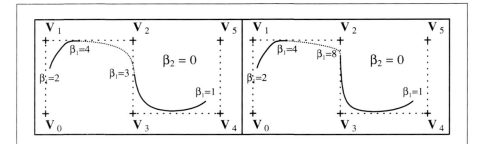

Figure 16.4. Less abrupt variation of β_1 can be used to smooth out the kink visible in the lower right frame of Figure 16.3, if that is desirable.

16.3   Tension

Since this scheme interpolates the β_i, the discussion of tension in [Barsky81a, Barsky87a, Barsky87b] is equally applicable here. We already know that the effect of increasing β_2 is to draw the curve towards the control graph. Let us examine the path followed by a particular joint, say the joint between segments $(i - 1)$ and i. The difference

$$\mathbf{Q}_i(0) - \mathbf{V}_{i-2} = \mathbf{Q}_{i-1}(1) - \mathbf{V}_{i-2} = \frac{\mathbf{C}_i - c_i \, \mathbf{V}_{i-2}}{c_i + \beta_{2,i}}$$

is the vector from the $(i - 2)^{nd}$ control vertex to this joint, where

$$\mathbf{C}_i = 2\,\beta_{1,i}^3\, \mathbf{V}_{i-2} + 4\,\beta_{1,i}\,(\beta_{1,i} + 1)\,\mathbf{V}_{i-1} + 2\,\mathbf{V}_i$$

$$c_i = 2\,\beta_{1,i}^3 + 4\,\beta_{1,i}^2 + 4\,\beta_{1,i} + 2.$$

Altering $\beta_{2,i}$ merely changes the length of this vector: values approaching $-c_i$ "push" the joint arbitrarily far away from $\mathbf{V}_{i-2}$. Large positive or negative values draw the joint arbitrarily close to $\mathbf{V}_{i-2}$, pulling the two segments meeting at that joint flat against the control polygon. Hence $\beta_{2,i}$ serves as a tension parameter, just as for uniformly-shaped Beta-spline curves. (See Figure 16.6.)

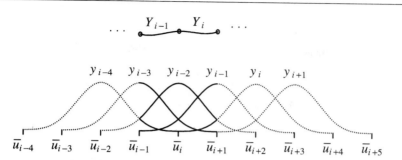

Figure 16.5. This illustration may help in keeping track of the indices. The ith interval runs from $\bar{u}_i$ to $\bar{u}_{i+1}$. The ith control vertex (actually the ith y coordinate here) scales the basis function whose support begins at $\bar{u}_i$. The ith uniform cubic B-spline $B_i(\bar{u})$ peaks at $\bar{u}_{i+2}$; the peak of ith Beta-spline $G_i(\bar{u})$ may be displaced left or right of $\bar{u}_{i+2}$ by decreasing or increasing β_1.

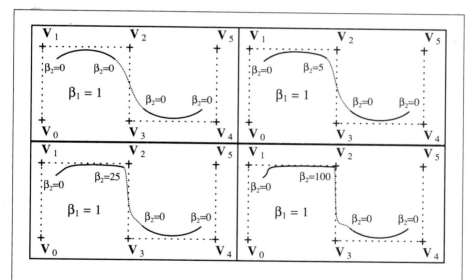

Figure 16.6. The value of β_2 at the joint nearest to V_2 is increased from 0 to 100 in three steps, pulling the joint towards V_2. In the limit this joint converges to V_2.

Again, wildly disparate values of β_2 for adjacent control vertices can produce kinks. These can be removed, if that is desirable, by smaller adjustments in neighboring β values, as shown in Figure 16.7, or by using an interpolation formula determined by more than two β values.

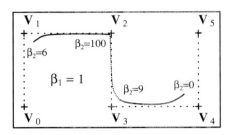

Figure 16.7. Altering the value of β_2 at a joint affects only the two curve segments that meet there. Making one such β_2 very large in comparison with its neighbors, as in Figure 16.5, causes these two segments to be abruptly pulled close to the control graph. The value of β_2 at adjacent joints can be adjusted to smooth out the curve.

For comparison with Figures 14.4 and 14.6, Figure 16.8 gives some examples of continuously-shaped basis functions.

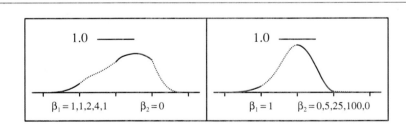

Figure 16.8. The effect of interpolating β values on the basis functions. On the left β_1 changes value from joint to joint, while on the right β_2 changes value.

Notice that each point on a continuously-shaped Beta-spline curve $\mathbf{Q}(u)$ also lies on the uniformly-shaped curve $\mathbf{R}(u)$ defined by the same control vertices and the values of β_1 and β_2 at that point on $\mathbf{Q}(u)$. The behavior of $\mathbf{Q}(u)$ as β_2 is varied can therefore be inferred from the behavior of the corresponding uniformly-shaped curves. Thus the β2 values can locally force a curve to converge to the control graph if they are increased arbitrarily.

16.4   Convex Hull

Like the uniformly-shaped Beta-spline curves, continuously-shaped Beta-spline curves possess a convex hull property in that the ith segment lies within the convex hull of control vertices $\mathbf{V}_{i-3}$, $\mathbf{V}_{i-2}$, $\mathbf{V}_{i-1}$ and $\mathbf{V}_i$, so long as both β_1 and β_2 are nonnegative. The argument, as we will see, is straightforward. Recall that because each basis function is nonzero over four intervals, we have

$$\mathbf{Q}_i(u) = \mathbf{V}_{i-3}b_{-3}(u) + \mathbf{V}_{i-2}b_{-2}(u) + \mathbf{V}_{i-1}b_{-1}(u) + \mathbf{V}_i\, b_{-0}(u). \tag{16.6}$$

Now for any given value of u, $\beta_1(u)$ and $\beta_2(u)$ yield some particular value of β_1 and β_2. By simply summing equations (14.5) we see that for every such β_1, β_2 and u

$$b_{-0}(u) + b_{-1}(u) + b_{-2}(u) + b_{-3}(u) = 1.$$

Next we must verify that these basis segments are nonnegative for all u in the interval $[0,1]$. If we rewrite equations (14.5) in the form

$$b_{-0}(u) = \frac{1}{\delta}\left[\, 2u^3 \,\right]$$

$$b_{-1}(u) = \frac{1}{\delta}\left[\, 2\beta_1^2 u^2(3-u) + 2\beta_1 u\,(3-u^2) \right.$$

$$\left. + \beta_2 u^2(3-2u) + 2(1-u^3) \,\right]$$

$$b_{-2}(u) = \frac{1}{\delta}\left[\, 2\beta_1^3 u\,((1-u)(2-u)+1) + 2\beta_1^2(u^3-3u^2+2) \right.$$

$$\left. + 2\beta_1(u^3-3u+2) + \beta_2(2u^3-3u^2+1) \,\right]$$

$$b_{-3}(u) = \frac{1}{\delta}\left[\, 2\beta_1^3(1-u)^3 \,\right]$$

where

$$\delta = \beta_2 + 2\beta_1^3 + 4\beta_1^2 + 4\beta_1 + 2 \neq 0$$

for $\beta_1 \geq 0$, $\beta_2 \geq 0$, and $u \in [0,1]$, it is easy to see by inspection that $b_{-0}(u)$, $b_{-1}(u)$, and $b_{-3}(u)$ are nonnegative. For $b_{-2}(u)$, elementary consideration of the zeros of the derivatives $3u(u-2)$, $3(u-1)(u-1)$ and $6u(u-1)$ of $u^3 - 3u^2 + 2$, $u^3 - 3u + 2$, and $2u^3 - 3u^2 + 1$ yields the same conclusion. Since β_1 and β_2 are actually interpolated by (16.5), it is necessary to show that

$$\beta_i(u) = \beta_{i-1} + (\beta_i - \beta_{i-1})[10u^3 - 15u^4 + 6u^5] \geq 0$$

if $\beta_{i-1} \geq 0$, $\beta_i \geq 0$, and $u \in [0,1]$. Consider

$$\beta_i^{(1)}(u) = 30(\beta_i - \beta_{i-1})u^2(1-u)^2.$$

Clearly the slope changes sign only at $u = 0$ and $u = 1$. Since

$$\beta_i(0.5) = \frac{\beta_i + \beta_{i-1}}{2} \geq 0 \quad \text{if} \quad \beta_{i-1}, \beta_i \geq 0,$$

$\beta_i(u)$ must be nonnegative on $[0,1]$ so long as the β_i are nonnegative.

Hence as long as $\beta_{1,i} \geq 0$ and $\beta_{2,i} \geq 0$, $\mathbf{Q}_i(u)$ lies within the convex hull of $\mathbf{V}_{i-3}$, $\mathbf{V}_{i-2}$, $\mathbf{V}_{i-1}$ and $\mathbf{V}_i$.

16.5   End Conditions

Just as for the uniform cubic B-splines, a properly defined continuously-shaped Beta-spline curve segment is the linear combination of four basis functions, as in equation (16.6). Thus $m+1$ control vertices $\mathbf{V}_0, \ldots, \mathbf{V}_m$ can be used to define $m-2$ segments, which we index as $\mathbf{Q}_3(u), \cdots, \mathbf{Q}_m(u)$. The Beta-spline curve begins at

$$\mathbf{Q}_3(0) = \frac{1}{\delta(0)}\left[2\beta_{1,i}^3 \mathbf{V}_0 + (\delta(0) - 2\beta_{1,i}^3 - 2)\mathbf{V}_1 + 2\mathbf{V}_2 \right].$$

(The ending point of the curve is analyzed in an analogous manner.) Thus the curve does not, in general, begin at a control vertex, or even at a point along the line segment from $\mathbf{V}_0$ to $\mathbf{V}_1$. (See Figure 16.9 for example.) To obtain better control of the beginning of the curve, one therefore often treats the ends of the curve specially.

Let $\mathbf{Q}(\overline{u})$ be a continuously-shaped Beta-spline curve with $\beta_1 = \beta_{1,i}$ and $\beta_2 = \beta_{2,i}$ at the joint between the ith and $(i+1)^{st}$ segments. Let $\mathbf{R}(\overline{u})$ be a uniformly-shaped Beta-spline curve defined by the same control vertices, but with $\beta_1 = \beta_{1,i}$ and $\beta_2 = \beta_{2,i}$ throughout. By the definition of $\mathbf{Q}(\overline{u})$ we must have $\mathbf{Q}(\overline{u}) = \mathbf{R}(\overline{u})$, $\mathbf{Q}^{(1)}(\overline{u}) = \mathbf{R}^{(1)}(\overline{u})$ and $\mathbf{Q}^{(2)}(\overline{u}) = \mathbf{R}^{(2)}(\overline{u})$ at the joint in question.

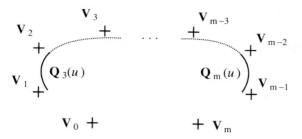

Figure 16.9. It is hard to say more than that a typical Beta-spline curve begins and ends "in the vicinity" of the first and last control vertices. For example it does not, in general, interpolate any of them.

Hence the analysis of end conditions in [Barsky81a, Barsky87b] applies immediately to continuously-shaped Beta-spline curves. In fact these techniques for controlling Beta-spline end conditions are identical to the techniques discussed earlier for uniform cubic B-splines (which are a special case of the Beta-splines), although the analysis is more complicated. We will summarize them here, but will not give a detailed development.

- *A double first vertex.* We define an additional segment at the beginning of the curve by

$$\mathbf{Q}_2(u) = \mathbf{V}_0 [b_{-3}(u) + b_{-2}(u)] + \mathbf{V}_1 b_{-1}(u) + \mathbf{V}_2 b_{-0}(u).$$

$\mathbf{Q}_2(u)$ begins at a point lying along the line segment from $\mathbf{V}_0$ to $\mathbf{V}_1$, at which point it is tangent to that line and has zero curvature.

- *A triple first vertex.* We define two additional segments at the beginning of the curve by

$$\mathbf{Q}_1(u) = \mathbf{V}_0 [b_{-3}(u) + b_{-2}(u) + b_{-1}(u)] + \mathbf{V}_2 b_{-0}(u)$$

$$\mathbf{Q}_2(u) = \mathbf{V}_0 [b_{-3}(u) + b_{-2}(u)] + \mathbf{V}_1 b_{-1}(u) + \mathbf{V}_2 b_{-0}(u).$$

The curve then begins at $\mathbf{Q}_1(0) = \mathbf{V}_0$ and the first segment of the curve is a short straight line. The behavior of the second segment $\mathbf{Q}_2(u)$, which has a double first vertex, is described above.

The analysis of double and triple vertices is equally applicable on the interior of a curve. Triple interior vertices are particularly interesting since they can result in a corner, as in Figure 16.10.

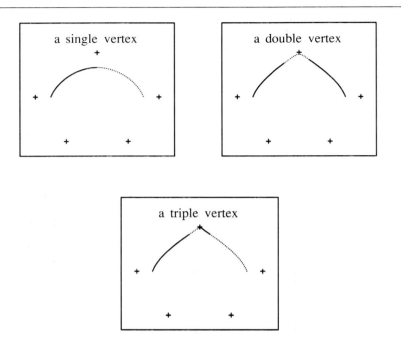

Figure 16.10. β_1 is one and β_2 is zero at all joints; these are in fact simply uniform cubic B-spline curves, although a corner results at a triple vertex for any values of β_1 and β_2 unless the control vertices immediately preceding and following the vertex are both collinear with it. The double control vertex is not interpolated, while the triple vertex is.

This corner is not a violation of G^2 continuity because, or at least in the sense that, the first parametric derivative vector has the value (0,0) at the joint that coincides with the interpolated control vertex where the corner occurs, so that the unit tangent vector is not defined. Multiple vertices give a tension-like effect. Figure 16.11 to compares the effect of repeating a vertex with the effect of altering β_2 there.

An alternative way of controlling the beginning of a curve is to define a *phantom vertex* $\mathbf{V}_{-1}$ and a corresponding initial segment

$$\mathbf{Q}_2(u) = \mathbf{V}_{-1} b_{-3}(u) + \mathbf{V}_0 b_{-2}(u) + \mathbf{V}_1 b_{-1}(u) + \mathbf{V}_2 b_{-0}(u)$$

in such a way as to satisfy some requirement. We may ask that:

- $\mathbf{Q}_2(0)$ interpolate some furnished point (generally resulting in nonzero curvature);
- $\mathbf{Q}_2(0)$ interpolate $\mathbf{V}_0$ (at which point the curvature is then zero);

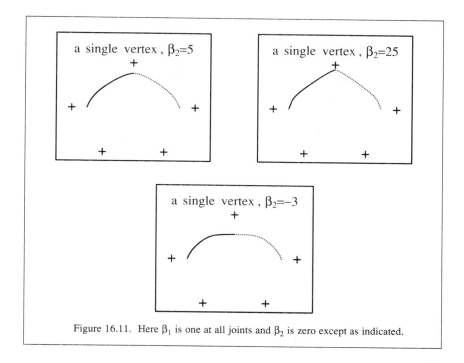

Figure 16.11. Here β_1 is one at all joints and β_2 is zero except as indicated.

- $\mathbf{Q}_2^{(1)}(0)$ have some specified value (generally resulting in nonzero curvature);

- $\mathbf{Q}_2^{(2)}(0)$ have some specified value (generally resulting in nonzero curvature);

- $\mathbf{Q}_2^{(2)}(0)$ be zero, resulting in zero curvature at $\mathbf{Q}_2(0)$.

All these techniques involve extending the curve by one or two segments at either end. This implies the existence of additional joints and associated β values. Hence the sequence of control vertices is extended to specify behavior at the ends of the curve, and additional β_1 and β_2 values must be specified as well. These may take any value without affecting the behavior described above. In practice it is probably easiest simply to replicate β values as well as vertices.

The curves we have discussed so far are *open* curves, which is to say that the two endpoints do not, in general, coincide. A G^2-continuous *closed* curve whose endpoints do meet and which is G^2-continuous is obtained if the first three control vertices are identical to the last three and the same values of β_1 and β_2 are used at the joint between the beginning and the ending of the curve. (See Figure 16.12 for an example.)

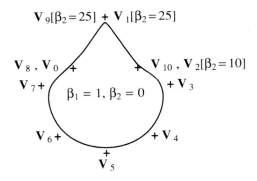

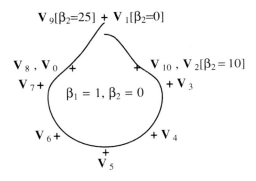

Figure 16.12. On the top is a continuously-shaped Beta-spline curve in which the first three and the last three control vertices are identical and the values of β_1 and β_2 at the second and penultimate control vertices are also identical; a closed G^2 continuous curve results. The bottom curve is defined identically except that the second and penultimate control vertices, whose positions coincide, have distinct values of β_2; a discontinuity results.

Although it may appear that the joint near V_1 in the top curve of Figure 16.12 is a corner, by zooming in on the joint Figure 16.13 shows that in fact curvature continuity is maintained.

Again, the arguments establishing these results appear in [Barsky81a, Barsky87b] and the details have therefore been omitted.

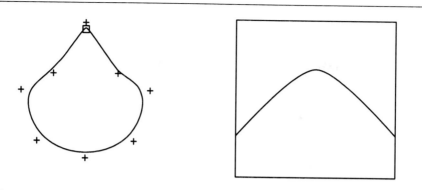

Figure 16.13. On the right is a magnified image of the indicated portion of the curve shown on the left.

16.6 Evaluation

Using factorizations given in [Barsky81a, Barsky87b], the Beta-spline basis segments (14.5) can be evaluated in 28 multiplication/divisions and 21 addition/subtractions. If a *single point* on $\mathbf{Q}(\overline{u})$ is to be determined, the evaluation of the right hand side of (4.10) in d dimensions then requires $4d$ multiplications and $3d$ additions. The total cost of evaluating a point on a uniformly-shaped 2D Beta-spline curve is therefore 36 multiplication/divisions and 27 addition/subtractions; a 3D uniformly-shaped Beta-spline curve requires 40 multiplication/divisions and 30 addition/subtractions.

For a continuously-shaped Beta-spline curve, equation (16.5) can be evaluated in 6 multiplications and 4 addition/subtractions if it is factored into the form

$$H(\beta_{i-1}, \beta_i, u) = \beta_{i-1} + (\beta_i - \beta_{i-1})[10 + (6u - 15)u]u^3.$$

Since both $\beta_1(\overline{u})$ and $\beta_2(\overline{u})$ must be computed, both $H(\beta_{1,i-1}, \beta_{1,i}, u)$ and $H(\beta_{2,i-1}, \beta_{2,i}, u)$ must be evaluated. However, since $[10 + (6u - 15)u]u^3$ need only be evaluated once, the total cost of interpolation is 7 multiplications and 6 addition/subtractions. The additional cost for a single evaluation by this technique of a continuously-shaped Beta-spline curve, beyond that required to evaluate a uniformly-shaped curve, is therefore about 20%.

More often we wish to evaluate a sequence of points along each segment to render a curve. If we compute these points by repeatedly evaluating the basis functions as described above, then a uniformly-shaped 2D Beta-spline segment can be evaluated at r values of u in $16 + 20r$ multiplication/divisions and $14 + 13r$ addition/subtractions while its 3D counterpart requires $16 + 24r$ multiplication/divisions and $14 + 16r$ addition/subtractions. The corresponding cost to evaluate a 2D continuously shaped Beta-spline curve is $36r$

multiplication/divisions and $2+31r$ addition/subtractions, while in 3D the cost is $41r$ multiplication/divisions and $2+34r$ addition/subtractions. The difference between the evaluation of uniformly- and continuously-shaped Beta-spline curves results from the need to re-evaluate the coefficients of the polynomials forming the basis segments, owing to the fact that β_1 and β_2 are no longer constant, as well as from the cost of actually performing the interpolation [Barsky81a,Barsky87b].

If, instead, we first sum the terms in equations (4.11) so as to compute the coefficients of $X(\bar{u})$ and $Y(\bar{u})$, and then use Horner's rule (nested multiplication), then the evaluation of a 2D uniformly-shaped Beta-spline segment at r points requires $49+6r$ multiplication/divisions and $38+6r$ addition/subtractions while the 3D curve requires $65+9r$ multiplication/divisions and $50+9r$ addition/subtractions. A modified version of this algorithm which computes continuously-shaped Beta-spline curves requires $55r$ multiplication/divisions and $2+48r$ addition/subtractions in 2D and $75r$ multiplication/divisions and $2+63r$ addition/subtractions in 3D.

A third alternative is to use forward differencing techniques. For large values of r the evaluation of a 2D uniformly-shaped curve in this way is almost a factor of 17 faster than the evaluation of a continuously-shaped curve using Horner's rule, although it is subject to cumulative roundoff error. While forward differencing in principle is applicable to the continuously-shaped Beta-splines as well, it is impractical since each coordinate is the quotient of an 18th and a 15th degree polynomial. Where cost is a crucial factor it may be desirable to fix β_1 at one and manipulate β_2 alone. Doing so significantly reduces the expense of evaluating equations (14.5) after interpolating β_2; each coordinate is then the quotient of an 8th and a 5th degree polynomial.

There are other possibilities. Uniformly-shaped Beta-splines are translates of one another, and need only be evaluated for the first segment drawn. Their values may be saved and used again to draw all the other segments. In the case of continuously-shaped Beta-splines, each joint is associated with distinct values of β_1 and β_2, so that in general each basis function has a different shape and must be individually evaluated. The rendering of curves by subdivision was touched upon in Chapter 10. For Beta-splines this is covered more fully in [Barsky/DeRose85] and [Barsky/et al.87].

An existing curve can be altered much more efficiently than a new curve can be drawn. If a control vertex is moved then only four segments of the curve must be recomputed, since the basis function that the vertex weights is nonzero on only four successive intervals. Because the vertex is usually moved several times in succession, it is advantageous to save the basis segments as they are first evaluated to avoid recomputing them. Moreover, the portions of the computation for each segment that are actually dependent on the vertex being moved may be segregated from those portions of the computation that are not, and which therefore need not be recomputed.

Altering a β parameter necessitates recomputing only two intervals, although all the basis segments in each must be re-evaluated.

16.7 Continuously-Shaped Beta-spline Surfaces

Continuously shaped Beta-spline curves can be elegantly generalized to define surfaces that preserve G^2 continuity at the boundaries between adjacent patches. The generalization we will present allows the user to specify a bias and tension parameter at each corner of a patch; patches that share a corner make use of the same β values at that corner. The technique is to generalize the univariate interpolation formula (16.5) to a bivariate formula in such a way that:

- the β values at the four corners of a patch are interpolated;
- two patches which share an edge will have the same β values along that edge;
- the first and second partial derivatives of $\beta_1(u,v)$ and $\beta_2(u,v)$ across a patch boundary will be zero.

This last property will allow us to ignore (at boundaries) all but one of the terms that arise in computing the partial derivatives of a Beta-spline surface in which $\beta_1(u,v)$ and $\beta_2(u,v)$ are allowed to vary, so that the properties of a uniformly shaped Beta-spline surface will be inherited by our continuously shaped surface.

Our first consideration is to develop a bivariate interpolation formula. It is at least plausible that we would like lines of constant u or of constant v on a continuously-shaped surface to be continuously-shaped curves. Along such curves we would then expect β_1 and β_2 to vary as they do along continuously-shaped Beta-spline curves. For convenience let us write equation (16.5) in two pieces as

$$s = 10u^3 - 15u^4 + 6u^5$$

$$H(\beta_{i-1},\beta_i;u) = (1-s)\beta_{i-1} + s\,\beta_i$$

and along the top and bottom boundaries of the patch interpolate the β values

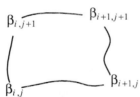

with our customary formula to obtain

$$\beta_{top} = H(\beta_{i-1,j}, \beta_{i,j};u) = (1-s)\beta_{i-1,j} + s\,\beta_{i,j}$$

$$\beta_{bot} = H(\beta_{i-1,j-1}, \beta_{i,j-1};u) = (1-s)\beta_{i-1,j-1} + s\,\beta_{i,j-1}.$$

This yields values of β at parametric distance u from the left edge along the top and bottom of the patch. To interpolate in the v direction across the interior of the patch it is again natural to use the formula

---

$$H(\beta_{bot}, \beta_{top}; v) = (1-t)\beta_{bot} + \beta_{top}$$

with

$$t = 10v^3 - 15v^4 + 6v^5.$$

Substituting, we obtain the desired bivariate interpolation formula

$$\beta_{i,j}(u,v) = (1-s)(1-t)\beta_{i-1,j-1} + s(1-t)\beta_{i,j-1}$$
$$+ (1-s)t\,\beta_{i-1,j} + st\,\beta_{i,j} \qquad (16.7)$$

with

$$s = 10u^3 - 15u^4 + 6u^5$$

$$t = 10v^3 - 15v^4 + 6v^5.$$

(We emphasize that s and t are used here for notational convenience.) $\beta_{i,j}(u,v)$ has some rather attractive properties:

- it interpolates $\beta_{i-1,j-1}$, $\beta_{i,j-1}$, $\beta_{i-1,j}$ and $\beta_{i,j}$;
- along any of the four borders of a patch it reduces to the univariate interpolating formula (16.5);
- the first and second partial derivatives of $\beta_{i,j}(u,v)$ with respect to v for $v = 0$ and $v = 1$ (i.e., across a vertical patch boundary) are zero, as are the first and second partial derivatives with respect to u for $u = 0$ and $u = 1$.

Now let us define a continuously-shaped Beta-spline surface patch $\mathbf{Q}_{i,j}$ by equation (14.8) except that we let β_1 and β_2 be functions of u and v, using equation (16.7) to interpolate between β values associated with the corners of each patch. To simplify the notation we will actually discuss $\mathbf{Q}_{3,3}$ and $\mathbf{Q}_{3,4}$, which are defined by the control vertex mesh

$\mathbf{V}_{0,4}$	$\mathbf{V}_{1,4}$	$\mathbf{V}_{2,4}$	$\mathbf{V}_{3,4}$
$\mathbf{V}_{0,3}$	$\mathbf{V}_{1,3}$	$\mathbf{V}_{2,3}$	$\mathbf{V}_{3,3}$
$\mathbf{V}_{0,2}$	$\mathbf{V}_{1,2}$	$\mathbf{V}_{2,2}$	$\mathbf{V}_{3,2}$
$\mathbf{V}_{0,1}$	$\mathbf{V}_{1,1}$	$\mathbf{V}_{2,1}$	$\mathbf{V}_{3,1}$
$\mathbf{V}_{0,0}$	$\mathbf{V}_{1,0}$	$\mathbf{V}_{2,0}$	$\mathbf{V}_{3,0}$.

(The generalization for an arbitrary patch is straightforward.) Since the $b_r(u)$ and $b_s(v)$ are now functions of $\beta_1(u,v)$ and $\beta_2(u,v)$, we write equation (14.9) for $\mathbf{Q}_{3,4}$ as

$$\mathbf{Q}_{3,4}(u,v) = \tag{16.8}$$

$$[\ \mathbf{V}_{0,4}\,b_{-3}(\beta_1,\beta_2;u) + \mathbf{V}_{1,4}\,b_{-2}(\beta_1,\beta_2;u) + \mathbf{V}_{2,4}\,b_{-1}(\beta_1,\beta_2;u) + \mathbf{V}_{3,4}\,b_{-0}(\beta_1,\beta_2;u)\ ]\ b_{-0}(\beta_1,\beta_2;v)$$

$$+\ [\ \mathbf{V}_{0,3}\,b_{-3}(\beta_1,\beta_2;u) + \mathbf{V}_{1,3}\,b_{-2}(\beta_1,\beta_2;u) + \mathbf{V}_{2,3}\,b_{-1}(\beta_1,\beta_2;u) + \mathbf{V}_{3,3}\,b_{-0}(\beta_1,\beta_2;u)\ ]\ b_{-1}(\beta_1,\beta_2;v)$$

$$+\ [\ \mathbf{V}_{0,2}\,b_{-3}(\beta_1,\beta_2;u) + \mathbf{V}_{1,2}\,b_{-2}(\beta_1,\beta_2;u) + \mathbf{V}_{2,2}\,b_{-1}(\beta_1,\beta_2;u) + \mathbf{V}_{3,2}\,b_{-0}(\beta_1,\beta_2;u)\ ]\ b_{-2}(\beta_1,\beta_2;v)$$

$$+\ [\ \mathbf{V}_{0,1}\,b_{-3}(\beta_1,\beta_2;u) + \mathbf{V}_{1,1}\,b_{-2}(\beta_1,\beta_2;u) + \mathbf{V}_{2,1}\,b_{-1}(\beta_1,\beta_2;u) + \mathbf{V}_{3,1}\,b_{-0}(\beta_1,\beta_2;u)\ ]\ b_{-3}(\beta_1,\beta_2;v)\ .$$

$\mathbf{Q}_{3,3}$ is similarly defined by

$$\mathbf{Q}_{3,3}(u,v) = \tag{16.9}$$

$$[\ \mathbf{V}_{0,3}\,b_{-3}(\beta_1,\beta_2;u) + \mathbf{V}_{1,3}\,b_{-2}(\beta_1,\beta_2;u) + \mathbf{V}_{2,3}\,b_{-1}(\beta_1,\beta_2;u) + \mathbf{V}_{3,3}\,b_{-0}(\beta_1,\beta_2;u)\ ]\ b_{-0}(\beta_1,\beta_2;v)$$

$$+\ [\ \mathbf{V}_{0,2}\,b_{-3}(\beta_1,\beta_2;u) + \mathbf{V}_{1,2}\,b_{-2}(\beta_1,\beta_2;u) + \mathbf{V}_{2,2}\,b_{-1}(\beta_1,\beta_2;u) + \mathbf{V}_{3,2}\,b_{-0}(\beta_1,\beta_2;u)\ ]\ b_{-1}(\beta_1,\beta_2;v)$$

$$+\ [\ \mathbf{V}_{0,1}\,b_{-3}(\beta_1,\beta_2;u) + \mathbf{V}_{1,1}\,b_{-2}(\beta_1,\beta_2;u) + \mathbf{V}_{2,1}\,b_{-1}(\beta_1,\beta_2;u) + \mathbf{V}_{3,1}\,b_{-0}(\beta_1,\beta_2;u)\ ]\,b_{-2}(\beta_1,\beta_2;v)$$

$$+\ [\ \mathbf{V}_{0,0}\,b_{-3}(\beta_1,\beta_2;u) + \mathbf{V}_{1,0}\,b_{-2}(\beta_1,\beta_2;u) + \mathbf{V}_{2,0}\,b_{-1}(\beta_1,\beta_2;u) + \mathbf{V}_{3,0}\,b_{-0}(\beta_1,\beta_2;u)\ ]\,b_{-3}(\beta_1,\beta_2;v)\ .$$

We will discuss the behavior of these patches at their common (''horizontal'') boundary, which is $\mathbf{Q}_{3,4}(u,0)$ and $\mathbf{Q}_{3,3}(u,1)$. (The argument for common ''vertical'' boundaries is analogous, and is therefore omitted.)

First, of course, we must verify that the curves $\mathbf{Q}_{3,4}(u,0)$ and $\mathbf{Q}_{3,3}(u,1)$ are actually identical. For any fixed u we may rewrite (16.8) and (16.9) as

$$\mathbf{Q}_{bot}(v) = \mathbf{W}_0\,b_{-3}(v) + \mathbf{W}_1\,b_{-2}(v) + \mathbf{W}_2\,b_{-1}(v) + \mathbf{W}_3\,b_{-0}(v) \tag{16.10}$$

and

$$\mathbf{Q}_{top}(v) = \mathbf{W}_1\,b_{-3}(v) + \mathbf{W}_2\,b_{-2}(v) + \mathbf{W}_3\,b_{-1}(v) + \mathbf{W}_4\,b_{-0}(v) \tag{16.11}$$

where

$$\mathbf{W}_4 = \mathbf{V}_{0,4}\,b_{-3}(u) + \mathbf{V}_{1,4}\,b_{-2}(u) + \mathbf{V}_{2,4}\,b_{-1}(u) + \mathbf{V}_{3,4}\,b_{-0}(u)$$

$$\mathbf{W}_3 = \mathbf{V}_{0,3}\,b_{-3}(u) + \mathbf{V}_{1,3}\,b_{-2}(u) + \mathbf{V}_{2,3}\,b_{-1}(u) + \mathbf{V}_{3,3}\,b_{-0}(u)$$

$$\mathbf{W}_2 = \mathbf{V}_{0,2}\,b_{-3}(u) + \mathbf{V}_{1,2}\,b_{-2}(u) + \mathbf{V}_{2,2}\,b_{-1}(u) + \mathbf{V}_{3,2}\,b_{-0}(u) \tag{16.12}$$

$$\mathbf{W}_1 = \mathbf{V}_{0,1}\,b_{-3}(u) + \mathbf{V}_{1,1}\,b_{-2}(u) + \mathbf{V}_{2,1}\,b_{-1}(u) + \mathbf{V}_{3,1}\,b_{-0}(u)$$

$$\mathbf{W}_0 = \mathbf{V}_{0,0}\,b_{-3}(u) + \mathbf{V}_{1,0}\,b_{-2}(u) + \mathbf{V}_{2,0}\,b_{-1}(u) + \mathbf{V}_{3,0}\,b_{-0}(u)\ .$$

As we have seen, along the common border $\beta_{2,3}(u,0)$ and $\beta_{2,2}(u,1)$ both reduce to $H(\beta_{2,1},\beta_{2,2};u)$. Hence the β_1 and β_2 which appear in (16.8) and (16.9) are identical, so that (16.10) and (16.11) are simply two successive segments on a uniformly-shaped Beta-spline curve. Hence $\mathbf{Q}_{bot}(1) = \mathbf{Q}_{top}(0)$, that is, $\mathbf{Q}_{3,3}(u,1) = \mathbf{Q}_{3,4}(u,0)$ as desired.

Tangent and curvature continuity between patches follow similarly if we apply the argument used earlier. Recall that the partial derivatives of $\beta_1(u,v)$ and $\beta_2(u,v)$ with respect to v for $v = 0$ and $v = 1$ are zero. If we fully expand equations (16.8) or (16.9), a typical term has the form

$$\frac{c\,[\beta_1(u,v)]^m\,[\beta_2(u,v)]^n\,u^p\,v^q}{[\beta_2(u,v)] + 2\,[\beta_1(u,v)]^3 + 4\,[\beta_1(u,v)]^2 + 4\,[\beta_1(u,v)] + 2}\,.$$

If we then compute the first partial derivative of this term with respect to v we find, after repeated application of the product, quotient and chain rules, that the only resulting term that does not contain a product with at least one of

$$\frac{d}{dv}\,\beta_1(u,v) \quad \text{and} \quad \frac{d}{dv}\,\beta_2(u,v)\,,$$

both of which are known to be zero by construction, is

$$\frac{c\,q\,[\beta_1(u,v)]^m\,[\beta_2(u,v)]^n\,u^p\,v^{q-1}}{[\beta_2(u,v)] + 2\,[\beta_1(u,v)]^3 + 4\,[\beta_1(u,v)]^2 + 4\,[\beta_1(u,v)] + 2}\,.$$

This is exactly the derivative that would have been obtained if β_1 and β_2 had not been functions of v. Therefore the first partial derivative of (16.8) with respect to v, for any u and $v = 0$, is exactly

$$\mathbf{Q}_{top}^{(1)}(0) \;=\; \mathbf{W}_1\,b_{-3}{}^{(1)}(0) + \mathbf{W}_2\,b_{-2}{}^{(1)}(0) + \mathbf{W}_3\,b_{-1}{}^{(1)}(0) + \mathbf{W}_4\,b_{-0}{}^{(1)}(0)$$

and the first partial derivative of (16.9) with respect to v, for any u and $v = 1$, is exactly

$$\mathbf{Q}_{bot}^{(1)}(1) \;=\; \mathbf{W}_0\,b_{-3}{}^{(1)}(1) + \mathbf{W}_1\,b_{-2}{}^{(1)}(1) + \mathbf{W}_2\,b_{-1}{}^{(1)}(1) + \mathbf{W}_3\,b_{-0}{}^{(1)}(1)\,.$$

These are simply the derivatives of two successive segments of a uniformly-shaped Beta-spline curves for particular values of β_1 and β_2, and we already know that such a curve has tangent continuity at its joints. Hence our surface has tangent continuity along its "horizontal" boundaries. The same argument works, *mutatis mutandis,* for the "vertical" boundaries as well, and generalizes to arbitrary patch boundaries, so that our surface is everywhere G^1 continuous.

An analogous argument suffices to establish the continuity of the curvature vector.

Alternatively, G^2 continuity can be directly verified using MACSYMA by evaluating the Beta-spline constraint equations if (16.7) is used to compute the values of β_1 and β_2. The algebra involved is, however, rather extensive.

The material in Chapters 17, 18, and 19 provides an alternative approach to defining nonuniformly-shaped Beta-spline curves and surfaces. In most respects these definitions will be as flexible as the continuously-shaped Beta-spline. In one respect, however, they will be less general. When they are used to define a tensor-product surface, they will not be capable of associating a different set of β values to each different patch corner as is shown in Figure 16.14. They are restricted to associating β values with each $\bar{u}_i$ knot and, separately, with each $\bar{v}_j$ knot. Consequently, the effect of varying a β value will be felt across the entire surface, along a $\bar{u} = \bar{u}_i$ or $\bar{v} = \bar{v}_j$ parametric line.

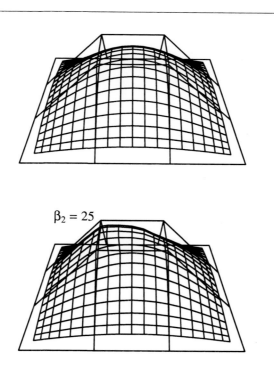

$\beta_2 = 25$

Figure 16.14. On the top is a Beta-spline surface in which $\beta_1 = 1$ and $\beta_2 = 0$ — a uniform bi-cubic B-spline surface. On the bottom the β_2 value at the joint corresponding to the indicated control vertex has been increased to 25. The twelve boundary vertices in the control graph have been "doubled" so as to define a total of 9 patches; otherwise the sixteen control vertices shown would define only a single patch lying close to the four central control vertices.

17

An Explicit
Formulation for
Cubic Beta–splines

In this chapter we wish to obtain basis functions for the G^2 cubic splines without appealing to reparametrizations of the sort used in Chapter 16. The desired result is pictured in Figure 17.1.

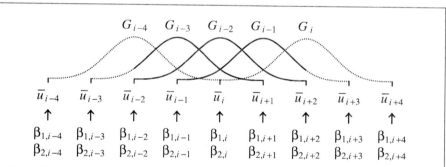

Figure 17.1. The Beta-splines in general. Various knot spacings as well as various values for β_1 and β_2 should be allowed. There should be 4-segment locality for each Beta-spline. We also expect the locality of effect due to changes in β_1 and/or β_2 at any knot, $\bar{u}_i$, to cover 4 segments, as indicated.

We will be able to provide explicit formulas for the basis segments of the ith Beta-spline, $G_i(\bar{u})$, in the case where the knots are spaced a unit apart, that is when

$$\bar{u}_{i+1} = \bar{u}_i + 1,$$

but with arbitrary nonnegative values of β_1 and β_2 at each knot. (See Figure 17.2.) We begin by establishing that this special case is all we need.

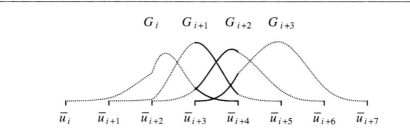

Figure 17.2. The four basis functions $G_i(\overline{u})$, $G_{i+1}(\overline{u})$, $G_{i+2}(\overline{u})$ and $G_{i+3}(\overline{u})$ that are nonzero on the particular interval $[\overline{u}_{i+3}, \overline{u}_{i+4})$. The knots are equally spaced, but a variety of different β_1 and β_2 values have been used.

17.1   Beta-splines with Uniform Knot Spacing

The general problem to be solved in constructing $G_i(\overline{u})$ is that of constructing segment polynomials $p_{left}(\overline{u})$ and $p_{right}(\overline{u})$ that meet at a knot $\overline{u}_i$ with G^2 continuity. Beyond providing $p_{left}(\overline{u}_i) = p_{right}(\overline{u}_i)$, which is easy to accomplish, we must arrange that

$$\beta_{1,i}\, p_{left}^{(1)}(\overline{u}_i) \;=\; p_{right}^{(1)}(\overline{u}_i) \tag{17.1}$$

and

$$\beta_{1,i}^2\, p_{left}^{(2)}(\overline{u}_i) + \beta_{2,i}\, p_{left}^{(1)}(\overline{u}_i) \;=\; p_{right}^{(2)}(\overline{u}_i) \tag{17.2}$$

for given values of $\beta_{1,i}$ and $\beta_{2,i}$.

Consider making two changes of variables, one for p_{left}:

$$u \;=\; \frac{\overline{u} - \overline{u}_{i-1}}{\overline{u}_i - \overline{u}_{i-1}} \quad \text{or} \quad \overline{u} \;=\; u\,(\overline{u}_i - \overline{u}_{i-1}) + \overline{u}_{i-1},$$

and the other for p_{right}:

$$u \;=\; \frac{\overline{u} - \overline{u}_i}{\overline{u}_{i+1} - \overline{u}_i} \quad \text{or} \quad \overline{u} \;=\; u\,(\overline{u}_{i+1} - \overline{u}_i) + \overline{u}_i.$$

If we define $\hat{p}_{left}(u)$ and $\hat{p}_{right}(u)$ by

$$p_{left}(u) \; = \; p_{left}(u\,(\bar{u}_i - \bar{u}_{i-1}) + \bar{u}_{i-1}) \; = \; \hat{p}_{left}(\bar{u})$$

and

$$p_{right}(u) \; = \; p_{right}(u\,(\bar{u}_{i+1} - \bar{u}_i) + \bar{u}_i) \; = \; \hat{p}_{right}(\bar{u}),$$

then the chain rule would give for example,

$$D_{\bar{u}}^{(1)}\,p_{left}(\bar{u})\,\big|_{\bar{u}=\bar{u}_i} \; = \; \frac{1}{\bar{u}_i - \bar{u}_{i-1}}\,D_u^{(1)}\,\hat{p}_{left}(u)\,\big|_{u=1}.$$

That is, the first derivatives at the knot would become

$$p_{left}^{(1)}(\bar{u}_i) \; = \; \frac{1}{\bar{u}_i - \bar{u}_{i-1}}\,\hat{p}_{left}^{(1)}(1)$$

and

$$p_{right}^{(1)}(\bar{u}_i) \; = \; \frac{1}{\bar{u}_{i+1} - \bar{u}_i}\,\hat{p}_{right}^{(1)}(0).$$

This shows that it would be sufficient to construct segment polynomials

$$\hat{p}_{left}(u) \quad \text{for } 0 \le u \le 1$$

and

$$\hat{p}_{right}(u) \quad \text{for } 0 \le u \le 1$$

so that

$$\beta_{1,i}\,\frac{1}{\bar{u}_i - \bar{u}_{i-1}}\,\hat{p}_{left}^{(1)}(1) \; = \; \frac{1}{\bar{u}_{i+1} - \bar{u}_i}\,\hat{p}_{right}^{(1)}(0)\,;$$

that is,

$$\hat{\beta}_{1,i}\,\hat{p}_{left}^{(1)}(1) \; = \; \hat{p}_{right}^{(1)}(0), \tag{17.3}$$

where

$$\hat{\beta}_{1,i} \; = \; \beta_{1,i}\,\frac{\bar{u}_{i+1} - \bar{u}_i}{\bar{u}_i - \bar{u}_{i-1}}. \tag{17.4}$$

This means that, if we have an explicit formula for each segment polynomial $\hat{p}_{left}(u)$ and $\hat{p}_{right}(u)$ on the unit interval, which satisfy (17.3), then $p_{left}(\overline{u})$ and $p_{right}(\overline{u})$ will satisfy (17.1) for a value of $\beta_{1,i}$ related to $\hat{\beta}_{1,i}$ according to (17.4). Likewise, to obtain (17.2), it is sufficient to find $\hat{p}_{left}(u)$ and $\hat{p}_{right}(u)$ on the unit interval so that

$$\hat{\beta}_{1,i}^2 \, \hat{p}_{left}^{(2)}(\overline{u}_i) + \hat{\beta}_{2,i} \, \hat{p}_{left}^{(1)}(\overline{u}_i) = \hat{p}_{right}^{(2)}(\overline{u}_i) \tag{17.5}$$

with $\hat{\beta}_{1,i}$ as given in (17.4) and

$$\hat{\beta}_{2,i} = \beta_{2,i} \, \frac{(\overline{u}_{i+1} - \overline{u}_i)^2}{\overline{u}_i - \overline{u}_{i-1}}. \tag{17.6}$$

Any cubic Beta-spline curve with arbitrary interval spacing, β_1's and β_2's can therefore be represented as a *uniform* cubic Beta-spline curve for an appropriately modified set of β_1's and β_2's.

17.2   Formulas

The specific formulas for the segment polynomials of a cubic Beta-spline with uniform knot spacing were first given in [Goodman85]. They reappeared in [Goodman/Unsworth85] and [Goodman/Unsworth86], with the addition of a recurrence based formula in the former of these two references.

Establishing formulas for the segment polynomials of the Beta-splines is a straightforward process of forming linear equations and finding solutions. Figure 17.2 presents the picture on which the basic analysis takes place. The segment intervals shown as solid curves are, for $\overline{u}_{i+3} \leq \overline{u} < \overline{u}_{i+4}$

$s_{i+3,-0}(\overline{u})$ for $G_{i+3}(\overline{u})$

$s_{i+2,-1}(\overline{u})$ for $G_{i+2}(\overline{u})$

$s_{i+1,-2}(\overline{u})$ for $G_{i+1}(\overline{u})$

$s_{i,-3}(\overline{u})$ for $G_i(\overline{u})$.

By assuming unit spacing of the knots, by comparing

$s_{i+3,-0}(\overline{u})$

and

$$f(\overline{u}) = s_{i+2,-1}(\overline{u}) + s_{i+1,-2}(\overline{u}) + s_{i,-3}(\overline{u})$$

on $[\overline{u}_{i+3}, \overline{u}_{i+4})$ and $[\overline{u}_{i+4}, \overline{u}_{i+5})$, by observing that

---

$$f(\bar{u}) + s_{i+3,-0}(\bar{u}) = 1$$

identically on $[\bar{u}_{i+3}, \bar{u}_{i+4})$, by recalling that $s_{i+3,-0}(\bar{u})$ is zero and has zero first and second derivatives at $\bar{u}_{i+3}$, and by using the equations for G^2 continuity at the knots, it is possible to set up enough equations for the coefficients of

$$f(\bar{u}) = d_0 + d_1 u + d_2 u^2 + d_3 u^3$$

and

$$s_{i+3,-0}(\bar{u}) = c_0 + c_1 u + c_2 u^2 + c_3 u^3,$$

where $u = \bar{u} - \bar{u}_{i+3}$, to determine $s_{i+3,-0}(\bar{u})$. The remaining segments are obtained in a similar manner.

The formulas given in the references result in the following segment polynomials for $G_i(\bar{u})$.

For $u = \bar{u} - \bar{u}_i$, $\bar{u}_i \le \bar{u} < \bar{u}_{i+1}$:

$$s_{i,-0}(u) = \frac{a_{i+2}}{d_{i+1}} u^3 \;;$$

for $u = \bar{u} - \bar{u}_{i+1}$, $\bar{u}_{i+1} \le \bar{u} < \bar{u}_{i+2}$:

$$s_{i,-1}(u) = \frac{a_{i+2}}{d_{i+1}} + 3\frac{a_{i+2}\beta_{1,i+1}}{d_{i+1}} u + 3\frac{a_{i+2}(a_{i+1} - \beta_{1,i+1})}{d_{i+1}} u^2$$
$$+ \frac{(a_{i+2}\beta_{1,i+1} + a_{i+1}\beta_{1,i+2}^2 - 2a_{i+1}a_{i+2})}{d_{i+1}} u^3 - \frac{a_{i+3}}{d_{i+2}} u^3 \;;$$

for $u = \bar{u} - \bar{u}_{i+2}$, $\bar{u}_{i+2} \le \bar{u} < \bar{u}_{i+3}$:

$$s_{i,-2}(u) = \frac{a_{i+2}\beta_{1,i+3}^3}{d_{i+2}} + 3\frac{a_{i+2}\beta_{1,i+3}^2}{d_{i+2}}(1-u) + 3\frac{a_{i+2}(a_{i+3} - \beta_{1,i+3}^2)}{d_{i+2}}(1-u)^2$$
$$+ \frac{(a_{i+3}\beta_{1,i+2} + a_{i+2}\beta_{1,i+3}^2 - 2a_{i+2}a_{i+3})}{d_{i+2}}(1-u)^3$$
$$- \frac{a_{i+1}\beta_{1,i+2}^3}{d_{i+1}}(1-u)^3 \;;$$

for $u = \bar{u} - \bar{u}_{i+3}, \bar{u}_{i+3} \le \bar{u} < \bar{u}_{i+4}$:

$$s_{i,-3}(u) = \frac{a_{i+2}\beta_{1,i+3}^3}{d_{i+2}} (1-u)^3,$$

where the knots are a unit distance apart, and

$$a_j = \beta_{1,j}^2 + \beta_{1,j} + \frac{1}{2}\beta_{2,j}$$

$$d_j = a_j (\beta_{1,j+1}^3 + \beta_{1,j+1}^2) + a_{j+1}(\beta_{1,j} + 1) + a_j a_{j+1}$$

for each j.

17.3   Recurrence

Strictly speaking, the contents of this section do not provide a true recurrence for the Beta-splines; i.e., a relationship of the form

$$G_{i,k}(\bar{u}) = L_i(\bar{u}) G_{i,k-1}(\bar{u}) + R_{i+1}(\bar{u}) G_{i+1,k-1}(\bar{u}),$$

which would relate the kth-order, G^{k-2} Beta-splines to the $k - 1^{\text{st}}$-order, G^{k-3} Beta-splines. However, it is possible, in the case of the cubic Beta-splines [Goodman85a], to develop a representation of the form

$$G_{i,4}(\bar{u}) = L_i(\bar{u}) B_{i,3}(\bar{u}) + R_{i+1}(\bar{u}) B_{i+1,3}(\bar{u})$$

that involves the quadratic B-splines. This has been done for the special case in which $\beta_{1,i} = 1$ for all i (allowing nonuniform knot spacing and arbitrary values for $\beta_{2,i}$). The functions $L_i(\bar{u})$ and $R_{i+1}(\bar{u})$ must provide the discontinuities in the second derivative of $G_{i,4}(\bar{u}) = G_i(\bar{u})$, and so it turns out that these functions must be piecewise linear. Figure 17.3 sketches the situation.

Formulas for the functions L and R can be worked out from the picture by equating polynomial coefficients. It is necessary to write out the segments in terms of powers of $\bar{u}$ and to derive equations on the coefficients from the relationship between segments represented by the β_2 discontinuity in the second derivative of G_i. For the special case under consideration ($\beta_1 = 1$), the Beta-spline is C^1, which also provides relationships between the segments. The formulas for the quadratic B-spline segments are as follows. For $\bar{u}_i \le \bar{u} < \bar{u}_{i+1}$:

$$B_{i,3}(\bar{u}) = \frac{(\bar{u} - \bar{u}_i)^2}{(\bar{u}_{i+2} - \bar{u}_i)(\bar{u}_{i+1} - \bar{u}_i)};$$

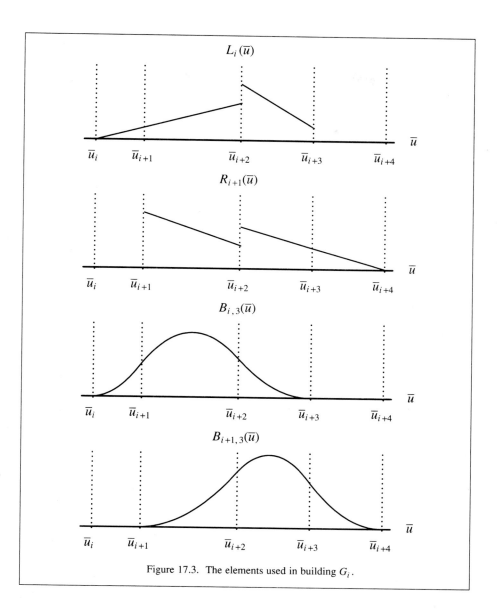

Figure 17.3. The elements used in building G_i.

for $\bar{u}_{i+1} \leq \bar{u} < \bar{u}_{i+2}$:

$$B_{i,3}(\bar{u}) = \frac{(\bar{u}-\bar{u}_i)\left[1-\dfrac{\bar{u}-\bar{u}_{i+1}}{\bar{u}_{i+2}-\bar{u}_{i+1}}\right]}{\bar{u}_{i+2}-\bar{u}_i} + \frac{\left[1-\dfrac{\bar{u}-\bar{u}_{i+1}}{\bar{u}_{i+3}-\bar{u}_{i+1}}\right](\bar{u}-\bar{u}_{i+1})}{\bar{u}_{i+2}-\bar{u}_{i+1}} \; ;$$

for $\bar{u}_{i+2} \leq \bar{u} < \bar{u}_{i+3}$:

$$B_{i,3}(\bar{u}) = \left[1-\frac{\bar{u}-\bar{u}_{i+1}}{\bar{u}_{i+3}-\bar{u}_{i+1}}\right]\left[1-\frac{\bar{u}-\bar{u}_{i+2}}{\bar{u}_{i+3}-\bar{u}_{i+2}}\right].$$

Next come the formulas for the segments of $L_i(\bar{u})$. For $\bar{u}_i \leq \bar{u} < \bar{u}_{i+2}$:

$$\frac{L_i(\bar{u})}{1+\tau_{i+2}} = \frac{\bar{u}-\bar{u}_i}{\sigma_{i+1}} \; ;$$

for $\bar{u}_{i+2} \leq \bar{u} < \bar{u}_{i+3}$:

$$\frac{L_i(\bar{u})}{1+\tau_{i+2}} =$$

$$\left[\frac{(\bar{u}_{i+2}-\bar{u}_i)+(\bar{u}_{i+2}-\bar{u}_{i+1})\,\tau_{i+1}}{\sigma_{i+1}} + \frac{(\bar{u}_{i+2}-\bar{u}_{i+1})\,\tau_{i+3}}{\sigma_{i+2}}\right]\left[\frac{\bar{u}_{i+3}-\bar{u}}{\bar{u}_{i+3}-\bar{u}_{i+2}}\right]$$

$$+ \left[\frac{\bar{u}_{i+4}-\bar{u}_{i+1}+3\,(\bar{u}_{i+3}-\bar{u}_{i+1})\,\tau_{i+3}}{\sigma_{i+2}}\right]\left[\frac{\bar{u}-\bar{u}_{i+2}}{\bar{u}_{i+3}-\bar{u}_{i+2}}\right].$$

Finally come the formulas for the segments of $R_i(\bar{u})$. (Note that we define R_i, but use R_{i+1}.) For $\bar{u}_i \leq \bar{u} < \bar{u}_{i+1}$:

$$\frac{R_i(\bar{u})}{1+\tau_{i+1}} = \left[\frac{\bar{u}_{i+3}-\bar{u}_{i+1}+(\bar{u}_{i+2}-\bar{u}_{i+1})\,\tau_{i+2}}{\sigma_{i+1}} + \frac{(\bar{u}_{i+2}-\bar{u}_{i+1})\,\tau_i}{\sigma_i}\right]\left[\frac{\bar{u}-\bar{u}_i}{\bar{u}_{i+1}-\bar{u}_i}\right]$$

$$+ \left[\frac{\bar{u}_{i+2}-\bar{u}_{i-1}+3\,(\bar{u}_{i+2}-\bar{u}_i)\,\tau_i}{\sigma_i}\right]\left[\frac{\bar{u}_{i+1}-\bar{u}}{\bar{u}_{i+1}-\bar{u}_i}\right] \; ;$$

for $\bar{u}_{i+1} \leq \bar{u} < \bar{u}_{i+3}$:

$$\frac{R_i(\bar{u})}{1+\tau_{i+1}} = \frac{\bar{u}_{i+3}-\bar{u}}{\sigma_{i+1}}.$$

In the above formulas σ_j and τ_j for each index j are defined as

$$\tau_j = \beta_{2,j} \frac{(u_{j+1}-u_j)(u_j-u_{j-1})}{2(u_{j+1}-u_{j-1})}$$

and

$$\sigma_j = u_{j+2}-u_{j-1}+(u_{j+2}-u_j)\tau_j+(u_{j+1}-u_{j-1})\tau_{j+1}+(u_{j+1}-u_j)\tau_j\tau_{j+1}.$$

The special case in which $\beta_{1,i}=1$ for all i is sufficient to handle general Beta-splines. In brief outline, the process of transforming from the general situation to the $\beta_1=1$ situation is as follows.

- Start with the general situation involving $\bar{u}$, $\bar{u}_i$, $\beta_{1,i}$, and $\beta_{2,i}$.

- Transform to the uniform knot spacing by setting $u=(\bar{u}-\bar{u}_i)/(\bar{u}_{i+1}-\bar{u}_i)$ for each interval $[\bar{u}_i,\bar{u}_{i+1})$. (If we were to produce Beta-splines in this setting, we would want to use

$$\hat{\beta}_{1,i} = \beta_{1,i} \frac{\bar{u}_{i+1}-\bar{u}_i}{\bar{u}_i-\bar{u}_{i-1}}$$

and

$$\hat{\beta}_{2,i} = \beta_{2,i} \frac{(\bar{u}_{i+1}-\bar{u}_i)^2}{\bar{u}_i-\bar{u}_{i-1}}$$

to construct basis functions equivalent to those originally desired.)

- Choose $\ddot{u}_0$ arbitrarily, and choose knots $\ddot{u}_1,\ldots,\ddot{u}_{m+4}$ so that the knot spacing $\ddot{u}_{i+1}-\ddot{u}_i$, $\ddot{u}_i-\ddot{u}_{i+1}$ produces

$$\ddot{\beta}_{1,i} = \hat{\beta}_{1,i} \frac{\ddot{u}_i-\ddot{u}_{i-1}}{\ddot{u}_{i+1}-\ddot{u}_i} = 1.$$

Construct Beta-splines using the $\ddot{u}$ knot spacing and β_2 parameters given by

$$\ddot{\beta}_{2,i} = \hat{\beta}_{2,i} \frac{\ddot{u}_i-\ddot{u}_{i-1}}{(\ddot{u}_{i+1}-\ddot{u}_i)^2}.$$

17.4   Examples

Generally speaking the explicit Beta-splines behave much as the uniformly- and continuously-shaped Beta-splines do. Figures 17.4–13 illustrate this. It is illuminating to see how changes in the basis functions shown in Figures 17.5, 17.7 and 17.11 produce the curves shown in Figures 17.4, 17.6, 17.8 and 17.10.

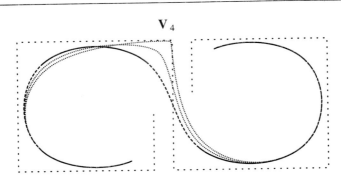

Figure 17.4. The solid/dashed line is a uniform cubic B-spline curve (β_1 and β_2 have the values 1 and 0 at every joint). The dotted curves result when the value of β_2 at the joint nearest $\mathbf{V}_4$ is set to 2, 10 and 100, respectively. Increasing values of β_2 draw the joint in question towards $\mathbf{V}_4$. For clarity the control graph is shown, but not the control vertices.

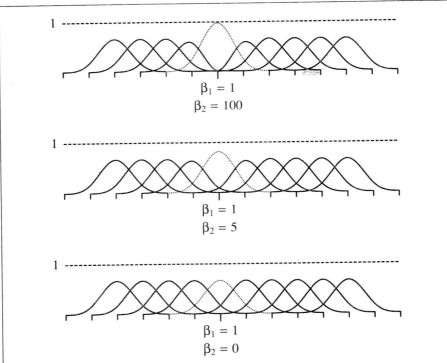

$$\beta_1 = 1$$
$$\beta_2 = 100$$

$$\beta_1 = 1$$
$$\beta_2 = 5$$

$$\beta_1 = 1$$
$$\beta_2 = 0$$

Figure 17.5. The Beta-splines corresponding to the four curves of Figure 17.4. β_1 and β_2 have the values 1 and 0 at all knots except the one explicitly labeled.

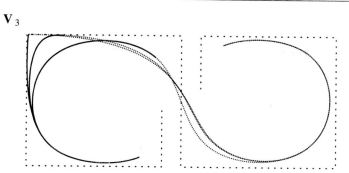

V₃

Figure 17.6. Starting from the same uniform cubic B-spline curve as appears in Figure 17.4, we successively increase β_1 at the joint between the solid and dotted portions of the curve, so that it has the values 1, 10 and 200. As β_1 is increased the joint is pulled towards V_3.

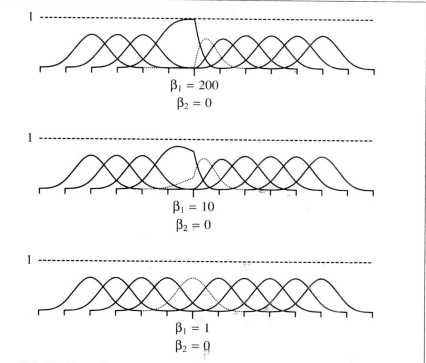

$$\beta_1 = 200$$
$$\beta_2 = 0$$

$$\beta_1 = 10$$
$$\beta_2 = 0$$

$$\beta_1 = 1$$
$$\beta_2 = 0$$

Figure 17.7. The Beta-splines corresponding to the four curves of Figure 17.6. β_1 and β_2 have the values 1 and 0 at all knots except the one explicitly labeled.

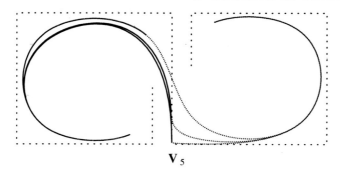

V$_5$

Figure 17.8. Symmetric behavior occurs if we set β_1 to the values 1 , 1/10, and 1/200 , respectively, with $\beta_2 = 0$. This time the joint is pulled towards **V**$_5$.

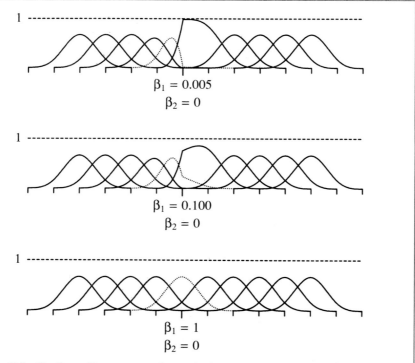

$$\beta_1 = 0.005$$
$$\beta_2 = 0$$

$$\beta_1 = 0.100$$
$$\beta_2 = 0$$

$$\beta_1 = 1$$
$$\beta_2 = 0$$

Figure 17.9. The Beta-splines corresponding to the four curves of Figure 17.8. β_1 and β_2 have the values 1 and 0 at all knots except the one explicitly labeled.

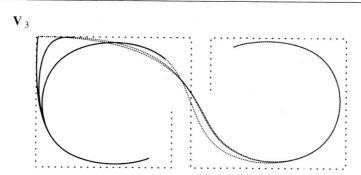

V_3

Figure 17.10. The β_1 values here are the same as in Figure 17.6 except that the value of β_2 at the joint in question is 10 in each case instead of 0. Again the joint is pulled towards V_3. Recall that increasing β_2 at that joint has the effect of pulling the curve towards V_4.

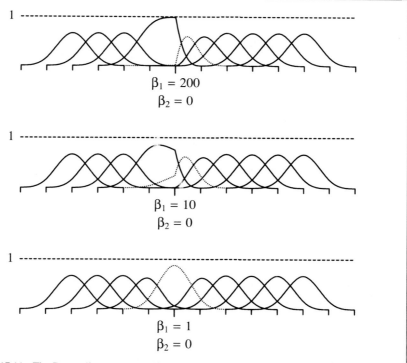

$\beta_1 = 200$
$\beta_2 = 0$

$\beta_1 = 10$
$\beta_2 = 0$

$\beta_1 = 1$
$\beta_2 = 0$

Figure 17.11. The Beta-splines corresponding to the four curves of Figure 17.10. β_1 and β_2 have the values 1 and 0 at all knots except the one explicitly labeled.

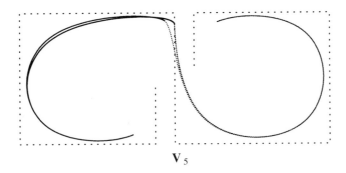

V₅ ... $\mathbf{V}_5$

Figure 17.12. The β_1 values here are the same as in Figure 17.8 except that the value of β_2 at the joint in question is 10 in each case instead of 0. Note that in this case the joint does not converge to $\mathbf{V}_5$. Tensing the curve toward $\mathbf{V}_4$ by setting a high value on β_2 at the joint has inhibited the convergence.

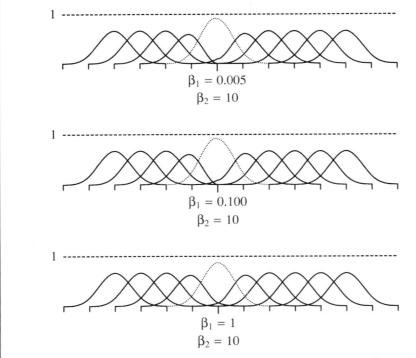

Figure 17.13. The Beta-splines corresponding to the four curves of Figure 17.12. β_1 and β_2 have the values 1 and 0 at all knots except the one explicitly labeled.

Discretely–Shaped
Beta–splines

The material of Chapter 17 provided an explicit formulation for general Beta-splines. A Beta-spline recurrence was also outlined. This chapter will cover a divided-difference formulation for these Beta-splines. Our approach is analogous to the development of cubic B-splines sketched in Chapter 6.

18.1   A Truncated Power Basis for the Beta-splines

Our first task is to define an analog of the one-sided function. The function $(\bar{u} - t)_+^3$ itself will not do, because its first and second derivatives are continuous across all knots. What we want is a function that undergoes a jump in its first and second derivatives as it crosses each knot, sufficient to satisfy the geometric continuity constraints (14.1), (14.2) and (14.3). Consider a function of the form

$$p(\bar{u}) + a_{i,i+1}(\bar{u} - \bar{u}_{i+1})_+^1 + b_{i,i+1}(\bar{u} - \bar{u}_{i+1})_+^2,$$

as is shown in Figure 18.1. The first and second derivatives of $p(\bar{u})$ from the left at $\bar{u}_{i+1}$ are simply $p^{(1)}(\bar{u}_i)$ and $p^{(2)}(\bar{u}_i)$. Its first and second derivatives from the right at $\bar{u}_{i+1}$ are

$$p^{(1)}(\bar{u}_{i+1}) + a_{i,i+1}$$

$$p^{(2)}(\bar{u}_{i+1}) + 2 b_{i,i+1}.$$

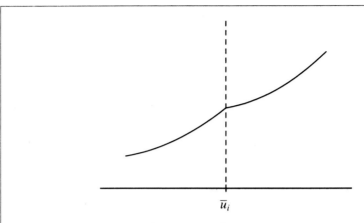

Figure 18.1. Adding $a\,(\overline{u}-\overline{u}_i)_+^1$ and $b\,(\overline{u}-\overline{u}_i)_+^2$ to $p\,(\overline{u})$ creates a new function with discontinuities in the first and second derivative.

Thus there is a jump of $a_{i,i+1}$ in the first derivative and of $2b_{i,i+1}$ in the second derivative. If we want to satisfy equation (14.2) then we must have

$$\beta_{1,i+1}\,p^{(1)}(\overline{u}_{i+1}) \; = \; p^{(1)}(\overline{u}_{i+1}) + a_{i,i+1}$$

or

$$a_{i,i+1} \; = \; (\beta_{1,i+1}-1)\,p^{(1)}(\overline{u}_{i+1}). \tag{18.1}$$

To satisfy equation (14.3) we must have

$$\beta_{1,i+1}^2\,p^{(2)}(\overline{u}_{i+1}) + \beta_{2,i+1}\,p^{(1)}(\overline{u}_{i+1}) \; = \; p^{(2)}(\overline{u}_{i+1}) + 2\,b_{i,i+1}$$

or

$$b_{i,i+1} \; = \; \frac{1}{2}[\,(\beta_{1,i+1}^2-1)p^{(2)}(\overline{u}_{i+1}) + \beta_{2,i+1}\,p^{(1)}(\overline{u}_{i+1})\,]. \tag{18.2}$$

These equations tell us how to modify an arbitrary function so that it will satisfy our G^2 continuity conditions as it crosses a knot. To construct a one-sided basis for the Beta-splines, we begin with the one-sided function $(\overline{u}-\overline{u}_i)_+^3$, since it introduces the necessary third derivative discontinuity at $\overline{u}_i$, and we modify it as above each time we cross a knot. Consider the function

$$g_i(\overline{u}) \; = \; (\overline{u}-\overline{u}_i)_+^3 + a_{i,i+1}(\overline{u}-\overline{u}_{i+1})_+^1 + \cdots + a_{i,m+3}(\overline{u}-\overline{u}_{m+3})_+^1$$

$$+ b_{i,i+1}(\overline{u}-\overline{u}_{i+1})_+^2 + \cdots + b_{i,m+3}(\overline{u}-\overline{u}_{m+3})_+^2.$$

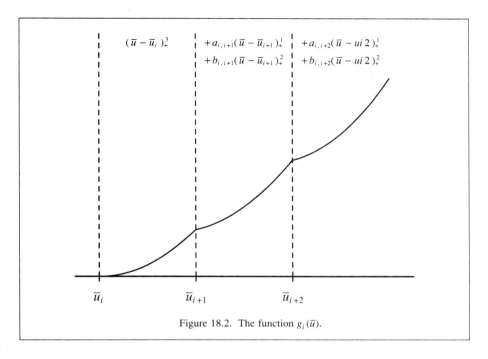

Figure 18.2. The function $g_i(\overline{u})$.

Since equations (14.1), (14.2) and (14.3) will necessarily be satisfied by any linear combination of functions individually satisfying these equations, it is sufficient to ensure that the functions $g_i(\overline{u})$ each do so.

The function $(\overline{u} - \overline{u}_i)^3_+$ itself has zero value, as well as zero first and second derivatives, at $\overline{u}_i$ and at all knots left of $\overline{u}_i$, and so trivially satisfies our G^2 constraints for all $\overline{u} \le \overline{u}_i$. It is therefore sufficient to define the $a_{i,j}$ and $b_{i,j}$ from left to right, for $i < j \le m + 3$, using equations (18.1) and (18.2). Thus when computing $a_{i,i+1}$ and $b_{i,i+1}$, $g_i(\overline{u})$ is simply $(\overline{u} - \overline{u}_i)^3_+$. The values $a_{i,i+1}$ and $b_{i,i+1}$ are given by (18.1) and (18.2). More generally, when computing $a_{i,j}$ and $b_{i,j}$, $\overline{u}$ is at the knot $\overline{u}_j$ and $g_i(\overline{u})$ has the value

$$(\overline{u} - \overline{u}_i)^3 + \sum_{k=i+1}^{j-1} a_{i,k}(\overline{u} - \overline{u}_k)^1 + \sum_{k=i+1}^{j-1} b_{i,k}(\overline{u} - \overline{u}_k)^2,$$

the preceding a_i's and b_i's having already been computed. Consequently the first derivative from the left of $g_i(\overline{u})$ at $\overline{u}_j$ is

$$3(\overline{u}_j - \overline{u}_i)^2 + \sum_{k=i+1}^{j-1} a_{i,k} + 2\sum_{k=i+1}^{j-1} b_{i,k}(\overline{u}_j - \overline{u}_k)^1$$

and the second derivative from the left of $g_i(\bar{u})$ at $\bar{u}_j$ is

$$6(\bar{u}_j - \bar{u}_i)^1 + 2 \sum_{k=i+1}^{j-1} b_{i,k} \, .$$

Equations (18.1) and (18.2), with a suitable change of indices, then yield $a_{i,j}$ and $b_{i,j}$. The following algorithm computes the $a_{i,j}$ and $b_{i,j}$.

$\qquad$**for** $i \leftarrow 0$ **step** 1 **until** $m+2$ **do**

$\qquad\qquad Sa \leftarrow 0$

$\qquad\qquad Sb \leftarrow 0$

$\qquad\qquad$**for** $j \leftarrow i+1$ **step** 1 **until** $\min(i+4, m+3)$ **do**

$$p_{left}^{(1)} \leftarrow 3(\bar{u}_j - \bar{u}_i)^2 + Sa + 2 \sum_{k=i+1}^{j-1} b_{i,k}(\bar{u}_j - \bar{u}_k)$$

$$p_{left}^{(2)} \leftarrow 6(\bar{u}_j - \bar{u}_i) + Sb$$

$$a_{i,j} \leftarrow (\beta_{1,j} - 1)\, p_{left}^{(1)}$$

$$b_{i,j} \leftarrow \frac{1}{2}\left[(\beta_{1,j}^2 - 1)\, p_{left}^{(2)} + \beta_{2,j}\, p_{left}^{(1)} \right]$$

$$Sa \leftarrow Sa + a_{i,j}$$

$$Sb \leftarrow Sb + 2\, b_{i,j}$$

$\qquad\qquad$**endfor**

$\qquad$**endfor**

The outer loop steps through the $g_i(\bar{u})$ in turn. For each $g_i(\bar{u})$ the inner loop computes the $a_{i,j}$'s and $b_{i,j}$'s; Sa and Sb keep a running total of the $a_{i,j}$'s and $b_{i,j}$'s that have been computed thus far. The "min" expression will be explained in Section 18.3.

It is not hard to see that the functions $g_i(\bar{u})$ form a basis for the G^2 splines over some particular knot sequence and associated shape parameters $\beta_{1,i}$ and $\beta_{2,i}$ — the argument is very much analogous to that given in the case of C^2 splines for the one-sided cubics, and is therefore omitted.

18.2   A Local Basis for the Beta-splines

The $g_i(\overline{u})$ have the same deficiencies, namely rapid growth and non-locality, as the one-sided basis for the C^2 splines. The obvious next step is to see whether some form of differencing can be applied to the $g_i(\overline{u})$ so as to obtain a local basis.

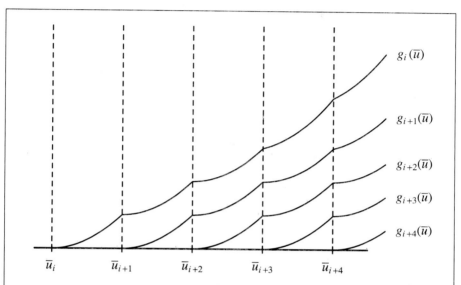

Figure 18.3.   The basis functions shown can be combined to form a G^2 function which replaces $g_i(\overline{u})$.

As in constructing the B-splines, the cubic term in each $g_i(\overline{u})$ can easily be canceled for $\overline{u}$ sufficiently far to the right.   We need only compute

$$g_{i+1}(\overline{u}) - g_i(\overline{u}), \tag{18.3}$$

$$g_{i+2}(\overline{u}) - g_{i+1}(\overline{u}), \tag{18.4}$$

and so on.   To cancel the quadratic terms in (18.3) and (18.4) by computing a further difference we need to arrange for the coefficient of $\overline{u}^2$ in (18.3) and (18.4) to have the same value.   Unfortunately, these coefficients depend not only on the knot spacing (as was true for the B-splines), but also on the particular knot interval containing $\overline{u}$ since we pick up an additional $a_{i,j}$ and $b_{i,j}$ each time we move rightwards across a knot.   In particular, if $\overline{u}_j \le \overline{u} < \overline{u}_{j+1}$ and $i < j$ then

$$g_i(\overline{u}) = \overline{u}^3 + \overline{u}^2 \left[(b_{i,i+1} + \cdots + b_{i,j}) - 3\overline{u}_i \right]$$

$$+ \overline{u} \left[(a_{i,i+1} + \cdots + a_{i,j}) - 2(b_{i,i+1}\overline{u}_{i+1} + \cdots + b_{i,j}\overline{u}_j) + 3\overline{u}_i^2 \right]$$

$$+ \left[(b_{i,i+1}\overline{u}_{i+1}^2 + \cdots + b_{i,j}\overline{u}_j^2) - (a_{i,i+1}\overline{u}_{i+1} + \cdots + a_{i,j}\overline{u}_j) - \overline{u}_i^3 \right],$$

while the one-sided basis used for the B-splines is simply

$$(\overline{u} - \overline{u}_i)^3 = \overline{u}^3 + \overline{u}^2 \left[-3\overline{u}_i \right] + \overline{u} \left[+3\overline{u}_i^2 \right] + \left[-\overline{u}_i^3 \right]$$

for all $\overline{u} > \overline{u}_i$. Thus for $(\overline{u} - \overline{u}_i)_+^3$ the coefficient of $\overline{u}^2$ is a constant: if we divide $(\overline{u} - \overline{u}_{i+1})_+^3 - (\overline{u} - \overline{u}_i)_+^3$ by $-3(\overline{u}_{i+1} - \overline{u}_i)$ then the coefficient of the quadratic term is simply 1, no matter what the value of i. For $g_i(\overline{u})$ the coefficient of $\overline{u}^2$ alters each time we move to the right across a knot. Hence we cannot divide $g_{i+1}(\overline{u}) - g_i(\overline{u})$ by any single constant and expect that the coefficient will be constant. In general it will change each time we cross a knot.

This difficulty can be overcome, however. For the B-splines we needed to take a fourth difference to obtain a local function, and the $B_i(\overline{u})$ became zero for $\overline{u} \geq \overline{u}_{i+4}$. At each step we arranged for the leading coefficients to be identical for $\overline{u} \geq \overline{u}_{i+4}$ so that they would cancel when performing the next difference.

For the Beta-splines, we will normalize the leading coefficients after each difference so that for $\overline{u}_{i+4} \leq \overline{u} < \overline{u}_{i+5}$ these coefficients will be identical. In particular, for the fourth difference they will be identically zero on this interval. From the equation for $g_i(\overline{u})$ above it is apparent that we will need the constants

$$A_{i,i} = (b_{i,i+1} + b_{i,i+2} + b_{i,i+3} + b_{i,i+4}) - 3\overline{u}_i$$

$$B_{i,i} = (a_{i,i+1} + a_{i,i+2} + a_{i,i+3} + a_{i,i+4})$$
$$- 2(b_{i,i+1}\overline{u}_{i+1} + b_{i,i+2}\overline{u}_{i+2} + b_{i,i+3}\overline{u}_{i+3} + b_{i,i+4}\overline{u}_{i+4}) + 3\overline{u}_i^2$$

$$C_{i,i} = (b_{i,i+1}\overline{u}_{i+1}^2 + b_{i,i+2}\overline{u}_{i+2}^2 + b_{i,i+3}\overline{u}_{i+3}^2 + b_{i,i+4}\overline{u}_{i+4}^2)$$
$$- (a_{i,i+1}\overline{u}_{i+1} + a_{i,i+2}\overline{u}_{i+2} + a_{i,i+3}\overline{u}_{i+3} + a_{i,i+4}\overline{u}_{i+4}) - \overline{u}_i^3$$

$$A_{i,i+1} = (b_{i+1,i+2} + b_{i+1,i+3} + b_{i+1,i+4}) - 3\overline{u}_{i+1}$$

$$B_{i,i+1} = (a_{i+1,i+2} + a_{i+1,i+3} + a_{i+1,i+4})$$
$$- 2(b_{i+1,i+2}\overline{u}_{i+2} + b_{i+1,i+3}\overline{u}_{i+3} + b_{i+1,i+4}\overline{u}_{i+4}) + 3\overline{u}_{i+1}^2$$

$$C_{i,i+1} = (b_{i+1,i+2}\overline{u}_{i+2}^2 + b_{i+1,i+3}\overline{u}_{i+3}^2 + b_{i+1,i+4}\overline{u}_{i+4}^2)$$
$$- (a_{i+1,i+2}\overline{u}_{i+2} + a_{i+1,i+3}\overline{u}_{i+3} + a_{i+1,i+4}\overline{u}_{i+4}) - \overline{u}_{i+1}^3$$

$\cdots$

$$A_{i,i+4} = -3\,\overline{u}_{i+4}$$

$$B_{i,i+4} = +3\,\overline{u}_{i+4}^2$$

$$C_{i,i+4} = -\overline{u}_{i+4}^3 .$$

Then we may write

$$g_j(\overline{u}) = \overline{u}^3 + A_{i,i}\overline{u}^2 + B_{i,i}\overline{u} + C_{i,i} \qquad \text{for} \quad \overline{u}_{i+4} \le \overline{u} < \overline{u}_{i+5} .$$

Similarly we have

$$g_{i+1}(\overline{u}) = \overline{u}^3 + A_{i,i+1}\overline{u}^2 + B_{i,i+1}\overline{u} + C_{i,i+1} \qquad \text{for} \quad \overline{u}_{i+4} \le \overline{u} < \overline{u}_{i+5}$$

$$g_{i+2}(\overline{u}) = \overline{u}^3 + A_{i,i+2}\overline{u}^2 + B_{i,i+2}\overline{u} + C_{i,i+2} \qquad \text{for} \quad \overline{u}_{i+4} \le \overline{u} < \overline{u}_{i+5}$$

$$g_{i+3}(\overline{u}) = \overline{u}^3 + A_{i,i+3}\overline{u}^2 + B_{i,i+3}\overline{u} + C_{i,i+3} \qquad \text{for} \quad \overline{u}_{i+4} \le \overline{u} < \overline{u}_{i+5}$$

$$g_{i+4}(\overline{u}) = \overline{u}^3 + A_{i,i+4}\overline{u}^2 + B_{i,i+4}\overline{u} + C_{i,i+4} \qquad \text{for} \quad \overline{u}_{i+4} \le \overline{u} < \overline{u}_{i+5} .$$

From these we form the four functions $\Delta_i^1 g_i(\overline{u})$, $\Delta_i^1 g_{i+1}(\overline{u})$, $\Delta_i^1 g_{i+2}(\overline{u})$ and $\Delta_i^1 g_{i+3}(\overline{u})$ defined by

$$\Delta_i^1 g_j(\overline{u}) = \frac{g_{j+1}(\overline{u}) - g_j(\overline{u})}{A_{i,j+1} - A_{i,j}} \qquad \text{for all } \overline{u} \text{ and } j = i,\, i+1,\, i+2,\, i+3$$

$$= \overline{u}^2 + \frac{B_{i,j+1} - B_{i,j}}{A_{i,j+1} - A_{i,j}}\overline{u} + \frac{C_{i,j+1} - C_{i,j}}{A_{i,j+1} - A_{i,j}} \qquad \text{for } \overline{u}_{i+4} \le \overline{u} < \overline{u}_{i+5}$$

$$= \overline{u}^2 + D_{i,j}\overline{u} + E_{i,j} ,$$

thus implicitly defining the $D_{i,j}$ and $E_{i,j}$. The index i with which we subscript Δ reminds us that we are eventually going to replace $g_i(\overline{u})$ with an appropriate linear combination $G_i(\overline{u})$ of $g_i(\overline{u})$, $g_{i+1}(\overline{u})$, $g_{i+2}(\overline{u})$, $g_{i+3}(\overline{u})$ and $g_{i+4}(\overline{u})$, computed in such a way as to ensure that $G_i(\overline{u})$ will be zero on $\overline{u}_{i+4} \le \overline{u} < \overline{u}_{i+5}$.
We can now cancel the quadratic term by forming the three functions $\Delta_i^2 g_i(\overline{u})$, $\Delta_i^2 g_{i+1}(\overline{u})$ and $\Delta_i^2 g_{i+2}(\overline{u})$ as

$$\Delta_i^2 g_j(\overline{u}) = \frac{\Delta_i^1 g_{j+1}(\overline{u}) - \Delta_i^1 g_j(\overline{u})}{D_{i,j+1} - D_{i,j}} \qquad \text{for all } \overline{u} \text{ and } j = i,\, i+1,\, i+2$$

$$= \overline{u} + \frac{E_{i,j+1} - E_{i,j}}{D_{i,j+1} - D_{i,j}} \qquad \text{for } \overline{u}_{i+4} \le \overline{u} < \overline{u}_{i+5}$$

$$= \overline{u} + F_{i,j} \qquad \text{for } \overline{u}_{i+4} \le \overline{u} < \overline{u}_{i+5}$$

and then cancel the linear term by forming the two functions $\Delta_i^3 g_i(\bar{u})$ and $\Delta_i^3 g_{i+1}(\bar{u})$ as

$$\Delta_i^3 g_j(\bar{u}) = \frac{\Delta_i^2 g_{j+1}(\bar{u}) - \Delta_i^2 g_i(\bar{u})}{F_{i,j+1} - F_{i,j}} \quad \text{for all } \bar{u} \text{ and } j = i, i+1$$

$$= 1 \quad \text{for } \bar{u}_{i+4} \leq \bar{u} < \bar{u}_{i+5}.$$

Finally we compute the function

$$\Delta_i^4 g_i(\bar{u}) = -[\Delta_i^3 g_{i+1}(\bar{u}) - \Delta_i^3 g_i(\bar{u})] \quad \text{for } \bar{u}_{i+4} \leq \bar{u} < \bar{u}_{i+5},$$

with which we replace $g_i(\bar{u})$. The pattern of this computation is shown in the following diagram.

$g_i(\bar{u})$ $\qquad$ $g_{i+1}(\bar{u})$ $\qquad$ $g_{i+2}(\bar{u})$ $\qquad$ $g_{i+3}(\bar{u})$ $\qquad$ $g_{i+4}(\bar{u})$

$\quad\Delta_i^1 g_i(\bar{u})$ $\qquad$ $\Delta_i^1 g_{i+1}(\bar{u})$ $\qquad$ $\Delta_i^1 g_{i+2}(\bar{u})$ $\qquad$ $\Delta_i^1 g_{i+3}(\bar{u})$

$\qquad\quad\Delta_i^2 g_i(\bar{u})$ $\qquad$ $\Delta_i^2 g_{i+1}(\bar{u})$ $\qquad$ $\Delta_i^2 g_{i+2}(\bar{u})$

$\qquad\qquad\Delta_i^3 g_i(\bar{u})$ $\qquad$ $\Delta_i^3 g_{i+1}(\bar{u})$

$\qquad\qquad\qquad\Delta_i^4 g_i(\bar{u})$

Now $\Delta_i^4 g_i(\bar{u})$ is defined for any value of $\bar{u}$, but we have only ensured that it is zero when $\bar{u}$ lies between $\bar{u}_{i+4}$ and $\bar{u}_{i+5}$, or is less than $\bar{u}_i$. To arrange for locality we simply define our Beta-splines $G_i(\bar{u})$ to be

$$G_i(\bar{u}) = \begin{cases} 0 & \bar{u} < \bar{u}_i \;\; or \;\; \bar{u} \geq \bar{u}_{i+4} \\ \\ \Delta_i^4 g_i(\bar{u}) & \bar{u}_i \leq \bar{u} < \bar{u}_{i+4}. \end{cases}$$

Since by construction $\Delta_i^4 g_i(\bar{u})$ is zero on $[\bar{u}_4, \bar{u}_5)$, the extension to the right by zero leaves us with a function satisfying the G^2 continuity constraints.

Discretely-shaped Beta-spline curves are now defined by

$$\mathbf{Q}(\bar{u}) = \sum_i \mathbf{V}_i G_i(\bar{u}) = \sum_i (x_i G_i(\bar{u}), y_i G_i(\bar{u})). \tag{18.5}$$

The ith curve segment is

$$\mathbf{Q}_i = \sum_{r=-3}^{0} \mathbf{V}_{i+r} G_{i+r}(\bar{u})$$

$$= \mathbf{V}_{i-3} G_{i-3}(\bar{u}) + \mathbf{V}_{i-2} G_{i-2}(\bar{u}) + \mathbf{V}_{i-1} G_{i-1}(\bar{u}) + \mathbf{V}_i G_i(\bar{u}).$$

18.3 Evaluation

The inner loop of the computational algorithm given in Section 18.1 can be explained easily, if the upper limit is set to $m+3$. All possible differences will have been handled. However, if one simply pre-computes the coefficients $a_{i,j}$, $b_{i,j}$, $A_{i,j}$, $B_{i,j}$, $C_{i,j}$, $D_{i,j}$, $E_{i,j}$, $F_{i,j}$, one can compute the difference $\Delta_i^4 g_i(\overline{u})$ directly whenever a point on the curve is required. Doing so does not require an $a_{i,j}$ or $b_{i,j}$ for any value of j other than $i+1$, $i+2$, $i+3$ or $i+4$. This is the reason for having the expression $\min(i+4, m+3)$ as the upper limit of the inner loop.

Moreover, since differencing and differentiation commute, we may compute derivatives of the $G_i(\overline{u})$ by differencing derivatives of the $g_i(\overline{u})$, and so obtain a power representation of the basis segments that can be evaluated by using Horner's rule or forward differences.

We end this section with one word of caution. The process described is a *differencing* process, and as such, it can suffer cancellation difficulties if the knot spacing is permitted to become too small. However, if confluent knots are avoided, the process provides a computational alternative to the explicit formula.

18.4 Equivalence

We begin by reminding ourselves that the functions that we have managed to construct by this differencing process have 4-segment locality (support). Linear independence of these functions is established in [Bartels/Beatty84], as is positivity of these functions on their support. We clearly have the number of functions needed to equal the dimensionality of the Beta-spline space ($m+1$ basis functions for knots $0, \ldots, m+4$). We conclude that we have constructed basis which has 4-segment local support and is nonnegative.

The divided-difference construction can be programmed in MACSYMA [Bogen83], and the symbolic result can be tested for summation to one. This has been done successfully for uniform knot spacing, and summation to one has been verified. In view of Section 17.1, this is sufficient to establish the general case.

Goodman [Goodman85] has established that there is a unique system of basis functions (Beta-splines) that are 4-segment local, that are nonnegative, and that sum to one. We conclude, for the uniform knot case, that we have computed this system by our differencing process. Since the transformation to general knot spacing is by a linear change of variables, to which the differencing process will be insensitive, we further conclude that the differencing process computes the basis functions in the general case. That is, the material in this chapter provides another computational approach to providing the Beta-splines given in Chapter 17.

18.5 Beta2-splines

In many applications the ability to manipulate β_2 may be sufficient [Barsky85], and because they can be evaluated more efficiently, we therefore list the basis segments on the interval $[\bar{u}_i, \bar{u}_{i+1})$ for the special case in which the knots are spaced one unit apart and the β_1 values all have the value one. (These are the four segments drawn as solid curves in Figure 17.2.)

$$s_{i,-0}(u) \;=\; \frac{2\,(\beta_{2,i+2}+4)\,u^3}{\delta 1}$$

$$
\begin{aligned}
s_{i-1,-1}(u) \;=\; & -\frac{2\,(\beta_{2,i+1}+4)}{\delta 1\,\delta 2}\Big[\,\beta_{2,i}\,\beta_{2,i+1}\,\beta_{2,i+2}+8\,\beta_{2,i}\,\beta_{2,i+1} \\
& +3\,\beta_{2,i+1}\,\beta_{2,i+2}+8\,\beta_{2,i}\,\beta_{2,i+2} \\
& +44\,\beta_{2,i}+24\,\beta_{2,i+1}+28\,\beta_{2,i+2}+144\,\Big]\,u^3 \\
& +\frac{(\beta_{2,i+1}+4)}{\delta 2}\Big[\,3\,(\beta_{2,i}+2)\,u^2+6\,u+2\,\Big]
\end{aligned}
$$

$$
\begin{aligned}
s_{i-2,-2}(u) \;=\; & -\frac{2\,(\beta_{2,i}+4)}{\delta 2\,\delta 3}\Big[\,\beta_{2,i-1}\,\beta_{2,i}\,\beta_{2,i+1}+3\,\beta_{2,i-1}\,\beta_{2,i}+8\,\beta_{2,i}\,\beta_{2,i+1} \\
& +8\,\beta_{2,i-1}\,\beta_{2,i+1} \\
& +28\,\beta_{2,i-1}+24\,\beta_{2,i}+44\,\beta_{2,i+1}+144\,\Big]\,(1-u)^3 \\
& +\frac{(\beta_{2,i}+4)}{\delta 3}\Big[\,3\,(\beta_{2,i+1}+2)\,(1-u)^2+6\,(1-u)+2\,\Big]
\end{aligned}
$$

$$s_{i-3,-3}(u) \;=\; \frac{2\,(\beta_{2,i-1}+4)\,(1-u)^3}{\delta 3}$$

where

$$\delta 1 \;=\; (\beta_{2,i+1}\,\beta_{2,i+2}+8\,\beta_{2,i+1}+8\,\beta_{2,i+2}+48)$$

$$\delta 2 \;=\; (\beta_{2,i}\,\beta_{2,i+1}+8\,\beta_{2,i}+8\,\beta_{2,i+1}+48)$$

$$\delta 3 \;=\; (\beta_{2,i-1}\,\beta_{2,i}+8\,\beta_{2,i-1}+8\,\beta_{2,i}+48).$$

By inspection it is clear that so long as the β_2 values are not too negative, the above representation for Beta-splines over a uniform knot sequence is necessarily well defined — the denominators cannot vanish, even though the differencing representation of the Beta-splines admits of this possibility.

The formulas given here for the basis segments of the Beta2-splines are equivalent to those obtainable from the formulas given in Section 17.2 with all of the β_1's set to one.

18.6 Examples

Figure 18.4 demonstrates the tension-like effects produced by manipulating β_1 and β_2. Figure 18.5 is produced by varying several shape parameters simultaneously.

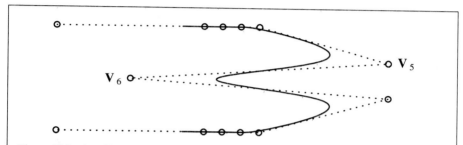

Figure 18.4. A uniform Beta-spline curve. Actually this is a C^2 spline curve since β_1 and β_2 have the values 1 and 0 throughout the curve, which should be compared with the curves in Figure 18.5.

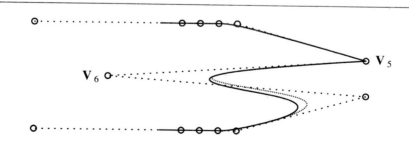

Figure 18.5. The solid curve here is obtained from the curve of Figure 18.4 by increasing β_1 at V_5 from 1 to 10,000. The dotted curve is obtained by instead increasing β_2 at V_5 from 0 to 10,000. In both cases a further increase in the shape parameter produces no observable change in the figure.

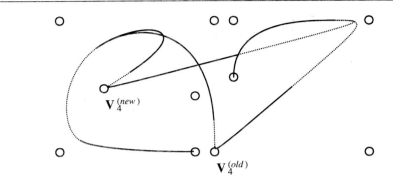

Figure 18.6. Here we see the effect produced by moving one of the control vertices defining a curve. Notice that only four curve segments are altered. The control graph has been omitted here to enhance visibility of the curves.

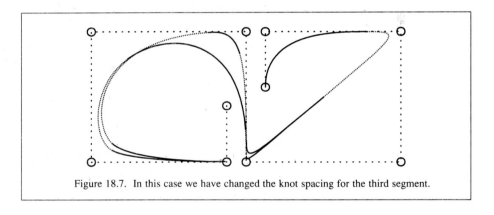

Figure 18.7. In this case we have changed the knot spacing for the third segment.

Figures 18.6 and 18.7 illustrate the locality provided by the Beta-splines.

One sees also how the curves lie within the convex hull of their corresponding control vertices; Figures 18.8 and 18.9 illustrate the failure of a curve to lie within the convex hull of its control points when a β_2 value is sufficiently negative.

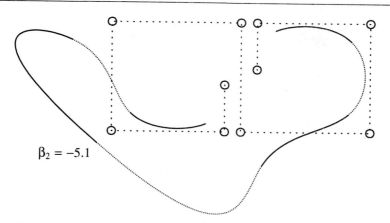

$\beta_2 = -5.1$

Figure 18.8. For large enough negative values of β_2 the curve may pass outside the convex hull. β_1 has the value 1 and β_2 the value 0 at every joint except the one explicitly indicated.

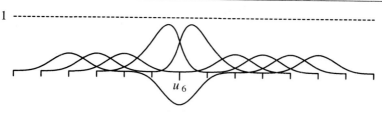

u_6

Figure 18.9. These are the unscaled basis functions with which the curve of Figure 18.8 is defined. Notice the negative basis function centered over the knot at which $\beta_2 = -5.1$. This is not a violation of the convex hull property established in the text, which holds only for nonnegative values of β_1 and β_2.

19

B-spline
Representations
for Beta-splines

In Chapter 18, we observed that the discontinuities in the first and second derivatives required by G^2 continuity can be obtained through the use of the truncated power functions

$$(\bar{u} - \bar{u}_i)_+^3 , \ (\bar{u} - \bar{u}_i)_+^2 , \ \text{and} \ (\bar{u} - \bar{u}_i)_+^1 . \tag{19.1}$$

These same truncated power functions, on the other hand, are hidden within the differencing process that produces the B-splines associated with knots of multiplicity 3.

Moreover, the B-splines are a basis for all piecewise polynomials, given an appropriate knot vector. This suggests that we could represent cubic Beta-splines by triple-knot B-splines — triple-knot because we need C^0, and not C^2, parametric continuity. Such a representation is of interest because it would make possible the evaluation and subdivision of Beta-splines using B-spline algorithms, though perhaps preserving a Beta-spline interface to the user. The latter is preferable because a third as many control vertices are involved, and there are no constraints on their movement; constraints would be required if one tried to manipulate directly the B-spline control vertices defining a Beta-spline curve.

Further, as the final remarks in Section 9.6 point out, the segment polynomials of those B-splines are simply the Bernstein polynomials. If the triple-knot B-spline representations are possible, then so must be Bézier representations.

The validity of these ideas for general orders of splines is to be found in [Höllig86]. In this chapter we will outline the representation of cubics.

19.1 Linear Equations

Figure 19.1 presents the situation we expect to establish. The top axis shows a cubic Beta-spline, $G_i(\bar{u})$. The bottom axis shows all the triple-knot, cubic B–splines, $B_i(\bar{u})$, that will be needed to represent this Beta-spline. In particular, the first segment of $G_i(\bar{u})$ is simply a multiple of $(\bar{u} - \bar{u}_i)^3$ and the last segment of $G_i(\bar{u})$ is simply a multiple of $(\bar{u}_{i+4} - \bar{u})^3$, which justifies the leftmost and rightmost B-splines that appear.

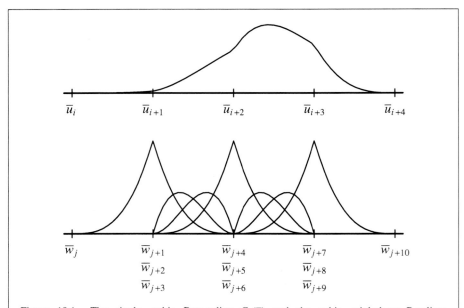

Figure 19.1.   The single, cubic Beta-spline $G_i(\bar{u})$ and the cubic, triple-knot B-splines $B_j(\bar{u})$, . . . , $B_{j+6}(\bar{u})$ that will be used to represent it. The segment of $G_i(\bar{u})$ from $\bar{u}_i$ to $\bar{u}_{i+1}$ is exceedingly flat.

Algebraically, the representation will be

$$G_i(\bar{u}) = c_{i,j} B_j(\bar{u}) + c_{i,j+1} B_{j+1}(\bar{u}) + c_{i,j+2} B_{j+2}(\bar{u}) + c_{i,j+3} B_{j+3}(\bar{u})$$
$$+ c_{i,j+4} B_{j+4}(\bar{u}) + c_{i,j+5} B_{j+5}(\bar{u}) + c_{i,j+6} B_{j+6}(\bar{u}).$$

(19.2)

Counting from the leftmost knot, $\bar{u}_0 = \bar{w}_0$, it will be seen that the relationship between the $\bar{u}$ knots and the $\bar{w}$ knots is

$$\overline{u}_0 \quad \overline{u}_1 \quad \cdots \quad \overline{u}_i \quad \cdots \quad \overline{u}_{m+k}$$

$$\overline{w}_0 \quad \overline{w}_3 \quad \cdots \quad \overline{w}_{3i} \quad \cdots \quad \overline{w}_{3(m+k)}$$
$$\overline{w}_1 \quad \overline{w}_4 \quad \cdots \quad \overline{w}_{3i+1} \quad \cdots \quad \overline{w}_{3(m+k)+1}$$
$$\overline{w}_2 \quad \overline{w}_5 \quad \cdots \quad \overline{w}_{3i+2} \quad \cdots \quad \overline{w}_{3(m+k)+2} .$$

Furthermore, the B-splines starting at $\overline{w}_0$ and $\overline{w}_1$ will not be needed to construct $G_0(\overline{u})$. The "peaked" B-spline that starts the first segment of $G_0(\overline{u})$ is the B-spline beginning at $\overline{w}_2$. Consequently, the relationship between i and j will be

$$j = 3i + 2 .$$

The component B-splines for $G_i(\overline{u})$ are listed below in terms of the knots $\overline{u}_i$ for the Beta-spline.

For $\overline{u}_i \leq \overline{u} < \overline{u}_{i+1}$:

$$B_j(\overline{u}) = \frac{(\overline{u} - \overline{u}_i)^3}{(\overline{u}_{i+1} - \overline{u}_i)^3} .$$

For $\overline{u}_{i+1} \leq \overline{u} < \overline{u}_i$:

$$B_j(\overline{u}) = \frac{(\overline{u}_{i+2} - \overline{u})^3}{(\overline{u}_{i+2} - \overline{u}_{i+1})^3} ,$$

and similarly for $B_{j+3}(\overline{u})$, replacing $\overline{u}_i$ by $\overline{u}_{i+1}$, and $B_{j+6}(\overline{u})$, replacing $\overline{u}_i$ by $\overline{u}_{i+2}$. Figure 19.2 shows this.

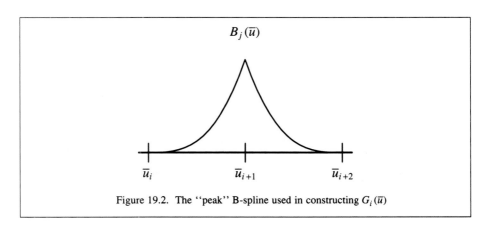

$$B_j(\overline{u})$$

$$\overline{u}_i \qquad \overline{u}_{i+1} \qquad \overline{u}_{i+2}$$

Figure 19.2. The "peak" B-spline used in constructing $G_i(\overline{u})$

For $\bar{u}_{i+1} \le \bar{u} < \bar{u}_{i+2}$:

$$B_{j+1}(\bar{u}) = \frac{3(\bar{u} - \bar{u}_{i+1})(\bar{u}_{i+2} - \bar{u})^2}{(\bar{u}_{i+2} - \bar{u}_{i+1})^3},$$

and similarly for $B_{j+4}(\bar{u})$, replacing $\bar{u}_{i+1}$ by $\bar{u}_{i+2}$, as shown in Figure 19.3.

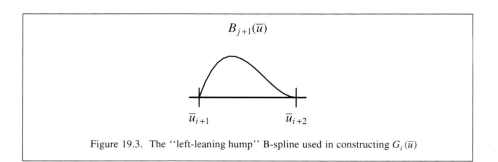

$B_{j+1}(\bar{u})$

$\bar{u}_{i+1}$ $\bar{u}_{i+2}$

Figure 19.3. The "left-leaning hump" B-spline used in constructing $G_i(\bar{u})$

For $\bar{u}_{i+1} \le \bar{u} < \bar{u}_{i+2}$:

$$B_{j+2}(\bar{u}) = \frac{3(\bar{u} - \bar{u}_{i+1})^2(\bar{u}_{i+2} - \bar{u})}{(\bar{u}_{i+2} - \bar{u}_{i+1})^3},$$

and similarly for $B_{j+5}(\bar{u})$, replacing $\bar{u}_{i+1}$ by $\bar{u}_{i+2}$. Figure 19.4 shows this.

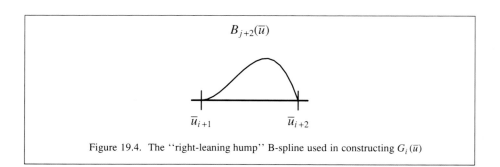

$B_{j+2}(\bar{u})$

$\bar{u}_{i+1}$ $\bar{u}_{i+2}$

Figure 19.4. The "right-leaning hump" B-spline used in constructing $G_i(\bar{u})$

Using the representation given by (19.2), we obtain the segments for $G_i(\bar{u})$ listed below.

For $\bar{u}_i \leq \bar{u} < \bar{u}_{i+1}$:

$$G_i(\bar{u}) = \frac{c_{0,i}\,(\bar{u} - \bar{u}_i)^3}{(\bar{u}_{i+1} - \bar{u}_i)^3}\;;$$

for $\bar{u}_{i+1} \leq \bar{u} < \bar{u}_{i+2}$:

$$G_i(\bar{u}) = \frac{c_{0,i}\,(\bar{u}_{i+2} - \bar{u})^3}{(\bar{u}_{i+2} - \bar{u}_{i+1})^3} + \frac{3\,c_{1,i}\,(\bar{u} - \bar{u}_{i+1})(\bar{u}_{i+2} - \bar{u})^2}{(\bar{u}_{i+2} - \bar{u}_{i+1})^3}$$

$$+ \frac{3\,c_{2,i}\,(\bar{u} - \bar{u}_{i+1})^2(\bar{u}_{i+2} - \bar{u})}{(\bar{u}_{i+2} - \bar{u}_{i+1})^3} + \frac{c_{3,i}\,(\bar{u} - \bar{u}_{i+1})^3}{(\bar{u}_{i+2} - \bar{u}_{i+1})^3}\;;$$

for $\bar{u}_{i+2} \leq \bar{u} < \bar{u}_{i+3}$:

$$G_i(\bar{u}) = \frac{c_{3,i}\,(\bar{u}_{i+3} - \bar{u})^3}{(\bar{u}_{i+3} - \bar{u}_{i+2})^3} + \frac{3\,c_{4,i}\,(\bar{u} - \bar{u}_{i+2})(\bar{u}_{i+3} - \bar{u})^2}{(\bar{u}_{i+3} - \bar{u}_{i+2})^3}$$

$$+ \frac{3\,c_{5,i}\,(\bar{u} - \bar{u}_{i+2})^2(\bar{u}_{i+3} - \bar{u})}{(\bar{u}_{i+3} - \bar{u}_{i+2})^3} + \frac{c_{6,i}\,(\bar{u} - \bar{u}_{i+2})^3}{(\bar{u}_{i+3} - \bar{u}_{i+2})^3}\;;$$

for $\bar{u}_{i+3} \leq \bar{u} < \bar{u}_{i+4}$:

$$G_i(\bar{u}) = \frac{c_{6,i}\,(\bar{u}_{i+4} - \bar{u})^3}{(\bar{u}_{i+4} - \bar{u}_{i+3})^3}\;.$$

Using the conditions for G^2 continuity, we can form equations for the coefficients $c_{i,\ell},\ \ell = 0, \ldots, 6$. For example,

$$\beta_{1,i+3}\, G_i^{(1)}(\bar{u}_{i+3}^-) = G_i^{(1)}(\bar{u}_{i+3}^+),$$

which produces

$$\beta_{1,i+3}\, c_{i,j+5}\, B_{j+5}^{(1)}(\bar{u}_{i+3}^-) + c_{i,j+6}\, B_{j+6}^{(1)}(\bar{u}_{i+3}^-) = c_{i,j+6}\, B_{j+6}^{(1)}(\bar{u}_{i+3}^+),$$

taking account of the fact that certain of the B-splines have a zero derivative at $\bar{u}_{i+3}$. Next, the specific formulas for the derivatives of the segment polynomials are to be substituted, and an equation for the c's results.

The conditions of G^2 continuity,

$$\beta_1\, G_i^{(1)}(\bar{u}^+) = G_i^{(1)}(\bar{u}^-)$$

and

$$\beta_1^2 \, G_i^{(2)}(\bar{u}^+) + \beta_2 \, G_i^{(1)}(\bar{u}^+) \;=\; G_i^{(2)}(\bar{u}^-)$$

for $\bar{u} = \bar{u}_{i+1}$, $\bar{u}_{i+2}$, and $\bar{u}_{i+3}$, yield the following six equations.

$$-\frac{3\,c_{i,1}}{\bar{u}_{i+2}-\bar{u}_{i+1}} + \frac{3\,c_{i,0}}{\bar{u}_{i+2}-\bar{u}_{i+1}} + \frac{3\,\beta_{1,i+1}\,c_{i,0}}{\bar{u}_{i+1}-\bar{u}_i} \;=\; 0$$

$$-\frac{3\,c_{i,4}}{\bar{u}_{i+3}-\bar{u}_{i+2}} + \frac{3\,c_{i,3}}{\bar{u}_{i+3}-\bar{u}_{i+2}} + \beta_{1,i+2}\left(\frac{3\,c_{i,3}}{\bar{u}_{i+2}-\bar{u}_{i+1}} - \frac{3\,c_{i,2}}{\bar{u}_{i+2}-\bar{u}_{i+1}}\right) \;=\; 0$$

$$\frac{3\,c_{i,6}}{\bar{u}_{i+4}-\bar{u}_{i+3}} + \beta_{1,i+3}\left(\frac{3\,c_{i,6}}{\bar{u}_{i+3}-\bar{u}_{i+2}} - \frac{3\,c_{i,5}}{\bar{u}_{i+3}-\bar{u}_{i+2}}\right) \;=\; 0$$

$$-\frac{6\,c_{i,2}}{(\bar{u}_{i+2}-\bar{u}_{i+1})^2} + \frac{12\,c_{i,1}}{(\bar{u}_{i+2}-\bar{u}_{i+1})^2}$$
$$-\frac{6\,c_{i,0}}{(\bar{u}_{i+2}-\bar{u}_{i+1})^2} + \frac{3\,\beta_{2,i+1}\,c_{i,0}}{\bar{u}_{i+1}-\bar{u}_i} + \frac{6\,\beta_{1,i+1}^2\,c_{i,0}}{(\bar{u}_{i+1}-\bar{u}_i)^2} \;=\; 0$$

$$-\frac{6\,c_{i,5}}{(\bar{u}_{i+3}-\bar{u}_{i+2})^2} + \frac{12\,c_{i,4}}{(\bar{u}_{i+3}-\bar{u}_{i+2})^2} - \frac{6\,c_{i,3}}{(\bar{u}_{i+3}-\bar{u}_{i+2})^2}$$
$$+\,\beta_{2,i+2}\left[\frac{3\,c_{i,3}}{\bar{u}_{i+2}-\bar{u}_{i+1}} - \frac{3\,c_{i,2}}{\bar{u}_{i+2}-\bar{u}_{i+1}}\right]$$
$$+\,\beta_{1,i+2}^2\left[\frac{6\,c_{i,3}}{(\bar{u}_{i+2}-\bar{u}_{i+1})^2} - \frac{12\,c_{i,2}}{(\bar{u}_{i+2}-\bar{u}_{i+1})^2} + \frac{6\,c_{i,1}}{(\bar{u}_{i+2}-\bar{u}_{i+1})^2}\right] \;=\; 0$$

$$-\frac{6\,c_{i,6}}{(\bar{u}_{i+4}-\bar{u}_{i+3})^2} + \beta_{2,i+3}\left[\frac{3\,c_{i,6}}{\bar{u}_{i+3}-\bar{u}_{i+2}} - \frac{3\,c_{i,5}}{\bar{u}_{i+3}-\bar{u}_{i+2}}\right]$$
$$+\,\beta_{1,i+3}^2\left[\frac{6\,c_{i,6}}{(\bar{u}_{i+3}-\bar{u}_{i+2})^2} - \frac{12\,c_{i,5}}{(\bar{u}_{i+3}-\bar{u}_{i+2})^2} + \frac{6\,c_{i,4}}{(\bar{u}_{i+3}-\bar{u}_{i+2})^2}\right] \;=\; 0.$$

There are seven c's to be determined by these six equations and by one additional, linear restriction. As in Chapter 4, where we needed a 16th equation, we derive our 7th here by imposing the condition that four adjacent Beta-splines sum to one. There are two ways in which to do this. The first is suggested by Figure 19.5.

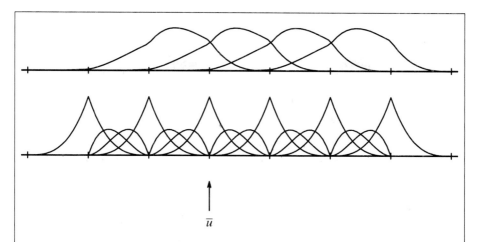

Figure 19.5. Four successive Beta-splines, the B-splines from which they can be constructed, and a value of $\overline{u}$ ($\overline{u} = \overline{u}_{i+3}$) at which summation to one is to be imposed for a segment interval ($[\overline{u}_{i+3}, \overline{u}_{i+4})$).

We may take the six equations above for $G_i(\overline{u})$ and combine them with the corresponding six equations for $G_{i+1}(\overline{u})$ and $G_{i+2}(\overline{u})$ to obtain 18 equations in 21 unknowns. Imposing summation to one on the interval $[\overline{u}_{i+3}, \overline{u}_{i+4})$ adds three more equations to the composite, for a total of 21 equations, by the following considerations. The only B-splines that are nonzero on this interval are

$$B_{j+6}(\overline{u}), \quad B_{j+7}(\overline{u}), \quad B_{j+8}(\overline{u}), \quad \text{and} \quad B_{j+9}(\overline{u}),$$

where $j = 3i + 2$. We expect to have

$$G_i(\overline{u}) + G_{i+1}(\overline{u}) + G_{i+2}(\overline{u}) + G_{i+3}(\overline{u}) = 1$$

throughout this interval. Hence, using the B-spline representations of these G's and collecting terms

$$(c_{i,6} + c_{i+1,3} + c_{i+2,0}) B_{j+6}(\overline{u}) + (c_{i+1,4} + c_{i+2,1}) B_{j+7}(\overline{u})$$

$$+ (c_{i+1,5} + c_{i+2,2}) B_{j+8}(\overline{u}) + (c_{i+1,6} + c_{i+2,3} + c_{i+3,0}) B_{j+9}(\overline{u}) = 1.$$

But

$$1\, B_{j+6} + 1\, B_{j+7} + 1\, B_{j+8} + 1\, B_{j+9} = 1,$$

and these four B-splines are linearly independent, which means that

$$c_{i,6} + c_{i+1,3} + c_{i+2,0} = 1$$

$$c_{i+1,4} + c_{i+2,1} = 1$$

$$c_{i+1,5} + c_{i+2,2} = 1$$

and

$$c_{i+1,6} + c_{i+2,3} + c_{i+3,0} = 1.$$

The last of these equations can be ignored (B_{j+9} disappears when $\bar{u} = \bar{u}_{i+3}$), and the first three equations may be used as normalizing conditions.

The 21 equations are to be solved as a unit. They represent the inherent work required to modify the representation of all the Beta-splines that change whenever there is a change in the bias or tension at the knot $\bar{u}_{i+3}$. Solving these equations is exactly the updating required due to the 4-segment locality of the cubics.

The 21 equations are sparse and highly structured. If proper use is made of the structure, the essential work in solving these equations is somewhat less than that of solving three arbitrary 7×7 equation systems.

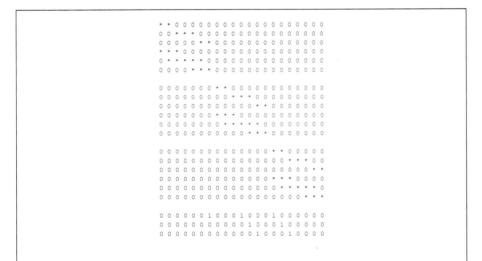

Figure 19.6. The structure of the linear equations representing the complete determination of the 3 successive cubic Beta-splines that are nonzero over the knot $\bar{u} = \bar{u}_{i+3}$ and are influenced by changes in β_1 and β_2 at that knot.

The second way of imposing the normalization on the Beta-spline $G_i(\bar{u})$ that will cause it to sum to one with its neighbors, is to make use of the explicit representation of $G_i(\bar{u})$ given in Chapter 17. The formula given in that chapter for $s_{i,-0}(u)$, suitably transformed to the interval $[\bar{u}_i, \bar{u}_{i+1})$ and evaluated at $\bar{u} = \bar{u}_{i+1}$, gives the value of $G_i(\bar{u}_{i+1})$, which must also be equal to

$$c_{i,0} B_j(\bar{u}_{i+3}) \;=\; c_{i,0} 1 \;=\; c_{i,0}.$$

This will produce a seventh equation to use with the six that define the representation of $G_i(\bar{u})$.

19.2 Examples

We show three examples of the conversion of cubic Beta-splines to cubic, triple-knot B-splines.

Figure 19.7 shows the result of using uniform knots, $\bar{u}_i = i$, and of setting $\beta_1 = 1$ and $\beta_2 = 0$ at every knot position. The resulting Beta-spline curve represents, in fact, a uniform cubic B-spline curve, which is then re-represented as a triple-knot B-spline curve. The B-spline coefficients $c_{i,\ell}$ are

For G_0:	0.166667	0.333333	0.666667	0.666667	0.666667	0.333333	0.166667
For G_1:	0.166667	0.333333	0.666667	0.666667	0.666667	0.333333	0.166667
For G_2:	0.166667	0.333333	0.666667	0.666667	0.666667	0.333333	0.166667
For G_3:	0.166667	0.333333	0.666667	0.666667	0.666667	0.333333	0.166667
For G_4:	0.166667	0.333333	0.666667	0.666667	0.666667	0.333333	0.166667
For G_5:	0.166667	0.333333	0.666667	0.666667	0.666667	0.333333	0.166667

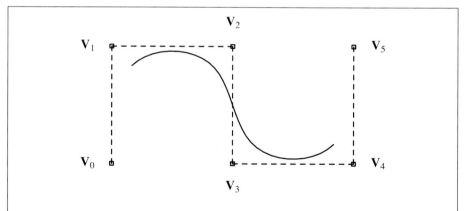

Figure 19.7. A curve produced from triple-knot B-splines representing Beta-splines representing uniform B-splines.

Figure 19.8 shows the result of using uniform knots and β_2's all equal to zero, but the value 8 for all β_1's. The B-spline coefficients $c_{i,\ell}$ are

For G_0:	0.00152207	0.0136986	0.123288	0.219178	0.986301	0.876712	0.7793
For G_1:	0.00152207	0.0136986	0.123288	0.219178	0.986301	0.876712	0.7793
For G_2:	0.00152207	0.0136986	0.123288	0.219178	0.986301	0.876712	0.7793
For G_3:	0.00152207	0.0136986	0.123288	0.219178	0.986301	0.876712	0.7793
For G_4:	0.00152207	0.0136986	0.123288	0.219178	0.986301	0.876712	0.7793
For G_5:	0.00152207	0.0136986	0.123288	0.219178	0.986301	0.876712	0.7793

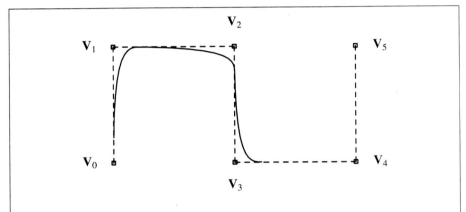

Figure 19.8. A curve produced from triple-knot B-splines representing uniform-knot Beta-splines that have $\beta_2 = 0$ and $\beta_1 = 8$ at all knots.

Figure 19.9 shows the result of using uniform knots and β_1's all equal to one, but with all β_2's set to 10. The B-spline coefficients $c_{i,\ell}$ are

For G_0:	0.0909091	0.181818	0.818182	0.818182	0.818182	0.181818	0.0909091
For G_1:	0.0909091	0.181818	0.818182	0.818182	0.818182	0.181818	0.0909091
For G_2:	0.0909091	0.181818	0.818182	0.818182	0.818182	0.181818	0.0909091
For G_3:	0.0909091	0.181818	0.818182	0.818182	0.818182	0.181818	0.0909091
For G_4:	0.0909091	0.181818	0.818182	0.818182	0.818182	0.181818	0.0909091
For G_5:	0.0909091	0.181818	0.818182	0.818182	0.818182	0.181818	0.0909091

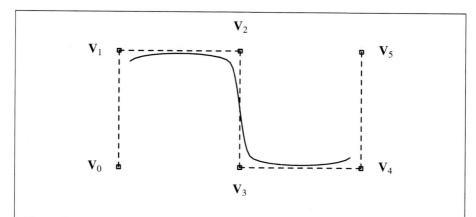

Figure 19.9. A curve produced from triple-knot B-splines representing uniform-knot Beta-splines that have $\beta_1 = 1$ and $\beta_2 = 10$ at all knots.

Finally, Figure 19.10 shows the result of choosing random knots and random nonnegative values for β_1's and β_2's. The knots used are

$$0, 1.2, 1.4, 2.5, 3.4, 5, 6.1, 6.7, 8, 10.4 \, .$$

The β_1 values are

$$3, 2, 9, 4, 0.5, 2, 1, 6, 1, 3 \, .$$

The β_2 values are

$$9, 16, 12, 15, 8, 0, 6, 11, 1, 7 \, .$$

The B-spline coefficients $c_{i,\ell}$ are

For G_0:	0.0272178	0.0362905	0.0556454	0.0742283	0.994084	0.697	0.533872
For G_1:	0.000117145	0.0059158	0.303	0.427679	0.835719	0.0857276	0.0403424
For G_2:	0.0384488	0.164281	0.914272	0.929261	0.942585	0.545707	0.315936
For G_3:	0.0303963	0.0574152	0.454293	0.529349	0.632551	0.127309	0.0449326
For G_4:	0.154715	0.367449	0.872691	0.915435	0.93875	0.866428	0.804541
For G_5:	0.0396326	0.0612504	0.133572	0.193323	0.970083	0.548055	0.355495

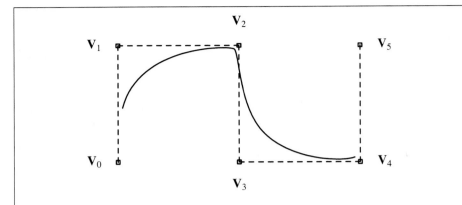

Figure 19.10. A cubic, triple-knot B-spline curve representing a cubic, randomly shaped, nonuniform Beta-spline curve.

20

Rendering and Evaluation

There are several ways to obtain values of B-splines and their derivatives. We will look at some of these in this chapter, also covering the evaluation of discrete B-splines and the refinement of control vertices. With this background, we can then discuss some of the methods that have been proposed in the literature to render B-spline curves and surfaces graphically.

For uniform cubic B-spline curves, we often look upon evaluation as a vector-matrix-vector product involving the 4×4 basis-change matrix that gives the B-spline segment polynomials in terms of the powers of $u = (\bar{u} - \bar{u}_i)/(\bar{u}_{i+1} - \bar{u}_i)$; that is,

$$
\begin{bmatrix} 1 & u & u^2 & u^3 \end{bmatrix} \frac{1}{6} \begin{bmatrix} 1 & 4 & 1 & 0 \\ -3 & 0 & 3 & 0 \\ 3 & -6 & 3 & 0 \\ -1 & 3 & -3 & 1 \end{bmatrix} \begin{bmatrix} \mathbf{V}_{i-3} \\ \mathbf{V}_{i-2} \\ \mathbf{V}_{i-1} \\ \mathbf{V}_i \end{bmatrix}.
\tag{20.1}
$$

This product may be grouped in either of two promising ways.

On the one hand, we may first carry out the vector-matrix product on the left. This will yield, for each given u, a vector of B-spline values

$$
\begin{bmatrix} 1 & u & u^2 & u^3 \end{bmatrix} \frac{1}{6} \begin{bmatrix} 1 & 4 & 1 & 0 \\ -3 & 0 & 3 & 0 \\ 3 & -6 & 3 & 0 \\ -1 & 3 & -3 & 1 \end{bmatrix} = \begin{bmatrix} B_{i-3}(u) & B_{i-2}(u) & B_{i-1}(u) & B_i(u) \end{bmatrix},
\tag{20.2}
$$

which may then applied to the vector of control vertices to produce a value on the ith segment of the curve

$$\mathbf{Q}_i(u) \;=\; \left[\, B_{i-3}(u)\; B_{i-2}(u)\; B_{i-1}(u)\; B_i(u)\, \right] \begin{bmatrix} \mathbf{V}_{i-3} \\ \mathbf{V}_{i-2} \\ \mathbf{V}_{i-1} \\ \mathbf{V}_i \end{bmatrix}. \tag{20.3}$$

In fact, since all B-splines are translates of each other in the uniform case, the vector of B-splines values produced in (20.2) can be tabulated and then applied to all 4-tuples of successive control vertices to produce a corresponding point on every segment of the curve $\mathbf{Q}(u)$.

On the other hand, the matrix-vector product on the right of (20.1) may be carried out first to produce, for any given 4-tuple of control vertices, a vector of transformed control vertices

$$\frac{1}{6} \begin{bmatrix} 1 & 4 & 1 & 0 \\ -3 & 0 & 3 & 0 \\ 3 & -6 & 3 & 0 \\ -1 & 3 & -3 & 1 \end{bmatrix} \begin{bmatrix} \mathbf{V}_{i-3} \\ \mathbf{V}_{i-2} \\ \mathbf{V}_{i-1} \\ \mathbf{V}_i \end{bmatrix} = \begin{bmatrix} \mathbf{T}_{i-3} \\ \mathbf{T}_{i-2} \\ \mathbf{T}_{i-1} \\ \mathbf{T}_i \end{bmatrix}. \tag{20.4}$$

These may be used for any sequence of values of u within the interval $[0,1)$ to produce points on the single curve segment $\mathbf{Q}_i(u)$:

$$\mathbf{Q}_i(u) \;=\; \left[\, 1\; u\; u^2\; u^3\, \right] \begin{bmatrix} \mathbf{T}_{i-3} \\ \mathbf{T}_{i-2} \\ \mathbf{T}_{i-1} \\ \mathbf{T}_i \end{bmatrix}. \tag{20.5}$$

The material in Section 20.5 provides a convenient way to step through (20.5) for a succession of values of u, at least for splines of relatively low order k.

Surfaces, of course, merely add some complexity:

$$\mathbf{Q}_{i,j}(u,v) \;=\; \left[\, 1\; u\; u^2\; u^3\, \right] \frac{1}{6} \begin{bmatrix} 1 & 4 & 1 & 0 \\ -3 & 0 & 3 & 0 \\ 3 & -6 & 3 & 0 \\ -1 & 3 & -3 & 1 \end{bmatrix}$$

$$\times \begin{bmatrix} \mathbf{V}_{i-3,j-3} & \mathbf{V}_{i-2,j-3} & \mathbf{V}_{i-1,j-3} & \mathbf{V}_{i,j-3} \\ \mathbf{V}_{i-3,j-2} & \mathbf{V}_{i-2,j-2} & \mathbf{V}_{i-1,j-2} & \mathbf{V}_{i,j-2} \\ \mathbf{V}_{i-3,j-1} & \mathbf{V}_{i-2,j-1} & \mathbf{V}_{i-1,j-1} & \mathbf{V}_{i,j-1} \\ \mathbf{V}_{i-3,j} & \mathbf{V}_{i-2,j} & \mathbf{V}_{i-1,j} & \mathbf{V}_{i,j} \end{bmatrix}$$

$$\times \frac{1}{6} \begin{bmatrix} 1 & -3 & 3 & -1 \\ 4 & 0 & -6 & 3 \\ 1 & 3 & 3 & -3 \\ 0 & 0 & 0 & 1 \end{bmatrix} \begin{bmatrix} 1 \\ v \\ v^2 \\ v^3 \end{bmatrix},$$

but they do not change the essential ingredients.

For general B-splines, the interpretation given by (20.3) and (20.4) extends to a process that can be expressed as follows:

- Select $\bar{u}$.

- Determine $\bar{u}$'s segment interval.

- Compute $\mathbf{B}$, the corresponding k B-spline values, using the recurrence.

- Retrieve $\mathbf{V}$, the corresponding k control vertices.

- Compute the dot product $\mathbf{B} \cdot \mathbf{V}$.

- The result is $\mathbf{Q}(\bar{u})$, a point on the curve.

The k B-spline values, of course, can be used only once, rather than once for each segment as in the uniform case. The material in Section 20.1 will cover evaluation by recurrence in more detail.

To extend the interpretation given by (20.4) and (20.5) to general B-splines, it is necessary to convert the segment polynomials of the B-splines into their representation in terms of powers of u in order to provide a basis-change matrix. That is, the coefficients of the segment polynomials, expressed in terms of $\bar{u} - \bar{u}_i$, must be found explicitly. This, we will see, involves differentiating general B-splines, a topic which is covered in Section 20.3, as well as evaluating them.

20.1 Values of B-Splines

Suppose that a value of $\bar{u}$ is given within a designated parameter range

$$\bar{u}_{k-1} \leq \bar{u} < \bar{u}_{m+1},$$

and let δ be the unique index for which

$$\bar{u}_\delta \leq \bar{u} < \bar{u}_{\delta+1}.$$

Recall that all the first-order B-splines (step functions) will be zero for this index except $B_{\delta,1}(\bar{u})$:

$$B_{\delta,1}(\bar{u}) = 1.$$

It is of interest to consider what nonzero values would occur if the recurrences for each of the values $B_{\delta,k}(\bar{u}), \ldots, B_{\delta-k+1,k}(\bar{u})$ were carried out. These nonzero values can be arranged in a table:

				0
		0		$B_{\delta-k+1,k}(\bar{u})$
	0	$B_{\delta-2,3}(\bar{u})$		$B_{\delta-k+2,k}(\bar{u})$
0	$B_{\delta-1,2}(\bar{u})$	$B_{\delta-1,3}(\bar{u})$	$\cdots$	$\vdots$
$B_{\delta,1}(\bar{u})$	$B_{\delta,2}(\bar{u})$	$B_{\delta,3}(\bar{u})$		$B_{\delta,k}(\bar{u})$
0	0	0		0

The zeros are included at the top and bottom of each column to serve as a reminder that the B-splines coming in sequence before and after those shown are nil at the given value of $\bar{u}$.

These nonzero values can be produced columnwise from left to right, and elementwise in each column from top to bottom. Each entry is produced from the computation indicated in Figure 20.1.

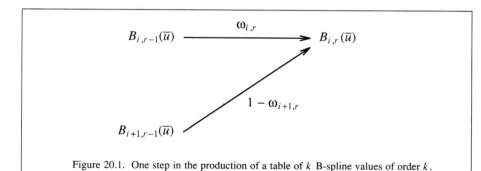

Figure 20.1. One step in the production of a table of k B-spline values of order k.

The quantity $\omega_{i,r}$ that appears in Figure 20.1 stands for the linear factor

$$\omega_{i,r} = \frac{\bar{u} - \bar{u}_i}{\bar{u}_{i+r-1} - \bar{u}_i},$$

and consequently,

$$1 - \omega_{i+1,r} = \frac{\overline{u}_{i+r} - \overline{u}}{\overline{u}_{i+r} - \overline{u}_{i+1}}.$$

The second formula would require a special interpretation if $\overline{u}_{i+r} = \overline{u}_{i+1}$. However, the only ratios required to produce the ω's needed for this table are

$$\frac{\overline{u} - \overline{u}_\delta}{\overline{u}_{\delta+1} - \overline{u}_\delta}$$

to obtain the second column from the first,

$$\frac{\overline{u} - \overline{u}_{\delta-1}}{\overline{u}_{\delta+1} - \overline{u}_{\delta-1}} \quad \text{and} \quad \frac{\overline{u} - \overline{u}_\delta}{\overline{u}_{\delta+2} - \overline{u}_\delta}$$

to obtain the third column from the second, and so on. It is easy to see that all these ratios have denominators that are positive, since

$$\overline{u}_\delta < \overline{u}_{\delta+1} \leq \cdots \leq \overline{u}_{\delta+k-1}.$$

The computational algorithm that results from these observations follows.

$bval_0 \leftarrow 1$

for $r \leftarrow 2$ **step** 1 **until** k **do**

$\quad i \leftarrow \delta - r + 1$

$\quad bval_{r-1} \leftarrow 0$

$\quad$ **for** $s \leftarrow r - 2$ **step** -1 **until** 0 **do**

$\quad\quad i \leftarrow i + 1$

$\quad\quad omega \leftarrow (\overline{u} - \overline{u}_i) / (\overline{u}_{i+r-1} - \overline{u}_i)$

$\quad\quad bval_{s+1} \leftarrow bval_{s+1} + (1 - omega) \times bval_s$

$\quad\quad bval_s \leftarrow omega \times bval_s$

$\quad$ **endfor**

endfor

The result of this computation is that the value of $B_{\delta-s,k}(\overline{u})$ is stored in $bval_s$ for $s = 0, \ldots, k-1$.

It should be observed that the numerators of the ratios are given by

$$\overline{u} - \overline{u}_\delta, \quad \overline{u} - \overline{u}_{\delta-1}, \ldots, \quad \overline{u} - \overline{u}_{\delta+k-1}.$$

These numbers are computed several times over during the course of the computation. If space is available, they could be computed in advance and stored. Finally, it should be understood that the indices i and s are not both necessary. The use of i merely permits the code to follow the text of the discussion above more closely.

20.2   Sums of B-Splines

Linear combinations of B-splines are the objects of primary concern in rendering and evaluation. This is because they constitute the x, y, and z coordinates of curves and surfaces; for example,

$$X(\overline{u}) = \sum_i x_i B_{i,k}(\overline{u}),$$

or

$$X(\overline{u},\overline{v}) = \sum_j d_j(\overline{u}) B_{j,k}(\overline{v}),$$

where for each j and each fixed value of $\overline{u}$

$$d_j(\overline{u}) = \sum_i x_{i,j} B_{i,k}(\overline{u}),$$

and similarly for Y and Z. In this section we will use the following general notation for any such linear combination:

$$s(\overline{U}) = \sum_{i=0}^{m} C_i B_{i,K}(\overline{U}). \tag{20.6}$$

We have used C's for the coefficients, we have replaced $\overline{u}$ by $\overline{U}$, and we are using K for the order of the B-splines, all for reasons that will become clear in Section 20.4.

For any given value of $\overline{U}$, the corresponding value of (20.6) can be obtained from the B-spline recurrence without dealing with the values of the individual B–splines. Consider the following:

$$\sum_{i=0}^{m} C_i B_{i,K}(\overline{U}) = \sum_{i=0}^{m} C_i \left[\frac{\overline{U} - \overline{u}_i}{\overline{u}_{i+K-1} - \overline{u}_i} B_{i,K-1}(\overline{U}) \right.$$

$$\left. + \frac{\overline{u}_{i+K} - \overline{U}}{\overline{u}_{i+K} - \overline{u}_{i+1}} B_{i+1,K-1}(\overline{U}) \right]$$

$$= \sum_{i=0}^{m} C_i \frac{\overline{U} - \overline{u}_i}{\overline{u}_{i+K-1} - \overline{u}_i} B_{i,K-1}(\overline{U})$$

$$+ \sum_{i=0}^{m} C_i \frac{\overline{u}_{i+K} - \overline{U}}{\overline{u}_{i+K} - \overline{u}_{i+1}} B_{i+1,K-1}(\overline{U}).$$

The index in the second sum can be shifted, and the two sums can be recombined, to give

$$\sum_{i=0}^{m+1} \left[\frac{\overline{U} - \overline{u}_i}{\overline{u}_{i+K-1} - \overline{u}_i} C_i + \frac{\overline{u}_{i+K-1} - \overline{U}}{\overline{u}_{i+K-1} - \overline{u}_i} C_{i-1} \right] B_{i,K-1}(\overline{U}),$$

where the values of C_{-1} and C_{m+1} are taken to be zero.

If we set

$$C_i^{[K]} = C_i \quad \text{for } i = 0, \dots, m$$

and

$$C_i^{[K-1]} = \frac{\overline{U} - \overline{u}_i}{\overline{u}_{i+K-1} - \overline{u}_i} C_i^{[K]} + \frac{\overline{u}_{i+K-1} - \overline{U}}{\overline{u}_{i+K-1} - \overline{u}_i} C_{i-1}^{[K]} \quad \text{for } i = 0, \dots, m+1, \tag{20.7}$$

then we have

$$s(\overline{U}) = \sum_{i=0}^{m+1} C_i^{[K-1]} B_{i,K-1}(\overline{U}).$$

This clearly produces yet another recurrence.

■ Theorem

Let $\overline{U}$ be a given fixed value in the parameter range. Let δ be the unique index such that

$$\overline{u}_\delta \leq \overline{U} < \overline{u}_{\delta+1}.$$

Then the value

$$s(\overline{U}) = \sum_{i=0}^{m} C_i B_{i,K}(\overline{U})$$

is given by

$$s(\overline{U}) = C_\delta^{[1]},$$

where

$$C_i^{[K]} = C_i \quad \text{for} \quad i = 0, \ldots, m$$

and

$$C_i^{[r-1]} = \frac{\overline{U} - \overline{u}_i}{\overline{u}_{i+r-1} - \overline{u}_i} C_i^{[r]} + \frac{\overline{u}_{i+r-1} - \overline{U}}{\overline{u}_{i+r-1} - \overline{u}_i} C_{i-1}^{[r]} \quad \text{for} \quad i = 0, \ldots, m + K - r \tag{20.8}$$

for $r = K, \ldots, 2$.

The convention is adopted that values of zero are adjoined as necessary at both ends of the index range i to handle values of C that might not otherwise be defined; that is,

$$0 = C_{-1}^{[K]} = C_{-1}^{[K-1]} = \cdots$$

$$0 = C_{m+1}^{[K]} = C_{m+2}^{[K-1]} = \cdots.$$

The convention that terms containing ratios with zero denominators are equal to zero is, of course, also in force.

■

The above is stated as if the location of the value of $\overline{U}$ could have been anywhere in the parameter range. In fact, we have assumed that

$$\overline{u}_\delta \le \overline{U} < \overline{u}_{\delta+1},$$

and this means that many B-spline values occurring in the above expressions are zero. The original sum will reduce to

$$s(\overline{U}) = \sum_{i=\delta-K+1}^{\delta} C_i B_{i,K}(\overline{U}).$$

At the first stage of the recurrence the following will be produced, at least formally:

$$s(\overline{U}) = \sum_{i=\delta-K+2}^{\delta} C_i^{[K-1]} B_{i,K-1}(\overline{U}).$$

The values of $B_{\delta-K+1,K-1}(\overline{U})$ and $B_{\delta-K+2,K-1}(\overline{U})$, however, will both be zero for the given value of $\overline{U}$. At each stage of the recurrence, only

$$B_{\delta,r}(\overline{U}), \ldots, B_{\delta-r+1,r}(\overline{U})$$

will be nonzero. If the zero values of the B-splines are taken into account, the only coefficients that enter into the recurrence can be arranged into the type of table that appeared in Section 20.1:

				0
			0	$C_{\delta-K+1}^{[K]}$
		0	$C_{\delta-2}^{[3]}$	$C_{\delta-K+2}^{[K]}$
	0	$C_{\delta-1}^{[2]}$	$C_{\delta-1}^{[3]}$ $\cdots$	$\vdots$
$C_{\delta}^{[1]}$	$C_{\delta}^{[2]}$	$C_{\delta}^{[3]}$		$C_{\delta}^{[K]}$
0	0	0		0

In this case, Figure 20.2 presents the basic step of computation.

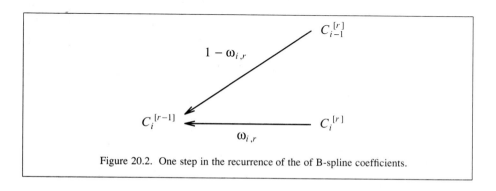

Figure 20.2. One step in the recurrence of the of B-spline coefficients.

The value of $\omega_{i,r}$ is given by

$$\omega_{i,r} = \frac{\overline{U} - \overline{u}_i}{\overline{u}_{i+r-1} - \overline{u}_i}.$$

The values in the table can be produced columnwise from right to left, and elementwise in each column from bottom to top. It is easy to verify that the ω's needed for this table are the same as the ones in Section 20.1; namely,

$$\frac{\overline{U} - \overline{u}_\delta}{\overline{u}_{\delta+1} - \overline{u}_\delta},$$

which will provide the last computational transition, producing the leftmost column from the next to the leftmost,

$$\frac{\overline{U} - \overline{u}_{\delta-1}}{\overline{u}_{\delta+1} - \overline{u}_{\delta-1}} \quad \text{and} \quad \frac{\overline{U} - \overline{u}_\delta}{\overline{u}_{\delta+2} - \overline{u}_\delta},$$

which will provide the next-to-last transition, and so on.

Assuming that the array *coef* is initialized with

$$coef_s = C_{\delta-s} \quad \text{for } s = 0, \ldots, K-1,$$

the algorithm that results from the observations we have just made is as follows:

> **for** $r \leftarrow K$ **step** -1 **until** 2 **do**
>
> $\quad i \leftarrow \delta$
>
> $\quad$ **for** $s \leftarrow 0$ **step** 1 **until** $r-2$ **do**
>
> $\qquad omega \leftarrow (\overline{U} - \overline{u}_i) / (\overline{u}_{i+r-1} - \overline{u}_i)$
>
> $\qquad coef_s \leftarrow omega \times coef_s + (1 - omega) \times coef_{s+1}$
>
> $\qquad i \leftarrow i - 1$
>
> $\quad$ **endfor**
>
> **endfor**

The result of this computation is that the value of

$$C_\delta B_{\delta,K}(\overline{U}) + \cdots + C_{\delta+K-1} B_{\delta+K-1,K}(\overline{U})$$

will be stored in $coef_0$.

20.3 Derivatives of B-splines

Many of the evaluation and rendering processes used in dealing with parametric curves and surfaces in computer graphics require the knowledge of parametric derivatives, i.e.

$$\frac{d^\ell}{d\bar{u}^\ell}\, \mathbf{Q}(\bar{u}), \quad \frac{\partial^\ell}{\partial\bar{u}^\ell}\, \mathbf{Q}(\bar{u},\bar{v}), \quad \frac{\partial^\ell}{\partial\bar{v}^\ell}\, \mathbf{Q}(\bar{u},\bar{v}).$$

For parametric curves and surfaces generated by B-splines, these derivatives require evaluation of the derivatives of individual B-splines:

$$D_{\bar{u}}^{(r)}\, B_{i,k}(\bar{u}) = B_{i,k}^{(r)}(\bar{u}).$$

When the segment polynomials of $B_{i,k}(\bar{u})$ are known explicitly, finding derivatives is no more than a simple exercise in calculus. For example, with uniform knot spacing, $\bar{u}_{i+1} = \bar{u}_i + 1$, the cubic B-spline has the first derivative

$$B_{i,4}^{(1)}(\bar{u}) = \begin{cases} b_{-0}^{(1)}(u) = \dfrac{1}{2}\,u^2 & \text{for } \bar{u}_i \le \bar{u} < \bar{u}_{i+1} \\ & \text{and } u = \bar{u} - \bar{u}_i \\[2mm] b_{-1}^{(1)}(u) = \dfrac{1}{6}\,(3 + 6u - 9u^2) & \text{for } \bar{u}_{i+1} \le \bar{u} < \bar{u}_{i+2} \\ & \text{and } u = \bar{u} - \bar{u}_{i+1} \\[2mm] b_{-2}^{(1)}(u) = \dfrac{1}{6}\,(-12u + 9u^2) & \text{for } \bar{u}_{i+2} \le \bar{u} < \bar{u}_{i+3} \\ & \text{and } u = \bar{u} - \bar{u}_{i+2} \\[2mm] b_{-3}^{(1)}(u) = \dfrac{1}{6}\,(-3 + 6u - 3u^2) & \text{for } \bar{u}_{i+3} \le \bar{u} < \bar{u}_{i+4} \\ & \text{and } u = \bar{u} - \bar{u}_{i+3}. \end{cases}$$

In general situations, however, the individual B-splines are available only through their definitions as divided differences or as the results of a recurrence process. The segment polynomials are not tabulated; hence they can not be called upon to provide derivatives.

We will show how the derivatives of a B-spline can be obtained from the B-spline recurrence. Indeed, it is by using the derivatives, obtained from the recurrence, that the coefficients of the segment polynomials can be tabulated. Since some rendering and evaluation schemes work more efficiently in terms of segment polynomials, this will be an important result.

We remarked in the development of Chapter 7 that differentiation with respect to $\bar{u}$ can pass through divided-differencing with respect to t. Consequently,

$$D_{\bar{u}}^{(1)}\, B_{i,k}(\bar{u}) = D_{\bar{u}}^{(1)}\, (-1)^k\, (\bar{u}_{i+k} - \bar{u}_i)\, [\bar{u}_i(k){:}t\,]\, (\bar{u} - t)_+^{k-1}$$

$$= (-1)^k\, (\bar{u}_{i+k} - \bar{u}_i)\, [\bar{u}_i(k){:}t\,]\, D_{\bar{u}}^{(1)}\, (\bar{u} - t)_+^{k-1}$$

$$= (-1)^k\, (\bar{u}_{i+k} - \bar{u}_i)\, [\bar{u}_i(k){:}t\,]\, (k-1)\, (\bar{u} - t)_+^{k-2}.$$

If we ignore the terms $(-1)^k$ and $(k-1)$ for a moment, what remains can be written as:

$$(\bar{u}_{i+k} - \bar{u}_i)\,[\bar{u}_i(k):t\,]\,(\bar{u}-t)_+^{k-2} \tag{20.9}$$

$$= (\bar{u}_{i+k} - \bar{u}_i)\,\frac{[\bar{u}_{i+1}(k-1):t\,]\,(\bar{u}-t)_+^{k-2} - [\bar{u}_i(k-1):t\,]\,(\bar{u}-t)_+^{k-2}}{\bar{u}_{i+k} - \bar{u}_i}.$$

This is true directly from the definition of the divided difference $[\bar{u}_i(k):t\,]$, if $\bar{u}_{i+k} > \bar{u}_i$ (as we generally assume to be the case), but it is also true if $\bar{u}_{i+k}$ and $\bar{u}_i$ have the same value. To see this, note that the equality $\bar{u}_{i+k} = \bar{u}_i$ will make the left side of (20.9) equal to

$$(\bar{u}_{i+k} - \bar{u}_i)\,[\bar{u}_i(k):t\,]\,(\bar{u}-t)_+^{k-2} = 0 \cdot \frac{1}{k!} D_t^{(k)}\,(\bar{u}-t)_+^{k-2}\,\big|_{t=\bar{u}_i} = 0.$$

For the right side of (20.9) we may consider $\bar{u}_{i+k} = \bar{u}_i$ to be the limiting case of $\bar{u}_{i+k} \to \bar{u}_i$. Since we should have canceled out the term $(\bar{u}_{i+k} - \bar{u}_i)$, this will make this side equal to

$$[\bar{u}_{i+1}(k-1):t\,]\,(\bar{u}-t)_+^{k-2} - [\bar{u}_i(k-1):t\,]\,(\bar{u}-t)_+^{k-2}$$

$$= \frac{1}{(k-1)!} D_t^{(k-1)}\,(\bar{u}-t)_+^{k-2}\,\big|_{t=\bar{u}_{i+1}}$$

$$- \frac{1}{(k-1)!} D_t^{(k-1)}\,(\bar{u}-t)_+^{k-2}\,\big|_{t=\bar{u}_i},$$

which is zero, since both terms in the difference will be equal in the limit. The result is that both sides of (20.9) are zero, hence the equality it expresses is valid. The case in which $\bar{u}_{i+k} = \bar{u}_i$ would be pertinent to the discussion of a recurrence for B-spline derivatives that will appear below. However, we will not be setting up a formal argument for the derivative recurrence, so the case in which $\bar{u}_{i+k} = \bar{u}_i$ will remain merely an observation.

Applying (20.9) to the differentiation result and then applying the divided difference definition of $k-1^{\text{st}}$-order B-splines to the result gives the following:

$$D_{\bar{u}}^{(1)}\,B_{i,k}(\bar{u}) = (-1)(k-1)(-1)^{k-1}\,[\bar{u}_{i+1}(k-1):t\,]\,(\bar{u}-t)_+^{k-2}$$

$$- (-1)(k-1)(-1)^{k-1}\,[\bar{u}_i(k-1):t\,]\,(\bar{u}-t)_+^{k-2} \tag{20.10}$$

$$= (k-1)\left[\frac{B_{i,k-1}(\bar{u})}{\bar{u}_{i+k-1} - \bar{u}_i} - \frac{B_{i+1,k-1}(\bar{u})}{\bar{u}_{i+k} - \bar{u}_{i+1}}\right].$$

For higher derivatives this result could be repeated recursively, but the expressions which result rapidly become quite complicated. A more productive approach, to be found in [DeBoor78] and [Schumaker81], involves looking at the derivatives of linear combinations of B-splines; that is,

$$\sum_{i=0}^{m} E_i B_{i,L}(\overline{u}).$$

We have used E's for the coefficients and L for the order of the spline for reasons that will become clear in Section 20.4. Since the x, y, and z components of any B-spline curve or surface will be functions of this form, we frequently want to work with linear combinations, rather than with the individual B-splines themselves. If the derivatives of only a single B-spline are wanted, this can be handled by noting that, for any specific index, s,

$$B_{s,L}(\overline{u}) = \sum_{i=0}^{m} E_i B_{i,L}(\overline{u})$$

$$\text{for } E_0 = \cdots = E_{s-1} = E_{s+1} = \cdots = E_m = 0 \text{ and } E_s = 1.$$

Applying the derivative result, (20.10), to a linear combination gives:

$$D_{\overline{u}} \sum_{i=0}^{m} E_i B_{i,L}(\overline{u}) = \sum_{i=0}^{m} (L-1) E_i \left[\frac{B_{i,L-1}(\overline{u})}{\overline{u}_{i+L-1} - \overline{u}_i} - \frac{B_{i+1,L-1}(\overline{u})}{\overline{u}_{i+L} - \overline{u}_{i+1}} \right].$$

By rearranging the summation to collect terms which are common to each B-spline, we obtain

$$D_{\overline{u}} \sum_{i=0}^{m} E_i B_{i,L}(\overline{u}) = \sum_{i=0}^{m+1} (L-1) \frac{E_i - E_{i-1}}{\overline{u}_{i+L-1} - \overline{u}_i} B_{i,L-1}(\overline{u}).$$

Notice that this sum calls for values of E_{-1} (for $i = 0$) and E_{m+1} (for $i = m + 1$). These fictitious coefficients were introduced to unify the summation; we define them to have the value zero.

By taking this approach, we can define

$$E_i^{[0]} = E_i \quad \text{for } i = 0, \ldots, m$$

and

$$E_i^{[1]} = (L-1) \frac{E_i^{[0]} - E_{i-1}^{[0]}}{\overline{u}_{i+L-1} - \overline{u}_i} \quad \text{for } i = 0, \ldots, m+1,$$

and we have the start of a recurrence which can be carried on to higher derivatives.

■ **Theorem**

Let $0 \le \ell < L$. Then

$$D_{\bar{u}}^{(\ell)} \sum_{i=0}^{m} E_i B_{i,L}(\bar{u}) = \sum_{i=0}^{m+\ell} E_i^{[\ell]} B_{i,L-\ell}(\bar{u})$$

where

$$E_i^{[0]} = E_i \quad \text{for } i = 0, \ldots, m$$

and for each $r = 1, \ldots, \ell$,

$$E_i^{[r]} = (L-r) \frac{E_i^{[r-1]} - E_{i-1}^{[r-1]}}{\bar{u}_{i+L-r} - \bar{u}_i} \tag{20.11}$$

$$\text{for } i = 0, \ldots, m+r.$$

The convention is adopted that values of zero are adjoined as necessary at both ends of the index range i to handle values of E which might not otherwise be defined in (20.11); that is,

$$E_{-1}^{[0]} = E_{-1}^{[1]} = \cdots = 0$$

$$E_{m+1}^{[0]} = E_{m+2}^{[1]} = \cdots = 0.$$

The convention that terms containing ratios with zero denominators are taken as equal to zero is also in force; that is,

$$E_i^{[r]} = 0 \quad \text{if } \bar{u}_{i+L-r} = \bar{u}_i.$$

■

The theorem above is stated for general $\bar{u}$. In a computational setting we will want the value of a derivative at some specific $\bar{u}$ in the parameter range. At any specific value of $\bar{u}$, however, many of the terms in the linear combination will disappear, because the corresponding values of the B-splines will be zero. Taking this into account results in the simplified recurrence:

■ Derivative Value Recurrence

Begin with the coefficients E_i of the linear combination

$$s(\bar{u}) = \sum_{i=0}^{m} E_i \, B_{i,L}(\bar{u}).$$

Let $\bar{u}$ and δ be given, with

$$\bar{u}_\delta \leq \bar{u} < \bar{u}_{\delta+1},$$

and let ℓ be given in the range $0 \leq \ell < L$.
Set

$$E_i^{[0]} = E_i \quad \text{for} \quad i = \delta - L + 1, \ldots, \delta.$$

For each $r = 1, \ldots, \ell$, let

$$E_i^{[r]} = (L - r) \, \frac{E_i^{[r-1]} - E_{i-1}^{[r-1]}}{\bar{u}_{i+L-r} - \bar{u}_i} \tag{20.12}$$

$$\text{for} \quad i = \delta - L + r + 1, \ldots, \delta.$$

Then the ℓth derivative of $s(\bar{u})$ at the specific value of $\bar{u}$ in question is given by the linear combination

$$s^{(\ell)}(\bar{u}) = \sum_{i=\delta-L+\ell+1}^{\delta} E_i^{[\ell]} \, B_{i, L-\ell}(\bar{u}).$$

■

Assuming that the array $coef_s$ is initialized with

$$coef_s = E_{\delta-s} \quad \text{for } s = 0, \ldots, L - 1,$$

then the algorithm that follows will transform the contents of the array so that, upon completion,

$$coef_s = E_{\delta-s}^{[\ell]} \quad \text{for } s = 0, \ldots, L - \ell - 1.$$

for $r \leftarrow 1$ **step** 1 **until** ℓ **do**

    $i \leftarrow \delta$

    for $s \leftarrow 0$ **step** 1 **until** $L - r - 1$ **do**

        $coef_s \leftarrow (L - r) \times (coef_s - coef_{s+1}) / (\overline{u}_{i+L-r} - \overline{u}_i)$

        $i \leftarrow i - 1$

    endfor

  endfor

The value of $s^{(\ell)}(\overline{u})$ can then be computed using the algorithm from Section 20.2 with $\overline{U} = \overline{u}$, $K = L - \ell$, and $C_i = E_i^{[\ell]}$.

20.4   Conversion to Segment Polynomials

In this section we will return to our more conventional notation.

Consider any linear combination; e.g., the x, y, or z components of a curve, any of which has the form

$$s(\overline{u}) = \sum_{i=0}^{m} c_i \, B_{i,k}(\overline{u}). \tag{20.13}$$

Given a fixed value of $\overline{u}$, consider the breakpoint interval

$$\overline{u}_\delta \leq \overline{u} < \overline{u}_{\delta+1}.$$

Within such an interval, any linear combination (20.13) becomes simply a polynomial; hence, it can be expressed as

$$s(\overline{u}) = \sum_{j=0}^{k-1} a_j(\delta) (\overline{u} - \overline{u}_\delta)^j \tag{20.14}$$

for some collection of coefficients $a_j(\delta)$. We will present a computational scheme for making the conversion from the B-spline representation of $s(\overline{u})$, (20.13), which is valid for all $\overline{u} \in [\overline{u}_{k-1}, \overline{u}_{m+1})$, to the power representation, (20.14), whose coefficients $a_j(\delta)$ are only valid on the specific breakpoint interval $\overline{u}_\delta \leq \overline{u} < \overline{u}_{\delta+1}$. The reason for wishing to make this conversion derives from the observation that representation (20.14) can be evaluated more efficiently than (20.13). The conversion is costly, however, so it will only be interesting when we are faced with the

---

task of evaluating $s(\overline{u})$ several times in succession on a breakpoint interval. In [Schumaker81] it is observed that two or more values of $s(\overline{u})$ on a breakpoint interval would already make the conversion worthwhile for cubic splines.

Recall from Section 6.1 that the coefficients $a_j(\delta)$ are essentially the derivatives of $s(\overline{u})$ at $\overline{u}_\delta$:

$$a_j(\delta) = \frac{1}{j!} \cdot \frac{d^j}{du^j} s(\overline{u})\big|_{\overline{u} = \overline{u}_\delta} = \frac{1}{j!} D_{\overline{u}}^{(j)} s(\overline{u})\big|_{\overline{u} = \overline{u}_\delta}.$$

Also note that

$$D_{\overline{u}}^{(\ell)} s(\overline{u}) = D_{\overline{u}}^{(\ell)} \sum_{j=0}^{k-1} a_j(\delta)(\overline{u} - \overline{u}_\delta)^j$$

$$= \sum_{j=\ell}^{k-1} a_j(\delta)(j)\cdots(j - \ell + 1)(\overline{u} - \overline{u}_\delta)^{j-\ell},$$

and

$$D_{\overline{u}}^{(\ell)} s(\overline{u})\big|_{\overline{u} = \overline{u}_\delta} = a_\ell(\delta)\ell!.$$

A consequence of this is that it is only necessary to "dovetail" recurrences (20.12) and (20.8) to produce

$$a_0(\delta), \ldots, a_{k-1}(\delta).$$

■ **Segment Polynomial Conversion Recurrence**

Let a breakpoint interval $[\overline{u}_\delta, \overline{u}_{\delta+1})$ be given. Let

$$c_i^{[0]} = c_i \quad \text{for } i = \delta - k + 1, \ldots, \delta.$$

For each $r = 0, \ldots, k - 1$ in turn:

(1) Let $C_i = c_i^{[r]}$ for $i = \delta - k + r + 1, \ldots, \delta$.

(2) Use the algorithm of recurrence (20.8) with $\overline{U} = \overline{u}_\delta$, $K = k - r$, and coefficients C_i to obtain a value $C_\delta^{[1]}$.

(3) Set $a_r(\delta) = \frac{1}{r!} C_\delta^{[1]}$.

(4) Let $E_i = c_i^{[r]}$ for $i = \delta - k + r + 1, \ldots, \delta$.

(5) If $r < k - 1$, use the algorithm of recurrence (20.12) with $\ell = 1$ and $L = k - r$ to produce $c_i^{[r+1]}$ for $i = \delta - k + r + 2, \ldots, \delta$.

■

20.5 Rendering Curves: Horner's Rule and Forward Differencing

Given that we now know how to convert from the B-spline representation of a segment to the usual polynomial form, let us suppose that our problem is to evaluate piecewise cubic polynomials so that we can display the curve they define. Let us consider the polynomial

$$p(u) = a + bu + cu^2 + du^3. \tag{20.15}$$

If $p(u)$ is to be approximated by N line segments then we will need to evaluate $p(u)$ at $N+1$ values of u. Direct application of equation (20.15) requires $6(N+1)$ multiplications and $3(N+1)$ additions. However, we can rearrange this equation to obtain

$$p(u) = a + u(b + u(c + du)). \tag{20.16}$$

Evaluating $p(u)$ at $N+1$ values of u using (20.16), which is called *Horner's rule* or *nested multiplication*, requires $3(N+1)$ multiplications and $3(N+1)$ additions — an improvement. Indeed, Horner's rule is optimal with respect to the number of arithmetic operations if we are evaluating $p(u)$ at a single u value [Aho74].

We can do even better if we are evaluating $p(u)$ at a sequence of equally spaced u's. Suppose that we wish to evaluate $p(u)$ at the $N+1$ positions

$$u = i \cdot h \quad \text{for } i = 0, 1, \ldots, N,$$

where h is the *step size*. If we were dealing with a linear polynomial, say

$$q(u) = a + bu$$

we would simply observe that

$$q(u+h) - q(u) = a + b(u+h) - a - bu = bh$$

so that we could efficiently generate $N+1$ points (u_i, y_i) by computing

$$u_0 \leftarrow 0$$

$$y_0 \leftarrow a$$

for $i \leftarrow 1$ **step** 1 **until** N **do**

$$u_i \leftarrow u_{i-1} + h$$

$$y_i \leftarrow y_{i-1} + bh$$

endfor

Of course, to avoid redundant computation of bh we would precompute it outside the loop:

$$u_0 \leftarrow 0$$

$$y_0 \leftarrow a$$

$$\Delta_1 \leftarrow bh$$

for $i \leftarrow 1$ **step** 1 **until** N **do**

$$u_i \leftarrow u_{i-1} + h$$

$$y_i \leftarrow y_{i-1} + \Delta_1$$

endfor

This technique can be generalized to polynomials of higher order. Suppose that $r(u)$ is a quadratic polynomial, say

$$r(u) = a + bu + cu^2.$$

Then

$$\Delta_1(u) = r(u+h) - r(u)$$

$$= a + b(u+h) + c(u^2 + 2hu + h^2) - a - bu - cu^2$$

$$= (bh + ch^2) + (2ch)u$$

so that

$$r(u+h) = r(u) + \Delta_1(u)$$

where

$$\Delta_1(u) = (bh + ch^2) + (2ch)u.$$

However, the technique used to evaluate $q(u+h)$ can't be applied immediately because $\Delta_1(u)$ is a function of u, and therefore changes value at each iteration of the loop. We could, of course, simply evaluate $\Delta_1(u)$ at $u=0, h, 2h, 3h, \ldots Nh$ and use the results to compute $r(u)$ at each of these points. Notice, however, that $\Delta_1(u)$ is a linear polynomial. We already know how to evaluate a linear polynomial efficiently for such a sequence — we simply compute $\Delta_1(0) = bh + ch^2$ and then add

$$\Delta_2(u) = \Delta_1(u+h) - \Delta_1(u) = 2ch^2$$

to $\Delta_1(ih)$ to obtain $\Delta_1(ih+h)$. Altogether, then, our computation now looks like this:

$$u_0 \leftarrow 0$$

$$y_0 \leftarrow a$$

$$\Delta_1 \leftarrow bh + ch^2$$

$$\Delta_2 \leftarrow 2ch^2$$

for $i \leftarrow 1$ **step** 1 **until** N **do**

$$u_i \leftarrow u_{i-1} + h$$

$$y_i \leftarrow y_{i-1} + \Delta_1$$

$$\Delta_1 \leftarrow \Delta_1 + \Delta_2$$

endfor

Let us recapitulate. When $r(u)$ is a quadratic, the value $\Delta_1(u) = r(u+h) - r(u)$ that must be added to $r(u)$ to obtain $r(u+h)$ is not a constant — it changes value as we move from u to $u+h$. Fortunately though, $\Delta_1(u)$ itself is easy to update after we have reached $u+h$ so as to obtain the increment that will be needed to compute $u+2h$ from $u+h$; we simply need to increment Δ_1 by Δ_2, which is the constant $2ch^2$.

We may extend this approach to our cubic polynomial $p(u)$ in much the same way. In this case

$$\Delta_1(u) = p(u+h) - p(u) = (bh + ch^2 + dh^3) + (2ch + 3dh^2)u + (3dh)u^2$$

$$\Delta_2(u) = \Delta_1(u+h) - \Delta_1(u) = (2ch^2 + 6dh^3) + (6dh^2)u$$

$$\Delta_3(u) = \Delta_2(u+h) - \Delta_2(u) = 6dh^3.$$

Suppose that we know $\Delta_1(u)$, $\Delta_2(u)$ and $\Delta_3(u)$. Then these equations tell us that

$$p(u+h) = p(u) + \Delta_1(u)$$

$$\Delta_1(u+h) = \Delta_1(u) + \Delta_2(u)$$

$$\Delta_2(u+h) = \Delta_2(u) + \Delta_3(u)$$

$$\Delta_3(u+h) = 6dh^3.$$

Having obtained $p(u+h)$, $\Delta_1(u+h)$, $\Delta_2(u+h)$ and $\Delta_3(u+h)$, the same equations tell us how to compute $p(u+2h)$, $\Delta_1(u+2h)$, $\Delta_2(u+2h)$ and $\Delta_3(u+2h)$, and so on since they are valid for any u, and in particular are valid for $u' = u+h$:

$$p(u' + h) = p(u') + \Delta_1(u')$$

$$\Delta_1(u' + h) = \Delta_1(u') + \Delta_2(u')$$

$$\Delta_2(u' + h) = \Delta_2(u') + \Delta_3(u')$$

$$\Delta_3(u' + h) = 6dh^3.$$

Thus we may use the following algorithm to compute the desired $N + 1$ points on $p(u)$, beginning from $p(0)$, $\Delta_1(0)$, $\Delta_2(0)$ and $\Delta_3(0)$:

$$u_0 \leftarrow 0$$

$$y_0 \leftarrow a$$

$$\Delta_1 \leftarrow bh + ch^2 + dh^3$$

$$\Delta_2 \leftarrow 2ch^2 + 6dh^3$$

$$\Delta_3 \leftarrow 6dh^3$$

for $i \leftarrow 1$ **step** 1 **until** N **do**

$$u_i \leftarrow u_{i-1} + h$$

$$y_i \leftarrow y_{i-1} + \Delta_1$$

$$\Delta_1 \leftarrow \Delta_1 + \Delta_2$$

$$\Delta_2 \leftarrow \Delta_2 + \Delta_3$$

endfor

Aside from initialization, this method of computing the y_i requires no multiplications and only $3N$ additions (plus N additions to compute the u_i). This is a substantial improvement, especially when multiplications are expensive.

Of course, we are actually interested in parametric polynomials. Thus a 2D curve is represented by

$$\mathbf{Q}(u) = (X(u), Y(u))$$

where $X(u)$ and $Y(u)$ are each cubic polynomials of the parameter u. Typically u varies between 0 and some maximum value u_{max}; for the time being we will assume that $u_{max} = 1$, as is the case for each segment of a uniform cubic B-spline curve. Evaluation of the curve is then performed by forward differencing the equations

$$X(u) = a_x + b_x u + c_x u^2 + d_x u^3$$

$$Y(u) = a_y + b_y u + c_y u^2 + d_y u^3$$

simultaneously, using the same step size h:

$$x_0 \leftarrow a_x$$

$$\Delta x_1 \leftarrow b_x h + c_x h^2 + d_x h^3$$

$$\Delta x_2 \leftarrow 2c_x h^2 + 6d_x h^3$$

$$\Delta x_3 \leftarrow 6d_x h^3$$

$$y_0 \leftarrow a_y$$

$$\Delta y_1 \leftarrow b_y h + c_y h^2 + d_y h^3$$

$$\Delta y_2 \leftarrow 2c_y h^2 + 6d_y h^3$$

$$\Delta y_3 \leftarrow 6d_y h^3$$

for $i \leftarrow 1$ **step** 1 **until** N **do**

$$x_i \leftarrow x_{i-1} + \Delta x_1$$

$$\Delta x_1 \leftarrow \Delta x_1 + \Delta x_2$$

$$\Delta x_2 \leftarrow \Delta x_2 + \Delta x_3$$

$$y_i \leftarrow y_{i-1} + \Delta y_1$$

$$\Delta y_1 \leftarrow \Delta y_1 + \Delta y_2$$

$$\Delta y_2 \leftarrow \Delta y_2 + \Delta y_3$$

endfor

A 3D cubic curve

$$\mathbf{Q}(u) = (X(u), Y(u), Z(u))$$

would be computed analogously.

We should note that forward differencing is not to be used without caution, owing to the cumulative error that arises from the finiteness of our arithmetic. This is particularly a problem on machines that lack floating point hardware, as is usually true of the microprocessors one finds integrated with displays. To see why this is so, suppose that each of x_0, Δ_1, Δ_2 and Δ_3 is at most one unit in error. After i iterations, Δ_3 is still correct within one unit because it is a constant.

The possible error in Δ_2, however, is larger. At each iteration of the loop its error may increase by one unit because we are adding Δ_2 to it, so that at the end of j iterations it may be in error by as much as $1+j$.

The maximum error in Δ_1 after k steps is its initial error, plus the sum of the amounts by which Δ_2 may be in error at each step of the iteration. Hence the maximum possible error in Δ_1 is given by

$$1 + \sum_{j=1}^{k} (1+j) = 1 + k + \frac{k(k+1)}{2}.$$

Finally, the maximum error in x or y after N steps is its initial error plus the error that may have been contributed at each iteration by Δ_1. This amounts to

$$1 + \sum_{k=1}^{N} \left[1 + k + \frac{k(k+1)}{2} \right] = \frac{11N + 6N^2 + N^3}{6}.$$

If we are working on a 512×512 raster display, the coefficients a, b, c and d require at least 9 bits of accuracy, and since they can differ in sign, will require more. Two to three additional bits of subpixel accuracy are desirable for antialiasing. If $N = 2^6$ then the total error might be as much as 0.73×2^{16}, requiring that we maintain at least 16 bits of extra fractional precision to avoid an error of more than one pixel, for a total of about 28 bits. If $N = 2^8$ then the total error might be as much as 0.68×2^{22} and we cannot be sure of preserving the 12 or more bits of accuracy we desire, even on a 32 bit machine.

There are two obvious ways of dealing with this problem. We could use multiple precision arithmetic, or we may scale Δ_1 and Δ_2 so as to provide "guard" bits, and shift them away before adding them to y_i and Δ_1, respectively. In this way the error that is added to y_i does not, practically speaking, grow as the computation proceeds.

Suppose that we maintain Δ_1 and Δ_2 scaled up by $N = 2^n = 1/h$ and shift them right by n (written $\gg n$) before adding them to y_i and Δ_1, respectively, so that (roughly speaking) errors will be restricted to the bits that are discarded. Notice that there is no reason to scale up Δ_3 since it is a constant.

$$y_0 \leftarrow a$$

$$\Delta_1 \leftarrow b + c \gg n + d \gg 2n$$

$$\Delta_2 \leftarrow 2c \gg n + 6d \gg 2n$$

$$\Delta_3 \leftarrow 6d \gg 3n$$

for $i \leftarrow 1$ **step** 1 **until** N **do**

$\quad y_i \leftarrow y_{i-1} + \Delta_1 \gg n$

$\quad \Delta_1 \leftarrow \Delta_1 + \Delta_2 \gg n$

$\quad \Delta_2 \leftarrow \Delta_2 + \Delta_3$

endfor

Now the maximum possible error in y_i is approximately 2^n. If we assume that we will never want $n > 8$, and maintain y_i with 10–12 fractional bits of precision, our computation will be satisfactorily accurate using 32 bit integer arithmetic. If $n \leq 6$ then we can even squeeze the computation into 16 bits.

Of course, a machine with floating point hardware performs this scaling for us automatically, and if $N \leq 2^8$ we are unlikely to have problems with cubic polynomials. Nevertheless, it is apparent that cumulative error could become a problem, even on machines with floating point hardware, if we were to try differencing significantly higher degree polynomials.

Finally, suppose that we have an order k spline curve. Initial values of the Δ_i needed to perform forward differencing on the interval $\bar{u}_\delta < \bar{u}_{\delta+1}$ can be computed by direct evaluation of the curve at k points $\bar{u}_\delta + j*h$, $j = 0, \ldots, k-1$. For example, Δ_1 is simply $Y(\bar{u}_\delta + h) - Y(\bar{u}_\delta)$; if t_0 is $Y(\bar{u}_\delta + h) - Y(\bar{u}_\delta)$ and t_1 is $Y(\bar{u}_\delta + 2h) - Y(\bar{u}_\delta + h)$, then Δ_2 is $t_1 - t_0$, and so on. The following pseudo-code computes y_0 and the Δ_i for $Y(\bar{u})$ at the left end of the interval $\bar{u}_\delta < \bar{u}_{\delta+1}$.

for $j \leftarrow 0$ **step** 1 **until** $k-1$ **do** $t_j \leftarrow Y(\bar{u}_\delta + j*h)$

$y_0 \leftarrow t_0$

for $i \leftarrow 1$ **step** 1 **until** $k-1$ **do**

$\quad$ **for** $j \leftarrow 0$ **step** 1 **until** $k-2$ **do**

$\quad\quad t_j \leftarrow t_{j+1} - t_j$

$\quad$ **endfor**

$\quad \Delta_i \leftarrow t_0$

endfor

Thus one can avoid conversion to the power series representation, and the computation of derivatives.

20.6 The Oslo Algorithm — Computing Discrete B-splines

The evaluation of the discrete B-splines (α's) closely parallels the material in Section 20.1. The conversion of the control vertices $\mathbf{V}$ into the refined control vertices $\mathbf{W}$ by means of the Oslo recurrence closely parallels the material in Section 20.2. So we will be brief.

The only significant difference between the material in Section 20.1 and the material that needs to be covered to present an algorithm for producing the values of $\alpha_{\delta-k+1,k}(j), \ldots, \alpha_{\delta,k}(j)$ concerns the need to worry about the <u>extended</u> parameter range

$$\bar{u}_0 \leq \bar{u} < \bar{u}_{m+1}.$$

The discrete B-spline recurrence requires values of $\alpha_{i,k}(j)$ for all $\bar{w}_j$ for $j = 0, \ldots, m+n$; that is, for all $\bar{w}_j$ in this extended range. The value of $\bar{w}_j$ plays the same role in the recurrence for $\alpha_{i,k}(j)$ that $\bar{u}$ plays in the recurrence for $B_{i,k}(\bar{u})$. Hence, the basic algorithm of Section 20.1 must be modified. It makes the assumption that the value of $\bar{u}$ lies to the right of $\bar{u}_{k-1}$.

For any given value of $\bar{u}$ within $[\bar{u}_0, \bar{u}_{m+k})$, $\bar{u}$ will lie within some segment interval

$$\bar{u}_\delta \leq \bar{u} < \bar{u}_{\delta+1}$$

defined by the original knot sequence $\{\bar{u}_i\}_0^{m+k}$, as well as within a segment interval

$$\bar{w}_\gamma \leq \bar{u} < \bar{w}_{\gamma+1}$$

defined by the refined knot sequence $\{\bar{w}_j\}_0^{m+n+k}$. These two segment intervals must, of course, be nested:

$$\bar{u}_\delta \leq \bar{w}_\gamma < \bar{w}_{\gamma+1} \leq \bar{u}_{\delta+1}.$$

Within the segment interval $[\bar{u}_\delta, \bar{u}_{\delta+1})$ the only nonzero B-splines of $\mathbf{S}(\mathbf{P}^k, \{\bar{u}_i\}_0^{m+k})$ are

$$B_{i,k}(\bar{u}) \text{ for } i = \delta, \delta-1, \ldots, \text{last\_i},$$

where $\text{last\_i} = \max(0, \delta-k+1)$. Likewise, within the segment interval $[\bar{w}_\gamma, \bar{w}_{\gamma+1})$ the only nonzero B-splines of $\mathbf{S}(\mathbf{P}^k, \{\bar{w}_j\}_0^{m+n+k})$ are

$$N_{j,k}(\bar{u}) \text{ for } j = \gamma, \gamma-1, \ldots, \text{last\_j},$$

where $last\_j = \max(0, \gamma - k + 1)$. This means that we only have to consider the representations

$$
\sum_{i=last\_i}^{\delta} \mathbf{V}_i B_{i,k}(\bar{u}) = \sum_{i=last\_i}^{\delta} \mathbf{V}_i \sum_{j=last\_j}^{\gamma} \alpha_{i,k}(j) N_{j,k}(\bar{u})
$$

$$
= \sum_{j=last\_j}^{\gamma} \left[\sum_{i=last\_i}^{\delta} \alpha_{i,j}(j) \mathbf{V}_i \right] N_{j,k}(\bar{u})
$$

$$
= \sum_{j=last\_j}^{\gamma} \mathbf{W}_j N_{j,k}(\bar{u}),
$$

from which we have

$$
\mathbf{W}_j = \sum_{i=last\_i}^{\delta} \alpha_{i,j}(j) \mathbf{V}_i .
$$

It is instructive to interpret this, for a moment, in matrix-vector terms. We have

$$
\left[\mathbf{V}_{last\_i} \cdots \mathbf{V}_\delta \right]
\begin{bmatrix}
\alpha_{last\_i,k}(last\_j) & \cdots & \alpha_{last\_i,k}(\gamma) \\
\cdot & \cdot & \cdot \\
\cdot & \cdot & \cdot \\
\cdot & \cdot & \cdot \\
\alpha_{\delta,k}(last\_j) & \cdots & \alpha_{\delta,k}(\gamma)
\end{bmatrix}
$$

$$
= \left[\mathbf{W}_{last\_j} \cdots \mathbf{W}_\gamma \right].
$$

The recurrence for the discrete B-splines is a mechanism for computing the values of the α's in the jth column of the matrix. The recurrence for the control vertices is a mechanism for bypassing the explicit computation of the α's to produce the jth element of the $\mathbf{W}$ vector.

Given the two knot sequences $\{\bar{u}_i\}_0^{m+k}$ and $\{\bar{w}_j\}_0^{m+n+k}$, the complete conversion of

$$
\sum_i \mathbf{V}_i B_{i,k}
$$

into

$$\sum_j \mathbf{W}_j \, N_{j,k}$$

would require that one begin with $\bar{u}_0 = \bar{w}_0$, and for each δ in sequence such that

$$\bar{u}_\delta \; < \; \bar{u}_{\delta+1}$$

find, in turn, each γ in sequence such that

$$\bar{u}_\delta \leq \bar{w}_\gamma < \bar{u}_{\delta+1} \quad \text{and} \quad \bar{w}_\gamma < \bar{w}_{\gamma+1} \, ,$$

and then produce $\mathbf{W}_j$ for each $j = last\_j, \ldots, \gamma$. If this is done in order, however, from $i = 0, \ldots, m$ and $j = 0, \ldots, m+n$, some potential efficiencies will become apparent. When $\bar{w}_\gamma$ is a multiple knot, for instance,

$$\bar{w}_\lambda < \bar{w}_{\lambda+1} = \cdots = \bar{w}_\gamma < \bar{w}_{\gamma+1} \, ,$$

we will have produced

$$\mathbf{W}_{\lambda-k+1} \, , \ldots , \; \mathbf{W}_\lambda$$

(or alternatively columns of $\alpha(j)$'s for $j = \lambda - k + 1, \ldots, \lambda$) when dealing with the segment interval $[\bar{w}_\lambda, \bar{w}_{\lambda+1})$, and the segment interval $[\bar{w}_\gamma, \bar{w}_{\gamma+1})$ will be expected to produce

$$\mathbf{W}_{\gamma-k+1} \, , \ldots , \; \mathbf{W}_\lambda, \mathbf{W}_{\lambda+1} \, , \ldots , \; \mathbf{W}_\gamma .$$

Clearly, only $\mathbf{W}_{\lambda+1}, \ldots, \mathbf{W}_\gamma$ need to be computed. Specifically, when $\bar{w}_\gamma$ is a single knot, only $\mathbf{W}_\gamma$ needs to be produced, and the matrix of the matrix-vector expression above reduces to a single column. When $\bar{w}_\gamma$ is a double knot, only $\mathbf{W}_{\gamma-1}$ and $\mathbf{W}_\gamma$ need to be computed. Generally, when $\bar{w}_\gamma$ is a knot of multiplicity μ, only $\mathbf{W}_{\gamma-\mu+1}, \ldots, \mathbf{W}_\gamma$ need to be computed.

Other observations lead to the realization that certain of the α's will be zero under certain circumstances. Such questions of structure, and the computational efficiencies that they offer, are studied in detail in [Lyche86]. We will be content here with establishing simple computational schemes for producing $\mathbf{W}_j$ for a given j, knowing that $\bar{u}_\delta \leq \bar{w}_j < \bar{u}_{\delta+1}$, or for producing the corresponding values $\alpha_{last\_j,k}(j), \ldots, \alpha_{\delta,k}(j)$.

The table of nonzero values encountered in producing $\alpha_{last\_j,k}(j), \ldots, \alpha_{\delta,k}(j)$ from the recurrence for discrete B-splines exactly follows that for the continuous B-splines, save that the value $\bar{w}_{j+r-1}$ plays the role of $\bar{u}$ at every stage, and save that the table is "chopped off at the top" if $\delta < k - 1$. This means that the α's can be computed by a minor modification of the algorithm given in Section 20.1:

$aval_0 \leftarrow 1$

for $r \leftarrow 2$ **step** 1 **until** k **do**

    $rm1 \leftarrow r - 1$

    $last \leftarrow \min(rm1, \delta)$

    $i \leftarrow \delta - last$ $\{\, \delta - r + 1 \; except \; near \; i = 0 \,\}$

    if ($last < rm1$) **then**

        $aval_{last} \leftarrow aval_{last} \times (\overline{w}_{j+r-1} - \overline{u}_i) / (\overline{u}_{i+r-1} - \overline{u}_i)$

    else

        $aval_{last} \leftarrow 0$

    endif

    for $s \leftarrow last - 1$ **step** -1 **until** 0 **do**

        $i \leftarrow i + 1$

        $omega \leftarrow (\overline{w}_{j+r-1} - \overline{u}_i) / (\overline{u}_{i+r-1} - \overline{u}_i)$

        $aval_{s+1} \leftarrow aval_{s+1} + (1 - omega) \times aval_s$

        $aval_s \leftarrow omega \times aval_s$

    endfor

endfor

The result of this computation is that the value of $\alpha_{\delta - s, k}(j)$ is stored in $aval_s$ for $s = 0, \ldots, last$, where $last = \min(k - 1, \delta)$.

The production of the control vertex $\mathbf{W}_j$ by the Oslo recurrence parallels the computational algorithm of Section 20.2 in the same way in which the production of the α's parallels the computational algorithm of Section 20.1. Assume that the array $\mathbf{C}$ is initialized with

$$\mathbf{C}_s = \mathbf{V}_{\delta - s} \quad \text{for } s = 0, \ldots, \; last,$$

where $last = \min(k - 1, \delta)$. Then the Oslo algorithm becomes

for $r \leftarrow k$ **step** -1 **until** 2 **do**

$\quad rm\,2 \leftarrow r - 2$

$\quad i \leftarrow \delta$

$\quad last \leftarrow \min(rm\,2, \delta)$ $\qquad \{r-2 \text{ except near } i = 0\}$

$\quad$ **for** $s \leftarrow 0$ **step** 1 **until** $last - 1$ **do**

$\qquad omega \leftarrow (\overline{w}_{j+r-1} - \overline{u}_i)/(\overline{u}_{i+r-1} - \overline{u}_i)$

$\qquad \mathbf{C}_s \leftarrow omega \times \mathbf{C}_s + (1 - omega) \times \mathbf{C}_{s+1}$

$\qquad i \leftarrow i - 1$

$\quad$ **endfor**

$\quad omega \leftarrow (\overline{w}_{j+r-1} - \overline{u}_i)/(\overline{u}_{i+r-1} - \overline{u}_i)$

$\quad$ **if** $(last < rm\,2)$ **then**

$\qquad \mathbf{C}_s \leftarrow omega \times \mathbf{C}_s$

$\quad$ **else**

$\qquad \mathbf{C}_s \leftarrow omega \times \mathbf{C}_s + (1 - omega) \times \mathbf{C}_{s+1}$

$\quad$ **endif**

endfor

The result of this computation is that $\mathbf{W}_j$ will be stored in $\mathbf{C}_0$.

20.7 Partial Derivatives and Normals

To perform solid area shading and hidden surface processing on raster devices, the simplest approach to take is to obtain a "wire frame" approximation to a spline surface. One way this may be done is by using the points $\mathbf{Q}(\overline{u}_i, \overline{v}_j)$ generated from the grid of values

$$\overline{u}_i = \overline{u}_0 + i\,\Delta\overline{u} \quad \text{and} \quad \overline{v}_i = \overline{v}_0 + i\,\Delta\overline{v}$$

for some arbitrary choice of $\Delta\overline{u}$ and $\Delta\overline{v}$. These are the positions in space at which the lines of constant parameter on the surface intersect, and these positions may be taken as the vertices of polygons used to approximate the surface. We have rendered most of the spline surfaces in our figures by this method.

Another way of obtaining a wire-frame approximation is to use the vertices $\mathbf{W}_{i,j}$ of a suitably refined control graph as the polygonal mesh.

After a wire-frame approximation has been obtained, by whatever means, standard polygonal techniques can be used to determine visibility, compute shading (if desired), and render the polygons. With respect to shading, however, a word of caution is in order. Since the surface $\mathbf{Q}(\overline{u})$ is not planar, the rectangles formed in the obvious way from the points $\mathbf{Q}(\overline{u}_i, \overline{v}_j)$ or $\mathbf{W}_{i,j}$ are not necessarily planar. It is sometimes advisable to render shaded, spline-generated polyhedral surfaces by dividing each rectangle into two triangles along one of the diagonals.

For smooth shading computations one may, of course, simply average the polygon normals for each of the polygons sharing a vertex. However, it is straightforward to compute the cross product of the partial derivatives with respect to u and v, so as to obtain an accurate normal vector at each polygon. The example of uniform cubic B-splines is instructive with respect to some of the computational issues involved in doing this.

From equation (4.28) we can see that to compute

$$\frac{\partial}{\partial v} \mathbf{Q}_{i,j}(u,v)$$

we simply evaluate a point on each of four uniform cubic B-spline curves to obtain what we called $\mathbf{W}_0$, $\mathbf{W}_1$, $\mathbf{W}_2$ and $\mathbf{W}_3$ in equation (4.28), and then we use these to scale $b_{-3}^{(1)}(v)$, $b_{-2}^{(1)}(v)$, $b_{-1}^{(1)}(v)$, and $b_{-0}^{(1)}(v)$. To compute

$$\frac{\partial}{\partial u} \mathbf{Q}_{i,j}(u,v)$$

we factor out $b_{-0}^{(1)}(u)$, $b_{-1}^{(1)}(u)$, $b_{-2}^{(1)}(u)$, and $b_{-3}^{(1)}(u)$ instead and proceed analogously.

It is worth pointing out that there are a variety of ways to give the user effective cues about the shape of a surface, and "realistic" shading is only one of them. Robin Forrest compares a number of others in [Forrest79].

20.8 Locality

The locality evidenced by uniform cubic B-splines has two advantages.

- It allows the designer of a complex curve to alter the shape of that curve in one region without affecting the shape of remote portions of the curve that have already been satisfactorily defined; the same is true of surfaces.

- Because only a part of the curve changes when a control vertex is moved, only a part of the curve must be recomputed. This facilitates real-time interaction.

Recall that the uniform cubic B-splines are translates of one another; that is, they are identically shaped. If we choose to approximate each curve segment by s consecutive chords whose endpoints are equally spaced $h = 1/s$ apart in u, then it is sufficient to compute values of the four basis segments at

$$u = 0, h, 2h \cdots, (s-1)h, sh = 1$$

and store them in arrays $b_{-3}[k]$, $b_{-2}[k]$, $b_{-1}[k]$ and $b_{-0}[k]$ before beginning to draw the curve. We then simply look up these values as we compute, and draw each segment using

$$\mathbf{Q}_i(kh) = \sum_{r=-3}^{r=0} \mathbf{V}_{i+r} \, b_r[k]$$

$$= \mathbf{V}_{i-3} b_{-3}[k] + \mathbf{V}_{i-2} b_{-2}[k] + \mathbf{V}_{i-1} b_{-1}[k] + \mathbf{V}_i \, b_{-0}[k].$$

These precomputed values can also be used when we alter the position of some control vertex $\mathbf{V}_i$ and need to recompute the four segments $\mathbf{Q}_i(u)$, $\mathbf{Q}_{i+1}(u)$, $\mathbf{Q}_{i+2}(u)$ and $\mathbf{Q}_{i+3}(u)$. Since we usually need to recompute these four segments several times as we move $\mathbf{V}_i$, it is advantageous to add together the terms not involving $\mathbf{V}_i$ so that we need only perform a single multiplication and addition to obtain each new coordinate. For example, on the ith segment we would precompute

$$C[k] = \mathbf{V}_{i-3} b_{-3}[k] + \mathbf{V}_{i-2} b_{-2}[k] + \mathbf{V}_{i-1} b_{-1}[k]$$

as soon as the user had selected $\mathbf{V}_i$ for alteration, and then compute

$$\mathbf{Q}_i(kh) = C[k] + \mathbf{V}_i \, b_{-0}[k]$$

each time we wanted to redraw this segment.

These observations extend to surfaces in the obvious way.

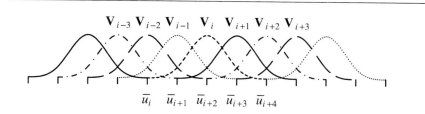

$$\mathbf{V}_{i-3} \ \mathbf{V}_{i-2} \ \mathbf{V}_{i-1} \ \mathbf{V}_i \ \mathbf{V}_{i+1} \ \mathbf{V}_{i+2} \ \mathbf{V}_{i+3}$$

$$\bar{u}_i \quad \bar{u}_{i+1} \quad \bar{u}_{i+2} \quad \bar{u}_{i+3} \quad \bar{u}_{i+4}$$

Figure 20.3. It is occasionally helpful to recall our indexing conventions. The ith interval is $[\bar{u}_i, \bar{u}_{i+1})$. It is determined by $\mathbf{V}_{i-3}$, $\mathbf{V}_{i-2}$, $\mathbf{V}_{i-1}$ and $\mathbf{V}_i$. On the other hand, $\mathbf{V}_i$ contributes to $\mathbf{Q}_i$, $\mathbf{Q}_{i+1}$, $\mathbf{Q}_{i+2}$ and $\mathbf{Q}_{i+3}$.

20.9 Scan-Line Methods

One would prefer to work directly with the curved boundaries of these spline surfaces, rather than approximating them with straight line segments as one does by reducing them to polygons. There are two sources of complication in this approach, both resulting from the way in which scan-line algorithms are organized.

First, because patch boundaries are parametric curves, altering $\bar{u}$ or $\bar{v}$ by a fixed amount does not result in movement of the same distance everywhere along the surface, or even in the same direction. Hence there is no simple incremental way to compute the intersection of an edge with scan-line n from its intersection with scan-line $n - 1$. Instead one has to use iterative numerical techniques. A typical approach is to solve for a zero of $Y(0,\bar{v}) - n = 0$, $Y(1,\bar{v}) - n = 0$, $Y(\bar{u},0) - n = 0$, or $Y(\bar{u},1) - n = 0$ (depending on which boundary is involved) by performing Newton iteration, using the known intersection of $Y(\bar{u})$ with scan-line $n - 1$ as the initial guess. Given that we know the values $(\bar{u}_l,\bar{v}_l)$ and $(\bar{u}_r,\bar{v}_r)$ at which the left and right edges of a patch intersect the current scan-line, an analogous technique must be used to compute the values of $(\bar{u},\bar{v})$ corresponding to each interior pixel on that scan-line.

A second and more serious problem, arising because the patches are themselves curved, is that the apparent visible boundary of a patch on the display screen need not be an actual boundary of the patch. These are called *silhouette edges*, and to perform the sort of scan conversion described above one must first identify the silhouette edges. A given boundary also need not be monotonic; it may intersect a scan-line more than once. Moreover, if we are generating a picture in top to bottom order, the highest point on a curved patch need not occur at a vertex, as it does for a polygon. Completely acceptable methods for dealing with these problems have yet to be developed. The state of the art is ably discussed in [Lane/et al.80] and [Schweitzer/Cobb82].

20.10 Ray-Tracing B-spline Surfaces

In this section we outline a method for intersecting rays with B-spline surfaces, based on the recurrence properties of B-splines [Cohen/et al.80] and on the fractal intersection algorithm of Kajiya [Kajiya83].

The material presented here is a brief account of that in [Sweeney84, Sweeney/Bartels86]. The method given there requires the aid of two preprocessing steps. The first step employs control-vertex refinement to produce local information about the surface suitable for use in starting Newton's iteration. The second step builds a tree of nested bounding boxes to be used for a version of hierarchical intersection testing that derives from Kajiya's work on ray-tracing fractals.

20.10.1   Refinement Preprocessing

The first step in preprocessing a spline surface involves using the Oslo algorithm to replace the representation of the surface in terms of given control vertices by a refined representation in terms of more control vertices. The easiest version of this refinement process, which is the one presented in [Sweeney84], restricts the surfaces to those generated by uniform bicubic B-splines and carries out Oslo refinement only by the introduction of d equally spaced subintervals within each segment interval. For example, Figures 12.13, 12.14, 12.15, and 12.16 give an instance of $d = 2$, and Figure 12.17 gives an instance of $d = 4$. General B-splines could be used, of course, and more general refinements are possible. Moreover, the "subdivided refinements" mentioned in connection with Figures 12.15, 12.16, and 12.17 appearing in Section 12.4 could be employed. That is, an entire surface can be regarded as the union of two or more smaller surfaces, with separate control graphs derived from the single graph of the entire surface, and each of the smaller surfaces can be independently refined. Subdivided refinements provide the flexibility of dynamically adjusting a control graph to account for surface areas of local high or low variation.

The control vertices must be refined in advance of the ray-tracing process sufficiently so that:

- The projection of each refined facet

$$
\begin{array}{ll}
\mathbf{W}_{r,s+1} & \mathbf{W}_{r+1,s+1} \\
\mathbf{W}_{r,s} & \mathbf{W}_{r+1,s}
\end{array}
\qquad (20.17)
$$

  covers no more than a few hundred pixels on the screen.

- The refined knots $\bar{w}_{r+2}$ (for parameter $\bar{u}$) and $\bar{t}_{s+2}$ (for parameter $\bar{v}$) associated with a control vertex $\mathbf{W}_{r,s}$ resulting from the refinement constitute acceptably good starting guesses for the Newton iteration, which is used to locate a ray's intersection with the spline surface.

20.10.2   Tree Construction

The refinement process described above constitutes a first step in the preprocessing of each spline surface. The second step in preprocessing involves building a tree of nested rectilinear bounding boxes containing the refined vertices. (Rectilinear bounding boxes — boxes whose sides are aligned with the coordinate planes — are advocated in [Sweeney84] because intersections of rays with such boxes are easy to compute. [Weghorst/et al.84] contains further discussions on building nested structures of bounding volumes for the purposes of ray tracing.) The smallest bounding boxes in the tree, the leaf bounding boxes, must satisfy two containment requirements:

- Each leaf of the tree should represent a small bounding box that is centered on one particular refined vertex or facet and is large enough to guarantee the inclusion of a piece of the underlying surface.

- The union of the leaf boxes should include the entire surface.

Each other bounding box in the tree (that is, any box associated with an interval node) must provide nested containment of all boxes associated with its children nodes.

A rectilinear bounding box is defined by two points $(x_{min}, y_{min}, z_{min})$ and $(x_{max}, y_{max}, z_{max})$. A secure way of meeting the requirements just stated is to build the bounding box at each leaf around one of the facets (20.17) with x_{max}, x_{min}, y_{max}, y_{min}, z_{max}, and z_{min} set just large enough to contain the convex hull of the 16 vertices associated with this facet:

$$
\begin{array}{cccc}
\mathbf{W}_{r-1,s+2} & \mathbf{W}_{r,s+2} & \mathbf{W}_{r+1,s+2} & \mathbf{W}_{r+2,s+2} \\[2mm]
\mathbf{W}_{r-1,s+1} & \mathbf{W}_{r,s+1} & \mathbf{W}_{r+1,s+1} & \mathbf{W}_{r+2,s+1} \\[2mm]
\mathbf{W}_{r-1,s} & \mathbf{W}_{r,s} & \mathbf{W}_{r+1,s} & \mathbf{W}_{r+2,s} \\[2mm]
\mathbf{W}_{r-1,s-1} & \mathbf{W}_{r,s-1} & \mathbf{W}_{r+1,s-1} & \mathbf{W}_{r+2,s-1} \; .
\end{array}
$$

An alternative to this is the construction advocated in [Sweeney84], where a box is built around a single vertex $\mathbf{W}_{r,s}$, and $x_{min}, \ldots, z_{max}$ are set large enough to include the four surrounding vertices

$$
\begin{array}{ccc}
 & \mathbf{W}_{r,s+1} & \\
\mathbf{W}_{r-1,s} & \mathbf{W}_{r,s} & \mathbf{W}_{r+1,s} \; . \\
 & \mathbf{W}_{r,s-1} &
\end{array}
\tag{20.18}
$$

A predefined overlap is included in the setting of $x_{min}, \ldots, z_{max}$ to include a volume beyond that containing the vertices (20.18). For a sufficiently large overlap, the containment requirements set out above will hold well enough to serve the purposes of ray-tracing.

Next, a pair of values for $\bar{u}, \bar{v}$ is associated with each leaf box. This pair of parameter values should give a point on the surface centered within the box. For example (recalling that the knots $\bar{w}_r$ are those which result in refining along the $\bar{u}$ parameter axis and the knots $\bar{t}_s$ are those which result in refining along the $\bar{v}$ axis), the pair of values

$$
\bar{u} = \frac{1}{2}(\bar{w}_{r+2} + \bar{w}_{r+3})
$$

$$\overline{v} = \frac{1}{2}(\overline{t}_{s+2} + \overline{t}_{s+3})\ \ \ \ \ \ \ \ \ (20.19)$$

are reasonable ones to store for a bounding box defined on the sixteen vertices around the facet (20.17), while the pair of values

$$\overline{u} = \overline{w}_{r+2}$$

$$\overline{v} = \overline{t}_{s+2}\ \ \ \ \ \ \ \ \ (20.20)$$

is reasonable for the scheme which uses four vertices about (20.18) plus over ap. Such a $(\overline{u},\overline{v})$ pair will serve as the starting values of a Newton process to be described below.

Finally, each internal node of the tree should represent a bounding box that is just large enough to contain the bounding boxes of its four children.

The leaves can be organized into a tree by a procedure that recursively subdivides the $\overline{u}, \overline{v}$ parameter rectangle. At each level of recursion, the procedure allocates a node of the tree (the *current node*) and connects to it the four nodes to be allocated at the next level. The current node is associated with a rectangular section of the $\overline{u}, \overline{v}$ range (in particular the root node is associated with the entire $\overline{u}, \overline{v}$ rectangle), and the current node's rectangular section is quartered by halving its sides to produce the subrectangles given to the current node's children.

The recursion terminates when the current node's rectangular section of the $\overline{u}, \overline{v}$ plane contains only the pair of values (20.19), in case the sixteen-vertex leaf box is used, or the pair of values (20.20) in the other case. The current node is tagged as a leaf node, and a leaf bounding box is calculated as described above.

As the procedure returns through the recursion, the parent nodes are tagged as internal nodes, and ever larger bounding boxes are calculated to contain the bounding boxes of the children.

The memory requirements for a spline surface are determined largely by the size of the tree of bounding boxes, and this is dictated, in turn, by the number of given control vertices and the level of refinement.

20.10.3 Intersection Processing

Kajiya [Kajiya83] has reported on a method for finding the intersection of rays with fractals and other surfaces he calls *height fields*. His algorithm has the property that it correctly handles surfaces that intersect rays at more than one spot. The algorithm is not limited to height fields but can be applied to any three dimensional surface.

Recall that the leaf nodes of the tree of bounding boxes contain starting values for a Newton iteration. Kajiya's algorithm, as applied to the subdivision trees described above, selects candidate leaf nodes for further processing by Newton's iteration, or else it rejects the ray as having no intersection with the surface if the ray fails to intersect any bounding box at some level of depth in the tree.

Briefly, for each ray, one may maintain a linked list of active nodes. Attached to those nodes are various subtrees of the tree of bounding boxes described above. With each node is associated a distance from the ray origin to the closest intersection with the bounding box of the root of the attached subtree. One may maintain the list of active nodes sorted by increasing distance (or perhaps in a heap). The algorithm would proceed as follows:

- Choose the first (closest) node on the active node list, and remove it.

- If the root of the attached subtree is interior to the tree, consider in turn each of its four children.

- If the ray hits the bounding box of a child, then attach the child to an active node and sort the node into the the active node list.

- If the root of the attached subtree is a leaf, use the contained $(\bar{u}, \bar{v})$ parameter values to initiate a Newton process.

This algorithm will terminate when the active node list is empty (failure), or when the distance to the surface, as returned by the Newton iteration routine, is less than the distance to the first (closest) node on the active node list (success).

20.10.4   The Newton Iteration

A ray tracing process for spline surfaces is described in [Joy/Bhetanabhotla86] that makes use of a *minimization* version of the Newton (actually: quasi-Newton) method. We present a root-finding version of ray-tracing using Newton's method here.

The goal of an intersection computation is that of finding a pair of parameter values $\bar{u}, \bar{v}$ such that a point $Q(\bar{u}, \bar{v})$ on the surface is also a point contained in a given ray. The two unknowns, $\bar{u}$ and $\bar{v}$, can be expressed as the roots of a pair of polynomial equations by the technique of formulating the desired intersections as the locus of all points on the surface that lie simultaneously in two planes containing the ray. (This formulation was borrowed from [Kajiya82] although the rest of the intersection process to be described is entirely different from the one he presented.) We have

Plane 1: $(A_1, B_1, C_1) \cdot (x, y, z) = D_1$

Plane 2: $(A_2, B_2, C_2) \cdot (x, y, z) = D_2,$

where

$$(x, y, z) = (X(\bar{u}, \bar{v}), Y(\bar{u}, \bar{v}), Z(\bar{u}, \bar{v})) = Q(\bar{u}, \bar{v}).$$

In particular, for a ray given parametrically as

$$(x_a, y_a, z_a) + t\,(x_b, y_b, z_b),$$

we have

$$(A_1, B_1, C_1) = (x_a, y_a, z_a) \times (x_b, y_b, z_b)$$

$$(A_2, B_2, C_2) = (A_1, B_1, C_1) \times (x_b, y_b, z_b)$$

$$D_1 = (A_1, B_1, C_1) \cdot (x_a, y_a, z_a)$$

$$D_2 = (A_2, B_2, C_2) \cdot (x_a, y_a, z_a).$$

Using

$$\mathbf{Q}(\bar{u}, \bar{v}) = \sum_{i=0}^{m} \sum_{j=0}^{n} \mathbf{V}_{i,j}\, B_{i,4}(\bar{u})\, B_{j,4}(\bar{v}),$$

this gives two equations in two unknowns to be solved:

$$E_k(\bar{u}, \bar{v}) = \sum_{i=0}^{m} \sum_{j=0}^{n} \left[(A_k, B_k, C_k) \cdot \mathbf{V}_{i,j} \right] B_{i,4}(\bar{u})\, B_{j,4}(\bar{v}) - D_k = 0 \qquad (20.21)$$

for $k = 1, 2$.

Let $\bar{u}^{[0]}, \bar{v}^{[0]}$ stand for the values stored in a leaf node. Newton's method starts with these values as an approximation to the solution of (20.21) and refines them

$$\bar{u}^{[0]} \to \cdots \to \bar{u}^{[l]} \to \bar{u}^{[l+1]} \to \cdots$$

$$\bar{v}^{[0]} \to \cdots \to \bar{v}^{[l]} \to \bar{v}^{[l+1]} \to \cdots$$

by taking each $\bar{u}^{[l]}, \bar{v}^{[l]}$ and solving the 2×2 system

$$\begin{bmatrix} \dfrac{\partial E_1}{\partial \bar{u}} & \dfrac{\partial E_1}{\partial \bar{v}} \\ \dfrac{\partial E_2}{\partial \bar{u}} & \dfrac{\partial E_2}{\partial \bar{v}} \end{bmatrix} \begin{bmatrix} \Delta \bar{u}^{[l]} \\ \Delta \bar{v}^{[l]} \end{bmatrix} = \begin{bmatrix} E_1(\bar{u}^{[l]}, \bar{v}^{[l]}) \\ E_2(\bar{u}^{[l]}, \bar{v}^{[l]}) \end{bmatrix}$$

to produce the (usually) more accurate solution of (20.21) given by

$$\bar{u}^{[l+1]} = \bar{u}^{[l]} - \Delta \bar{u}^{[l]}$$

and

$$\overline{v}^{[l+1]} = \overline{v}^{[l]} - \Delta \overline{v}^{[l]}.$$

The partial derivatives

$$\frac{\partial E_k}{\partial \overline{u}}$$

for $k = 1, 2$ are given by

$$\frac{\partial E_k}{\partial \overline{u}} = \sum_{i=0}^{m} \sum_{j=0}^{n} \left[(A_k, B_k, C_k) \cdot \mathbf{V}_{i,j} \right] B_{i,4}^{(1)}(\overline{u}) B_{j,4}(\overline{v})$$

and similarly for

$$\frac{\partial E_k}{\partial \overline{v}}.$$

Note that control vertices used in the iteration should be the original, unrefined set $\mathbf{V}_{i,j}$ to reduce computation.

The Newton iteration can be terminated, and $\overline{u}^{[l+1]}, \overline{v}^{[l+1]}$ can be taken as defining an intersection, if

$$\left| E_1 \left[\overline{u}^{[l+1]}, \overline{v}^{[l+1]} \right] \right| + \left| E_2 \left[\overline{u}^{[l+1]}, \overline{v}^{[l+1]} \right] \right| < tolerance.$$

Failures should be registered (that is, a ray strike should be regarded as not occurring) if the Newton iterates $\overline{u}^{[l+1]}, \overline{v}^{[l+1]}$ wander outside the bounds of the parametric intervals; *i.e.*

$$\overline{u}^{[l+1]} < \overline{u}_{k-1} \text{ or } \overline{u}^{[l+1]} > \overline{u}_{m+1} \text{ or } \overline{v}^{[l+1]} < \overline{v}_{k-1} \text{ or } \overline{v}^{[l+1]} > \overline{v}_{p+1}$$

or if

$$l > allowance$$

and the value of

$$\left| E_1 \left[\overline{u}^{[l+1]}, \overline{v}^{[l+1]} \right] \right| + \left| E_2 \left[\overline{u}^{(l+1)}, \overline{v}^{(l+1)} \right] \right|$$

has increased over that of the preceding iteration step.

Two examples of images produced by this ray-tracing process are to be found in Plates XII and XIII.

21

Selected
Applications

We close with a brief discussion of selected applications, touching upon picture processing, animation, free-form curve input, least-squares approximation, and interpolation.

In Section 21.1 we will introduce a basis for describing cubic segment polynomials that automatically enforces C^1 continuity at the joints and facilitates the interpolation of control vertices. This basis also makes it trivial to impose any desired tangent vector upon a parametric spline curve at each joint. The application chosen to illustrate this will be the use of cubic C^1 splines as a method of key-frame inbetweening for computer animation.

A special class of splines that makes the solution of interpolating problems trivial to solve, borrowing methods discussed in Section 21.1, is the class of "cardinal-spline bases." An example of these will be presented briefly in Section 21.2.

Section 21.2 will have the secondary purpose of illustrating how problems solved using one representation of a spline can be solved in a different way using another representation. The cardinal-spline representation provides a solution to the interpolation problem, which was solved in the initial chapters using a segment-polynomial representation. Section 21.3 will solve the interpolation problem again, this time using B-splines. A sample application in picture processing will be given.

Extensions of the control-vertex construction process that we have been using will also be explored: if the control vertices are replaced by certain vector functions, the result is a constructive process whose products are called *Catmull-Rom splines*. These will be presented in Section 21.4.

Finally, Section 21.5 will illustrate the use of B-splines in another form of control vertex approximation: least squares fitting. We will present an application of this form of approximation to the job of capturing and editing gestures made with a tablet or mouse.

A point we would like to emphasize is that different spline representations are suitable for different tasks: B-splines and Beta-splines are not *always* the representation of choice. Then, too, it is useful to distinguish between the representation used to interface with the user and the representation used computationally, inside a program.

In any given situation the choice between techniques might be based on some combination of convenience, ease of use, efficiency, numerical accuracy, or compactness of storage. Thus, for example, one might design a surface using a Beta-spline representation for ease of use, but convert to a Bézier representation for output because it provides more efficient rendering via subdivision [Barsky/et al.87].

That any given spline can be represented in many ways is illustrated by the cover of the January, 1985 issue of *Computer Graphics* [Stone85], reproduced in this volume as Plate XIV. In this image the outline of a flamingo is defined in three equivalent ways: one (designated as "interpolating") uses what is essentially a segment-polynomial representation; one (labeled "B-spline") shows the B-spline control graph defining the same piecewise curve; and the third (labeled "Bézier") shows the equivalent Bézier polygon for the curve. A discussion of the practical ramifications of converting between spline representations can be found in [Barsky/Thomas81].

21.1 The Hermite Basis and C^1 Key-Frame Inbetweening

Material in this section derives from [Kochanek/et al.82] and [Kochanek/Bartels84].

One of the oldest techniques used in computer animation is the automatic generation of *inbetweens* (intermediate frames) based on a set of *key frames* supplied by the animator. This same method is frequently used in computer assisted special effects where camera and positions of objects are defined only at key points in the action, leaving the calculation of intermediate positions to the computer.

Linear interpolation has been used in many such systems, but it produces undesirable side effects that give the animation a mechanical look, often referred to as the "computer signature." The most objectionable characteristic of this type of animation is a lack of smoothness in the motion. The key frames may be clearly visible in the animation because of sudden changes in the direction of motion (Figure 21.1). Discontinuities in the speed of motion may also be visible with linear interpolation, for example when the animator requests a different number of frames between successive keys (Figure 21.2). A third common problem is distortion, which may occur whenever the movement has a rotational component (Figure 21.3).

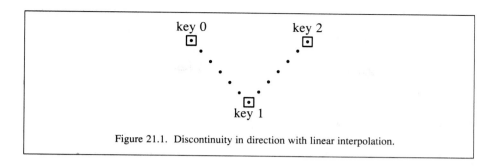

Figure 21.1. Discontinuity in direction with linear interpolation.

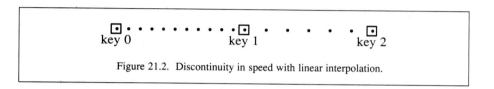

Figure 21.2. Discontinuity in speed with linear interpolation.

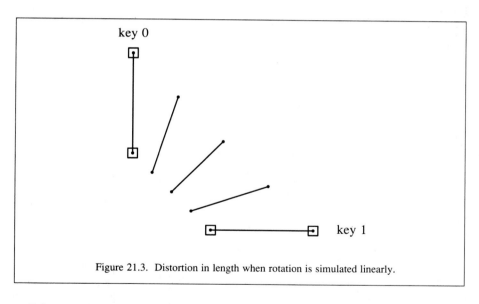

Figure 21.3. Distortion in length when rotation is simulated linearly.

Inbetweening systems usually begin with the assumption that each of the objects in the ith key frame in a sequence can be described by a collection of *key points* (e.g., the two designated endpoints of the line segment in key 0 shown in Figure 21.3, which completely define the segment) and that to each such point in one key frame there will be a corresponding point in all the other key frames of a motion sequence (e.g., the same two endpoints which reappear in key 1 of Figure 21.3 to specify a later position of the line segment.) If we choose one such point at the ith key frame,

$$\mathbf{P}_i = (x_i, y_i, z_i),$$

called the ith *key position*, then the corresponding points in all the key frames constitute a sequence of key positions

$$\cdots, \mathbf{P}_{i-1}, \mathbf{P}_i, \mathbf{P}_{i+1}, \cdots,$$

that we want to interpolate using a simple smooth curve to ameliorate the problems described above. In Figure 21.3, for example, the top endpoint of the line segment in key 0 could be the chosen key position, $\mathbf{P}_0$; hence, the key position, $\mathbf{P}_1$, would be the right-hand endpoint of the line segment in key 1, and the sequence we must interpolate is merely

$$\mathbf{P}_0, \mathbf{P}_1.$$

The result of the interpolation should be a parametric curve $\mathbf{Q}(\overline{u})$ with segments

$$\mathbf{Q}_i(u) = (X_i(u), Y_i(u), Z_i(u)) \quad \text{for } 0 \leq u \leq 1,$$

where

$$\mathbf{Q}_i(0) = (X_i(0), Y_i(0), Z_i(0)) = (x_i, y_i, z_i) = \mathbf{P}_i$$

and

$$\mathbf{Q}_i(1) = (X_i(1), Y_i(1), Z_i(1)) = (x_{i+1}, y_{i+1}, z_{i+1}) = \mathbf{P}_{i+1}.$$

The positions in the inbetween frames on each such segment will be given by $\mathbf{Q}_i(u)$ for some sequence of u-values between 0 and 1. The entire curve $\mathbf{Q}(\overline{u})$ defines the *trajectory* followed by the point whose key positions we have interpolated. The *motion dynamics* of the the point's transit over this trajectory will be determined by the sequence of $\overline{u}$-values chosen. The discussion given here covers only the trajectory aspects of inbetweening; there is much work left to be done on the motion dynamics.

If we decide to use cubic splines with C^1 continuity at each joint, and we consider each of the segments in turn, we recall from Chapter 3 that each of the component polynomials $X_i(u)$, $Y_i(u)$, and $Z_i(u)$ can be defined uniquely by Hermite interpolation. Two constraints are given directly by the interpolation conditions and the other two constraints are given by specifying derivatives at $u = 0$ and $u = 1$. Thus, $\mathbf{Q}_i(u)$ is completely determined by

---

$$\mathbf{P}_i \quad \text{and} \quad \mathbf{D}_i = \left[\frac{dX_i(0)}{du}, \frac{dY_i(0)}{du}, \frac{dZ_i(0)}{du} \right]$$

and

$$\mathbf{P}_{i+1} \quad \text{and} \quad \mathbf{D}_{i+1} = \left[\frac{dX_i(1)}{du}, \frac{dY_i(1)}{du}, \frac{dZ_i(1)}{du} \right].$$

This is shown in Figure 21.4.

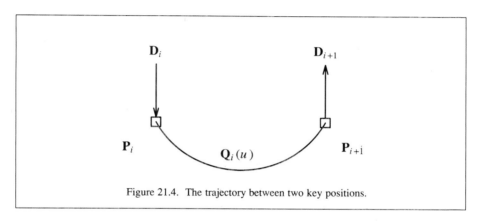

Figure 21.4. The trajectory between two key positions.

An automatic inbetweening system may choose $\mathbf{D}_i$ and $\mathbf{D}_{i+1}$ using some geometric information derived from the surrounding keys, or by human input, or by some combination of both.

The specification of $X_i(u)$, $Y_i(u)$, and $Z_i(u)$ is most conveniently made in terms of the *Hermite interpolation basis functions*, which are shown in Figure 21.5. These functions have the following properties.

	h_{00}	h_{10}	h_{01}	h_{11}
function value at $u = 0$	1	0	0	0
function value at $u = 1$	0	1	0	0
derivative at $u = 0$	0	0	1	0
derivative at $u = 1$	0	0	0	1

Consider any expression of the form

$$p(u) = a\, h_{00}(u) + b\, h_{10}(u) + c\, h_{01}(u) + d\, h_{11}(u),$$

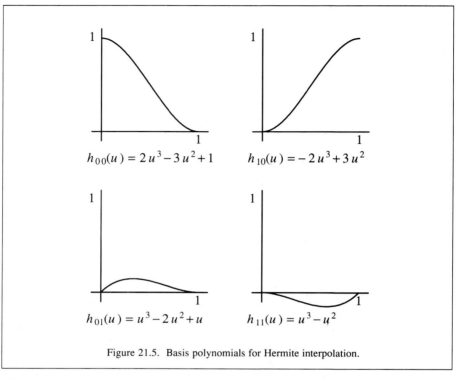

Figure 21.5. Basis polynomials for Hermite interpolation.

$$h_{00}(u) = 2u^3 - 3u^2 + 1 \qquad h_{10}(u) = -2u^3 + 3u^2$$

$$h_{01}(u) = u^3 - 2u^2 + u \qquad h_{11}(u) = u^3 - u^2$$

where a, b, c, and d are arbitrary coefficients. Note that $h_{00}(u)$ alone determines the function value of $p(u)$ at the start of the interval; that is, $p(0) = a$. Similarly, $h_{10}(u)$ determines $p(u)$ at the end of the interval; that is, $p(1) = b$. The derivatives of $p(u)$ at the beginning and end of the interval are determined by $h_{01}(u)$ and $h_{11}(u)$, respectively; that is, $p^{(1)}(0) = c$ and $p^{(1)}(1) = d$. These observations lead to the representation

$$\mathbf{Q}_i(u) = (X_i(u), Y_i(u), Z_i(u))$$

$$= h_{00}(u)\mathbf{P}_i + h_{10}(u)\mathbf{P}_{i+1} + h_{01}(u)\mathbf{D}_i + h_{11}(u)\mathbf{D}_{i+1}.$$

In matrix form this expression reduces to

$$\mathbf{Q}_i(u) = \mathbf{u} \cdot \mathbf{H} \cdot \mathbf{C}$$

$$= \begin{bmatrix} 1 & u & u^2 & u^3 \end{bmatrix} \cdot \begin{bmatrix} 1 & 0 & 0 & 0 \\ 0 & 0 & 1 & 0 \\ -3 & 3 & -2 & -1 \\ 2 & -2 & 1 & 1 \end{bmatrix} \cdot \begin{bmatrix} \mathbf{P}_i \\ \mathbf{P}_{i+1} \\ \mathbf{D}_i \\ \mathbf{D}_{i+1} \end{bmatrix} . \qquad (21.1)$$

Note that the vector $\mathbf{u}$ changes only from one frame in the animation to the next. Within a given frame it applies to the x, y, and z components of all key positions which are being interpolated. The matrix $\mathbf{H}$ contains the coefficients of the Hermite interpolation basis functions and is therefore constant for all frames and all key positions. In practice, $\mathbf{u} \cdot \mathbf{H}$ need only be calculated once per frame for each collection of key positions that are moving as a unit. By contrast, each $\mathbf{C}$, which is a 4×3 matrix, corresponds to a single key position and is independent of the $\mathbf{C}$ associated with any of the other key positions being interpolated. It does not change from one frame to another (except at a key frame), and this independence implies that all key positions can be interpolated ''in parallel.''

To give an example, the product $\mathbf{u} \cdot \mathbf{H}$ would be the same for both the top (key 0), respectively right (key 1), and the bottom (key 0), respectively left (key 1), endpoint of the line segment in Figure 21.3. However, there would be one version of $\mathbf{C}$ for the top/right endpoint and another for the bottom/left endpoint. If the animation sequence included a circle whose motion differed from that of the line segment, $\mathbf{H}$ would remain the same, but a different version of $\mathbf{u}$ and $\mathbf{C}$ would be needed.

Using this formulation as a framework, we offer some suggestions about finding values for the components of $\mathbf{D}_i$ and $\mathbf{D}_{i+1}$ (the derivative vectors at the key positions) purely from local geometric information. The derivative vector at $\mathbf{P}_i$ may be calculated as

$$\mathbf{D}_i = \frac{1}{2} (\mathbf{P}_{i+1} - \mathbf{P}_{i-1}) = \frac{1}{2} \left[(\mathbf{P}_{i+1} - \mathbf{P}_i) + (\mathbf{P}_i - \mathbf{P}_{i-1}) \right], \tag{21.2}$$

which is simply the average of the *source chord* $\mathbf{P}_i - \mathbf{P}_{i-1}$ and the *destination chord* $\mathbf{P}_{i+1} - \mathbf{P}_i$. We will refer to this average as the *default* (Figure 21.6). This method of providing a derivative, or the more general formula

$$\mathbf{D}_i = a (\mathbf{P}_{i+1} - \mathbf{P}_i) + (1 - a) (\mathbf{P}_i - \mathbf{P}_{i-1})$$

for values of a between zero and one, generates what are called *Catmull-Rom splines* by some, although we will see in Section 21.4 that this method is actually just a particular instance of the family of splines defined by Catmull and Rom, and are called *cardinal splines* by others, (not to be confused with the cardinal basis spline to be discussed in 21.2).

At the beginning of a motion sequence, i.e., at $\mathbf{P}_0$, some arbitrary choice for the source chord must be made. Similarly, the destination chord must be specified arbitrarily at the end of the sequence. Alternatively a specification of the beginning and ending derivative vectors can be made without regard to any chords.

A standard smooth motion through a given set of keys does not always produce the effect desired by the animator. In certain cases a wider, more exaggerated curve may be desired, while in other cases the desired path may be much tighter. This suggests that some sort of ''tension'' in the trajectory as it passes through a key position, such as that shown in Figure 21.7, would be desirable.

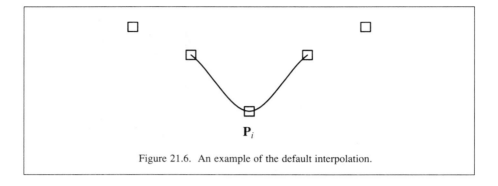

Figure 21.6. An example of the default interpolation.

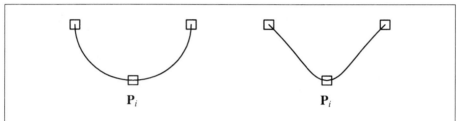

Figure 21.7. Two interpolations, the one on the right being more tense at $\mathbf{P}_i$ than the one at the left.

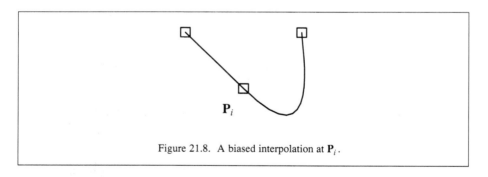

Figure 21.8. A biased interpolation at $\mathbf{P}_i$.

The animator may wish to have a trajectory anticipate or overshoot a key position by a certain amount. This suggests that the sort of "bias" illustrated in Figure 21.8 would be useful.

Even continuity in the direction and speed of motion is not always desirable. Animating a bouncing ball, for example, actually requires the introduction of a discontinuity in the motion at the point of impact. Variation of "continuity" is illustrated in Figure 21.9.

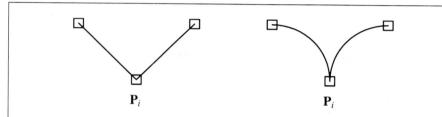

Figure 21.9. Two interpolations; the one on the right being more discontinuous at $\mathbf{P}_i$ than the one on the left.

We can introduce *tension, continuity,* and *bias* parameters by separating each derivative vector at the ith key position into an *incoming* and an *outgoing* part, respectively the *source derivative* $\mathbf{DS}_i$ and the *destination derivative* $\mathbf{DD}_i$ as indicated in Figure 21.10.

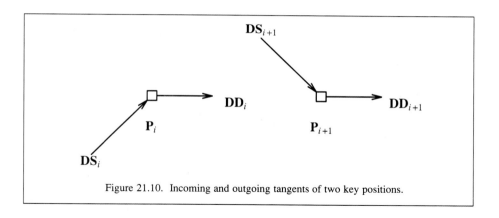

Figure 21.10. Incoming and outgoing tangents of two key positions.

These replace the single derivative vector in the default spline at each $\mathbf{P}$. Furthermore, the default average (21.2) is relaxed in favor of a more selective average of the source and destination chord.

A tension parameter t_i to control how sharply the curve bends may be implemented as a scale factor which changes the length of both the incoming and outgoing parts of the derivative vector equally at $\mathbf{P}_i$:

$$\mathbf{DS}_i \;=\; \mathbf{DD}_i \;=\; (1-t_i)\,\frac{1}{2}\,\Big[(\mathbf{P}_{i+1}-\mathbf{P}_i)+(\mathbf{P}_i-\mathbf{P}_{i-1})\Big]. \tag{21.3}$$

Setting $t_i = 0$ produces the default; the derivative vector is the average of the two adjacent chords. Increasing the tension to $t_i = 1$ (Figure 21.11) reduces the length of the derivative vector to zero and tightens the curve to a corner.

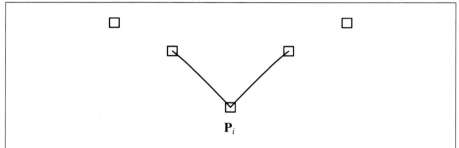

Figure 21.11. An interpolation at $\mathbf{P}_i$ with $t_i = 1$. The value of t is zero at all other points $\mathbf{P}$.

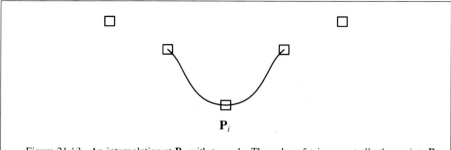

Figure 21.12. An interpolation at $\mathbf{P}_i$ with $t_i = -1$. The value of t is zero at all other points $\mathbf{P}$.

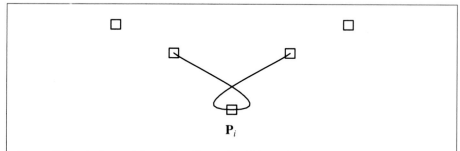

Figure 21.13. An interpolation at $\mathbf{P}_i$ with $t_i = 4$, which results in a loop. The value of t is zero at all other points $\mathbf{P}$.

Reducing the tension to $t_i = -1$ increases the derivative vector to twice its default length and produces more slack in the curve (Figure 21.12).

The value of t_i can be set at other values for more pronounced effects. For example, $t_i > 1$ will produce loops (Figure 21.13).

The principal reason for using splines in key frame animation is to avoid discontinuities in the direction and speed of motion which are produced by linear interpolation. However, in animation, discontinuities are sometimes necessary to create realistic effects such as punching, bouncing, etc. A common technique to introduce such a discontinuity into an otherwise continuous spline is to repeat a key position or to simply terminate the spline at a key and start an entirely independent spline to interpolate the next sequence of key frames.

Neither of these approaches is very satisfactory because the discontinuity cannot be controlled. While it is true that, mathematically speaking, a spline's derivative is either continuous or discontinuous, the artist's view is quite different. He or she would like to have more control over continuity than a simple on/off switch. In fact, from the animator's point of view, two curve segments which have very different derivative vectors at their joint appear ''more discontinuous'' than two curve segments which have fairly similar derivative vectors.

Using c_i to denote a continuity parameter, we may allow the source and destination components of the derivative vector to differ from each other according to,

$$\mathbf{DS}_i = \left[\frac{1-c_i}{2}(\mathbf{P}_i - \mathbf{P}_{i-1}) + \frac{1+c_i}{2}(\mathbf{P}_{i+1} - \mathbf{P}_i) \right] \qquad (21.4)$$

$$\mathbf{DD}_i = \left[\frac{1+c_i}{2}(\mathbf{P}_i - \mathbf{P}_{i-1}) + \frac{1-c_i}{2}(\mathbf{P}_{i+1} - \mathbf{P}_i) \right]. \qquad (21.5)$$

Note that with $c_i = 0$ we obtain $\mathbf{DS}_i = \mathbf{DD}_i$, which produces a spline with derivative vector continuity at the keys. (In fact, this choice reproduces the default interpolation.) As the magnitude $|c_i|$ of c_i increases, the two derivative vectors become increasingly distinct. When $c_i = -1$, the source derivative vector $\mathbf{DS}_i$ reduces to the source chord, and the destination derivative vector $\mathbf{DD}_i$ reduces to the destination chord, producing a pronounced corner in the curve, if the two chords are not collinear and of equal length. In fact, Figure 21.11 is exactly reproduced with this setting. As c_i is made more negative, the corner becomes more acute, and the curve buckles inward. Figure 21.14 shows this buckling when $c_i = -2$.

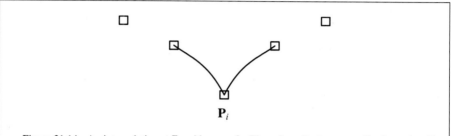

Figure 21.14. An interpolation at $\mathbf{P}_i$ with $c_i = -2$. The value of c is zero at all other points $\mathbf{P}$.

For positive values of c_i corners pointing in the opposite direction are produced (Figure 21.15).

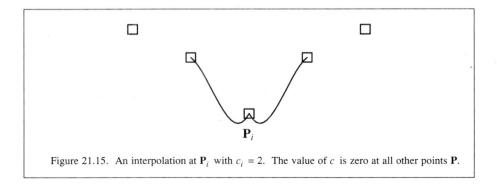

Figure 21.15. An interpolation at $\mathbf{P}_i$ with $c_i = 2$. The value of c is zero at all other points $\mathbf{P}$.

Finally, we can introduce a bias parameter b_i to control the direction of the path as it passes through $\mathbf{P}_i$. Both incoming and outgoing parts of the derivative are formed as an average of the incoming and outgoing chords, but the bias assigns different weights to the two chords when forming the average.

$$\mathbf{DS}_i = \mathbf{DD}_i = \frac{1+b_i}{2}(\mathbf{P}_i - \mathbf{P}_{i-1}) + \frac{1-b_i}{2}(\mathbf{P}_{i+1} - \mathbf{P}_i). \tag{21.6}$$

Note that with $b_i = 0$ the two chords are weighted equally, and the default interpolation is produced. When $b_i = -1$, the derivative vector is completely determined by the destination chord, and when $b_i = 1$, the derivative vector is completely determined by the source chord. The more negative b_i is made, the more the trajectory "bends" to one side of $\mathbf{P}_i$ (Figure 21.16).

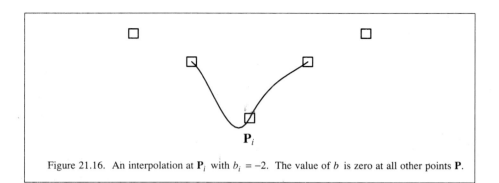

Figure 21.16. An interpolation at $\mathbf{P}_i$ with $b_i = -2$. The value of b is zero at all other points $\mathbf{P}$.

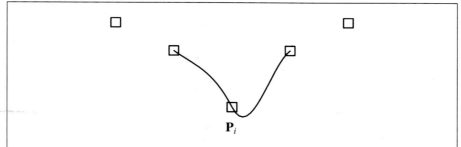

Figure 21.17. An interpolation at $\mathbf{P}_i$ with $b_i = 2$. The value of b is zero at all other points $\mathbf{P}$.

The more positive b_i is made, the more the trajectory bends to the other side of $\mathbf{P}_i$ (Figure 21.17).

The bias parameter easily simulates the traditional animation effect of following through after an action by "overshooting" the key position or exaggerating a movement by "undershooting" a key position.

Combining the tension, continuity, and bias control parameters we obtain the following general equations for the source and destination derivative vectors at the key position $\mathbf{P}_i$.

$$\mathbf{DS}_i = \frac{(1-t_i)(1-c_i)(1+b_i)}{2} (\mathbf{P}_i - \mathbf{P}_{i-1})$$

$$+ \frac{(1-t_i)(1+c_i)(1-b_i)}{2} (\mathbf{P}_{i+1} - \mathbf{P}_i) \qquad (21.7)$$

$$\mathbf{DD}_i = \frac{(1-t_i)(1+c_i)(1+b_i)}{2} (\mathbf{P}_i - \mathbf{P}_{i-1})$$

$$+ \frac{(1-t_i)\cdot(1-c_i)\cdot(1-b_i)}{2} \cdot (\mathbf{P}_{i+1} - \mathbf{P}_i) \qquad (21.8)$$

This composite formula provides considerable flexibility in the construction of trajectories (Figure 21.18).

The approach described in this section for specifying curve segments has recently been extended to surface patches in [Du/et al.87a] and generalized and improved further in [Du/et al.87b].

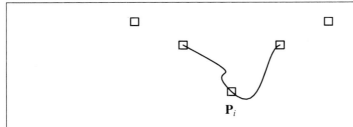

Figure 21.18. An interpolation at $\mathbf{P}_i$ with $b_{i-1} = 2$, $b_i = 1$, $b_{i+1} = 0$, $c_{i-1} = 2$, $c_i = 0$, $c_{i+1} = 2$, $t_{i-1} = 0$, $t_i = -1$, and $t_{i+1} = 0$.

21.2   A Cardinal Basis Spline for Interpolation

We will use the term *cardinal basis* (or, more completely *cardinal basis for interpolation*) to describe a basis for splines that serves to make a given interpolation problem trivial in the same sense that the Lagrange polynomials

$$P_i(\overline{u}) = \prod_{\substack{j=0 \\ j \neq i}}^{M} \left[\frac{\overline{u} - \overline{u}_j}{\overline{u}_i - \overline{u}_j} \right] \quad \text{for } i = 0, \ldots, M$$

make the polynomial interpolation problem trivial. These polynomials have the property that

$$P_i(\overline{u}_j) = \begin{cases} 1 & \text{if } i = j \\ 0 & \text{if } i \neq j \, , \end{cases}$$

and the result of this is that the coefficients c_j which provide the interpolation

$$\sum_{i=0}^{M} c_i P_i(\overline{u}_j) = y_j \quad \text{for } j = 0, \ldots, M$$

are simply given by $c_i = y_i$ for all i.

Sometimes not only the data but also the certain derivatives must also be interpolated. If values and first derivatives s_j are both to be interpolated at $\overline{u}_0, \ldots, \overline{u}_M$, for example, one can take a partial collection of basis functions

$$P_0(\overline{u}), \ldots, P_M(\overline{u})$$

satisfying

$$P_i(\overline{u}_j) = \begin{cases} 1 & \text{if } i = j \\ 0 & \text{if } i \neq j \end{cases}$$

and

$$P_i^{(1)}(\bar{u}_j) = 0$$

for all i, j and complete it with a collection of basis functions

$$D_0(\bar{u}), \ldots, D_M(\bar{u})$$

satisfying

$$D_i(\bar{u}_j) = 0$$

and

$$D_i^{(1)}(\bar{u}_j) = \begin{cases} 1 & \text{if } i = j \\ 0 & \text{if } i \neq j \end{cases}$$

for all i, j. The result will be that

$$\sum_{i=0}^{M} c_i P_i(\bar{u}_j) + \sum_{i=0}^{M} d_i D_i(\bar{u}_j) = y_j$$

and

$$\sum_{i=0}^{M} c_i P_i^{(1)}(\bar{u}_j) + \sum_{i=0}^{M} d_i D_i^{(1)}(\bar{u}_j) = s_j$$

for given data y_j and s_j, $j = 0, \ldots, M$, if we simply set $c_i = y_i$ and $d_i = s_i$.

Including higher derivatives in the general picture is accomplished in the obvious way. Once the idea of a cardinal basis for interpolation is grasped, it is easy to imagine ways in which such bases can be tailor-made for a variety of interpolation problems. We will present two examples here: a C^2 cardinal spline basis for Hermite interpolation and a C^2 cardinal basis for simple interpolation. The functions $h_{00}(u)$, $h_{10}(u)$, $h_{01}(u)$, and $h_{11}(u)$ which we used in Section 21.1 to achieve cubic C^1 spline interpolation are not, themselves, cubic C^1 splines. That is, while they may constitute basis functions for the segment polynomials of the spline curves we constructed, they are <u>not</u> basis splines. An appropriate name for them is *blending functions*, since they "blend" together given data values and corresponding derivative values into a cubic C^1 spline.

The term "blending functions" is generally used to denote a linearly independent collection of functions which, like the Hermite basis polynomials of Section 21.1, serve to create piecewise functions that have at their joints given values and a number of given consecutive derivatives (first, second, third, etc.). Such functions are used frequently in graphics. The simplest are the *linear blending functions*

$$L_0(u) = 1 - u \quad \text{and} \quad L_1(u) = u \quad \text{for } 0 \leq u \leq 1,$$

which constituted the segment polynomials for the uniform linear B-splines (the hat functions of Chapter 4).

The linear B-splines are an example of the fact that blending functions can also be basis splines. The hat functions clearly "blend" given data values together into an interpolating linear C^0 spline. Such splines (those which act simultaneously as blending functions and basis functions) are called *cardinal basis splines*. Given this idea, the construction of a basis of such splines, a *cardinal basis*, is a straightforward exercise. For example, taking the hint from the fact that the hat functions are merely the linear blending functions "placed back-to-back," it is easy to see that translates of the two cubic C^1 functions shown in Figure 21.19 could be used to form a cardinal basis for cubic C^1 Hermite interpolation.

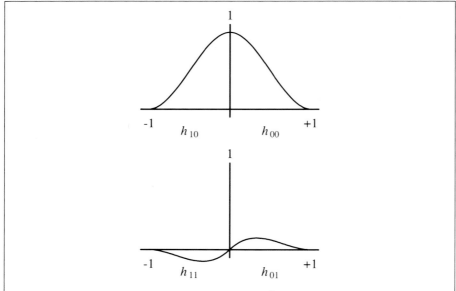

Figure 21.19. The two distinct members of the cubic, C^1, cardinal spline basis, suitable for use in piecewise cubic Hermite interpolation.

In closing we present two members of a cardinal cubic C^2 basis that are suited for the interpolation of data values. These basis elements produce interpolating splines satisfying the end conditions used by [Forsythe/et al.77] and discussed in Chapter 3 (see Figure 3.5). They are generated by interpolating the data values

1,0,0 ,..., 0,0,0

0,1,0 ,..., 0,0,0

0,0,1 ,..., 0,0,0

and so on, finishing with

0,0,0 ,..., 0,1,0

0,0,0 ,..., 0,0,1 .

That is, the first basis function is the spline satisfying the Forsythe, Malcolm and Moler end conditions that interpolates

1,0,0 ,..., 0,0,0 ,

the second basis function is the spline satisfying the Forsythe, Malcolm and Moler end conditions that interpolates

0,1,0 ,..., 0,0,0 ,

and so on. It is easy to see that if each is multiplied by a control vertex then their sum interpolates all the control vertices.

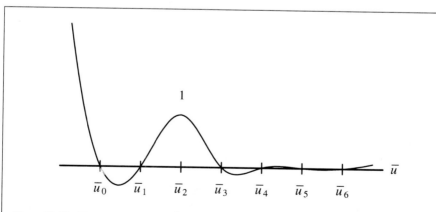

Figure 21.20. The cardinal, cubic, C^2 basis spline, with Forsythe, Malcolm and Moler end conditions, suitable for interpolating a data value at $\bar{u}_2$.

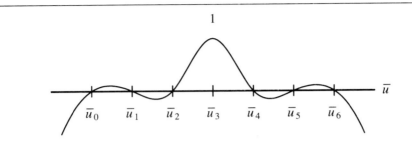

Figure 21.21. The cardinal, cubic, C^2 basis spline, with Forsythe, Malcolm and Moler end conditions, suitable for interpolating a data value at $\bar{u}_3$.

21.3 Interpolation Using B-splines

We will begin the discussion using curves, for which [Wu/et al.77] and [Barsky/Thomas81] amplify what we will present in graphics terminology. Then we will move on to surfaces, for which [Barsky/Greenberg80] and [Boehm85] provide an amplification in graphical terms. A very thorough discussion in [deBoor78] is given in mathematical terms, and backed up with computer code. The supplementary discussion in [Cox78, Cox82] is also helpful.

Let us begin with a special case: given some points $\mathbf{P}_p$, find control vertices $\mathbf{V}_i$ such that at each <u>knot</u> $\bar{u}_p$ in the range $[\bar{u}_{k-1}, \bar{u}_{m+1}]$ the curve attains a specified point. (Later we will comment on the more general situation in which we might require the points $\mathbf{P}_p$ to be "touched" by the surface at other values of $\bar{u}$ than the knot values.) This means we want to compute $\mathbf{V}_i$ such that

$$\mathbf{Q}(\bar{u}_p) = \sum_{i=0}^{m} \mathbf{V}_i B_{i,k}(\bar{u}_p) = \mathbf{P}_p \tag{21.9}$$

for all $p = k - 1, \ldots, m + 1$.

If $\mathbf{V}_i = (x_i, y_i, z_i)$ and $\mathbf{P}_p = (r_p, s_p, t_p)$, then (21.9) can be written in terms of individual components as follows (using the y components for illustration):

$$Y(\bar{u}_p) = \sum_{i=0}^{m} y_i B_{i,k}(\bar{u}_p) = s_p \quad \text{for } p = k - 1, \ldots, m + 1.$$

This constitutes a system of $m - k + 3$ equations in $m + 1$ unknowns:

$$
\begin{bmatrix}
B_{0,k}(\bar{u}_{k-1}) & \cdots & B_{m,k}(\bar{u}_{k-1}) \\
 & \cdot & \\
 & \cdot & \\
 & \cdot & \\
B_{0,k}(\bar{u}_{m+1}) & \cdots & B_{m,k}(\bar{u}_{m+1})
\end{bmatrix}
\begin{bmatrix}
y_0 \\ \cdot \\ \cdot \\ \cdot \\ y_m
\end{bmatrix}
=
\begin{bmatrix}
s_{k-1} \\ \cdot \\ \cdot \\ \cdot \\ s_{m+1}
\end{bmatrix}. \tag{21.10}
$$

We are short $k-2$ equations. For cubic splines k is 4, and we are short 2 equations, just as we were in Sections 3.1 and 3.2, and any of the end conditions of those sections may be considered here. For example, the two extra equations

$$
\sum_{i=0}^{m} y_i B_{i,4}^{(2)}(\bar{u}_{k-1}) = 0
$$

and

$$
\sum_{i=0}^{m} y_i B_{i,4}^{(2)}(\bar{u}_{m+1}) = 0
$$

may be added to provide a system of equations defining the B-spline representation of the natural cubic interpolating spline. The references [Cox78, Cox82] offer variations on this approach.

In the B-spline formulation of the interpolation problem, however, an alternative way of selecting extra conditions becomes evident. We may choose auxiliary data values associated with knots in the range $[\bar{u}_0, \bar{u}_{k-2}]$ and in the range $[\bar{u}_{m+2}, \bar{u}_{m+k}]$ to form the extra equations needed to fill out system (21.10). For example, in the cubic case, we could select values s_{k-2} and s_{m+2} as "boundary values" to produce the full, nonsingular system of equations. This amounts to selecting two additional points $\mathbf{P}_{k-2}$ and $\mathbf{P}_{m+2}$ to be interpolated on extensions of the curve at $\mathbf{Q}(\bar{u}_{k-2})$ and at $\mathbf{Q}(\bar{u}_{m+2})$.

$$
\begin{bmatrix}
B_{0,k}(\bar{u}_{k-2}) & \cdots & B_{m,k}(\bar{u}_{k-2}) \\
B_{0,k}(\bar{u}_{k-1}) & \cdots & B_{m,k}(\bar{u}_{k-1}) \\
 & & \\
 & \cdot & \\
 & & \\
B_{0,k}(\bar{u}_{m+1}) & \cdots & B_{m,k}(\bar{u}_{m+1}) \\
B_{0,k}(\bar{u}_{m+2}) & \cdots & B_{m,k}(\bar{u}_{m+2})
\end{bmatrix}
\begin{bmatrix}
y_0 \\ \\ \cdot \\ \cdot \\ \cdot \\ \\ y_m
\end{bmatrix}
=
\begin{bmatrix}
s_{k-2} \\ s_{k-1} \\ \\ \cdot \\ \\ s_{m+1} \\ s_{m+2}
\end{bmatrix}. \tag{21.11}
$$

These auxiliary data values can be chosen at will, though the shape of the resulting curve will depend, nonlocally, upon the specific values chosen.

An interesting candidate for auxiliary values are ones that are not derived from points $\mathbf{P}_{k-1}$ and $\mathbf{P}_{m+2}$ but are chosen, instead, to approximate the standard first-derivative and second-derivative end conditions. Considering only the cubic case for illustration, and only the value $\bar{u} = \bar{u}_{k-2}$, suppose we wished to approximate the natural end condition:

$$\sum_{i=0}^{m} y_i B_{i,4}^{(2)}(\bar{u}_{k-1}) = 0.$$

We can use the fact that, by Taylor expansion,

$$B_{i,k}(\bar{u}_{k-2}) \approx B_{i,k}(\bar{u}_{k-1}) + (\bar{u}_{k-2} - \bar{u}_{k-1}) B_{i,k}^{(1)}(\bar{u}_{k-1}) + \frac{1}{2} (\bar{u}_{k-2} - \bar{u}_{k-1})^2 B_{i,k}^{(2)}(\bar{u}_{k-1}).$$

Setting $B_{i,k}^{(2)}(\bar{u}_{k-1})$ to zero yields

$$B_{i,k}(\bar{u}_{k-2}) \approx B_{i,k}(\bar{u}_{k-1}) + (\bar{u}_{k-2} - \bar{u}_{k-1}) B_{i,k}^{(1)}(\bar{u}_{k-1}).$$

If this approximate equality is multiplied by y_i and the result is summed up for $i = 0, \ldots, m$, we obtain

$$\sum_{i=0}^{m} y_i B_{i,k}(\bar{u}_{k-2}) \approx \sum_{i=0}^{m} y_i B_{i,k}(\bar{u}_{k-1}) + \sum_{i=0}^{m} y_i (\bar{u}_{k-2} - \bar{u}_{k-1}) B_{i,k}^{(1)}(\bar{u}_{k-1}).$$

Observe that the first summation on the right is equal to s_{k-1}, from (21.10), so we may take

$$s_{k-2} = s_{k-1} + \sum_{i=0}^{m} y_i (\bar{u}_{k-2} - \bar{u}_{k-1}) B_{i,k}^{(1)}(\bar{u}_{k-1})$$

as an auxiliary value that defines an approximately natural cubic interpolating spline — for surfaces, this observation is essentially what underlies the material in [Barsky/Greenberg80].

Note that system (21.11) will have zero entries in the matrix except in a band $k-1$ entries wide along the main diagonal; this follows from the locality of the B-splines. For the uniform cubic B-splines, the matrix of (21.11) reduces to

$$\frac{1}{6} \begin{bmatrix} 4 & 1 & & & & & \\ 1 & 4 & 1 & & & & \\ & 1 & 4 & 1 & & & \\ & & 1 & 4 & 1 & & \\ & & & \cdot & \cdot & \cdot & \cdot \\ & & & & 1 & 4 & 1 \\ & & & & & 1 & 4 \end{bmatrix},$$

which is similar to those in sections 3.1 and 3.2.

It is possible, of course, to use any selection of knots (that is, any varieties of B-splines) to set up the matrix of (21.11). The uniform knot selection that leads to the simple 1-4-1 matrix above for cubics is only a special case.

It is also worthwhile noting that other $\bar{u}$ values than those of the knots can be used to set up the equations. In that case we would be asking for the control vertices $\mathbf{V}_i$ that would cause the curve $\mathbf{Q}(\bar{u})$ to pass through given points $\mathbf{P}_p$ at some selected parameter positions $\bar{u} = a_p$

$$\mathbf{Q}(a_p) = \sum_{i=0}^{m} \mathbf{V}_i \, B_{i,k}(a_p) = \mathbf{P}_p \,.$$

As in the case where $\bar{u}$ was set to successive knot values, one may select $m - k + 3$ values a_p and fill out the remaining $k - 2$ linear system by some boundary condition equations. The simplest boundary conditions in this context, however, and the one we will use for the sake of discussion, would arise from selecting $k - 2$ more points $\mathbf{P}_p$ and $k - 2$ more values $\bar{u} = a_p$ at which to require interpolation. In this case it is natural to index the values as follows,

$$a_0 < a_1 < \cdots < a_m \,,$$

which gives the equations

$$\mathbf{Q}(a_p) = \sum_{i=0}^{m} \mathbf{V}_i \, B_{i,k}(a_p) = \mathbf{P}_p$$

for all $p = 0, \ldots, m$.

We would expect to choose the values a_p, for the most part, within the legal parameter range, perhaps venturing outside a short way for the sake of obtaining some boundary information; e.g., as we used $\bar{u} = \bar{u}_{k-2}$ in equation (21.11). The resulting matrix system that corresponds to (21.11) would be

$$\begin{bmatrix} B_{0,k}(a_0) & \cdots & B_{m,k}(a_0) \\ B_{0,k}(a_1) & \cdots & B_{m,k}(a_1) \\ & \cdot & \\ & \cdot & \\ & \cdot & \\ B_{0,k}(a_{m-1}) & \cdots & B_{m,k}(a_{m-1}) \\ B_{0,k}(a_m) & \cdots & B_{m,k}(a_m) \end{bmatrix} \begin{bmatrix} y_0 \\ \cdot \\ \cdot \\ \cdot \\ y_m \end{bmatrix} = \begin{bmatrix} s_0 \\ s_1 \\ \cdot \\ \cdot \\ \cdot \\ s_{m-1} \\ s_m \end{bmatrix} . \tag{21.12}$$

The values of the a_p cannot be chosen in an entirely arbitrary fashion, of course. A trivial example to show that some restrictions are necessary comes from choosing all the values of a_p to be in the interval $(\bar{u}_{k-1}, \bar{u}_k)$. Since all the B-splines $B_{i,k}$ with $i \geq k$ are zero at these values of a_p, the matrix in (21.12)

---

would have rows k through m filled with nothing but zero entries. The following theorem, due to Schoenberg and Whitney and cited in [deBoor78], provides the necessary and sufficient condition for selecting the values of the a_p.

■ **Theorem**

The matrix in (21.12) is nonsingular if and only if

$$\overline{u}_p \leq a_p < \overline{u}_{p+k}$$

for all $p = 0, \ldots, m$.

■

The same discussion may be carried out for surfaces. In this case we would expect to provide points in parameter space

$$(\overline{u}, \overline{v}) = \mathbf{A}_p$$

and corresponding points in object space

$$(x, y, z) = \mathbf{P}_p;$$

for example, as is indicated in Figure 21.22.

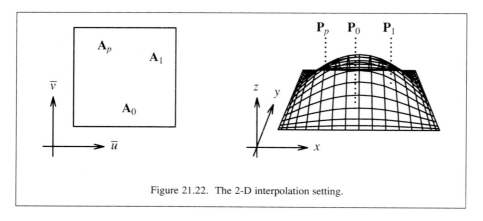

Figure 21.22. The 2-D interpolation setting.

In this setting we would be trying to find control vertices $\mathbf{V}_{i,j}$ such that

$$Q(\mathbf{A}_p^{(\overline{u})}, \mathbf{A}_p^{(\overline{v})}) = \sum_{i=0}^{m} \sum_{j=0}^{n} \mathbf{V}_{i,j} B_{i,k}(\mathbf{A}_p^{(\overline{u})}) B_{j,l}(\mathbf{A}_p^{(\overline{v})}) = \mathbf{P}_p,$$

where $A_p^{(\bar{u})}$ and $A_p^{(\bar{v})}$ are, respectively, the $\bar{u}$ and $\bar{v}$ coordinates of the parametric point A_p. Note that we can allow the order of the B-splines in the $\bar{v}$ direction to be different, possibly, from those in the $\bar{u}$ direction. We can provide up to $L = (m+1) \times (n+1)$ data points and corresponding parameter pairs, making up the difference between the number of points we provide and L by imposing some sort of boundary conditions. In the special case that we provide all L points, the system of equations to be solved would have the matrix format

$$
\begin{bmatrix}
B_{0,k}(A_0^{(\bar{u})})B_{0,l}(A_0^{(\bar{u})}) & \cdots & B_{m,k}(A_0^{(\bar{u})})B_{n,l}(A_0^{(\bar{u})}) \\
B_{0,k}(A_1^{(\bar{u})})B_{0,l}(A_1^{(\bar{u})}) & \cdots & B_{m,k}(A_1^{(\bar{u})})B_{n,l}(A_1^{(\bar{u})}) \\
& & \\
& \cdot & \\
& \cdot & \\
& \cdot & \\
B_{0,k}(A_{L-1}^{(\bar{u})})B_{0,l}(A_{L-1}^{(\bar{u})}) & \cdots & B_{m,k}(A_{L-1}^{(\bar{u})})B_{n,l}(A_{L-1}^{(\bar{u})}) \\
B_{0,k}(A_L^{(\bar{u})})B_{0,l}(A_L^{(\bar{u})}) & \cdots & B_{m,k}(A_L^{(\bar{u})})B_{n,l}(A_L^{(\bar{u})})
\end{bmatrix}
\begin{bmatrix}
V_{0,0} \\
\\
\cdot \\
\cdot \\
\cdot \\
\\
V_{m,n}
\end{bmatrix}
=
\begin{bmatrix}
s_0 \\
s_1 \\
\cdot \\
\cdot \\
\cdot \\
s_{L-1} \\
s_L
\end{bmatrix}. \quad (21.13)
$$

Until now we have assumed that the parameter points A_p are "scattered." However, if the interpolation can be arranged according to a regular grid of $\bar{u}, \bar{v}$ values, then a significant savings results. Instead of having to solve the single $L \times L$ system of equations (21.13), it is possible to find the control vertices $V_{i,j}$ by successively solving smaller systems. Specifically, suppose the parametric points are arranged according to the scheme

$$
\begin{array}{llll}
A_0 = (a_0, b_0), & A_1 = (a_0, b_1), & \cdots & A_n = (a_0, b_n), \\
A_{n+1} = (a_1, b_0), & A_{n+2} = (a_1, b_1), & \cdots & A_{2n+1} = (a_1, b_n), \\
\cdot & \cdot & & \cdot \\
\cdot & \cdot & & \cdot \\
\cdot & \cdot & & \cdot \\
A_L = (a_m, b_0), & A_L = (a_m, b_1), & \cdots & A_L = (a_m, b_n)
\end{array}
$$

for $L = (m+1) \times (n+1)$. Then the interpolation equations become

$$
Q(a_f, b_g) = \sum_{i=0}^{m} \sum_{j=0}^{n} V_{i,j} B_{i,k}(a_f) B_{j,l}(b_g) = P_{f,g}
$$

for given points $P_{f,g}$, where $f = 0, \ldots, m$ and $g = 0, \ldots, n$, and the matrix system (21.13) becomes

$$
\begin{bmatrix}
B_{0,k}(a_0)B_{0,l}(b_0) & \cdots & B_{m,k}(a_0)B_{n,l}(b_0) \\
B_{0,k}(a_0)B_{0,l}(b_1) & \cdots & B_{m,k}(a_0)B_{n,l}(b_1) \\
 & & \vdots \\
 & & \vdots \\
 & & \vdots \\
B_{0,k}(a_m)B_{0,l}(b_{n-1}) & \cdots & B_{m,k}(a_m)B_{n,l}(b_{n-1}) \\
B_{0,k}(a_m)B_{0,l}(b_n) & \cdots & B_{m,k}(a_m)B_{n,l}(b_n)
\end{bmatrix}
\begin{bmatrix}
\mathbf{V}_{0,0} \\
\\
\vdots \\
\\
\\
\\
\mathbf{V}_{m,n}
\end{bmatrix}
=
\begin{bmatrix}
s_{0,0} \\
s_{0,1} \\
\vdots \\
\\
\\
s_{m,n-1} \\
s_{m,n}
\end{bmatrix} .
$$

For each fixed g the system becomes

$$
\mathbf{Q}(a_f,b_g) = \sum_{i=0}^{m} \left[\sum_{j=0}^{n} \mathbf{V}_{i,j} B_{j,l}(b_g) \right] B_{i,k}(a_f) = \mathbf{P}_{f,g}
$$

$$
= \sum_{i=0}^{m} \mathbf{W}_{i,g} B_{i,k}(a_f) = \mathbf{P}_{f,g} ,
$$

where we have defined $\mathbf{W}_{i,g}$ by

$$
\mathbf{W}_{i,g} = \sum_{j=0}^{n} \mathbf{V}_{i,j} B_{j,l}(b_g) .
$$

This represents a succession of 1-D interpolation problems, for $g = 0, \ldots, n$, all of which have the common system matrix

$$
\begin{bmatrix}
B_{0,k}(a_0) & \cdots & B_{m,k}(a_0) \\
 & \cdot & \\
 & \cdot & \\
 & \cdot & \\
B_{0,k}(a_m) & \cdots & B_{m,k}(a_m)
\end{bmatrix} .
$$

This matrix will be nonsingular if and only if the values a_f satisfy the conditions of the Schoenberg and Whitney theorem. One application of a forward elimination process followed by $n+1$ backward substitutions, one for each value of g, will suffice to find the $\mathbf{W}$'s. For each i, the $\mathbf{V}$'s, in turn, satisfy the equations

$$
\sum_{j=0}^{n} \mathbf{V}_{i,j} B_{j,l}(b_g) = \mathbf{W}_{i,g} \quad \text{for } g = 0, \ldots, n .
$$

This represents a second succession of 1-D problems with the common system matrix

$$\begin{bmatrix} B_{0,l}(b_0) & \cdots & B_{n,l}(b_0) \\ \cdot & \cdot & \cdot \\ \cdot & \cdot & \cdot \\ \cdot & \cdot & \cdot \\ B_{0,l}(b_n) & \cdots & B_{n,l}(b_n) \end{bmatrix}.$$

Again, the Schoenberg and Whitney theorem will tell us what values of b_g can be allowed. One application of a forward elimination process followed by $m+1$ backward substitutions, one for each $i = 0, \ldots, m$, will suffice to find the $\mathbf{V}$'s.

To illustrate the use of the material outlined in this section we display the following three pictures. The first, Plate XV, shows a milk drop striking a surface. The data for this picture was obtained as a 256×256 raster of 256 grey levels. The grey levels were then imagined to be one-dimensional points $\mathbf{P}_{f,g}$, for $f = 0, \ldots, 255$ $g = 0, \ldots, 255$, floating in the range

$$0.0 \le \mathbf{P}_{f,g} \le 255.0$$

and associated with the knots

$$\bar{u}_f = f + 2 \quad \text{and} \quad \bar{v}_g = g + 2.$$

The totality of knots in $\bar{u}$ and $\bar{v}$ was taken to be

$$\{0,1,2,3, \ldots, 257,258,259,260\},$$

the grey levels corresponding to the bordering raster points; i.e., those along the horizontal and vertical pixel lines corresponding to $\bar{u} = 2$, $\bar{u} = 258$, $\bar{v} = 2$, and $\bar{v} = 258$ were taken to be the auxiliary data values, and the points $\mathbf{P}_{f,g}$ were interpolated. In effect, the one pixel perimeter around the raster image was taken for interpolational "boundary" values, and the remaining 254×254 pixels were taken as interpolational "central-data" values. Plate XVI shows what can be achieved by evaluating the "surface" that results over various grids of equally spaced points. Any values that fell outside the interval [0,255] were cut down (or up) to size. Both magnification and compression of the picture are possible. Even distortions can be obtained if the "surface" is evaluated at unevenly spaced points. To provide a comparison between interpolation and control vertex approximation, Plate XVII displays the same sequence of evaluations of the bicubic spline produced by taking the grey levels as control vertices and merely constructing the "surface"

$$\sum_i \sum_j \mathbf{P}_{i,j} B_{i,4}(\bar{u}_i) B_{i,4}(\bar{v}_j).$$

As in the interpolating case, uniform cubic B-splines were used. A further discussion of the use of raster image data as control vertices for picture processing is to be found in [Klassen/Bartels86]. Further discussions of the use of B-splines in picture filtering applications are given in [Hou/Andrews78], [Ferrari/et al.86] and [Heckbert86].

21.4 Catmull-Rom Splines

The material in this section derives from [DeRose/Barsky84].

It has usually been our practice to define a curve in the form

$$\mathbf{Q}(\overline{u}) = \sum_{i=0}^{m} \mathbf{V}_i \, B_{i,k}(\overline{u}),$$ (21.14)

but Catmull and Rom have noted in [Catmull/Rom74] that a more general formulation would be

$$\mathbf{Q}(\overline{u}) = \frac{\sum_{i=0}^{m} \mathbf{P}_i(\overline{u}) \, W_i(\overline{u})}{\sum_{i=0}^{m} W_i(\overline{u})},$$ (21.15)

where the W_i are a set of basis splines and the $\mathbf{P}_i$ are vector-valued functions. The summation in the denominator was included in the formulation to provide a normalization in case the W_i did not sum to one, which is necessary for translation invariance. While

$$W_0(\overline{u}), \ldots, W_m(\overline{u})$$

can be any basis splines, it is most reasonable to select a set with local support. The reason for this is that the flexibility of the class of Catmull-Rom splines is kept under control by specifying the functions $\mathbf{P}_i$ so as to have "useful" values on the support W_i. We may ignore values of $\mathbf{P}_i$ outside this support, which makes the task of specifying them so as to achieve some useful effect manageable. These remarks imply that the B-splines and the Hermite cardinal spline basis are reasonable choices for the basis splines, since they have local support, while the interpolating cardinal splines are a less reasonable choice. The following assumptions will be made:

- The functions $W_i(\overline{u})$ are nonzero over the parametric interval from $\overline{u}_i$ to $\overline{u}_{i+d}$ (excluding $\overline{u}_{i+d}$ but possibly including $\overline{u}_i$).

- The functions $\mathbf{P}_i$ satisfy $\mathbf{P}_i(\overline{u}_q) = \mathbf{V}_q$ for $q = i, i+1, \ldots, i+r$.

Our usual construction of curves is of the form (21.15), if we choose

$$W_i(\bar{u}) = B_{i,k}(\bar{u})$$

(for which $d = k$), and if we choose

$$\mathbf{P}_i(\bar{u}) = \mathbf{V}_i \quad \text{for all } \bar{u}$$

(for which $r = 0$).

In general it is the interaction of the <u>width</u> of the support, d, of the basis functions, W_i, and the <u>number</u> of control vertices, r, interpolated by the vector-valued functions, $\mathbf{P}_i$, which dictates the character of the resulting curve. The example $W = B$ and $\mathbf{P} = \mathbf{V}$ given above demonstrates that the curves we have usually been studying, which have the character of <u>approximating</u> the control vertices $\mathbf{V}_i$, are a special case of the Catmull-Rom splines. We now show that, if r is increased, any curve of the form (21.15) can be made to <u>interpolate</u> the control vertices. Observe that the only functions W that are nonzero over the interval $[\bar{u}_q, \bar{u}_{q+1})$ are

$$W_{q-d+1}(\bar{u}), \ldots, W_q(\bar{u}).$$

Hence, for

$$\bar{u}_q \le \bar{u} < \bar{u}_{q+1},$$

(21.15) reduces to

$$\mathbf{Q}(\bar{u}) = \frac{\displaystyle\sum_{i=q-d+1}^{q} \mathbf{P}_i(\bar{u}) W_i(\bar{u})}{\displaystyle\sum_{i=q-d+1}^{q} W_i(\bar{u})},$$

and at $\bar{u} = \bar{u}_q$

$$\mathbf{Q}(\bar{u}_q) = \frac{\displaystyle\sum_{i=q-d+1}^{q} \mathbf{P}_i(\bar{u}_q) W_i(\bar{u}_q)}{\displaystyle\sum_{i=q-d+1}^{q} W_i(\bar{u}_q)}. \tag{21.16}$$

Now, if $r \ge d - 1$, then

$$\mathbf{P}_i(\bar{u}_q) = \mathbf{V}_q,$$

and (21.16) reduces to

$$Q(\overline{u}_q) = \frac{\mathbf{V}_q \sum\limits_{i=q-d+1}^{q} W_i(\overline{u}_q)}{\sum\limits_{i=q-d+1}^{q} W_i(\overline{u}_q)} = \mathbf{V}_q .$$

Any vector-valued functions $\mathbf{P}_i$ satisfying the condition that

$$\mathbf{P}_i(\overline{u}_q) = \mathbf{V}_q$$

for $q = i, i+1, \ldots, i+r$ will serve to define a Catmull-Rom spline. Catmull and Rom themselves chose to use

$$\mathbf{P}_i(\overline{u}) = \sum_{j=0}^{r} \mathbf{V}_{i+j} L_j(\overline{u}),$$

where L_j is the classical *Lagrange polynomial*:

$$L_j(\overline{u}) = \prod_{\substack{p=0 \\ p \neq j}}^{r} \left[\frac{\overline{u} - \overline{u}_p}{\overline{u}_j - \overline{u}_p} \right],$$

but one might choose to replace the Lagrange polynomials with the interpolating cardinal spline basis, with step functions, or with other convenient functions. In [DeRose/Barsky84] the Lagrange polynomials are replaced with functions specially chosen to introduce *shape parameters* of the sort already mentioned in Section 21.1 and in the chapters on Beta-splines.

21.5   B-splines and Least Squares Fitting

Often it is most natural to begin constructing a curve by simply sketching a rough approximation of it, perhaps with tablet and stylus or puck. The tablet is periodically sampled to obtain tens or hundreds of data points representing the curve. (See Figure 21.23 for an example.) This data is generally somewhat noisy, both because of electronic glitches in the puck and because the user's hand motions are jittery. Hence we would like to approximate the data by a piecewise polynomial curve having a relatively small number of segments, the exact number depending on the complexity of the curve.

What we will do is perform a *least squares fit* of the data by a B-spline curve, which can then be manipulated in the usual way to fine tune its shape. Our treatment follows that of [Forsythe/et al.77]; our examples are movement lines generated by an interactive editor for Benesh Dance Notation [Dransch85]. A more general treatment of least squares approximations by parametric cubic splines is given by [Plass/Stone83].

Suppose that we are given $p+1$ points $\mathbf{P}_i = (x_i, y_i)$. We want to find a set of $m+1$ control vertices $\mathbf{V}_j$ that minimize the distance between the cubic B-spline curve they define and the data points. If we use enough control vertices (namely

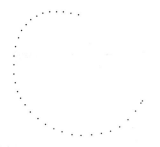

Figure 21.23. The data for a simple Benesh movement line, generated by a tablet and puck. This is actually filtered data; sample points were thrown away if they were less than three pixels in x or y from the previously accepted data point.

$m = p$) we can arrange to actually interpolate the data points; instead we select a smaller value of m, yielding a curve that ''adequately'' represents the data. We assume that m is given.

For the sake of efficiency we will make some simplifying assumptions whose legitimacy is discussed later. Recall that

$$\mathbf{Q}(\overline{u}) = (X(\overline{u}), Y(\overline{u}))$$

$$= \sum_{j=0}^{m} \mathbf{V}_j B_{j,4}(\overline{u})$$

$$= \sum_{j=0}^{m} (X_j B_{j,4}(\overline{u}), Y_j B_{j,4}(\overline{u})),$$

where the position of the jth control vertex is represented by (X_j, Y_j) so as to distinguish it from any of the data points (x_i, y_i) that we are fitting. What we will actually minimize is the expression

$$\sum_{i=0}^{p} |Q(\overline{U}_i) - \mathbf{P}_i|^2 = \sum_{i=0}^{p} \left[(X(\overline{U}_i) - x_i)^2 + (Y(\overline{U}_i) - y_i)^2 \right] = R, \qquad (21.17)$$

where $\overline{U}_i$ is some parameter value associated with the ith data point. The choice of this parameter value is discussed below. Since equation (21.17) is quadratic its minimum occurs for those values of X_j and Y_j such that

$$\frac{\partial}{\partial X_\ell} R = 0$$

$$\frac{\partial}{\partial Y_\ell} R = 0,$$

where l ranges between 0 and m. As usual we will consider just the Y_j, with the X_j treated analogously.

If we compute a typical such partial derivative we obtain

$$\frac{\partial}{\partial Y_\ell} R = \sum_{j=0}^{m} \left[\sum_{i=0}^{p} B_{j,4}(\overline{U}_i) B_{\ell,4}(\overline{U}_i) \right] Y_j - \sum_{i=0}^{p} y_i B_{\ell,4}(\overline{U}_i) = 0.$$

If we do this for each Y_ℓ, we have a set of $m+1$ simultaneous linear equations in $m+1$ unknowns, which can be solved by the usual techniques. (Although the authors of [Forsythe/et al.77] warn that in general this system of equations is prone to numerical error, in fact our particular formulation is safe because we are using B-splines rather than the power functions.)

We have still to indicate how the $\overline{U}_i$ are associated with the data points. We let

$$S = \sum_{i=1}^{p} |\mathbf{P}_i - \mathbf{P}_{i-1}|,$$

so that S is the total length of the line segments connecting the data points, and then we set

$$\overline{U}_0 = 3$$

$$\overline{U}_{i+1} = \overline{U}_i + (m-2)\frac{|\mathbf{P}_{i+1} - \mathbf{P}_i|}{S}.$$

As a result the spacing between the parametric values $\overline{U}_i$ is proportional to the Euclidean distance between their associated data points. This does not, of course, ensure that $Q(\overline{U}_i)$ is the point at which the curve is closest to the ith data point, but in practice it produces better results than uniform spacing.

For the application discussed in [Dransch85] it was important that the first and last data points be interpolated, and that the user have explicit control over the endpoints of the curve when manipulating control vertices. Hence the initial and final knots (3 and $m+1$) were given multiplicity four, Y_0 was given the value y_0, and Y_m was given the value y_p. This leaves $m-1$ equations

$$\sum_{j=1}^{m-1} \left[\sum_{i=0}^{p} B_{j,4}(\overline{U}_i) B_{\ell,4}(\overline{U}_i) \right] Y_j$$

$$= \sum_{i=0}^{p} y_i B_{\ell,4}(\overline{U}_i) - \sum_{i=0}^{p} B_{0,4}(\overline{U}_i) B_{\ell,4}(\overline{U}_i) Y_0 - \sum_{i=0}^{p} B_{n,4}(\overline{U}_i) B_{\ell,4}(\overline{U}_i) Y_m .$$

$$= \sum_{i=0}^{p} y_i B_{k,4}(\overline{u}_i) - \sum_{i=0}^{p} B_{0,4}(\overline{u}_i) B_{k,4}(\overline{u}_i) y_0 - \sum_{i=0}^{p} B_{n,4}(\overline{u}_i) B_{k,4}(\overline{u}_i) y_m .$$

in the $m-1$ unknowns Y_1 through Y_{m-1}.

Figures 21.24, 21.25 and 21.26 show one, three and five segment cubic B-spline curves fit to the data of Figure 21.23 using this technique. The curves of Figures 21.28–30 show the results of fitting the more complicated data shown in Figure 21.27.

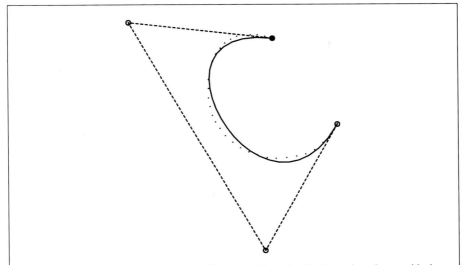

Figure 21.24. A one segment cubic B-spline curve, fit to the 34 data points shown with dots. Multiplicity 4 knots are used at either end to force interpolation of the ending data points; otherwise the parametric spacing is proportional to the Euclidean spacing between data points. The control graph is shown with a dashed line to avoid confusion with the data points.

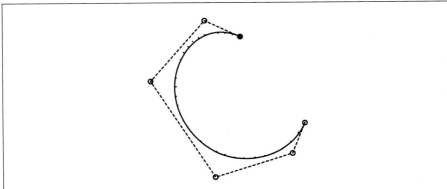

Figure 21.25. A three segment cubic B-spline curve, fit to the data of Figure 21.23. Compare the resulting curve to that of Figure 21.24.

Figure 21.26. A five segment cubic B-spline curve, fit to the data of Figure 21.23. Compare the resulting curve to those of Figures 21.24 and 21.25.

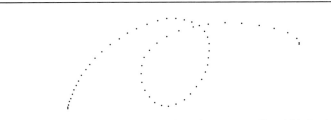

Figure 21.27. The data for a more complex Benesh movement line. This is also filtered data. Even so there is a marked change in the spacing between data points as the user's hand changes speed at the ends of the curve. There are 60 data points.

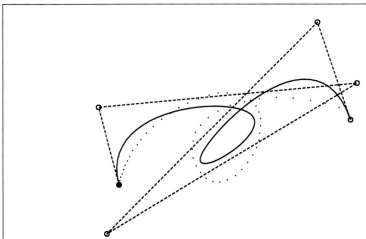

Figure 21.28. A three segment cubic B-spline curve, fit to the data of Figure 21.27.

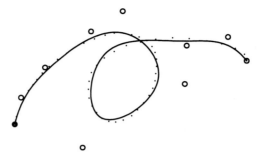

Figure 21.29. A seven segment cubic B-spline curve, fit to the data of Figure 21.27. The control graph has been omitted to avoid clutter.

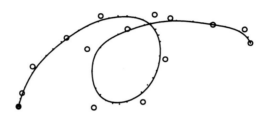

Figure 21.30. A 12 segment cubic B-spline curve, fit to the data of Figure 21.27. We are well past the point of needing more segments, since we have begun to mimic jitter in the user's hand. A curve of fewer segments should be used and reshaped slightly by moving a few of the control vertices.

The quality of the fit, as measured by the sum-square of the residuals R, can generally be improved by intelligently selecting where the joints between successive segments occur, and by adjusting the knot values $\bar{u}_i$ associated with each data point $\mathbf{P}_i$. Techniques for doing so are discussed in [Plass/Stone83]. Doing so is, of course, more expensive. In an interactive environment it may well be preferable to rapidly compute a somewhat inferior fit and adjust it by manipulating control vertices.

There are a variety of means other than the use of multiple knots for obtaining interpolation of the endpoints, as discussed in Section 4.6. Also, the initial fit by an open curve will generally be quite close to the data points at either end, and for some applications that may be sufficient.

As a final note of reference, some work on the much more difficult problem of fitting spline surfaces to input data using least squares is to be found in [Schmitt/et al.86]. One of the interesting aspects of this approach is that it demonstrates a novel use of adaptive subdivision, which has been discussed in several earlier chapters.

References

[Aho/et al.74]   Alfred V. Aho, John E. Hopcroft, and Jeffrey D. Ullman (1974), *The Design and Analysis of Computer Algorithms*, Addison-Wesley, Reading, Massachusetts.

[Barnhill/Riesenfeld74]   Robert E. Barnhill and Richard F. Riesenfeld (eds.) (1974), *Computer Aided Geometric Design*, Academic Press, New York [proceedings of the first International Conference on Computer Aided Geometric Design, held at the University of Utah, March 18-21].

[Barsky81a]   Brian A. Barsky (1981), The Beta-spline: A Local Representation Based on Shape Parameters and Fundamental Geometric Measures, PhD dissertation, Department of Computer Science, University of Utah, Salt Lake City, Utah 84112, December.

[Barsky81b]   Brian A. Barsky (1981), Computer-Aided Geometric Design: A Bibliography with Keywords and Classified Index, *IEEE Computer Graphics and Applications*, **1**(3), July, 67-109 [also reprinted in *ACM Computer Graphics* **16**(1), May, 1982, 119-159].

[Barsky82]   Brian A. Barsky (1982), End Conditions and Boundary Conditions for Uniform B-spline Curve and Surface Representations, *Computers in Industry* **3**(1 & 2), March & June, 17-29 [the Steven A. Coons memorial issue].

[Barsky84a]   Brian A. Barsky (1984), Exponential and Polynomial Methods for Applying Tension to an Interpolating Spline Curve, *Computer Vision, Graphics, and Image Processing* **27**(1), July, 1-18.

[Barsky84b]   Brian A. Barsky (1984), A Description and Evaluation of Various 3-D Models, *IEEE Computer Graphics and Applications* **4**(1), January, 38-52.

[Barsky85]   Brian A. Barsky (1985), Arbitrary Subdivision of Bézier Curves, Technical Report UCB/CSD 85/265, Computer Science Division, University of California, Berkeley, California 94720, November.

[Barsky87a]   Brian A. Barsky (1987), The Beta-spline: A Curve and Surface Representation for Computer Graphics and Computer Aided Geometric Design [to appear in a book from the International Summer Institute, June, 1986, Stirling, Scotland, Rae A. Earnshaw and David F. Rogers (eds.), Springer-Verlag, New York].

[Barsky87b]   Brian A. Barsky (1987), *Computer Graphics and Geometric Modelling Using Beta-splines*, Springer-Verlag, Heidelberg [to appear].

[Barsky/Beatty82]   Brian A. Barsky and John C. Beatty (1982), Varying the Betas in Beta-splines, Technical Report CS-82-49, University of Waterloo, Waterloo, Ontario, Canada N3l 3G1, December [also available as Technical Report UCB/CSD 82/112 from the Computer Science Division of the University of California, Berkeley, California 94720].

[Barsky/Beatty83a]   Brian A. Barsky and John C. Beatty (1983), Local Control of Bias and Tension in Beta-splines, *ACM Transactions on Graphics* **2**(2), April, 109-134 [also available in *Computer Graphics — SIGGRAPH '83 Conference Proceedings*, **17**(3), July, 193-218].

[Barsky/Beatty83b]   Brian A. Barsky and John C. Beatty (1983), Controlling the Shape of Parametric B-spline and Beta-spline Curves, *Proceedings of the Graphics Interface '83 Conference*, May, 223-232.

[Barsky/DeRose84]   Brian A. Barsky and Tony D. DeRose (1984), Geometric Continuity of Parametric Curves, Technical Report UCB/CSD 84/205, Computer Science Division, University of California, Berkeley, California 94720, October.

[Barsky/DeRose85]   Brian A. Barsky and Tony D. DeRose (1985), The Beta2-spline: A Special Case of the Beta-spline Curve and Surface Representation, *IEEE Computer Graphics and Applications* **5**(9), September, 46-58 [and errata in *IEEE Computer Graphics and Applications* **7**(3), March, 1987, page 15].

[Barsky/et al.87]   Brian A. Barsky, Tony D. DeRose, and Mark D. Dippé (1987), An Adaptive Subdivision Method with Crack Prevention for Rendering Beta-spline Objects, Technical Report UCB/CSD 87/348, Computer Science Division, University of California, Berkeley, California 94720, March 1987.

[Barsky/Greenberg80]   Brian A. Barsky and Donald P. Greenberg (1980), Determining a Set of Control Vertices to Generate an Interpolating Surface, *Computer Graphics and Image Processing* **14**(3), November, 203-226.

[Barsky/Thomas81]   Brian A. Barsky and Spencer W. Thomas (1981), TRANSPLINE — A System for Representing Curves Using Transformations Among Four Spline Formulations, *The Computer Journal* **24**(3), August, 271-277.

[Bartels83]   Richard H. Bartels (1983), Splines in Interactive Computer Graphics, in *Proceedings of the 1983 Dundee Conference on Numerical Analysis*, Lecture Notes in Mathematics Number 1066, David F. Griffiths (ed.), Springer-Verlag, New York, 1-29.

[Bartels/Beatty84]   Richard H. Bartels and John C. Beatty (1984), Beta-splines With A Difference, Technical Report CS-83-40, Computer Science Department, University of Waterloo, Waterloo, Ontario, Canada N2L 3G1, May.

[Bézier70]   Pierre E. Bézier (1970), *Emploi des machines à commande numérique*, Masson et Cie, Paris [translated by A. Robin Forrest and Anne F. Pankhurst (1972) as *Numerical Control — Mathematics and Applications*, John Wiley & Sons, New York].

[Bézier74]   Pierre E. Bézier (1974), Mathematical and Practical Possibilities of UNISURF, in *Computer Aided Geometric Design*, Robert E. Barnhill and Richard F. Riesenfeld (eds.), Academic Press, New York, 127-152.

[Bézier77]   Pierre E. Bézier (1977), Essai de Définition Numérique des Courbes et des Surfaces Expérimentales, PhD dissertation, l'Université Pierre et Marie Curie, Paris, February.

[Boehm80]   Wolfgang Boehm (1980), Inserting New Knots into B-spline Curves, *Computer-Aided Design* **12**(4) July, 199-202.

[Boehm85]   Wolfgang Boehm (1985), On the Efficiency of Knot Insertion Algorithms, *Computer-Aided Geometric Design* **2**(1-3) September, 141-143 [in the special issue *Surfaces in CAGD '84*].

[Boehm/et al.84]   Wolfgang Boehm, Gerald Farin, and Juergen Kahmann (1984), A Survey of Curve and Surface Methods in CAGD, *Computer Aided Geometric Design* **1**(1) July, 1-60.

[Boehm/Prautzsch85]   Wolfgang Boehm and Hartmut Prautzsch (1985), The Insertion Algorithm, *Computer-Aided Design* **17**(2), March, 58-59.

[Bogen83]   Richard Bogen (1983), *MACSYMA Reference Manual — Version Ten*, The Mathlab Group, Laboratory for Computer Science, Massachusetts Institute of Technology, Cambridge, Massachusetts 02139, January.

[deBoor72]   Carl de Boor (1972), On Calculating with B-splines, *Journal of Approximation Theory* **6**(1), July, 50-62.

[deBoor78]   Carl de Boor (1978), *A Practical Guide to Splines*, Applied Mathematical Sciences Volume 27, Springer-Verlag, New York.

[deCasteljau59]   Paul de Casteljau (1959), Courbes et Surfaces à Pôles, Citröen, Paris.

[Catmull74]   Edwin E. Catmull (1974), A Subdivision Algorithm for Computer Display of Curved Surfaces, PhD dissertation, Department of Computer Science, University of Utah, Salt Lake City, Utah 84112, December.

[Catmull75]   Edwin E. Catmull (1975), Computer Display of Curved Surfaces, *Proceedings of the Conference on Computer Graphics, Pattern Recognition, and Data Structures*, May, 11-17 [also available in *Tutorial and Selected Readings in Interactive Computer Graphics*, Herbert Freeman (ed.), IEEE Catalog No. EHO 156-0].

[Catmull/Clark78]   Edwin E. Catmull and James H. Clark (1978), Recursively Generated B-spline Surfaces on Arbitrary Topological Meshes, *Computer-Aided Design* **10**(6), November, 350-355.

[Catmull/Rom74]   Edwin E. Catmull and Raphael J. Rom (1974), A Class of Local Interpolating Splines, in *Computer Aided Geometric Design*, Robert E. Barnhill and Richard F. Riesenfeld (eds.), Academic Press, New York, 317-326.

[Chaikin74]   George M. Chaikin (1974), An Algorithm for High-Speed Curve Generation, *Computer Graphics and Image Processing* **3**(4), December, 346-349.

[Clark79]   James H. Clark (1979), A Fast Scan-Line Algorithm for Rendering Parametric Surfaces, *Computer Graphics* **14**(3), August, 7-12 [addendum to the *SIGGRAPH '79 Conference Proceedings* — ''papers to be published in the *CACM*''].

[Cline74]   Alan K. Cline (1974), Scalar- and Planar-Valued Curve Fitting Using Splines Under Tension, *Communications of the ACM* **17**(4), April, 218-220.

[Cohen88]   Elaine Cohen, (1988), A New Local Basis for Designing with Tensioned Splines, *ACM Transactions on Graphics*, to appear.

[Cohen/et al.80]   Elaine Cohen, Tom Lyche, and Richard Riesenfeld (1980), Discrete B-splines and Subdivision Techniques in Computer-Aided Geometric Design and Computer Graphics, *Computer Graphics and Image Processing* **14**(2), October, 87-111.

[Coons64]   Steven A. Coons (1964), Surfaces for Computer Aided Design, Project MAC, Massachusetts Institute of Technology, Cambridge, Massachusetts 02139.

[Coons67]   Steven A. Coons (1967), Surfaces for Computer-Aided Design of Space Forms, Technical Report MAC-TR-41, Massachusetts Institute of Technology, Cambridge, Massachusetts 02139 [available as AD-663 504 from the National Technical Information Service, Springfield, Virginia 22161].

[Cox72]   Maurice G. Cox (1972), The Numerial Evaluation of B-splines, *Journal of the Institute of Mathematics and its Applications* **10**(2), October, 134-149.

[Cox78]   Maurice G. Cox (1978), The Incorporation of Boundary Conditions in Spline Approximation Problems, in *Proceedings of the 1977 Dundee Conference on Numerical Analysis*, Lecture Notes in Mathematics Number 630, G. A. Watson (ed.), Springer-Verlag, New York, 51-63.

[Cox82]   Maurice G. Cox (1982), Practical Spline Approximation, in *Proceedings of the S. E. R. C. Numerical Analysis Summer School and Workshop*, Lecture Notes in Mathematics Number 965, P. R. Turner (ed.), Springer-Verlag, New York, 79-112.

[DeRose85]   Tony D. DeRose (1985), Geometric Continuity: a Parametrization-Independent Measure of Continuity for Computer-Aided Geometric Design, PhD dissertation, Computer Science Division, University of California at Berkeley, Berkeley, California 94720, August.

[DeRose/Barsky84]   Tony D. DeRose and Brian A. Barsky (1984), Geometric Continuity and Shape Parameters for Catmull-Rom Splines (Extended Abstract), in *Proceedings of the Graphics Interface '84 Conference*, May, 57-64. [An expanded version of this paper has been accepted by the *ACM Transactions on Graphics*.]

[DeRose/Barsky85]   Tony D. DeRose and Brian A. Barsky (1985), An Intuitive Approach to Geometric Continuity for Parametric Curves and Surfaces, in *Computer-Generated Images—The State of the Art*, Nadia Magnenat-Thalmann and Daniel Thalmann (eds.), Springer-Verlag, New York, 159-175.

[Doo78]   D. W. H. Doo (1978), A Subdivision Algorithm for Smoothing down Irregularly Shaped Polyhedrons, in *Proceedings of the Interactive Techniques in Computer-Aided Design Conference*, Bologna, Italy, 157-165.

[Doo/Sabin78]   D. W. H. Doo and Malcolm A. Sabin (1978), Behaviour of Recursive Division Surfaces Near Extraordinary Points, *Computer-Aided Design* **10**(6), November, 356-360.

[Dransch85]   Detlef Dransch (1985), An Editor for Benesh Dance Notation, Master's thesis, Computer Science Department, University of Waterloo, Waterloo, Ontario, Canada N2L 3G1, August.

[Du/et al.87a]   Wen-Hui Du, Francis J. M. Schmitt, and Brian A. Barsky (1987), Modelling Free-Form Surfaces Using Brown's Interpolant with Control Parameters, in *Proceedings of the International Conference on Computer-Aided Drafting, Design, and Manufacturing Technology*, Beijing, China, April, 21-25, 240-247.

[Du/et al.87b]   Wen-Hui, Du, Brian A. Barsky, and Francis J.M. Schmitt (1987), New Formulation Using Brown's Interpolant with Control Parameters, SIAM Conference on Applied Geometry, July 20-24.

[Dyn/Micchelli85]   Nira Dyn and Charles A. Micchelli (1985), Piecewise Polynomial Spaces and Geometric Continuity of Curves, Technical Report RC 11390 (#51284), IBM T. J. Watson Research Center, Yorktown Heights, New York 10598, September.

[Farin82]   Gerald Farin (1982), Visually C^2 Cubic Splines, *Computer-Aided Design*, **14**(3), May, 137-139.

[Faux/Pratt79]   Ivor D. Faux and Michael J. Pratt (1979), *Computational Geometry for Design and Manufacture*, John Wiley & Sons, New York.

[Ferrari/et al.86]   Leonard A. Ferrari, P. V. Sankar, Jack Sklansky, and Sidney Leeman (1986), Efficient Two-Dimensional Filters Using B-spline Functions, *Computer Vision, Graphics, and Image Processing* **35**(2), August, 152-169.

[Foley/vanDam82]   James D. Foley and Andries van Dam (1982), *Fundamentals of Interactive Computer Graphics*, Addison Wesley, Reading, Massachusetts.

[Forrest72]   A. Robin Forrest (1972), Interactive Interpolation and Approximation by Bézier Polynomials, *Computer Journal* **15**(1), February, 71-79.

[Forrest79]   A. Robin Forrest (1979), On the Rendering of Surfaces, *Computer Graphics—SIGGRAPH '79 Conference Proceedings* **13**(2), August, 253-259.

[Forsythe/et al.77]   George E. Forsythe, Michael A. Malcolm, and Cleve B. Moler (1977), Computer Methods for Mathematical Computations, Prentice-Hall, Englewood Cliffs, New Jersey.

[Fournier/Barsky85]   Alain Fournier and Brian A. Barsky (1985), Geometric Continuity with Interpolating Bézier Curves (Preliminary Report), in *Computer-Generated Images—The State of the Art*, Nadia Magnenat-Thalmann and Daniel Thalmann (eds.), Springer-Verlag, New York, 153-158.

[Goldman82]   Ronald N. Goldman (1982), Using Degenerate Bézier Triangles and Tetrahedra to Subdivide Bézier Curves, *Computer-Aided Design* **14**(6), November, 307-311.

[Goodman85]   Tim N. T. Goodman (1985), Properties of Beta-splines, *Journal of Approximation Theory* **44**(2), June, 132-153.

[Goodman/Unsworth85]   Tim N. T. Goodman and Keith Unsworth (1985), Generation of β-spline Curves Using a Recurrence Relation, in *Fundamental Algorithms for Computer Graphics*, Springer-Verlag, New York, 325-357 [NATO ASI Series, Series F, Volume 17].

[Goodman/Unsworth86]   Tim N. T. Goodman and Keith Unsworth (1986), Manipulating Shape and Producing Geometric Continuity in β-spline Curves, *IEEE Computer Graphics and Applications* **6**(2), February, 50-56 [special issue on Parametric Spline Curves and Surfaces].

[Gordon/Riesenfeld74]   William J. Gordon and Richard F. Riesenfeld (1974), B-spline Curves and Surfaces, in *Computer Aided Geometric Design*, Robert E. Barnhill and Richard F. Riesenfeld (eds.), Academic Press, New York, 95-126.

[Heckbert86]   Paul S. Heckbert (1986), Filtering by Repeated Integration *Computer Graphics—SIGGRAPH '86 Conference Proceedings*, **4**(20), August, 315-321.

[Höllig86]   Klaus Höllig (1986), Geometric Continuity of Spline Curves and Surfaces, University of Wisconsin, Madison, Wisconsin 53706 [available in the notes of SIGGRAPH '86 Course #5: *Extension of B-spline Curve Algorithms to Surfaces*].

[Hosaka/Kimura80]   Mamoru Hosaka and Fumihiko Kimura (1980), A Theory and Methods for Free Form Shape Construction, *Journal of Information Processing* **3**(3), 140-151.

[Hou/Andrews78]   Hsieh S. Hou and Harry C Andrews (1978), Cubic Splines for Image Interpolation and Digital Filtering *IEEE Transactions on Acoustics, Speech, and Signal Processing* **26**(6), December, 508-517.

[Joe87]   Barry Joe (1987), Discrete Beta-splines, *Computer Graphics—SIGGRAPH '87 Conference Proceedings*, to appear.

[Joy/Bhetanabhotla86]   Kenneth I. Joy and Murthy N. Bhetanabhotla (1986), Ray Tracing Parametric Surface Patches Utilizing Numerical Techniques and Ray Coherence, *Computer Graphics—SIGGRAPH '86 Conference Proceedings* **20**(3), August, 279-286.

[Kajiya82]   James T Kajiya (1982), Ray Tracing Parametric Patches, *Computer Graphics—SIGGRAPH '82 Conference Proceedings* **16**(3), July, 245-254.

[Kajiya83]   James T. Kajiya (1983), New Techniques for Ray Tracing Procedurally Defined Objects, *ACM Transactions on Graphics* **2**(3), July, 161-181.

[Klassen/Bartels86]   R. Victor Klassen and Richard H. Bartels (1986), Using B-splines for Re-Sizing Images, Technical Report CS-85-55, Computer Science Department, University of Waterloo, Waterloo, Ontario, Canada N2L 3G1, November.

[Knapp79]   Lewis C. Knapp (1979), A Design Scheme Using Coons Surfaces with Nonuniform B-spline Curves, PhD dissertation, Computer and Information Science, Syracuse University, Syracuse, New York 13210, December.

[Kochanek/Bartels84]   Doris H. U. Kochanek and Richard H. Bartels (1984), Interpolating Splines with Local Tension, Continuity and Bias Control, *Computer Graphics—SIGGRAPH '84 Conference Proceedings* **18**(3), July, 33-41.

[Kochanek/et al.82]   Doris H. U. Kochanek, Richard Bartels, and Kellogg S. Booth (1982), A Computer System for Smooth Keyframe Animation, Technical Report CS-82-42, Computer Science Department, University of Waterloo, Waterloo, Ontario, Canada N2L 3G1, December.

[Koparkar/Mudur83]   P. A. Koparkar and S. P. Mudur (1983), A New Class of Algorithms for the Processing of Parametric Curves, *Computer-Aided Design* **15**(1), January, 41-45.

[Lane/Carpenter79]   Jeffrey M. Lane and Loren C. Carpenter (1979), A Generalized Scan Line Algorithm for the Computer Display of Parametrically Defined Surfaces, *Computer Graphics and Image Processing* **11**(3), November, 290-297.

[Lane/et al.80]   Jeffrey M. Lane, Loren C. Carpenter, J. Turner Whitted, and James F. Blinn (1980), Scan Line Methods for Displaying Parametrically Defined Surfaces, *Communications of the ACM* **23**(1), January, 23-34.

[Lane/Riesenfeld80]   Jeffrey M. Lane and Richard F. Riesenfeld (1980), A Theoretical Development for the Computer Generation of Piecewise Polynomial Surfaces, *IEEE Transactions on Pattern Analysis and Machine Intelligence* **2**(1), January, 35-46.

[Lane/Riesenfeld81]   Jeffrey M. Lane and Richard F. Riesenfeld (1981), Bounds on a Polynomial, *BIT* **21**(1), March, 112-117.

[Lee85]   Eugene T. Y. Lee (1985), Some Remarks Concerning B-splines, *Computer Aided Geometric Design* **2**(4), December, 307-311.

[Lyche/Mørken86]   Tom Lyche and K. Mørken (1986), Making the Oslo Algorithm More Efficient, *SIAM Journal on Numerical Analysis* **23**(3), June, 663-675.

[Manning74]   J. R. Manning (1974), Continuity Conditions for Spline Curves, *The Computer Journal* **17**(2), May, 181-186.

[Marsden70]   Martin J. Marsden (1970), An Identity for Spline Functions with Applications to Variation-Diminishing Spline Approximation, *Journal of Approximation Theory* **3**(1), March, 7-49.

[Mortenson85]   Michael E. Mortenson (1985), *Geometric Modeling*, John Wiley & Sons, New York.

[Newman/Sproull79]   William M. Newman and Robert F. Sproull (1979), *Principles of Interactive Computer Graphics*, second edition, McGraw-Hill, New York.

[Nielson74]   Gregory M. Nielson (1974), Some Piecewise Polynomial Alternatives to Splines Under Tension, in *Computer Aided Geometric Design*, Robert E. Barnhill and Richard F. Riesenfeld (eds.), Academic Press, New York, 209-235.

[Nielson86]   Gregory M. Nielson (1986), Rectangular ν-Splines, *IEEE Computer Graphics and Applications* **6**(2), February, 35-40 [special issue on Parametric Curves and Surfaces].

[Nydegger72]   Robert W. Nydegger (1972), A Data Minimization Algorithm of Analytical Models for Computer Graphics, Master's thesis, Computer Science Department, University of Utah, Salt Lake City, Utah 84112, June.

[Penna/Patterson86]   Michael A. Penna and Richard R. Patterson (1986), *Projective Geometry and its Applications to Computer Graphics*, Prentice-Hall, New Jersey.

[Piegl85]   Leslie Piegl (1985), Recursive Algorithms for the Representation of Parametric Curves and Surfaces, *Computer-Aided Design* **17**(5), June, 225-229.

[Pilcher73]   David T. Pilcher (1973), Smooth Approximation of Parametric Curves and Surfaces, PhD dissertation, Computer Science Department, University of Utah, Salt Lake City, Utah 84112, August.

[Plass/Stone83]   Michael Plass and Maureen Stone, Curve-Fitting with Piecewise Parametric Cubics, *Computer Graphics—SIGGRAPH '83 Conference Proceedings* **17**(3), July, 229-239.

[Prautzsch84]   Hartmut Prautzsch (1984), A Short Proof of the Oslo Algorithm, *Computer Aided Geometric Design* **1**(1), July, 95-96.

[Prautzsch85]   Hartmut Prautzsch (1985), Letter to the Editor, *Computer Aided Geometric Design* **2**(4), December, page 329.

[Ramer72]   Urs Ramer (1972), An Iterative Procedure for the Polygonal Approximation of Plane Curves, *Computer Graphics and Image Processing* **1**(3), November, 244-256.

[Riesenfeld73]   Richard F. Riesenfeld (1973), Applications of B-spline Approximation to Geometric Problems of Computer-Aided Design, PhD dissertation, Department of Systems and Information Science, Syracuse University, Syracuse, New York 13210, May.

[Riesenfeld75]   Richard F. Riesenfeld (1975), On Chaikin's Algorithm, *Computer Graphics and Image Processing* **4**(3), September, 304-310.

[Riesenfeld/et al.81]   Richard F. Riesenfeld, Elaine Cohen, Russell D. Fish, Spencer W. Thomas, Elizabeth S. Cobb, Brian A. Barsky, Dino L. Schweitzer, and Jeffrey M. Lane (1981), Using the Oslo Algorithm as a Basis for CAD/CAM Geometric Modelling, in *Proceedings of the Second Annual NCGA National Conference*, National Computer Graphics Association, P.O. Box 3412, McLean, Virginia 22103, June, 345-356.

[Rogers/Adams76]   David F. Rogers and J. Alan Adams (1976), Mathematical Elements for Computer Graphics, McGraw-Hill, New York.

[Sabin70]   Malcolm A. Sabin (1970), Parametric Splines in Tension, Technical Note VTO/MS/160, British Aircraft Corporation, Weybridge, Surrey, England, July 23.

[Schmitt/et al.86]   Francis J. M. Schmitt, Brian A. Barsky, and Wen-Hui Du (1986), An Adaptive Subdivision Method for Surface-Fitting from Sampled Data, *Computer Graphics—SIGGRAPH '86 Conference Proceedings* **20**(3), August, 179-188.

[Schumaker81]   Larry L. Schumaker (1981), *Spline Functions: Basic Theory*, John Wiley & Sons, New York.

[Schweikert66]   Daniel G. Schweikert (1966), An Interpolation Curve Using a Spline in Tension, *Journal of Mathematics and Physics* **45**, 312-317.

[Schweitzer/Cobb82]   Dino Schweitzer and Elizabeth S. Cobb (1982), Scanline Rendering of Parametric Surfaces, Data, *Computer Graphics—SIGGRAPH '82 Conference Proceedings* **16**(3), July, 179-188.

[Smith83]   Alvy Ray Smith (1983), Spline Tutorial Notes, Technical Memo 77, Lucasfilm, Ltd. [appeared in the notes of *SIGGRAPH '83 Course #7: Introduction to Computer Animation*].

[Stone85]   Maureen Stone (1985), One Curve, Three Definitions, *Computer Graphics* **19**(1), January, cover picture.

[Sweeney84]   Michael A. J. Sweeney (1984), The Waterloo CGL Ray Tracing Package, Master's thesis, Computer Science Department, University of Waterloo, Waterloo, Ontario, Canada N2L 3G1, September.

[Sweeney/Bartels86] Michael A. J. Sweeney and Richard H. Bartels (1986), Ray Tracing Free-Form B-spline Surfaces, *IEEE Computer Graphics and Applications* **6**(2), February, 41-49 [special issue on Parametric Spline Curves and Surfaces].

[Tiller83] Wayne Tiller (1983), Rational B-splines for Curve and Surface Representations, *IEEE Computer Graphics and Applications* **3**(6), September, 61-69.

[Weghorst/et al.84] Hank Weghorst, Gary Hooper, and Donald Greenberg (1984), Improved Computational Methods for Ray Tracing, *ACM Transactions on Graphics* **3**(1), January, 52-69.

[Wu/et al.77] Sheng-Chuan Wu, John F. Abel, and Donald P. Greenberg (1977), An Interactive Computer Graphics Approach to Surface Representation, *Communications of the ACM* **20** (10), October, 703-712.

[Wang84] Guo-Zhao Wang (1984), The Subdivision Method for Finding the Intersection Between Two Bézier Curves or Surfaces, Zhejiang University Journal, Zhejiang University, Hangzhou, Zhejiang, People's Republic of China [Special Issue on Computational Geometry (in Chinese)].

Index